Visual Basic® .NET Programming with Peter Aitken

Peter Aitken

President and CEO
Roland Elgey

Publisher
Al Valvano

Associate Publisher
Katherine R. Hartlove

Acquisitions Editor
Jawahara Saidullah

Product Marketing Manager
Jeff Johnson

Project Editor
Marcus Huff

Technical Reviewer
Chris Crane

Production Coordinator
Meg E. Turecek

Cover Designer
Carla J. Schuder

Visual Basic® .NET Programming with Peter Aitken

Limits of Liability and Disclaimer of Warranty
The author and publisher of this book have used their best efforts in preparing the book and the programs contained in it. These efforts include the development, research, and testing of the theories and programs to determine their effectiveness. The author and publisher make no warranty of any kind, expressed or implied, with regard to these programs or the documentation contained in this book.

The author and publisher shall not be liable in the event of incidental or consequential damages in connection with, or arising out of, the furnishing, performance, or use of the programs, associated instructions, and/or claims of productivity gains.

Trademarks
Trademarked names appear throughout this book. Rather than list the names and entities that own the trademarks or insert a trademark symbol with each mention of the trademarked name, the publisher states that it is using the names for editorial purposes only and to the benefit of the trademark owner, with no intention of infringing upon that trademark.

The Coriolis Group, LLC
14455 North Hayden Road
Suite 220
Scottsdale, Arizona 85260

(480) 483-0192
FAX (480) 483-0193
www.coriolis.com

Library of Congress Cataloging-in-Publication Data
Aitken, Peter G.
Visual Basic.Net programming with Peter Aitken / by Peter Aitken.
p. cm.
Rev. ed. of: Visual Basic 6 programming blue book. c1998.
Includes index.
ISBN 1-57610-961-5
1. Microsoft Visual BASIC. 2. BASIC (Computer program language)
I. Aitken, Peter G. Visual Basic 6 programming blue book. II. Title.
QA76.73.B3 A3827 2001
005.2'768 -- dc21 2001042211
CIP

Printed in the United States of America
10 9 8 7 6 5 4 3 2 1

The Coriolis Group, LLC • 14455 North Hayden Road, Suite 220 • Scottsdale, Arizona 85260

A Note from Coriolis

Coriolis Technology Press was founded to create a very elite group of books: the ones you keep closest to your machine. In the real world, you have to choose the books you rely on every day very carefully, and we understand that.

To win a place for our books on that coveted shelf beside your PC, we guarantee several important qualities in every book we publish. These qualities are:

- *Technical accuracy*—It's no good if it doesn't work. Every Coriolis Technology Press book is reviewed by technical experts in the topic field, and is sent through several editing and proofreading passes in order to create the piece of work you now hold in your hands.
- *Innovative editorial design*—We've put years of research and refinement into the ways we present information in our books. Our books' editorial approach is uniquely designed to reflect the way people learn new technologies and search for solutions to technology problems.
- *Practical focus*—We put only pertinent information into our books and avoid any fluff. Every fact included between these two covers must serve the mission of the book as a whole.
- *Accessibility*—The information in a book is worthless unless you can find it quickly when you need it. We put a lot of effort into our indexes, and heavily cross-reference our chapters, to make it easy for you to move right to the information you need.

Here at The Coriolis Group we have been publishing and packaging books, technical journals, and training materials since 1989. We have put a lot of thought into our books; please write to us at **ctp@coriolis.com** and let us know what you think. We hope that you're happy with the book in your hands, and that in the future, when you reach for software development and networking information, you'll turn to one of our books first.

Coriolis Technology Press
The Coriolis Group
14455 N. Hayden Road, Suite 220
Scottsdale, Arizona
85260

Email: ctp@coriolis.com
Phone: (480) 483-0192
Toll free: (800) 410-0192

Look for these related books from The Coriolis Group:

Visual Basic .NET Black Book

By Steven Holzner

Visual Studio .NET: The .NET Framework Black Book

By Julian Templeman and David Vitter

C# Core Language Little Black Book

By Bill Wagner

Also published by Coriolis Technology Press:

Windows XP Professional - The Ultimate User's Guide

By Joli Ballew

Mac OS X Version 10.1 Black Book

By Mark R. Bell and Debrah Suggs

C# Black Book

By Matthew Telles

About the Author

Peter Aitken has been writing about computers and programming for over 10 years, with some 30 books well as hundreds of magazine and trade publication articles to his credit. His recent book titles include *Office XP Development With VBA*, *XML the Microsoft Way*, *Windows Script Host*, and *Teach Yourself Visual Basic .NET Internet Programming in 21 Days*. For several years he was a Contributing Editor at *Visual Developer Magazine* where he wrote a popular Visual Basic column, and he is regular contributor to Microsoft Office Solutions magazine and the DevX Web site. Peter is the proprietor of PGA Consulting, providing custom application and Internet development to business, academia, and government since 1994. You can reach him at **peter@pgacon.com**.

Acknowledgments

This book lists only one author, but could not have been created without the skilled help of the following people at The Coriolis Group: Kathy Hartlove, Jawahara Saidullah, Don Eamon, Marcus Huff, and Meg Turecek. Thanks, everyone.

Contents at a Glance

Table of Contents

Introduction

For many years, Microsoft Visual Basic has been the world's most popular programming language. There are good reasons for this wide acceptance. From its very beginning over ten years ago, Visual Basic has brought unmatched flexibility and ease of programming to the Windows platform. Many features that are now standard in other programming languages were first seen in Visual Basic. In its previous six versions, Visual Basic evolved into an extremely powerful development tool that was equally at home in business, academia, engineering, or everywhere else in which Windows applications were being created.

The latest version of Visual Basic, called Visual Basic .NET (say "dot-net"), is the most significant evolutionary change yet in the language. At its heart is the totally new .NET framework, a rich and powerful set of classes that provides support for just about any imaginable area of programming—desktop, Internet, database, graphics, and so on. The .NET framework itself is independent of any specific language, and Visual Basic is one of three languages that Microsoft provides for use with .NET (the others being C# and C++).

Learning to program in Visual Basic .NET consists of two related parts: learning the Visual Basic language and learning the .NET framework. This book covers both in a logically organized and clearly presented manner. I start at the beginning, explaining the concepts and goals of Visual Basic .NET and describing how the various parts relate to one another. Then I cover the details of using Visual Studio, the sophisticated development environment that you will use to create and test your applications. The next two chapters provide complete coverage of the Visual Basic language: keywords, syntax, data storage, and so on. Two later chapters cover Visual Basic's new object-oriented programming capabilities. The remainder of this book's chapters delves into a wide variety of specific programming topics, such as creation of desktop and Web applications, database access, graphics, and custom controls. Throughout the book, the emphasis is on clear explanation and helpful code examples.

This book is actually the fourth edition of a very popular Visual Basic book that I wrote for the Coriolis Group. The first two editions covered Visual Basic versions 4 and 5, and were called *Visual Basic Programming Explorer*. The third edition was titled *Visual Basic Programming Blue Book*, and it covered version 6 of the Visual Basic language. From the beginning, my goal in these books was to emphasize clear, concise explanations and working code examples to help the reader quickly master the fundamentals of Visual Basic programming. Based on the books' success and on feedback from readers, I was successful. I hopefully have continued this tradition with this new book.

Who This Book Is For

I wrote this book for the beginning to intermediate-level programmer. It will be suitable for anyone who falls into one of the following three categories:

- You are totally new to programming, and Visual Basic .Net is your first language.
- You have worked with previous versions of Visual Basic, and you are moving up to .NET.
- You have worked with other languages, such as Java or C++, and you want to learn Visual Basic .NET.

I do not recommend this book for advanced programmers. One of the book's goals is the clear and concise explanation of fundamental concepts and techniques, and if you are already familiar with these topics, you are likely to find those parts of the book of little value.

About the CD-ROM

You'll find a CD-ROM bound into this book. It contains the Microsoft .NET Software Development Kit, the book's source code, as well as other goodies that you may find useful. For the complete details, as well as instructions on how to install the CD-ROM contents, browse to the file README.HTM in the CD-ROM's root directory.

Updates and Feedback

Despite the best efforts of author and editors, it is unavoidable that a few errors may make it into the printed book. This is particularly true for books such as this one, which are written using a pre-release version of software. Given the realities of publishing schedules, it would be impossible to check everything against the final commercial version of Visual Basic .Net and still get the book into readers' hands in a timely manner. Therefore, it is possible that last-minute changes to Visual Basic .Net will affect some of the book's demonstration programs. If you have a problem running any of the sample code, check the book's website at **www.pgacon.com/vbnet.htm** for corrections and updated code. At this site, you can also report errors you found and send me feedback or other comments you may have. Please note, however, that I can respond only to book-related topics. I simply don't have the time to help you set up your computer, do your programming homework, or explain how to get a job as a programmer.

Peter G. Aitken
Chapel Hill, North Carolina
October 2001

Chapter 1
Introduction to Visual Basic

As you start your exploration of the Visual Basic programming language, you may be comforted to know that Visual Basic has a well-deserved reputation as being relatively easy to learn. In fact, programming techniques that got their start with Visual Basic have proven so effective that they are now found in many other languages. Note, however, that I said "relatively easy." Visual Basic may be easier to learn than C++ or Java, but that does not mean mastering it is a trivial task. Any language that has the power and flexibility demanded by today's development needs is unavoidably complex. There's no avoiding the fact that the aspiring Visual Basic programmer has a lot to learn. Your task will be easier if you have an understanding of the overall picture—what the parts of Visual Basic are, and how they fit in and work with one another—before getting to the details. That's the topic of this chapter.

The Visual Basic Programming Model

To understand the approach that Visual Basic takes to programming, look closely at some of the programs you use every day. On my system, for example, I have three programs running at present: Microsoft Word for word processing, Microsoft Outlook for email, and Jasc Software's Paint Shop Pro for graphics. These are very different programs that perform very different tasks, but a moment's examination will reveal many similarities. For example, each of these programs displays in a screen window whose size and position can be changed. The windows all have a menu, a title bar, minimize and close buttons, and many other common features. Behind the visual interface, all three programs must perform a

Differences between the New and the Old Visual Basic

The current version of Visual Basic (called Visual Basic .NET) represents some very significant changes from the previous version, Visual Basic 6. If you are just getting started with Visual Basic, these changes will not concern you. However, if you have some experience with a previous version of Visual Basic, or need to migrate some existing Visual Basic 6 projects to Visual Basic .NET, you can refer to Appendices A and B for an overview of changes and information on project migration.

---

variety of common tasks, such as sending output to the printer and reading information from disk files. I could mention many more examples, but I think you'll agree—all Windows programs have a lot in common.

When Visual Basic was first introduced many years ago, its genius was to not only recognize the fact that all Windows programs have a lot in common, but to do something about it. Rather than requiring the programmer to do it all, Visual Basic provided many of the things that programmers commonly needed in a prepackaged, tested, and ready-to-use form. These ready-to-use software modules are called *components*. Visual Basic may have been the first to do so, but essentially all modern programming languages use the component-based approach.

Programming with Components

When you create a program in Visual Basic, you are not starting from scratch, writing the code to create all the functionality that your program requires from the ground up. Such an approach would be unimaginably complex and time consuming. Imagine building a house and having to dig up clay to make bricks, cut down trees to make doors, and melt sand to make window glass. No thanks! The only rational way to build a house is to use premade components for most of the tasks. You'll use ready-made bricks from the brickyard, doors that are already cut and assembled, and windows that are put together and ready to pop into place. You still need to put the components together, of course, but their availability saves a huge amount of time and effort.

Visual Basic works in essentially the same way. The Visual Basic programming environment consists of not only the Visual Basic language, but also a huge array of software components that have been created and tested to perform specific tasks. Some of these components represent elements that are displayed on the screen, such as windows, menus, and buttons. Others have no visual display but work behind the scenes to perform tasks such as reading and writing disk files. The main task of a Visual Basic programmer is to stitch these components together to create the needed functionality.

What components are available? In many ways, this entire book is an answer to that question. Almost any programming task you can imagine—and a few you can't imagine—are provided for by Visual Basic components. They range from the very simple to the very complex. Here are some examples of the tasks that components can handle:

- Displaying a button that the user can click
- Downloading a Web page from the Internet
- Playing a sound on the system speakers
- Reading information from a disk file

Your job as a programmer is largely one of selecting the proper components and then writing the code to integrate the components into a finished program. As sophisticated as Visual Basic components are, they cannot read your mind! You must tell them, often by means of code, how to behave and what to do. For example, if you need a button that the user can click, Visual Basic provides a component for that purpose. However, it is up to you to specify what color the button should be, where you want it located on-screen, and the text that should be displayed on it (among other things).

Classes and Objects

Most Visual Basic components are provided as classes. I have been using the term *component* as a general term used to refer to any reusable and self-contained piece of software, but the term *class*, and the related term *object*, have specific meanings. I'll be going into these meanings, and other aspects of object-oriented programming, in more detail in Chapters 9 and 10. For the present, an introduction will be sufficient.

A class is a blueprint for an object. It is exactly analogous to a furniture designer's drawings being a blueprint for a chair. Given a class, you can create as many objects from it as you need—just like, given blueprints for a chair, you can build as many chairs as you need. An object is said to be an *instance* of its class, and the process of creating an object from a class is called *instantiation*.

Let's look at a specific example. Suppose you are writing a program that will require the user to enter his or her name, phone number, and email address. Visual Basic provides a class called **TextBox** that is designed specifically for entering and editing text information. Your program will create three instances of the **TextBox** class—that is, three **TextBox** objects—one for each piece of information that the user will enter. The three **TextBox** objects are completely independent of one another. After you have created an object, you work with it by means of its properties and methods.

Properties

A property is an attribute of an object—in other words, a bit of information stored by the object. Many properties control the appearance and behavior of an object. Continuing with the **TextBox** object, for example, you would specify its position, size, color, and font by setting the relevant properties. Other properties provide your program with information about an object. If the user enters text into a **TextBox** object, your program would read that text by means of a property.

Every class has its own set of properties. Some properties are part of many different classes. Thus, any object that displays on the screen will have the **Location** property to specify its location on the screen. Other properties are more specialized and are part of only one or a few classes.

Methods

A *method* represents an action that can be carried out by an object. For example, the **TextBox** object has the **Clear()** method, which erases any text that is displayed in the box. Each class has its own set of methods, as required by the class's purpose. To differentiate method names from property names, method names are traditionally written followed by a pair of parentheses.

Rolling Your Own

So far, I have been talking about those components, or classes, that are part of Visual Basic. However, that is only part of the story. In addition to having all of these powerful predefined classes at your disposal, you can create your own custom classes. This is an extremely powerful and versatile technique that is applicable in a wide range of programming scenarios. A class that you create exists as a software component, just like the predefined classes, and can be used and reused with the same flexibility. What's more, Visual Basic's object-oriented capabilities mean that you can base a custom class on an existing class, and the new class will automatically have all the features and capabilities of the class it is based on. You can then customize the new class as desired.

Events

Another central part of Visual Basic programming is the concept of an event. An *event* is something that happens to which the program might want to respond. Many events are related to user actions, such as mouse clicks or keyboard input. Using the **TextBox** object as an example again, when the user is entering or editing text in the box, a **KeyPress()** event occurs every time the user presses a key. Likewise, if the user moves the mouse pointer over the object, a **MouseEnter()** event occurs. You can respond to or ignore these and other events, as dictated by the needs of the program. The important point is that the detection of events is performed automatically—it is built into Visual Basic.

The Software Component Mindset

Software components sound like a good idea, and anyone can see the advantages of using them (not that you really have a choice!). But to derive the maximum benefit from components, you will have to develop a specific way of thinking when creating Visual Basic programs. This attitude is something I call the *software component mindset*. It goes beyond thinking, "Oh yeah, maybe I can use a software component here." Rather, it's the habit of starting at the very beginning, when the structure of your Visual Basic program begins to take shape in your mind, with the goal of using as many software components as possible. Another way of looking at it is that instead of selecting components based on the structure of your program, you will design the structure of your program based on the available components.

Not only do you want to maximize the use of existing components in your program, you also want to remain aware of creating your own components. Almost all of the programs you write will include certain tasks for which you will not be able to use an existing component. You'll have to write those software components yourself. With a bit of planning, you can create components for such tasks, and these components will be available to you in the future. After a while, you'll find yourself with a small library of software components that perform the functions you need most often in your programs.

A necessary part of the software component mindset is having a good idea of what components are available. You can't keep all the details in your head—at least I can't—but unless you have at least a general idea of what components are available and what they can do, you may end up doing unnecessary work. As I know from personal experience, few things are more disheartening than putting in several days writing custom Visual Basic code only to discover that there was a component that could have been used for the task!

The .NET Framework

One of the most important tools at the Visual Basic programmer's disposal is Microsoft's .NET (pronounced *dot-net*) Framework. Almost all of the components that Visual Basic provides are .NET Framework classes. This framework is the result of Microsoft's realization that the Internet is becoming increasingly central to almost all areas of programming. Previously, the class frameworks that were available to programmers using Visual Basic and other languages had been designed primarily for creating standalone or client/server applications. (A client-server app is one that utilizes a local area network to distribute processing and/or data between two or more computers.) Internet capabilities had been added on as needed, but they were not integrated into the basic design of the framework. As programmers demanded more and more Internet functionality in their programs, the limitations of the old frameworks became painfully obvious.

.NET is Microsoft's response to this situation. It was designed from the ground up to have Internet capabilities as an integral part of the framework rather than as an afterthought. This does not mean that the new Visual Basic is limited to creating only Internet applications—it remains a powerful tool for creating standalone applications. The .NET Framework, however, provides a rich set of Internet capabilities that you can call on if you need them. The .NET Framework provides other advantages as well, such as cross-language integration, but its Internet features are generating the most excitement.

It would not be correct to think of the .NET Framework as a part of Visual Basic. The framework is language-independent, and Visual Basic is one of several languages that Microsoft has designed to use .NET (the others being C#, C++, and Jscript). You'll learn more about the .NET Framework in later chapters.

The Role of Code

What's the role of Basic code in Visual Basic? Isn't programming supposed to require writing lots of code? So far, I've been talking about everything except code—classes, objects, properties, and so on. Where's the code?

Don't worry—you'll be writing plenty of code for your Visual Basic programs. While some programs require less code than others, some code is always needed to tie the program's components together and to direct them in performing the real work of the program. Code is also required when a component does not exist for a particular task and you need to create a custom class. Code ties all the program's components together, linking them to one another, to the user, and to the outside world.

Project Types

Visual Basic offers several different types of projects. When you first start a project, you must select the proper project type for the task you want to accomplish. The variety of project types is an indication of the flexibility that Visual Basic and the .NET framework provide to the programmer. You'll learn more about these project types in subsequent chapters. For now, Table 1.1 provides you with a brief description of each type.

Your First Visual Basic Project

Before getting into the details of VB .NET, you will benefit from seeing a complete, if simple, Windows application. By walking through the steps of creating this application, you'll develop a better feel for what's involved than you could by reading alone. This project will

Table 1.1 Visual Basic's project types.

Project Type	Description
Windows Application	A local Windows application whose user interface consists of Windows forms. Most of the Windows programs that you use fall into this category.
Web Application	An application whose user interface consists of Web pages that are viewed in a browser.
Class Library	Classes for use in other applications.
Windows Control Library	Controls for use in Windows applications. A control is a component with a visual interface.
Web Service	A software service that will be available to other applications via the Web.
Windows Service	A software service that will be available to other Windows applications.
Console Application	A console, or command-line, application. A console application has no visual interface and provides for text input and output only.

perform a very simple task—adding two numbers—but it serves to demonstrate many of the tasks that will be involved in any Windows application you create. You may not understand all of the details, but that's okay—you'll learn them in later chapters. The goal is to give you a hands-on feel for what it is like to create a program using VB .NET.

Starting the Project

The first step is to create a new, blank Windows application project. You do this in the New Project dialog box, shown in Figure 1.1. Depending on your Visual Studio settings, this dialog box may be displayed automatically when you start Visual Studio. If not, you display it by pressing Ctrl+N or by selecting New from the File menu, then selecting Project.

After the New Project dialog box is open, follow these steps to create a new Windows application:

1. Under Project Types, select Visual Basic Projects.
2. In the Templates box, select the Windows Application icon.
3. In the Name box, type a name for the project. I suggest FirstWindowsApp.
4. (Optional) In the Location box, specify a location for the project files. I suggest that you accept the default location unless you have a specific reason for changing it. Visual Studio will create a folder using the name that you specified in Step 3, and all project files will be placed in this folder.
5. Click OK.

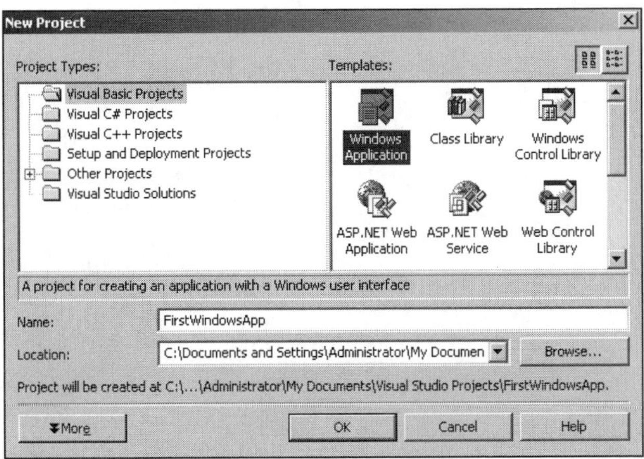

Figure 1.1
Starting a new Windows application in the New Project dialog box.

When the project is created, it will display a blank form ready for you to start designing. The screen, shown in Figure 1.2, also contains the following elements:

- On the left is the Toolbox, containing the Windows forms controls that you can place on your form.
- At the upper right is the Solution Explorer, listing the project's components. In this case, there is only one component, Form1.vb, representing the project's one form. The Solution Explorer also lists the project's references and assembly information, which you can ignore for now.
- At the lower right is the Properties window, listing the properties of the currently selected object (Form1 in this case).

Visual Studio uses a lot of clever techniques to make the most of the available screen real estate, such as overlapping windows and tabs. If you ever have trouble finding a window that you think should be visible, you can usually display it by selecting the appropriate command from the View menu. Chapter 2 will present more information on working with Visual Studio windows.

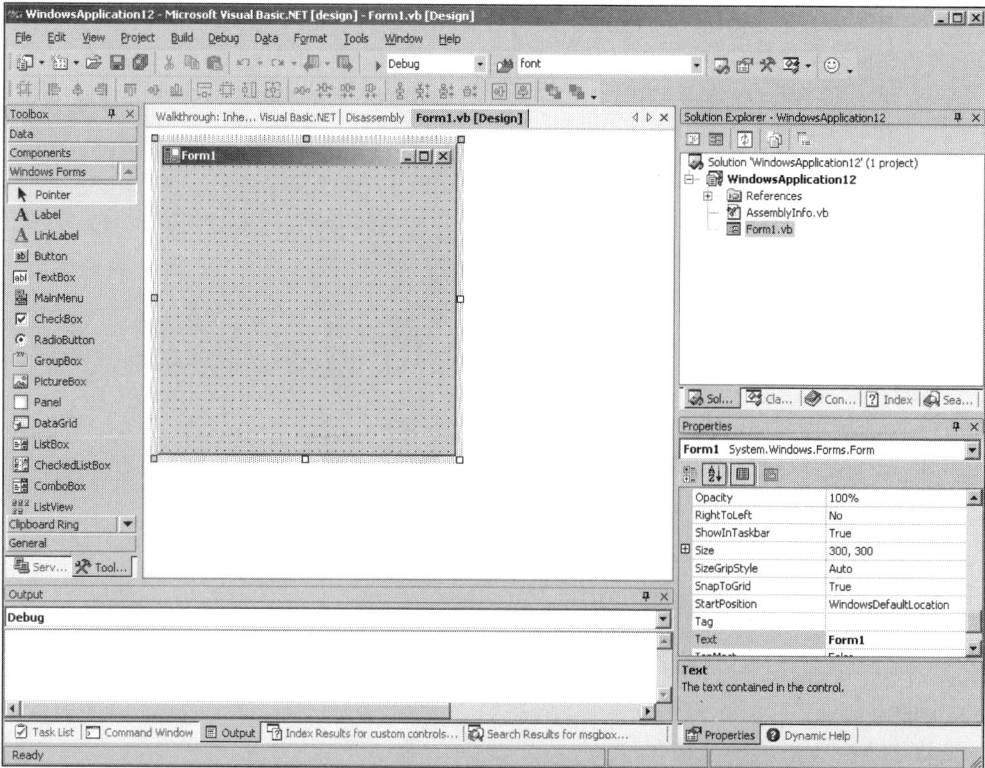

Figure 1.2
A blank Windows application project.

Setting Form Properties

The next task is to set some form properties so the form will appear and behave in the desired manner:

1. Set the **FormBorderStyle** to **FixedSingle**. This results in a form that has a single border and cannot be resized by the user while the program is running (although you can still set its size during design).
2. Set the **MaximizeBox** property to **False**. This disables the form's maximize box, which is appropriate for this project as there will never be a reason for the user to maximize this form.
3. Set the **StartPosition** property to **CenterScreen** so that the form will display in the center of the screen when the application runs. The user will still be able to move it, however.
4. Set the **Text** property to **Adder**. This is the text that displays in the form's title bar.

Now that the form properties are set, it is a good time to save the form by clicking the Save or Save All button on the Visual Studio toolbar.

Designing the Visual Interface

The first part of creating this demonstration project will be to design the visual interface. This consists of adding the needed controls to the form and setting the properties of the form and controls to meet the requirements of the project. This project will require eight controls, as follows:

- Three Text Box controls, two to input the numbers being added and one to display the sum.
- Three Label controls to identify the three Text Box controls.
- Two buttons, one to perform the addition, the other to quit the program.

To add a text box, click the TextBox icon in the Toolbox, then drag on the form to place the control. Repeat this three times, positioning the controls one above the other. Don't be concerned with their exact size or position, as these can be changed later. Note that each text box is assigned a default name in the form TextBox1, TextBox2, and so on. This name is displayed in the control, but be aware that a control's name and the text it displays are two separate properties that just happen to be the same initially.

The next step is to change some properties of the text boxes. To work with an object's properties you must select the object by clicking it with the mouse or by selecting it from the drop-down list at the top of the Properties window. The selected object displays small boxes, called *handles*, around its perimeter. Change the properties of the Text Box control as follows:

- Change the **Text** property of all three controls to a blank string.
- Set the **Name** property of the top text box to **txtNum1**, of the middle text box to **txtNum2**, and of the bottom text box to **txtSum**.
- Change the **ReadOnly** property of the bottom text box to **True**. This prevents the user from changing the text in the control while the program is running. A read-only text box displays with a gray background by default.

Now it's time to add the three Label controls. Use the same technique as you used for the Text Box controls, clicking the Label icon in the Toolbox and dragging on the form to place the labels. Place one Label control to the left of each text box. Change the **Text** property of the controls so that from top to bottom the three Label controls read "Number 1:", "Number 2:", and "Sum:".

The final controls to be added are two buttons. Place then next to each other, below the other controls on the form. For the left button, change the **Text** property to **Add** and the **Name** property to **btnAdd**. For the right button, set the **Name** property to **btnQuit** and the **Text** property to **Quit**.

At this time, you should adjust the position and size of the controls to create an attractive visual interface. You can also adjust the size of the form if desired. The basics of moving and resizing controls and forms are:

- To move a control, point at it with the mouse. The mouse pointer will change to a four-headed arrow. Then, drag the control to the new position. You'll note that the default is for controls to align to the grid on the form (which does not display when the program runs), making it easy to line controls up with each other.
- To resize a control or form, select it. (To select the form, click on the form between the controls.) Then, point at one of the handles displayed around the selected object; the mouse pointer will change to a two-headed arrow. Drag the handle to the desired size.

Don't forget to save the form as you work on it. At this point, the visual design of your form is complete and it will look something like Figure 1.3.

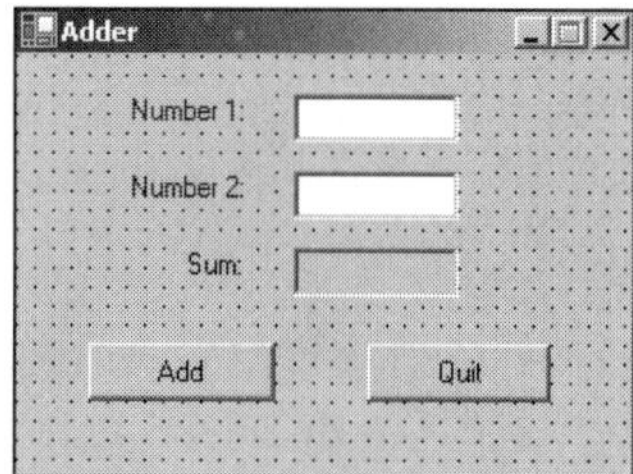

Figure 1.3
The completed form for the Adder project.

You can run the project at this time (press F5 or select Start from the Debug menu). The form will display on the screen, and you'll be able to enter data in the two upper Text Box controls, but that's all. The buttons will not do anything, and you'll have to quit the application by clicking the Close button (the "X") at the right end of the title bar. To bring functionality to the visual interface, you must add some Visual Basic code.

Adding the Code

Before starting to add code to a Windows application, it is always a good idea to do a little planning. What exactly does the code need to do? What actions will the user take? For the current project, the planning is quite simple, but for more complex programs there will be many things to consider. Planning ahead can save you a lot of time down the road!

For the current project, there are two actions to consider:

- When the user clicks the Add button, the program should add the numbers in the first two text boxes and display the result in the third text box.
- When the user clicks the Quit button, the program should terminate.

This sounds simple enough, but perhaps you have noticed that something is missing. For the addition action, it is assumed that the user has entered a number in each of the first two text boxes. What happens if the user has not done so? Perhaps he left one or both text boxes blank, or entered some text instead of a number. Clearly, this would prevent the program from working properly, so the code you will write needs to take this eventuality into account. Therefore, the first action listed above should be modified as follows:

- When the user clicks the Add button, verify that both text boxes contain numbers.
- If not, display a message to the user.
- Otherwise, add the numbers and display the result in the third text box.

Because the user action that we are dealing with is a mouse click, the appropriate place for the code is in the **Click()** event procedures of the two buttons. I'll deal with the Add button first. To create and display its **Click()** event procedure, double-click the button on the form. Visual Studio opens the form's code window and inserts the empty skeleton of the **Click()** event procedure, as shown in Figure 1.4. In the figure, I have used the line continuation character to break the first line of the event procedure into two lines so it would all be visible in the editing window. Before adding the code needed for our project, let's examine some aspects of the code in this window.

First, note that the event procedure is named **btnAdd_Click**, reflecting VB .NET's event procedure naming convention that uses the object name and the event name separated by an underscore. It is not this name, however, that connects the procedure to the object and event; that is done by the **Handles** keyword. Thus, you could rename the procedure and as

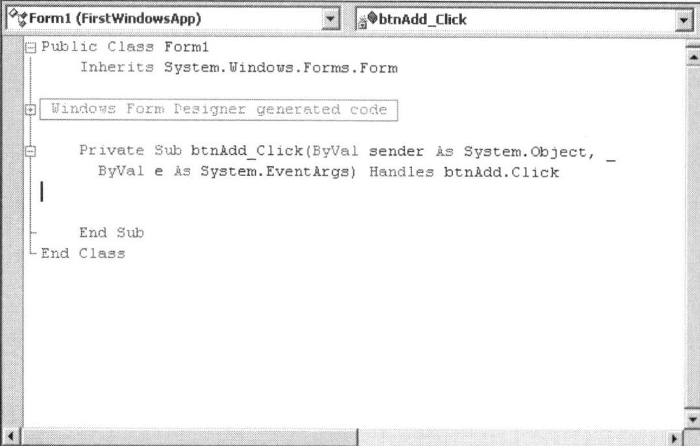
Form1 (FirstWindowsApp)
btnAdd_Click
Public Class Form1
Inherits System.Windows.Forms.Form
Windows Form Designer generated code
Private Sub btnAdd_Click(ByVal sender As System.Object, _
ByVal e As System.EventArgs) Handles btnAdd.Click
End Sub
End Class

Figure 1.4
Creating the **Click** event procedure for the Add button.

long as the **Handles** keyword still specifies btnAdd.Click, the procedure will still be connected to the **Click** event for the control named btnAdd. The event procedure is passed two arguments: **sender** identifies the source of the event and **e** contains information about the event.

If you examine this code further, you'll see that the form is in fact a class that subclasses **System.Windows.Forms.Form**. This means that your form is based on the **Form** class that is defined in VB .NET. There is a hidden section of code labeled "Windows Form Designer generated code" that performs the various actions that are related to the visual interface you designed, such as creating and placing the various controls on the form and setting their properties. In other words, as you design your visual interface, adding controls, setting properties, and so on, the Form Designer is translating your actions into code that is placed in the form class. When your program runs, it is this code that actually creates the form and controls that the user works with. You can view this code by clicking the + that is adjacent to the label. However, you should not make any changes in this section.

Creating Event Procedures

You can simply type an event procedure into the code editor, but it's a lot easier to use the Visual Studio tools. When you are designing a form, double-clicking an element (a control or the form) opens the editing window for the "default" event procedure for that element. This is the event procedure that Microsoft thinks programmers use most often, and it is different for different controls—**Click** for Button controls, **TextChanged** for Text Box controls, and so on. You can access all event procedures using the drop-down boxes at the top of the code editing window. Select the control or form in the left list, then select the event from the right list. Either of these techniques will display the event procedure for editing (if it already exists) or create a new, empty skeleton of the event procedure (if it does not already exist).

Now we can get to the code for our project. To verify that the user has entered a number in the text boxes, we will use the **IsNumeric()** function. Passed an expression, which in this case will be the text in the text box, the function returns True if the expression can be evaluated as a number, False if not. Thus, if **IsNumeric()** returns True for the text in both text boxes, we know that the user has entered numbers. The outline of the code is as follows:

```
If IsNumeric(txtNum1.Text) And IsNumeric(txtNum2.Text) Then
   ' Data is OK, perform the addition.
Else
   ' Data not OK, display a message.
End If
```

Another factor we must consider is that the data in a text box is a string and not a number. Thus, if the user enters "45", it is a string consisting of the characters "4" and "5"—it is not a number with the value 45. To perform addition, it is necessary to convert these strings to numeric values using the **Val** function. Passed a string representation of a number, **Val** returns the corresponding numeric value. Therefore, the addition step will look like this:

```
txtSum.Text = Val(txtNum1.Text) + Val(txtNum2.Text)
```

Note that the conversion of the result from a number to text, for display in the txtSum text box, is handled automatically.

We can now complete the event procedure for the Add button's **Click()** event. In addition to the material already discussed, this code makes use of the **MsgBox()** function to display a message to the user. The code for this event procedure is shown in Listing 1.1.

Listing 1.1 The event procedure for the Add button's Click event.

```
Private Sub btnAdd_Click(ByVal sender As System.Object, _
  ByVal e As System.EventArgs) Handles btnAdd.Click

    If IsNumeric(txtNum1.Text) And IsNumeric(txtNum2.Text) Then
        txtSum.Text = Val(txtNum1.Text) + Val(txtNum2.Text)
    Else
        MsgBox("You must enter a number in both text boxes.")
    End If

End Sub
```

The final step in creating this sample Windows application is the event procedure for the Quit button. Code in this event procedure has only one task to carry out—terminating the program. This is easily done using the form's **Close()** method. Because this is the only form in the application, when it is closed, the application is terminated. The code makes use of the **Me** keyword, which is a useful shortcut that refers to the object that the code is executing in. Thus, the code

```
Me.Close()
```

will close the form in which it is located. Listing 1.2 shows the full code for the Quit button's **Click()** event procedure.

Listing 1.2 The event procedure for the Quit button's Click() event.

```
Private Sub btnQuit_Click(ByVal sender As System.Object, _
      ByVal e As System.EventArgs) Handles btnQuit.Click

    Me.Close()

End Sub
```

Running the Project

The demonstration Windows application is now finished, and you can build and execute it by pressing F5 or by selecting Start from the Debug menu. Figure 1.5 shows the program executing. If you made any errors in the code, the compiler will point them out to you for correction. When you build the program, Visual Studio creates an executable file named FirstWindowsApp.exe. You can run the program from this executable using the usual Windows techniques, such as double-clicking the file name in Windows Explorer. You could also copy this executable file to any other computer and execute it there, as long as the .NET framework is installed.

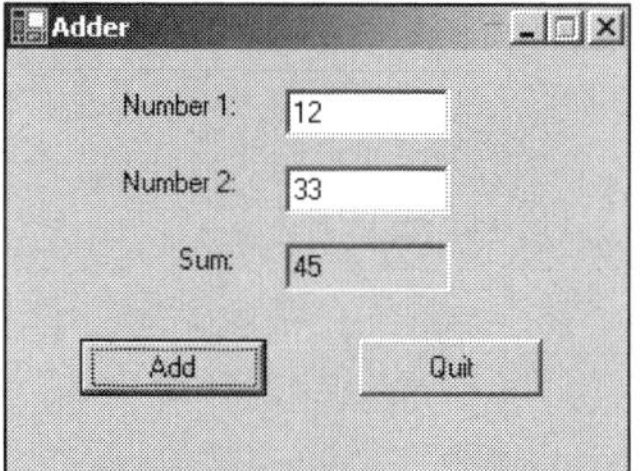

Figure 1.5
The demonstration program executing.

What Next?

This chapter has presented an overview of the Visual Basic programming model and the types of projects that you can create. In following chapters, you'll start learning the details of using the Visual Studio programming environment, the Visual Basic language, and the .NET framework. First, I'd like to finish this chapter with a few suggestions and reminders about Visual Basic programming:

- *Plan ahead*—As with all types of programming, creating a Visual Basic program will always go more smoothly if you spend some time planning. Think about what you need to do in the context of Visual Basic's available tools. This sort of planning is more difficult when you're just starting out with Visual Basic, because you are unfamiliar with its capabilities. But as you gain expertise, planning ahead should become a top priority.

- *Think like a user*—Design your program from the user's perspective. Don't base the design on what's easy for you to program. What data will the user want to see? How will he or she want it displayed? What tasks (and in what order) will the user need to perform? Many technically talented programmers have seen their work collect dust on users' shelves because they neglected to follow this advice.
- *Think components*—After you have some idea of what your program will do, start looking for existing classes that can handle parts of the job. When you're doing it yourself, try to encapsulate your interface and code elements in classes that you can reuse in future projects.
- *Learn by doing*—Programming is like surgery (except for the pay, of course!): You can read every book on the market, but you'll never learn how to do it until you actually do it. That's the approach I take in this book, and so should you. Yes, you should definitely read the rest of this book, but you should also spend as much time as possible working with Visual Basic. You'll be pleasantly surprised at how quickly your programming skills improve.
- *Learn from other Visual Basic programs*—Take time to examine other Visual Basic programs. You never know when you might trip over an idea or technique that you can use in your own work. Sources for Visual Basic programs include the samples provided with the Visual Basic package, Visual Basic programming forums provided by online services, and books and magazines.

Summary

This first chapter got you off to a good start on the road to becoming a proficient VB .NET programmer. You learned about the Visual Basic programming model and the central role that components—classes and objects—play. This includes components that are part of Visual Basic as well as those you design yourself. You also learned the fundamentals of how VB related to the .NET framework and the different types of projects that you can create. Finally, you worked through creating your first Visual Basic project. Although this was a pretty simple project, I hope that it gave you some idea of the power and ease of use that Visual Basic brings to your development needs.

Chapter 2
Using Visual Studio

Visual Studio is the development environment designed by Microsoft for creating applications based on the .NET framework. It supports three languages—Visual Basic, of course, as well as the new C# (C sharp) language and the older C++ language. Technically speaking, you don't have to use Visual Studio to create .NET applications; you could use any text editor and run the compilers from the command line (although the .NET framework must be installed, of course). However, in my opinion, no one in their right mind would do this. Visual Studio offers such a wide range of powerful and time-saving tools that I can't imagine anyone wanting to do without them. This chapter shows you how to find your way around the Visual Studio environment and use its tools.

Parts of the Screen

Learning the parts of the Visual Studio screen can be a daunting task. First of all, so many screen components are available that it can be difficult to keep track of them all. Second, the screen is highly customizable as regards to the size and placement of the screen elements and which ones are displayed at a particular time. Finally, the screen will change depending on what you are doing at the moment. This means that no fixed screen appearance or layout can be used as a reference. Your screen is likely to look different from mine even though it has the same screen elements available. However, when you start Visual Studio for the first time, the screen elements are arranged in the default pattern, as shown in Figure 2.1. We can use this default screen to introduce you to some of the more important elements of the Visual Studio screen.

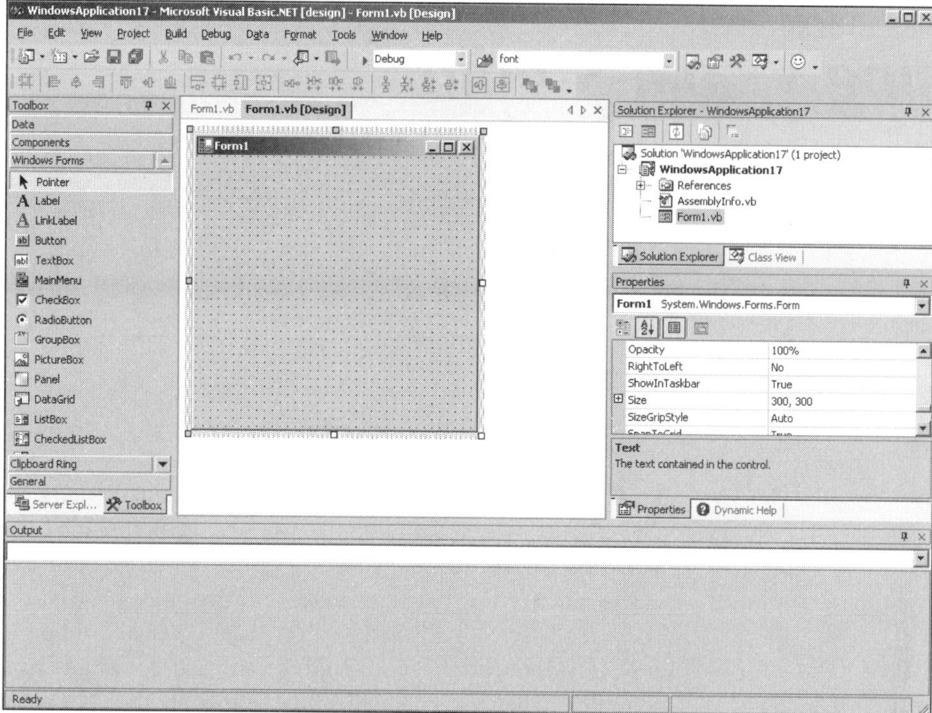

Figure 2.1
The main windows on the Visual Studio screen.

Menu and Toolbars

The menu and toolbars provide access to the various Visual Studio commands that you use while developing a project. They work in the same way as the menu and toolbars in other Windows applications. You can determine the function of a toolbar button by resting the mouse cursor over it for a moment. A ToolTip will then appear that describes the button's function.

Visual Studio automatically hides and displays specialized toolbars as you work to make available the commands you will most likely need. You can rearrange the toolbars to suit your personal preferences, moving them to different screen locations or letting them "float"

Customizing the Screen

Several options for customizing the screen are available from the Visual Studio Start screen. By selecting the My Profile link, you can select one of several options for both the Window layout and the Keyboard scheme. For example, if you are used to working with Visual Basic version 6, you can select that option to have the Visual Studio screen arranged in a manner similar to Visual Basic 6.

Use Those Pop-up Menus

The Visual Studio development environment makes heavy use of pop-up menus (sometimes called context menus). These menus, which appear when you right-click on a screen element, contain the commands that are appropriate for the item you clicked. Every pop-up menu command is also available elsewhere—on the main menus or toolbars, for example—so you never need to use these menus. They can, however, be a great convenience. I will generally not mention specific pop-up menu commands, because you should be able to find them on your own.

---

over the main window. To do this, point at the vertical hatched line at the left end of a toolbar; when the mouse pointer changes to a four-headed arrow, drag the toolbar to its new location.

You can control which toolbars are displayed. Visual Studio provides over two dozen specialized toolbars, each containing commands related to a specific type of task—debugging, for example, or working with XML. To display or hide toolbars, right-click on any toolbar to display a list of all available toolbars. Those that are already displayed have a checkmark next to their name. To display or hide a toolbar, click its name to check or uncheck it.

Editing/Design Window

The editing/design window is where you'll perform most of your development work. This area displays two main types of windows. The first, as shown in Figure 2.1, is a design window where you create the visual interface of your project (as you'll learn in subsequent chapters). The other type is a code editor window in which you edit your project's source code. If more than one window is open, you switch between them by clicking the tabs displayed at the top, or by selecting from the Window menu.

This part of the Visual Studio screen can also display online help information. This will be covered later in the chapter.

Toolbox

The Toolbox displays various items, or components, that you can use in your applications. At least two tabs are always available in the Toolbox: General and Clipboard Ring. Depending on what you are doing, additional tabs will be displayed and hidden automatically. For example, when you are designing a form (as in Figure 2.1), the Windows Forms tab displays the various components you can use on your form, and the Components tab displays other components that are available for use in your project.

To switch between tabs in the Toolbox, click the button at the top or bottom of the Toolbox corresponding to the tab you want to display. When a tab contains more items than can be displayed at once, you can scroll up and down using the arrow buttons in the Toolbox.

Output Window

The output window displays a variety of messages from the Visual Studio environment. These include status messages, error messages when you're building your project, and the output of debugging statements in your code. As you work with Visual Studio, you'll learn to use these messages to keep yourself informed of the status of your project.

Solution Explorer and Class View

The window labeled Solution Explorer in Figure 2.1 actually provides two different windows on separate tabs. These windows offer an organized view of your project. One window, which is the Solution Explorer proper (on the Solution Explorer tab), organizes the project by files, with one entry for each file in your project, including AssemblyInfo.vb, a file that holds information about the assembly (explained later in this chapter). There is also a References entry, which does not correspond to a file but rather to external components that are used by your project without actually being a part of it (more on references later).

In the Solution Explorer, you can manipulate and work with your project files. The buttons displayed at the top of the Solution Explorer window let you view a file in the code editor or, if appropriate for the file type, in the Form Designer. You can also refresh the file list, which is appropriate only for a multiple-author project when some of the files may be viewed by another programmer. You can also click the Show All Files button, which updates the display to show all the project files, including those that you are usually not directly concerned with during development. This includes project files that are automatically managed by Visual Studio as well as the project's output files.

The second view available is the Class View tab, which organizes your project by classes. This view might look superficially like the file view in the Solution Explorer, particularly if your project is organized with a single class definition in each file. If, however, you have multiple classes per file, you'll see each class with its own entry in this view.

In Class View, the project information is arranged in a tree-like structure, as shown in Figure 2.2. Click the + sign next to an item to expand a branch of the tree; click the - sign to collapse a branch. For example, under each class you can display, as shown in the figure, the class constructor (the **New()** procedure), the **InitializeComponent()** method, contained components, and more.

In Class View, you can change how the class listing is sorted by using the button on the toolbar. In addition, you can right-click any item in the list to display a pop-up menu of actions that you can take with that item, such as viewing its definition.

The way things are organized in the Solution Explorer and Class View can sometimes be confusing to new users. It should become clearer after you learn about the various parts that make up a VB .NET project, as I'll explain later in this chapter.

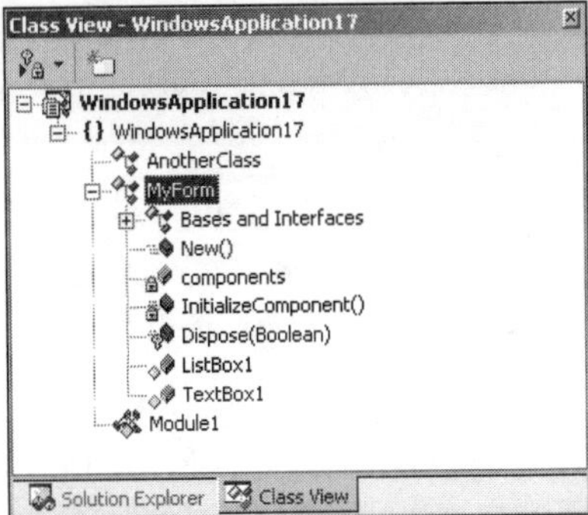

Figure 2.2
In Class View, the Solution Explorer organizes your project by class.

Properties Window

The Properties window displays the properties of the currently selected object in Visual Studio. This object may be a component in the Form Designer, in which case the Properties window automatically displays the properties of the selected object. It can also be a file in the Solution Explorer, in which case you must right-click the file name and select Properties from the pop-up menu. In any case, the drop-down list at the top of the Properties window displays the name of the object whose properties are displayed, and in some cases, it also lets you select a different object. Within the main list, the left column displays the property name and the right column displays its setting.

The Properties window toolbar contains two buttons that control how the properties are listed. Click the Categorized button to list properties organized by category—for example, appearance properties are listed together in one group and behavior properties in another. Click the Alphabetic button to list all properties alphabetically by name.

The Properties window offers an optional description pane, which can be displayed beneath the list of properties (as shown in Figure 2.1). This pane displays a brief description of the currently highlighted property. You can hide and display this pane as desired by right-clicking in the Properties window's toolbar and selecting Description from the pop-up menu.

To change a property setting, select the property in the property list. If the property has a + sign to the left of its name, it is a compound property. Click the + sign to display the property's component parts. Then, how you set a property depends on the type of property:

- If the property value displays a button with an ellipsis (...), it means you set the property in a dialog box. Click the button to open the dialog box. Make the desired changes in the dialog box and then close it.
- If the property value displays a button with a downward-pointing arrow, it means you select the property value from a list of permitted values. Click the button to display the list and make the desired selection.

- If the property value displays no button—just text or a number—it means you can enter your own property value. Click the value, edit the text as desired, and then click outside the value to save your setting.

Some properties are Boolean, which means that they can have the value **True** or **False**. You can quickly toggle these properties, from **True** to **False** or from **False** to **True**, by double-clicking the property name. Note that the Properties window uses a boldface font to display the values of those properties that have been changed from their default values.

The toolbar in the Properties window has a Property Pages button (this is the rightmost button). It is available only when the current object has property pages, which are special dialog boxes used to set properties that cannot be set in the Properties window. You'll see property pages in action in some of the book's sample programs.

Projects, Solutions, and Assemblies

To work efficiently in Visual Studio, you need to understand three of its core concepts: projects, solutions, and assemblies. Let's look at projects and solutions first because they are related.

Projects

A *project* is a container that lets you organize and work with all the various items that go into creating a single application. The output of a project might be an executable file (EXE), a dynamic link library (DLL), or an ASP.NET Web page (ASPX), among others, but the important concept is that one project corresponds to one application. Project definitions are stored in files with the .vbproj extension.

A project can be very simple, consisting of a single source code file plus a few support files that are created by Visual Studio. A project can also be extremely complex, containing multiple source code files, references to libraries, database connections, and disk folders. The items contained in a project fall into two general categories. Some represent specific files and folders that are located on your hard disk. Others represent links, or references, to items that are used by your project but that are not actually part of your project. For example, look at the project components displayed in the Solution Explorer shown in Figure 2.3. You can see three main entries there:

- *References*—This section contains links, or references, to five items: **System**, **System.Data**, **System.Drawing**, **System.Windows.Forms**, and **System.XML**. These items are used by your project without actually being part of it (they are part of VB .NET). Some references are added automatically by Visual Studio, others you add manually (as you'll learn soon).

- *AssemblyInfo.vb*—This file contains information about the project assembly. I'll explain more about assemblies later in this chapter.

- *Form1.vb*—This is the project's source code file.

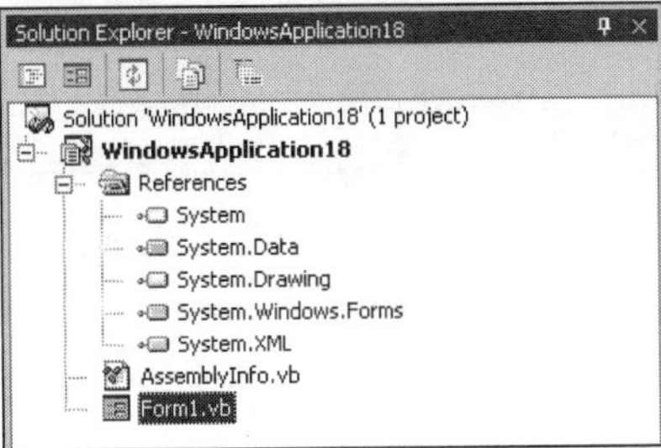

Figure 2.3
A project's items include both references and files.

VB .NET supports several different types of projects. You were introduced to these project types in Chapter 1, and you'll learn more about them throughout the remainder of this book. When you start a new project, you choose a project template that corresponds to the type of application you want to create. A new project contains the file types and configuration settings that are appropriate for that type of project. This information is kept in a project definition file. As you work with a project, you might need to add items, such as forms, modules, and classes. You add items using the commands on the Project menu. As you work through this book, you'll learn what the various items are and when you would need to add them to a project.

Solutions

A *solution* is similar to a project in that it serves as a container, however, it has a larger scope than a project. Although a solution can contain one or more projects, the reverse is not true. Every project you create in VB .NET is contained in a solution, and very often, particularly as you are learning to program, each of your solutions will contain only a single project. As the complexity of your development work advances, you'll probably find yourself working with multiproject solutions.

What is the point of being able to group two or more projects in a solution? After all, a project corresponds to a final application—isn't that what matters? Sometimes this is true; a single application is all you need, and you'll be working with a solution that contains only one project. At other times, however, your development goals require multiple applications. For example, a complex Web-based application might require you to create a Web application, a Web control library, and a Web service. You need three distinct applications, or projects. The ability to manage all three projects together inside a solution provides significant convenience for the programmer.

You can start a new solution in two ways. One method is to create a new project, which automatically creates a solution to contain the project. The other method is to select File | New | Blank Solution to create an empty solution. To add a project to the current solution, select File | Add Project and then select either New Project or Existing Project.

Solutions are stored in files with the .sln extension. These files do not actually contain the entire solution, of course, but they hold information about the projects and other files that the solution contains.

In addition to projects, a solution can contain two other types of items that are not associated with a particular project:

- *Solution items*—Files, references, and other items that are associated with the solution. They may be referenced by projects, but are not included in the final build. Examples of solution items include bitmap images, XML schemas, and HTML pages. Solution items are organized in the Solution Items folder in the Solution Explorer.
- *Miscellaneous items*—Files that are not part of the solution but that you want to view and work with at the same time you are working on the solution. Examples could be a note from your client outlining application specifications or a text file in which you keep reminders to yourself. Miscellaneous items are organized in the Miscellaneous Files folder in the Solution Explorer.

Figure 2.4 shows the Solution Explorer displaying a solution that contains some solution items and miscellaneous files.

To add a solution item, highlight the solution name in the Solution Explorer. Then follow these steps:

- To add a new item, select Add New Item from the Project menu, and then select the type of item to add. A new, blank item of the specified type is added to the solution.
- To add an existing item, select Add Existing Item from the Project menu, and then browse to locate the desired item.

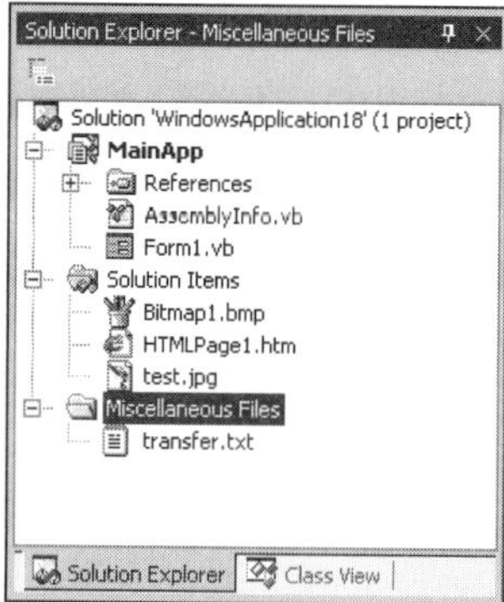

Figure 2.4
A solution can contain solution items and miscellaneous files that are not part of any project.

The display of miscellaneous files in the Solution Explorer is controlled by Visual Studio option settings. You can specify whether the Miscellaneous Files folder is displayed and how many files, if any, are "remembered" between sessions. Here are the steps to follow:

1. Select Options from the Tools menu to display the Options dialog box.
2. In the left pane, select Documents under the Environment category (see Figure 2.5).
3. Select or deselect the Show Miscellaneous Files In Solution Explorer option, as desired.
4. Enter the number of files to be "remembered" in the Miscellaneous Files Project Saves Last *XXX* Items box.
5. Click OK.

To add a miscellaneous file, select File | Open | File. Navigate to the desired file and open it. If it is a file type that Visual Studio supports, such as text or bitmap, it will be opened in Visual Studio for viewing and modification. If it is a nonsupported file type, such as a Microsoft Word document, it will be opened in its native application.

Assemblies

An *assembly* comprises the fundamental unit of deployment for VB .NET applications. An assembly can consist of one file or multiple files, but in either case the important consideration is that an assembly is self-contained and self-describing. In addition to being crucial for application deployment, assemblies play important roles in security considerations, versioning, and scope boundaries.

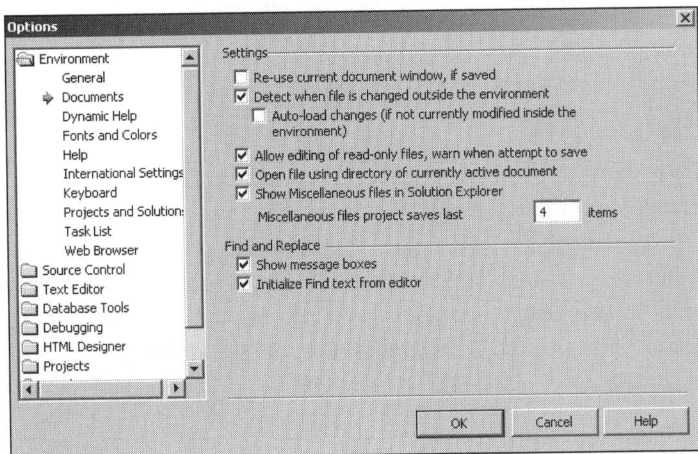

Figure 2.5
Setting options for the display of miscellaneous files.

Each assembly contains a *manifest*. The manifest provides information, or metadata, about the assembly, including the following:

- The assembly name and version number
- The types exposed by the assembly (that is, its classes and their members)
- The names and version numbers of other assemblies that this one depends on (if any)
- Security information

Each assembly also contains one or more modules. Each module contains compiled code as well as metadata about the module contents. An assembly can also contain resources, such as bitmaps.

In many situations, particularly for the beginning-level programmer, Visual Studio performs all the assembly management that is needed. For example, when you build a Windows application like the one that was presented in Chapter 1, the output of the build process is an assembly contained in an EXE file. Complex projects and unusual deployment situations might call for customized assemblies, and Visual Studio provides the tools needed for these tasks, but these advanced topics are beyond the scope of this book.

Visual Studio Options

Visual Studio provides a large number of configuration options that control the appearance and behavior of the development environment. There are way too many options to cover them all in this book, and in any case many of the options are related to advanced aspects of the Visual Studio environment that you need not be concerned with at present. In this section, I will offer an overview of the options, describe how you change them, and provide specific details on a few that you need to know about.

The Options Dialog Box

You set all Visual Studio options in the Options dialog box, which you access by selecting Options from the Tools menu. Figure 2.6 shows this dialog box, and as you can see, a lot is crowded into this single box! In the left-hand pane is a list of option categories: Environment, Source Control, and so on. Under each category is a list of subcategories (shown for the Environment category in the figure). The current subcategory has an arrow displayed next to its name (General in Figure 2.6). The remainder of the dialog box displays the options for the selected subcategory.

The Options dialog box has three buttons:

- *OK*—Saves any changes you have made and closes the dialog box.
- *Cancel*—Undoes any changes you have made and closes the dialog box. Options revert to the settings that were in effect when you opened the dialog box.
- *Help*—Displays help information about the currently displayed options.

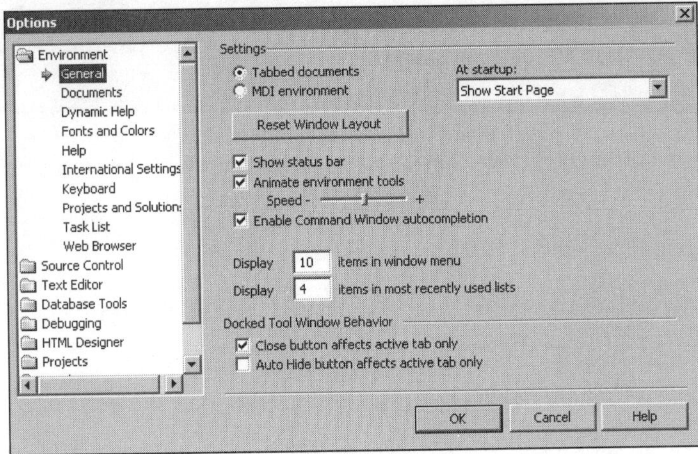

Figure 2.6
You use the Options dialog box to set all Visual Studio options.

Startup Options

One option you should know about is located in the Environment, General category. This option specifies what you first see when Visual Studio starts. The available settings appear in the At Startup drop-down list. Your choices include the following:

- *Show Start Page*—Displays the Visual Studio Start Page from which you can select to open a recent solution, create a new project, or browse to any one of several Web sites that may be of interest to VB .NET developers.
- *Load Last Loaded Solution*—Visual Studio automatically loads and displays the solution you were working on most recently.
- *Show Open Project Dialog Box*—Visual Studio displays the Open Project dialog box, which you can use to locate and open an existing project.
- *Show New Project Dialog Box*—Visual Studio displays the New Project dialog box, which you can use to create a new project.
- *Show Empty Environment*—Visual Studio opens with no solution loaded.

Another useful tool in the Environment, General category is the Reset Window Layout button. Given the high degree to which you can customize the Visual Studio windows, you might at times want to reset them to the original sizes and positions—the defaults that were in effect when Visual Studio was first installed. That's what this button does.

Project and Solution Options

The Environment, Projects and Solutions category includes a couple of options you might want to change. The Project Location setting determines the default location where project and solution files are stored. The Build and Run options affect the saving of files when you build or run your project. You can specify that all files are saved automatically, that the user is prompted to save files, or that files are not saved.

Text Editor Options

The Text Editor category contains options that control the operation of the editor you use for your source code and other text files. There are several subcategories:

- *General*—Options that affect editing of all text files regardless of type.
- *All Languages*—Options that affect the editing of source code files, regardless of language, but do not affect editing of non-source code text files.
- *Basic, C#, etc.*—Options that are in effect only for the specific type of source code file.

Some of the options you can set for editing Basic source code are described in Table 2.1.

Other options control indenting and the use of tabs in your source code. You'll find these options in the Text Editor, Basic, Tabs category. For Indenting, you have these options:

- *None*—There is no automatic indenting. You must use the Tab key or the spacebar to indent lines of code.
- *Block*—When you press Enter, the new line of code is indented to the same level as the previous line.
- *Smart*—When you press Enter, the new line is indented according to the logical structure of the Basic language. Thus, code within logical blocks, such as **For...Next** loops, is indented with respect to the loop statements.

Visual Basic-Specific Options

Three options specific to the Visual Basic language are located in the Text Editor, Basic, VB Specific category. They are described in Table 2.2.

Table 2.1 Options for editing source code.

Option	Description
Auto List Members	When you are editing code, the editor displays lists of items, such as class members, for you to select from as appropriate.
Hide Advanced Members	The auto-lists display only members that are normally used in source code and hides the other members.
Parameter Information	When you're entering a call to a procedure, this option displays information about the procedure's parameters (if the information is available).
Enable Virtual Space	Lets you move the editing cursor into the "virtual" space that follows the end of a line of text. Otherwise, the cursor moves to the start of the next line.
Word Wrap	Lines of code that would extend past the right edge of the editor window are wrapped to the next line.

Table 2.2 Visual Basic-specific editor options.

Option	Description
Automatic Insertion Of End Constructs	Some VB statements always come in two parts, a beginning part and an end part. When this option is enabled and you type the beginning part of such a statement, the editor automatically inserts the ending part.
Pretty Listing (Reformatting) Of Code	When this option is enabled, the editor automatically aligns your code at the proper indention levels according to the formatting standards for the Visual Basic language.
Enter Outlining Mode On File Open	When this option is enabled, the text editor automatically enters outlining mode when you open a file. Outlining mode is explained later in this chapter.

Creating and Opening Projects

Visual Studio provides a variety of ways for you to create a new project or solution or open an existing project or solution. To some extent, the method you use depends on the Visual Studio option that controls what is displayed when Visual Studio starts, as explained in the section "Startup Options" earlier in this chapter. Assuming that you are not using one of those startup screens, you can use the commands described here.

To open an existing project or a solution while closing any project or solution that is currently open in Visual Studio, select File | Open | Project. Browse to locate the project or solution file that you want to open. Note that opening a project has the same effect as opening the solution that the project is a part of.

To add an existing project to the current solution, select File | Add Project | Existing Project. Browse to locate the project file that you want to add.

To add a new project to the current solution, select File | Add Project | New Project. In the Add New Project dialog box, select the project type, assign it a name, and click OK.

Editing Code

The Visual Studio text editor that you use to edit your Visual Basic source code works, in many respects, like any other text editor, so I won't go into much detail on its basic functions. The editor inserts any text you type at the location of the blinking cursor, and you can move this cursor using the keyboard movement keys or the mouse. Insert mode allows you to move existing code over to make room for new code on the same line; in overwrite mode, new code overwrites existing code. In insert mode, the cursor displays as a blinking vertical line between letters; in overwrite mode, it displays as a blinking box. To toggle between these modes, press the Insert key.

You can also select text using the standard techniques: dragging over it with the mouse, or by holding down the Shift key while pressing the cursor movement keys. Text can be cut or copied to the Clipboard and then pasted at a new location.

Outline Mode

The Visual Studio editor has a feature that lets you define sections of code and then hide or display them as desired. Code that is hidden is said to be collapsed, and displays as an ellipsis (...) adjacent to a + sign. Click the + sign to expand the collapsed code; the + sign then changes to a - sign, which you click to collapse the code again. These sections can be nested, with one outline section containing several additional outline sections.

To define an outline section and collapse it, first select the text and then choose Edit | Outlining | Hide Selection. Other commands on this menu include the following:

- *Toggle Outlining Expansion*—Toggles the current outline section (the one the cursor is in) between collapsed and expanded.
- *Toggle All Outlining*—Toggles all outline sections. If some sections are currently collapsed, they all become expanded. If some are collapsed and some are expanded, all become collapsed.
- *Stop Outlining*—Removes all outlining information from the current document and expands all sections.
- *Stop Hiding Content*—Removes all outlining information from the currently selected text.
- *Start Automatic Outlining*—Outline sections are created automatically based on the structure of the language of your source code. Use the Stop Outlining command to turn off automatic outlining.
- *Collapse To Definitions*—This command is available only if you are editing a source code document (as opposed to a plain text file). It creates outlining regions based on the structure of your code, collapses the regions, and displays them with a descriptive label. For example, in a Visual Basic source code file, each procedure is collapsed and displayed with just its name showing, as illustrated in Figure 2.7.

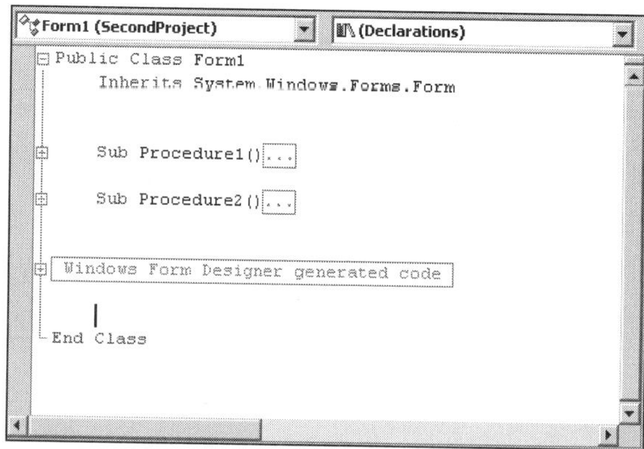

Figure 2.7
The Collapse To Definitions command collapses all procedures and displays only their names.

You can obtain capabilities similar to outlining by using Visual Basic's **#Region** directive to enclose code. Some of the code that is automatically generated by the Visual Studio environment is set off in this way. The syntax is as follows:

```
#Region identifier

' Code goes here.

#End Region
```

A region can be expanded or contracted by clicking the + or - sign next to the identifier.

Using the Clipboard Ring

The standard Windows Clipboard can hold a single item, be it text, graphics, or something else. Whenever you cut or copy something, the new item replaces whatever was on the Clipboard previously. Visual Studio expands the utility of the Windows Clipboard by providing a tool called the *Clipboard Ring*. The Clipboard Ring, which is on one of the tabs in the Toolbox window, holds the last 12 text items that have been cut or copied. Figure 2.8 shows the Clipboard Ring, in this case containing three items.

To retrieve items from the Clipboard Ring and paste them into your text documents, you can use either of the following techniques:

- Drag an item from the Clipboard Ring to the desired location in your document.
- Press Ctrl+Shift+V repeatedly. Each press pastes the next item from the Clipboard Ring into your document, replacing the previously pasted one. When the desired item has been pasted, press Ctrl+V.

After the Clipboard Ring is full, old items are deleted as new ones are added. To delete a specific item from the Clipboard Ring, right-click it and select Delete from the pop-up menu.

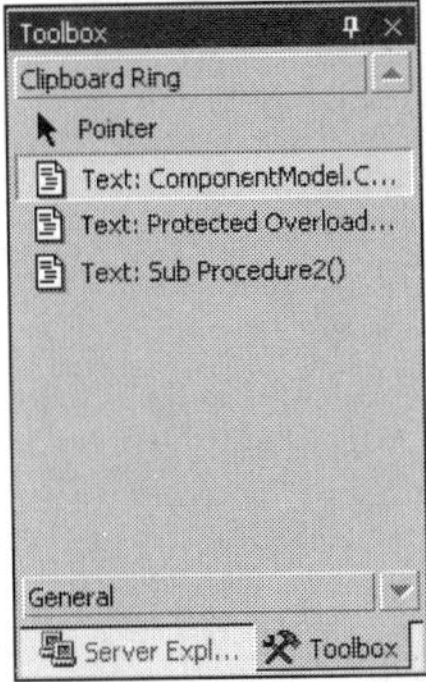

Figure 2.8
The Clipboard Ring can hold the last 12 text items that were cut or copied.

Locating Errors as You Work

The Visual Studio compiler checks your code for errors when you build your project, as you'll learn later in this chapter. As you are working, however, the compiler can work in the background, looking for and marking errors even before the project is built. When questionable code is found, it is underlined with a wavy blue line. If you rest the mouse pointer over such code, a pop-up window will appear with a brief description of the error. You can use this feature to catch and respond to errors as you are working, or you can ignore it and deal with errors when they are caught at build time.

Building and Running Projects

The process of building a project refers to the compilation of your source code, converting it into the executable code that is required for the application to be run. To build your project, select Build Solution from the Build menu, or press Ctrl+Shift+B. During the build process, Visual Studio closely examines your code and detects and flags various kinds of errors that exist. If your code is error-free, the Visual Studio output window will display the result with a message something like this:

```
Build: 1 succeeded, 0 failed, 0 skipped
```

Errors that can occur include misspelled member names, incorrect procedure parameters, references to undeclared variables, and so on (you'll learn all about errors in Chapter 5).. There are many ways in which your code can be in error, but fortunately the Visual Studio environment makes it fairly easy to detect and fix errors. When one or more errors are detected, the message in the output window indicates that the build has failed. Then, the Task List displays a list of errors. This list has three columns:

- The left column displays a description of the error.
- The middle column displays the path and name of the file where the error is located.
- The right column displays the line number where the error is located.

If you double-click an error entry in the Task List, you are taken directly to the location of the error so you can fix it. After you think you have fixed the error(s), build the project again. By repeating this process, you can locate, fix, and verify any and all errors in your code.

Building your project is a process that you will repeat many times as you develop your application. Most of the time you will do what is called a *debug* build, by selecting the Solution Configuration option displayed on the toolbar. When your project is complete and fully debugged and tested and you are ready to create the final build for distribution, you will change this option to Release to instruct the compiler to perform a release build. Compared with a debug build, a release build takes longer to perform, but the resulting executable code is smaller and runs faster.

To run your project, select Start from the Debug menu. Visual Studio builds your project, if necessary (that is, if it has been modified since the last build) and, if no build errors occur, executes the application. Executing an application from within the Visual Studio environment is the same in many ways as executing it as a standalone. The main difference is that you have Visual Studio's debugging tools at your disposal to help you locate bugs in your program. Debugging will be covered in Chapter 25.

Working with Windows

You might be content to use the default window layout provided by Visual Studio, but if not, there are several ways to customize the screen. You should feel free to experiment because you can always return to the default arrangement by selecting Tools | Options, then under the Environment, General category, clicking the Reset Window Layout button.

By default, the various windows on the screen are *docked*, which means that windows do not overlap but adjust to each other's sizes and positions to fill the main Visual Studio window. To change the relative sizes of windows, point at the border between them; the mouse pointer will change to two parallel lines with arrows pointing up and down (for a horizontal border) or left and right (for a vertical border). Then, drag the border to the desired position and release the mouse button.

To hide a window, click the X in its upper right-hand corner, or right-click the window's title bar and select Hide from the pop-up menu. To display a hidden window, select the appropriate command from the View menu.

Visual Studio windows have an auto-hide feature, which causes the window to hide itself and display as a rectangular icon when it is not in use. To display the window again, move the mouse pointer over the window's icon. To turn the auto-hide feature on or off, right-click the window's title bar and select Auto Hide from the pop-up menu, or click the thumbtack icon on the title bar.

Windows can be made to float, displaying "on top" of other screen elements. To float a window, right-click its title bar and select Floating. A window that is floating can be moved around the screen by dragging its title bar and can be resized by dragging its border. To change a floating window back to a dockable window, select Dockable from the title bar menu and then drag the window to the desired docking position.

Getting Help

One of the best features of the Visual Studio environment, at least in my opinion, is the extensive online help that is available. This information covers Visual Basic and the other Visual Studio languages, the .NET framework, Visual Studio itself, and a host of related topics. When you access help information, it displays on a tab that shares space with the main designer/text editor window. The help information is designed like a set of Web pages, with links between related topics that make it easy to locate related information. As you move from topic to topic, you can use the Back and Forward buttons on the toolbar to navigate among topics you have viewed previously. Help information can be accessed in five different ways, which we'll look at in the following sections.

Dynamic Help

The Dynamic Help system keeps track of what you are doing and automatically displays a list of relevant help topics. The default location for Dynamic Help is on a tab that shares space with the Properties window. As you work, the contents of this window change to display links to help information that is related to what you are doing. Click a link to display the help topic. If the Dynamic Help window is not displayed, you can display it by selecting Dynamic Help from the Help menu.

Contents

The Table of Contents for the help system provides a hierarchical entry point to the help information. The Contents topics are organized in a tree structure, with branches that you can expand or collapse by clicking the + and - signs that are shown (see Figure 2.9). The information displayed in Contents can be filtered using the list box that is displayed at the top of the Contents window. By selecting the Visual Basic And Related filter, for example, you can avoid having to sift through information that is relevant only to the C# and C++ languages. If you cannot find the information you think should be available, check your filter setting to be sure it is set appropriately.

Index

The index, shown in Figure 2.10, provides an alphabetical listing of all help topics, in much the same way as a back-of-book index. Start typing the word or phrase of interest in the Look For box and the index automatically scrolls to the matching topics. Select a topic

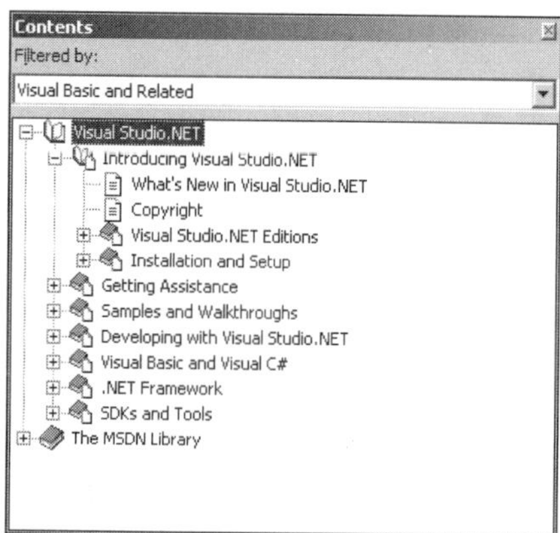

Figure 2.9
Help Contents provides a tree-structured listing of help topics.

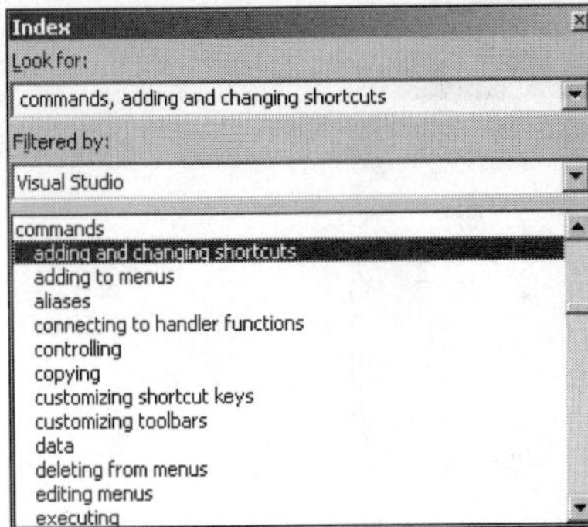

Figure 2.10
The help index provides an alphabetical listing of all help topics.

from the list to display the corresponding information. If more than one help topic exists for the selected index entry, the topic titles will be displayed in the Index Results window. Double-click the desired topic to display its information. Like with Contents, you can filter the index by subject area.

Search

The Search capability lets you search all the help information for specific information. In the Search window (shown in Figure 2.11), you enter the search term in the Look For window, select filtering and other search options, and then click the Search button. The results of the search appear in the Search Results window (see Figure 2.12). Each "hit" displays its title, the general topic area it belongs to, and a numerical ranking that indicates how good a match there was (with a rank of 1 being the best match). Double-click a topic in this list to display its information.

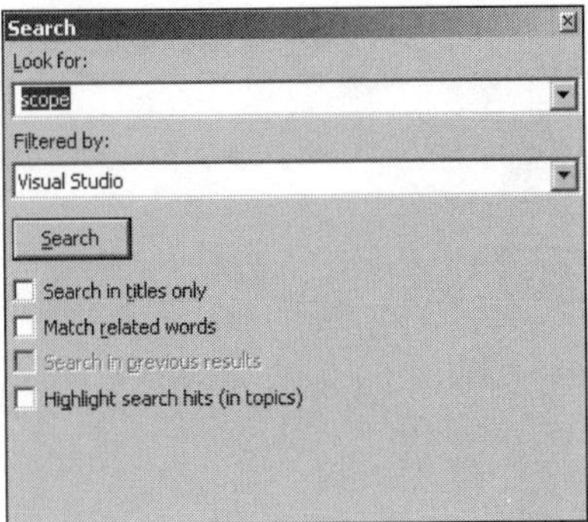

Figure 2.11
Use the Search window to search online help for specific subjects.

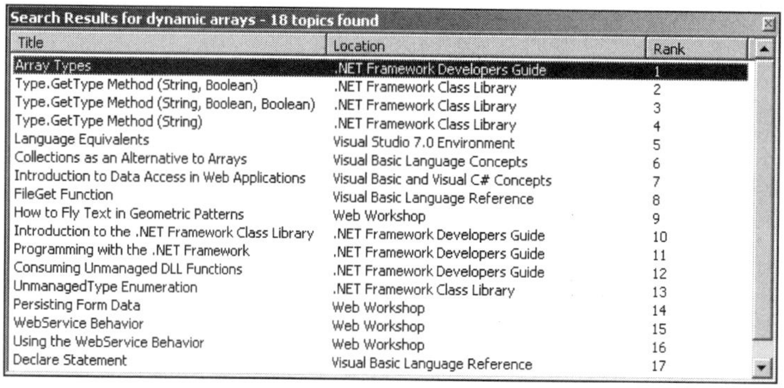

Title	Location	Rank
Array Types	.NET Framework Developers Guide	1
Type.GetType Method (String, Boolean)	.NET Framework Class Library	2
Type.GetType Method (String, Boolean, Boolean)	.NET Framework Class Library	3
Type.GetType Method (String)	.NET Framework Class Library	4
Language Equivalents	Visual Studio 7.0 Environment	5
Collections as an Alternative to Arrays	Visual Basic Language Concepts	6
Introduction to Data Access in Web Applications	Visual Basic and Visual C# Concepts	7
FileGet Function	Visual Basic Language Reference	8
How to Fly Text in Geometric Patterns	Web Workshop	9
Introduction to the .NET Framework Class Library	.NET Framework Developers Guide	10
Programming with the .NET Framework	.NET Framework Developers Guide	11
Consuming Unmanaged DLL Functions	.NET Framework Developers Guide	12
UnmanagedType Enumeration	.NET Framework Class Library	13
Persisting Form Data	Web Workshop	14
WebService Behavior	Web Workshop	15
Using the WebService Behavior	Web Workshop	16
Declare Statement	Visual Basic Language Reference	17

Figure 2.12
The results of a search are displayed in the Search Results window, ranked by relevance.

Context-Sensitive Help

At almost any time when you are working in Visual Studio, pressing F1 activates context-sensitive help, displaying information that is related to what you are doing. For example, if you are working in the Form Designer and a control is selected, pressing F1 brings up help information on that control class. Likewise, if you are editing code and the cursor is on a VB language keyword, F1 brings up information on that language element.

Summary

The Visual Studio development environment provides the programmer with a huge array of tools. Every aspect of developing your application can be done from within Visual Studio. In this chapter, I have covered the most important tools, those that every programmer will almost surely need. There's a lot more to Visual Studio, however, and only you can determine whether these additional features will be useful to you. By exploring Visual Studio and using the online help information that explains how to use Visual Studio, you can tap into the full capabilities of the development environment.

Chapter 3

Visual Basic Syntax: Fundamentals and Data Storage

Someday, you might be able to create a complete applications program by doing nothing more than combining a few software components, but that day has yet to arrive. By now, I hope you are convinced of the power and flexibility of the classes that are available to the Visual Basic programmer. Despite all this power, Visual Basic still requires some glue to stick the components together into a functioning program. That glue is Basic code.

What exactly is Basic? The name is an acronym for Beginner's All-Purpose Symbolic Instruction Code, a language that was originally developed for instructional purposes many moons ago at Dartmouth College. Although the original Basic may have been ideal as a teaching aid, for many years it had a reputation among programmers for being slow and inflexible. The reason for this negative connotation was that Basic *was* slow and inflexible. "Greasy kid stuff," snorted the serious programmers as they went off to struggle with C or FORTRAN.

Over the years, however, Basic gradually improved. With Microsoft QuickBasic leading the way, followed by early versions of Visual Basic, the language evolved from being suited only for students and hobbyists to a powerful tool that was up to the task of creating full-fledged business and scientific applications.

With the current version of Visual Basic, however, the Basic language has undergone a major transformation. The foundation of Microsoft's development tools is the .NET framework, and it was unavoidable that the language had to evolve to meet the requirements of .NET. If you are just getting started with Basic, this will not matter to you, but anyone who has previous experience with

QuickBasic or a previous version of Visual Basic will notice quite a few changes. If you are interested, these differences are detailed in Appendix A.

I won't be covering the complete Basic language here. That could be—and, in fact, has been—the subject of complete books. Instead, I'll cover what I feel are the real basics (no pun intended) of the language: the tools you will need to get started working with Visual Basic. In this chapter, you will learn about syntax fundamentals and the techniques that Visual Basic provides for storage of data. The next chapter explains how to use program control statements and how to write your own procedures. Then, as more advanced language topics arise during the remainder of this book, I'll provide you with more detailed information.

Syntax Fundamentals

Visual Basic code consists of statements, or instructions, that tell the operating system and computer hardware to carry out the tasks of your program. In your source code, statements are written one per line. By default, statements are executed in order, one at a time, from the top down. As you'll see, however, this top-down order is rarely followed for more than short sections of code because Visual Basic has many statements that modify the order of execution. The following are some fundamental rules regarding Visual Basic source code:

- No special character is used to mark the end of a line. To start a new line, simply press Enter.
- Blank lines and indentation are ignored.
- Capitalization does not matter. You'll see, however, that the Visual Studio editor enforces certain capitalization guidelines.

You need to be aware of one possible exception to the rule that Visual Basic statements are each on their own line. By separating statements with a colon (:), you can place two or more statements on the same line. I suggest that you avoid this practice because it makes your code harder to read. You should know about it, however, in case you see it used in code written by someone else.

Comments

A comment is a section of your Visual Basic code that is ignored by the compiler. Programmers use comments to document the operation of the code, to leave reminders for themselves, and to perform similar tasks. Visual Basic has two styles of comments:

- Any line that starts with the keyword **Rem** is a comment.
- Any text that follows a single quote character is a comment.

Here are some examples:

```
' This is a comment.
Rem This is a comment too.
x = 5 ' This is also a comment.
```

The only place where **Rem** or a single quote do not mark a comment is inside quoted text (text that is inside double quotation marks).

Visual Basic Code Line Wrapping

Some lines of Visual Basic code can be rather long. Although the Visual Basic editor is able to handle long lines, it can be a nuisance to have your lines of code running off the right edge of the editor window where you can't see them without scrolling. You can avoid this problem by using the line continuation character to break a long line of code into two or more lines. All you need to do is type a space followed by an underscore, then press Enter. All code on the new line will be treated by Visual Basic as part of the first line. The only restriction is that you cannot place the line continuation character in a literal string within double quotation marks. It is a good idea, although not required, to indent continued lines with respect to the first part of the line to make it clear that they are not themselves new lines.

Data Storage

Almost every program works with data, or information, of one kind or another. Whether the data is a chunk of text to be edited, a graphic image, or a table of numbers, the program needs a place to keep the data while the program is executing. I'm not talking about persistent storage of information in disk files, although that's an important topic in its own right.

During execution, a program stores its data in *variables* and, to a lesser degree, *constants*. A variable derives its name from the fact that the information it holds can change, or vary, during program execution. In contrast, the information stored in a constant does not change. Visual Basic offers a wide range of variable types and constants to suit all your programming needs.

Variables

A variable is a named location where you can store data. Variables are stored in RAM (random access memory) while the program is running. A variable has a name that is used to refer to the variable in code. A variable also has a type, which is related to the kind of data stored in the variable.

Variable Types

All variables have a type, which you declare when the variable is declared. Visual Basic offers several different variable types, each designed to hold a specific type of data. Table 3.1 summarizes these data types. Note that each Visual Basic data type has a corresponding .NET data type. The Visual Basic data type names and the .NET data type names are nothing more than synonyms for each other.

Many of Visual Basic's data types are used to store numeric values. Different types of numeric variables are available to match the different kinds of values that a program might need to store. The primary distinction is between integer types, which cannot have a fractional part, and floating point types, which can. Within the integer types exist unsigned types (**Byte** and **Char**) that can hold only positive values (and 0), and the signed types (**Short**, **Integer**, **Long**) that can hold positive or negative values. Among the floating point data types, the differences are mainly in the largest and smallest values that can be stored.

Why not have just a single data type for all numbers? The reason is that memory requirements and processing time varies for different data types. Numbers of type **Short**, for example,

Table 3.1 Visual Basic's data types.

Visual Basic Data Type	.NET Data Type	Storage Space in Bytes	Values
Boolean	**System.Boolean**	4	True or False.
Byte	**System.Byte**	1	Integers 0 to 255.
Char	**System.Char**	2	Integers 0 to 65535.
Date	**System.DateTime**	8	Date/time values between January 1, 0001 and December 31, 9999.
Decimal	**System.Decimal**	12	Floating point values with 29 digits, with anywhere from 0 to 28 of the digits to the right of the decimal point. Range is approximately +/- 7.9E28.
Double	**System.Double**	8	Floating point values approximately -1.7E308 to -4.9E-324 for negative values, 4.9E-324 to 1.7E308 for positive values.
Integer	**System.Int32**	4	Integers -2,147,483,648 to 2,147,483,647.
Long	**System.Int64**	8	Integers approximately -9E18 to 9E18.
Object	**System.Object**	4	Object references or any other data type.
Short	**System.Int16**	2	Integers -32,768 to 32,767.
Single	**System.Single**	4	Approximately -3.4E38 to -1.4E-45 for negative values, 1.4E-45 to 3.4E38 for positive values.
String	**System.String**	Twice the number of characters plus 10.	Any text from 0 to approximately 2 billion characters in length.

Exponential Notation

Exponential notation is commonly used to represent very large and very small values. The format is xEy, meaning x times 10 to the y power. For example, the value 2134 would be written 2.134E3, and the value 0.00055 would be written 5.5E–4. The Visual Basic compiler understands exponential notation as well, so you can use it in your code.

can be manipulated faster and take up less memory than numbers of type **Double**. By carefully matching data types to the requirements of your program, you maximize efficiency and minimize memory use. For small amounts of data, this difference is negligible, but it can become significant for large data sets.

Variable Names

Every variable must have a name that is unique within its scope (variable scope will be covered later in this chapter). Visual Basic variable naming rules are as follows:

- The maximum length is 255 characters.
- The first character must be a letter.
- Subsequent characters can be letters, the digits 0 through 9, or the underscore character.
- Names are not case-sensitive.
- VB .NET keywords cannot be used.

When selecting names for your variables, I strongly recommend that you use descriptive names. This means simply that the name of a variable should describe the data it holds. For example, if your program deals with the population genetics of bats and you need a variable to hold the number of bats, you should use a name such as **Bat_Count** or **NumberOfBats**. You could legally name the variable **XY**, **J89**, or **BillClinton**, and Visual Basic wouldn't care. But when working on the program later, you'll find that descriptive variable names make a big difference in the readability of your code. It's a good habit to cultivate right from the get-go.

Some programmers believe that descriptive variable naming should be taken a step further so that the name of each variable identifies not only its contents, but also its data type. This is typically done with a type of prefix called Hungarian notation. Using this prefix, the name of an integer variable might be preceded with an i for integer. For your bat count, therefore, you would have a variable named **iNumberOfBats**. The idea behind Hungarian notation is the ability to discern the variable type immediately whenever you see a variable name in code.

In my opinion, the inconvenience of using Hungarian notation in Visual Basic outweighs its benefit. The Visual Studio code editor has a feature that makes it a cinch to determine the type of any variable. Simply rest the mouse pointer on the variable name, and a small window pops up showing the variable type. With such easy access to variable types, why bother with the awkward and inconvenient variable names created by Hungarian notation? It's your choice, however, so you should use the technique that suits your style.

Declaring Variables

Every variable must be declared in your program before it can be used. Declaring a variable sets aside storage space for it, specifies the data type of the variable, and optionally assigns an initial value to the variable. To declare a variable, you use the **Dim** statement. The syntax is as follows:

```
Dim name As type
```

Here's a specific example:

```
Dim X As Integer
```

The variable name is listed, followed by the **As** keyword and the type name. You can have one or more variables in a single **Dim** statement, as shown in these two examples:

```
Dim X As Integer, Y As Single, Z As Date
Dim A, B, C As String
```

In the second example, all three variables are assigned type **String**. You can have as many **Dim** statements as you need, each on its own line. Note that the type specification is optional. If the type specification is omitted, the variable defaults to type **Object**.

Where do you place your variable declaration statements? This question has no single answer. In general, variable declarations go either at the beginning of a module or at the beginning of a procedure, depending on the desired scope of the variable. You'll learn more when I cover the topic of variable scope later in this chapter. I am postponing my discussion of scope because you need to know some other aspects of Visual Basic syntax before you can fully understand scope.

Type Declaration Characters

VB .NET supports a holdover from earlier versions of Visual Basic that permits the type of a variable to be specified by a *type declaration character* at the end of the variable name. Thus, the declaration

```
Dim Name$
```

would result in the variable **Name$** being type **String** because **$** is the string declaration character. Other type declaration characters include % for type **Integer**, # for type **Double**, and **!** for type **Single**. You should never use this technique in your own code. It is supported only for backward compatibility purposes.

You can assign an initial value to a variable when it is declared. The syntax is as follows:

```
Dim name As type = InitialValue
```

InitialValue is an expression specifying the variable's initial data value. If you do not assign an initial value to a variable, initial values are assigned as specified in Table 3.2.

Implicit Variable Declaration

Visual Basic's default is to require explicit declaration of all variables using the **Dim** statement, as described in the previous section. If the compiler encounters a variable name that has not been declared, it generates an error. You can use an option that enables *implicit* variable declaration where you do not need to declare a variable with **Dim** but can just start using it in your code. To enable implicit variable declaration within a Visual Basic module, place the **Option Explicit Off** statement at the beginning of the module. However, I strongly recommend that you never do this.

Why am I so adamant about *always* declaring your variables? Why wouldn't the use of implicit declaration be easier? Though it might appear easier at first, it always seems to lead to problems. Here's why. Let's say you've created a variable, but at some point in the code the name is misspelled. With implicit declaration, Visual Basic simply creates a new variable using the misspelled name (as far as Visual Basic is concerned, you are creating a new variable). Because the program is using this new variable instead of the one it should be using, you are almost sure to get program errors that are extremely hard to track down. If explicit declaration were required, however, Visual Basic would immediately flag the misspelled variable name as an undeclared variable. The problem would never arise.

Another reason to avoid implicit variable declaration is that all implicitly declared variables are of type **Object**. This type can hold any kind of data, but you will be denied the storage and processing efficiencies that come from using a specific variable type that is tailored to your data.

The bottom line is that you should never rely on implicit declaration—it is bad programming practice, plain and simple, and I do not know why it is even supported in Visual Basic. Explicit variable declaration is Visual Basic's default, and it can also be specified by placing the **Option Explicit On** statement at the start of a module.

Table 3.2 Default initial values of variables.

Variable Type	Default Initial Value
Any numeric type	0
String	An empty string
Object	The special value **Nothing**
Boolean	False
Date	Midnight on 01/01/01

Static Variables

Any variable declared within a procedure or method is called a *local* variable. By default, local variables that are declared with the **Dim** statement are temporary, being created when the procedure is called and then destroyed when the procedure terminates. A result of this is that local variables will not "remember" their value between calls to the procedure. If you want a local variable to retain its value between procedure calls, you must declare it using the **Static** keyword in place of **Dim**. Look at this example:

```
Public Sub MySub()

    Static X As Integer
    Dim Y As Integer

    X = X + 1
    Y = Y + 1

End Sub
```

If you call this procedure 5 times, Y will have the value 1 each time because it is initialized to 0 and then has 1 added to it. X, on the other hand, will have the values 1, 2, 3, 4, 5 as the procedure is called repeatedly because, being a static variable, it "remembers" its value each time.

*The **Object** Data Type*

The **Object** data type can be thought of as Visual Basic's universal data type. In many ways, it is like the **Variant** type that was supported in earlier versions of Visual Basic. While the **Object** type is intended primarily for holding references to objects, it can also hold numeric and string data. More important, the **Object** type is "smart" and can automatically deal with situations involving strings and numerical values. For instance, look at this code:

```
Dim X As Integer
X = "17"
```

This will not compile because "17" is string data and cannot be assigned to a type **Integer** variable because that type can hold only numeric data. Likewise, the following code will fail because it attempts to assign a numeric value to a type **String** variable:

```
Dim Y As String
Y = 17
```

The **Object** type, however, can hold either string or numeric data and automatically make conversions as needed. The following code and comments will illustrate:

```
Dim ob ' Object type by default.
ob = "22" ' ob now contains the string "22"
ob = ob + 5 ' ob now contains the value 27
ob = ob & " Oak Street" ' ob now contains the string "27 Oak Street"
```

In addition to data, a type **Object** variable can contain the following special values:

- The value **Nothing** when the variable has been declared but has not yet been assigned a value.
- The value **DBNull** to indicate that the variable does not contain meaningful data.

Given the flexibility of the **Object** data type, you may be tempted to use it frequently in your programs. I advise against this. Use of this data type should be restricted to those situations where it is really needed, and not just as a convenience.

Object References

Because VB .NET is so heavily object oriented, you will find that you often need to work with object references in your code. An object reference is a variable that "points" to an object. You use the variable to access the object and work with its properties and methods. This is true for objects that are based on classes that are part of the .NET framework, as well as for objects based on classes you create yourself.

The first step in creating an object reference is to declare a variable of the proper type. You do this using the **Dim** statement:

```
Dim varname As classname
```

Varname is the variable name, following the standard naming rules (presented earlier in this chapter). **Classname** is the name of the class, qualified by its namespace if necessary (more on this shortly). For example, the following code declares a variable of type **VBCodeProvider** (You needn't be concerned with what this class does, because I am only using it for an example):

```
Dim obj1 As VBCodeProvider
```

This first step declares a variable to hold the object reference, but does not actually create, or instantiate, the object. The second step does this, using the following syntax:

```
varname = New classname()
```

After this second step has been performed, **varname** refers to an instance of the class (an object) and can be used in code. Between steps one and two, **varname** refers to nothing.

VB .NET provides a shortcut syntax that combines these two steps into a single one, with the following syntax:

```
Dim varname As New classname()
```

Both the two-step and the one-step syntax have the same effect, and programmers generally use the one-step method if only because it saves a bit of typing. The one situation where the two-step method is required is when you want the object variable to have global scope, which requires declaring it (step one) at the module level, but you want to instantiate the object in a procedure. You'll learn about variable scope later in the chapter.

A third syntax for creating an object reference is as follows:

```
Dim varname As classname = New classname()
```

This has exactly the same effect as the one-step method already presented, and is rarely used. I mention it only so you will understand it should you see it.

*Namespaces and the **Imports** Statement*

Namespaces are central to VB .NET, providing a way to organize classes and to prevent possible conflicts between class names. You'll learn more about namespaces in Chapter 6, but for the present, you need to know how namespaces are related to creating object references.

Every .NET Framework class exists in a namespace. To fully identify a class, you must specify not only the class name but also its namespace. (Each class's namespace is identified in the .NET documentation.) For example, the **XmlTextWriter** class is in the **System.Xml** namespace. This means that the class's fully qualified name is **System.Xml.XmlTextWriter**, and you can always refer to the class by this name. Here's an example:

```
Dim myTW As New System.Xml.XmlTextWriter
```

To save typing and to make the code more concise, you can *import* a namespace, making all of its classes available without referring to the namespace. The **Imports** statement is used to import a namespace, as shown here:

```
Imports namespace
```

You place the **Imports** statement at the very beginning of a module, before any other code, except for **Option** directives. You can have as many **Imports** statements as needed, one per line. Continuing with the previous example, you could import the **System.Xml** namespace as follows:

```
Imports System.Xml
```

Then, you could refer to the classes in this namespace without the namespace qualification:

```
Dim myTW As New XmlTextWriter
```

Note that importing a namespace does not mean you cannot use it in fully qualified class names, just that you do not have to.

Dereferencing Objects

When your code is finished using an instance of an object, you should dereference the object by setting the variable to the special value **Nothing**:

```
Dim varname As New classname
...
' Code to use the object here.
...
varname = Nothing
```

When an object no longer has any references, it becomes fair game for VB .NET's garbage collection process, which will remove it from memory and free up the associated resources. Note that, when an object reference goes out of scope, it is automatically dereferenced. For example, if you declare and create an instance within a procedure or method, that instance will be dereferenced when execution leaves the procedure or method.

Early versus Late Binding

The term *binding* is used to refer to when your code starts interacting with an object—when the code "knows" the details of the class, such as its methods and properties. The object references described previously in this section represent *early binding* because the compiler knows the type of an object reference before the program runs. Look at this object declaration:

```
Dim myTW As XmlTextWriter
myTW = New XmlTextWriter
```

As soon as you write this code, the Visual Studio compiler "knows" that the variable **myTW** is going to reference an object of type **XmlTextWriter**. Because the compiler also has information about the class members, it can check your code during compilation and catch errors such as calling a non-existent method or passing the wrong type or number of parameters. In addition, Visual Studio's IntelliSense feature makes your code editing a lot easier. Continuing with this example, when you enter "myTW" in code followed by a period, the editor displays a drop-down list of class members from which you can select.

Late binding is when the program does not know the type of an object reference until the code actually executes. You implement late binding by use of the **Object** data type for object references. When a variable is declared as type **Object**, the compiler does not know what class it will refer to until the program runs and a reference is actually assigned to the variable. In fact, a variable of type **Object** could hold references to many different types of objects during the course of program execution. For example:

```
Dim myObj As Object

myObj = New XmlTextReader
...
myObj = New VBCodeProvider
```

The use of late binding has three consequences:

- It makes your program slower. Late binding requires that certain steps be carried out during program execution. With early binding, these steps are carried out during program compilation.
- It increases the chance of runtime errors. With late binding, errors such as calling a method with the wrong parameters can only be caught at runtime. Early binding permits such errors to be caught during compilation.
- It disables IntelliSense. When using a late-bound object reference, you must refer to the documentation for information on its members rather than have the convenience of IntelliSense helping you.

It should be clear why early binding is the preferred method. Late binding offers a degree of flexibility that is useful in certain specialized situations, but otherwise should be avoided. In fact, VB .NET's default is to prohibit late binding. This is one of the things controlled by the Option Strict setting. By default, this option is set to On, which means that late binding is not permitted. You can change the setting for the entire project as follows:

1. Display the property pages for your project by right-clicking the project in the Solution Explorer and selecting Properties from the menu.
2. Under Common Properties, select Build (see Figure 3.1).
3. Select the desired Option Strict setting.
4. Click OK.

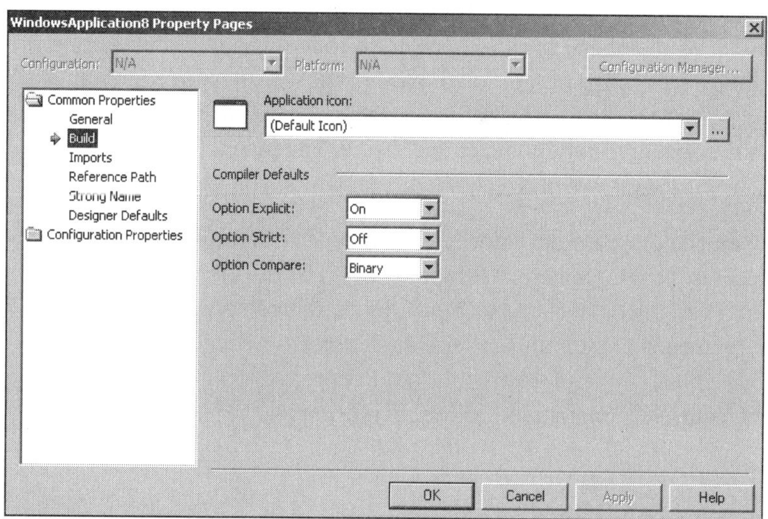

Figure 3.1
Specifying the global Option Strict setting in the project's property pages.

You can also specify the Option Strict setting for individual modules by including either **Option Strict On** or **Option Strict Off** at the beginning of the module (before any **Imports** statements). Using either of these statements overrides whatever Option Strict setting is in effect for the entire project, but just for the one module.

When Option Strict is turned on, you are also prohibited from declaring variables without the **As** clause. In other words, you must specify a type for every variable.

Constants

A constant is a piece of program data that cannot change during program execution. The values of constants are set when the source code is written. Visual Basic supports two types of constants: literal and symbolic.

Literal Constants

A *literal constant* is nothing more than a number, string, or date typed directly into your source code. In the following lines of code,

```
Dim MyString As String, MyNumber As Integer
...
MyString = "New York"
MyNumber = 123
```

"New York" and **123** are literal constants. You type them in while you are editing your source code, and they (of course) do not change during program execution. Any characters enclosed in quotation marks are considered to be text, or string, data. Numbers are not enclosed in quotes and can be written in several different ways:

- As a regular decimal (base 10) number with or without a decimal point and minus sign (for example, 123 and –2.95).
- As a hexadecimal (base 16) number with the &H prefix (for example, &HFF22).
- As an octal (base 8) number with the &O prefix (for example, &O12).
- In exponential notation, as described earlier in this chapter (for example, 1.25E6).

Dates can also be represented by literal constants. Date formats will be covered in Chapter 15.

Symbolic Constants

Visual Basic's other type of constant is the so-called *symbolic constant*. It has a name and a data type, just like a variable, and generally follows the same rules. Here is the difference: A symbolic constant is assigned a value when it is declared, and this value cannot change during program execution. To create a symbolic constant, use the **Const** keyword in the declaration statement:

```
Const ConstName As type = value
```

ConstName is the constant name and follows the same rules as variable names. ***Type*** is the data type of the constant. ***Value*** is an expression specifying the value of the constant. The **As *type*** part of the declaration is optional. If you omit that part, Visual Basic will assign the constant a type based on ***value***.

Here are some examples of declaring symbolic constants:

```
Const MAXIMUM As Integer = 100
Const CITY = "New York"
```

Visual Basic does not differentiate between constant names and variable names. This means that a constant name must be unique within its scope—in other words, you cannot have a variable and a constant with the same name in the same scope. To help the clarity of your source code, I recommend that constant names be all uppercase, and variable names be a mix of upper- and lowercase. Visual Basic does not care about case, but following this convention will make it immediately clear, for example, that **MAXIMUM** is a constant and **NumberOfSales** is a variable.

What is the purpose of symbolic constants? Why not just type in literal constants wherever they are needed? One major advantage is being able to change the value of a symbolic constant throughout the program simply by editing its declaration statement. Another advantage is that the constant's name can help in making the program easier to read. You might think that you could achieve the same thing with a variable, but that opens the possibility of the value inadvertently being changed in code.

Arrays

An **array** contains multiple variables that all have the same name and are differentiated by an index value, in parentheses, following the array name. To declare an array, use the **Dim** statement with the following syntax:

```
Dim ArrayName(maxindex) As Type
```

ArrayName is the name of array, which must follow the same rules as simple Visual Basic variables. ***Maxindex*** is an optional integer expression specifying the highest index in the array. If ***maxindex*** is omitted, the array has an indeterminate size that must be set before the array can be used. ***Type*** is the data type of the array and can be any Visual Basic data type. Here is an example:

```
Dim Months(12) As Double
```

This statement declares an array named **Months** that has 13 elements, with each element a type **Double**. Why 13 elements? Array indexes always start at 0, so an array with a maximum index of *n* will have *n+1* elements.

You can use an array element anywhere that a simple variable of the same type could be used. To specify which of the array's elements you are accessing, use the element number, as in this example:

```
Months(2) = 5.54
```

If you try to access an array element that does not exist—**Months(13)** in this example—an error is generated. The maximum number of elements in an array is the same as the maximum value of a type **Long** variable, or approximately 9E18.

Multidimensional Arrays

The arrays discussed so far are one-dimensional, meaning that they have a single index. You can also declare multidimensional arrays with two or more indexes. The declaration syntax is essentially the same, the only difference being that the number of elements in each dimension is specified. This statement, for example, creates a two-dimensional array with 10 elements in the first dimension and 5 in the second dimension:

```
Dim Data(10,5) As Integer
```

This array has a total of 66 elements, **Data(0, 0)** through **Data(10, 5)**. You can create arrays with three, four, or more dimensions, although they are useful only in special situations.

Changing Array Size

You can use the **ReDim** statement to change the size (number of elements) of an existing array. If the array was originally declared without specifying its size, you must use **ReDim** to assign an initial size before using the array. For multidimensional arrays, you can change the size of each dimension but not the number of dimensions. The syntax is:

```
ReDim ArrayName(NewMaxIndex)
```

ArrayName is the name of the array whose size you are changing, and ***NewMaxIndex*** specifies the new number of dimensions and elements using the same syntax as when an array is originally declared using **Dim**. Here's an example:

```
' Create an array with 21 elements.
Dim MyArray(20) As Byte
...
' Increase the array size to 51 elements.
ReDim MyArray(50)
```

When you use **ReDim**, the default is for any data in the array to be lost. To keep existing data in the array, use the **Preserve** keyword as shown here:

```
ReDim Preserve ArrayName(NewMaxIndex)
```

When you are using the **Preserve** keyword with a multidimensional array, you can change the size of only its last dimension. If you try to change the size of another dimension, an error occurs. For example:

```
Dim MyArray(5, 10) As Integer
...
ReDim Preserve MyArray(5, 20) ' Legal
ReDim Preserve MyArray(10, 10) ' Illegal
```

The UBound Function

The **UBound()** function is used to determine the maximum index of an array. The syntax is as follows:

```
UBound(ArrayName, Dimension)
```

ArrayName is the name of an existing array. ***Dimension*** is an optional integer expression specifying which dimension of a multidimensional array is of interest; 1 is the first dimension, 2 the second, etc. If the ***Dimension*** argument is omitted, 1 is the default. The function returns the largest legal index for the array, which is 1 less than its number of elements. Here are some examples:

```
Dim MyArray(20, 15)
x = UBound(MyArray) ' Returns 20.
y = UBound(MyArray, 2) ' Returns 15
```

The **UBound()** function can be very useful when you are using **ReDim** to change the size of an array but do not know its present size. For example, suppose you are using an array to hold data being entered by the user. Each time the user enters another item, you want to increase the array size by 1. The following line of code does the trick:

```
ReDim Preserve MyArray(UBound(MyArray) + 1)
```

Note that it is necessary to add 1 to the value returned by **UBound()** because the function returns the largest legal index of the array, which is 1 less than the new desired maximum index.

Structures

Visual Basic structure lets you combine variables of different types into a single unit designed for the specific needs of your programs. Structures are similar in some respects to a data construct called user-defined types (UDTs). Although earlier versions of VB supported UDTs, they have been replaced by the much more powerful structures in VB .NET. Structures go well beyond the simple storage of data and can include data validation code, methods, and events. Because they are a part of VB .NET's object-oriented programming capabilities, structures will be covered in Chapter 10.

Enumerations

An enumeration is used to associate integer values with names. These names then serve as constants within the program, but with certain advantages over regular constants declared with the **Const** keyword. You can declare enumerations in classes, modules, and structures. To declare an enumeration, use the **Enum...End Enum** statement:

```
Enum EnumName
...
End Enum
```

EnumName is the name of the enumeration and follows Visual Basic's standard variable naming rules. Within the body of the statement, you list the enumeration members in the desired order. Here's an example:

```
Enum OrderStatus
    Backordered
    InProgress
    Shipped
End Enum
```

This code creates an enumeration named **OrderStatus** with three members. By default, the members are assigned sequential values starting with 0. In this example, **Backordered** will have the value 0, **InProgress** will have the value 1, and so on. To start at a value other than 0, you would assign the desired starting value to the first member:

```
Enum OrderStatus
    Backordered = 1
    InProgress
    Shipped
End Enum
```

Now, **InProgress** is 2 and **Shipped** is 3. You can assign nonsequential values also:

```
Enum OrderStatus
    Backordered = -1
    InProgress = 15
    PgaShipped = 123
End Enum
```

Why use an enumeration instead of named constants, as shown here:

```
Const Backordered = 0
Const InProgress = 1
Const Shipped = 2
```

Naming Enumeration Members

To avoid conflicts with other variable or constant names, it is standard practice to create enumeration member names that all start with the same series of lowercase letters. In the examples, I did not follow this convention, but in a large complex program, this practice can greatly improve the readability of your source code. The prefix could identify the class the enumeration is defined in, or it could identify the enumeration itself. Thus, for the **OrderStatus** enumeration used in the example, the prefix "os" could be used for the members: **osBackordered**, **osInProgress**, and so on.

In terms of using the constant names, you have no advantage. The advantage to using an enumeration lies in the fact that it becomes a data type you can use for variables and for the parameters and return values of procedures. Thus, you could declare a variable as follows:

```
Dim StateOfOrder As OrderStatus
```

You could also declare a procedure to take the enumeration type as a parameter:

```
Public Sub SetStatus (X As OrderStatus)
...
End Property
```

Or, use an enumeration as the return value of a function:

```
Public Function GetOrderStatus(OrderNumber As Integer) As OrderStatus
...
End Function
```

Two additional advantages of using enumerations are as follows:

- They can be viewed in the Visual Basic Object Browser.
- The AutoList feature will display a list of enumeration members while you are writing code.

Variable Scope

Every variable and constant in a Visual Basic program has a *scope* associated with it. Sometimes referred to as *visibility*, a variable's scope refers to the parts of the program where the variable is available. For example, if a variable is declared inside a procedure, its scope is limited to that procedure, and outside the procedure, the variable might as well not exist. In fact, a program can have two or more variables with the same name but different scopes—the two variables will be completely independent of each other.

A variable also has a *lifetime*, referring to when the variable is created and destroyed. A variable retains its data throughout its lifetime. Even though a variable might have gone out of scope, it will "remember" the data stored in it as long as its lifetime has not ended. Lifetime is related to, but not the same as, scope. The concept of lifetime is not applicable to constants.

The scope of a variable is determined by the location where it is declared and by keywords used in the declaration statement.

Block-Level Scope

A variable that is declared within a block of code (a set of statements terminated by an **End**, **Loop**, or **Next** statement) has scope that is limited to the block. Here's an example:

```
If City = "Rome" Then
    Dim Message As String
    Message = "The city is in Italy."
    MsgBox(Message)
End If
```

The scope of the variable **Message** is limited to the **If...End If** block. Note, however, that a block-level variable's lifetime is not limited to the block, but the entire procedure where the block is located. Thus, if execution reenters the block, the variable will "remember" its previous value. For this reason, block-level variables should always be explicitly initialized.

Procedure-Level Scope

A variable declared within a procedure (but outside any block) has scope limited to that procedure. Procedure-level variables are sometimes called *local* variables. A local variable's lifetime is the same as its scope, while execution is within the procedure. When execution leaves the procedure, the variable is destroyed. If the procedure is called again, the variable is created anew and initialized. Static variables, which were covered previously in this chapter, are the only exception to this rule.

Module-Level Scope

A variable with module-level scope is visible to all code in the module, class, or structure where it is declared (including code within procedures). It is not visible to other code—in another module, for example. A module-level variable is created by declaring it in the module but outside any procedure. You can declare the variable with the **Dim** statement or with the **Private** statement, which has exactly the same effect. Look at the following declarations:

```
Dim X As Integer
Private Y As Integer
```

If these are placed in a module, outside any procedure, both **X** and **Y** will have module-level scope.

Project-Level Scope

A variable with project-level scope is visible to all procedures throughout the entire project. To create a variable with project-level scope, declare it at the module level (outside any procedure) using the **Public** keyword:

```
Public X As Integer
```

Class-Level Scope

A variable declared within a class but outside any class methods has scope throughout that class. For example:

```
Class MyClass
  Dim Count As Long
...
End Class
```

The scope of variables within classes can be modified as needed with certain keywords. You'll learn all the details of class variables in Chapters 9 and 10.

Shadowing

With different levels of scope, it is possible to have more than one variable of the same name in a program. For example, a module could contain a module-level variable named **X** as well as a local variable named **X**. Within the procedure where the local **X** is declared, both variables are in scope. Which one will be accessed if code in the procedure references **X**? The rule is that the variable with the narrower scope will be accessed. This is called *shadowing*. Look at this code:

```
' At the module level.
Private X As Integer

Sub Test1()
    Dim X As Integer
    ' The next line references the local X, not the module-level X.
    X = 12
End Sub

Sub Test2()
    ' The next line references the module-level X because
    ' there is no local X to shadow it.
    X = 12
End Sub
```

Generally speaking, if code in a procedure needs to access the value of a module- or project-level variable, the value should be passed as an argument to the procedure. This eliminates the chance that the variable will be shadowed by a local variable.

Same-Name Variables

If public or module-level variables from different modules have the same name, you can differentiate between them by qualifying the variable name with the module name. Suppose that a public variable named **Total** is declared in **Module1**, and a private module-level variable also named **Total** is declared in **Module2**. Code in **Module2** can reference the public **Total** that is declared in **Module1** as follows:

```
Module1.Total
```

Here's an example. This code is in **Module2**:

```
Private Total

Sub Test()
    ' The next line references the Total declared in module (Module2).
    Total = 123
    ' The next line references the Total declared in Module1.
    Module1.Total = 456
End Sub
```

Choosing Variable Scope

The rule for selecting a scope for a variable is simple: Use the narrowest scope possible for the situation at hand. This conserves memory resources and lessens the chance of bugs caused by inadvertently referring to the wrong variable.

Expressions and Data Manipulation

Now that you know how to store data in your program, you'd probably like to know what you can do with the data. The answer is, "Lots." Some of the most important data-manipulation tasks involve Visual Basic's *operators*. An operator is a symbol or word that instructs Visual Basic to manipulate data in a certain way. Operators fall into several categories. The

---

What's an Expression?

You'll see the term *expression* used frequently, and you're probably wondering just what exactly it refers to. It is quite simple, actually. An expression is anything that evaluates to a number, a string, or a logical (True/False) value. Thus, the literal constant **5** is an expression, as is **5 + 2**.

---

arithmetic and string operators, which manipulate number and string data, are covered in this section. The comparison and logical operators are used to work with logical expressions, and they will be covered in the next chapter.

Arithmetic Operators

The arithmetic operators—seven in all—perform mathematical manipulations. Four of them are the common operations of addition, subtraction, division, and multiplication. The other three operations may be less well known. Table 3.3 lists the arithmetic operators.

Integer division, represented by the \ symbol, divides two numbers and returns an integer result, discarding any fractional part of the answer. Thus, **7 \ 2** evaluates to 3, as does **6 \ 2**. No rounding occurs; any fractional part of the answer is simply discarded. Thus, both **21 \ 10** and **29 \ 10** evaluate to 2.

The *exponentiation* operator raises a number to a power. The symbol for this operation is **^**. In Visual Basic, therefore, **X ^ Y** means the same as the more common notation X^Y. If **X** is negative, then **Y** must be an integer; otherwise, both **X** and **Y** can be floating point values.

The *modulus* operator, represented by the keyword **Mod**, divides two numbers and returns only the remainder. The expression **7 Mod 2** evaluates to 1, **23 Mod 4** evaluates to 3, and **25 Mod 5** evaluates to 0. Any fractional part of the answer is truncated, so **23.5 Mod 4** evaluates to 3, not 3.5.

String Operators

The only operator that works with string data is called the *concatenation* operator, represented by the symbol **&**. Concatenation simply means to tack one string onto the end of another. For example, if **MyString** is a string variable, then executing the statement

```
MyString = "Visual " & "Basic"
```

results in the string **"Visual Basic"** being stored in the variable. You can also use the **+** symbol for string concatenation. It is provided for compatibility with old Visual Basic programs, but it's best to stick with **&** for new programs.

Table 3.3 The arithmetic operators.

Operation	Symbol	Example	Result
Addition	+	2 + 5	7
Subtraction	-	18 - 10	8
Multiplication	*	2 * 5	10
Division	/	10 / 2	5
Integer division	\	5 \ 2	2
Exponentiation	^	4 ^ 3	64
Modulus	Mod	10 Mod 4	2

Is That All?

Is concatenation all that Visual Basic can do with strings? Not by a long shot. It performs other string manipulations, not with operators, but with the **String** class and the built-in string procedures. These will be covered in Chapter 14.

Assignment Operators

The most basic assignment operator is **=**. Its action is to assign the value of the expression on the right side to the variable on the left side. For example:

```
X = 5
```

After this statement executes, the variable **X** will have the value **5**. Visual Basic also supports some other assignment operators, which I call the compound assignment operators. These compound operators let you perform an operation and assignment in one step. It is common in programming to manipulate the data stored in a variable and then store the end result back in the same variable. For example,

```
X = X + 1
```

Using a compound assignment operator, you could write:

```
X += 1
```

The general form of the compound operators is:

```
variable op = expression
```

This shorthand has the same effect as the following, less convenient format:

```
variable = variable op expression
```

Op can be any of the following operators: **+**, **-**, **/**, *****, ****, **^**, **&**. The first six of these work with numeric values, and the last one works with string data.

Operator Precedence

What happens if an expression contains more than one operator? What difference does it make? An example will illustrate. Consider this expression:

```
5 + 3 * 2
```

What does it evaluate to? If we perform the addition first, it evaluates to **16** (**5 + 3 = 8, 8 * 2 = 16**); but if we perform the multiplication first, the result is **11** (**3 * 2 = 6, 5 + 6 = 11**).

Which is correct? Because of such potentially ambiguous expressions, Visual Basic includes strict rules of operator precedence. This is just a fancy way of determining which operations are performed first. The precedence of Visual Basic's operators is given in Table 3.4. Operators with low precedence numbers are performed first.

Returning to the original example, we can see that the expression **5 + 3 * 2** will evaluate to 11, because multiplication has a higher precedence than addition and thus will be performed first. For operators that have the same precedence level, such as multiplication and division, the order of execution is always left to right.

What if the order of execution specified by the operator precedence rules isn't what you want? Let's say you would like to add variables **A** and **B**, then multiply the sum by variable **C**. Can this be done? Yes. Parentheses come to the rescue. By including parentheses in an expression, you force operators inside parentheses to be evaluated first, regardless of precedence. If you write

```
A + B * C
```

the precedence rules will cause the multiplication to be performed first, and the result will not be what you want. If, however, you write the expression like this

```
(A + B) * C
```

the parentheses force the addition to be performed first, and the expression evaluates properly. You can use as many parentheses in an expression as you need, as long as they always come in pairs; each left parenthesis *must* have a matching right parenthesis. If you create an expression with an unmatched parenthesis, Visual Basic displays an error message when you try to move the editing cursor off the line. When parentheses are nested (one set inside another set), execution starts with the innermost set and proceeds outward.

You can use parentheses in an expression even when they are not needed to modify the order of operator precedence. Particularly with long, complex expressions, parentheses can help make the expression easier to read and understand.

Table 3.4 Operator precedence.

Operator	Precedence
Exponentiation ^	1
Multiplication (*), division (/)	2
Integer division (\)	3
Modulus (MOD)	4
Addition (+), subtraction (-)	5
String concatenation (&)	6

Summary

This chapter introduced you to Visual Basic syntax. Although this is a fairly clear and easy syntax to learn, you must follow it exactly if your code is to run. You also learned about VB's tools for data storage and manipulation, which can be used for string and number data as well as for object references. Some special purpose data storage tools, such as arrays and enumerations, are available when your project needs them. The chapter also covered the important concept of variable scope, which lets you compartmentalize your data to minimize the chances of unintended interactions. Finally, you learned about using the arithmetic operators to manipulate numbers. There's more to learn about the Visual Basic language, but with this chapter, you are off to a good start.

Chapter 4

Visual Basic Syntax: Program Control and Procedures

As you saw in the previous chapter, a lot of Visual Basic syntax is concerned with the storage of data. Program control and organization is another aspect of Visual Basic that is equally important. You can use Visual Basic program control statements to control which sections of code execute, when they execute, and how many times they execute. Visual Basic procedures are used to organize your code into independent, self-contained units. These aspects of Visual Basic syntax are the topics of this chapter.

Program Control Statements

You've seen that Visual Basic code consists of a series of statements, one to a line. When a chunk of code executes, the normal execution order begins with the first statement and then executes all the statements in order, top to bottom. Sometimes, however, this just won't do. One of the most powerful programming tools available to you is the ability to control program execution—to determine which Basic statements execute, when they execute, and how many times they execute. Before I show you how to do this, however, you need to know about logical expressions and Visual Basic's comparison and logical operators.

Logical Expressions

Computer programs often need to deal with yes/no questions. When a question or an expression has only these two possible outcomes, it is called a *logical expression*, or sometimes a *Boolean expression*. In computer programming, the two possible values of a logical expression are referred to as **True** and **False**. As an example, consider the question, "Is the value stored in the variable **X** larger than the value stored in the variable **Y**?" Clearly, either it is (answer = **True**) or it is not (answer = **False**). Visual Basic has the built-in keywords **True** and **False** to represent these logical values. Visual Basic also has a special data type, **Boolean**, designed specifically to hold logical values. To ask the sorts of questions that have logical True/False answers, you use the comparison operators.

Comparison Operators

Visual Basic provides a number of operators you can use to construct logical expressions by asking questions about the data in your programs. Specifically, these *comparison operators* perform comparisons between expressions, returning a value of **True** or **False**, depending on the result of the comparison. Table 4.1 lists the comparison operators.

You can see that if **X** is equal to 10 and **Y** is equal to 5, then the expression **X < Y** will evaluate as **False** and **X <> Y** will evaluate as **True**. Assuming both **Q** and **Z** have been declared as type **Boolean**, we can use the value of a logical expression like this:

```
Q = X < Y
Z = X <> Y
```

which would result in the variable **Q** having the value **False** and **Z** having the value **True**. More often, however, logical expressions are used in program control, as you'll see soon. But first, we need to take a look at how to combine two or more logical expressions to arrive at a single True/False answer.

Logical Operators

The logical operators are used to combine two or more logical expressions into a single True or False answer. Why would you want to do this? Here's an example from everyday life. Suppose that you receive a call inviting you to join a group of friends for dinner. If Mary is coming along, you'd like to go, because you're a bit sweet on her; otherwise, you'll pass. This is a single logical condition and easy to understand. Now, assume for a moment that you also like Helen; if she's coming with the group, you'd also like to go. But if both Mary and

Table 4.1 The comparison operators.

Operator	Comparison	Example	Meaning
=	Equal to	**X = Y**	Is **X** equal to **Y**?
>	Greater than	**X > Y**	Is **X** greater than **Y**?
<	Less than	**X < Y**	Is **X** less than **Y**?
>=	Greater than or equal to	**X >= Y**	Is **X** greater than or equal to **Y**?
<=	Less than or equal to	**X <= Y**	Is **X** less than or equal to **Y**?
<>	Not equal to	**X <> Y**	Is **X** not equal to **Y**?

Helen are coming, the situation will get a bit too complicated, so you again will pass. In this situation, we have two True/False questions ("Is Mary coming?" and "Is Helen coming?"), and you need to combine these two questions in order to answer the single True/False question: "Are you going?"

Similar situations arise in computer programming. For example, you need an answer to the question: "Are **X** and **Y** both greater than 0?" Here's where the logical operators come in, letting you combine and manipulate logical expressions to get the answer you need. The four logical operators (shown in Table 4.2) are each designated by a keyword. As you review this table, assume that **X** and **Y** are both logical expressions.

Using these operators, you can cast the earlier question using the comparison operators and the logical operators. The expression

```
(X > 0) And (Y > 0)
```

will evaluate as **True** if, and only if, both **X** and **Y** are greater than 0. Likewise, if you need to know whether at least one of these two variables is greater than 0, you would write:

```
(X > 0) Or (Y > 0)
```

Getting back to the dinner invitation, you can see that the **Xor** operator is what is needed:

```
I am going = (Mary coming?) Xor (Helen coming?)
```

Of course, you can use the comparison and logical operators to ask questions about object properties, too. Let's say you have two Check Box controls on a form and want to determine if one or both of them are checked. Here's the expression to do so:

```
(Check1.Value = True) Or (Check2.Value = True)
```

I have been talking about comparison and logical operators for a while now, but I haven't really demonstrated how they can be useful. Don't worry; that's the next topic—how to use logical expressions in conjunction with Visual Basic's decision and loop structures to control program execution.

Table 4.2 The logical operators.

Operator	Example	Evaluation
And	**X And Y**	**True** if both **X** and **Y** are **True**; **False** otherwise
Or	**X Or Y**	**True** if **X** or **Y**, or both of them, are **True**; **False** only if both **X** *and* **Y** are **False**
Xor (exclusive Or)	**X Xor Y**	**True** if **X** and **Y** are different (one **True** and the other **False**); **False** if both are **True** or both are **False**
Not	**Not X**	**True** if **X** is **False**, **False** if **X** is **True**

Decision Structures

Visual Basic's *decision structures* control program execution based on whether certain logical conditions are met. In other words, program statements are either executed or not executed, based on the evaluation of logical expressions. These logical expressions typically evaluate the state of program data or user input, so the execution of the program can be controlled according to the specific needs of the application.

If...Then...Else

The **If...Then...Else** structure executes a block of one or more statements only if a specified logical expression evaluates as **True**. Optionally, you can include a second block of statements that is executed only if the logical expression is **False**. An **If...Then...Else** structure has the following form (in these examples, **X** stands for any logical expression):

```
If X Then
   ...
   Statements to be executed if X is TRUE go here.
   ...
Else
   ...
   Statements to be executed if X is FALSE go here.
   ...
End If
```

The **Else** keyword and the block of statements between it and the **End If** keyword are optional. If no statements are to be executed when **X** is **False**, you can write the structure as follows:

```
If X Then
   ...
   Statements to be executed if X is TRUE go here.
   ...
End If
```

If your blocks of statements are only single statements, you can use the concise single-line form of the **If...Then...Else** structure:

```
If X then Statement1 Else Statement2
```

For more involved situations, you can include the **ElseIf** keyword to create what are effectively nested **If...Then...Else** structures:

```
If X Then
   ...
   Statements to be executed if X is TRUE go here.
```

```
   ...
ElseIf Y Then
   ...
   Statements to be executed if Y is TRUE go here.
   ...
Else
   ...
   Statements to be executed if both X and Y are FALSE go here.
   ...
End If
```

You can have as many **ElseIf** statements as you like. Keep in mind, however, that at most one of the blocks of statements in an **If...Then...Else** structure will be executed. In the preceding example, if both **X** and **Y** are **True**, only the statements associated with the **X** condition are executed. The rule is that only the statements associated with the first **True** condition are executed. Note, however, that for situations that would require more than one or two **ElseIf** clauses, you are usually better off using the **Select Case** structure, which is covered next.

You might have noticed the indentation style in the previous code samples; within each block, all statements are indented with respect to the statements that mark the beginning and the end of the block. This is not required by Visual Basic, but in my opinion it makes the code more readable.

Select Case

The **Select Case** structure is more appropriate than the **If...Then...Else** structure when you have more than a couple of conditions to be tested. The syntax is as follows:

```
Select Case TestExpression
   Case Comparison1
      ...
      Block1
      ...
   Case Comparison2
      ...
      Block2
      ...
   Case Else
      ...
      ElseBlock
      ...
End Select
```

TestExpression is any numeric or string expression. **Select Case** goes through the list of **Case** statements, comparing ***TestExpression*** with each ***Comparison*** until a match is found.

At that point, the statements in the associated block are executed. If no match is found, the statements associated with the optional **Case Else** statement are executed. If no **Case Else** statement and no match are found, none of the statements are executed. The number of **Case** statements allowed in a **Select Case** structure has no limit.

In the simplest situation, each ***Comparison*** is a numeric or string expression against which ***TestExpression*** is compared for equality. You can also use the **To** keyword to check ***TestExpression*** against a range of values and the **Is** keyword in conjunction with one of the comparison operators to make a relational comparison. Thus, if you want a match when ***TestExpression*** is between 1 and 5, you would write

```
Case 1 To 5
```

and if you want a match when ***TestExpression*** is greater than 10, you would write

```
Case Is > 10
```

You can use multiple ***Comparison*** expressions that are associated with one **Case** statement by separating them with commas. For example, here's a **Case** statement that would match ***TestExpression*** if it is equal to -1 or -2, between 8 and 12, or greater than 100:

```
Case -1, -2, 8 To 12, Is > 100
```

Loop Structures

You've seen that Basic's decision structures determine whether a block of statements is executed. In contrast, Basic's loop structures control how many times a block of statements is executed. You can accomplish "looping" in one of two ways: by executing a block of statements a fixed number of times or by executing the block repeatedly until a specified condition is met.

For...Next

In its most common use, the **For...Next** loop executes a block of statements a fixed number of times. The syntax is as follows:

```
For Counter = Start To Stop
   ...
   statement block
   ...
Next Counter
```

Counter is a numeric variable that can be any type, although you would generally use type **Integer** unless you have a specific reason to use another type. ***Start*** and ***Stop*** are the values that specify the start and stop of the loop; they can be any numeric expressions. A **For...Next** loop begins by setting ***Counter*** equal to ***Start***. It then follows these steps:

1. **Counter** is compared with **Stop**. If **Counter** is greater than **Stop**, execution passes to the first statement after the **For...Next** loop. If **Counter** is not greater than **Stop**, go to Step 2.
2. The statements in the loop are executed.
3. **Counter** is incremented by 1.
4. Return to Step 1.

Note that if **Stop** is equal to **Start**, the loop executes only once; if **Stop** is less than **Start**, it does not execute at all.

Here's an example of a **For...Next** loop that will execute the number of times specified by the variable **X**:

```
For Count = 1 to X
   ...
Next X
```

You are not limited to starting the loop at 1, of course. You can also use the **Step** keyword to specify that the **Counter** variable be incremented by a value other than 1 with each cycle of the loop. Here's a loop that will execute four times, with the **Counter** variable taking the values 4, 7, 10, and 13:

```
For I = 4 To 13 Step 3
   ...
Next I
```

You can use negative **Step** values to count backward, which, of course, requires that the **Stop** value be smaller than **Start**. You can also use fractional values as long as the **Counter** variable is a floating point type. The following loop will count backward from 4 to 1 by increments of 0.25 (4, 3.75, 3.5, ... , 1.25, 1):

```
For I = 4 To 1 Step -0.25
   ...
Next I
```

Never Change the Counter Variable

Basic will not prevent you from changing the value of the **Counter** variable inside the loop. This practice should be avoided, however. It can lead to pesky program bugs and code that is difficult to understand.

If you want to terminate a loop early—that is, before the ***Counter*** variable exceeds ***Stop***—you can use the **Exit For** statement. This is an extremely useful statement, because it lets you specify a variety of conditions that will terminate the loop in addition to the loop's own count programming. Here's a loop that will execute 10 times or until the variable **X** is less than 0:

```
For I = 1 to 10
   ...
   If X < 0 Then Exit For
   ...
Next I
```

Strictly speaking, you do not have to include the name of the ***Counter*** variable in the **Next** statement. Visual Basic will automatically associate each **Next** statement with the immediately preceding **For** statement. I suggest, however, that you develop the habit of always including the ***Counter*** variable name with **Next**, to improve readability of the code.

Do...Loop

The **Do...Loop** structure is the most flexible of Visual Basic's loops. It allows the loop to execute repeatedly until a specified condition is either **True** or **False**, and it allows the condition to be evaluated either at the start or the end of the loop. In its simplest form, a **Do...Loop** loop executes as long as a condition is **True**:

```
Do While Condition
   ...
   statement block
   ...
Loop
```

Condition is any logical expression. When execution first reaches the **Do** statement, ***Condition*** is evaluated. If it is **False**, execution passes to the statement following the **Loop** statement. If ***Condition*** is **True**, the block of statements is executed, execution returns to the **Do** statement, and ***Condition*** is evaluated again. You can also replace the **While** keyword with the **Until** keyword to continue execution for as long as ***Condition*** is **False**, as shown here:

```
Do Until Condition
   ...
   statement block
   ...
Loop
```

Both of the previous examples perform the comparison at the start of the loop, which means it is possible for the statement block *not* to be executed—even once. For example, if ***Condition*** is **False** to begin with, a **Do While...Loop** loop will not execute even once. If you want to be sure the loop executes at least once, you can place ***Condition*** at the end of the loop. As before, you can use either the **While** or the **Until** keyword:

```
Do
   ...
   statement block
   ...
Loop While Condition

Do
   ...
   statement block
   ...
Loop Until Condition
```

To terminate the loop early, use **Exit Do**. Here's a loop that will execute until **Y** is greater than 0 or **X** is less than 0:

```
Do
   ...
   If X < 0 Then Exit Do
   ...
Loop Until Y > 0
```

You may be thinking that the same result could be obtained by writing the loop like this:

```
Do
   ...
Loop Until Y > 0 Or X < 0
```

You are correct, but a subtle difference exists between these two loops. In the first example, the statements between the **If X < 0** statement and the **Loop** statement are not executed during the last loop iteration, when **X** becomes less than 0. In the second example, all of the statements in the loop are executed during the last execution.

While...End While

The **While...End While** loop executes a block of statements as long as a specified condition is **True**. The syntax is as follows:

```
While Condition
    ...
    Statement block
    ...
End While
```

Note that exactly the same thing can be accomplished with a **Do...Loop** structure:

```
Do While Condition
    ...
    Statement block
    ...
Loop
```

Because of its added flexibility, I recommend that you use **Do...Loop** rather than the **While...End While** structure.

Nested and Infinite Loops

A *nested loop* is a loop contained within another loop. No limit is placed on nesting of loops in Visual Basic, although nesting beyond four or five levels is rarely necessary or even advisable. If your program seems to need such deep nesting, you should probably reexamine its structure to see if you can accomplish the same task more simply. The only restriction on nesting loops is that each inner loop must be enclosed entirely within the outer loop. The following example is illegal, because the **For...Next** loop is not contained entirely within the **Do...Loop** loop:

```
Do While X > 0
   For I = 1 to 10
      ...
Loop
   Next I
```

The next example, however, is okay:

```
Do While X > 0
   For I = 1 to 10
      ...
   Next I
Loop
```

An *infinite loop* is one that executes forever (or until you halt the program). Clearly, if a loop's terminating condition is never met, it will loop indefinitely. This situation can arise from faulty program logic or from unexpected user input. Keep a sharp eye out for this sort of problem. If your program seems to "hang" during execution, you might want to examine your loops.

With...End With

The **With...End With** statement provides a convenient shorthand when you want to execute a series of statements on a single object. The syntax is as follows:

```
With object
    ...
    statements
    ...
End With
```

Within the block, the reference to ***object*** is implicit and need not be written. For example, look at this code:

```
With TextBox1
    .Height = 250
    .Width = 600
    .Text = "Hello World"
    .Show()
End With
```

This code is exactly equivalent to the following:

```
TextBox1.Height = 250
TextBox1.Width = 600
TextBox1.Text = "Hello World"
TextBox1.Show()
```

When used simply as a shorthand, the **With...End With** statement is at best a minor convenience. It is more useful when included in procedures that take an object as a parameter. Here, for example, is a procedure that will change several font-related properties of any object that is passed to it:

```
Public Sub ChangeFont(ob As Object)

With ob
    .Font.Bold = True
    .Font.Italic = True
    .ForeColor = RGB(255, 0, 0)
End With

End Sub
```

For Each...Next

The **For Each...Next** statement loops through all the elements in a collection or an array. You do not need to know ahead of time how many elements the collection or array contains, because the statement automatically loops once for each element. The syntax is as follows:

```
For each Item in Group
...
```

```
statements
...
Next
```

Item is a variable declared to be a data type that is appropriate for the elements in the collection or array. Typically, this will be the same data type as the collection or array, or type **Object**. **Group** is a reference to the collection or array that you are looping through. The statements in the loop execute one time for each element in *Group*. With each iteration, the variable **Item** provides a reference to the current element.

The following example calculates the sum of all the values in the array **data**, assumed to be of type **Double**:

```
Dim x As Double
Dim sum As Double = 0

For Each x In data
    sum += x
Next
```

The collections that you'll access with **For Each...Next** are typically the many collections that are part of the .NET framework. You'll learn about these collections as needed throughout the book.

Procedures

A *procedure* is a self-contained section of code that has been assigned a name. Visual Basic has several types of procedures, summarized here:

- **Event** procedures are used to respond when a specific event occurs, such as a keystroke.
- **Property** procedures are used to create class properties.
- **Sub** and **Function** procedures are used by the developer to organize and simplify source code.

Event and **Property** procedures are covered elsewhere in the book. In this section, I explain how to create your own **Sub** and **Function** procedures. But first, I will give you two reasons why you would want to create your own procedures.

What about Methods?

You may have heard that methods are an important part of object-oriented programming, and that is correct. In essence, a method is nothing more than a **Sub** or **Function** procedure that is inside a class. You'll learn about class methods in Chapter 9, but for the most part, the details are the same, as you will learn here for **Sub** and **Function** procedures that are not inside a class.

First of all, you have no alternative. The way Visual Basic works, almost all code must be inside a procedure. The only exceptions are variable and constant declarations and some other code elements that are placed at the module level. Everything your program does will be accomplished by procedure-level code.

Second, procedures are an essential part of good programming practice. Over the years, programmers have realized that organizing source code into independent, self-contained units can have many benefits. These benefits include reduction of errors and bugs as well as increased programmer productivity through code reuse. Suppose that you are a programmer at a bank and have written the code to perform some complex depreciation calculations. By putting that code in a procedure, you isolate it from the rest of the program, thereby reducing or eliminating the possibility of unexpected interactions with other code. Also, you make the code reusable. If next month you are writing another program that needs to perform the same depreciation calculations, you can use the original procedure and save yourself time and effort.

Visual Basic's two types of procedures have a great deal in common. I will cover **Sub** procedures in detail first, and then explain the few ways in which **Function** procedures differ.

Sub Procedures

A **Sub** procedure is a section of Visual Basic code that is assigned a name. The syntax for creating a **Sub** procedure is as follows:

```
Sub SubName(argument_list)
...
'Procedure code goes here.
...
End Sub
```

SubName is the name of the procedure, following the same naming rules as Visual Basic variables. Procedures should be given names that describe the task they perform. ***Argument_list*** is an optional list of arguments—information that is passed to the procedure when it is called. If a procedure has no arguments, follow its name with an empty set of parentheses.

When a **Sub** procedure is called, the code it contains is executed. When execution reaches the **End Sub** statement, execution returns to the program location from where the procedure was called. To exit a **Sub** procedure before the **End Sub** statement is reached, use the **Exit Sub** statement. You can have any number of **Exit Sub** statements in a procedure, and you can put almost any Visual Basic code in a procedure. You cannot, however, define one procedure within another procedure.

Procedure Arguments

A procedure can take one or more arguments. When you define the procedure, you must specify the number and data types of the arguments. Each argument is declared using the syntax as follows:

```
name As type
```

Name is the argument name, and ***type*** is a Visual Basic data type or the name of a user-defined type, an enumeration, a structure, or a class. If **As *type*** is omitted, the argument defaults to type **Object**. If the procedure takes more than one argument, separate them by commas. The following declaration specifies that the procedure takes one type **Integer** argument and one type **String** argument:

```
Sub MySub(X As Integer, S As String)
...
End Sub
```

Arguments work as follows. When your program calls a procedure, it must pass a value for each of the procedure's arguments. Using the above procedure as an example, it could be called as follows:

```
Call MySub(123, "Hello")
```

Inside the procedure, the argument **X** will have the value **123**, and the argument **S** will have the value **"Hello"**. It is actually uncommon to use literal values like this as arguments—it is much more common to use variables or expressions, but the idea is the same.

To specify that an argument is an array, use an empty set of parentheses following the name. This procedure takes an array of type **Double** as its one argument:

```
Sub MySub(Data() As Double)
...
End Sub
```

When you call a procedure, you must pass the right number and type of arguments or an error will occur. The only exception is when the procedure is defined to take optional arguments. To pass an array, use the array name without parentheses.

Optional Arguments

You can specify that one or more of a procedure's arguments are optional and need not be included when the procedure is called. The syntax for an optional argument is as follows:

```
Optional name = defaultvalue
```

Name is the argument name, and ***defaultvalue*** is an expression that specifies the value the argument will have when the procedure is called without passing the argument. The equal sign and default value are optional; if they are omitted, the argument will be undefined if not passed by the caller. In a procedure definition, optional arguments must always come at the end of the argument list. Here's an example:

```
Sub MySub(Name As String, Optional Country As String = "USA", _
    Optional Age As Integer)
...
End Sub
```

Passing Arguments ***ByVal*** *and* ***ByRef***

Visual Basic's default is to pass arguments by value. This means that when a procedure is called and a variable is passed as an argument, Visual Basic makes a copy of the variable and passes the copy to the procedure. Because the code in the procedure does not have access to the original variable, it cannot change its value. You can explicitly indicate that an argument is to be passed by value using the **ByVal** keyword:

```
Sub MySub(ByVal X As Integer)
...
End Sub
```

Because passing by value is Visual Basic's default, however, use of the **ByVal** keyword is unnecessary.

You can also pass an argument by reference using the **ByRef** keyword. When a variable is passed to a procedure by reference, the actual variable, and not just a copy, is passed. The code in the procedure can change the value of the variable. To illustrate, look at the following procedure:

```
Sub MySub(ByRef X As Integer, Y As Integer)

X = 100
Y = 200

End Sub
```

Now, suppose that the procedure is called as follows:

```
A = 5
B = 5
Call MySub(A, B)
```

After execution returns from the procedure, the variable **A** will have the value **100** as assigned in the procedure. Because the procedure's first argument was passed by reference, the code in the procedure could access and modify the variable **A**. The variable **B**, on the other hand, will have its original value of **5**. Because the procedure's second argument was passed by value, the code in the procedure could not access and modify the variable.

Parameter Array Arguments

When you do not know how many arguments will be passed to a procedure, you can use the **ParamArray** keyword to specify an optional array of arguments to a procedure. The size of this array is unlimited, letting you pass as many argument values as needed to the procedure.

In a procedure declaration, the argument identified by the **ParamArray** keyword must be the last one in the argument list, following any optional arguments that are present. The following example defines a procedure that takes a **ParamArray** argument:

```
Private Sub MySub(X As Integer, ParamArray Names() As String)
...
End Sub
```

Inside the procedure, the code needs a way to determine if the **ParamArray** argument was passed because it is optional. If the array was passed, the procedure code also needs a way to tell how many elements the array contains. Both tasks are accomplished with the **Ubound()** function, which has the following syntax:

```
Ubound(arrayname)
```

The return value is one of the following:

- The highest legal index of the array if the array exists (was passed as an argument)
- The value –1 if the array does not exist (was not passed as an argument)

The following code snippet shows how code in a procedure can determine if the **ParamArray** argument was passed:

```
Private Sub MySub(X As Integer, ParamArray Names() As String)

Dim size As Long

size = Ubound(Names)

If size = -1 Then
    ' No Names array was passed.
Else
    ' The Names array was passed, with
    ' elements 0 thru size.
End If

End Sub
```

*Calling **Sub** Procedures*

When you want to execute the code in a procedure, you *call* it in one of two ways. The first is by using the **Call** keyword followed by the procedure name, with an argument list. The second is to use the procedure name by itself (again, with the argument list). These two methods of calling a procedure are equivalent. For example:

```
Call MySub(X, Y)
MySub(X, Y)
```

Function Procedures

A **Function** procedure is like a **Sub** procedure in most ways. It differs in that it returns a value to the calling program. To define a function, the syntax is as follows:

```
Function FuncName(argumentlist) As type
...
End Function
```

The rules for the function name and the argument list are the same as for **Sub** procedures, as was presented earlier in this chapter. ***Type*** specifies the return type—that is, the type of the data that the function returns to the calling program. It can be any Visual Basic data type or the name of a user-defined type, an enumeration, a structure, or a class.

The value returned by the function can be specified in two ways. One is to assign the value to the function name. For example, here is a function that adds two numbers together and returns the result:

```
Function Add(X As Double, Y As Double) As Double

Add = X + Y

End Function
```

The other way to return a value is to use the **Return** statement. The same function is shown here using the **Return** statement:

```
Function Add(X As Double, Y As Double) As Double

Return X + Y

End Function
```

Note that neither the **Return** statement nor the assignment of a value to the function name causes execution to exit the function. This occurs only when execution reaches the **End**

Function statement that marks the end of the function, or when an **Exit Function** statement is encountered.

*Calling **Function** Procedures*

A **Function** procedure is called differently than a **Sub** procedure. Because a function returns a value, it can be treated like an expression and used anywhere an expression would be used. For example, using the **Add()** function presented above:

```
Sum = Add(5, 8)
Result = Add(10, 50) / Add(-5, 33)
```

Summary

The information that was covered in this chapter is essential to almost every aspect of VB .NET programming. The ability to control the execution of code, in response to program conditions and/or user input, is a central part of most programs. Likewise, loop statements are important for many different kinds of programming tasks. Finally, putting code in procedures—both **Sub** and **Function** procedures—is a key part of the VB .NET programming model. With the information in this and the previous chapter under your belt, your development as a VB .NET programmer is well on its way.

Chapter 5
Runtime Error and Exception Handling

Runtime errors, or exceptions—the two terms are synonymous—are an unavoidable problem that the programmer must face. Although careful programming can minimize the chance of exceptions, you can never eliminate them entirely because many of the causes of exceptions are beyond your control. However, you can *handle* exceptions, which permits your program to respond to them in a user-friendly way. That's the topic of this chapter.

What Are Exceptions?

An exception, sometimes called a runtime error, is a problem that crops up while the program is executing. In VB .NET terminology, a program is said to *throw* an exception. Many situations can cause exceptions, including the following:

- Trying to open a nonexistent file for reading
- Attempting to instantiate a class that is not available
- Writing to a removable media drive when no media is inserted

I could provide many more examples, but I think that you get the idea. It's important to be aware that exceptions are different from two other types of errors that a VB .NET program can experience. A *syntax error* is when you make an error in your code, such as misspelling a variable name or passing the wrong type of arguments to a procedure. VB .NET catches these errors during program development, so they never can cause a problem in the finished program. A *bug*, sometimes called a *logic error*, causes your program to behave in unexpected or incorrect ways (but without causing an exception). A financial program producing incorrect results, or a graphics program drawing the wrong shapes, are examples of bugs. You'll learn how to track down and fix bugs in Chapter 25.

By default, a VB .NET program does not include exception handling. When an unhandled exception occurs, the program stops running and displays a message to the user. A less polite way of saying this is that the program crashes. This can result in an extremely annoyed user and also has the potential for data loss. Clearly, you do not want this to happen.

Some exceptions can be prevented by careful coding. For example, the "file not found" exception can be prevented by always checking for the existence of a file before trying to open it for reading. Other exceptions cannot be prevented by even the most skilled programmer, so you must handle them in your code. VB .NET offers two methods of exception handling: structured and unstructured.

Exception handling occurs at the level of the procedure. This means that each procedure in your program should contain exception-handling code designed to catch the types of exceptions that the procedure might generate. If a procedure generates an unhandled exception, it is passed up the call stack to the caller. In other words, if procedure A calls procedure B, and procedure B generates an unhandled exception, it is passed up to procedure A for handling. A given procedure can contain structured exception-handling code or unstructured exception-handling code, but not both.

Structured Exception Handling

Structured exception handling is the preferred method of dealing with exceptions. The term *structured* means that the code that has the potential for causing an exception, as well as the code designed to handle the exception, are organized in structured blocks. You use the **Try...Catch...Else** statement for this purpose. The syntax is as follows:

```
Try

' Executable statements that may cause an exception are placed here.

Catch [optional filters]

' Statements that are to be executed when an exception occurs go here.
' The optional filters permit the code to respond only to specific
' types of exceptions. You can place multiple Catch blocks in a
' Try statement.

Finally

' Code placed here is executed after the code in the Try block
' or in the Catch block is executed. This block is optional.

End Try
```

If the **Catch** statement does not include any filter, it will respond to any and all exceptions generated in the **Try** block. To have access to information about the exception, a nonfiltered **Catch** statement is usually written like this:

```
Catch e As Exception
```

Because all exception types derive from the **System.Exception** class, this "filter" will catch any and all exceptions while permitting code in the **Catch** block to use the expression **e** to access information about the exception.

Code that is inside the **Try** portion of a **Try...End Try** block is said to be *protected* because exceptions thrown by that code can be caught. Note, however, that code in the **Catch** and the **Finally** portions of a **Try...End Try** block are not protected. If the code in either of these sections has the potential to throw an exception, you can protect the code using nested **Try...End Try** blocks:

```
Try

Catch e As SomeException
    Try

    Catch ex As SomeOtherException

    Finally

    End Try
Finally
    Try

    Catch ex As YetAnotherException

    Finally

    End Try

End Try
```

Filtering Catch Expressions

Most often, you will want to use filtering to enable different responses to different exceptions. One type of filter is based on the type of exception thrown. The syntax of the **Catch** statement is as follows:

```
Catch e As ExceptionType
```

ExceptionType identifies the type of exception to be caught by this **Catch** block. The identifier **e** is used to access information about the exception in code; you can use any legal variable name here, although **e** is traditional. The .NET framework includes several dozen types of exceptions, which will be discussed in more detail later in the chapter. For now, it's enough to know that you must identify the types of exceptions that code in the **Try** block might throw, and then construct your **Catch** filters accordingly. Here's an example that will catch two types of exceptions:

```
Try
...
Catch e As IOException

' Code here will execute if a type IOException occurs

Catch e As PathTooLongException

' Code here will execute if a type PathTooLongException occurs

Finally
...
End Try
```

You can write **Catch** blocks to deal with certain specific exceptions and also include a **Catch** block to deal with all other exceptions. The following code, which is a modification of the previous example, does this:

```
Try
...
Catch e As IOException

' Code here will execute if a type IOException occurs

Catch e As PathTooLongException

' Code here will execute if a type PathTooLongException occurs

Catch e As Exception

' Code here executes for all other types of exceptions.

Finally
...
End Try
```

As in this example, multiple **Catch** blocks should be ordered from most specific to least specific. If a more general filter is placed before a more specific filter, it will catch those exceptions that were supposed to be caught by the second filter.

Catch block filtering can also be based on any Boolean expression, using the **When** keyword. The syntax is as follows:

```
Catch When expression
```

This **Catch** block will execute when an exception occurs and **expression** is **True**. Note that only a single **Catch** block will be executed, even if there is more than one matching filter. If no matching **Catch** block is found, the exception is passed up the call stack, as I explained earlier in the chapter.

The Exception Class and Its Derived Classes

All exceptions in VB .NET derive from the **System.Exception** class, either directly or indirectly. There is a hierarchy of exception classes, organized by type of error. A small portion of this hierarchy is shown in Figure 5.1. You can make use of this hierarchy to fine-tune your program's exception catching. For example, the following **Catch** phrase will catch only a single type of exception, **DivideByZeroException**:

```
Catch e As DivideByZeroException
```

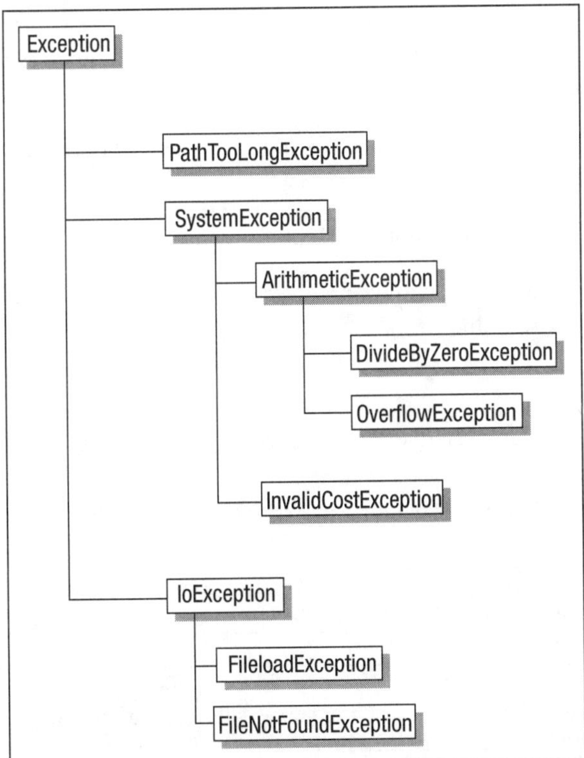

Figure 5.1
This diagram shows a small part of the hierarchy of exception-related classes.

This phrase, however, will catch both **DivideByZeroException** and **OverFlowException**:

```
Catch e As ArithmeticException
```

Finally, this phrase will catch **DivideByZeroException**, **OverFlowException**, and **InvalidCostException** (plus many more exceptions that are derived from **SystemException** but are not included in the diagram):

```
Catch e As SystemException
```

All exception classes have a base set of members that provide information about the exception. Table 5.1 describes the exception members. Many derived exception classes have additional members that provide information specific to the type of exception. For example, the **FileLoadException** class, which is thrown when an error occurs loading a file, has the **FileName** property, which provides the name of the file. Details on these specific exception members will be provided as needed throughout the book.

An Exception-Handling Example

The program presented in this section demonstrates the use of structured exception handling. It deals with file input/output, which is one of the most important areas in which exception handling should be used. The program tries to open a file named data.txt on the A: drive. Two exceptions could occur:

- If the floppy disk in the A: drive does not include a file of that name, a **FileNotFoundException** occurs.
- If the drive doesn't contain a disk, an **IOException** occurs.

The program catches both errors and displays an appropriate error message to the user. Here are the steps required to create this program:

1. Create a new Windows application project.
2. Add a Button control to the form and change its **Text** property to "Open File".

Table 5.1 Members of the System.Exception class and its derived classes.

Property	Description
HelpLink	Specifies the Uniform Resource Name (URN) or Uniform Resource Locater (URL) of the help file associated with this exception.
Message	A short description of the exception.
Source	The name of the application or object that caused the exception.
StackTrace	Identifies the stack trace—the sequence of procedure calls leading up to the location in code where the exception occurred.

3. Insert the statement **Imports System.IO** at the beginning of the class module. This makes the file-related classes in this namespace available to the program.

4. In the Button's **Click** event procedure, add the code shown in Listing 5.1.

When you run the program, click the button. Depending on the state of the A: drive, you will see the appropriate error message.

Listing 5.1 Code in the Click event procedure.

```
Private Sub Button1_Click(ByVal sender As System.Object, ByVal e As_
System.EventArgs) Handles Button1.Click

    Dim fs As FileStream

    Try
        fs = New FileStream("a:\data.txt", FileMode.Open)
    Catch ex As FileNotFoundException
        MsgBox("The file could not be found.")
        Exit Sub
    Catch ex As IOException
        MsgBox("An error occurred: " & ex.Message)
        Exit Sub
    End Try

End Sub
```

Throwing Exceptions

The **Throw** statement is used to throw an exception. The effect as far as your program is concerned is exactly the same as if the system had thrown the exception. Why would you want to throw an exception? One situation is to create and use custom exceptions so that your program can make use of VB .NET's exception-handling mechanism to handle program-specific error conditions. Custom exceptions are covered in the next section. The other time you would use **Throw** is inside a **Catch** block, when your code's response to a caught exception is to throw a new exception (or re-throw the original exception). This is often the case when you are handling exceptions in components. You might want the code in the component to take some action in response to the exception, while at the same time passing the exception back up the call stack for additional handling.

The syntax of the **Throw** statement is as follows:

```
Throw ex
```

The ***ex*** argument is an exception of a type derived from **System.Exception**. If the **Throw** statement is within a **Catch** block, you can omit the ***ex*** argument and the **Throw** statement will re-throw the current exception that is being handled.

When you create a new **Exception** object, the class constructor takes a string argument that becomes the **Message** property of the exception. For example, the following code throws a **FileNotFoundException** class with the specified **Message** property:

```
Throw New FileNotFoundException("The specified file does not exist.")
```

Let's look at a more specific example. Suppose you have created a class that performs various file input/output tasks. You need to catch exceptions that will occur when a file is not found. The class offers the option of handling exceptions locally or passing them up the call stack for handling; this option is controlled by the flag **HandleExceptionsLocally**. The following code fragment shows how you would handle an exception that occurs when a file is not found, either handling it locally (by displaying a message) or throwing a new exception that will be passed up the call stack:

```
Try
    Dim fs As New FileStream(filename, FileMode.Open)
Catch e As FileNotFoundException
    If HandleExceptionsLocally Then
        MsgBox("The file was not found.")
    Else
        Throw New FileNotFoundException(filename & " was not found.")
    End If
End Try
```

Unstructured Exception Handling

VB .NET's unstructured exception handling is a holdover from the previous version of Visual Basic. It is markedly inferior to the structured exception handling, and I think that it was retained only to make it easier to migrate projects from the old version of Visual Basic to VB .NET. The exceptions that can be handled are the same as for structured error handling. However, the way you go about it is quite different.

The On Error Statement

Within a procedure that requires error handling, you use the **On Error** statement to specify the exact code location where execution is supposed to pass when an error occurs. Here's an example. The statement

```
On Error Goto ErrorHandler
```

tells Visual Basic that when an error occurs, execution passes to the line of code identified by the label **ErrorHandler**. Labels that identify locations in code consist of a name followed by a colon, as shown in these three examples:

```
ErrorHandler:
IfError:
GreenGrapes:
```

The rules for line labels are the same as for Basic variable names—the only difference is the colon at the end. Each procedure's error-handling code is traditionally placed at the end of the procedure, between the last "regular" statement in the procedure and the **End Sub** or **End Function** statement at the end. You must place an **Exit Sub** or **Exit Function** statement just before the label identifying the error-handling code to prevent execution from falling into the error-handling code. Here are the basics:

```
Sub MySub()

On Error Goto Errorhandler

' Procedure statements go here.

Exit Sub

Errorhandler:

' Error handling code goes here.

End Sub
```

The line label identifying the error-handling code must be in the same procedure as the **On Error Goto** statement that specifies it. This means that error-handling code is local to procedures.

You can use two variants of the **On Error** statement. The statement

```
On Error Goto 0
```

causes error trapping to be disabled; the program will respond to errors in the default manner as described earlier in this chapter. The statement

```
On Error Resume Next
```

instructs the program to ignore the error temporarily and to continue executing with the statement immediately following the one that caused the error. This does not mean that you are ignoring the error (a bad idea, to be sure) but that you are deferring handling of the error for the moment. This technique is used in situations where the information needed to diagnose the error accurately is not immediately available.

The Resume Statement

After code in your error handler has dealt with the error, you use the **Resume** statement to specify where program execution is to resume. **Resume** can be used only within error-handling code; otherwise, an exception occurs. Several variants of **Resume** are available. When used by itself, it means, "Try again to execute the statement that caused the error." This is appropriate in situations where the cause of the error has been fixed. In other circumstances, however, this is not possible. If you want execution to continue somewhere other than the statement that caused the error, you have the following two choices:

- **Resume Next** continues execution immediately after the statement that caused the error.
- **Resume *label*** continues execution with the program line identified by ***label***. The line identified by *label* must be in the same procedure as the **Resume** statement (the same procedure where the error occurred).

The Err Object

Unstructured error handling relies on the **Err** object. Each program automatically has a single **Err** object associated with it. **Err** has global scope, meaning it can be accessed from anywhere in a program. At any moment, **Err** contains (in its properties) information about the most recent exception that has occurred. The properties you'll need most often are the following:

- **Number**—A type **Long** value identifying the specific error that occurred.
- **Description**—A brief text description of the error.
- **Source**—A string identifying the name of the object or application that generated the error.

In your error-handling code, you will test the properties of the **Err** object and take appropriate action based on the nature of the exception. You can see that in some ways the **Err** object is like an **Exception** object. In fact, the **Err** object has an **Exception** property that retrieves the **Exception** object corresponding to the latest error. In my opinion, however, if you want to work with **Exception** objects, you will be using the structured exception handling statements, so the **Err** object will not come into play.

Using On Error Resume Next

As I have already mentioned, executing the **On Error Resume Next** statement defers error trapping. If this statement is in effect when an error occurs, execution continues with the statement immediately following the one that caused the error. This type of deferred error trapping is most useful when the program is accessing objects, because it permits you unambiguously to identify the object that caused the error. The basic sequence of code is as follows:

1. Execute **On Error Resume Next**.
2. Access or manipulate the object.
3. Immediately test **Err.Number** to see if an error has occurred; if so, handle it.

The following code snippet shows an example:

```
On Error Resume Next
' Code here that might cause an error.
If Err.Number > 0 Then
' Handle the error.
End If
```

Summary

There are numerous possibilities for runtime errors, or exceptions, to occur in a VB .NET program. Even with the most careful programming, you cannot reduce the chance of exceptions to zero because some of them are caused by factors outside your control, such as hardware problems. An unhandled exception causes the program to quit, and that should be avoided at all times. By using **Try...Catch** blocks, you can protect sections of code that have the potential to thrown an exception, enabling your program to deal with the problem in a graceful manner. Exception handling may not be the most fun or glamorous part of programming, but it is very important.

Chapter 6
Visual Basic and the .NET Framework

Some readers might have noticed that the latest version of Visual Basic is not called version 7, which is what you would expect based on the fact that the previous release was version 6. Rather, it is called Visual Basic .NET. This strange-sounding name is the result of the intimate relationship between the Visual Basic language and Microsoft's new .NET (dot-net) Framework. In this chapter, I will explain the origins of the .NET Framework, some of its inner workings, why it is so important for developers, and how Visual Basic fits in.

The information in this chapter falls into the technical background category. There's nothing here that you need to know in order to start writing programs using VB .NET. If you're like me, however, and like to know the background and theory of the tools you are using, I think you'll find this short chapter quite interesting.

Why .NET?

The .NET Framework is Microsoft's new platform for the development and implementation of applications programs. It has been under development for at least a couple of years, and it represents the biggest change for developers since the shift to Windows many years ago. Much of the impetus for the development of the .NET Framework came from the rapid expansion of the Internet and its ever-increasing importance to program developers and computer users. Previous frameworks had their origins in the pre-Internet world, and as the need for Internet programming tools increased, these capabilities were tacked on as afterthoughts rather than being designed in from the start. The resulting tools worked—usually—but they were cumbersome and prone to errors, and they placed heavy demands on the time and creativity of the programmers.

The main idea behind the .NET framework was to create an integrated set of programming tools that was designed from the ground up to be Internet-aware and Internet-capable. However, you should not get the idea that the .NET framework is only for Internet programming. It casts a very broad net (pardon the pun!) and in addition to Web programming brings together all aspects of Windows programming, ranging from the simplest command-line utility all the way up to complex, multiuser, distributed database applications.

.NET is just getting started. At present, it consists of the following two products:

- The .NET framework is available for the Windows operating system. In order to run or develop programs written for .NET, a system must have the framework installed.
- Visual Studio .NET is a development environment, also for the Windows operating system, that provides for development of .NET applications in three languages: Visual Basic, C# (C sharp), and Visual C++. Visual Studio is not required to run .NET programs, and is optional for developing them.

Microsoft's vision for .NET is much broader than might be suggested by this. Although .NET provides extremely powerful capabilities for creating traditional computer applications, its design goes much further. The ultimate goal is to permit globally distributed systems that include not only personal computers but also personal digital assistants, cell phones, and any other devices that would benefit from a remote link. Versions of .NET will eventually be available for all of these platforms, permitting them to interact seamlessly.

Inside the .NET Framework

Frameworks are nothing new in the world of computing, although they have often been called by other names. What exactly is a framework? In the broadest possible terms, a framework serves as a wrapper for a computer's operating system. Why is this desirable?

On any computer, the operating system has the most direct relationship with the computer hardware. It "operates" the computer, hence its name. The operating system, whether it be Windows, Linux, or anything else, contains the code that interacts directly with the hardware devices, including the video display adapter, the hard disk, the network interface, and so on. When a program wants something done—read some data from a disk file, for example—it issues a command to the operating system, which then carries out the actual task. This is illustrated in Figure 6.1.

The operating system provides device independence, which means that the commands a program uses are the same regardless of the specific hardware installed. Thus, the command to read a disk file is the same whether the file is on a floppy disk, a hard disk, or a CD-ROM. This

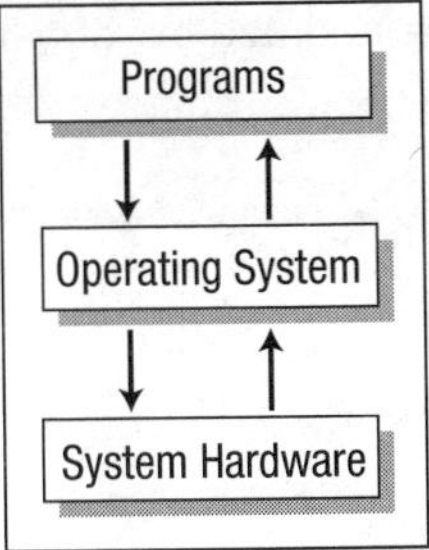

Figure 6.1
The operating system provides an interface between programs and the system hardware.

hardware independence is what makes it possible for a program written for the Windows operating system to run on any system that has that operating system installed.

The first frameworks arose as attempts to simplify the task of the program developer. The operating system commands were unavoidably cryptic and complex, being tied so closely with the hardware. Commonly needed tasks, such as displaying screen windows, were possible but required some fairly difficult and time-consuming programming. Microsoft and other publishers of development tools realized that they could write the code needed to perform a variety of commonly needed tasks and make this functionality available to the programmer in an easy-to-use form. This was the rationale behind the first version of Visual Basic, as well as numerous other tools. Creating a screen window required nothing more than issuing a simple menu command—the framework did all the work behind the scenes, serving as an interface between the program and the operating system (see Figure 6.2).

.NET does a terrific job of simplifying the programmer's job. More than any previous framework from Microsoft (and possibly from anyone), it provides a rich and comprehensive set of ready-to-use components. Because .NET is object-oriented from the ground up, components

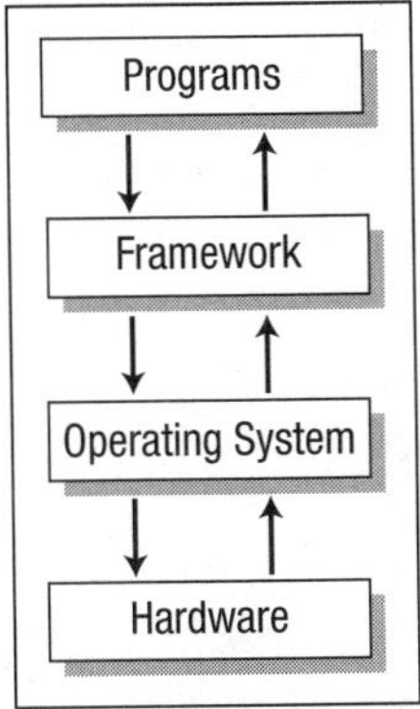

Figure 6.2
A framework provides an interface between applications program development and the operating system.

are all provided as classes. Thus, not only can you use these classes unmodified in your applications, but by using inheritance, overloading, and the other powerful tools of object-oriented programming, you can extend the framework classes to suit your own specialized needs. Don't worry if you do not understand some of these terms now—they will be explained in later chapters.

However, the .NET vision goes well beyond providing components to simplify the programmer's life. Just as an operating system can provide hardware independence, a framework has the potential to provide operating system independence. In the future, Microsoft plans to create versions of the .NET framework for other operating systems, including Linux and Macintosh as well as handheld devices such as Palm Pilots. This will, in theory at least, permit the same programs to run on any device that is supported by .NET. The concept, called *cross-platform compatibility*, is illustrated in Figure 6.3.

Let's look at the three main parts of the .NET framework: the Common Language Runtime, the .NET framework classes, and ASP.NET.

The Common Language Runtime

The Common Language Runtime (CLR) is often considered to be the heart of .NET. The concept of a "runtime" has been around for a while, referring to helper code that was installed on target systems and was called as needed by programs while they were running. Older versions of Visual Basic, for example, installed a runtime in the form of a DLL file named VBRUN*xxxx*.DLL (where *xxxx* referred to the version). This runtime was required for any Visual Basic program to run.

The CLR, however, goes well beyond the traditional runtime concept of providing execution support. It also provides many other services that simplify program development and deployment. These include the following:

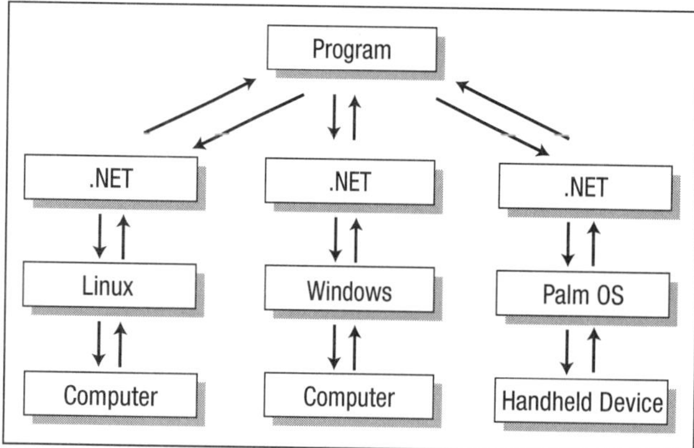

Figure 6.3
.NET offers the future promise of cross-platform compatibility.

- *Memory and process management*—When a program executes, a lot of complicated "plumbing" is at work behind the scenes. Objects must be created and destroyed; memory must be allocated and freed; execution threads must be started and stopped. The CLR simplifies many of these tasks, as compared with non-CLR code, and also makes some of them unnecessary. In particular, memory management is automated and need no longer be the concern of the programmer. Through automatic garbage collection, unused memory is freed up periodically. This automated memory management prevents memory leaks and invalid memory references, two of the most frequent application errors.

- *Intermediate language compilers*—Programs written for the CLR are compiled, during program development, to Microsoft Intermediate Language (MSIL). When the program runs, the MSIL is compiled into native code for execution. This final compilation is performed by the intermediate language compiler, sometimes called the just-in-time (JIT) compiler. The compilation from MSIL to native code is typically performed only once, when the program runs for the first time, and the output is cached for future use. The use of intermediate language and JIT compilers opens the door for true platform independence. If you use platform-specific versions of the CLR, the same MSIL code could be run on different platforms.

- *Common type system*—One of the necessities for smooth multiple-language support is for the various languages to use the same system for storing data. In the past, this was not the case—Visual C++ stored strings differently than did Visual Basic, for example. The CLR implements a system in which all commonly used data types are identical across languages. Now, Visual Basic code can interact with C# or C++ code without the many problems caused in the past by differing data representations. The same will be true of any languages written in the future for the CLR. Every type supported by the common type system is an object, being derived from the base **System.Object** class.

- *Metadata management*—For the CLR to manage the various elements that make up an application, it must have access to information about those elements. This includes version information, class and member definitions, security attributes, and information required for debugging. The CLR requires that elements be self-describing, meaning that they contain all of this information rather than having it stored externally—in the Windows Registry, for example. This information is called *metadata*. It is stored in a binary format, but .NET provides tools to export the data as a COM type library or as XML. In addition to enabling many of the automatic functions of the CLR, this metadata makes for greatly simplified program distribution and deployment (as you will learn in Chapter 25).

Managed vs. Unmanaged Code

Code that is written to the specifications of the CLR is called *managed code*. Code that is written without regard for the CLR requirement is called *unmanaged code*. Although unmanaged code can execute in the CLR, it does so with few, if any, of the CLR services.

- *Security*—In today's ever-more interconnected computing environment, security is a vital concern. These concerns fall into two general areas. Code-access security prevents the execution of unauthorized or malicious code by enforcing various degrees of trust based on the origins of the code and other information. Role-based security prevents unauthorized access to programs or program functions based on permissions assigned to different users. The CLR implements both types of security, and although the details of these security tools are beyond the scope of this book, you can find full information in Visual Studio's online documentation.

The .NET Class Framework

Much of the functionality available to the VB .NET programmer is provided by the .NET Class Framework (sometimes called the .NET Base Classes). This is a rich set of classes, interfaces, and structures that provides support for data storage, access to system services, input/output, security, and a whole host of other things that the programmer needs. All components in the .NET framework are CLR-compliant, with all the attendant benefits as described earlier in this chapter.

The class framework is arranged hierarchically, using the concept of namespaces. A *namespace* is nothing more than an identifier that is used to group related items together. The root namespace for the entire framework is **System**. This root namespace contains the classes for all of the base data types (**Integer**, **Char**, **Array**, and so on) as well as for the **Object** type that is the base for all .NET components. The **System** namespace also contains classes for exception handling, garbage collection, and other fundamental runtime activities.

Within the **System** namespace are numerous second-level namespaces, and some of those contain third-level namespaces. Each of these namespaces contains components that are related in terms of the functions they perform. Table 6.1 lists and briefly describes these namespaces. Some of the namespaces will be explored in more detail in later chapters, but many will not. Using this table as a guide, you can turn to the VB .NET online documentation for more information on any .NET component you want to use.

Table 6.1 Namespaces in the .NET framework.

Category	Namespace	Functionality
Component model documents	**System.CodeDom**	Manipulation and compiling of source code
Component model	**System.ComponentModel**	Implementation of components; licensing considerations
Configuration	**System.Configuration**	Access to application configuration data
Data	**System.Data**	Access to data sources, management of data
Data	**System.Xml**	XML processing
Data	**System.Xml.Serialization**	Object-to-XML mapping
Framework services	**System.Diagnostics**	Application diagnostics
Framework services	**System.DirectoryServices**	Access to Active Directory services

(continued)

Table 6.1 Namespaces in the .NET framework *(continued)*.

Category	Namespace	Functionality
Framework services	**System.Management**	Tools that work with the Web-Based Enterprise Management (WBEM) standards
Framework services	**System.Messaging**	Microsoft Message Queue (MSMQ) access and management, and the sending and receiving of messages
Framework services	**System.ServiceProcess**	Installation and execution of Windows-based service applications
Framework services	**System.Timers**	Access to system timers
Globalization and localization	**System.Globalization**	Support for internationalization and globalization of code and resources
Globalization and localization	**System.Resources**	Access to and management of resources; support for localization
Net	**System.NET**	Sending and receiving of data over a network; programming interfaces for common network protocols
Common tasks	**System.Collections**	Creation and management of collections of objects, such as lists, queues, arrays, and dictionaries
Common tasks	**System.IO**	Basic input/output tasks, including file I/O, memory I/O, and isolated storage
Common tasks	**System.Text**	Character encoding, character conversion, and string manipulation
Common tasks	**System.Text. RegularExpressions**	Support for regular expressions
Common tasks	**System.Threading**	Multithreaded programming support
Reflection	**System.Reflection**	Access to type metadata; creation and invocation of types
Rich, client-side GUI	**System.Drawing**	Two-dimensional graphics
Rich, client-side GUI	**System.Windows.Forms**	User-interface components for Windows-based applications
Runtime infrastructure services	**System.Runtime. CompilerServices**	Support for compilers
Runtime infrastructure services	**System.Runtime. InteropServices**	Support for unmanaged code
Runtime infrastructure services	**System.Runtime. Remoting**	Support for creating distributed applications
Runtime infrastructure services	**System.Runtime. Serialization**	Object serialization and deserialization, including SOAP encoding support
.NET Framework security	**System.Security**	Access to the .NET Framework security system
.NET Framework security	**System.Security. Cryptography**	Cryptographic services
Web Services	**System.Web**	Web server and client management, communication, and design; Web Forms support
Web Services	**System.Web.Services**	Client- and server-side support for SOAP-based Web services

User Interfaces

From the perspective of the developer, some of the most important and interesting parts of VB .NET are related to user interfaces. These parts of the .NET framework were discussed in the previous section—specifically, the **System.Windows.Forms** and **System.Web** namespaces. Because of their importance, however, they merit separate coverage. The .NET framework includes support for two kinds of sophisticated visual user interfaces: Windows Forms and Web Forms.

Windows Forms are used to create "traditional" Windows applications that execute locally on a desktop system (possibly involving a local area network). The user interface consists of screen windows, or forms, that contain a variety of controls, such as menus, buttons, and text boxes. Most of the programs you see running on the Windows operating system fall into this category. The program files exist locally and are executed locally. From the user's perspective, the end result of a Windows program created with the .NET framework is not much different from one created with earlier technologies, such as Visual Basic version 6. Under the hood, however, the .NET framework classes provide a simpler and more powerful set of tools for the programmer, and a more robust end product.

Web Forms are used to create a user interface that displays in a browser (typically this will be Microsoft Internet Explorer). The program code exists and is executed on a Web server, and information is transmitted in both directions between the server and the client via the Internet. A Web Form application is like a Windows Form application in some ways—you can place controls on the form (in this case, a Web page) to provide user interactivity. However, the underlying logic is different, and the two types of applications are suited for different purposes.

You'll learn about Windows Form applications in Chapters 7 and 8, and about Web Forms applications in Chapters 20 and 21. Chapter 20 also provides an overview of the factors to take into account when deciding which type of application to use for a specific project.

Other Interface Types

In addition to Windows Forms and Web Forms, VB .NET offers several other types of interfaces. Only one of these other interface types is a user interface. The others are called *programmatic interfaces* because rather than interfacing with the user, they interface with other software. They include the following:

- *Console application*—Provides a simple text-only visual interface that runs at the command prompt (sometimes called the DOS Box or the MS-DOS Window). Program input and output are limited to unformatted text. Console applications are covered in Chapter 12.

- *Web Service application*—Provides a software component that can be accessed over the Internet. The component provides a service, such as credit card processing or financial calculations, and returns the result to the calling program. Web Services are covered in Chapter 23.

- *Windows Service application*—Runs in the background, typically for extended periods, and performs tasks, such as monitoring system performance or user activity. Windows Service applications are an advanced topic that is not covered in this book.

Finally, there are three other types of VB .NET projects: Class Library, Windows Control Library, and Web Control Library. These projects are used to create libraries of software components for use in other programs.

Value Types and Reference Types

All data types in VB .NET are either a value type or a reference type. Although the way you use these two types is often similar or identical, you should be aware of some important underlying differences. In simplest terms, a value type actually contains its data, whereas a reference type contains a pointer to where its data is located.

Here's an analogy: Imagine that your mother sent you her favorite recipe for chicken, and you wrote the recipe on an index card. That is analogous to a value type, because the card contains the actual data. Then, suppose you found a terrific recipe in a cookbook, and to serve as a reminder, you wrote the name of the cookbook and the page number on an index card. This is analogous to a reference type because the index card refers to, but does not contain, the actual data.

In VB .NET, the following are value types:

- All numeric data types
- All structures, even if their members are reference types
- Types **Boolean**, **Char**, and **Date**
- All enumerations

The following are reference types:

- All arrays, even if the array elements are value types
- Type **String**
- All class types

String—Value or Reference Type?

Technically, type **String** (represented by the **String** class) is a reference type. In some ways, however, it acts like a value type. This will be explained when I cover the **String** class in Chapter 14.

The following code is an example of using a value type:

```
Dim X As Integer
Dim Y As Integer
X = 10
Y = X
```

After this code executed, you have two separate and independent variables, **X** and **Y**, each containing the value **10**. If you later change the value of **X**, **Y** is not affected (and vice versa).

In contrast, look at this code, which is similar but uses a reference type:

```
Dim X As MyClass
Dim Y As New MyClass
X = Y
```

After this code executes, there is a single instance of **MyClass** in memory, and both **X** and **Y** refer to it. If you make changes to **X**, they are reflected in **Y**:

```
X.BackColor = "Red"
```

Now, **Y.BackColor** is also **"Red"**.

Namespaces

I have already mentioned namespaces in reference to the .NET framework classes. The use of namespaces provides for the organization of components and unambiguous reference to them. Two different components can have the same name, as long as they are in different namespaces.

Any .NET component is always available in your programs by making use of its fully qualified name—that is, its name, including the namespace. You can also import one or more namespaces into a program module, which means that its members can usually be referred to without full qualification. I say "usually" because naming conflicts can occur when two or more classes from different namespaces have the same name. In this case, you must use the fully qualified name even when the namespace has been imported. For example, the following fully qualified name will always refer to the **XmlDocument** object in the **System.Xml** namespace:

```
Dim myXmlDoc As System.Xml.XmlDocument
```

You can import the namespace by placing an **Imports** statement at the beginning of a module (before any other statements):

```
Imports System.Xml
```

Now, you can refer to members of that namespace by their name alone:

```
Dim myXmlDoc As XmlDocument
```

You can also define an alias for an imported namespace. The syntax is as follows:

```
Imports alias = Namespace
```

Now, ***alias*** is a synonym for the namespace. For example:

```
Imports XMLStuff = System.Xml
```

After the alias has been assigned, the following two statements are equivalent:

```
Dim X As System.Xml.XmlDocument
Dim Y As XMLStuff.XmlDocument
```

Where Does Visual Basic Fit In?

After reading this chapter, you might feel that the .NET framework is where the real action is—and there's no doubt that the framework is central to anything the VB .NET programmer does. Where, then, does the Visual Basic language fit in?

It's true that learning to program in VB .NET is probably 80 percent learning about .NET and 20 percent learning the Visual Basic language. Visual Basic is not alone in having a reduced relative importance as a discrete language. The exact same thing will be true for any other language written to run on .NET. This does not, however, reduce the real importance—in fact, the necessity—of the Visual Basic language. Without VB (or another .NET language), the .NET framework is nothing more than a useless set of sophisticated tools. Think of masons, who have hundreds of types of ready-made bricks at their disposal. These bricks are the components in the .NET framework. Without the mortar to put them together (that's Visual Basic) and the skill to do so (this is where you come in), all the fancy bricks in the world are useless.

Summary

It's clear why the new release of Visual Basic is called Visual Basic .NET, given how tightly the language and the .NET framework are integrated. With the .NET framework, Microsoft has provided a rich and powerful set of classes to meet just about any imaginable programming need, from the desktop to the database to the Internet. These framework classes are your servants, and Visual Basic is the language you use to tell them what to do. To be a proficient Visual Basic .NET programmer, you need to know both the language and the framework.

Chapter 7
Creating Windows Applications

Windows applications are one of the three broad categories of user interfaces that VB .NET supports (the other two are console applications and Web applications, covered in Chapters 12 and 20). A Windows application is a program that runs locally (or, in some cases, over a local area network, or LAN). Most or all of the programs you use every day would be called Windows applications in VB .NET terminology—your word processor, personal finance program, and email client are just a few examples.

The cabability to create Windows applications is a central part of VB .NET. Despite the increasing importance of the Web, local Windows applications continue to be the mainstay of Windows development and will continue to be vitally important for the foreseeable future. This chapter and the next show you how to create Windows applications using VB .NET. This chapter focuses on forms, which provide the screen windows that are central to any Windows application. The next chapter deals with the controls that make up a form's user interface.

Forms and Controls

Two concepts are at the heart of all Windows applications: forms and controls. As with all things in the .NET framework, they are classes—specifically the **Form** and **Control** classes, respectively. They are both part of the **System.Windows.Forms** namespace.

A form—or Windows Form to give it its full name—is nothing more than a rectangular screen window, the same sort of window

---

What's in a Name(space)?

The **UserControl** class discussed in this section is not the only .NET class that uses this name. The **System.Web.UI** namespace also contains a **UserControl** class that is used for creating Web applications. This is an excellent example of the utility of namespaces. However, it is also an illustration of the occasional need to use the fully qualified class name and the **Imports** statement to ensure that your class references are unambiguous.

---

that you use every day when you work with your Windows programs. A form can be resized, moved around the screen, and minimized on the taskbar. A control is an element, such as a button or a text box, which is placed on a form to make up your program's user interface. A program may have only a single form, or it may have dozens.

Each form is an instance of a class that inherits from the **System.WinForms.Form** class. Thus, when you design a form for your program, you are actually designing a class. Your class starts out inheriting all the functionality of the **System.WinForms.Form** class, and you then add to it as required by the needs of your program.

Likewise, each .NET framework control is based on the **System.Windows.Forms.Control** class. These are controls that you can use in your Windows applications; you'll find them in the Windows Forms section of the Visual Studio Toolbox. All of these controls are based, either directly or indirectly, on **System.Windows.Forms.Control**.

You can also create you own controls, which involves creating a new class that subclasses (inherits from) **System.Windows.Forms.UserControl**. Creating custom controls is covered in Chapter 11. For now, discussion will be limited to the controls that are part of the .NET framework.

The **Form**, **Control**, and **UserControl** classes have a lot in common. This becomes clear when you examine the .NET inheritance hierarchy for these classes, shown in somewhat simplified form in Figure 7.1. The **Control** class inherits indirectly from the **Object** class, which is the base class for all .NET classes. Let's take a look at the classes in this hierarchy.

The Control Class

The **Control** class is a parent class of all components that provide a visual representation on the screen. It implements the base functionality for defining a screen rectangle that the user can interact with. This includes the following:

- Controlling the base appearance of the object, such as its default font and background color
- Determining the size and location of the rectangle on screen, and whether it is visible

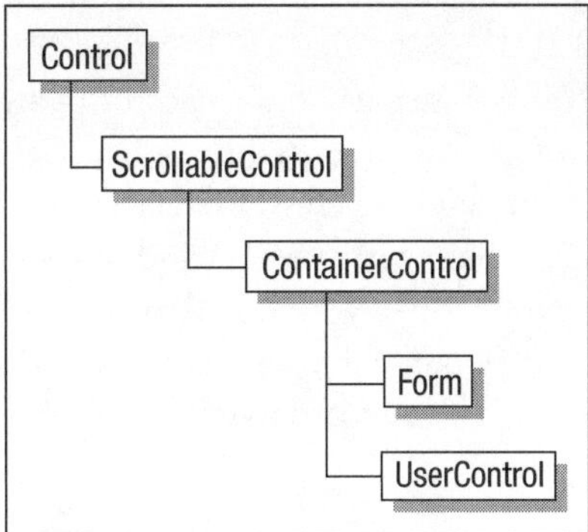

Figure 7.1
The simplified inheritance hierarchy for the **Form** and **UserControl** classes.

- Responding to user input by means of keyboard- and mouse-related events
- Processing operating system messages

You will rarely subclass the **Control** class directly, although it is not an abstract class so you can do so.

The ScrollableControl Class

The **ScrollableControl** class adds the functionality for scrolling. This means that a component can hold more content than is visible at one time, with different parts being brought into view by scrolling. The members that this class implements almost all relate to scrolling, such as specifying whether scrollbars are displayed and the distance to scroll when the user clicks the scrollbars. As with the **Control** class, the **ScrollableControl** class is rarely, if ever, used directly as a base class.

The ContainerControl Class

The **ContainerControl** class implements the capability to act as a container—in other words, to contain child controls. It is obvious why a form would need to contain child controls, but why would one control need to contain other controls? First of all, when you create your own custom controls, you will usually design them by combining two or more controls into a single control, which requires the capability to manage child controls. Second, some of .NET's predefined controls are designed to create functional groupings of other controls, again requiring the capability to act as a container. The members implemented by the **ContainerControl** class relate to managing child controls, such as keeping track of which child control is currently active (has the focus).

The Form Class

The **Form** class, of course, inherits all the members of its base class and so possesses all the capabilities of the **ContainerControl** class, which in turn has inherited the capabilities of the **ScrollableControl** class, and so on back to the ultimate base class, **Object**. The **Form** class adds some of the functionality that you usually associate with screen windows, such as a title bar and a system menu. With the **Form** class, you finally have a class that you will use a lot. As mentioned earlier, every Windows form that you create for a program is based on the **Form** class. Much of the remainder of this chapter will be devoted to explaining how to use this class in your projects.

The UserControl Class

Like the **Form** class, the **UserControl** class inherits all the members of its ancestor classes, which are the same as for the **Form** class. This means that in many ways the **UserControl** class is like the **Form** class: It has the capability to respond to user input, to scroll, to contain other controls, and so on. It adds very little to its inherited members and is designed to provide a base class on which to build self-contained components that present a single interface to their containers. Custom controls that you create will be based on this class.

The Form Class

This section provides information on how to work with forms. Specifically, it details the class members (properties, methods, and events) that the VB .NET programmer will need most often. A complete coverage of all the members of the **Form** class is beyond the scope of this book, but you can find the details in the .NET framework documentation.

When you add a form to your project, it has certain default properties that control its appearance and behavior. These default settings might be fine, and it is not at all uncommon for a form to be used without any changes to its properties (except for the **Text** property, which controls the caption displayed in the form's title bar). When you have to, however, you can work with the **Form** class's properties to customize the appearance and behavior of the form to suit the needs of your application. The relevant properties are presented here, arranged by category. Please note that there is some overlap between the categories–for example, some properties that control a form's behavior also have an influence on its appearance.

Form properties can be set at design time using the property window or at runtime in code. These two methods are actually equivalent, because when you set a property to a value other than the default using the property window, the result is to add the corresponding line of code to the **Form** class, in the **Windows Form Designer Generated Code** section. Property settings are done in the **InitializeComponent()** procedure, and if you want to write code to change the form's initial properties, rather than relying on the property window, this is the place to do it. Some properties can also be set in the form constructor (that is, the

New() procedure), but it is advisable to use the **InitializeComponent()** procedure for all such code to set the form's initial properties.

Form Behavior

There are several properties that affect the behavior of a form. Some of these properties also affect its appearance, but are covered in this section.

Form Border Style

The border style of a form, set by its **FormBorderStyle** property, determines the appearance of the form's border as well as whether the form can be resized and moved by the user and whether it displays a title bar. The possible settings for this property are described in Table 7.1.

When setting the **FormBorderStyle** property in code, use the **FormBorderStyle** enumeration, which includes the constants listed in Table 7.1. Here's an example:

```
Form1.FormBorderStyle = FormBorderStyle.FixedDialog
```

This enumeration is part of the **System.Windows.Forms** namespace.

Form Buttons

A form can display several buttons in its title bar that are used to perform various actions, such as closing the form. You control the display of these buttons with the form properties described in Table 7.2. All of these properties are True/False values, with a setting of **True** displaying the corresponding button. Note that the display of certain buttons is dependent on the form's **FormBorderStyle** property, as described earlier in this chapter. For example, if **FormBorderStyle** is set to **FixedToolWindow**, the form cannot have a Maximize or Minimize button regardless of the settings of the related properties.

Table 7.1 Settings for the Form class's FormBorderStyle property.

Border Style	Border	Move?	Resize?	Title Bar?
None	No border	No	No	No
FixedSingle	Single	Yes	No	Yes
Fixed3D	3-dimensional	Yes	No	Yes
FixedDialog	Single*	Yes	No	Yes
Sizable (the default)	Single	Yes	Yes	Yes
FixedToolWindow	Single	Yes	No	Yes**
SizableToolWindow	Single	Yes	No	Yes**

** The **FixedSingle** and **FixedDialog** styles look identical, although according to the documentation, the **FixedDialog** style is supposed to have a thicker border.*

*** The title bar of the **FixedToolWindow** and **SizableToolWindow** styles is somewhat thinner than a normal title bar, and it lacks the Minimize, Maximize, and Control Menu buttons.*

Table 7.2 Properties that control form buttons.

Property	Description
MinimizeBox	Displays a Minimize button at the right end of the title bar. Clicking this button hides the form.
MaximizeBox	Displays a Maximize button at the right end of the title bar. Clicking this button expands the form to fill the screen.
ControlBox	Displays a Control Menu button at the left end of the title bar. Clicking this button displays the form's Control menu.
HelpButton	Displays a Help button (a small box with a question mark) at the right end of the title bar. A Help button cannot display if either the Maximize or Minimize button is displayed. Use of the Help button is covered later in this chapter.

Form Appearance

Certain aspects of a form's appearance are under the programmer's control. You can, for example, display an image in the form as a background and specify the font for text that is displayed on the form. These properties are described in Table 7.3, with additional explanation for some properties in the accompanying text.

The **ForeColor** property determines the color that will be used for graphic objects, such as lines, that are drawn on the form. More important, this property is inherited by all controls on the form. Thus, if you set the form's **ForeColor** property, all of the controls on the form will use that same foreground color unless you set their **ForeColor** property explicitly. The same is true of the **BackColor** property. Note that the **BackColor** property has no effect on the appearance of the form if a background image is used, but it still affects controls on the form. Both the **ForeColor** and **BackColor** properties are set using the **Color** structure, explained later in this chapter.

The **BackgroundImage** property can be used to specify an image to display in the form, behind any controls it has. If the image is smaller than the form, it is tiled to fill the form. In the property window, you can browse to select an image file from your disk. In code, this property is specified as an **Image** object, which will be explained in more detail in Chapter 17.

Table 7.3 Appearance-related properties of the Form class.

Property	Description
ForeColor	The foreground color of the form.
BackColor	The background color of the form.
BackgroundImage	The image displayed in the form's background.
Cursor	The appearance of the mouse cursor while over the form.
Font	The font used for text on the form. See the section "Working with Fonts" in Chapter 8 for more details.
Text	The text displayed in the form's title bar.

The **Cursor** property specifies the appearance of the mouse cursor when it's over the form. You set this property using the **Cursors** class, part of the **System.Windows.Forms** namespace. This class has various static properties, each of which defines a particular type of cursor. Those you will use most often are described in Table 7.4. You can find out about other **Cursors** class members in the online help. Here's a code snippet that displays the Wait cursor (an hourglass) during some lengthy process and then sets it back to the default when the process is complete. Note the use of the **Me** keyword to refer to the current object—in this case, the form in which the code is running.

```
Me.Cursor = Cursors.WaitCursor

' Long process occurs here.

Me.Cursor = Cursors.Default
```

Form Size and Position

A form has properties that control its size and position on the screen. It also has properties that specify its minimum and maximum sizes, its initial position when first displayed, and its state. Table 7.5 describes these size- and position-related properties. Some of these properties make use of the **Point** and **Size** structures, which are explained later in this section.

Table 7.4 Commonly used members of the Cursors class.

Property	Description
Arrow	The standard arrow cursor (pointing northwest)
Cross	The crosshair cursor
Default	The default cursor, usually the same as **Arrow**
Hand	The hand cursor
Help	The help cursor (an arrow with a question mark)
Ibeam	The vertical I-beam cursor (typically used when editing or selecting text)
No	The No cursor (a red circle with a slash through it)
UpArrow	An upward-pointing arrow
WaitCursor	The Wait cursor (an hourglass)

Table 7.5 Size- and position-related properties of the Form class.

Property	Description
Height, **Width**	Integers specifying the height and width of the form.
Left, **Top**	Integers specifying the position of the form's left and top edges with respect to its container.
Location	A **Point** structure specifying the location of the form's top-left corner with relation to its container (usually the screen) in pixels.
MaximumSize	A **Size** structure specifying the form's maximum permitted vertical and horizontal dimensions, in pixels. Set to **0, 0** to impose no maximum size.

(continued)

Table 7.5 Size- and position-related properties of the Form class *(continued)*.

Property	Description
MinimumSize	A **Size** structure specifying the form's minimum permitted vertical and horizontal dimensions, in pixels. Set to **0, 0** to impose no minimum size.
Size	A **Size** structure specifying the form's vertical and horizontal dimensions, in pixels.
StartPosition	Specifies the initial position of the form. See Table 7.6 for possible settings from the **FormStartPositon** enumeration.
WindowState	The state of the window as specified by the **FormWindowState** enumeration: **Maximized**, **Minimized**, or **Normal**.

Table 7.6 Settings for the StartPosition property (from the FormStartPosition enumeration).

Enumeration Member	Description
CenterParent	Centered within the parent form
CenterScreen	Centered on the screen
Manual	As set by the **Location** property
WindowsDefault Bounds	Size and position set by the operating system defaults
WindowsDefault Location	Position set by the operating system default; size set by the **Size** property

Note that there is some duplication of function in the properties: the **Width** and **Height** properties duplicate the function of the **Size** property, and the **Left** and **Top** properties duplicate the function of the **Location** property. This is an intentional arrangement. The **Width**, **Height**, **Left**, and **Top** properties actually control the form's size and position, and the **Size** and **Location** properties provide another way to access these properties using the **Size** and **Point** structures. Thus, if you set the **Location** property, you are actually setting the **Top** and **Left** properties. Likewise, if you read the **Size** property, you are actually retrieving the values of the **Height** and **Width** properties packaged in a **Size** structure.

When using these properties, you must realize that some interactions occur between them. For example, if during design you set a form's **WindowState** property to **Maximized**, when the form is first displayed, any **Size** property you have assigned will be ignored.

*The **Point** Structure*

The **Point** structure represents a point on a two-dimensional plane. It contains two coordinates, X and Y, for the horizontal and vertical components of the location. No assumptions are made about the units of coordinates, which is decided by the user of the **Point** structure. In the context of form properties, the units are screen pixels.

The **Point** structure has several constructors. The one you'll use most often initializes the coordinates with two values passed to the structure:

```
Sub New(X As Integer, Y As Integer)
```

For example, you could create a new **Point** structure initialized to the coordinates 100,200 as follows:

```
Dim p As New Point(100,200)
```

If you are setting a property that uses a **Point** structure, you do not have to create a reference to the **Point** object but can do the assignment directly, as shown in this example, which moves the indicated form to the top-left corner of the screen:

```
Form1.Location = New Point(0, 0)
```

Because **Point** is a structure, and hence a value type, you cannot set its members directly. Thus, the following will not compile:

```
Form1.Location.X = 250
```

You need to use the **Left** or **Top** property if you want to set the horizontal or vertical position separately. For example, this code moves the form 50 pixels to the right:

```
Form1.Left += 50
```

Members of the **Point** structure are described in Table 7.7.

*The **Size** Structure*

The **Size** structure represents the size of a rectangular region as a width and height. As with the **Point** structure, no assumptions are made about the unit of measurement. This structure has two constructors. One initializes the structure with separate width and height values, as shown here:

```
Sub New(Width As Integer, Height As Integer)
```

The other constructor initializes the **Size** structure with data from a **Point** structure:

```
Sub New(sz As Point)
```

Table 7.7 Frequently needed members of the Point structure.

Member	Description
IsEmpty	Returns **True** if the structure is empty, **False** if not
X	The X (horizontal) coordinate
Y	The Y (vertical) coordinate
Equals(*p*)	Returns **True** if the point has the same coordinates as the point ***p***
Op_Equality(*X*, *Y*)	Returns **True** if the point has the coordinates ***X*, *Y***

The result of using this second form of the constructor is that the **Size** structure represents a rectangle with one corner at coordinates 0,0 and the other corner at the coordinates specified by the **Point** structure.

The following code snippet sets the size of the form to be 250 pixels on a side:

```
Form1.Size = New Size(250, 250)
```

The following line of code increases the size of the form (referenced by the **Me** keyword) by 10 percent each time it is run:

```
Me.Size = New Size(Me.Size.Width * 1.1, Me.Size.Height * 1.1)
```

Like **Point**, **Size** is a value type and its members cannot be set directly:

```
Me.Size.Width += 100  ' Does not compile!
```

Frequently needed members of the **Size** structure are described in Table 7.8.

Form Layout and Design

Several of the **Form** class's properties are relevant only during design mode. In other words, they have no effect on the form's appearance or behavior when the program runs, but only while you are designing it. These properties can be set during form design, but not in code. They are as follows:

- *DrawGrid*—A Boolean value specifying whether a design grid is drawn on the form.
- *GridSize*—A type **Size** specifying the size of the grid.
- *SnapToGrid*—A Boolean value specifying whether controls on the form snap to the grid.

Other Form Properties

This section covers a number of **Form** class properties that do not fit into any of the earlier categories.

Table 7.8 Frequently needed members of the Size structure.

Member	Description
IsEmpty	Returns **True** if the structure is empty, having 0 **Width** and **Height**
Width	The horizontal dimension
Height	The vertical dimension
Equals(*sz*)	Returns **True** if the size has the same dimensions as the size ***sz***

Tag

The **Tag** property provides a place for the programmer to store arbitrary information. The data type is **Object**, so this property can hold essentially any type of data. The setting of this property has no effect on the form—it is provided only as a convenience for the programmer. The default property value is **Nothing**.

AcceptButton

The **AcceptButton** property identifies a Button control on the form that will be the form's default, or "Accept," button. This button will be triggered (as if the user had clicked it) when the user presses Enter while the form is active. In the property window, you can select from a list of Button controls that exist on the form when setting this property. In code, assign the button's reference to this property. Here is an example, assuming this code is running in a form named **Form1**:

```
Dim button1 As New Button()
button1.text = "OK"
button1.Location = New Point(50,100)
Form1.AcceptButton = button1
```

In some situations, a control on the form might intercept the input when the user presses Enter. For example, if the user is entering text in a text box that has its **Multiline** property set to **True**, pressing Enter starts a new line of text. In such situations, the default button will not be activated.

CancelButton

The **CancelButton** property identifies a Button control that will be the form's "Cancel" button, triggered when the user presses Esc. In other respects, this property works just like the **AcceptButton** property.

Icon

The **Icon** property is used to specify the form's icon, which is displayed in the taskbar as well as being the button (in the form's title bar) for the Control menu. If you do not explicitly specify an icon, the default form icon will be used. In the property window, you can browse your disk for icon files (*.ico) to use for this property. The data type of this property is **Icon**. Visual Studio provides a comprehensive library of icons, and you can create your own custom icons using one of the many icon editors that are available.

ShowInTaskbar

This is a Boolean property that determines whether the form is represented by an icon in the taskbar. The default setting is **True**. If you set this property to **False**, it will not have an icon in the taskbar but the user will still be able to switch to and from the form using Alt+Tab.

TopMost

TopMost is a Boolean property that determines whether the form is a top-most form that displays "on top" of all other forms even when it does not have the focus. The default setting is **False**.

AutoScroll

The **AutoScroll** property is relevant only when the contents of the form are larger than the form itself. If **AutoScroll** is **True**, the form automatically displays scrollbars when needed, permitting the user to scroll hidden parts of the form into view. The default setting is **False**.

Form Events

The **Form** class can detect a wide variety of events, both generated by the user and generated by the system. Because form events have a lot of overlap with control events, they are discussed together later in this chapter.

Form Methods

The **Form** class has numerous methods that perform some action on the form or its contents. There are too many methods to cover them all in this book, so this section is limited to those methods that a programmer will use most frequently. They are summarized in Table 7.9.

Table 7.9 Frequently used methods of the Form class.

Method	Description
Activate	Activates the form and gives it the focus. If the form is part of the active application, it is brought to the front. If not, the form's title bar flashes. The form must be visible for this method to have any effect.
BringToFront	Brings the form to the front of the Z-order.
Close	Closes and destroys the form. If you close a form and then redisplay it, it will be reinitialized. When all of an application's forms are closed, the application terminates.
Contains(*ctrl*)	Returns **True** if the specified control is contained by the form.
GetChildAtPoint(*pt*)	Returns a reference to the child control located at the position specified by ***pt*** (which is a type **Point**). Returns a null reference (the value **Nothing**) if no control is located at the specified position.
Hide	Hides the form but does not destroy it.
Refresh	Forces the form to repaint itself and any child controls.
Reset*XXXX*	Resets the property specified by ***XXXX*** to its default value. Possible values of ***XXXX*** include **BackColor**, **Cursor**, **Font**, **ForeColor**, and **Text**.
SendToBack	Sends the control to the back of the Z-order.
Show	Makes the form visible.
ShowDialog	Shows the form as a modal dialog box. See the text for an explanation of *modal*.

The Z-order

The Windows operating system often has a number of overlapping windows on the screen. The Z-order refers to the order of those windows. If you think of a messy desk as an analogy, the sheet of paper on top of the pile is at the top of the Z-order, and the sheet at the bottom of the pile is at the back of the Z-order.

You can use two methods to show a form: **Show()** and **ShowDialog()**. The former method displays the form as a non-modal window. This means that other parts of the application remain accessible while the form is displayed. For example, if the application was displaying its main form and a second form was displayed using **Show()**, the user would be able to switch back to the first form while the second form was still displayed.

In contrast, **ShowDialog()** displays the form as a modal window. This means that the user cannot switch away from the form to any other part of the application—the form must be explicitly closed first. In addition, the **ShowDialog()** method returns a value indicating which button the user selected in the form. Using modal forms will be explained in more detail later in the chapter, in the section "Working with Forms."

Designing Forms

Much of the effort that goes into creating a Windows application is involved with form design. This is an important part of application development; a well-designed user interface makes a program easy and intuitive to use. In contrast, a bad user interface can make things very difficult for the user. I can't tell you how to design your forms—that will depend on the specific needs of your program. I can, however, show you how to use the form design tools in Visual Studio.

Adding Controls to a Form

The three methods you can use to add a control to a form are as follows:

- Double-click a control in the Toolbox. This adds a default size control to the form at the position of the currently selected control. If no control is selected, the new control is placed in the top-left corner of the form.
- Click a control in the Toolbox, then drag on the form to place the control. The size and position of the control are determined by your dragging.
- Select a control that is already on the form by clicking it. Copy the control to the Clipboard by pressing Ctrl+C, and then paste the copy onto the form by pressing Ctrl+V. You can use the Copy and Paste commands on the Edit menu if you prefer. When you copy and paste an existing control, the new control inherits all of the property settings of the copied control (except for the **Name** property, which is changed).

Selecting Controls

Many of the things you will do with controls require that you select the control or controls to work with. You can select a single control in one of two ways: by clicking on the control or by selecting it from the drop-down list at the top of the property window. The selected control displays a shaded border with small boxes that are called *handles*. In Figure 7.2, the OK button is selected.

To select multiple controls, select one control and then hold down the Shift key while clicking the other controls you want to select. You can also drag over a group of controls to select them. This latter method works only when the Pointer tool is active in the Toolbox. When multiple controls are selected, each one displays a border and handles. You will notice that one control (the last one selected) has black handles, while all the others have white handles. This is important when using the alignment and sizing tools, described later in this chapter.

To select the form, click anywhere on the form between the controls.

Sizing and Arranging Controls

You can change the size and position of controls by setting the corresponding properties in the property window, but it's a lot easier to use the Form Designer's layout tools. To move a control, or a group of selected controls, point at the control(s) with the mouse; the mouse pointer will change to a four-headed arrow. Then, drag to the new location. To resize a selected control, point at one of its handles; the mouse pointer will change to a two-headed arrow. Drag the control to the new size. A control might display some of its handles in gray, which means that these handles are not available for resizing. For example, a TextBox control with its **Multiline** property set to **False** has a fixed height based on its font, and you cannot change its height during design. You can, however, change its width. Therefore, its handles display as shown in Figure 7.3.

The Form Designer provides various commands that make certain layout tasks easier. For example, you can align controls with one another, make their sizes the same, and so on.

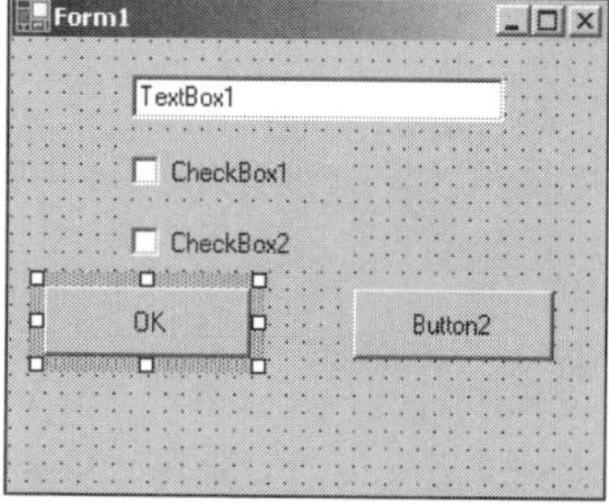

Figure 7.2
The selected control is displayed with a border and handles, in this case the OK button.

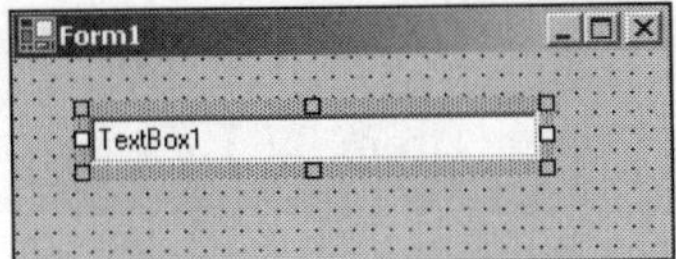

Figure 7.3
Gray handles on a selected control mean you cannot resize the control in those directions.

The Magical Undo Command

Any editing action that you take can be reversed using the Undo command on the Edit menu. Undo has several "levels," and each time you select the Undo command, the Form Designer reverses one more action. Use the Redo command to reverse an Undo.

Many of these layout tasks would be very difficult to do manually. The basic procedure is to select the controls you want to change, selecting the "model" control last (so it displays black handles). All the other controls will be adjusted to match the model control. Then, select one or more commands from the Format menu as follows (or use the buttons on the Layout toolbar):

- Select Align to align controls with one another. Then select Lefts, Centers, or Rights to move controls horizontally so their left edges, centers, or right edges align. Select Tops, Middles, or Bottoms to move controls vertically so their top edges, middles, or bottom edges align. Select Size To Grid to align all controls to the design grid.
- Select Make Same Size to change the control size. Then select Width to make the controls the same width, Height to make the controls the same height, or Both to adjust both width and height. Select Size To Grid to adjust all control sizes, both height and width, to the design grid.
- Select Horizontal Spacing or Vertical Spacing to change the horizontal or vertical spacing between the controls. Then select Make Equal, Increase, Decrease, or Remove as needed.
- Select Center In Form, then select Horizontally or Vertically to center the control(s) in the form.

Locking Controls

When designing a form, particularly when working on a large, complex form, you might want to lock controls to prevent inadvertent changes. A locked control cannot be selected, and therefore its size and position cannot be changed in the Form Designer. You can still work with its properties, however. Here are the steps to take:

- To lock a single control, set its **Locked** property to **True**.

- To lock a group of controls, select the controls and then set the **Locked** property to **True**.
- To lock all controls, and the form as well, select Lock Controls from the Format menu.

To unlock controls, set the **Locked** property back to **False**. If you used the Lock Controls command to lock the entire form, you must unlock the controls individually.

The Z-Order

The controls on a form have a Z-order that works in the same way as the Z-order for forms on the screen. If you do not have overlapping controls on a form, the Z-order is irrelevant. When controls do overlap, the Z-order determines which controls display on top of or behind other controls. To illustrate, look at Figure 7.4. On this form, **TextBox1** is at the top, or front, of the Z-order, and **TextBox2** is at the back of the Z-order.

When you add controls to a form, the Z-order is determined by the order in which controls are added. Each control you add is at the top of the Z-order until you add another control. To change the Z-order, select a control, select Order from the Format menu, and then select Bring To Front or Send To Back. Other than moving a control to the front or the back, you cannot assign specific positions in the Z-order.

The Tab Order

When a program is running, the user can select a control on the form by clicking it or by pressing Tab or Shift+Tab. The latter technique moves the focus forward or backward through the controls according to the *tab order*. Each control on the form has a **TabIndex** property that determines its position in the tab order. This property is automatically assigned, starting with 0, as controls are added to the form during design. The control with **TabIndex 0** will receive the focus automatically when the form is first displayed.

If you need to change the tab order, you can change the **TabIndex** property of individual controls. It is much easier, however, to use the Tab Order command on the View menu. When you select this command, the **TabIndex** setting of each control is displayed in its upper-left corner, as shown in Figure 7.5. Click the controls in order to establish the desired tab order. Then, select Tab Order from the View menu again to save the changes.

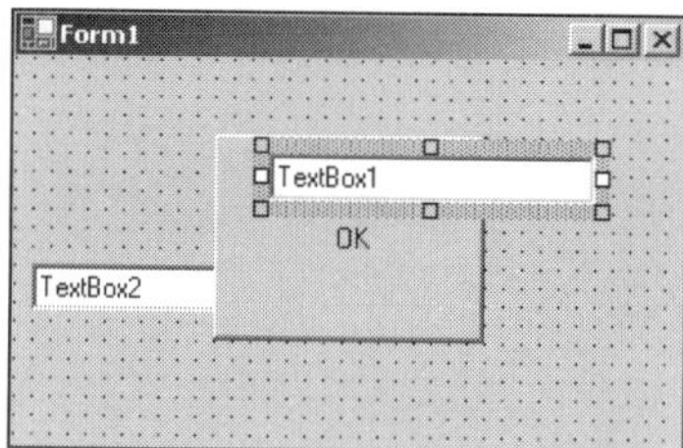

Figure 7.4
The display of overlapping controls is determined by the Z-order.

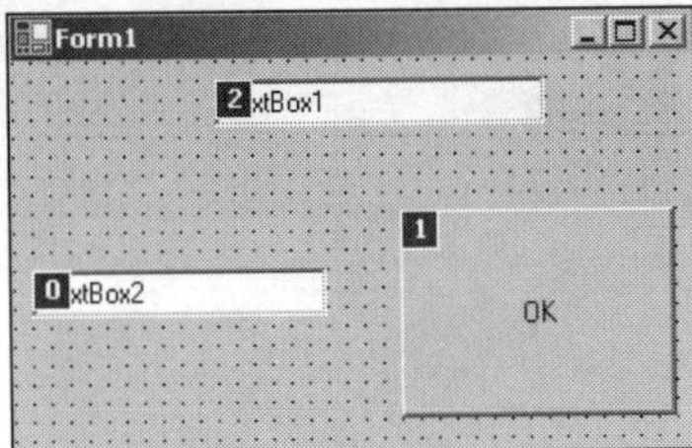

Figure 7.5
Using the View Tab Order command to set the tab order.

Two other properties affect tabbing. If the **TabStop** property is set to **False**, the control cannot be given the focus by tabbing (although it can be given the focus with the mouse). If the **Enabled** property is **False**, the control cannot receive the focus by any means.

Adding Menus to Your Forms

A Windows form can use two types of menus. A main menu is the standard type of menu that you see displayed across the top of many Windows applications. A context menu is displayed when the user right-clicks a screen element. Windows applications support both types of menus, by means of the **MainMenu** and **ContextMenu** controls. You'll learn how to use these controls in the next chapter.

Working with Forms

Some simpler Windows applications have only a single form and are very simple to work with. The form is displayed automatically when the program starts, and it is closed (hence ending the program) when the user clicks the Close button in the title bar or the **Me.Close()** statement is executed in the form's code. Projects with multiple forms are more complex.

The Startup Form

When you start a new Windows application project, it has a single form that is by default the project's startup form—the form that is automatically displayed when the project is executed. If you add other forms to the project, you can make another form the startup form as follows:

1. In the Solution Explorer, right-click the project name, then select Properties from the pop-up menu.
2. In the property page, select General under Common Properties (as shown in Figure 7.6).
3. Open the Startup Object list and select the form that you want to be the startup form.
4. Click OK.

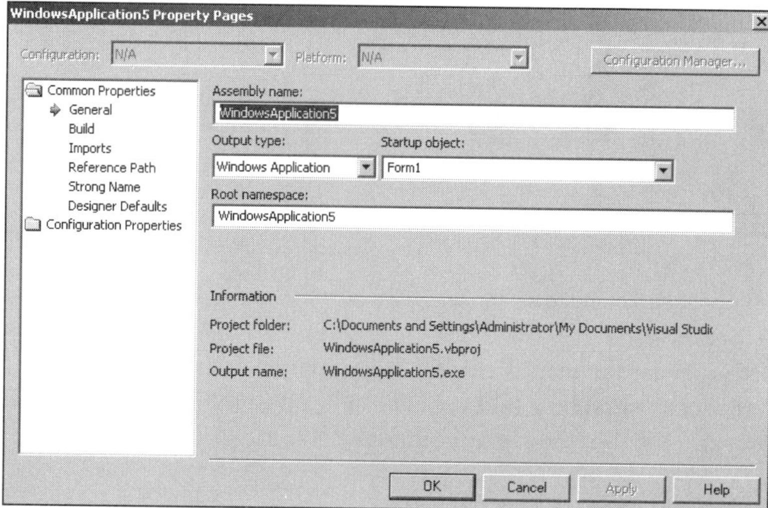

Figure 7.6
Selecting the startup form in the project's property page.

Displaying and Hiding Forms

After the startup form is displayed, other forms in the project must be displayed and hidden as needed by means of code, using the **Show()**, **ShowDialog()**, **Hide()**, and **Close()** methods. Let's look at some examples.

To display a form other than the startup form, create an instance of it and then call its **Show** or **ShowDialog()** method. For instance, suppose that a project has two forms named **Form1** and **Form2**, with **Form1** being the startup form. The following code, executed in **Form1** (perhaps in the **Click()** event procedure for a Button control), will display **Form2** (while leaving **Form1** displayed in the background):

```
Dim f2 As New Form2()
f2.Show()
```

After you have finished using **Form2**, the following code, executing in **Form2**, will close it:

```
Me.Close()
```

Suppose, however, you want to hide **Form1** while **Form2** is displayed, then redisplay it when **Form2** is closed. It's easy enough to hide **Form1** by calling its **Hide()** method. However, in order for code in **Form2** to redisplay **Form1**, it requires a reference to the instance of **Form1**. You can accomplish this in several ways, including defining a property of **Form2** to hold a reference to the form that displayed it, or using a **Sub Main()** (explained later in this chapter) to create global references to all forms. I prefer to overload the form constructor, permitting a reference to the calling form to be passed when the second form is instantiated. This is done as follows:

1. In the second form, create a variable with module scope to hold the reference to the calling form. It will be type **Object**; for example:

```
Dim theCaller As Object
```

2. Create an overloaded constructor for the second form that takes one type **Object** argument. In the constructor, assign the argument value to the variable created in Step 1. The best way to create a new constructor is to copy the existing one and then modify it, because two lines of code must be present in a form constructor:

```
Public Sub New(ByVal caller As Object)

    ' The next 2 lines are required in a form constructor.
    MyBase.New()
    InitializeComponent()

    theCaller = caller

End Sub
```

3. In the first form, the code to instantiate and display the second form and hide the first form will look like this:

```
Dim f2 As New Form2(Me)
f2.Show()
Me.Hide()
```

4. Finally, the code in **Form2** to hide it and redisplay **Form1** (or whatever form displayed **Form2**) is the following:

```
Me.Hide()
If Not IsNothing(theCaller) Then theCaller.Hide()
theCaller = Nothing
```

This technique will be demonstrated further in a short program presented at the end of this chapter.

Using Sub Main

A VB .NET project offers you the option of starting execution in a **Sub** procedure named **Main()** rather than by displaying a startup form. When you use this technique, no form is displayed automatically, but rather form display is controlled by code in **Main()**. This can be very useful in situations where a different form might be displayed based on conditions. Code in **Main()** can perform such tasks as querying a database or accessing a Web service, and then can decide which form to display based on the information obtained. To use a **Sub Main()** in your program, follow these steps:

1. Follow the steps described earlier for selecting the startup form. However, in the drop-down list, do not select a form; instead, select Sub Main.
2. Select Add Project from the Project menu to add a module to the project. You can also use an existing module if you like.
3. In the module, add **Sub Main()** as follows:

   ```
   Sub main()

   End Sub
   ```

4. Within **Sub Main()**, add the code to instantiate and display forms as needed, as well as code to carry out any other actions required at this time by your program.

I'll present a short demonstration of using **Sub Main()** at the end of the chapter.

Using Modal Forms

You learned earlier that the **ShowDialog** method displays a form modally, which means that the user cannot switch to any other part of the program until the modal form is closed. This technique is used primarily with dialog boxes that are designed to get information from the user. You would not want the user to be able to switch to another form while the dialog box remains open. Also, the **ShowDialog()** method returns information when the modal form is closed, identifying the button that the user clicked.

Returning information from a modal form makes use of the **DialogResult** property, which is a member of the **Form** and **Button** classes. This property can be set to one of the following members of the **DialogResult** enumeration:

```
Abort
Cancel
Ignore
No
None
OK
Retry
Yes
```

Here's how it works. If a form is displayed with the **ShowDialog()** method, when the form is closed (by calling its **Close** method, for example) the return value of the **ShowDialog()** method is the value that was assigned to the form's **DialogResult** property. The calling code can examine this return value and take appropriate action. Suppose that **Form2** has an OK button and a Cancel button. Then, in the **Click()** event procedures for these buttons, you would place the following code:

In the OK button's **Click()** event procedure, the code would look something like this:

```
Me.DialogResult = DialogResult.OK
Me.Close()
```

In the Cancel button's **Click()** event procedure, the code would look something like this:

```
Me.DialogResult = DialogResult.Cancel
Me.Close()
```

In the form that displays **Form2**, the code would look something like this:

```
Dim f2 As New Form2()
Dim retval As DialogResult
retval = f2.ShowDialog()
If retval = DialogResult.OK Then

' Code here to handle the user clicking OK.

ElseIf retval = DialogResult.Cancel Then

'Code here to handle the user clicking Cancel.

End If
```

Even greater convenience is gained by using the **DialogResult** property of the **Button** class. If this property is set to any value other than **DialogResult.None** (the default), when the user clicks the button, the form is automatically closed and the property value is returned by the **ShowDialog()** method.

Events in Forms and Controls

Every form and control can detect a variety of events, including events generated by the user as well as events generated by code or by the system. An event will be detected only if you have created an event handler for it. This is an extremely powerful aspect of VB .NET programming, making it simple for the programmer to write responsive applications. Many dozens of events are available, and I can only touch upon the more important ones. Some events, particularly those that are mouse- and keyboard-related, are explained in detail in Chapter 8. Table 7.10 describes the more commonly used events that are available to your programs.

Table 7.10 Commonly needed events of the Form class and controls.

Event	Occurs when
Activated*	The form is activated by the user or by code.
Click	The object is clicked with the mouse.
Closed*	The form is closed.
Closing*	The form is closing.
Deactivate	The form loses the focus (is deactivated) by the user or by code.
DoubleClick	The object is double-clicked.
DragDrop	A drag-drop operation is completed.
DragEnter	An object is dragged over the form or control.
DragLeave	An object is dragged over and then off the form or control.
DragOver	An object is being dragged over the form or control.
GotFocus	When the object receives the focus.
KeyDown	When the user presses a key while the object has the focus.
KeyPress	When the user presses and releases a key while the object has the focus.
KeyUp	When the user releases a key while the object has the focus.
LostFocus	When the object loses the focus.
MouseDown	When the user presses the mouse button over the object.
MouseEnter	When the mouse pointer enters the object.
MouseHover	When the mouse pointer hovers over the object.
MouseLeave	When the mouse pointer leaves the object.
MouseMove	When the mouse pointer moves over the object.
MouseUp	When the user releases the mouse button over the object.
Move	When the object is moved.
Paint	When the object is redrawn (for example, after being uncovered by another window).
Resize	When the object's size is changed.
TextChanged	When the **Text** property is changed.

* ***Form*** *class only*

To have your program respond to an event, you must write an event handler for it. Visual Studio makes it easy to create event handlers by automatically creating the skeleton of the procedure for you. Here are the steps to follow:

1. In the code editor window, open the drop-down list at the top left of the window and select the object that will receive the event. For the form, select (Base Class Events).
2. Open the drop-down list at the top right of the window, which will display a list of all events for the selected object. Events that already have an event procedure are in bold. Figure 7.7 shows the event list displayed for a Button control.
3. Select the desired event. If an event procedure already exists for that event, it will be displayed for editing. If not, a new, empty event procedure will be displayed for editing.

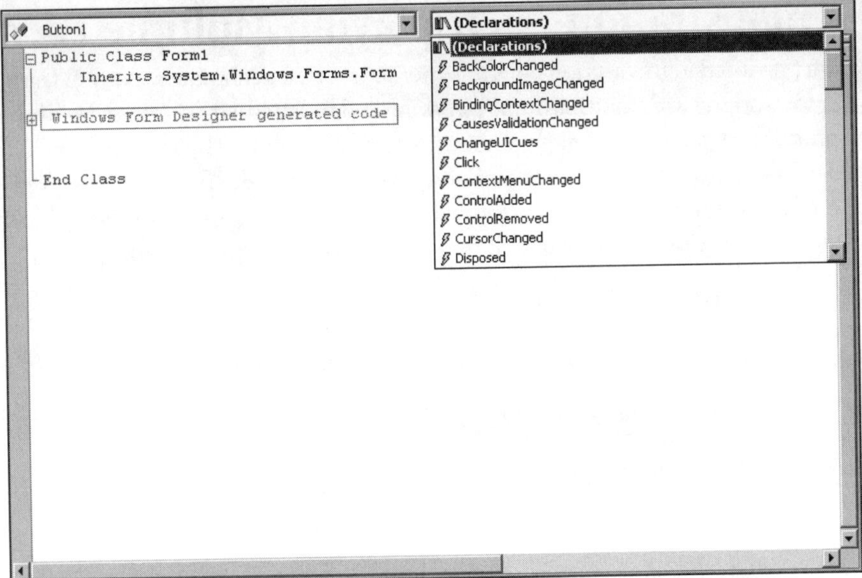

Figure 7.7
Selecting an event procedure for a control.

Every event procedure has the same fundamental syntax, as shown here:

```
Private Sub ProcName(arguments) Handles ObjectName.EventName
```

ProcName is the name of the procedure. Visual Studio assigns default names in the form ***ObjectName_EventName***, but you can change this if desired. Unlike with earlier versions of Visual Basic, the name of the event procedure is not what connects it to the event.

Arguments is a list of the arguments passed to the event procedure. This differs for different events, but typically includes one type **Object** argument that identifies the object that received the event, and a second argument that contains information about the event.

ObjectName is the name of the object receiving the event.

EventName is the name of the event.

It is the **Handles** clause that actually connects the event handler to a specific object and event. By including two or more object-event pairs, separated by commas, after the **Handles** keyword, you can have a single procedure handle multiple events. For example, the following event procedure would handle the **Click** event for **Button1** and **Button2**:

```
Private Sub MyClickHandler(ByVal Sender As Object, _
    ByVal e As System.EventArgs) Handles Button1.Click, Button2.Click
```

You'll learn more about events associated with specific controls in the next chapter.

Form Demonstration 1: Displaying Multiple Forms

The program presented in this section pulls together some of the techniques that you learned in this chapter for working with multiple forms, showing and hiding them as dictated by the needs of your program. The demonstration program consists of two forms. The startup form contains two buttons. One button displays the second form while leaving the first form displayed. The other button displays the second form and hides the first form. The second form has only a single button, which hides the second form and, if necessary, redisplays the first form.

To create this project, follow these steps:

1. Create a new Windows application named **MultiFormDemo**.
2. Place two Button controls on the form.
3. Change the **Text** property of **Button1** to "Show Form2 and hide me".
4. Change the **Text** property of **Button2** to "Show Form2 but don't hide me".
5. Use the Project | Add Windows Form Command to add a second form to the project. Accept the default name **Form2**.
6. Place a Button control on the second form and change its **Text** property to "Close Me".
7. Open the code editor window for **Form2** and add the following code to the class, after the **Inherits** statement and before the **Windows Form Designer** code:

```
Private theCaller As Object

    Public Sub New(ByVal caller As Object)
        MyBase.New()
        InitializeComponent()
        theCaller = caller
    End Sub
```

8. Still in **Form2**, create a **Click()** event procedure for **Button1**. Add the code shown here (this includes the entire event procedure):

```
Private Sub Button1_Click(ByVal sender As Object, _
            ByVal e As System.EventArgs) Handles Button1.Click
        Me.Hide()
        If Not IsNothing(theCaller) Then
            theCaller.Show()
          the(Caller = Nothing)
        End If
    End Sub
```

9. Return to **Form1** and display its code editor window. Create a **Click()** event procedure for **Button1** and edit it as follows:

```
Private Sub Button1_Click(ByVal sender As Object, _
            ByVal e As System.EventArgs) Handles Button1.Click
        Dim f2 As New Form2(Me)
        f2.Show()
        Me.Hide()
    End Sub
```

10. Still in **Form1**, create a **Click()** event procedure for **Button2** and edit it as follows:

```
Private Sub Button1_Click(ByVal sender As Object, _
            ByVal e As System.EventArgs) Handles Button1.Click
        Dim f2 As New Form2()
        f2.Show()
    End Sub
```

When you run the program, **Form1** will be displayed. Click either of the buttons to display **Form2**, and then click the button on **Form2** to return to **Form1**. This project can also demonstrate something about instances of forms: With **Form1** displayed, click the Show Form2 But Don't Hide Me button. You'll have both **Form2** and **Form1** on the screen. Make **Form1** active by clicking it, which is possible because **Form2** was not displayed modally. Click the same button again—you'll see a second copy of **Form2** displayed on the screen. This illustrates beautifully how a class (in this case your **Form2** file) is a blueprint from which you can create as many instances as you need.

Form Demonstration 2: Using Sub Main

The use of a **Sub Main()** can be useful, particularly in more complex projects that contain many forms. Code in **Sub Main()** can display one of several forms based on certain conditions. This technique is demonstrated by the program in this section. It has two forms, and the one that is displayed when the project starts is based on the date being even or odd. Here are the steps to follow:

1. Create a new Windows application project named **SubMainDemo**. The default form will be named **Form1**, which is fine.

2. Use the Project | Add Windows Form command to add a second form to the project. Accept the default name **Form2**.

3. Use the Project | Add Module command to add a module to the project, accepting the default module name.

4. Right-click the project name in the Solution Explorer and select Properties to display the property page for the project. On the General page, select Sub Main as the startup object, and then close the property page.

5. Open the code editor window for **Module1** and add the following code:

```
Sub main()
        Dim f As Form
        Dim d As Integer
        d = Day(Now)

        If d Mod 2 = 1 Then 'd is even
            f = New Form1()
        Else ' d is odd
            f = New Form2()
        End If
        f.ShowDialog()
    End Sub
```

The program is now ready to run. When you do so, you will see that if the current date is an even number, **Form1** is displayed; if the date is an odd number, **Form2** is displayed.

Summary

Creating Windows applications has never been faster or easier than with Visual Basic .NET. The .NET framework provides a new and unprecedented level of power and sophistication, offering the developer a rich set of classes for almost any imaginable programming need. Visual Basic's traditional excellence for interface design and coding let you pull all of your program's elements together quickly with little wasted effort. The result is higher quality applications and increased developer efficiency—things we all can appreciate.

Chapter 8
Controls for Windows Applications

A Windows application is based on forms and controls. A form, represented by the **Form** class, displays as a screen window, and controls that you place on the form provide the program's user interface. The previous chapter presented information on how to create and use forms. This chapter provides some general techniques for using controls and then presents specific information on individual controls in the .NET framework.

Working with Controls

The controls that are in the Visual Studio Toolbox for use on your Windows forms serve a wide variety of needs. Despite the differences between the various controls, they have certain members in common. This makes sense, when you think about it, because all of these controls are based, directly or indirectly, on the **Control** class. This section describes these common methods. Details of the individual controls are covered in the remainder of the chapter.

When you're working with controls, keep in mind this important aspect of the .NET framework: Many controls inherit certain properties from their parent—in this case, the form they are placed on. ("Inherit" is not the technically correct term in this situation, and "adopt" would be better, but the VB .NET documentation uses "inherit.") This means that if you set a property for the form, all controls will adopt that property value *unless* the property is explicitly set for that control. This applies mostly to properties that affect the appearance of a component, such as **ForeColor** and **BackColor**. Thus, if you want all controls on a form to use red as their foreground color, all you need to do is set the **ForeColor** property of the form to red and leave the **ForeColor** property of all controls at the default value.

Common Control Properties and Methods

Quite a few properties and methods are common to most or all controls. These properties and methods are members that are inherited from the **Control** class, from which all Windows controls inherit (using "inherit" here with its real meaning as part of object-oriented programming).

The ***Name*** *Property*

As with all components you use in your programs, a control has a **Name** property that uniquely identifies it within the form. When you add controls to a form, they are assigned default names that consist of the class name followed by a number, such as **TextBox1** and **Label2**. I suggest that you make it a habit to change the name of each control to something that is descriptive of its purpose. It can also be useful to use control name prefixes that identify the type of control, such as **txt** for a text box, **chk** for a checkbox, and so on. Thus, you might have text boxes named **txtFirstName** and **txtLastName**, and buttons named **btnOK** and **btnCancel**. I recommend retaining the default name only for controls that will not be referred to in code, such as Label controls.

Properties for Size and Position

Except for the few controls, such as ErrorProvider, that do not have a visual representation, all Windows controls have properties that specify their size and position on the form. For control position, these properties are **Location**, **Top**, and **Left**. A control's location is relative to its container (the form). For control size, these properties are **Size**, **Height**, and **Width**. These six properties work for controls as they do for forms, as described in Chapter 7.

The ***Anchor*** *Property*

The **Anchor** property specifies which edge or edges of its container a control is anchored to. Anchoring determines how the position and size of the control changes when the container is resized. By default, a control is anchored to the left and top edges of the container. When the container is resized, the control remains fixed at its location relative to the container's top-left corner, and its size does not change. This is illustrated in Figure 8.1.

Other anchoring possibilities are as follows:

- If a control is not anchored to either of a pair of opposing edges (top/bottom or left/right), it moves to retain its relative position between the edges but its size does not change.
- If a control is anchored to a pair of opposing edges (top/bottom or left/right), its size changes to retain a constant distance between the control and both of the edges.
- If a control is anchored to no edges, it moves to retain its relative position with all four edges, but its size does not change.

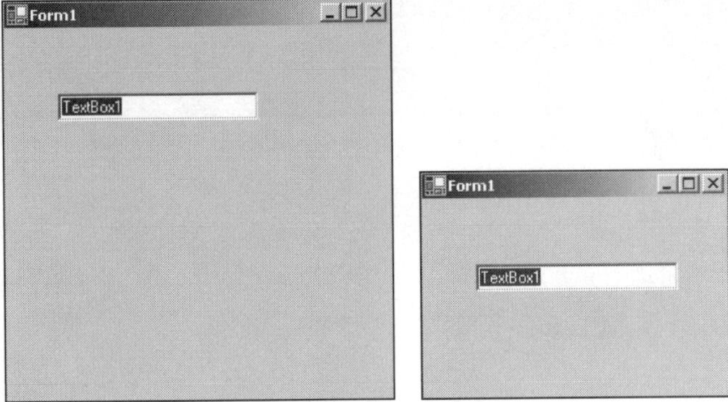

Figure 8.1
A control that is anchored to the container's top and left edges.

There are some constraints on the effects of anchoring. Certain controls, such as the ComboBox, have a fixed height that is based on the selected font. The height of such controls will not be changed when their parent is resized regardless of the anchoring setting.

In the Form Designer, you set a control's **Anchor** property graphically using the tool in the properties window. In code, you use the members of the **AnchorStyles** enumeration, which is part of the **System.Windows.Forms** namespace. The members are **Bottom**, **Left**, **None**, **Right**, and **Top**. To anchor a control to more than one edge, use the **Or** operator, as shown in this example:

```
Button1.Anchor = (AnchorStyles.Left Or AnchorStyles.Right)
```

*The **Dock** Property*

The **Dock** property lets you dock a control to one or all edges of its container. When a control is docked to an edge, its edge is aligned with that edge of its container (the form, usually). When the container is resized, the control's size changes as needed to match the edge's dimension. Figure 8.2 shows a form with a Button control that is docked to the bottom edge at two form sizes. This kind of docking is most appropriate for such controls as StatusBar. You can also dock a control on all four edges of the form; this is called *fill docking*. Fill docking results in the control automatically expanding as needed to fill the entire form. Fill docking could be used with a PictureBox control to ensure that it always fills the form.

In the Form Designer, you set a control's **Dock** property graphically using the tool in the property window. In code, you use the members of the **DockStyle** enumeration: **Bottom**, **Fill**, **Left**, **None**, **Right**, and **Top**. If you set the **Dock** property to a non-default setting, you must leave the **Anchor** property at its default, and vice versa. If you change the **Dock** property to a nondefault value, the **Anchor** property will automatically be changed back to its default value.

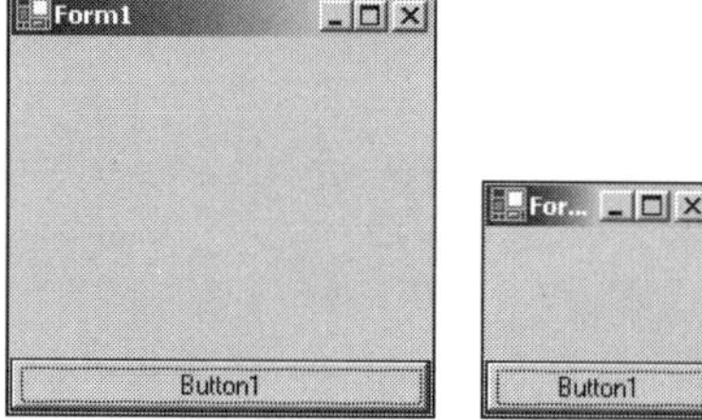

Figure 8.2
The Button control is docked to the form's bottom edge.

Appearance Properties

All visible controls have several properties that affect their appearance, as described in Table 8.1. You might recall that all of these properties are also members of the **Form** class, as discussed in the previous chapter.

In the form designed, you select values for the **ForeColor** and **BackColor** properties using a graphical palette in the properties window. In code, you use a **Color** structure, as explained later in this chapter.

*The **Enabled** Property*

Enabled is a Boolean property that specifies whether the control is enabled. When this property is set to **False**, the control is displayed grayed-out and the user cannot interact with it. When a control is disabled, it cannot respond to user events.

*The **Visible** Property*

The **Visible** property specifies whether the control is displayed. To hide a control, set this property to **False**. When a control is hidden, it cannot receive events.

*The **Tag** Property*

Most controls have the **Tag** property, which has data type **Object** so it can store essentially any type of data. This property is for the programmer's convenience, letting you associate any desired information with the control. The value of this property has no effect on the appearance or behavior of a control.

Table 8.1 Appearance-related control properties.

Property	Description
ForeColor	The foreground color of the control.
BackColor	The background color of the control.
BackgroundImage	The image displayed in the control's background.
Cursor	The appearance of the mouse cursor while over the control. See Chapter 7 for details.
Font	The font used for text on the control. See the section "Working with Fonts" later in this chapter for more details.
Text	The text displayed in the control.

*The **TabIndex** and **TabStop** Properties*

When a form is displayed, the user can move the focus from control to control by pressing Tab and Shift+Tab. The order in which the focus moves through the controls is determined by each control's **TabIndex** property, which is an index starting at 0. The focus moves first to the control with **TabIndex = 0**, then to the control with **TabIndex = 1**, and so on; Shift+Tab moves backwards in the order. The focus skips over any control with **TabStop** set to **False**. A few controls, such as Label, cannot receive the focus and have no **TabStop** property. These controls do have the **TabIndex** property, however. This means that if the user tries to tab to a Label control, the focus will move to the control that is just after it in the tab order.

The **TabIndex** property is assigned sequentially as you add controls to the form. You can change the tab order by manually changing the **TabIndex** property of individual controls, or by using the Tab Order command on the View menu. This latter technique was explained in Chapter 7.

*The **BringToFront()** and **SendToBack()** Methods*

The **BringToFront()** and **SendToBack()** methods affect the position of the control in the Z-order. **BringToFront()** moves the control to the front of the Z-order, which means that the control will display on top of any overlapping controls. **SendToBack()** moves the control to the back of the Z-order.

*The **Show()** and **Hide()** Methods*

The **Show()** and **Hide()** methods make the control visible or invisible, respectively. They work by setting the **Visible** property to **True** or **False**.

The Windows Form Controls

This section provides complete details and sample code for the Windows controls that are used most frequently. For the less-frequently used controls, a brief description is provided, and you can find the details in the VB .NET documentation. In these descriptions, the control's common properties and methods, as described earlier in this chapter, are not mentioned unless it is necessary.

Label

The Label control displays text that cannot be edited by the user. Its primary use is to provide an identifying label for another control, such as a text box. The text in a Label control can be changed by code, however, by means of the **Text** property. A Label control cannot receive the focus, but it still has a **TabIndex** property and can receive mouse-related events. The properties of the Label control are explained in Table 8.2, and Figure 8.3 shows a Label control (as well as some other controls).

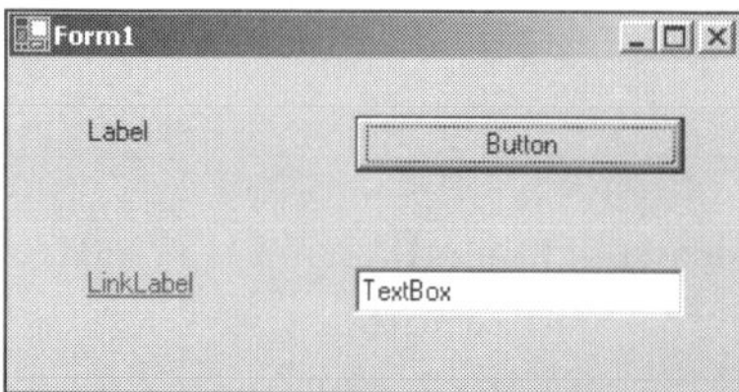

Figure 8.3
The Label, LinkLabel, TextBox, and Button controls.

Table 8.2 Properties of the Label control.

Property	Description
AutoSize	If this property is set to **True**, the control automatically resizes to display its entire contents. The default is **False**.
BorderStyle	Specifies the appearance of the control's borders. Can be set to one of the following **BorderStyle** enumerations: **Fixed3D**, **FixedSingle**, or **None**.
TextAlign	Specifies how text is aligned with respect to the four borders of the control. Can be set to any of the **ContentAlignment** members, as described later in this chapter. The default is **Left**.

LinkLabel

The LinkLabel control is specialized for the display of Web links. In addition to doing everything a Label control can do, it provides the capability to display some or all of its text as a link (underlined and in a different color) and to carry out some action when the link is clicked. The LinkLabel control has all of the members of the Label control plus the ones listed in Table 8.3. Figure 8.3 shows a LinkLabel control.

When first created, a LinkLabel has a single link that includes all of the text in the control (its **Text** property). In many situations, this is fine, but the control offers additional flexibility, letting you display text with only part of the text being the link.

To display a link that is part of the control's text, enter the text in the **Text** property first. Then, in the property window, open the **LinkArea** property and highlight the part of the text that will be the link. In code, you use the **LinkArea** structure that specifies what part of the control's text is the link. The constructor for the **LinkArea** has the following syntax:

```
Public Sub New(start As Integer, length As Integer)
```

Start is the character position where the link starts (the first character is at position 0), and ***length*** is the length of the link text. For example, the following code sets the LinkLabel control to display the indicated text with "my web site" as the link:

```
LinkLabel1.Text = "Visit my web site today!"
LinkLabel1.LinkArea = New LinkArea(6, 11)
```

Table 8.3 Special properties of the LinkLabel control.

Property	Description
ActiveLinkColor	References a **Color** structure that specifies the color that the link is displayed in when it is active (in the process of being clicked). The **Color** structure is described later in this chapter.
DisabledLinkColor	References a **Color** structure that specifies the color that a disabled link is displayed in (as specified by the **Enabled** property).
LinkArea	References a **LinkArea** structure that identifies the portion of the text that will be displayed as a link.
LinkColor	References a **Color** structure that specifies the color that the link is displayed in.
LinkVisited	Set to **True** to indicate the link has been visited.
VisitedLinkColor	References a **Color** structure that specifies the color that the link is displayed in when it has already been visited (as indicated by the **LinkVisited** property).

When the link in a LinkLabel control is clicked, its **LinkClicked()** event is fired. This is distinct from the **Click()** event, which occurs when any part of the control is clicked. The action that is taken when the link is clicked is up to the programmer—displaying a Web site in the system browser, displaying another form, and so on. The following code shows a **LinkClicked()** event procedure that will browse to the Microsoft Web site when the link is clicked, using the system default browser. Note that the code also sets the **LinkVisited** property to **True** so that the link will display in the color specified by the **VisitedLinkColor** property:

```
Private Sub LinkLabel1_LinkClicked(ByVal sender As Object, ByVal _
      e As System.Windows.Forms.LinkLabelLinkClickedEventArgs) _
      Handles LinkLabel1.LinkClicked

   LinkLabel1.LinkVisited = True
   System.Diagnostics.Process.Start("http://www.microsoft.com")

End Sub
```

This code uses the **System.Diagnostics.Process.Start()** method to launch the browser. The code relies on the fact that on most systems a particular browser is registered as the default application for Web pages. Thus, when you call the **Start()** method and pass it a Web page URL, the system "knows" what program to start.

The LinkLabel control has additional capabilities, specifically to display multiple links in a single control. You can refer to the VB .NET documentation for information on these advanced features.

Button

The Button control displays a button that the user can click to initiate some action. The caption displayed on a button is specified by its **Text** property. The alignment of the caption is specified by the **TextAlign** property, which can be set to a member of the **ContentAlignment** enumerations as described later in this chapter. If the caption is too long to fit within the width of the button, it will be wrapped to two or more lines. Figure 8.3 shows a Button control.

When the user selects a button, its **Click()** event is fired. You place the required code in this event procedure to carry out the associated action.

A form can contain one default Accept button and one Cancel button. A button that is designated as the Accept or Cancel button is automatically clicked when the user presses Enter or Esc, respectively. You create these buttons by setting properties of the form, specifically its **AcceptButton** and **CancelButton** properties. You'll find more details on these properties in Chapter 7.

The Button control has a **DialogResult** property that you can set to any of the following members of the **DialogResult** enumeration:

```
Abort
Cancel
Ignore
No
None
OK
Retry
Yes
```

This property is relevant only when the form containing the button has been displayed with the **ShowDialog()** method. Then, if the **DialogResult** property is set to any value other than **None**, clicking the button automatically closes the form and returns the property value to the calling code. You can learn more about this property in Chapter 7.

A Button control can display an image instead of, or in addition to, a text caption. You can set its image using either the **BackgroundImage** property or the **Image** property. If you specify images for both of these properties, the image specified by the **Image** property will display on top of the image specified by the **BackgroundImage** property. The alignment of the image specified by the **Image** property is controlled by the **ImageAlign** property, which can be one of the **ContentAlignment** enumeration members, as described later in this chapter.

To assign the **BackgroundImage** or **Image** property in code, use the **System.Drawing.Bitmap** class. For example, this code assigns Pic1.jpg as the image on **Button1**:

```
Button1.Image = New System.Drawing.Bitmap("Pic1.jpg")
```

You can specify the image file as a relative path, as in the previous example, or as an absolute path such as c:\data\images\pic1.jpg.

Another more flexible way to display images on a Button control is to set the Button control's **ImageList** property to refer to an ImageList control, which holds an indexed collection of images. By setting the Button control's **ImageIndex** property, you determine which of the images in the ImageList control is displayed on the button. The ImageList control is explained in detail later in this chapter.

TextBox

The TextBox control displays text that can be edited by the user. It is a very powerful control, and it finds use in many Windows applications. The text displayed by this control is not formatted, and the only appearance changes possible are to change the font and/or color of the text displayed. For display of formatted text, use the RichTextBox control (described later in the chapter). Figure 8.3 shows a TextBox control.

The TextBox control has two basic "personalities." When its **MultiLine** property is **False** (the default), the control displays a single line of text with a maximum length of 2,048 characters. If the text is wider than the control, part of the text will be hidden but can be brought into view with the standard cursor movement keys (Home, End, and so on) when the control has the focus. If the **AutoSize** property is **True**, the height of the text box cannot be changed and is determined by its font.

When the **MultiLine** property is **True**, the control can display multiple lines of text with a maximum capacity of approximately 32,000 characters. The height of the control can be adjusted as needed, and a vertical and/or horizontal scrollbar can be displayed. Lines of text are broken only where the text contains a CR/LF (carriage return/line feed). Otherwise, lines of text extend off the right side of the text box unless the **WordWrap** property is **True**, in which case long lines are broken at the right margin.

The properties of the TextBox control that you will use most often are described in Table 8.4.

Table 8.4 Commonly needed properties of the TextBox control.

Property	Description
AcceptsReturn	A **Boolean** value specifying whether the text box will accept Enter. See the text for details.
AcceptsTab	A **Boolean** value specifying whether the text box will accept tab characters. See the text for details.
AutoSize	A **Boolean** value specifying whether the height of the control automatically changes when the font size is changed.
MaxLength	The maximum number of characters that the text box can hold.
MultiLine	A **Boolean** value specifying whether the text box can display multiple lines of text.

(continued)

Table 8.4 Commonly needed properties of the TextBox control *(continued)*.

Property	Description
PasswordChar	Set this property to any single character, such as an asterisk, to have that character display in place of all other characters. The text box still holds the actual text, but this feature lets you hide a password from prying eyes.
ReadOnly	If this property is set to **True**, the user cannot modify the text that is displayed. The default is **False**.
ScrollBars	Specifies whether scrollbars are to be displayed in the text box. Set to one of the following values: **None**, **Horizontal**, **Vertical**, or **Both**. Applicable only when **MultiLine** is **True**.
TextAlign	Specifies how text is aligned with respect to the four borders of the control. Can be set to any of the **ContentAlignment** members, as described later in this chapter. The default is **Left**.
TextLength	The length (number of characters) of the text in the control.
WordWrap	A Boolean value specifying whether text automatically wraps to a new line when it reaches the right edge of the text box (applicable only if **MultiLine** is **True**).

When a user is working with a form, the Tab and Enter keys have special meanings. Pressing Tab moves the focus to the next control, and pressing Enter (Return) activates the default Button control (if one is defined). To have these keys accepted by the TextBox control so they can be used during text editing, you must set the **AcceptsTab** and/or **AcceptsReturn** properties to **True**. When these properties are **True** and the TextBox control has the focus, then the following is true:

- The focus can be moved to another control only by clicking that control.
- The default Button control must be clicked to be activated.

The TextBox control has a great deal of power built into it, and that power is available without any special programming on your part. You can select text (by highlighting it with the mouse or by pressing Shift while pressing an arrow key), cut and copy to the Clipboard, and paste from the Clipboard. The Clipboard commands are automatically available in the context menu that is displayed when the user right-clicks the text box. The control has several properties and methods that you can use programmatically to manipulate the text. Table 8.5 describes these properties and methods.

The following example will select the first five characters in the text box, cut that selection to the Clipboard, and then paste it at the end of the text:

```
TextBox1.Select(0, 5)
TextBox1.Cut()
TextBox1.SelectionStart = Len(TextBox1.Text)
TextBox1.Paste()
```

You'll see an example of using the TextBox control in a simple text editor later in this chapter.

Table 8.5 Properties and methods of the TextBox control relevant to text editing.

Property or Method	Description
Copy()	Copies the selected text to the Clipboard.
Cut()	Cuts the selected text to the Clipboard.
Paste()	Inserts text from the Clipboard at the insertion point.
Select(*start, length*)	Selects text in the text box starting at the specified character position and containing the specified number of characters. The first character has position 0.
SelectAll()	Selects all the text in the control.
SelectedText	Returns the currently selected text, or a zero-length string if no text is selected. If you set this property, the new text replaces the currently selected text.
SelectionLength	The number of characters in the current selection. If you set this property, the selection expands or contracts accordingly.
SelectionStart	The starting position of the current selection. If no text is selected, this property sets or returns the position of the insertion point (where new text will be inserted).

MainMenu

The MainMenu control is used to add a menu to a form. At runtime, the menu displays under the form's title bar, and it can have all of the features that are associated with the menus you see in commercial Windows applications. Within a MainMenu control, each submenu and each item on a submenu is represented by a MenuItem control. Windows forms menus offer a great deal of flexibility. You can create your entire menu structure at design time, and you can also modify the menu structure in code while the program is running to reflect changes in the program state.

Adding and Designing a Menu

To add a menu to a form, drag the MainMenu control from the Toolbox to the form. A single menu item displaying the text "Type Here" appears on the form, as shown in Figure 8.4.

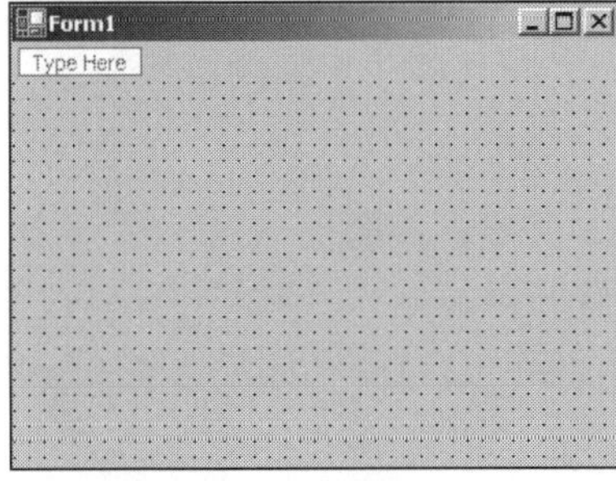

Figure 8.4
After you drag a MainMenu control onto a form, a menu item appears.

To enter the caption for the first submenu, click the box and type the caption. To define an access key for the menu, precede a letter in the caption with an ampersand. For example, if the caption will be "File" and you want the "F" to be the access key, you would enter "&File". An access letter is displayed underlined and permits the user to access menu items with the keyboard. If you want to display an ampersand in the caption, insert two ampersands.

As soon as you enter the first menu caption, two more "Type Here" boxes are displayed, one beneath and one next to the box you are typing in, as shown in Figure 8.5. The box under the current caption represents an item on the current submenu, and the box next to the current caption represents another submenu at the same level. As you enter captions, this process continues until you have entered the entire menu structure. As you work, each individual menu item is automatically assigned a name in the form **MenuItem1**, **MenuItem2**, and so on. These names are not visible but will be used to refer to the menu items in code. You can edit them, as I will explain soon.

As you work on the menu, follow these rules:

- To insert a new item above or to the left of an existing item, right-click a menu item and then select Add New from the context menu.
- To insert a separator line above an item on a submenu, select Insert Separator from the context menu.
- To edit the names assigned to the menu items, select Edit Names from the context menu. This command displays the menu captions along with the assigned names, as shown in Figure 8.6. When you have finished editing the menu item names, select Edit Names from the context menu again to hide the names.

The rules for naming menu items are the same as for any other controls. I have found it useful to adopt a menu-naming scheme that lets you identify a menu item just by its name. First, I use the "mnu" prefix for all menu item names. Then, the remainder of the name reflects the menu's caption and the captions of any "parent" menus. For example, the top level File menu would be named **mnuFile**, and the Open item on the File menu would be named **mnuFileOpen**.

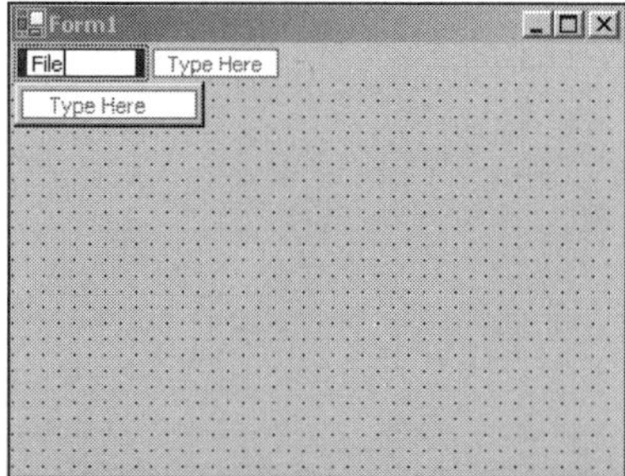

Figure 8.5
When you enter one menu caption, the menu editor displays two more caption boxes.

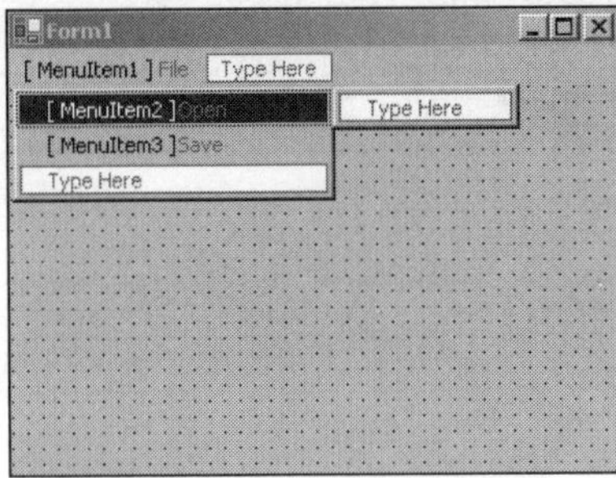

Figure 8.6
Editing the names assigned to the menu items.

Menu Item Properties

Each individual menu item has a set of properties that affect its appearance and behavior. When a menu item is selected in the Form Designer, these properties are accessible in the properties window. They can also be accessed in code. Table 8.6 explains the properties of menu items.

A menu item can have a shortcut key assigned to it by means of the **Shortcut** property. Pressing a shortcut key directly selects a menu command without opening the menu. This property can be set to a member of the **Shortcut** enumeration. These members are described in Table 8.7.

Obviously, you should assign a given shortcut key to only one menu command. Also, you should avoid using shortcut keys, such as Alt+F4, that are standard Windows shortcuts.

Table 8.6 Properties of the MenuItem control.

Property	Description
Checked	A **Boolean** value specifying whether a checkmark is displayed next to the menu caption.
DefaultItem	A **Boolean** value specifying whether this menu item is the default item. A submenu can have at most one default item, which is displayed in bold. When the submenu is double-clicked, the default item is automatically selected and the menu is closed.
Enabled	A **Boolean** value specifying whether the menu item is enabled. A disabled item is grayed out and cannot be selected.
RadioCheck	If this property is set to **True**, the menu item displays an adjacent radio button instead of a checkmark when the **Checked** property is **True**.
Shortcut	Set to a member of the **Shortcut** enumeration to assign a shortcut key to the menu item. See the text for more details.
ShowShortcut	A **Boolean** value specifying whether any shortcut key assigned to the menu item is displayed next to it. A shortcut key can still be used even if not displayed.
Text	The caption of the menu item.
Visible	A **Boolean** value specifying whether the menu item is visible.

Table 8.7 Members of the Shortcut enumeration are used to assign shortcut keys.

Shortcut key	Enumeration member
A function key F1 through F12	**F1–F12.**
The Ctrl and Shift keys plus another key	**CtrlShift*X*** where ***X*** is the key. For example, **CtrlShiftN** or **CtrlShiftF1.**
The Ctrl key plus another key	**Ctrl*X*** where ***X*** is the key. For example, **CtrlN** or **CtrlF1.**
The Alt key plus another key	**Alt*X*** where ***X*** is the key. For example, **AltX** or **AltF12.**
The Shift key plus another key	**Shift*X*** where ***X*** is the key. For example, **ShiftN** or **ShiftF1.**
The Insert, Delete, or Backspace keys	**Ins**, **Del**, or **Bksp**. Can be used in combination with **Shift**, **Ctrl**, **Alt**, and so on.

Menu Events

Menu commands are carried out by means of event procedures. I'll look at two events of interest:

- **Click()** occurs when the user chooses a menu item by clicking it with the mouse, by highlighting it with the keyboard and pressing Enter, or by means of a shortcut or access key. Code to carry out the action associated with the menu item is placed in the **Click()** event procedure.

- **Select()** occurs when the user rests the mouse cursor over the item or highlights it using the keyboard. This event is typically used to display a description of the menu item in the status bar or elsewhere.

You can create or display the **Click()** event procedure for a menu command by double-clicking the item in the Form Designer. You can also access menu item events using the lists at the top of the code editor window.

Working with Menus at Runtime

You have probably seen commercial Windows applications that seem to have "smart" menus. At any moment, only those menu commands that are appropriate for the current program state will be available. For example, when a program is in the process of downloading data, a Stop Download command will be available, but at other times the command will be hidden or disabled (by means of the menu item's **Visible** or **Enabled** properties).

When working with menus at runtime, you can choose between two general approaches. One method involves the actual addition and removal of menu items while the program is running. Although this is possible, it is an advanced technique that is beyond the scope of this book. Interested readers can find the relevant information in the Visual Studio online documentation. The second method requires that the entire menu be created during program design, with every menu item that the program will ever need. Then, at runtime, menu items are displayed and hidden, or enabled and disabled, as dictated by the state of the program.

When and how will your program make the needed changes to the menu? The ideal time is just as the menu is displayed. Suppose your program has a File menu that contains a Save command. You want the Save command to be enabled only if the current document has been modified and therefore needs saving. Otherwise, if the document has not been changed since the last time it was saved, you want the Save command to be disabled. The place to do this is the **Select()** event procedure for the File menu, which is fired every time the menu is opened. Assume that your program maintains a flag named **FileNeedsSaving** that is **True** if the file has been changed and **False** otherwise. Here is the code you would write:

```
Private Sub mnuFile_Select(ByVal sender As System.Object, _
        ByVal e As System.EventArgs) Handles MenuItem1.Select
    mnuFileSave.Enabled = FileNeedsSaving
End Sub
```

With this code in place, every time the user opens the File menu, the Save command will be enabled or disabled based on the state of the document.

CheckBox

The CheckBox control displays a caption with an adjacent box that can be checked or unchecked to turn an option on or off. Optionally, the control can display as a button that is either depressed (on) or raised (off). The user toggles a checkbox by clicking it or by pressing the spacebar when the control has the focus. A checkbox can also be in an indeterminate state, displaying a grayed-out checkmark or a flat button to indicate that the option setting is not specified. Figure 8.7 shows both normal and button-style CheckBox controls. Table 8.8 explains the properties of the CheckBox control.

When the user changes the state of a CheckBox control using either the mouse or the keyboard, its **Click()** event fires. Code in this event procedure can examine the **CheckState** property to determine the new state of the checkbox. This assumes that the control's **AutoCheck** property is **True**, which is almost always the case. Only in special situations will you need to set **AutoCheck** to **False**, which requires that your code handle all the

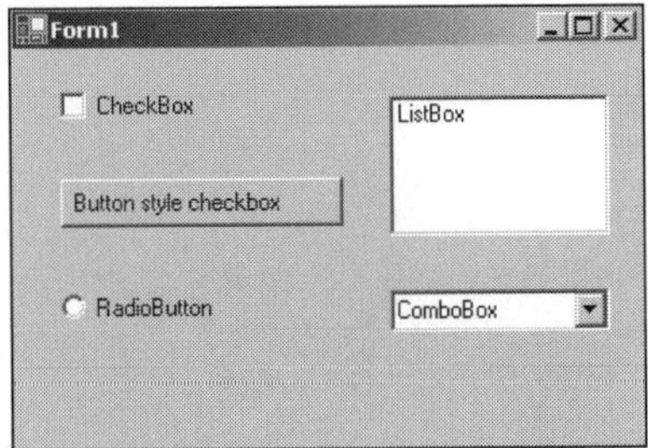

Figure 8.7
The CheckBox, RadioButton, Button, ListBox, and ComboBox controls.

Table 8.8 Properties of the CheckBox control.

Property	Description
Appearance	Set to **Normal** or **Button** to specify the appearance of the control.
AutoCheck	A **Boolean** value specifying whether the **CheckState** value changes automatically when the **Click** event occurs. The default is **True**.
CheckAlign	Specifies the alignment of the box with respect to the caption. Can be set to any of the **ContentAlignment** members, as described later in this chapter. The default is **Left**.
Checked	Returns **True** if the checkbox is in the **Checked** or **Indeterminate** state, **False** otherwise.
CheckState	Specifies the state of the checkbox as a **CheckState** enumeration: **Checked**, **UnChecked**, or **Indeterminate**.
Text	The text displayed in the control's caption.
ThreeState	A **Boolean** value specifying whether the user can set the control to the **Indeterminate** state. If the property is set to **False** (the default), the user can only toggle the control between **Checked** and **Unchecked**, and the **Indeterminate** state can be set only in code. If it's set to **True**, the user can cycle the control between the three states.

details of changing the control state. For example, you might want to prevent the user from changing an option based on certain program conditions.

CheckBox controls are typically used to display and set options that are yes/no or on/off. In many cases, the control itself is used to store the option setting, without the need for a separate flag variable to store the information. For example, your program might have an option that specifies whether data files are to be overwritten without prompting. You would create a CheckBox control named **chkOverwrite** for this option. You would not need any code in the CheckBox control's **Click()** event procedure because the control will store the option setting (assuming that **AutoClick** is **True**). Then, in the section of the program that saves data, you would have code like the following:

```
If chkOverwrite.CheckState = CheckState.Checked Then
' Code here to save data without prompting.
Else
' Code here to prompt the user.
End If
```

RadioButton

A RadioButton control displays a caption with an adjacent small dot that can be "on" or "off" to specify the state of an option or other program setting. Figure 8.7 shows a RadioButton control. In most ways, it is like the CheckBox control, with two major differences:

- A RadioButton control cannot have an indeterminate state—it is either on or off.
- RadioButton controls always come in groups of two or more, and only one radio button in a group can be "on" at a time. In other words, you use the RadioButton control for

groups of mutually exclusive options. When one radio button in a group is turned on, the one that was on previously is turned off automatically.

You create a group of RadioButton controls in one of two ways:

- By placing the controls directly on the form. All RadioButton controls placed directly on the form constitute one group.
- By placing a Panel or GroupBox control on the form and then placing the RadioButton controls in it. All RadioButton controls that are placed in a GroupBox or Panel control constitute one group.

Note that when using the second technique, you must draw each RadioButton control directly on the Panel or GroupBox control in order for it to be part of the group. You cannot draw the RadioButton control elsewhere and then move it onto the GroupBox or Panel control.

Most of the properties of the CheckBox control apply to the RadioButton control as well. The **Checked** property specifies whether the control is on (**Checked = True**) or off.

To get a feel for how the RadioButton control works, follow these steps:

1. Start a new Windows application project.
2. Place a GroupBox control on the form, filling most of the area.
3. Draw three RadioButton controls on the GroupBox.
4. Set the **Checked** property of one of the RadioButton controls to **True**.
5. Run the project.

You'll see how VB .NET takes care of ensuring that only one radio button in a group is on at the same time.

ListBox

A ListBox control displays a list of text items from which the user can select one or more. If the list contains more items than are visible, the control displays a scrollbar that lets the user scroll through the list. The items in a ListBox control are usually text, but because the data type is **Object**, you can include other types of items. Figure 8.7 shows a ListBox control.

The user selects and deselects items in a list box by clicking with the mouse or by scrolling through the list and pressing the spacebar to select the current item (which is indicated by a dotted outline). Selected items are displayed in reverse (white text on a blue background). The ListBox control has the **SelectionMode** property, which determines how the user can select items in the control. The settings for this property are part of the **SelectionMode** enumeration, and they are described in Table 8.9.

Table 8.9 Settings of the SelectionMode property.

Settings	Description
One	Only one item can be selected.
None	No items can be selected.
MultiExtended	Multiple adjacent items can be selected.
MultiSimple	Multiple nonadjacent items can be selected.

When **SelectionMode** is set to **MultiExtended**, the user selects multiple items by selecting the first item and then holding down the Shift key and clicking the last item (or using the arrow keys). When **SelectionMode** is set to **MultiSimple**, the user must hold down the Shift key while clicking the individual items.

Loading a ListBox Control

After you have placed a ListBox control on a form, you can fill it with items in one of several ways. The first method is to use the properties window. When you select the **Items** property, Visual Studio displays the String Collection Editor, as shown in Figure 8.8. In this dialog box, you can enter, edit, and delete items, one per line.

The other methods are done in code. To add an item to the end of the existing list, use the **Items** collection's **Add()** method, as shown in this example:

```
ListBox1.Items.Add("Purple")
```

To add an item at a specific location in the list, use this syntax, which adds the item "Purple" at the third position (the list of items is 0-based):

```
ListBox1.Items.Add(2, "Purple")
```

To remove items from the list, use one of the following syntaxes:

```
ListBox1.Items.RemoveItem(1)                    ' Remove item at
                                                ' position 1 (the 2nd
                                                ' item).

ListBox1.Items.RemoveItem("Red")                ' Remove item "Red".

ListBox1.Items.RemoveItem(ListBox1.SelectedItem) ' Remove currently
                                                ' selected item.

ListBox1.Items.Clear()                          ' Remove all items.
```

By default, items in a list box are displayed in the order they were entered. If the **Sorted** property is **True**, items are sorted alphabetically. If you add an item to the list box, it is automatically placed in the proper sorted position regardless of the position you specified for it.

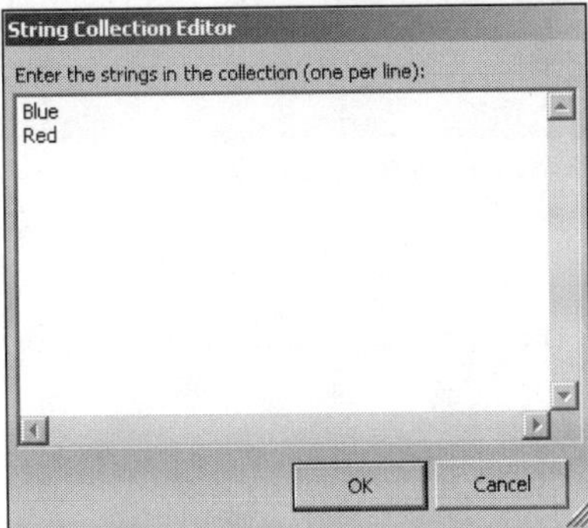

Figure 8.8
Entering ListBox items using the String Collection Editor.

Retrieving Selected Items

At runtime, code can retrieve the item or items that the user has selected in a ListBox control. First, see how many items are selected by testing the **SelectedItems.Count** property:

- If the property is **0**, no items are selected.
- If the property is **1**, a single item is selected.
- If the property is greater than **1**, multiple items are selected.

If one item is selected, the **SelectedIndex** and **SelectedItem** properties return the index and text of the selected item.

If multiple items are selected, you can access them by means of the **SelectedItems** property. This property references a **SelectedItems** collection that contains one **SelectedItem** object for each item that is selected in the list box. You can loop through this collection using a **For Each** loop, as shown here:

```
Dim item As object
For Each item In ListBox1.SelectedItems
    ' The item reference retrieves the item's text.
Next
```

A ListBox Demonstration

To demonstrate the use of a ListBox control, you can run the demonstration program presented here. The program has two ListBox controls, one containing a list of items and the other empty. When the program runs, the user selects one or more items in the first list box. Then, when the button is clicked, the selected items are copied to the second list box. Here are the steps to follow to create this project:

1. Create a new Windows application project.
2. Place two ListBox controls on the form, one next to the other.

3. Make the first ListBox control (with the name **ListBox1**) active. Use the properties window to set its **SelectionMode** property to **MultiSingle**.
4. Use the property window to add about half a dozen items to the first ListBox control.
5. Add a Button control to the form. It should look something like Figure 8.9.
6. Open the **Click()** event procedure for the button control, and add the code shown in Listing 8.1.

Listing 8.1 The Click() event procedure for the Button control in the ListBox demonstration.

```
Private Sub Button1_Click(ByVal sender As System.Object, _
            ByVal e As System.EventArgs) Handles Button1.Click

   Dim item As Object
   ListBox2.Items.Clear()

   For Each item In ListBox1.SelectedItems
        ListBox2.Items.Add(item)
    Next

End Sub
```

ComboBox

The ComboBox control can be thought of as a combination of a TextBox and a ListBox control. An example is shown in Figure 8.7. The user can select an item from the list or type a value. The ComboBox control has three styles, which are controlled by its **DropDownStyle** property. These styles affect the display of the list portion of the control and whether the user must select from the list or can enter any value. Settings for the **DropDownStyle** property are described in Table 8.10.

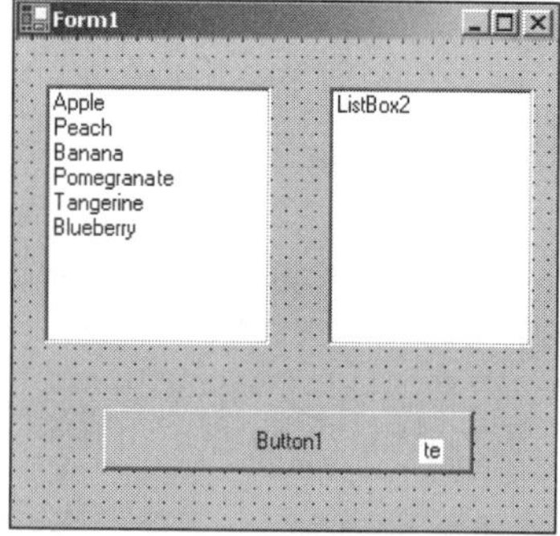

Figure 8.9
Designing the form of the ListBox demonstration program.

Table 8.10 Settings of the ComboBox control's DropDownStyle property.

Setting	Description
DropDown	The control displays as a text box with an arrow at the right end. The user can enter any text in the control or can click the arrow to display the list to select from. This is the default setting.
DropDownList	The control displays as a text box with an arrow at the right end. The user cannot enter text in the control but must click the arrow to display the list to select from.
Simple	The list is displayed at all times. Users can select from the list or enter their own text.

The techniques for adding items to the list portion of a ComboBox control are the same as for the ListBox control, and you can refer to that section of the chapter for information. The contents of the "text box" part of the control are specified by the **Text** property. When the user selects an item in the list portion of the control, that item is automatically copied to the text box portion. Unlike a ListBox control, the ComboBox control does not permit selection of more than one item at a time.

GroupBox

The GroupBox control is used to group other controls on a form. It can create functional groupings of RadioButton controls, and it can also create visual groupings of any other type of controls. By using one or more GroupBox controls, you can divide your form into functional areas, with related controls together in each group box.

The GroupBox control can display a caption in its upper-left corner, specified by the **Text** property. It can also display a background image, specified by the **BackgroundImage** property.

The GroupBox control acts as the container for all of its controls, and the position-related properties of the child controls (**Location**, **Top**, **Left**) specify a child's position relative to the group box and not relative to the form. Child controls adopt many of the properties of the group box. This is similar to the way controls that are placed directly on a form inherit some of the form's properties. Thus, all controls on a GroupBox control will inherit its **BackColor**, **ForeColor**, **Font**, and **Cursor** properties unless they are explicitly set for the control. Likewise, setting the GroupBox control's **Visible** and **Enabled** properties affects all the child controls. Finally, in design mode, deleting a GroupBox control also deletes all of its children.

Panel

A Panel control is very similar to a GroupBox control, serving to group other controls on a form. The Panel control differs in that it cannot display a caption but can display scrollbars. This permits a Panel control to serve as a scrollable area within a form, separate from scrolling the form itself. In other words, if the area in the panel that is occupied by child controls

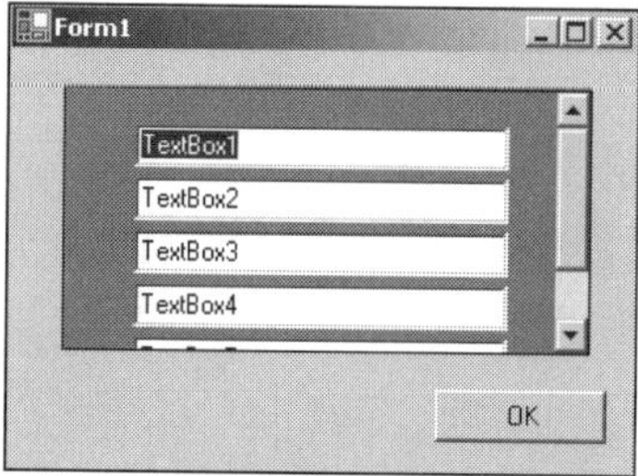

Figure 8.10
Using a Panel control to scroll controls into view.

is larger than the size of the panel itself, the user can use the scrollbars to bring hidden controls into view. With this technique, a relatively small form can contain more controls than would fit within it. Figure 8.10 shows a form that uses a Panel control to contain a long column of text boxes.

To use a Panel control to scroll controls in and out of view, you must set its **AutoScroll** property to **True**. Then, to place the controls within the panel, you can use one or more of these approaches:

- In the Form Designer, make the form and the Panel control very large. Place the controls as desired and then shrink the Panel control and form down to the desired sizes.
- Place the controls in the Panel control and then move them to their final positions by setting their **Top** and **Left** properties.

The Panel control has a few additional properties that you should know about, as explained in Table 8.11.

TabControl

The TabControl control lets you create a dialog box that contains multiple pages, or tabs. Each page is identified by a labeled tab, much like file folders. Figure 8.11 shows a form that uses a TabControl control. You have probably seen this control, or something similar, used in some of the commercial Windows applications that you use. It can be a great help when you want to fit a lot of functionality into a small form.

Table 8.11 Additional properties of the Panel control.

Property	Description
AutoScrollMargin	Specifies the horizontal and vertical margin to leave around the controls during scrolling.
AutoScrollMinSize	Specifies the minimum size of the scrolling area.
BorderStyle	Specifies the border style of the control. Can be one of the following: **None**, **FixedSingle**, **Fixed3D**.

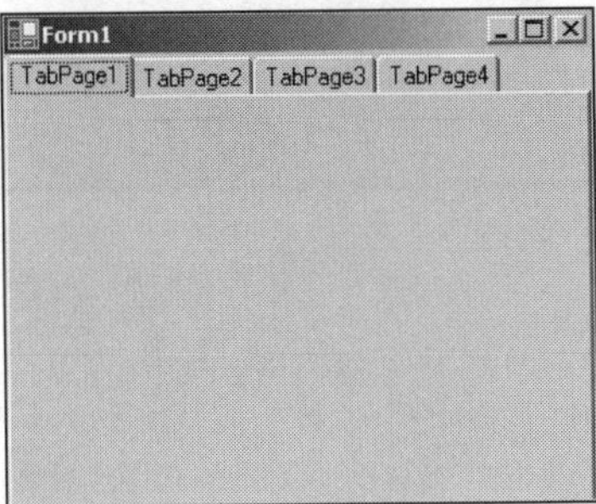

Figure 8.11
A form with a TabControl control that has four tabs.

Each page in a TabControl control is represented by a **TabPage** object. The control keeps track of all of its pages in its **TabPages** collection. When you first add a TabControl control to a form, it has no tabs. To add a tab, right-click the control and select Add Tab from the context menu. Repeat this step to add as many tabs as you will need. You can always add or remove tabs later. Each tab is added with a default caption in the form **TabPage1**, **TabPage2**, and so on.

To work with individual **TabPage** objects, you use the TabPage Collection Editor, which is shown in Figure 8.12. To display this editor, click the ellipsis next to the **TabPages** property in the property window. In the editor, the existing **TabPage** objects are listed in the Members list on the left, and the properties of the selected **TabPage** object are listed in the Properties pane on the right. The actions you can take in the editor are as follows:

- To delete a tab, select it in the Members list and click Remove.
- To add a new tab, click Add.

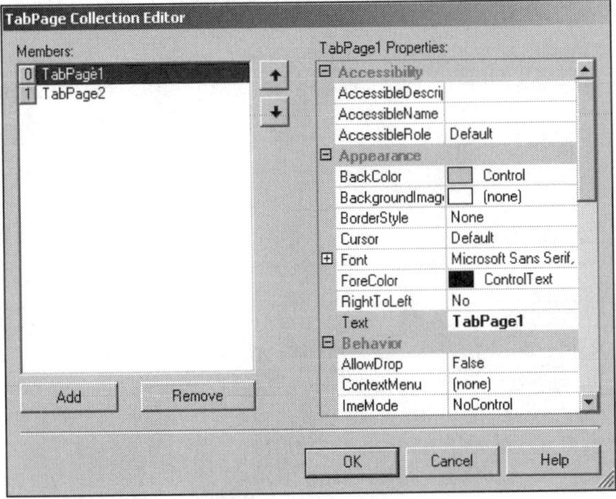

Figure 8.12
You use the TabPage Collection Editor to work with **TabPage** objects.

- To move a tab up or down in the order, select it and then click the arrow buttons.
- To modify a tab's properties, select the tab and then edit the properties in the Properties pane.

TabPage Properties

Each **TabPage** object has a set of properties that affects its appearance and behavior. It has many of the common properties that were described earlier in this chapter, such as **ForeColor**, **BackColor**, **Font**, and **Cursor**. Because a **TabPage** object serves as a container for the controls placed on it, many of these properties are "passed down" to the child controls. A **TabPage** object is a scrollable container, and the user can scroll controls into and out of view as needed. This is the same as was described for the Panel control earlier in the chapter. Other properties of this object are described in Table 8.12.

Adding Controls to a Tab

Adding controls to a **TabPage** object is no different from adding them to a form. Make the TabControl control active and select the desired page by clicking its tab. Then, drag controls onto the **TabPage** object in the usual manner. All of the Form Designer's layout tools are available, such as Snap To Grid and the alignment commands.

TabControl Properties

The TabControl control itself has a set of properties that affect its appearance and behavior. Some of them, such as **Cursor** and **Font**, will be "adopted" by all TabPage controls and in turn by their children. Other properties are described in Table 8.13.

Table 8.12 Properties of the TabPage object.

Property	Description
AutoScroll	Set to **True** to enable scrolling of controls.
AutoScrollMargin	Specifies the horizontal and vertical margin to leave around the controls during scrolling.
AutoScrollMinSize	Specifies the minimum size of the scrolling area.
BorderStyle	Specifies the **TabPage** object's border. Can be set to **None**, **FixedSingle**, or **Fixed3D**.
Text	The caption displayed on the page's tab.

Table 8.13 Properties of the TabControl control.

Property	Description
ItemSize	A **Size** structure that specifies the width and height of the tabs. If you want to change the width setting, **SizeMode** must be set to **Fixed**.
MultiLine	Applicable only when the control's tabs would be wider than the control width. If this property is **True**, the tabs are placed in two or more rows. If the property is set to **False** (the default), tabs remain in a single row and arrows are displayed at the end of the tab row to scroll the tabs left and right to bring them into view.

(continued)

Table 8.13 Properties of the TabControl control *(continued)*.

Property	Description
Padding	Specifies the padding, or space, around the tab captions.
SizeMode	Specifies how the tabs in the control are sized. Permitted settings are **Normal** (tabs are sized according to their caption), **Fixed** (all tabs are the same width), and **FillToRight** (when the control has two or more rows of tabs, each row is expanded as needed to fill the entire width of the control).

Working with the TabControl Control

When your program is running, the TabControl control pretty much takes care of itself. When a user clicks a tab, the corresponding page is made visible and its controls are accessible to the user. To access individual **TabPage** objects in code, you can simply refer to them by name. For example, the following line of code disables the **TabPage** object named **tpColorOptions**:

```
TpColorOptions.Enabled = False
```

When the user clicks a tab, the **Click()** event is raised for that **TabPage** object. You can use this event to make changes to the tab's controls as required by the state of the program.

Timer

The Timer control is used to trigger events at preset intervals. It has no visual representation, and when added to a form, it is displayed in the tray rather than on the form. The fundamentals of using the control are as follows:

1. Set the **Interval** property to the desired interval, in milliseconds. The maximum permitted setting is 64,767, or about 64 seconds.

2. In the control's **Tick()** event procedure, place the code that you want executed at the specified interval.

3. Set the **Enabled** property to **True** to begin timing.

4. Set the **Enabled** property to **False** to end timing.

Although the Timer control can be very useful, it does have some limitations. The timed intervals are not guaranteed to be exact, particularly when heavy demands have been placed on the system by the current or another program. Because the system clock "ticks" only 18 times a second, or approximately once per 55 milliseconds, the maximum accuracy of the Timer control is limited by that interval despite the fact that the **Interval** property can be set to the individual millisecond. Thus, the Timer control is not suitable when precise timing is required.

Although a single interval is limited to about 64 seconds, you can use the Timer control to time longer intervals by incrementing a counter when the interval times out. For example, Listing 8.2 shows a **Tick** event procedure that will execute the specified code every fifth time that the Timer control times out. If you set the **Interval** property to **60000** (one minute), the code will be executed every five minutes.

Listing 8.2 Using a counter to extend the Timer control's interval.

```
Private Sub Timer1_Tick(ByVal sender As System.Object, _
           ByVal e As System.EventArgs) Handles Timer1.Tick

    Static count As Integer
    count += 1

    If count = 5 Then
        count = 0
        ' Code to execute goes here.
    End If

End Sub
```

StatusBar

The StatusBar control displays an area, typically at the bottom of a form, that can display text and images to keep the user informed of the status of the application. At its simplest, a StatusBar control contains a single area in which you can display text messages. For more complex needs, a StatusBar control can be divided into two or more panels, with each panel displaying text or images. A StatusBar control can also detect user input by responding to **Click()** events.

When you add a StatusBar control to a form, its default is to be docked to the bottom of the form. You can change this if desired, but because people expect to see a status bar at the bottom of a screen window, there is rarely a good reason to dock it elsewhere.

To use a StatusBar control to display a single text message, first place the control on your form. Then, in code, change its **Text** property as needed.

To add panels to the StatusBar control, click the ellipsis next to the **Panels** property in the property window to display the StatusBarPanel Collection Editor, as shown in Figure 8.13. You can then do the following:

- To add a new panel, click Add.
- To delete a panel, select it in the Members list and click Remove.

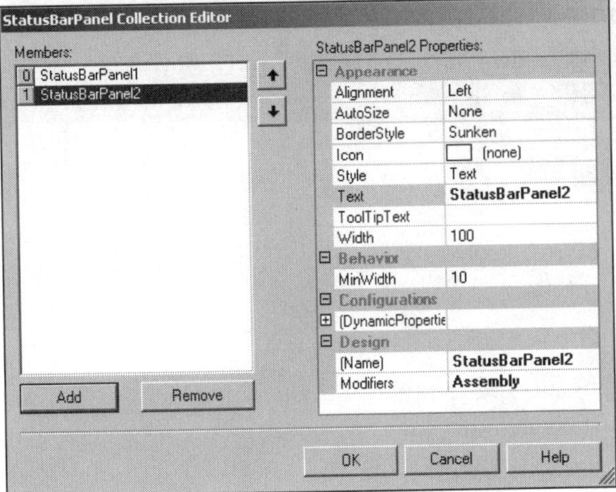

Figure 8.13
You use the StatusBarPanel Collection Editor to add and modify StatusBar panels.

- To move a panel up or down in the order, select it and then click the arrow buttons. Panels are displayed in the status bar in left-to-right order according to their position in the Members list.
- To modify a panel's properties, select the panel and then edit the properties in the Properties pane.

A StatusBar control can have panels, but they will not be displayed, either during design or at runtime, unless the **ShowPanels** property is set to **True**.

Each individual panel is represented by a **StatusBarPanel** object. This object has properties that control its appearance. They are described in Table 8.14.

Table 8.14 Properties of the StatusBarPanel object.

Property	Description
Alignment	Sets the alignment of the text or icon displayed in the panel: **Left**, **Right**, or **Center**.
AutoSize	Can be one of the following values: **None** (the default)—The panel does not resize automatically; **Contents**—The width of the panel is determined by its contents; **Spring**—The panel shares available space with other panels that have this property set to **Spring**.
BorderStyle	The appearance of the panel's border. Can be one of the following members of the **StatusBarPanelBorderStyle** enumeration: **None**, **Raised**, or **Sunken**.
Icon	Specifies an icon to display in the panel.
MinWidth	The minimum width of the panel.
Text	The text displayed in the panel.

Working with a StatusBar Control at Runtime

At runtime, you can add panels to the status bar by using the **Add()** method of the **Panels** collection. There are two ways to do this. One is to create an instance of the **StatusBarPanel** object, set its various properties, and then add it to the **StatusBar.Panels** collection:

```
Dim p As New StatusBarPanel
p.Text = "Panel Text"
p.BorderStyle = StatusBarPanelBorderStyle.Raised
StatusBar1.Panels.Add(p)
```

You can also use the **Add()** method by passing the text of the new panel, in which case all of its other properties will be left at their default value:

```
StatusBar1.Panels.Add("New Panel")
```

To reference an existing panel, you use the **Panels** collection. This collection's **Count** property returns the number of panels in the collection, and its **Item** property returns a reference to the panel at the specified index (the first panel is at index 0). Because **Item** is the default property for this collection, you can omit it. Thus, the following two lines of code do the same thing, setting the border style of the second panel in the status bar:

```
StatusBar1.Panels.Item(1).BorderStyle = _
        StatusBarPanelBorderStyle.Raised
StatusBar1.Panels(1).BorderStyle = _
        StatusBarPanelBorderStyle.Raised
```

To remove a panel from the collection, use the **Remove()** method. This code removes the first panel from the status bar (other panels "move up" in the index order when a panel is removed):

```
StatusBar1.Panels.Remove(0)
```

To remove all panels from the status bar, use the **Clear()** method:

```
StatusBar1.Panels.Clear()
```

Because **Panel** objects do not have a **Visible** property, no direct way to hide existing panels is available. You can, however, effectively hide a panel by setting its **Width** property to **0**. Note that the **MinWidth** property must also be set to **0** for this to work.

An icon displayed on a panel is represented by the **Icon** property, which references a **System.Drawing.Icon** object. To add an icon, or change the existing icon, at runtime, create an instance of this class and assign it to the panel's **Icon** property. Here's an example:

```
StatusBar1.Panels(1).Icon = New _
          System.Drawing.Icon("c:\icons\arrow.ico")
```

To delete an icon from a panel, set the **Icon** property to **Nothing**.

Detecting Click Events on Panels

When the user clicks a panel on a status bar, the StatusBar's **PanelClick()** event is fired. The individual panels to not themselves detect clicks. The **PanelClick()** event procedure has the following syntax:

```
Private Sub StatusBar1_PanelClick(ByVal sender As System.Object, _
    ByVal e As System.Windows.Forms.StatusBarPanelClickEventArgs) _
    Handles StatusBar1.PanelClick
```

You can see that this event procedure is passed an argument of type **StatusBarPanel-ClickEventArgs**. Code in the event procedure uses this argument to determine which panel was clicked and which mouse button was used. Specifically, the members are:

- **Button**. Returns a **MouseButtons** constant identifying the mouse button. Values are **Left, Middle, None, Right, Xbutton1**, and **Xbutton2**. The last two values are relevant for the new Microsoft Intellimouse Explorer, which has two "extra" buttons.
- **StatusBarPanel**. Returns a reference to the panel that was clicked. You can then use the **Text** property to identify the panel.

Here's an example of an event handler that detects various click events on the panels of a StatusBar control:

```
Private Sub StatusBar1_PanelClick(ByVal sender As System.Object, _
    ByVal e As System.Windows.Forms.StatusBarPanelClickEventArgs) _
    Handles StatusBar1.PanelClick

    If e.Button = MouseButtons.Left And e.StatusBarPanel.Text = "Network" Then
      ' Code here is executed if the user left-clicks the "Network" panel
    End If

    If e.Button = MouseButtons.Right And e.StatusBarPanel.Text = "Clock" Then
      ' Code here is executed if the user right-clicks the "Clock" panel
    End If

  End Sub
```

ImageList

The ImageList control is designed to let you manage a group of images. You can think of an ImageList control as an in-memory repository of images that your program can use for various purposes. This control always works "behind the scenes"; you never actually see it when your program is running, and it displays in the tray during form design. It does not display images, but rather it is used to make a set of images available to other controls that use them. Any control that has an **ImageList** property can make use of the images in an ImageList control.

An ImageList control can contain multiple images of different original sizes. Once in the ImageList control, however, all images are scaled to the same size. This size is specified by the ImageList control's **ImageSize** property; the default is 16×16 pixels.

The ImageList control supports image transparency. This means that you can define a specific color to be transparent, and wherever that color appears in an image, the image will be transparent. You set the transparent color using the ImageList control's **TransparentColor** property, which specifies a **Color** object (explained later in this chapter).

To add images to an ImageList control at design time, click the ellipsis next to the **Images** property in the property window. This displays the Image Collection Editor, as shown in Figure 8.14. You can add images of many different types, including bitmaps, icons, JPEG files, and Windows metafiles. In the Image Collection Editor, click Add to add an image, and then browse for the desired image file. Click Remove to remove an image, and use the arrow keys to change the position of an image in the list. You can view the properties of the selected image, but you cannot change them.

To add images to the ImageList control in code, use the **Add()** method of the **Images** property. You can add images represented by the following classes:

```
System.Drawing.Icon
System.Drawing.Bitmap
System.Drawing.Metafile
```

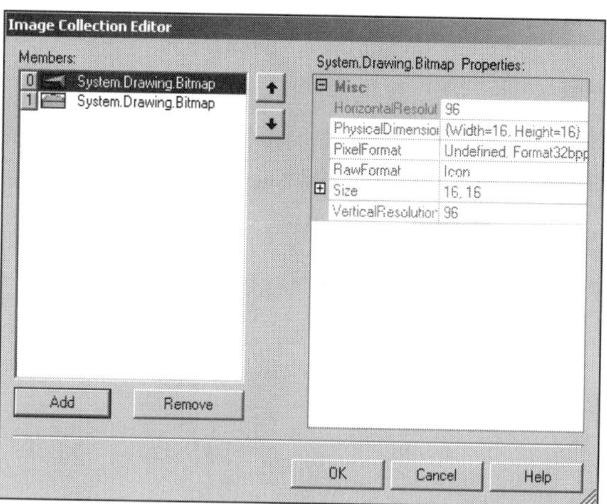

Figure 8.14
You use the Image Collection Editor to manage the images in an ImageList control.

Here's an example of adding a bitmap image to the ImageList control:

```
ImageList1.Images.Add(New System.Drawing.Bitmap("c:\flag.bmp")
```

To determine how many images an image list contains, read the **Images.Count** property. Because the images are indexed starting at 0, the available images will have indexes ranging from 0 to **Images.Count - 1**.

To associate an image list with a control, set the control's **ImageList** property to reference the ImageList control. To specify which image is displayed, set the control's **ImageIndex** property to the index of the desired image in the ImageList control.

Listing 8.3 contains a short program that demonstrates using an ImageList control to display images on a Button control. Here are the steps to follow to create the project:

1. Create a new Windows application project.
2. Add a Button control and an ImageList control to the form.
3. Add at least three images to the ImageList control. You can use your own images or the images provided with VB .NET (usually located in the \Program Files\Microsoft Visual Studio.NET\Common7\Graphics folder).
4. Set the **Text** property of the Button control to a blank string.
5. Set the **ImageList** property of the Button control to **ImageList1** (the name of the ImageList control).
6. Set the **ImageIndex** property of the Button control to **0**.
7. Put the code from Listing 8.3 into the Button's **Click()** event procedure.

When you run the program, the button will initially display the first image in the ImageList control. Each time you click the button, it cycles to the next image. When it reaches the end of the images, it cycles back to the first image.

Listing 8.3 Code for the Button control's Click() event procedure.

```
Private Sub Button1_Click(ByVal sender As System.Object, _
         ByVal e As System.EventArgs) Handles Button1.Click

    If Button1.ImageIndex < ImageList1.Images.Count - 1 Then
        Button1.ImageIndex += 1
    Else
        Button1.ImageIndex = 0
    End If

End Sub
```

ContextMenu

A context menu is a menu that displays when an object on the screen is right-clicked. Many context menus are available in Visual Studio. Typically, a context menu will contain a set of commands that is relevant to the object that was clicked. These commands might also be available on the main menu, but providing them on a context menu can make things more convenient for the user. A form can have as many context menus as you need, and each context menu can be associated with one or more controls as needed.

To add a context menu to a form, drag it from the Toolbox. A context menu does not display on the form, but rather in the tray. To add items to the menu, right-click the control in the tray and select Edit Menu. The context menu is displayed at the top of the form, as a box labeled "Context Menu." Click the box to start editing. You add items to a context menu using the exact same techniques as for a MainMenu control. In fact, almost all aspects of creating and using a context menu are the same as for a MainMenu control, so you can refer back to the MainMenu section of this chapter for details.

After you have created one or more context menus and written the appropriate code for the menu commands, you can assign a menu to any control that has a **ContextMenu** property. Note that the form also has this property. Then, when the program is running, right-clicking any control that has a context menu assigned will display that menu.

Other Controls

Space does not permit coverage of all of the Windows form controls provided by VB .NET. The controls that were not covered in this chapter are listed in Table 8.15, with a brief description of each. If the control is covered in another chapter, that chapter is referenced. Otherwise, you can refer to the VB .NET online help for information.

Table 8.15 Additional Windows form controls.

Control	Description	Covered in
CheckedListBox	Extends the ListBox control, permitting each item in the list to display an adjacent checkmark.	
PictureBox	Displays and manipulates graphical images.	Chapter 17
DataGrid	Displays data from a database table.	Chapter 19
HScrollBar and VScrollBar	Display vertical and horizontal scrollbars.	
ListView	Displays a list of items with icons. Can display one or more columns, and provides various features for sorting and other tasks. The file list in the Windows Explorer is a ListView control.	
TreeView	Displays a hierarchical tree of nodes, which can be opened and closed. The folder pane in Windows Explorer is a TreeView control.	

(continued)

Table 8.15 Additional Windows form controls *(continued)*.

Control	Description	Covered in
DateTimePicker	Lets the user select a date and/or time from a graphical interface.	
MonthCalendar	Lets the user select a date and/or time from a calendar-like interface.	
PrintDialog PrintPreviewDialog PrintPreviewControl PrintDocument PageSetupDialog	Set print options and control the printing process.	Chapter 17
OpenFileDialog	Displays a dialog box that permits the user to select a file to open.	Chapter 16
SaveFileDialog	Displays a dialog box that permits the user to set options for saving a file.	Chapter 16
Toolbar	Displays a toolbar with graphical buttons that the user can click to carry out actions.	
Splitter	Used to resize docked controls at runtime.	
DomainUpDown	Lets the user browse through a list of text items using the up and down buttons.	
NumericUpDown	Lets the user increment or decrement a numeric value by clicking the up and down arrows.	
TrackBar	Displays a scale with a "thumb" that the user can move with the mouse to adjust a numeric value or scroll through information. Sometimes called a Slider control.	
ProgressBar	Displays a graphical bar that visually indicates the progress of a time-consuming operation.	
RichTextBox	Similar to a TextBox control, but can display text with formatting such as underlining, different colors, hyperlinks, and embedded images.	
HelpProvider	Used to associate an HTML Help file with a Windows application.	
ToolTip	Displays pop-up help in a small balloon when the user points at a screen object.	
NotifyIcon	Displays an icon for background processes that do not have their own visual interface.	
FontDialog	Lets the user select a font.	
ColorDialog	Lets the user select a color.	
ErrorProvider	Displays a graphical indication that an error has occurred.	
CrystalReportViewer	Permits a Crystal Report to be viewed in an application.	

Working with the Mouse

Windows applications are mouse-oriented, and much of a user's interaction with a program will be done with the mouse. The .NET framework takes care of many mouse actions automatically, such as opening menus and changing the state of a CheckBox control. At other times, however, you'll need to deal with the mouse directly. There are two primary aspects to this: dealing with mouse-related events and implementing drag-and-drop.

Mouse-Related Events

Four events are associated with the mouse buttons: **MouseDown()**, **MouseUp()**, **Click()**, and **DoubleClick()**. These events occur regardless of whether the left or the right button was used (or the middle button, for three-button mice). A double-click is registered when two clicks occur within the interval specified by the system settings. When the user clicks an object, the events that occur are, in order:

```
MouseDown
Click
MouseUp
```

When the user double-clicks an object, events occur as follows:

```
MouseDown
Click
MouseUp
MouseDown
DoubleClick
MouseUp
```

When the mouse button is pressed over an object, that object *captures* the mouse. This means that the object receives subsequent mouse input up to and including the next **MouseUp()** event even if the mouse cursor has been moved off the object. For example, suppose you place the mouse cursor over a Label control, press the mouse button, move the cursor off the label so it is over the form, and then release the mouse button. The form receives no mouse events, while the label receives **MouseDown()** and **MouseUp()** events. Note that the Label control does not receive a **Click()** event because a click is defined as the mouse button being pressed and released on the same object.

As regards mouse movement, there are also four events:

- **MouseEnter()** fires when the cursor enters the object.
- **MouseHover()** fires when the cursor remains motionless over the object. This event fires at most once between a **MouseEnter()** and a **MouseLeave()** event.
- **MouseMove()** fires when the cursor moves while over the object. This event can fire multiple times between a **MouseEnter()** and a **MouseLeave()** event.
- **MouseLeave()** fires when the cursor leaves the object.

For some mouse events, both click-related and movement-related, there is no need for the event handler to receive information about the mouse, such as its position and the buttons that were used. These event handlers receive an argument of type **System.EventArgs**, which provides no useful information. This is the case with the following events:

```
Click
DoubleClick
MouseEnter
MouseLeave
MouseHover
```

For other events, however, it can be very useful to have this information. Thus, the following events receive an argument of type **System.Windows.Forms.MouseEventArgs**:

```
MouseDown
MouseUp
MouseMove
```

This type has members that provide information to code in the event procedure. These members are described in Table 8.16.

A simple program will illustrate the use of the information passed in the **MouseEventArgs** argument. Follow these steps to create the project:

1. Create a new Windows application project.
2. Create the **MouseDown()** event procedure for the form (this project has no controls).
3. Put the code from Listing 8.4 in the **MouseDown()** event procedure.

When you run the program, click anywhere on the form. The program will display a dialog box identifying the button you clicked and the coordinates. This is shown in Figure 8.15.

Table 8.16 Members of the MouseEventArgs class.

Member	Description
Button	Gets which mouse button was pressed. Can be one of the members of the **MouseButtons** enumeration: **Left**, **Middle**, **None**, **Right**, **Xbutton1**, or **Xbutton2**. The last two values are relevant for the new Microsoft Intellimouse Explorer, which has two "extra" buttons.
Clicks	Gets the number of times the mouse button was clicked.
Delta	Gets the number of detents the mouse wheel has rotated.
X	Gets the X coordinate of the mouse cursor. The value is in pixels relative to the client area of the form.
Y	Gets the Y coordinate of the mouse cursor. The value is in pixels relative to the client area of the form.

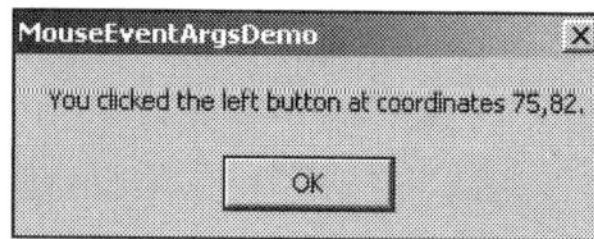

Figure 8.15
Demonstrating the **MouseEventArgs** class.

Listing 8.4 The Form1_MouseDown() event procedure for the MouseEventsArgs demonstration program.

```
Private Sub Form1_MouseDown(ByVal sender As Object, _
        ByVal e As System.Windows.Forms.MouseEventArgs) Handles
MyBase.MouseDown

    Dim s As String
    s = "You clicked the "

    Select Case e.Button
        Case MouseButtons.Left
            s &= "left "
        Case MouseButtons.Middle
            s &= "middle "
        Case MouseButtons.Right
            s &= "right "
    End Select

    s &= "button at coordinates "
    s &= e.X.ToString & "," & e.Y.ToString & "."

    MsgBox(s)

End Sub
```

Implementing Drag and Drop

The capability to drag data from one control and drop it on another control can be an important part of some user interfaces. The .NET Framework includes support for drag and drop, making it quite easy to implement. There are two main parts to the operation—starting the drag and performing the drop.

To initiate a drag operation, call the source control's **DoDragDrop()** method. Although not required, this method is typically called in the control's **MouseDown()** event procedure because that is how the user initiates drag operations. The syntax for the **DoDragDrop()** method is as follows:

```
DoDragDrop(data, effects)
```

Table 8.17. Members of the DragDropEffects enumeration.

Constant	Description
All	The data is copied, removed from the source, and scrolled in the target.
Copy	The data is copied to the target.
Link	The data is linked to the target.
Move	The data is moved to the target
None	The target cannot accept the data.
Scroll	The target is currently, or is about to start, scrolling.

The ***data*** argument is type **Object**, and is passed the data that you want to drag to the destination, and ***effects*** is a member of the **DragDropEffects** enumeration and specifies which drag/drop operations will be permitted. Settings for this argument are described in Table 8.17. The method provides a return value, also of type **DragDropEffects**, that identifies the final disposition of the data. This return value is often ignored, but can be useful in situations such as when you use drag/drop to move data, in which case you need to verify that the drag/drop operation completed before deleting the data from the source.

After the drag operation has commenced, potential target controls will respond to two drag-related events. First, the **DragEnter()** event occurs when something is dragged over the control (but not dropped). This event procedure has the following syntax:

```
Private Sub DragEnter(ByVal sender As Object, _
    ByVal e As System.Windows.Forms.DragEventArgs)
```

Code in the event procedure can use the **DragEventArgs** argument to check the format, or type, of the data that is being dragged. Specifically, you use the **DragEventArgs.Data.GetDataPresent()** method, as follows:

```
DragEventArgs.Data.GetDataPresent(format)
```

The method returns a True if the data being dragged is of the specified format. Values for *format* are from the **DataFormats** enumeration, and include the following:

- **Bitmap**—A Windows bitmap image
- **Html**—Hypertext Markup Language data
- **StringFormat**—The Windows Forms **String** class
- **Text**—Any text data
- **UnicodeText**—The Windows Unicode text format

Then, by setting the **DragEventArgs.Effect** property with one of the values from Table 8.17, you can specify what drop operation, if any, will be permitted on the control. For example, a PictureBox control might permit only image data to be dropped on it, while rejecting text data. On the other hand, a TextBox control would accept text data while rejecting image data. The mouse cursor's appearance changes automatically based on the operation(s) that are permitted. For a copy operation, for example, the cursor will change to an arrow with a dotted outline and a + sign when over a control that permits a copy. When the cursor is over a target that does not permit a drop operation, it displays as a "no" sign (a circle with a line through it).

The following code shows a **DragEnter()** event for a TextBox control that will permit text data to be moved or copied to it.

```
Private Sub TextBox1_DragEnter(ByVal sender As Object, _
        ByVal e As System.Windows.Forms.DragEventArgs) _
        Handles TextBox1.DragEnter

    If (e.Data.GetDataPresent(DataFormats.Text)) Then
        e.Effect = DragDropEffects.Move Or DragDropEffects.Copy
    End If

End Sub
```

Second, the target control must accept the dragged data in the **DragDrop()** event procedure. This procedure is also passed an argument of type **DragDropEventArgs**, and you retrieved the dragged data using the following method:

```
DragDropEventArgs.Data.GetData(format)
```

The *format* argument is one of the enumeration members from Table 8.17. Here is an example of a **DragDrop()** event procedure for a TextBox control that retrieves the text format data that was dropped on it and displays it in the control.

```
Private Sub TextBox1_DragDrop(ByVal sender As Object, _
        ByVal e As System.Windows.Forms.DragEventArgs) _
        Handles TextBox1.DragDrop

    TextBox1.Text = e.Data.GetData(DataFormats.Text)

End Sub
```

The program in Listing 8.5 demonstrates the use of drag and drop for both copying and moving data. To create this program, start a new Windows Application project. Then follow these steps:

1. Place a ListBox control on the form, and add several items to it using the properties window. Leave all other properties at their default values.
2. Add a TextBox control next to the ListBox control. Change its **Name** property to txtSource.

3. Place another TextBox control below the other controls. Change its **Name** property to txtDestination and its **AllowDrop** property to True.

4. Add the event procedures as shown in Listing 8.5.

When you run the program, you can use drag and drop to move items from the ListBox to the second TextBox, and to copy text from the first TextBox to the second TextBox. The program is shown after a few drag and drop operations have been performed, in Figure 8.16. There is one thing to note about this code, in the **MouseDown()** event procedure for the ListBox control: You cannot use the **SelectedItem** property to retrieve the item the user is dragging, because when the mouse has been depressed but not released, nothing is considered to be selected yet (which requires a **Click()** event). Yet, you can still obtain the selected item by determining the exact location of the mouse cursor and using the **IndexFromPoint()** method.

Listing 8.5 Event procedures for demonstrating drag and drop.

```
Private Sub ListBox1_MouseDown(ByVal sender As Object, _
        ByVal e As System.Windows.Forms.MouseEventArgs) _
        Handles ListBox1.MouseDown

    Dim Lbx As ListBox = sender
    Dim Pt As New Point(e.X, e.Y)
    Dim Idx As Integer
    Dim retval As DragDropEffects

    ' Determine which Listbox item was dragged.
    Idx = Lbx.IndexFromPoint(Pt)

    ' Start a drag-and-drop with that item.
    If Idx >= 0 Then
        retval = Lbx.DoDragDrop(Lbx.Items(Idx), DragDropEffects.Move)
        ' Make sure the move operation was completed.
```

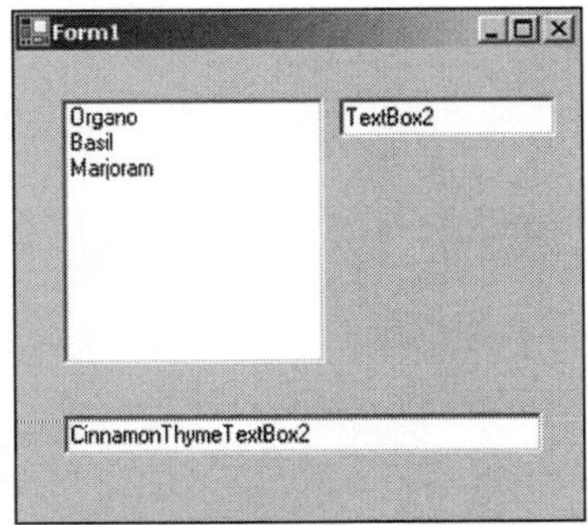

Figure 8.16
Demonstrating drag and drop.

```
        Debug.WriteLine(retval)
        If retval And DragDropEffects.Move Then
            Lbx.Items.RemoveAt(Idx)
        End If
    End If

End Sub

Private Sub txtDestination_DragEnter(ByVal sender As System.Object, _
        ByVal e As System.Windows.Forms.DragEventArgs) _
        Handles txtDestination.DragEnter

    ' If text is being dragged, permit a move or copy operation.
    If (e.Data.GetDataPresent(DataFormats.Text)) Then
        e.Effect = DragDropEffects.Move Or DragDropEffects.Copy
    End If

End Sub

Private Sub txtDestination_DragDrop(ByVal sender As System.Object, _
        ByVal e As System.Windows.Forms.DragEventArgs) _
        Handles txtDestination.DragDrop

    txtDestination.Text &= e.Data.GetData("Text")

End Sub

Private Sub txtSource_MouseDown(ByVal sender As System.Object, _
        ByVal e As System.Windows.Forms.MouseEventArgs) _
        Handles txtSource.MouseDown

    txtSource.DoDragDrop(txtSource.Text, DragDropEffects.Copy)

End Sub
```

Keyboard-Related Events

Any control that can have focus can receive keyboard input. The three keyboard-related events are as follows:

- ***KeyDown()***—When a key is pressed.
- ***KeyUp()***—When a key is released.
- ***KeyPress()***—When a key is pressed and released.

The **KeyDown()** and **KeyUp()** event procedures receive an argument of type **KeyEventArgs**, while the **KeyPress()** event receives an argument of type **KeyPressEventArgs**. The information passed in these arguments provides the event procedure with information about the key that was pressed, the state of the Shift, Ctrl, and Alt keys. Table 8.18 describes the members of the type **KeyEventArgs** object.

The **Keys** enumeration contains constants for any keyboard key. You can find the full list in online help. Here are some examples:

- *Keys.X*—Any letter (where X = A, B, …, Z).
- *Keys.DN*—A number key, where N is 0, 1, 2, …9. These are the number keys above the letter keys.
- *Keys.FN*—A function key (F1, F2, and so on) where N is 1…24.
- *Keys.NumpadN*—A numeric keypad number key, where N is 0, 1, …, 9.
- *Keys.Space*—The spacebar.
- *Keys.PageDown*—The PgDn key.

Note that these codes do not distinguish between upper- and lowercase letters. Thus, if the **KeyCode** property is **Keys.S**, you know that the S key was pressed, but you have to examine the **Shift** property to determine if the user entered "S" or "s". By using the **KeyCode** property and the **Alt**, **Control**, and **Shift** properties, you can detect any possible combination of keys, such as Ctrl+Alt+F4 or Shift+PgDn.

The **KeyPressEventArgs** class, passed to the **KeyPress()** event, has only two members that are of interest:

- *KeyChar*—The value of this property is a type **Char** corresponding to the key pressed.
- *Handled*—A Boolean value indicating whether the event was handled.

The **Handled** property can be quite useful. It is initially **False**, which means that the keystroke will be passed to Windows for the usual processing. If code in the event procedure

Table 8.18 Properties of the KeyEventArgs class.

Property	Description
Alt	A **Boolean** value indicating whether the Alt key was down
Control	A **Boolean** value indicating whether the Ctrl key was down
Shift	A **Boolean** value indicating whether the Shift key was down
KeyCode	A member of the **Keys** enumeration specifying the key that was pressed

sets **Handled** to **True**, the keystroke will not be passed on for further processing—in essence, the keystroke will be discarded.

You can use this feature to filter the characters that are permitted in certain controls, such as a text box. First, examine the **KeyChar** member. If it is one of the permitted characters, leave **Handled** at its default value of **False**, which permits the keystroke to be processed and entered in the text box. If it is a forbidden character, set **Handled** to **True** to prevent the character from reaching the text box.

Listing 8.6 shows an example. The program filters the character's input to a text box, permitting only digits and the hyphen (-) to be entered. This would be appropriate for a text box intended for entry of telephone numbers.

Listing 8.6 Filtering text-box input to permit only digits and the hyphen character.

```
Private Sub TextBox1_KeyPress(ByVal sender As Object, ByVal e _
      As System.Windows.Forms.KeyPressEventArgs) _
      Handles TextBox1.KeyPress

    Select Case e.KeyChar
        Case "0" To "9", "-"
        ' Do nothing - permitted character.
        Case Else
            e.Handled = True
    End Select

End Sub
```

Creating Access Keys for Controls

You saw earlier in the chapter that you can define an access key for a menu command by preceding a letter in the caption with an ampersand. The letter is then displayed underlined, and the user can select the command by pressing the Alt key plus the letter. You can also define access keys for other controls in the same manner. For example, if you set the **Text** property of a Button control to **&Quit**, the "Q" will be underlined and the user can select the button by pressing Alt+Q.

Controls that do not have captions, such as TextBox, PictureBox, and ListBox, cannot be assigned an access key directly. You can achieve the same effect by means of a Label control. A Label control cannot receive the focus, but it can be given an access key as described above. When the user presses the access key for a label, the focus moves to the control immediately after the label in the tab order. Suppose you create a Label control with the access key "X" and the **TabIndex** property of **5**. If you add a PictureBox control with **TabIndex = 6**, pressing Alt+X will move the focus to that picture box.

Working with Fonts

Many objects in VB .NET display text, and the appearance of the text is determined by the object's **Font** property. This property references a **Font** object, so in order to have full control over the text used in your programs, you need to understand this class.

When setting an object's **Font** property in the properties window, you work with the Font dialog box, shown in Figure 8.17. In this dialog box, you specify several things:

- The name of the font, which identifies the general appearance of the characters.
- The style, which can be normal, bold, italic, or bold italic.
- The size, specified in points (1 point = 1/72 inch).
- Whether the font is displayed with strikeout and/or underlining.

You can also work with font properties in code, reading or setting the properties as needed by your program. For example:

```
TextBox1.Font.Bold = True
```

The Color Structure

The **Color** structure, which is a member of the **System.Drawing** namespace, is used to specify colors for things such as the **ForeColor** and **BackColor** properties of controls. When you select colors in the property window, you can select visually from a color palette. In code, however, you need to know how to use the **Color** structure to specify the color you want.

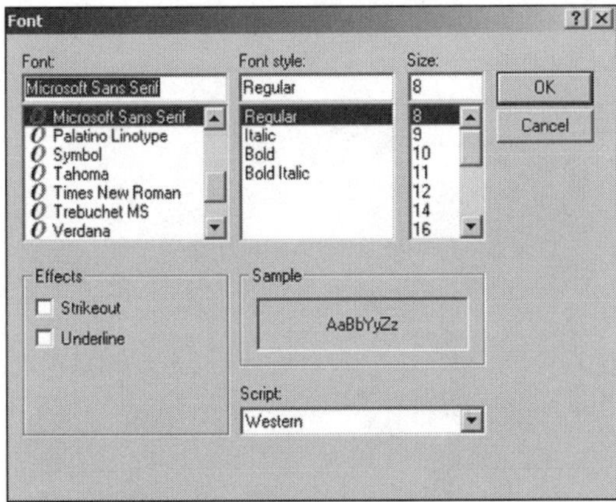

Figure 8.17
You select a font in the Font dialog box.

One way to use this structure is to use the system-defined colors that are structure members, as static properties. Many dozens of these predefined colors, each with a descriptive name, are available. Here are some examples:

```
Color.AntiqueWhite
Color.BlueViolet
Color.Khaki
Color.Thistle
```

Another way is to create a custom color based on red, green, and blue values. Each of these values can range from 0 to 255, and the resulting color is the result of the additive mix. Thus, an RGB value of 255,255,255 is white; 200,0,0 is medium red; 100,100,150 is bluish gray; and so on. To create a color based on RGB values, use the **Color** structure's **FromArgb()** method, which has the following syntax:

```
FromArgb(r, g, b)
```

The three arguments are type **Integer** values in the range 0–255 specifying the red, green, and blue components of the new color. Because **FromArgb** is a static method, you do not have to create an instance of the structure to call it. For example, the following code changes the foreground color of the text box to blue:

```
TextBox1.ForeColor = System.Drawing.Color.FromArgb(0, 0, 255)
```

The ContentAlignment Enumeration

Many control properties use values from the **ContentAlignment** enumeration to specify the alignment of text or other content within its container. The members of this enumeration are listed here; their meanings are self-evident:

```
BottomCenter
BottomLeft
BottomRight
MiddleCenter
MiddleLeft
MiddleRight
TopCenter
TopLeft
TopRight
```

Summary

The controls that you have available for your VB.NET Windows applications seem to cover all the bases. It's difficult to imagine a user interface task that could not be handled by these controls, used alone or in combination. Although all the Window Forms controls are different, they have lots of things in common, including many properties and events that are available for all or most of the controls. To create effective user interfaces for your programs, you need to know not only how to use the individual controls, but also what controls are available.

Chapter 9
Object-Oriented Programming with VB .NET, Part 1

From the ground up, Visual Basic and the .NET framework are object-oriented. This means that the language and the framework are themselves comprised of classes. Everything from the simplest data types provided by Visual Basic to the most complex screen windows supported by the .NET framework is a class. You have already learned about some of these classes, and you will learn about many more in the remainder of the book. The object-oriented nature of Visual Basic .NET also means that you can define your own classes, which is an extremely powerful technique. That's the topic of this chapter and the next.

OOP Fundamentals

Object-oriented programming, usually abbreviated as OOP, is not all that difficult to understand. However, you should get a few basics—including some specialized terminology—under your belt before delving into the details of how OOP is implemented in VB .NET.

At the heart of OOP is the idea that a program can be broken into functional units, with each unit walled off from the others. Each unit has carefully defined inputs and outputs that are used to interact with the rest of the program, but otherwise what goes on within the unit is completely isolated from what goes on in the rest of the program. As you might have guessed, these units are called objects. An object's inputs and outputs are called its *interface*.

The use of OOP has numerous advantages over the previous programming paradigm, which was called procedural programming. If you separate program functionality into discrete, isolated sections, the chance of unwanted and unexpected interactions between different sections of code is greatly reduced or eliminated, which in turn lessens the chance of program errors and bugs. Program maintenance is simplified, because changes made to one object will not affect other objects that the program uses. The job of the programmer is made a lot easier, too. These and other important advantages have made OOP the approach of choice for essentially all modern programming languages.

Classes and Objects

It is important to be aware of the difference in meaning between the terms *class* and *object*. A class is a plan, or blueprint, for an object. An object does not exist until a program creates it. The process of creating an object from a class is called *instantiating*. Sometimes an object is referred to as an instance of a class.

As an analogy, suppose that you have used your word processor to create a template for an employment application form. This template can be thought of as a class. Each time you print a copy of the template, you are creating an object—an instance of the class. You can print as many copies (objects) as you need. Initially, each object is the same, but when job applicants fill them in they will be different in some respects. You'll have identical objects containing different data.

To extend this to programming, consider the **DateTime** class that is provided by VB .NET for working with date and time information. Your program can create as many instances of this class as it needs. Each instance, or object, has a different name so the program can tell the instances apart. Each object will probably contain different data, as assigned by the program, but they all will have the same base capabilities that are defined by the **DateTime** class.

Capabilities of OOP

The capability to break a program down into separate functional units is central to OOP, but that's not all there is to it. Generally, for a language to be considered a true object-oriented language, it must support the following capabilities:

- *Encapsulation* is the technical term for walling off an object's functionality. The implementation of a class—in other words, what goes on inside the class—is encapsulated and is separate from the class's interface.
- *Abstraction* is the capability of a language to create an abstract representation of a real-world concept. This is how classes are typically used, as representations of concepts that are meaningful to the program. For example, an inventory program might define the Item class to represent each item in the inventory.

- *Polymorphism* means "many forms," and it refers to the capability of an object-oriented language to perform the same action on objects of different types (based on different classes). The same code can often handle different object types, which is a lot more efficient than writing specialized code for every type of object your program works with.
- *Inheritance* is the process by which a new class can be based on an existing class, and will automatically gain, or inherit, that class's interface and behaviors. When you define a new class, often you will not start from scratch but will base the new class on an existing class that already has some of the needed functionality. This procedure, which is called *subclassing*, results in the new class inheriting all the capabilities of the existing class. You then include additional features as needed.

These four features of OOP may sound rather dry and difficult to relate to real-world programming situations. After you start working with OOP, later in this chapter, you'll see how important they are.

Properties and Methods

A class interface consists of two types of elements: properties and methods. A property is a piece of data that is associated with an object, while a method is an action that the object can carry out. For example, suppose that you created a class called **Account** to represent an individual's bank account. This class might have properties such as **Name**, **Address**, and **Balance** that are used to hold the corresponding information, and methods such as **Deposit** and **Withdrawal** that are called to carry out the specified actions. A property can be read/write, which means that a program can both read and set (write) the property. A property can also be defined as write-only or read-only.

Creating Classes in VB .NET

I have divided the topic of creating classes into two sections. This first section covers the fundamentals of class definitions without considering the complications of subclassing (inheritance). The next section extends this material to consider the various aspects of subclassing.

To define a class, you use the **Class** and **End Class** statements. All of the code that defines the class implementation and interface are placed between these statements. The syntax is as follows:

```
Public Class ClassName
...
End Class
```

ClassName is the name of the class, following normal VB .NET variable naming rules. The **Public** keyword defines the class as having public access, meaning that the class is available

Don't Use MyClass

It can be tempting to use the class name **MyClass** when you are experimenting with classes in VB .NET. Don't do it! **MyClass** is a VB .NET keyword, and as such is off limits as a class name. If you try to use it, things will not work properly. I will explain the use of the **MyClass** keyword later in this chapter.

without restrictions. This is appropriate for most classes you will create. For special situations, other keywords can be used to restrict access to a class. These access modifiers will be covered later in this chapter in the section "Class Access Options."

Visual Studio provides a command for adding a class to your project—you select Add Class from the Project menu. This command displays the Add New Item dialog box with the Class item already selected, as shown in Figure 9.1. The default name for the class, and for the file it is located in, is assigned as **Class1**, **Class2**, and so on as you add more classes to your project. It is preferable to enter a descriptive name for the class in the Name box before clicking Open; then, the class and its file will have the assigned name.

Using the preceding technique to add classes to your project is fine, except that it always creates a new file for each class. This can become cumbersome in projects that include a lot of classes, and there is no reason you cannot define multiple classes in a single file. In fact, you can define a class just about anywhere in a VB .NET project. Generally, you will not define a class within another class, although this is permitted with nested classes (a specialized technique that is beyond the scope of this book). Simply type in the **Public Class ClassName** statement and press Enter, and the editor will automatically add the **End Class** statement for you.

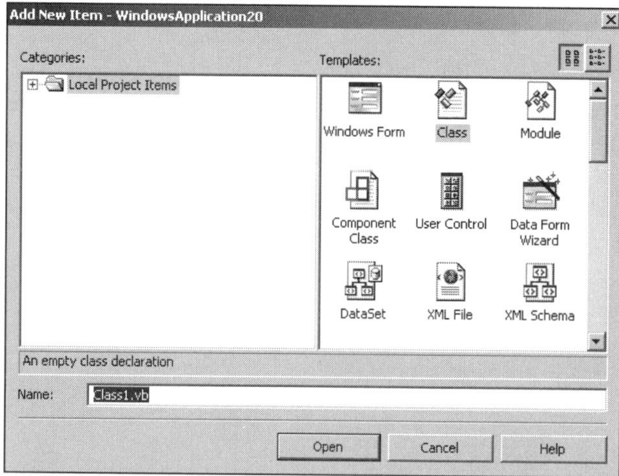

Figure 9.1
Adding a class with the Add New Item dialog

Namespaces and Classes

Namespaces are relevant to class definitions, just as they are to many other aspects of VB .NET programming. Namespaces provide a mechanism for organizing classes and for preventing conflicts between classes of the same name. The default namespace for any class is the project's root namespace, which is the same as the name of the project (unless you explicitly change it in the Project Properties dialog box). You can declare additional namespaces using the **Namespace...End Namespace** block with the following syntax:

```
Namespace name
...
End Namespace
```

Name is a unique name for the namespace. Anything within a **Namespace** block, including class definitions, belongs to that namespace and is addressed using that namespace. Here's an example of defining two classes in a namespace:

```
Namespace SomeNamespace

Public Class Class1
...
End Class

Public Class Class2
...
End Class

End Namespace
```

A given file can contain more than one **Namespace...End Namespace** block, and a project can contain two or more **Namespace...End Namespace** blocks with the same namespace located in different files. To refer to a class that is part of a namespace, you must include a reference to the namespace as well as the class name. For example, to declare a variable of type **Class1**, you would write the following:

```
Dim ob As SomeNamespace.Class1
```

The name of the root namespace can, but does not have to be, included:

```
Dim ob As RootNamespace.SomeNamespace.Class1
```

If you enter a blank string for the name of the root namespace in the Project Properties dialog box, the project will have no root namespace. For elements within a **Namespace...End Namespace** block, that namespace will be the root namespace. Elements not in a **Namespace...End Namespace** block will not be part of a namespace.

Note that the VB .NET editor's Auto List feature takes namespaces into account. If you type the beginning of a statement, such as "**Dim ob As**", the list that drops down will include those user-defined classes that are in the root namespace as well as any namespaces defined in the project with the **Namespace...End Namespace** block. Then, if you enter a namespace name followed by a period, another list will display the names of those classes defined in that namespace.

Class Properties

A property provides a data storage capability for a class. The simplest way to create a class property is to declare a class variable using the **Public** keyword. The name of the variable will be the name of the property. For example:

```
Public Class SomeClass

Public Count As Long

...

End Class
```

Now, the class **SomeClass** has a property named **Count** with the data type **Long**. You can use the property using the standard **Object.Property** syntax, as shown here:

```
Dim ob1 As New SomeClass
Dim ob2 As New SomeClass

ob1.Count = 22
ob2.Count = ob1.Count - 2
```

The other way to create a class property is to write a property procedure for it. This approach is a bit more involved than simply declaring a public variable, as just described, but it has several advantages that will become clear as you read this section. Creating a class property using this method involves two parts:

- Declaring a private class variable to hold the property value
- Writing a property procedure to provide the interface to the property value

The variable that holds the property value is declared using the **Private** keyword so it is not directly accessible from outside the class. Its data type can be any of VB .NET's available data types, as appropriate for the property data. There is nothing special about a property variable except that the class uses it to store the value of a property. Its name can be any legal VB .NET variable name, but I find it useful to use the same name as the property plus the "p" prefix to indicate it is a property variable. Thus, for a property named **Count**, the property variable will be **pCount**.

In its simplest form, the property procedure has the following syntax:

```
Public Property PropName() As type

Set(ByVal Value As type)
  VarName = Value
End Set

Get
  PropName = VarName
End Get

End Property
```

PropName is the name of the property, and ***type*** is the data type of the property (which must be the same data type as the property variable). ***VarName*** is the name of the property variable (declared elsewhere in the class). Here's how it works. When the program sets the property (assigns a value to it), the property procedure is called and the code between the **Set** and **End Set** statements is executed. The value assigned to the property is passed in the **Value** argument and is assigned to the property variable. When the program reads the property, the property procedure is called and the code between the **Get** and **End Get** statements is executed. The value of the property variable is returned to the program as the property value.

Listing 9.1 presents an example of defining a property. This code defines a class that has a single property named **Text**—not a particularly useful class, to be sure, but it illustrates the point.

Listing 9.1 A class with one property.

```
Public Class OneProperty

Private pText As String

Public Property Text As String

Set(ByVal Value As String)
  pText = Value
End Set

Get
  Text = pText
End Get

End Property

End Class
```

Read-Only and Write-Only Properties

A read-only property is one whose value can be set, but not read, by a program. To create a read-only property, use the **ReadOnly** keyword in the property definition, and then omit the **Set...End Set** block from the property procedure. Here's an example:

```
Public ReadOnly Property Name() As String

Get
  Name = pName
End Get

End Property
```

A write-only property is the converse of a read-only property—it can be set, but not read, by the program. To create a write-only property, use the **WriteOnly** keyword in the property definition, then omit the **Get...End Get** block from the property procedure, as shown here:

```
Public WriteOnly Property Color() As Integer

Set(ByVal Value As Integer)
  pColor = Value
End Set

End Property
```

An error occurs if a program tries to read a write-only property or to set a read-only property.

Properties with Parameters

In most cases, a property involves only a single piece of information passed between the program and the object, as in the properties you have seen so far. You also have the option to define properties that pass multiple data items, known as *parameters*. The set of parameters, if any, that a property takes is known as the property's *signature*. To define parameters for a property, include the parameter list in the property definition:

```
Public Property PropName(ParameterList) As type
...
End Property
```

The parameter list is identical in format to the argument list that passed to a procedure. It consists of a comma-delimited list of parameter names and types, as shown here, with **ByVal** being the default method of passing:

```
ByVal Param1 As type1 [, ByVal Param2 As type2 ...]
```

The following example defines a property that takes two parameters:

```
Public Property Item(ByVal Idx As Integer, ByVal Name As String) _
  As String
...
End Property
```

When a program refers to a property with parameters, either setting it or getting it, the proper number and type of parameters must be passed. Inside the property procedure, your code can use the parameters as needed. Perhaps the most common use is to create a property that is actually an array, using a parameter to pass the array index when setting or reading the property. Listing 9.2 shows an example of a class with a property that is an array. Note that this example omits checking the parameter value to ensure it is within the permitted array boundaries, something that a real-world program should do.

Listing 9.2 A class with a property that holds an array of data.

```
Public Class ArrayProperty

  Private pItem(100) As String

  Public Property Item(ByVal Idx As Integer) As String
    Get
      Item = pItem(Idx)
    End Get
    Set(ByVal Value As String)
      pItem(Idx) = Value
    End Set
  End Property

End Class
```

The following code fragment shows how you would use the class in Listing 9.2:

```
Dim ob As New ArrayProperty
Dim FirstName As String

ob.Item(1) = "Peter"
ob.Item(2) = "Paul"
ob.Item(3) = "Mary"
FirstName = ob.Item(1)
```

Default Properties

A class can have a single default property, which is created by using the **Default** keyword in the property definition. A default property cannot be declared as read-only or write-only, and it must have at least one parameter. The syntax is as follows:

```
Public Default Property PropName(ParamaterList) As type
...
End Property
```

An object's default property can be accessed by using the object name alone, without the property name. For example, if the class **Class1** has a nondefault property named **Text**, it would be accessed using the standard **ObjectName.PropertyName** syntax.

If, however, **Text** has been defined as the class's default property, you would use the object name alone. Listing 9.3 illustrates this, using the same class that was presented earlier in Listing 9.2 but this time defining the class's one property as the default property.

Listing 9.3 A class with a default property.

```
Public Class ArrayProperty

  Private pItem(100) As String

  Public Default Property Item(ByVal Idx As Integer) As String
    Get
      Item = pItem(Idx)
    End Get
    Set(ByVal Value As String)
      pItem(Idx) = Value
    End Set
  End Property

End Class
```

Continuing with the same example, this class would be used as follows. Note the changes due to the fact that **Item** is now the default property:

```
Dim ob As New ArrayProperty
Dim FirstName As String

ob(1) = "Peter"
ob(2) = "Paul"
ob(3) = "Mary"
FirstName = ob(1)
```

Overloading Properties

The principle of overloading permits a class to have two or more properties of the same name as long as they differ in their signature—the number and/or type of parameters they take. When a program refers to an overloaded property, the object "knows" which one to call based on the signature. When you overload a property name, obviously you cannot follow the suggestion to use the property name for the class variable where the property value is stored (because you'll need more than one), but will need to devise some other naming scheme.

To overload a property, use the **Overloads** keyword in the property definitions. Here's an example:

```
Public Overloads Property PropName(ParamList) As type
...
End Property
```

Overloading of properties is most common when you are subclassing and you want to create a new property using a property name already present in the base class. You'll see an example of overloading a base class property later in this chapter. For now, the class in Listing 9.4 shows how to overload a property when subclassing is not an issue. The following code fragment shows how you could use this class:

```
Dim ob As New Overloading

ob.Data = 123
ob.Data(1) = "Hello"
ob.Data(2) = "World"
```

Listing 9.4 A class with an overloaded property.

```
Public Class Overloading

Private pDataA(100) As String
Private pDataB As Integer

Public Overloads Property Data() As Integer

Get
  Data = pDataB
End Get
Set(ByVal Value As Integer)
  pDataB = Value
End Set

End Property

Public Overloads Property Data(ByVal Idx As Integer) As String

Get
  Data = pDataA(Idx)
End Get
```

```
Set(ByVal Value As String)
  pDataA(Idx) = Value
End Set

End Property

End Class
```

Class Methods

A method is nothing more than a procedure located in a class. VB .NET provides two types of methods: **function** procedures that return a value and **sub** procedures that do not. The syntax for creating methods is identical to the syntax for procedures described in Chapter 4. To review briefly, the syntax for a **sub** method is as follows:

```
Public Sub MethodName(argument_list)
...
'Method code goes here.
...
End Sub
```

The syntax for a function method is the same except that the return data type must be specified, and a return value must be assigned by code in the method:

```
Public Function MethodName(argument_list) As type
...
'Method code goes here.
MethodName = ReturnValue
...
End Function
```

The default for method arguments is passing by value. To pass an argument by reference, you must explicitly include the **ByRef** keyword. The **Public** keyword specifies that the method has public access and is available without restrictions. You can specify different types of method access by using other keywords. These access modifiers will be covered later in the chapter in the section "Class Access Options."

Listing 9.5 presents a simple example of a class with methods. You could use this class as shown in the following code fragment:

```
Dim MyMath As New SimpleMath
Dim x As Double
Dim y As Double
Dim z As Double
```

```
x = 1.234
y = MyMath.HalfOf(x)
z = MyMath.Twice(x)
```

Listing 9.5 A class with two methods.

```
Public Class SimpleMath
    Public Function HalfOf(ByVal Val As Double) As Double
        HalfOf = Val / 2
    End Function

    Public Function Twice(ByVal Val As Double) As Double
        Twice = Val * 2
    End Function
End Class
```

Method Overloading

Like properties, class methods can be overloaded, permitting a class to have two or more methods of the same name as long as their argument lists are different in data type and/or number of arguments. For example, a class might be designed to hold employee information, including the name and employee number of each individual. You want to have a search capability, permitting an individual's record to be located either by the person's name or by his or her employee number. Overloading will permit you to have two methods named Search, one that uses employee number and the other that uses employee name. This is shown here (assuming that **EmployeeData** is a data type defined elsewhere):

```
Public Overloads Function Search(ByVal EmpNo As Long) _
  As EmployeeData
...
'Code to search by employee number.
...
End Function

Public Overloads Function Search(ByVal EmpName As String) _
  As EmployeeData
...
'Code to search by employee name.
...
End Function
```

Class Constructors

Every class can have a *constructor*, a method that is called automatically when the class is instantiated. You use a constructor to perform any class initialization that is required. To create a constructor, give the class a **sub** method named **New**:

```
Class SomeClass

  Public Sub New()
  ' Initialization code goes here.
  End Sub

End Class
```

The constructor can be defined to accept parameters, which can be a very useful technique. This permits the object to be initialized with program-defined data when it is created. Listing 9.6 shows a simple class that uses this technique. The value of the **Name** property is set when the class is instantiated, using the constructor. You would instantiate and initialize this class as follows:

```
Dim ob As New UseConstructor("Fred")
```

You could also use this alternate syntax to accomplish the same end:

```
Dim ob As UseConstructor
...
ob = New UseConstructor("Fred")
```

You'll note that this constructor initializes data by directly setting the private variable that is used to hold the property. This is perfectly fine in many situations, but in others you will want to initialize through the property procedure. This is the case when the property procedure contains value-checking code, for example. To initialize through the property procedure, you would change the constructor as follows:

```
Public Sub New(ByVal Val As String)
    Me.Name = Val
  End Sub
```

Listing 9.6 Using a class constructor to initialize data.

```
Public Class UseConstructor

Private pName As String

  Public Sub New(ByVal Val As String)
    pName = Val
  End Sub

Public Property Name() As String
  Get
    Name = pName
  End Get
```

```
  Set(ByVal Value As String)
    pName = Value
  End Set
End Property

End Class
```

Like other methods, a class constructor can be overloaded using the **Overloads** keyword. This provides additional flexibility—for example, permitting a class to be initialized with different types of data. An overloaded constructor can also be used to make the initialization data optional by defining two constructors, one with and one without a parameter. Listing 9.7 shows this technique applied to the class that was shown earlier in Listing 9.6. With the overloaded constructor, the class data can be initialized or not when the object is instantiated, according to the needs of the program. If no initialization data is passed to the constructor, the **Name** property is set to a blank string.

Listing 9.7 Using an overloaded class constructor to provide for optional data initialization.

```
Public Class UseOverloadedConstructor

Private pName As String

  Public Overloads Sub New(ByVal Val As String)
    pName = Val
  End Sub

Public Overloads Sub New()
    pName = ""
End Sub

Public Property Name() As String
  Get
    Name = pName
  End Get
  Set(ByVal Value As String)
    pName = Value
  End Set
End Property

End Class
```

Object Termination

What happens when a program has finished using an object? Typically, this is marked by the removal of all references to the object. For example, if code in a procedure creates an object and refers to it with a local variable, then when execution exits the procedure, the variable used to reference the object goes out of scope. The object still exists in memory, but no references to it exist. Will the unused object remain in memory forever?

No, fortunately. The .NET framework has a garbage-collection mechanism that is designed to reclaim memory from unused objects. Garbage collection is called automatically at certain times, based on .NET framework rules and other factors. The garbage collector will look at all objects in memory, and those for which no references exist will be destroyed. The memory is then available for other uses.

The nature of .NET garbage collection is that the destruction of objects is not under direct control of our program. Even so, some cleanup tasks might need to be performed before an object is terminated. Code for such tasks can be placed in the class's **Finalize** method, which is called automatically just before garbage collection terminates the class. The syntax for this method is as follows:

```
Protected Overrides Sub Finalize()
...
End Sub
```

Note that the **Finalize** method is defined using the **Protected** and **Overrides** keywords, which will be explained later in this chapter.

What if you do not want to wait for **Finalize** to be called? Perhaps your class has some cleanup tasks that should be performed as soon as the program is finished with it, rather than waiting for garbage collection to occur. In this case, your only option is to define a method to perform cleanup, and then have the program code call it explicitly as needed. You can call this method any name you like, but the name **Dispose** is conventional.

Shared Methods

A shared method is available directly from a class without the need to create an instance of the class. Shared methods are known as static methods or class methods in some other programming languages. Methods defined without the **Shared** keyword are called *instance* methods because they can be called only from an instance of the class.

To create a shared method, include the **Shared** keyword in the method definition. Listing 9.8 shows an example of a class with two shared methods. Although this class has only shared methods, this is not required—a class can contain a mix of shared and instance methods.

Listing 9.8 A class with shared methods.

```
Class Math
  Public Shared Function Sum(ByVal x As Double, ByVal y As Double) _
      As Double
    Return x + y
  End Function
```

```
  Public Shared Function Difference(ByVal x As Double, _
      ByVal y As Double) As Double
    Return x - y
  End Function
End Class
```

To use a shared method, you need only to refer to the class name—you do not have to create an instance of the class. Using the **Math** class defined in Listing 9.8, a program could call the shared methods as follows:

```
x = Math.Sum(2, 3)
y = Math.Difference(10, 2)
```

A class that contains shared methods can be instantiated just like any other classes, and the shared methods can be called from an instance of the class as well as from the class name itself. For example:

```
Dim obj As New Math
x = obj.Sum(2, 3)
```

A shared method cannot include a reference to the **Me** keyword, nor can it be defined as **Overridable**, **NotOverridable**, or **MustOverride**. Shared methods are public by default.

As you may have noticed, many of the classes in the .NET framework implement shared methods. Generally speaking, shared methods are used when you want to encapsulate some related functionality in a class, when you have no need to store user data in class instances. For example, you might implement a set of financial functions as shared methods in a class called **Finance**. Users would never need to instantiate the class, but could use them directly as shown in the above example.

Shared Variables

A shared variable is one that is shared by all instances of a class. This is in contrast to a so-called instance variable where each instance of the class has a separate copy. You declare a shared variable using the **Shared** keyword, as in this example:

```
Shared Count As Long
```

Shared variables are private by default, but can be scoped as public by including the **Public** keyword:

```
Public Shared Count As Long
```

When you create instances of a class with one or more shared variables, only a single copy of each shared variable is shared by all the class instances. This can be very useful to permit data to be shared between instances of a class. Note that the sharing is between instances within a given program and does not extend to instances of the same class created in another program. Listing 9.9 provides a demonstration.

Listing 9.9 A class with one shared variable.

```
Class SharedVariableDemo

  Public Shared Info As String

End Class
```

Now look at the following code snippet:

```
Dim obj1 As New SharedVariableDemo()
Dim obj2 As New SharedVariableDemo()
Dim obj3 As New SharedVariableDemo()
obj1.Info = "Shared information!"
```

After this code executes, the expression **obj1.Info** will return "Shared information!" as you would expect, but the expressions **obj2.Info** and **obj3.Info** will also return the same thing. No matter how many instances of the class you create, they all share a single copy of each shared variable.

You can use a shared variable to create a shared property. Declare the variable with private access, and then write a property procedure to provide an interface to it. One useful way to take advantage of this approach is to keep track of how many instances of a given class have been created. The class in Listing 9.10 demonstrates this. The class has one shared variable to keep track of the instance count. Because this variable is private, the class also has a read-only property procedure to provide access to the value. In the class constructor, the value of the variable is increased by 1. In the class destructor, the value of the variable is decreased by 1.

To demonstrate this class, create a console application containing the code shown in Listing 9.11 (it must contain the class definition as well, of course). This code creates three instances of the class **InstanceCounter** and then displays the instance count as read from one of the instances. At this time, the value will be 3.

The code next calls the sub **Foo()**, which creates one local instance of the class and then displays the count again—here, it will be 4.

When execution returns from the sub **Foo()**, garbage collection is forced by calling **System.GC.Collect()**. Because the instance of the class that was created in **Foo()** is now out of scope, it will be destroyed by the garbage collection. Finally, when the instance count is again displayed, it will be 3 again.

Listing 9.10 A class that uses a shared variable.

```
Class InstanceCounter

 Private Shared pInstanceCount As Long

 Public Sub New()
   pInstanceCount += 1
 End Sub

 Protected Overrides Sub Finalize()
    pInstanceCount -= 1
 End Sub

 Public ReadOnly Property InstanceCount() As Long
    Get
      Return pInstanceCount
    End Get
 End Property

End Class
```

Listing 9.11 A console application to demonstrate the InstanceCounter class.

```
Sub Main()

  Dim obj1 As New InstanceCounter()
  Dim obj2 As New InstanceCounter()
  Dim obj3 As New InstanceCounter()

  Console.Write(obj1.InstanceCount)
  Console.WriteLine()
  Call Foo()
  ' Force garbage collection.
  System.GC.Collect()
  ' Wait for the user to press Enter to permit a
  ' pause for garbage collection to complete.
  Console.ReadLine()
  Console.Write(obj1.InstanceCount)
  ' Wait for the user to press Enter.
  Console.ReadLine()

End Sub

Private Sub Foo()
  Dim q As New InstanceCounter()
```

```
    Console.Write(q.InstanceCount)
    Console.WriteLine()

End Sub
```

Class Events

When you define a class, you have the option of defining one or more events that the class can raise. These class events are not the same as the user events—such as mouse clicks and key presses—that are used in other parts of VB .NET. Rather, they are events that are triggered in code in the class and can be detected by the host program. For example, a class that carries out a potentially time-consuming process could use an event to inform the host program of progress, and the host program could display a progress bar indicator to the user. Using events involves declaring the event, raising the event, and handling the event.

An event is declared in a class definition using the **Event** keyword. The event declaration serves to declare the name of the event as well as the number and types of arguments that the event has. The syntax is as follows:

```
Public Event EventName(ArgumentList)
```

EventName is the name of the event, following standard VB .NET variable naming rules. ***ArgumentList*** is a list of the arguments that the event takes. It has the same format as the argument list of other procedures except that optional arguments and **ParamArray** arguments are not permitted. If the event takes no arguments, use empty parentheses. Here is the declaration of an event that takes one type **Integer** argument:

```
Public Event MyEvent(PercentDone As Integer)
```

Although most events are declared with the **Public** keyword, you can also declare an event as shared by using the **Shared** keyword:

```
Shared Event MyEvent(PercentDone As Integer)
```

The reason for doing this is that shared methods can raise only shared events. A nonshared method can be raised by both shared and nonshared methods.

To raise an event, use the **RaiseEvent** statement. The syntax is as follows:

```
RaiseEvent EventName(ArgumentList)
```

EventName is the name of the event to raise, which must have been declared in the same module that the **RaiseEvent** statement is being called from. ***ArgumentList*** specifies the arguments required by the event. If the event takes no arguments, use empty parentheses.

Using DoEvents()

The **Application.DoEvents()** method lets your application handle other events while it is in the midst of processing code, such as another event handler. Without a call to **DoEvents()**, new events (such as repainting a screen window) will wait in the queue until the current process is terminated. In the example in Listing 9.12, without the call to **DoEvents()**, the user would not be able to do such things as drag the program's screen window to a new location while the **For** loops are executing.

Listing 9.12 presents a simple example of a class that raises an event. This class has a single method named **Process()** that mimics a task that takes a while to complete. The task is provided by nested **For** loops that take a few seconds to complete. The class's event, called **Progress()**, has a single argument that reflects the percentage of the task that is done at the time the event is raised. The code is written to raise this event every time the outer **For** loop iterates, so it will report 0 percent, 10 percent, and so on up to 100 percent complete. You'll see this class demonstrated later in this chapter when I cover event handlers.

Listing 9.12 A class that raises a "progress" event.

```
Public Class ClassWithEvent

Public Event Progress(ByVal PercentDone As Integer)

Public Sub Process()

Dim i As Integer
Dim j As Integer

For i = 0 To 100 Step 10
    Raise Event Progress (i)
    For j = 0 To 10000
        Application.DoEvents()
    Next
Next

End Sub

End Class
```

Raising an event is by itself pointless. Nothing will happen unless the host code responds to the event, or *handles* the event. Code that responds to an event is called an *event handler*. You can create event handlers in one of two ways. One method is easy and applicable to most situations; the other is a bit more difficult to use but is more flexible. I will cover them in turn.

*Handling Events Using **WithEvents** and Handles*

For most situations, the recommended way to create event handlers is by using the **WithEvents** and **Handles** keywords. First, the object that will raise the event(s) must be declared using the **WithEvents** keyword. For example, if **ClassWithEvents** is a class that raises events, you would declare an instance of it like this:

```
Public WithEvents obj As ClassWithEvents
```

Note that you cannot use the **New** keyword when declaring an object using **WithEvents**. The following is not permitted:

```
Public WithEvents obj As New ClassWithEvents
```

You must declare and instantiate the object separately:

```
Public WithEvents obj As ClassWithEvents
obj = New ClassWithEvents
```

Then, you must write an event handler for each event. An event handler is a regular VB .NET **Sub** procedure that is linked to one or more events by the **Handles** keyword. The syntax is as follows:

```
Sub HandlerName(ArgumentList) Handles EventList
```

HandlerName is the name of the event handler and can be any legal VB .NET name. It is customary, however, to assign names in the form ***ObjectName_EventName*** because this is the format used for other event handler names and makes it clear that the procedure is an event handler. ***ArgumentList*** is a list of arguments passed by the event, and must match the argument list in the event declaration. ***EventList*** is a list of one or more events that will be handled by this procedure. Each event is specified using the format ***ObjectName.EventName***. If the list contains more than one event, separate them by commas.

Here is an example of an event handler that will handle the **Progress** event for the objects named **obj1** and **obj2**. Assume that this event passes one type **Integer** argument:

```
Sub obj1_progress(PercentDone As Integer) Handles obj1.Progress, _
    obj2.Progress
' Code to handle the event goes here.
End Sub
```

To provide a demonstration of creating an event handler in this way, I will use the class **ClassWithEvent** that was presented earlier in Listing 9.12. Follow these steps to create the demonstration program:

1. Create a new Windows Application project in VB .NET.
2. Add the class definition from Listing 9.12 to the project.
3. Add a TextBox control to the project's form. Leave the control's name at the default value of **TextBox1**, and change its **Text** property to a blank string.
4. Add the following declaration to the form class definition:

```
Public WithEvents ob As ClassWithEvent
```

5. Add the following code to define the event handler:

```
Protected Sub ob_Progress(ByVal PercentDone As Integer) _
       Handles ob.Progress
    TextBox1.Text = PercentDone
End Sub
```

6. Create an event handler for the **Form1_Click()** event that will instantiate the class and call its **Process()** method when the user clicks the form:

```
Private Sub Form1_Click(ByVal sender As Object, _
    ByVal e As System.EventArgs) Handles MyBase.Click
        ob = New ClassWithEvent()
        ob.Process()
End Sub
```

When you run the program, click on the form to call the **Process()** method. As the method executes, it raises the **Progress()** event repeatedly. Each time this event fires, the event handler displays the latest "percent done" value in the text box. You'll see the value in the text box change from 0 to 10, 20, and so on up to 100.

*Handling Events Using **AddHandler***

Using the **WithEvents** and **Handles** keywords to set up event handlers works fine in most situations, as described in the previous section. You might run into some limitations, however. Specifically, this technique:

- Cannot be used with an object reference that is declared as a generic **Object** type. The object variable must be declared as the specific class type.
- Cannot be used to handle shared events.
- Cannot associate multiple event handlers with a given event.
- Cannot be used with arrays of object variables.

To overcome these limitations, you can use the **AddHandler** statement to associate an event handler with an event. When using this technique, you declare the object instance in the normal manner, without any special keywords. The event handler itself is a regular VB .NET **Sub** procedure with an argument list that matches that of the event that is being handled. Again, no special keywords are needed. Then, assign the event handler using the following syntax:

```
AddHandler ObjectName.EventName, AddressOf Me.HandlerName
```

ObjectName is the name of the object, ***EventName*** is the name of the event, and ***HandlerName*** is the name of the event-handling procedure. Note the use of the **Me** keyword, which provides a reference to the object the class is running in and which in this case contains the event handler procedure. **AddHandler** is very flexible. You can assign more than one event handler to an event, and you can also assign the same event handler to more than one event. To dissociate an event handler from an event, use the **RemoveHandler** statement, which has exactly the same syntax as **AddHandler**.

Now let's repeat the previous demonstration using the **ClassWithEvent** class, but this time assigning an event handler using the **AddHandler** statement. Here are the steps to follow:

1. Create a new Windows Application project in VB .NET.
2. Add the class definition from Listing 9.12 to the project.
3. Add a TextBox control to the project's form. Leave the control's name at the default value of **TextBox1**, and change its **Text** property to a blank string.
4. Add the following declaration to the form class definition:

   ```
   Public ob As New ClassWithEvent
   ```

5. Add the following code to define the event handler:

   ```
   Protected Sub ob_Progress(ByVal PercentDone As Integer)
           TextBox1.Text = PercentDone
   End Sub
   ```

6. Create an event handler for the **Form1_Click()** event that will assign the event handler and call the **Process()** method when the user clicks the form:

   ```
   Private Sub Form1_Click(ByVal sender As Object, _
       ByVal e As System.EventArgs) Handles MyBase.Click
           AddHandler ob.Progress, AddressOf Me.ob_Progress
           ob.Process()
   End Sub
   ```

The new demo will work exactly the same as the previous one.

Class Access Options

Classes and their variables, methods, and properties all have an *access* associated with them. Access, sometimes referred to as *scope*, has to do with an entity's accessibility—in other words, from which parts of a program the entity can be accessed. So far, you have seen classes, methods, and properties defined with public access, which is the default and places no restrictions on access. VB .NET offers other options that place various restrictions on access to an entity. You can use these more restrictive access options when you have no need for an entity to be publicly accessible, or when public access would cause problems. These modifiers are summarized in Table 9.1.

Some combinations of access modifiers and entities may not seem clear. For example, does the idea of a private method make any sense? Not really—if a procedure is available only within the class, it cannot be called a method. However, private procedures are commonly used, being called by other code within the class, and are sometimes referred to as helper procedures.

Table 9.1 Access modifier keywords.

Keyword	Description
Public	No restrictions on access in the current or other projects.
Private	Available only within its declaration context. A private class is available only within its own module (file). A private procedure is available only within its own class.
Protected	Available only within its own class and derived subclasses both within the project and outside the project.
Friend	Available within its own class and to client code and subclasses, but only within the current project.
Protected Friend	Available without restriction in the current project, but only to derived classes outside the project.

Summary

At the heart of object-oriented programming is the ability to define and use your own classes. VB .NET fully supports the tools of OOP, and while some of these techniques may seem a bit odd to someone who is new to OOP, you will soon get used to them and realize their full potential. This chapter started you on your way to learning VB .NET OOP, and the next chapter continues the journey.

Chapter 10
Object-Oriented Programming with VB .NET, Part 2

Object-oriented programming, or OOP, is at the heart of Visual Basic .NET. This includes the ability to define and use your own classes, an extremely powerful technique that you started learning about in the previous chapter. This chapter wraps things up, covering the remaining topics that you need to understand in order to create and use your own classes in VB .NET programs.

Structures

VB .NET supports another type of entity called a *structure*. In some ways, structures are like classes, but in other ways they are not. A structure can contain variables, properties, methods, and events, and structure members can be declared as having **Public**, **Private**, or **Friend** access. A structure can also implement an interface (covered later in this chapter). Finally, a structure can have a constructor that takes parameters. The ways in which structures differ from classes are as follows:

- A structure cannot inherit from another type (although all structures are implicitly based on the **System.Object** type, as are all VB .NET elements).
- A structure cannot be inherited from.
- A structure cannot have an explicitly defined constructor without parameters. There is an implicit parameter-less constructor that initializes all structure fields (variables) to their default values.

- A structure cannot have a destructor.
- Structure fields cannot be initialized at the same time they are declared.
- Structures are value types, whereas classes are reference types (you learned about value and reference types in Chapter 6).

From a practical point of view, these differences mean that structures are best suited for specialized data storage uses, where the lack of inheritance capabilities is not an issue. The system overhead is less for structures than for classes, so when you can use a structure instead of a class it is usually a good idea to do so.

To define a structure, use the following syntax:

```
Access Structure StructureName
...
End Structure
```

The optional **Access** keyword can be **Public**, **Private**, or **Friend** to specify the structure's access level (as explained earlier in this chapter). The access defaults to public if the **Access** keyword is omitted. ***StructureName*** is the name of the structure, following the standard VB .NET naming rules.

In its simplest and perhaps most common use, a structure is defined to serve as a compound data type. Its members are all fields (variables) that together make up a storage unit that is tailored to your program's needs. Here's an example:

```
Structure Person
    Dim FirstName As String
    Dim LastName As String
    Dim YearOfBirth As Short
End Structure
```

After you have defined a structure, you can use it like you would any other data type:

```
Dim ThePresident As Person
Dim Baseballteam(9) As Person
```

To access the fields of a structure, use the ***instancename.fieldname*** syntax:

```
ThePresident.FirstName = "George"
ThePresident.LastName = "Bush"
ThePresident.YearOfBirth = 1946
BaseballTeam(1).FirstName = "Babe"
BaseballTeam(1).LastName = "Ruth"
BaseballTeam(1).YearOfBirth = 1895
```

A structure can also be used as a parameter or return value of a procedure. A structure can contain arrays, other structures, and object references as fields. Note, however, that you can define a structure only at the module, namespace, or file level. Thus, a structure can be defined within a class, but not within another structure or in a procedure.

Interfaces

Every class has an interface that consists of its methods, properties, and events. Sometimes it is useful to declare an interface separately from a class. An interface declaration contains the names and parameters of the interface members, but no implementation (actual code). Let's look at declaring interfaces first, and then I will explain why you might want to do this.

You use the **Interface...End Interface** block to declare an interface, as shown here:

```
Public Interface Interface1
  Event Completed()
  Sub Calculate(Val As Double)
  Property Name() As String
  Function SubTotal(Rate As Single) As Single
End Interface
```

An interface declaration can include overloaded members as well as a default property:

```
Public Interface Interface1
  Default Property Amount() As Single
  Overloads Sub Init()
  Overloads Sub Init(Code As Integer)
End Interface
```

An interface can inherit from one or more other interfaces. The following interface will contain all the members of **Interface1** along with its own members:

```
Public Interface Interface2
  Inherits Interface1
  Function GetURL()
End Interface
```

Implementing Interfaces

Now you know how to declare an interface, but why bother? The point of interfaces is that a class or structure can implement an interface, which in turn means that the class or structure *must* provide all of the members in the interface. An interface can be thought of as a contract—when a class implements an interface, it agrees to implement all the interface members. The class can have additional members as well, as long as it implements all the members defined in the interface.

Let's look at a real-world example. You have written a program that uses an existing class. Your program depends on that class having certain properties, events, and methods. Then a programmer—perhaps you, perhaps someone else—decides to improve that class. This sounds great, but what if the class interface is changed so that a member no longer exists or takes different arguments? When your program tries to use the new class, it will not work—the code is broken. The terrific new features in the class are meaningless to you.

This potential problem is avoided by the use of a declared interface. By declaring an interface that contains all of the class's required members, then implementing the interface in the class definition, you guarantee that existing code will never be broken by changes to the class because it will always implement the required members.

Implementing an interface in a class requires two steps. First, you use the **Implements** keyword to specify that the class implements one or more interfaces:

```
Class MyClass
  Implements MyInterface
...
End Class
```

If the class implements more than one interface, you can list them in the same **Implements** statement, separated by commas. Or you can list them in separate **Implements** statements.

The next part of implementing an interface is creating the actual class members. This is essentially the same as the usual process of creating class members, as covered earlier in this chapter. The one difference is that each class member that implements an interface member must be marked as such using the **Implements** keyword. Here's an example:

```
Interface SomeInterface
  Function Total() As Single
End Interface

Class Class1
  Implements SomeInterface

  Function Name() As Single Implements SomeInterface.Total
  ...
  End Function

End Class
```

Name is the name of the function. Note that the name of the function or other member does not have to be the same as the name of the interface member (although it can be). The connection between the class member ***Name*** and the interface member **Total** is created by the **Implements** statement. When a program calls **Total**, this link will result in ***Name*** being called. When implementing an interface in a class, you must implement all the interface members or the compiler will report an error.

Using a Class That Implements an Interface

The process of declaring a class instance is changed from the usual when you want to make use of an interface that the class implements. Suppose you have a class ***ClassName*** that implements the interface ***InterfaceName***. To create an instance of the class using the interface, you would use the following code:

```
Dim obj As InterfaceName
obj = New ClassName
```

This results in the object exposing only those of its members that are part of the interface. If it has any public members that are not part of the interface, they remain hidden. You can use a class that implements an interface in the usual way, ignoring its interface, using the usual syntax as follows:

```
Dim obj As ClassName
obj = New ClassName
```

In this case, only the class's own public members will be exposed, and its interface will not be exposed.

Listing 10.1 shows an example of a class that can be used with its interface or on its own. The following code snippet shows how you could use it both ways:

```
Dim Math1 As OtherMath
Dim Math2 As SimpleMath
Math1 = New SimpleMath
Math2 = New SimpleMath

x = Math1.OneHalf(6) ' x = 3
y = Math2.HalfOf(6)  ' y = 3
```

Listing 10.1 A class that can be used with or without its interface.

```
Public Interface OtherMath
    Public Function OneHalf(ByVal Val As Double) As Double
    Public Function Double(ByVal Val As Double) As Double
End Interface
```

```
Public Class SimpleMath
    Implements OtherMath
    Public Function HalfOf(ByVal Val As Double) As Double _
      Implements OtherMath.OneHalf
        HalfOf = Val / 2
    End Function

    Public Function Twice(ByVal Val As Double) As Double _
      Implements OtherMath.Double
        Twice = Val * 2
    End Function
End Class
```

Inheritance

So far, you have seen how to create classes that might be considered standalone in that they do not subclass (inherit from) any other classes, nor are they designed with the possibility in mind that they will themselves be used as a base class. Because subclassing is central to the power of OOP, you really should not ignore these factors. In this section, I cover those aspects of VB .NET that are relevant when subclassing and when designing a base class. First, however, let's take a look at .NET's ultimate base class.

The Base Object Class

Everything in the .NET framework is an object, derived directly or indirectly from the **System.Object** class. In other words, every class, whether one that is a part of the .NET framework or one you define yourself, subclasses the **System.Object** class. Every class, therefore, inherits the members of the **System.Object** class, although in some cases they are overridden. For classes that you create, these members will be available as described in Table 10.1.

Table 10.1 Members of the System.Object class.

Member	Description
Equals(*obj*)	Returns True if the current object is the same as ***obj***, False if not.
GetHashCode()	Returns a type **Integer** representing the hash code for the current object (see the VB .NET documentation for more information.
GetType()	Returns a **Type** object that contains information about the current object (see the VB .NET documentation for more information).
ToString()	Returns a string representing the current object. For data types, such as **DateTime** or **Integer**, the string represents the data stored in the type. For other types, the default return value is in the form ***Namespace.Classname***.

The **Equals()** method is used to determine if two object references refer to the same object instance. The following code fragment illustrates:

```
Dim Same As Boolean
Dim ob1 As New SomeClass
Dim ob2 As New SomeClass
Same = ob1.Equals(ob2)
' At this point Same is False because ob1 and ob2 refer to
' two different instances of the class SomeClass.
ob1 = ob2
Same = ob1.Equals(ob2)
' At this point Same is True because ob1 and ob2 refer to
' the same instance of the class SomeClass.
```

Subclassing

When you create a class that is explicitly based on an existing class, it is called *subclassing*. To implement basic subclassing, all you need to do is use the **Inherits** keyword along with the name of class being subclassed. Here is a simple example:

```
Class NewClass
  Inherits Class1

End Class
```

The class doing the inheriting—in this case **NewClass**—is called the subclass (or sometimes the child class). The class being inherited from—**Class1**—is called the base class (or sometimes the superclass or the parent class). The base class can be a class you defined or a class that is part of VB .NET. In the simplest case, the result of the above code is simply that the subclass becomes a copy of a base class under a different name. It will have all the same methods, properties, variables, and so on. A base class can restrict the ways in which it can be subclassed, which will be covered later in the chapter, but you need not be concerned about that now.

Subclassing by itself is not much use. There's not much point in creating a copy of a class. The power of subclassing comes when you create a subclass that includes additional features. In other words, your new class will have all the features of its base class plus those features that you add to it.

Let's look at a simple example of inheritance. Suppose you have created a class designed to hold information about individual people: their first and last names and their phone numbers. This class, called **Person**, is shown in Listing 10.2. It has three properties, for the three needed pieces of information, plus one method named **GetAllInfo()** that returns the person's full name and phone number in one string. In addition, it has a constructor that allows initialization at the time of creation, as well as another constructor that permits creation without data initialization.

Listing 10.2 A class to hold information about a person.

```
Class Person
    Private pFirstName As String
    Private pLastName As String
    Private pPhoneNumber As String

    Overloads Sub New()
    End Sub

    Overloads Sub New(ByVal FirstName As String, _
           ByVal LastName As String, ByVal PhoneNumber As String)
      pFirstName = FirstName
      pLastName = LastName
      pPhoneNumber = PhoneNumber
    End Sub

    Property LastName() As String
      Get
        LastName = pLastName
      End Get
      Set(ByVal Value As String)
        pLastName = Value
      End Set
    End Property

    Property FirstName() As String
      Get
        FirstName = pFirstName
      End Get
      Set(ByVal Value As String)
        pFirstName = Value
      End Set
    End Property

    Property PhoneNumber() As String
      Get
        PhoneNumber = pPhoneNumber
      End Get
```

```
    Set(ByVal Value As String)
      pPhoneNumber = Value
    End Set
  End Property

  Public Function GetAllInfo() As String
    Dim buf As String
    buf = pFirstName & " " & pLastName
    buf &= ": " & pPhoneNumber
    GetAllInfo = buf
  End Function

End Class
```

Next, suppose that you need to create a class to hold information about your company's employees. The information that you want to store is first name, last name, phone number, date of hire, and employee number. You could create an **Employee** class from scratch, but because the existing **Person** class already contains most of the needed elements, this becomes a perfect place to use inheritance. By subclassing the **Person** class, you already have most of the needed functionality. All you need to do is the following:

1. Add properties for date of hire and employee number.
2. Modify the constructor to permit initialization of the new properties.

The resulting **Employee** class is shown in Listing 10.3. You should note two things about this subclass. First, you can see that the class constructor does not directly access the property variables in the base class (**pFirstName**, **pLastName**, and **pPhoneNumber**). Rather it performs the initialization by means of the corresponding properties. This is necessary because the property variables in the **Person** class are private and are therefore not directly available in the subclass. The property procedures, being public, are available.

Second, while the **Employee** class inherits the **GetAllInfo()** method from the **Person** class, it is not particularly useful because it returns only three of the five pieces of information about an employee. You could write another method to return all the employee information, but if you try to use the same name—**GetAllInfo()**—it will not work. The reason is that to create a method in a subclass that has the same name as a method in the base class, you must *override* the base class method, and this is permitted only if the base class method is marked with the **Overridable** keyword. You'll learn more about this later in this chapter.

Overloading Base Class Methods

A subclass can overload base class methods by using the **Overloads** keyword in the method definition. The only requirement, as with all overloading, is that the methods of the same name each have a different signature (number and type of arguments).

Listing 10.3 An Employee class that subclasses the Person class.

```
Class Employee
  Inherits Person

  Private pDateOfHire As Date
  Private pEmployeeNumber As Long

  Overloads Sub New()
  End Sub

  Overloads Sub New(ByVal FirstName As String, _
      ByVal LastName As String, ByVal PhoneNumber As String, _
      ByVal DateOfHire As Date, ByVal EmployeeNumber As Long)
    Me.FirstName = FirstName
    Me.LastName = LastName
    Me.PhoneNumber = PhoneNumber
    pDateOfHire = DateOfHire
    pEmployeeNumber = EmployeeNumber
  End Sub

  Property DateOfHire() As Date
    Get
      DateOfHire = pDateOfHire
    End Get
    Set(ByVal Value As Date)
      pDateOfHire = Value
    End Set
  End Property

  Property EmployeeNumber() As Long
    Get
      EmployeeNumber = pEmployeeNumber
    End Get
    Set(ByVal Value As Long)
      pEmployeeNumber = Value
    End Set
  End Property

End Class
```

Scoping in Subclasses

Earlier in this chapter, you learned about the access modifiers that can be applied to class members. These access modifiers become more important when using inheritance because they determine the extent to which members of a base class are accessible from a subclass. In particular, protected scope comes into play when creating base classes. Let's look at the various access options as they relate to subclassing.

When a class member is private, it is accessible only from within that class. It is not accessible from a subclass. A public member, on the other hand, is available in subclasses (as well as everywhere else). Look at these two class definitions:

```
Class Class1
  Private Var1 As String
  Public Var2 As String
End Class

Class Class2
  Inherits Class1
End Class
```

An instance of **Class2** will have a member named **Var2**, inherited from **Class1**, because it is declared as public in **Class1**. However, **Class2** will not have a member named **Var1**, because **Var1** is declared as private in **Class1**. The same thing would apply to class methods.

Public access is often too broad. You may want to give subclasses access to a base class member, but not provide any broader access. The protected access level was designed for just this purpose. A class member declared with the **Protected** keyword will be accessible within the class and all of its subclasses, but nowhere else. This includes subclasses within the project and in other projects.

It's important to note how friend access differs. A member declared with the **Friend** keyword is freely available within the project, both in subclasses and in other code. It is not accessible outside the project.

Base Class Design Considerations

When you are designing a class, you must take various factors into consideration that go beyond the class's own functionality. These factors have to do with the possibility that the class may be used as a base class.

Abstract Classes

An abstract class cannot be instantiated, but is designed to be used only as a base class. You declare a class as abstract using the **MustInherit** keyword, as shown here:

```
Public MustInherit Class MyAbstractClass
...
End Class
```

Abstract classes can have methods, properties, and other members just like nonabstract classes. You can think of an abstract class's members as providing the base functionality that will be present in any class derived from it. Typically, abstract classes also have methods that are declared with the **MustOverride** keyword. Such methods are not implemented in the abstract class, but must be implemented in any derived classes. Listing 10.4 shows an example of an abstract class named **Car**. Any subclass based on **Car** must implement methods named **Start()**, **GetGas()**, and **Speed()** as defined in the abstract class, with the same arguments and return values. All other details of the subclass implementation are left up to the developer.

Listing 10.4 An abstract class with MustOverride methods.

```
Public MustInherit Class Car
  Public MustOverride Sub Start()
  Public MustOverride Sub GetGas(Gallons As Integer)
  Public MustOverride Function Speed() As Single
End Class
```

Abstract classes with **MustOverride** members are very much like interfaces. For example, the interface in Listing 10.5 has much the same result as the abstract class in Listing 10.4. A class that subclasses the abstract class **Car** or implements the interface **Car** will be required to implement the three members **Start()**, **GetGas()**, and **Speed()**.

Listing 10.5 An interface that has the same effect as the abstract class in Listing 10.4.

```
Public Interface Car
  Sub Start()
  Sub GetGas(Gallons As Integer)
  Function Speed() As Single
End Interface
```

In choosing whether to use an abstract class or an interface, keep the following facts in mind:

- An abstract class can provide base functionality as well as specify class members that must be implemented. An interface can do only the latter.
- A class can implement multiple interfaces, but can inherit from only one abstract class (or any type of class, for that matter).
- A class that subclasses an abstract class can still implement one or more interfaces.

Noninheritable Classes

A class declared with the **NotInheritable** keyword is in some ways the opposite of an abstract class—it can be instantiated but cannot be subclassed. Here's an example:

```
Public NotInheritable Class SomeClass
...
End Class
```

Use **NotInheritable** when your class is not suitable for subclassing, or when you want others to be able to use your class but not base their own classes on it.

Overriding Methods

A method in a base class that is defined with the **Overridable** keyword can be overridden by a method of the same name in a subclass. In other words, the method in the subclass replaces the method in the base class. Methods are not overridable by default. In the subclass, use the **Overrides** keyword in the method that is overriding the base class method. Listing 10.6 illustrates overriding.

Listing 10.6 Demonstration of overriding a method.

```
Public Class Class1
  Public Overridable Sub DoSomething()
  ...
  End Sub
End Class

Public Class Class2
  Inherits Class1
  Public Overrides Sub DoSomething()
  ...
  End Sub
End Class
```

Note that a method defined with the **Overridable** keyword does not have to be overridden—it's an option depending on the needs of the subclass. Overridable methods are useful when you want to provide basic functionality in a base class but permit subclasses to implement their own functionality for the method as needed.

The **NotOverridable** keyword marks a method as not overridable. Because this is the default, it is generally not needed. The only situation where you will use it is when you are writing a method that itself overrides a method in the base class and you do not want it to be overridden. For example, suppose you rewrote **Class2** from Listing 10.6 as follows:

```
Public Class Class2
  Inherits Class1
  Public NotOverridable Overrides Sub DoSomething()
  ...
  End Sub
End Class
```

The result is that when you subclass **Class2**, the new class cannot override **DoSomething()**. Without the **NotOverridable** keyword, the "overridability" of the **DoSomething()** method would be inherited from **Class1** by all subclasses, no matter how far removed.

Special Object References

This section covers several special keywords that are used to provide specific object references that are required in certain situations.

The Me Keyword

The **Me** keyword always refers to the current object—the object containing the code where **Me** is used. For example, inside a method, you might have the following line of code:

```
Me.LastName = "Wong"
```

This would refer to the current object's **LastName** property. However, the implicit reference is always to the current object, so use of **Me** is usually optional. Thus, the following is equivalent to the above:

```
LastName = "Wong"
```

The one time **Me** is required when a variable is shadowed. Shadowing occurs when a procedure contains a variable that has the same name as a class-level variable. Here's an example:

```
Class Class1
  Private Index As Integer

  Sub SomeMethod()
    Dim Index As Integer
  End Sub

End Class
```

Inside **SomeMethod()**, the local variable **Index** shadows the class variable of the same name. Any reference to **Index** within the method will access the local index and not the class index. To access the class index when it is shadowed, qualify it with the **Me** keyword, as shown here:

```
Sub SomeMethod()

    Dim Index As Integer

    ' Sets the local Index
    Index = 12
    ' Sets the class Index
    Me.Index = 99

End Sub
```

The MyBase Keyword

The **MyBase** keyword refers to the base class of the current object. It is used to access an overridden method in the base class. This is demonstrated in Listing 10.7. You can see that **Class2** inherits from **Class1**, and overrides the method **Foo()**. If an instance of **Class2** is created and **Foo()** is called, it first executes its own code ("other code" in the listing) and then calls the base class's **Foo()**.

Listing 10.7 Demonstrating the MyBase keyword.

```
Class Class1
  Public Overridable Sub Foo()
  ...
  End Sub
End Class

Class Class2
  Inherits Class1

  Public Overrides Sub Foo()
    ' Other code.
    MyBase.Foo()
  End Sub
End Class
```

Note that **MyBase** refers only to the immediate base class of the current object. When multiple levels of inheritance exist, you cannot use **MyBase** to go "back" more than one level.

The MyClass Keyword

The **MyClass** keyword is used by code within a base class to refer to itself rather than to code in a derived class. It is applicable when a subclass overrides a method of the base class. Suppose a method in the base class calls the overridden method. Because all methods in VB .NET are virtual, this will result in the method in the subclass being called. Look at the example in Listing 10.8. Class B inherits from class A and overrides the method **ShowMessage()**. If you instantiate class B and call **Foo()**, it is the **Foo()** inherited from class A that is executed. However, when **Foo()** calls **ShowMessage()**, the call goes to the **ShowMessage()** implemented in class B.

Sometimes this is fine, but what if you want **Foo()** to call the **ShowMessage()** in class A? This is where **MyClass** comes in. If you modify the code in **Foo()** as follows:

```
MyClass.ShowMessage()
```

you'll see that the **ShowMessage()** in class A is called rather than the **ShowMessage()** in the subclass. Note that the **Me** keyword will not work for this purpose because **Me** refers to the object the code is in, whereas **MyClass** refers to the class the code is in.

Listing 10.8 Demonstrating the MyClass keyword.

```
Class A
  Public Sub Foo()
    ShowMessage()
  End Sub

  Public Overridable Sub ShowMessage()
    Console.Write("From class A")
  End Sub

End Class

Class B
  Inherits A

  Public Overrides Sub ShowMessage()
    Console.Write("From class B")
  End Sub

End Class
```

Summary

This chapter completes coverage of the tools that VB .NET provides for designing and using your own classes. This is a very important part of VB .NET programming, one that every developer should be familiar with. Due to the object-oriented nature of VB .NET and the .NET framework as a whole, it is really a good idea for you to take the object-oriented approach when designing your applications. I think that you will quickly come to realize all of the benefits.

Chapter 11
Creating Custom Controls

The Visual Basic .NET Toolbox contains a wide assortment of controls for use in your Windows applications. Although these tools meet a variety of needs, your project may sometimes call for something else. Fortunately, you are not limited to the controls in the .NET framework but also have the ability to design your own. That's the topic of this chapter.

Control Creation Basics

There are two general approaches to creating a custom control. Which one you select will depend on the needs of your project.

The first approach creates a new control that subclasses an existing control. The new control inherits the visual interface and all the functionality of the base class. Then, you add the additional functionality you need by means of properties, methods, and other additions. This approach is appropriate when an existing control has the visual interface and much of the functionality that you need. Although it is possible to design a new visual interface when subclassing an existing control, that is an advanced technique that will not be covered here. You can find the relevant information in the Visual Basic .NET documentation.

The second approach is used when you need a new visual interface for your control. You then create a new control class based on the **UserControl** class and create its visual interface in much the same way as you design a form. Thus, a UserControl control can combine the functionality of several existing Windows controls into a single control, along with code to customize the new control's behavior.

Using a Windows Control Library

When you create a custom control using either of these techniques, you use a Windows Control Library project. This type of VB .NET project is designed specifically for the creation of custom controls, and also to make them available for use in other projects. A control library can contain multiple controls, and the name of the project becomes the namespace that contains the controls.

The first step in creating a custom control is to create a new Windows Control Library project (or to open an existing one). Be sure to assign a meaningful name to the project, because this will be the namespace for all controls it contains. At this point, the steps diverge depending on whether you are subclassing an existing control or creating a user control. These steps are explained in the remainder of this chapter.

Subclassing an Existing Control

To create a new control based on an existing control, you must create or open a Windows Control Library project as described earlier in this chapter. If you create a new project, it will open with one new, blank UserControl control. If you open an existing project, you must add a new UserControl control by selecting Add UserControl from the Project menu. The next steps change the new control from a UserControl to one that subclasses an existing control:

1. In the Solution Explorer, select the new UserControl control and display its code. It will look like this (in this and other listings, the Windows Form Designer code is not shown):

```
Public Class UserControl1
    Inherits System.Windows.Forms.UserControl

End Class
```

2. Change the name of the class from the default name (e.g., **UserControl1**) to the name you want to use for your new control.

3. Edit the **Inherits** statement so the class inherits from an existing control rather than from the **UserControl** class. Your code will now look something like this:

```
Public Class MyTextBox
    Inherits System.Windows.Forms.TextBox

End Class
```

4. Be sure the new control is selected in the Solution Explorer, and then change its **File Name** property. This is the name assigned to the file where the control's code is stored, so you should choose a descriptive name. You can use any name you like, but I suggest using the same name you assigned to the class.

5. Select Save All from the File menu. You'll see that the entry in the Solution Explorer changes to reflect the new file name you assigned.

At this point, you will note that the Form Designer is no longer available. This is because your control will inherit the visual interface of its base class, so there are no modifications you can make in the Form Designer. You can make modifications to the new control's visual appearance in code, but that is beyond the scope of this book.

Your new control could be used at this time, but so far it is nothing more than an exact duplicate of its base class, so there is no point in doing so. The next steps are to customize the control by means of its properties, methods, and events.

Custom Properties

A custom control property can either be a totally new property or an override of an inherited property. In your custom control's code, you use the **MyBase** keyword to refer to the base class. This lets you override a property while still accessing the base class's property of the same name. Suppose that you are subclassing the CheckBox control and want to create a new property named **Value**. The base class's **Value** property would be referenced as **MyBase.Value**.

To create a new property, you follow the usual procedures for defining a class property. These procedures were covered in detail in Chapter 9. To review briefly, it requires that you write a property procedure for the property. In some cases, you will also be declaring a private instance variable to hold the property value. The second step is not required if the property value is stored elsewhere (such as in a base class property) or is calculated on-the-fly.

Take a look at two examples. This first example defines a new property called **Flavor**, of data type **String**:

```
Private pFlavor As String

Public Property Flavor() As String
    Get
        Flavor = pFlavor
    End Get
    Set(ByVal Value As String)
        pFlavor = Value
    End Set
End Property
```

This second example is intended to be used in a custom control that subclasses a TextBox control, or any other control that has a **Text** property but no **Length** property. It defines a read-only property named **Length** that returns the length (number of characters) in the **Text** property.

```
Public ReadOnly Property Length() As Long
    Get
        Length = Len(MyBase.Text)
    End Get
End Property
```

To override a property that exists in the base class, use the **Overrides** keyword in the property procedure definition. The new property can completely replace the property it overrides, or it can interact with the base class property (again, using the **MyBase** keyword). Here is an example of overriding the **Text** property in a control that subclasses the TextBox control. The result is that the text box always displays text in uppercase, whereas the text that is stored retains the original combination of upper- and lowercase. This works only when the **Text** property is assigned in code, and not when the user enters text directly in the control (although the latter could be programmed as well, if desired, but that's not done here):

```
Private pText As String

Public Overrides Property Text() As String
    Get
        Text = pText
    End Get
    Set(ByVal Value As String)
        pText = Value
        MyBase.Text = UCase(Value)
    End Set
End Property
```

Custom Methods

Creating custom methods follows the same general approach as creating custom properties. You can create totally new methods, or you can override existing methods. You can access base class methods by using the **MyBase** keyword, as needed. Note, however, that many methods of existing control classes are not overridable. If you try to override such a method, the VB .NET editor will inform you. Also, you can look in the online documentation to see which of your base control's methods are overridable. Methods that cannot be overridden are identified by the **NotOverridable** keyword in their syntax definition.

Custom Event Handlers

Creating a custom event handler in your derived class follows a somewhat different approach than creating custom properties and methods. You do not—in fact, you cannot—override the event handler in the base class. Rather, you make use of a set of overridable methods that are named using the format **On*XXXX*()**, where ***XXXX*** is the name of an event. For example, the TextBox control has **OnClick()**, **OnDoubleClick()**, and **OnMouseMove()** methods, among many others. Each of these methods is connected to the underlying event in both directions. This means the following:

- If the event occurs, the method is called (in addition to the regular event procedure).
- If the method is called, the event is triggered.

For the present purposes, the importance of the **On*XXXX*()** methods is that you can use them to override the base class events. For example, the following code in your custom control will override the base control's **Click()** event, displaying a message box when the custom control is clicked:

```
Protected Overrides Sub OnClick(ByVal e As EventArgs)

    MyBase.OnClick(e)
    MsgBox("Thanks for clicking me!")

End Sub
```

This example illustrates two things. First, each **On*XXXX*()** method has a *signature*—in other words, the type of its argument(s). The method you create to override the base class method must have the correct signature. Second, your method must call the corresponding method in the base class, using the **MyBase** keyword. This is necessary to ensure that the event is processed in the normal manner.

Here's an example of overriding the **OnMouseDown()** and **OnMouseUp()** methods. The result is that the custom control's foreground color changes to red when the mouse button is pressed, and it changes back to black when the button is released:

```
Protected Overrides Sub OnMouseDown(ByVal e As MouseEventArgs)
    MyBase.ForeColor = Color.Red
    MyBase.OnMouseDown(e)
End Sub

Protected Overrides Sub OnMouseUp(ByVal e As MouseEventArgs)
    MyBase.ForeColor = Color.Black
    MyBase.OnMouseDown(e)
End Sub
```

Using a Custom Control

When your control is complete, or at least ready for testing, you must build it by selecting the Build command from the Build menu. Assuming no syntax errors are found, the project will be built and the output will be a file named *xxxx*.dll, where *xxxx* is the project name. This DLL file will contain all the custom controls in your Windows Control Library project. The file will be located in the bin folder off the project folder.

To test your control, you will need to create a Windows Application project. You can have this new project loaded into Visual Studio at the same time as your Windows Control Library project, which simplifies the process of testing and modifying the control. To add this new project, follow these steps:

1. Select Add Project from the File menu, and then select New Project to display the Add New Project dialog box.
2. In the dialog box, select the Windows Application icon and enter a name for the new project (for example, TestControl).
3. Click OK.

Before you can use your custom control in the test project, you must add a reference to the control library and then add the control to the Toolbox. Here are the steps to follow to add the reference:

1. In the Solution Explorer, right-click the name of the test project.
2. Select Add Reference from the pop-up menu to display the Add Reference dialog box.
3. In the dialog box, select the Projects tab (see Figure 11.1). This tab will list all other open projects, in this case your control library project (named NewControls in the figure).
4. Double-click the project name to add it to the Selected Components list.
5. Click OK.

Use the following steps to add your new control(s) to the Toolbox:

1. Right-click the Toolbox.
2. Select Customize Toolbox from the pop-up menu to display the Customize Toolbox dialog box.
3. In the dialog box, select the .NET Framework Components tab (see Figure 11.2).
4. Click the Browse button and navigate to the DLL file that was created when you built your custom control project. Select the DLL file and then click the Open button.

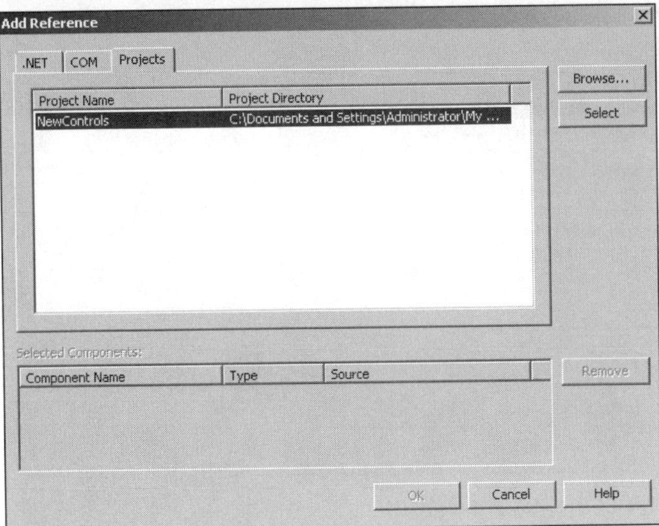

Figure 11.1
Adding a reference to the control library project to your test project.

5. The name of your control will appear in the list of .NET Framework Components. Click it to place a checkmark in the adjacent box.
6. Close the dialog box by clicking OK.

At this point, your custom control will appear in the Toolbox, and you are ready to use it in your test project as you would any other control.

After you have thoroughly tested your custom control, you can use it in Windows Application projects without having the control library project loaded into Visual Studio. If you have added the control to the Toolbox, it will remain there for future projects. You can remove a control from the Toolbox by right-clicking it and selecting Delete from the pop-up menu. You can later add a reference to the control to other projects and add the control to the Toolbox, using essentially the same techniques that were described previously. The only difference is when adding the reference—because the control project will not be loaded, it will not appear in the list on the Project tab in the Add Reference dialog box. You'll have to browse for the DLL file just as you would when adding the control to the Toolbox.

Setting the Startup Project

When you have two or more projects open in Visual Studio, one must be the startup project—the one that is executed when you press F5 or select Start from the Debug menu. In this case, your test project must be the startup project—a control project cannot be executed by itself. To set the startup project, right-click the desired project in the Solution Explorer and select Set As Startup Project from the pop-up menu.

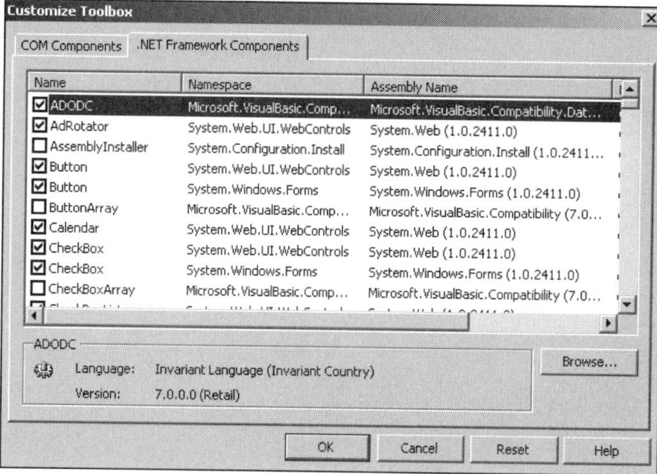

Figure 11.2
Adding a custom control to the Toolbox.

Custom Control Demonstration 1

This section walks you through all the steps involved in creating a custom control that subclasses a .NET framework control. The goal is to create a "number box" control that overcomes some of the shortcomings of the TextBox control for entry of numbers. Specifically, the control will have these characteristics:

- The control will permit entry of zero and positive integers only.
- The control will have a **Value** property that returns the contents of the control as a numeric value (rather than as a string, as the TextBox control does).

The first steps are to create a new Windows Control Library and create the fundamental class definition:

1. Create a new Windows Control Library project. Assign the name **NumberBox** to the project.
2. Open the code window for the default UserControl control that the project contains.
3. Edit the code to change the class name to **NumberBox**, and change the **Inherits** statement so the new class inherits from the **TextBox** class. The resulting code is shown in Listing 11.1.

Listing 11.1 Initial code entries to define the NumberBox class.

```
Public Class NumberBox
    Inherits System.Windows.Forms.TextBox

End Class
```

The next step is to add the code that will prevent the user from entering anything other than the digits 0 through 9 in the control. You learned the technique for doing this in Chapter 8. To review, it involves using the **KeyPress()** event to "catch" keystrokes when they are made. Permitted keys are passed through to the control, whereas forbidden keys are cancelled. The code for this will go in the **OnKeyPress()** method, overriding the base **TextBox** class's method of the same name. The code is shown in Listing 11.2.

Listing 11.2 Overriding the base class's OnKeyPress() method to trap all key strokes except digits.

```
Protected Overrides Sub OnKeyPress(ByVal e As KeyPressEventArgs)

    Select Case e.KeyChar
        Case "0" To "9"
            ' Permitted character - do nothing.
        Case Else
            ' Not a permitted character - cancel it.
            e.Handled = True
    End Select
    MyBase.OnKeyPress(e)

End Sub
```

The final step is to add the **Value** property. The problem is that the base class, **TextBox**, stores data as a type **String**, and the new control should permit the value of the data to be retrieved as a numeric value (specifically, type **Long**). Thus, code in the property procedure will have to convert from type **String** to type **Long** when the data is retrieved, and from type **Long** to type **String** when the property is set. These tasks are done with VB .NET's type conversion functions **CStr()** and **CLng()**. The final code for the **Value** property is shown in Listing 11.3.

Listing 11.3 The property procedure for the new control's Value property.

```
Public Property Value() As Long

    Get
        Value = CLng(MyBase.Text)
    End Get
    Set(ByVal newValue As Long)
        Me.Text = CStr(newValue)
    End Set

End Property
```

The new control is ready to build and test, using the procedures that were explained earlier in this chapter. When you use the control on a form, you will see that it has all the properties of the base TextBox control, plus the **Value** property that was added. When running, the control accepts only numbers, and you can retrieve its **Value** property as needed.

In a real-world situation, you might want to fine-tune this custom control some more. For example, as written, the control still permits access to its **Text** property in code, so nothing is preventing the host program from putting some non-numeric text in the control. Also, the control's **Value** property returns 0 if the control contains **0** and also if the control is empty—you might want to permit the control to differentiate between these two states.

Creating a UserControl Control

In many ways, creating a custom UserControl control is very much like designing a form. You have a rectangular container on which you place controls to create the visual interface. You put code in event procedures to handle the events received by these controls as well as by the container itself. You add property procedures to define custom properties for the component. The primary difference is that the container is a **UserControl** object and not a **Form** object. The final result is a self-contained control that can be used on a form, or on another user control, just like the controls that are provided as part of VB .NET.

Design Considerations

Many of the details of designing a UserControl control are the same as for designing a form, as covered in Chapters 7 and 8. For example, a UserControl control has **ForeColor**, **BackColor**, **Font**, **BackgroundImage**, and other properties that control its appearance and that are passed down to child controls. Controls that are placed on a user control can be docked to one, two, or more sides of the user control. Controls on a user control have a Z-order, just like controls on a form. Also, a user control has a design grid to which controls can be aligned, and the Form Designer's alignment and spacing tools work for user controls as they do for forms.

One difference between a user control and a form is that the former does not have a property to specify the display of a border. Therefore, a user control is by nature borderless. If you want to display a border around the perimeter of a user control, start your design by placing a Panel control on the user control. Dock the Panel control to all four sides of the UserControl control so it will automatically fill the entire container, and then set the panel's **Border** property as desired. Note that this prevents mouse events from reaching the user control itself (but not its child controls), so if your program needs to detect such events, you must use the panel control's event procedures.

UserControl Events

Events related to a custom UserControl control fall into three categories, which are illustrated in Figure 11.3. First of all, there are the events exposed by the base **UserControl** class, which can be detected by the container that the custom control is used in (a form, for example). These events include the usual mouse and keyboard events as well as many others, and the list of supported events is not much different from the list of events supported by the Form class. Note that these events reflect things that happen to the user control itself, and *not* things that happen to child controls it contains.

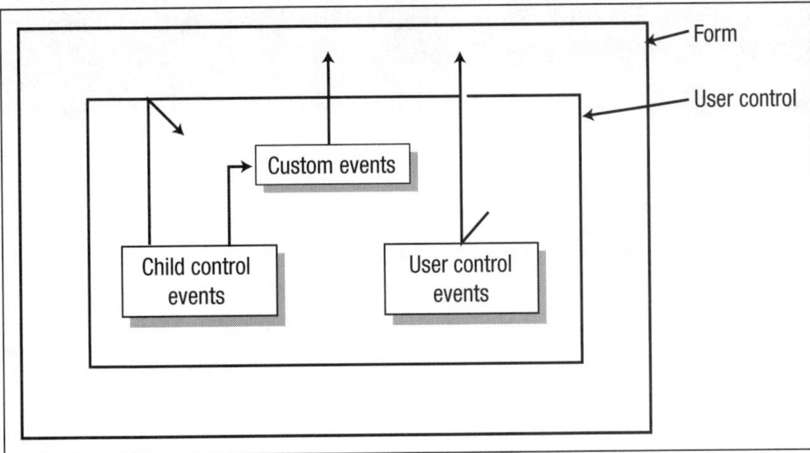

Figure 11.3
UserControl-related events.

The second category of UserControl-related events includes events that are related to the child controls the user control contains. For example, if the custom control contains a Button control, the button's **Click()** and other events will be detectable by code within the custom control. These events will not, however, be detectable outside the custom control—not directly, anyway. I'll explain this in the following paragraphs.

The third type of event we need to consider is a custom event that is raised by code within the UserControl control. This requires two steps. First, the event must be declared in the UserControl control with the **Event** statement. The syntax is

```
Event EventName(arguments)
```

EventName is the name you assign to the event, following the usual VB .NET naming rules. This name must be unique within its scope. ***arguments*** is an optional list of arguments that the event takes, following the same syntax as arguments lists for other procedures. For example, the following statement defines an event named **ButtonClick()** that takes one type **Integer** argument:

```
Event ButtonClick(ByVal x As Integer)
```

After an event is declared, code in the control can raise it whenever needed by means of the **RaiseEvent** statement. The syntax is

```
RaiseEvent EventName(arguments)
```

When you raise an event, the argument list must match the event declaration–in other words, the number and types of arguments passed must match the parameter list in the event syntax. An event that is declared and raised in this way can be detected by the

UserControl control's container (the form it is on), and it appears in the list of events for the user control along with the base class events.

The technique of raising events can be used to make events internal to the UserControl control—that is, the events of its child controls—visible outside the user control. For example, when code inside the user control detects a **Click()** event on a Button child control, it could raise the **ButtonClick()** event declared above, passing a numeric value to identify which button was clicked. This would permit code in the form containing the user control to detect these events. Of course, this is not the only use for raised events—you can use them for any signaling or information that needs to be passed from the user control to its container.

Testing a Custom User Control

A user control can be part of a Windows Application project, and you can add it by selecting Add UserControl from the Project menu. It can also be part of a Windows Control Library project. In either case, building the UserControl control automatically adds the control to the Toolbox. If you want to use a UserControl control that was created and tested previously, you can add it to the Toolbox by right-clicking the Toolbox and selecting Customize Toolbox to display the Customize Toolbox dialog box. Then, on the .NET Framework Components tab of the dialog box, you need to browse for the control's DLL file (the same as you do for a subclassed control, previously described in this chapter).

A Custom User Control Demonstration

The demonstration in this section walks you through the process of creating and testing a custom UserControl control. The objective is to create a self-contained control that permits the entry of three pieces of personal information: name, city, and email address. The control will also contain a Clear button that clears all the data fields. It will expose three properties, one for each piece of information. Finally, it will raise a **DataChanged()** event whenever any of its data has changed.

Designing the Visual Interface

First, you must create the new, blank control and then design its visual interface. Here are the steps to follow:

1. Create a new Windows Application project and name it **MyUserControl**.
2. Select Add UserControl from the Project menu, and in the Add New Item dialog box, assign the name **PersonalInfo** to the new UserControl control. At this point, the Form Designer will display a blank UserControl control, ready to be designed (see Figure 11.4).
3. Enlarge the UserControl control horizontally until it is about twice as wide as it is high.

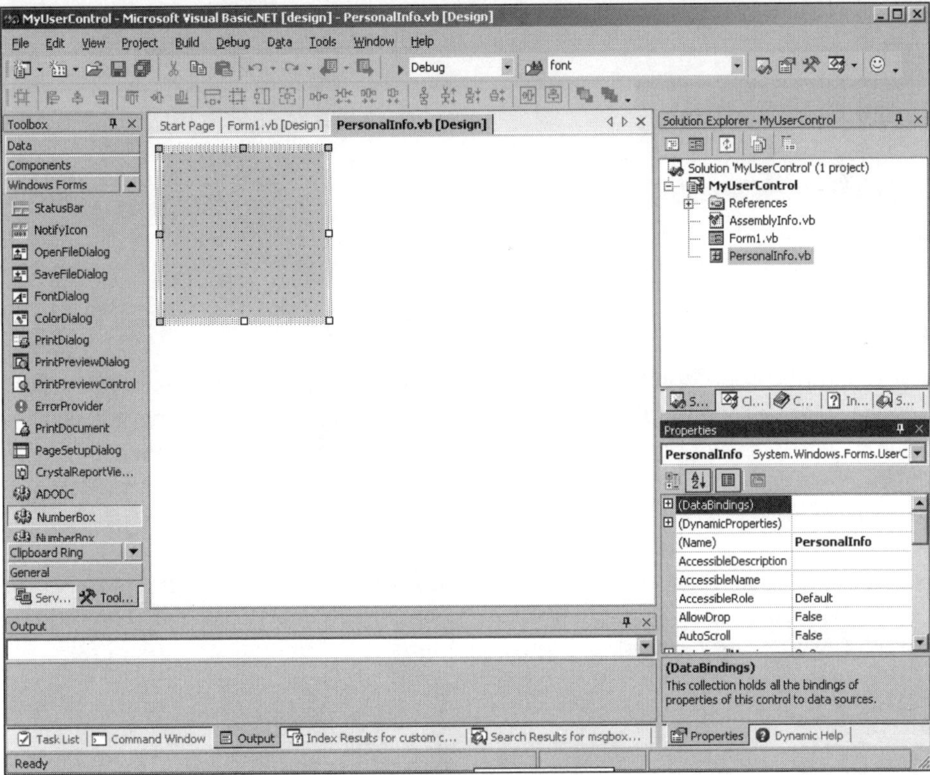

Figure 11.4
A new UserControl control ready for the addition of child controls.

4. Add a Panel control. Set its **Dock** property to **Fill** and its **BorderStyle** property to **FixedSingle**.

5. Add three Label controls, one above the other on the left side of the UserControl control. Change their **TextAlign** property to **MiddleRight**. Then, change their **Text** properties, working from the top down, to **Name:**, **City:**, and **Email:**.

6. Add three TextBox controls, one to the right of each Label control. Change the **Text** property of each one to a blank string. Then, change each one's **Name** property according to the adjacent Label control: **txtName**, **txtCity**, and **txtEmail**.

7. Add a Button control below the other controls. Change its **Name** property to **btnClear** and its **Text** property to **Clear**.

8. Adjust the control spacing and alignment, if needed, to achieve a neat appearance. At this point, your control will look something like Figure 11.5.

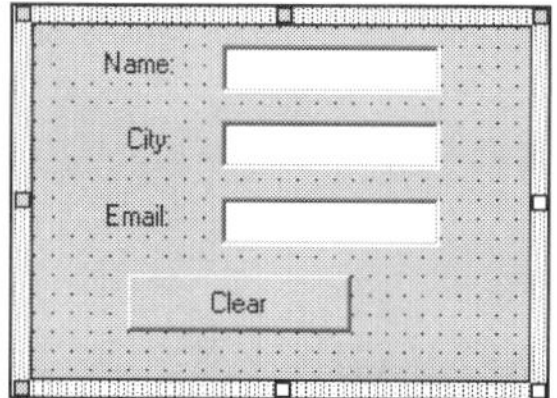

Figure 11.5
After designing the user control's visual interface.

Writing the Code

Now that the custom control's visual interface is complete, it's time to turn our attention to the code. First, declare the **DataChanged()** event by placing the following statement at the top of the UserControl control's module (just after the **Inherits** statement):

```
Event DataChanged()
```

Next, program the Clear button. When this button is clicked, the control should set all three TextBox controls to a blank string by calling their **Clear()** method. The code for the button's **Click()** event procedure is shown here:

```
Private Sub btnClear_Click(ByVal sender As System.Object, _
        ByVal e As System.EventArgs) Handles btnClear.Click
    txtName.Clear()
    txtCity.Clear()
    txtEmail.Clear()
End Sub
```

Shouldn't the **DataChanged()** event be raised here as well? That makes sense, but as you'll soon see, there is another way to do it.

The next step is to create the property procedures for the three pieces of information that the user control holds. It would make sense to call these properties **Name**, **City**, and **Email**. However, this causes a problem: The property **Name** already exists in the base class, so you cannot create a new property with the same name unless you use the **Shadows** keyword to hide the base class property. Because the **Name** property is important, it isn't a good idea to shadow it. Therefore, the UserControl property will be called **FullName** instead. The required property procedures are shown in Listing 11.4, and you should add them to the control.

Listing 11.4 Property procedures for the user control's three properties.

```
Public Property FullName() As String
    Get
        FullName = txtName.Text
    End Get
```

```
    Set(ByVal Value As String)
        txtName.Text = Value
    End Set
End Property

Public Property City() As String
    Get
        City = txtCity.Text
    End Get
    Set(ByVal Value As String)
        txtCity.Text = Value
    End Set
End Property

Public Property Email() As String
    Get
        Email = txtEmail.Text
    End Get
    Set(ByVal Value As String)
        txtEmail.Text = Value
    End Set
End Property
```

The final programming task is to raise the **DataChanged()** event as needed so the control's container will be able to detect when the data in any of the three TextBox controls has changed. The TextBox control provides the **TextChanged()** event that is fired any time the **Text** property of the control is modified. We can write a single procedure that handles the **TextChanged()** event for all three TextBox controls. That code is shown here:

```
Protected Sub TextBoxChange(ByVal Sender As Object, _
        ByVal e As EventArgs) Handles txtCity.TextChanged, _
        txtEmail.TextChanged, txtName.TextChanged

    RaiseEvent DataChanged()

End Sub
```

That's it—the control is finished. Use the Build command to build it, and, assuming no build errors occur, you are ready to test it.

Testing the Control

To test the control you just created, you can use the blank Windows Application project that is currently loaded. Display the form for this project, and then look in the Toolbox. Because you built the PersonalInfo control, it will already be added to the Toolbox. Use the usual form design techniques to add an instance of this control to the form. Add a Button control, also, below the custom control. Change its **Text** property to **Get Data**. In the **Click()** event procedure for this button, put the following code, which collects the input data from the three properties of the user control and displays it in a message box:

```
Private Sub Button1_Click(ByVal sender As System.Object, _
    ByVal e As System.EventArgs) Handles Button1.Click

    Dim s As String

    s = PersonalInfo1.FullName & " "
    s &= PersonalInfo1.City & " "
    s &= PersonalInfo1.Email
    MsgBox(s)

End Sub
```

Finally, to verify that the **DataChanged()** event is working, create an event procedure for it as shown here:

```
Private Sub PersonalInfo1_DataChanged() Handles _
          PersonalInfo1.DataChanged
    Debug.Write("X")
End Sub
```

The **Debug.Write()** method displays text in Visual Studio's output window. Thus, each time the contents of one of the custom control's text boxes changes, you'll see an "X" displayed in the output window.

The test program is shown executing in Figure 11.6. When you try it out, you'll see that the custom control behaves exactly as it was designed to do.

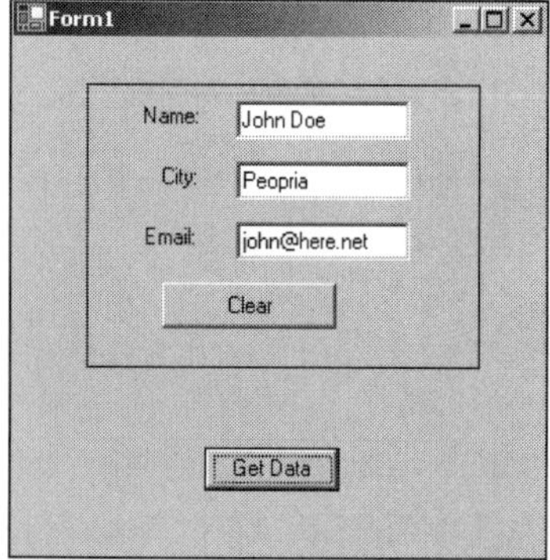

Figure 11.6
Testing the PersonalInfo custom control.

Summary

The ability to create your own custom controls is a very powerful feature of VB .NET. Despite the wide range of preexisting controls that are part of the .NET framework, occasionally you might need a custom control to meet the specific needs of your program. The two general approaches to this are subclassing an existing .NET framework control to customize its behavior and designing a new UserControl control with a custom visual interface. Either way, you should be able to come up with the exact control for your needs.

Chapter 12
Writing Console Applications

The ability for Visual Basic programmers to easily create console applications is new with VB .NET. You might think that these text-only, interface-less programs are a throwback to the days of DOS, with no relevance in the world of Windows and the Internet. As you'll see in this chapter, such an opinion would be misguided. Console applications definitely have a place in the programmer's toolbox, and they are fully supported as one of Visual Basic .NET's project types.

Console Fundamentals

The term *console* comes from the days when computers were hulking mainframes hidden away in air-conditioned rooms and users interacted with them by means of a keyboard and a video terminal. Together, the keyboard and the terminal were called a console. Input and output were text-only. In the early days of personal computers, the console paradigm still ruled. The computers were no longer remote, but the interface between user and computer was still one of text in, text out.

In today's world of sophisticated graphical interfaces, console applications may seem like a quaint relic of the past. They are not, however—they are very useful in certain circumstances. In recognition of this, Windows provides a console interface for use when needed, called variously the DOS box or the command prompt.

In what situations are console applications useful? The most important answer is that certain programs simply do not need any sort of visual interface. They have a task to perform that does not involve any interaction, or at most minimal interaction, with the user, so why bother with the overhead of a fancy interface? For example, you might want to write a program that copies all of the Excel files from your documents folder to a backup folder, and you want the program to run once a day. In this case, obviously, you have no need for a visual interface. Lacking a visual interface with menus, screen windows, and all the other elements, console applications are smaller, easier to write, and execute faster.

The potential uses for console applications become even wider when the technique of *redirection* is considered. To understand redirection, you need to know about the standard input and standard output streams. Provided by the operating system, these streams provide the means for a console application to input and output text. The standard input and output streams are by default connected to the console, so that's where a console application normally gets its input and sends its output. Using redirection, the standard input and output streams can be connected to something other than the console. The most useful type of redirection involves disk files—the program takes its input from a text file on disk, rather than from the keyboard, and its output goes to another disk file. Redirection provides for great flexibility in running console applications without user intervention.

Finally, you have considerable flexibility in how a console application is started. The traditional way—typing the program's name at the command prompt—certainly works. You can also start a console application by double-clicking the program name in Windows Explorer or by using the Run dialog box. Perhaps most important, a console application can be started from another program, as you'll see later in this chapter.

The Console Class

At the heart of any console application is the **Console** class. This class is part of the **System** namespace, and it provides members for reading from the standard input stream and writing to the standard output stream. The members that are required for input and output are described in Table 12.1.

When inputting data from the keyboard, the **Read()** method does not return until the user presses Enter. Then, repeated calls to **Read()** will return the numerical codes (ASCII) for the typed characters, one at a time, up to and including the codes for the CR/LF characters

Table 12.1 The input and output members of the Console class.

Member	Description
Read()	Returns a type **Integer** representing the next character available from the standard input. Returns–1 if no character is available.
ReadLine()	Returns a string containing all the characters from standard input up to, but not including, the next carriage return (CR), line feed (LF), or CR/LF combination.
Write(*exp*)	Writes ***exp*** to the standard output.
WriteLine(*exp*)	Writes ***exp*** followed by a newline character to the standard output.

that represent pressing Enter (13 for the carriage return, 10 for the line feed). This is demonstrated by the console application in Listing 12.1. When you run this program, you will see how the characters you enter are input one at a time by the **Read()** method. Sample program output is shown in Figure 12.1.

Listing 12.1 Demonstrating the Console.Read() method.

```
Sub Main()

    Dim i As Integer
    Console.WriteLine("Enter some text then press Enter:")
    Do While True
        i = Console.Read
        Console.WriteLine(i)
        If i = 10 Then Exit Do
    Loop
    Console.Write("Press Enter to end program.")
    Console.Read()

End Sub
```

Command-Line Arguments

A console application can have information passed to it when it is started by means of *command-line arguments*. A command-line argument is placed after the program name on the command line. For example, you could start the console application MyConsoleApp by typing the following at the command prompt:

```
myconsoleapp -c data.txt
```

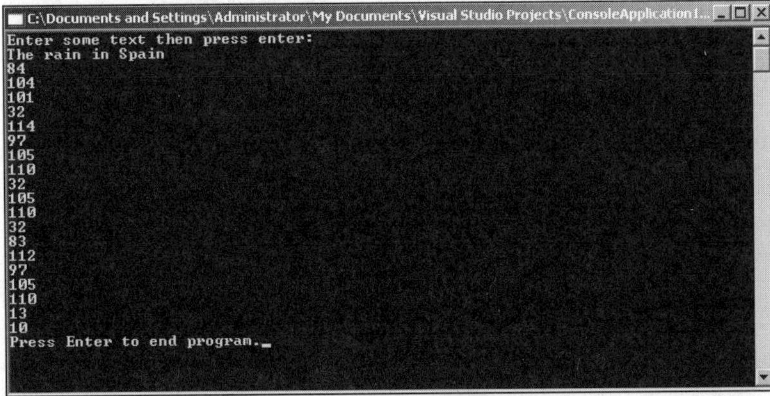

Figure 12.1
Running the demonstration program in Listing 12.1.

Spaces in Command-Line Arguments

Command-line arguments are separated from the program name and from one another by spaces. If an argument contains a space, enclose it in quotes, as in **myconsoleapp -c "c:\mydocuments\data.txt"**. This permits the second argument to be treated as a single argument rather than as two separate arguments.

The **-c** and the **data.txt** are command-line arguments and are available to code within the program. You can use command-line arguments to pass information to the program about what actions it is to carry out, what files it is to work with, and so on.

To access command-line arguments in your code, use the **Command()** function. This function returns a string containing all the text that was entered on the command line after the program name. It does not parse out the individual arguments—that is, something the program must do by looking for spaces and double quotes in the returned string. You can find an example of this in the VB .NET online help in the section on the **Command()** function.

You can work with command-line arguments from within the Visual Studio environment. By default, a console application runs without command-line arguments when executed from within Visual Studio. To add one or more arguments, follow these steps:

1. In the Solution Explorer, select the project.
2. Select View | Property Pages, or press Shift+F4, to open the project's property page.
3. On the left side of the property page, select Debugging under Configuration Properties, as shown in Figure 12.2.

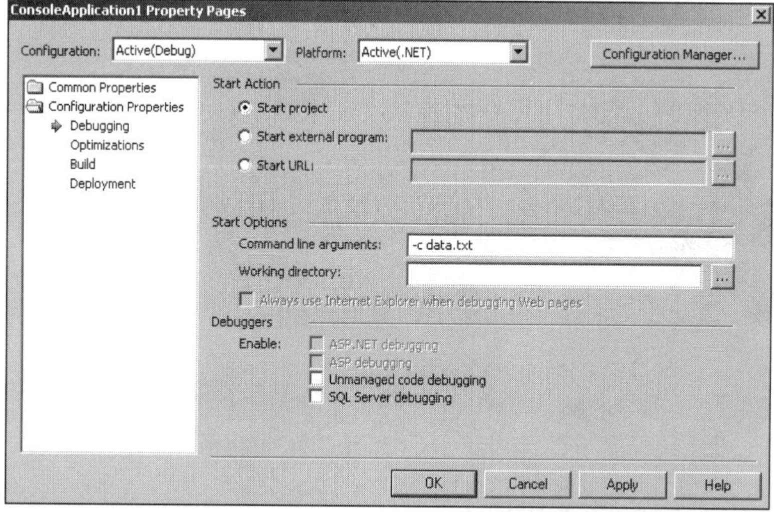

Figure 12.2
You can specify a program's command-line arguments in the project's property page.

4. In the box labeled Command Line Arguments, enter one or more arguments separated by spaces, remembering to enclose an argument in double quotes if it contains a space.

5. Click OK. When you run the project, the specified arguments will be passed to your program just as if they had been entered at the command prompt.

Redirecting Input and Output

To redirect the input or output of a console application, use the **Console.SetIn()** and **Console.SetOut()** methods. The syntax for these methods is as follows:

```
Console.SetIn(newIn As TextReader)
Console.SetOut(newOut As TextWriter)
```

TextReader and **TextWriter** are abstract classes and so cannot be implemented directly. You will use a derived class instead. For redirecting input and output to files, the technique is as follows:

1. Create a **FileStream** object for the desired file. Be sure the file mode is set appropriately depending on whether you will be reading from the file or writing to it.

2. Wrap the **FileStream** object in either a **StreamReader** object (for input) or a **StreamWriter** object (for output).

3. Pass the **StreamReader** object to the **Console.SetIn()** method, and pass the **StreamWriter** object to the **Console.SetOut()** method.

The program in Listing 12.2 demonstrates how to redirect both input and output to files. It doesn't do anything particularly useful; it simply reads lines of text from the input, appends a few exclamation points, and then writes to the output. It requires that a text file named Input.txt be present in the same folder as the application. After the program runs, a file named Output.txt will also be present, containing the program's output.

Listing 12.2 Redirecting a console application's input and output.

```
Imports System
Imports System.IO

Sub Main()
    Dim buf As String
    Dim inFile As New FileStream("Input.txt", FileMode.Open)
    Dim inStream As New StreamReader(inFile)
    Dim outFile As New FileStream("Output.txt", FileMode.CreateNew)
    Dim outStream As New StreamWriter(outFile)

    Console.SetIn(inStream)
    Console.SetOut(outStream)
```

```
    buf = Console.ReadLine()
    Do While Len(buf) > 0
        buf = buf & "!!!"
        Console.WriteLine(buf)
        buf = Console.ReadLine()
    Loop

    inStream.Close()
    outStream.Close()

    End Sub
```

Errors in Console Applications

Like any program, a console application can generate runtime errors. These should be handled with VB .NET's error-handling statements, which are covered in Chapter 5. You can use either unstructured error-handling statements (**On Error** and **Resume**) or the preferred structured ones (**Try**, **Catch**, **Finally**). In the demonstration program in Listing 12.2, for example, an error would occur if the file Input.txt could not be found or if the output file could not be created. Unhandled errors have the same consequences as in any type of VB .NET program: The user sees an error message and then is given the option of debugging the program. Clearly, unhandled errors are to be avoided.

Should an unhandled error occur, console applications have their own method of dealing with the error message. This operates in addition to the usual VB .NET response to unhandled errors, as described in the previous paragraph. Error messages in a console application are sent to an output stream called Standard Error. By default, Standard Error is connected to the console, so error messages appear on-screen. Redirecting Standard Input does not redirect Standard Error. However, you can redirect Standard Error by calling the **Console.SetError()** method. This method works exactly like the **Console.SetOut()** method described earlier in this chapter, and it is typically used to redirect error messages to a file.

Summary

Console applications may seem like a relic of the bad old days, but in certain situations, they can be quite useful. Not every program requires a graphical user interface, and when the user does not need to be involved, a console application provides an efficient and compact way to package your code.

Chapter 13

Creating MDI Applications

MDI stands for Multiple Document Interface, a type of program that permits the display of multiple documents, each in its own window. This type of application can be a useful approach for certain development needs. VB .NET fully supports MDI applications, and this chapter shows you how to create and work with them.

MDI Basics

When a Windows application has two or more forms, the default is for them to be largely independent of each other. In an MDI application, however, one form serves as the "parent" and the other forms are "children." The child forms are restricted to the client area of the parent form and cannot be moved outside this area. The parent form hosts the application's main menu and (if present) the toolbar. Each child form corresponds to a document, and the parent form can open as many children as it needs. One child document is active at a time, and the parent form has the capability to display, arrange, and close its child forms. When the parent is minimized, all the children are also minimized. A typical use for an MDI application would be a text editor that permits multiple text files to be open at one time, each in its own child form.

Figure 13.1 shows an MDI application with three open documents (which are blank). One of the documents is minimized and displays as an icon at the bottom of the main form.

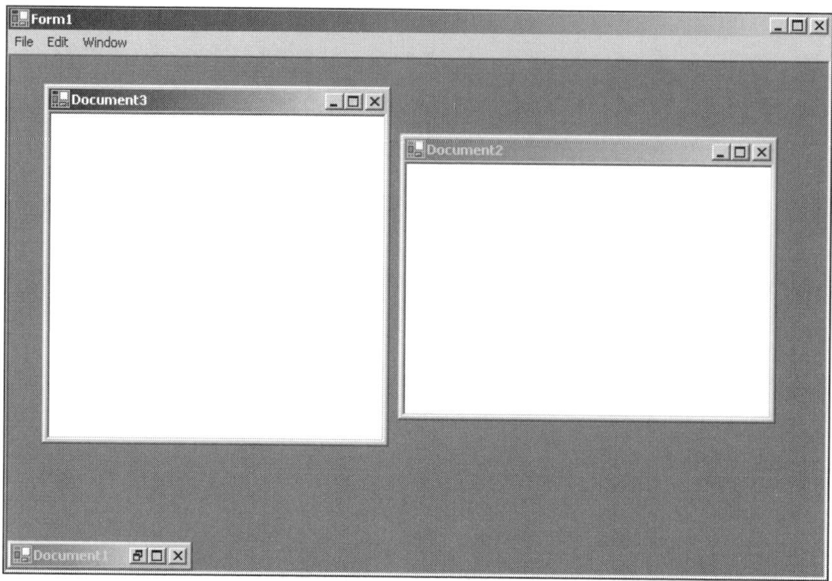

Figure 13.1
An MDI parent form serves as a container for child forms.

An MDI child form can have the usual assortment of controls and other components on it, just like a form that is not an MDI child. An MDI parent form can also contain controls, but because the main job of a parent is to serve as a container for the child forms, the controls on an MDI parent are usually limited to a MainMenu control and possibly a Toolbar control.

An MDI application can display forms that are not child forms. These could be dialog boxes for setting program options and the like. The child forms do not have to all be instances of the same class, although usually they are. When an MDI child form is minimized, it displays as an icon at the bottom of the parent form. When an MDI child form is maximized, it fills the client area of the parent form.

Menus in MDI Applications

Many MDI applications use child forms without menus, and all the needed menu functionality is provided by the parent form's menu. For more complex situations, however, you might want to define a menu for the child form class. A child form's menu does not display as part of the child form, but rather is merged with the parent form's menu. When the two menus contain conflicting items, the resulting merged menu will depend on various merge-related properties of the individual menu items. Please refer to the VB .NET documentation for more information on merging menus.

Creating MDI Forms

To create an MDI parent form, start a new Windows form in the usual manner and then set its **IsMDIContainer** property to **True**. You'll note that the edge of an MDI parent form displays the Windows System color that is set in the Windows Control Panel, and not the color specified by the form's **BackColor** property.

To create an MDI child form, you don't need to take any special steps at design time. Rather, the parent-child relationship is established at runtime using code that sets the child form's **MDIParent** property to refer to the parent form. If the child form class is named **ChildForm**, the procedure looks like this (the following code would execute in the parent form, so the **Me** keyword returns a reference to the parent form):

```
Dim MyNewChild as New ChildForm()
MyNewChild.MDIParent = Me
MyNewChild.Show()
```

The same technique can be used repeatedly to create as many child forms as are needed. Note that the **MDIParent** property is not available at design time so this must be done in code.

Maintaining a Child Window List

It is often useful for an MDI application to maintain a list of the child forms, or windows, that are open. Traditionally, this list is displayed on a Window menu and is used to switch between child windows. VB .NET can automatically maintain such a list. All you need to do is add a MainMenu control to the parent form, create a menu item named Window (or whatever you want, although "Window" is the traditional name for a menu that keeps track of MDI children), and set the menu item's **MdiList** property to **True**. The .NET framework will automatically maintain the list for you, adding and removing child windows as they are created and destroyed. The currently active window will be checked in the menu, and the user will be able to select from the menu to make another child window active. Note that if this menu contains other items, the window list appears at the bottom.

Working with Child Forms

An MDI parent has the **MdiChildren** property, which is used to obtain references to the individual child MDI forms. This property returns an array of **Form** objects, with one entry for each child form. You can use the **Array** object's **Length** property to determine the number of child forms. You can also loop through the array to locate a specific child—based on its title, for example. You can also loop through all child forms to perform various actions, such as saving all open form data to disk or closing all forms. For example, suppose that the child form class has a method named **Save()** that saves its data. The following code in the parent form will save the data for all child forms:

```
Dim f As Form
For Each f In Me.MDIChildren
    f.Save()
Next
```

At any time, code in the parent form can obtain a reference to the currently active child form from the **ActiveMDIChild** property. If no child form is currently active, this property returns the value **Nothing**.

Being able to reference individual child forms means that you can reference controls on those forms, too. Suppose that your child form class contains a RichTextBox control named RTB1. The following code would access the selected text in that control in the active child form, checking first to make sure that there is an active child form:

```
Dim selectedText As String
Dim activeForm As Form
activeForm = Me.ActiveMDIChild

If (Not activeForm Is Nothing) Then
    selectedText = activeForm.RTB1.SelectedText
End If
```

Arranging Child Forms

You can move and resize child forms as needed. You can also arrange them programmatically using the **LayoutMDI()** method. You call this method on the parent form, passing one of the members of the **MdiLayout** enumeration as described in Table 13.1. This method affects only those child forms that are not minimized.

Table 13.1 Members of the MdiLayout enumeration.

Member	Description
ArrangeIcons	MDI child icons are arranged within the parent form's client area.
Cascade	Child forms are overlapped with their title bars showing.
TileHorizontal	Child forms are tiled (not overlapping) in a horizontal arrangement.
TileVertical	Child forms are tiled (not overlapping) in a vertical arrangement.

An MDI Application Demonstration

The program that I develop in this section provides a good demonstration of using VB .NET's MDI capabilities to create a flexible and convenient user interface. It also demonstrates the power of some of the VB .NET components. The goal is to create a simple yet functional text editor that lets you have multiple files open at the sa1me time. The design goals are as follows:

- The user can open existing text files and create new ones.
- New documents are assigned a default name in the form document1, document2, and so on.
- When a new document is saved for the first time, the user has the choice of using its default name or assigning a new one. For subsequent saves, the document's existing name is always used.
- Standard Clipboard actions (copy, cut, and paste) are supported.
- MDI child windows can be cascaded or tiled.

Some new material will be included in this application, particularly the code that deals with the Clipboard and the code that deals with opening and saving files. However, this should not keep you from understanding how the code works. Here are some more features you could add to the editor (this would be great programming practice):

- Prompt to save changed documents before closing. The **Child** class already has a property, **IsDirty**, that you can use for this purpose. The program should check a document's **IsDirty** property both when the individual document is closed and when the entire program is closed.
- Prompt for verification before overwriting files.
- Add the standard shortcut keys to the menu commands—for example, Ctrl+O for Open and Ctrl+C for Copy.
- Let the user select the font for text display.

You can probably think of other enhancements. Although the text editor, as written, is not a complete application that you would want to use for your text-editing needs, it does serve to demonstrate some important programming tasks. It also illustrates the power of VB .NET and the .NET framework.

Creating the Project

To start the MDI Text Editor project, follow these steps:

1. Create a new Windows Application project and name it "MDIDemo".
2. Change the form's **IsMDIContainer** property to **True**, and change its **Text** property to "MDI Text Editor".
3. Add a MainMenu control to the form. Add three top-level menu items, with subitems as follows:
   - A File menu with New, Open, Save, and Exit commands.
   - An Edit menu with Copy, Cut, and Paste commands.
   - A Window menu with Cascade, Tile Vertically, and Tile Horizontally commands.
4. Set the **MdiList** property of the Window menu to **True**.
5. Select Add Windows Form from the Project menu to add a new form to the project. This will be the child form.
6. Change the **Name** property of the new form to **Child**.
7. Edit the new form's code as shown in Listing 13.1.
8. Display the code for the original (parent) form, and edit it as shown in Listing 13.2. Be sure that the event handlers for the menu commands are assigned properly, as indicated by the comments in the code. Depending on the order in which you add commands when editing the menu, your menu items might not have the same name as mine.

Listing 13.1 Code for the MDI child form.

```
Public Class Child
    Inherits System.Windows.Forms.Form

    Private pIsNamed As Boolean = False
    Private pIsDirty As Boolean

    Public Property IsNamed() As Boolean
        ' This property is true when the document has been
        ' assigned a real name (saved at least once), and false if
        ' it still has the default name.
        Get
            IsNamed = pIsNamed
        End Get
        Set(ByVal Value As Boolean)
            pIsNamed = Value
        End Set
    End Property
```

```
    Public Property IsDirty() As Boolean
        ' This property is true if the document has changed
        ' since the last save.
        Get
            IsDirty = pIsDirty
        End Get
        Set(ByVal Value As Boolean)
            pIsDirty = Value
        End Set
    End Property

    Private Sub RTB1_TextChanged(ByVal sender As Object, _
            ByVal e As System.EventArgs) Handles RTB1.TextChanged
        ' When the document text changes, mark it as dirty.
        IsDirty = True
    End Sub
End Class
```

Listing 13.2 Code for the MDI parent form.

```
Imports System.IO

Public Class Form1
    Inherits System.Windows.Forms.Form
    Private NewChildCount As Integer = 0

    Private Sub MenuItem3_Click(ByVal sender As System.Object, _
            ByVal e As System.EventArgs) Handles MenuItem3.Click
        ' File, New menu command.
        NewChildCount += 1
        Dim NewChild As New Child()
        NewChild.MdiParent = Me
        NewChild.Text = "Document" & CStr(NewChildCount)
        NewChild.Show()
    End Sub

    Private Sub MenuItem6_Click(ByVal sender As System.Object, _
            ByVal e As System.EventArgs) Handles MenuItem6.Click
        ' File, Open menu command.
        Dim sr As StreamReader
        OpenFileDialog1.Filter = "Text files *.txt | *.txt"
        If OpenFileDialog1.ShowDialog() = DialogResult.OK Then
            Try
                sr = File.OpenText(OpenFileDialog1.FileName)
                Dim newDoc As New Child()
                newDoc.RTB1.Text = sr.ReadToEnd
                sr.Close()
```

```
                newDoc.Text = OpenFileDialog1.FileName
                newDoc.MdiParent = Me
                newDoc.Show()
                newDoc.IsNamed = True
                newDoc.IsDirty = False
                ' The next three lines move the cursor
                ' to the start of the RTB.
                newDoc.RTB1.Select()
                newDoc.RTB1.SelectionStart = 0
                newDoc.RTB1.SelectionLength = 0
            Catch ex As IOException
                MsgBox("Error opening file.")
            End Try
        End If

    End Sub

    Private Sub MenuItem4_Click(ByVal sender As System.Object, _
            ByVal e As System.EventArgs) Handles MenuItem4.Click
        ' File, Exit menu command.
        Me.Close()
    End Sub

    Private Sub MenuItem12_Click(ByVal sender As System.Object, _
            ByVal e As System.EventArgs) Handles MenuItem12.Click
        ' Window, Cascade menu command.
        Me.LayoutMdi(MdiLayout.Cascade)
    End Sub

    Private Sub MenuItem13_Click(ByVal sender As System.Object, _
            ByVal e As System.EventArgs) Handles MenuItem13.Click
        ' Window, Tile Vertically menu command.
        Me.LayoutMdi(MdiLayout.TileVertical)
    End Sub

    Private Sub MenuItem14_Click(ByVal sender As System.Object, _
            ByVal e As System.EventArgs) Handles MenuItem14.Click
        ' Window, Tile horizontally menu command.
        Me.LayoutMdi(MdiLayout.TileHorizontal)
    End Sub

    Private Sub MenuItem7_Click(ByVal sender As System.Object, _
            ByVal e As System.EventArgs) Handles MenuItem7.Click
        ' File, Save menu command.
        Dim ad As Child = Me.ActiveMdiChild
```

```
        If (Not ad Is Nothing) Then
            If ad.IsNamed Then
                SaveDoc(ad, ad.Text)
            Else
                SaveFileDialog1.Filter = "Text files (*.txt) | *.txt"
                SaveFileDialog1.FileName = ad.Text & ".txt"
                If SaveFileDialog1.ShowDialog() = DialogResult.OK Then
                    SaveDoc(ad, SaveFileDialog1.FileName)
                    ad.Text = SaveFileDialog1.FileName
                End If
            End If
        End If
    End Sub

    Private Sub SaveDoc(ByVal doc As Child, ByVal Filename As String)
        Try
            Dim sw As New StreamWriter(Filename)
            sw.Write(doc.RTB1.Text)
            sw.Close()
            doc.IsNamed = True
            doc.IsDirty = False
        Catch ex As IOException
            MsgBox("There was an error saving the file")
        End Try
    End Sub

    Private Sub MenuItem9_Click(ByVal sender As System.Object, _
            ByVal e As System.EventArgs) Handles MenuItem9.Click
        ' Edit, Copy menu command.
        Dim activeChild As Child = Me.ActiveMdiChild
        If Not activeChild Is Nothing Then
            If activeChild.RTB1.SelectionLength > 0 Then
                Clipboard.SetDataObject(activeChild.RTB1.SelectedText)
            End If
        End If
    End Sub

    Private Sub MenuItem10_Click(ByVal sender As System.Object, _
            ByVal e As System.EventArgs) Handles MenuItem10.Click
        ' Edit, Cut menu command.
        Dim activeChild As Child = Me.ActiveMdiChild
        If Not activeChild Is Nothing Then
            If activeChild.RTB1.SelectionLength > 0 Then
                Clipboard.SetDataObject(activeChild.RTB1.SelectedText)
                activeChild.RTB1.SelectedText = ""
```

```
            End If
        End If
    End Sub

    Private Sub MenuItem11_Click(ByVal sender As System.Object, _
            ByVal e As System.EventArgs) Handles MenuItem11.Click
        ' Edit, Paste menu command.
        Dim activeChild As Child = Me.ActiveMdiChild
        If Not activeChild Is Nothing Then
            Dim data As IDataObject = Clipboard.GetDataObject()
            ' If the data is text, then set the text of the
            ' RichTextBox to the text in the Clipboard.
            If (data.GetDataPresent(DataFormats.Text)) Then
                activeChild.RTB1.SelectedText = _
                    data.GetData(DataFormats.Text).ToString()
            End If
        End If
    End Sub
End Class
```

When you run the project, you'll see that it provides many of the capabilities that you would want in a text editor—all for a relatively small investment of programming time and effort. Figure 13.2 shows what the program looks like.

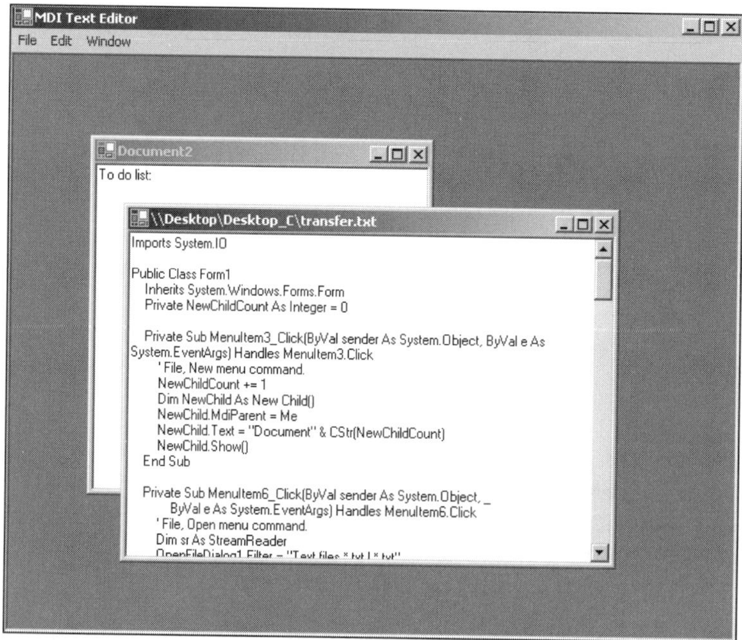

Figure 13.2
The MDI Text Editor executing.

In this sample program, note that the variable used to reference each child form is declared locally. This is okay because the parent form maintains a globally available list of references to all child forms.

Summary

This chapter showed you how to create and use MDI applications, in which a single parent window acts as a container for multiple child windows. This type of application is well suited to tasks that require the user to work with multiple documents at the same time. The capabilities built into the .NET framework classes make creating MDI applications a simple task, with most of the underlying functionality already in place.

Chapter 14

Working with Text and Numbers

The data that your program works with will almost always be in the form of text or numbers. Some of the more fundamental data manipulations can be done using the operators that you learned about in Chapters 3 and 4, such as adding numbers and concatenating strings. However, Visual Basic .NET is not limited to these simple manipulations. Using the members of the **String** and **Math** classes, you can perform a wide variety of data manipulations in your programs. This chapter also covers the use of the **Random** class for generating random numbers.

The String Class

Text data in VB .NET is represented by the **String** class (part of the **System** namespace). Thus, when you create a type **String** variable, you are actually creating an instance of the **String** class. Many of the things that you can do with text data are done by means of class members. The **String** class represents an immutable string, one that cannot be changed. This might sound strange at first, because being immutable is not consistent with the concept of a variable. What happens behind the scenes is that whenever you "change" a string, a new instance is created to replace the old instance:

```
' Create an instance of type String
Dim s As String = "Hello"
...
' Old instance destroyed, new instance created.
s = "goodbye"
```

To the programmer, this is transparent, and the result is that the **String** data type acts as you would expect.

Table 14.1 lists and briefly describes the most frequently used members of the **String** class. Detailed information on using these members is given in the following sections.

Chars

The **Chars** property returns, as a type **Char**, the single character at a specified position in the string. The syntax is

```
Chars(index)
```

In the preceding line, ***index*** is the position from which to retrieve a character. The first character has position 0. If ***index*** is greater than the length of the string, an exception of type **ArgumentException** occurs. Here is an example of using this property:

```
Dim s As String = "abcde"
Dim c As Char
c = s.Chars(1) ' c now contains "b"
```

Table 14.1 Members of the String class.

Member	Description
Chars	Returns the character at a specified position in the string.
Length	Returns the length of the string.
CompareTo()	Compares one string with another.
EndsWith()	Determines if the string ends with the specified text.
Equals()	Determines if two strings have the same value.
IndexOf()	Returns the position of the first occurrence in the string of specified text.
Insert()	Inserts text at a specified position in the string.
LastIndexOf()	Returns the position of the last occurrence in the string of specified text.
PadLeft()	Pads the beginning of the string with a space or other character to make the string a specified length.
PadRight()	Pads the end of the string with a space or other character to make the string a specified length.
Remove()	Deletes a specified number of characters from a specified position in the string.
Replace()	Replaces all instances of specified text in the string with new text.
StartsWith()	Determines if the string starts with the specified text.
SubString()	Retrieves a substring from the string.
ToLower()	Returns a copy of the string in lowercase.
ToUpper()	Returns a copy of the string in uppercase.
Trim()	Removes all spaces or other specified character from the start and end of the string.
TrimEnd()	Removes all spaces or other specified character from the end of the string.
TrimStart()	Removes all spaces or other specified character from the start of the string.

Length

The **Length** property returns the length of the string (number of characters), as a type **Integer**. If the string has not been initialized, an exception of type **NullReferenceException** occurs:

```
Dim s As String = "Hello"
Dim s2 As String
Dim len As Integer
len = s.Length      ' len is equal to 5.
len = s2.Length     ' Causes an exception.
```

CompareTo()

The **CompareTo()** method compares a string with another string. The syntax is

```
CompareTo(arg)
```

In this line, ***arg*** is another type **String** or an object that evaluates to a string. If ***arg*** cannot be evaluated as a string, an exception of type **ArgumentException** occurs. The method returns a signed integer as follows:

- A negative value (usually **–1**) if the string is less than ***arg***.
- Zero if the string is equal to ***arg***.
- A positive value (usually **1**) if the string is greater than ***arg***.

The nature of string comparisons is based on the code page in use, and also on the setting of **Option Compare**. If **Option Compare** is set to **Binary**, characters are compared based on their internal numerical representations. This leads to all uppercase letters being "less than" the corresponding lowercase letters, so **Apple** and **apple** would not be equal. If **Option Compare** is set to **Text**, uppercase and lowercase letters are equal. To change the default setting for the entire project, set the Option Compare option on the Common Properties – Build section of the project's property pages. To change the setting for a single module, place the **Option Compare Binary** or **Option Compare Text** statement at the start of the module, before any other code. This code demonstrates the two text-comparison options:

```
Dim s1 As String = "Banana"
Dim s2 As String = "banana"
Dim result As Integer
Result = s1.CompareTo(s2)  ' Result = 1 with Option Compare Binary.
                           ' Result = 0 with Option Compare Text.
```

EndsWith(), StartsWith()

These methods determine if a string ends with or begins with specified text. The syntax is

```
EndsWith(match)
StartsWith(match)
```

In this syntax example, ***match*** is the string you are looking for. The return value is a type **Boolean**. If ***match*** is a null reference, an exception of type **ArgumentNullException** occurs. Comparisons are case-sensitive regardless of the **Option Compare** setting (explained under **CompareTo()**). Here are some examples:

```
Dim s As String = "New York"
Dim result as Boolean
result = s.EndsWith("rk")     ' returns True.
result = s.StartsWith("New") ' returns True.
result = s.StartsWith("new") ' returns False.
```

Equals()

The **Equals()** method determines if two strings are equal. The syntax is

```
Equals(arg)
```

In this syntax line, ***arg*** is another type **String** or an object that evaluates to a string. If ***arg*** cannot be evaluated as a string, an exception of type **ArgumentException** occurs. The method returns **True** if the strings are the same (case-sensitive), **False** if not:

```
Dim s As String = "reed"
Dim result as Boolean
Result = s.Equals("seed")   ' returns False
```

IndexOf(), LastIndexOf()

The **IndexOf()** and **LastIndexOf()** methods return the position at which specified text is found within a string. The **IndexOf()** method starts at the beginning of the string and works forward, while the **LastIndexOf()** method starts at the end of the string and works backward. There are three syntax variants for each method:

```
IndexOf(arg)
LastIndexOf(arg)
IndexOf(arg, start)
LastIndexOf(arg, start)
IndexOf(arg, start, length)
LastIndexOf(arg, start, length)
```

Here, ***arg*** is a type **Char** or a type **String** specifying the text to look for. ***start*** is an optional type **Integer** specifying the position at which to start looking; if omitted, the default is **0**. ***length*** is an optional type **Integer** specifying how many characters to examine; if omitted, all characters from ***start*** to the end of the string are examined. The method returns the character position of the first match, or **–1** if no match is found. Matches are case-sensitive, as shown in these examples:

```
Dim s As String = "Mississippi"
Dim pos As Integer
pos = s.IndexOf("ss")        ' returns 2
pos = s.IndexOf("ss", 3)     ' returns 5
pos = s.LastIndexOf("ss")    ' returns 5
pos = s.LastIndexOf("Mi")    ' returns 0
pos = s.LastIndexOf("mi")    ' returns -1
```

Insert()

The **Insert()** method inserts text into a string at a specified position and returns the new string. The original string is not changed. The syntax is

```
Insert(pos, arg)
```

In this syntax example, ***pos*** is the position at which to insert the text, and ***arg*** is a type **String** specifying the text to insert. If ***pos*** is negative or greater than the length of the string, an exception of type **ArgumentOutOfRangeException** occurs. If ***arg*** is a null reference, an exception of type **ArgumentNullException** occurs.

```
Dim s As String = "V Basic"
Dim t As String
T = s.Insert(1, "isual")    ' t = "Visual Basic"
```

LastIndexOf()

For an explanation of **LastIndexOf**, see **IndexOf()**.

PadLeft(), PadRight()

The **PadLeft()** method adds a repeated character to the start of a string to make the string length equal to a specified value, and returns the new string. The **PadRight()** method does the same thing but pads at the end of the string. There are two overloads for these methods:

```
PadLeft(len)
PadRight(len)
PadLeft(len, char)
PadRight(len, char)
```

len is an integer specifying the final desired string length. ***char*** is an optional type **Char** specifying the character to pad with; if omitted, the space character is used. If ***len*** is equal to or less than the length of the string, the methods return the original string. If ***len*** is negative, an exception of type **ArgumentException** occurs.

```
Dim s As String = "Index"
Dim r1 As String
Dim r2 As String
r1 = s.PadLeft(10, ".")    ' r1 = ".....Index"
r2 = s.PadRight(5)         ' r2 = "Index     "
```

Remove()

The **Remove()** method deletes a specified number of characters from a specified position in a string and returns the resulting string. The syntax is

```
Remove(start, count)
```

start is a type **Integer** specifying the position at which to start removing characters, and ***count*** is a type **Integer** specifying how many characters to remove. If either argument is negative, or if the sum of ***start*** and ***count*** is greater than the length of the string, an exception of type **ArgumentOutOfRange** occurs.

```
Dim s As String = "abcdefg"
Dim r1 As String
Dim r2 As String
r1 = s.Remove(1, 3)      ' r1 = "aefg"
r2 = s.Remove(4, 5)      ' an exception occurs
```

Replace()

The **Replace()** method replaces all instances of specified text with new text and returns the result. The syntax is

```
Replace(old, new)
```

old is the text to replace; ***new*** is the new text. ***old*** and ***new*** can both be a type **Char** or type **String**. If there is no match for ***old***, the return value is the original string. Matches are case-sensitive.

```
Dim s As String = "Mississippi"
Dim r As String
r = s.Replace("ss", "xxx")    ' r = "Mixxxixxxippi"
```

StartsWith()

See **EndsWith()**.

SubString()

The **SubString()** method returns a portion of a string. There are two overloaded syntax forms:

```
SubString(start)
SubString(start, length)
```

start is a type **Integer** specifying the position in the string where the substring starts. ***length*** is an optional type **Integer** specifying the length of the substring; if omitted, the substring extends to the end of the string. If ***start*** or ***length*** is negative, or if ***start*** is greater than the length of the string, an exception of type **ArgumentOutOfRange** occurs.

```
Dim s As String = "Visual Basic Programming"
Dim r as String
R = s.SubString(7, 5)    ' r = "Basic"
```

ToLower(), ToUpper()

The **ToLower()** and **ToUpper()** methods return a string with all letters converted to lowercase or uppercase, respectively. Non-letter characters are not affected. These methods take no arguments.

```
Dim s As String = "Visual Basic"
Dim r1 As String
Dim r2 As String
r1 = s.ToLower()     ' r1 = "visual basic"
r2 = s.ToUpper()     ' r2 = "VISUAL BASIC"
```

Trim(), TrimEnd(), TrimStart()

These methods remove all white space characters (such as spaces and tabs) from the beginning and/or end of a string. The methods take no arguments.

```
Dim s As String = "     Peter      "
Dim r1 As String
Dim r2 As String
Dim r3 As String
r1 = s.Trim()            ' r1 = "Peter"
r2 = s.TrimStart()       ' r2 = "Peter      "
r3 = s.TrimEnd()         ' r3 = "     Peter"
```

Obsolete String Functions and Statements

The VB .NET language supports a number of string-manipulation functions and statements that are carryovers from the previous version of Visual Basic. These language elements offer no advantages over the members of the **String** class that were described earlier in this chapter, and they are provided solely for compatibility with older VB code. I will not provide details on these elements, because you should always use the **String** class members in new code. Table 14.2 lists and briefly describes these functions.

Table 14.2 Obsolete string-manipulation functions.

Action	Keyword
Compare two strings	**StrComp**
Convert a string to lowercase or uppercase	**LCase**, **UCase**
Create a string of a repeating character	**Space**, **String**
Find the length of a string	**Len**
Format a string	**Format**
Justify a string	**LSet**, **Rset**
Find one string in another	**InStr**, **InstrRev**
Extract part of a string	**Mid** function; **Left** and **Right** functions
Insert one string within another	**Mid** statement
Replace parts of strings	**Replace**
Trim leading and/or trailing spaces	**LTrim**, **RTrim**, **Trim**
Set string comparison rules	**Option Compare**
Work with ASCII and ANSI values	**Asc**, **Chr**
Convert strings	**StrConv**
Process arrays of strings	**Filter**, **Join**, **Split**

Working with Numbers

The .NET framework provides a rich set of methods for working with numbers. The methods are static members of the **Math** class, part of the **System** namespace. These members perform a variety of commonly needed mathematical tasks, such as obtaining square roots and performing trigonometric calculations. The members of the **Math** class are described in Table 14.3, and examples of their use are given where appropriate.

The **Math** class members are designed to be error-free, which means that you cannot cause an exception by passing inappropriate arguments. For example, it is not possible to take the square root of a negative number, but if you pass a negative argument to the **Sqrt()** method, it does not cause an error; instead, the method returns the special value **NaN** (for Not a Number). Other special values that might be returned are **PositiveInfinity** (for example, returned by **Log10(0)**) and **NegativeInfinity**.

Note that the .NET trigonometric functions work with angles that are expressed in radians rather than in degrees. One radian equals approximately 57.3 degrees.

Table 14.3 Members of the Math class.

Member	Description	Example
Abs(*x*)	Returns the absolute value of ***x***.	**Abs(–5)** returns **5**.
Acos(*x*)	Returns the angle whose cosine is ***x***.	
Asin(*x*)	Returns the angle whose sine is ***x***.	
Atan(*x*)	Returns the angle whose tangent is ***x***.	
Atan2(*x, y*)	Returns the angle whose tangent is ***y*** divided by ***x***.	
Ceiling(*x*)	Returns the smallest integer number that is greater than or equal to ***x***.	**Ceiling(4.5)** returns **5**. **Ceiling(–4.5)** returns **–4**.
Cos(*x*)	Returns the cosine of the angle ***x***.	
Cosh(*x*)	Returns the hyperbolic cosine of the angle ***x***.	
Exp(*x*)	Returns **e** (the base of the natural logarithms) raised to the power ***x***.	
Floor(*x*)	Returns the largest integer number that is less than or equal to ***x***.	**Floor(4.5)** returns **4**. **Floor(–4.5)** returns **–5**.
IEEERemainder(*x, y*)	Returns the remainder of ***x*** divided by divided by ***y***.	**IEEERemainder(13, 1.2)** returns **1**.
Log(*x*)	Returns the natural logarithm of ***x***.	
Log10(*x*)	Returns the base 10 logarithm of ***x***.	
Max(*x, y*)	Returns the larger of its two arguments.	
Min(*x, y*)	Returns the smaller of its two arguments.	
Pow(*x, y*)	Returns ***x*** raised to the ***y*** power.	
Round(*x*)	Returns the value ***x*** rounded to the nearest integer.	**Round(4.50)** returns **4.0**. **Round(4.51)** returns **5.0**.
Sign(*x*)	Returns **–1** if ***x*** is less than 0, **1** if ***x*** is greater than 0, and **0** if ***x*** is 0.	
Sin(*x*)	Returns the sine of the angle ***x***.	
Sinh(*x*)	Returns the hyperbolic sine of the angle ***x***.	
Sqrt(*x*)	Returns the square root of ***x***, or **NaN** if ***x*** is negative.	
Tan(*x*)	Returns the tangent of the angle ***x***.	
Tanh(*x*)	Returns the hyperbolic tangent of the angle ***x***.	

In addition to the methods described in the table, the **Math** class provides the following two constants:

- **Math:E**—The value of the constant **e**, the base of the natural logarithms
- **Math:PI**—The value of the constant **PI** (π), the ratio of a circle's circumference to its diameter

The Visual Basic language supports some obsolete mathematical functions that perform some of the same tasks that the **Math** class members do. They are provided only for compatibility with older Visual Basic programs, and you should not use them in your code. They are as follows (you can tell their function from the name):

Abs
Atn
Cos
Exp
Fix
Int
Log
Sgn
Sin
Sqr
Tan

Generating Random Numbers

Certain mathematical and statistical procedures require the use of random numbers. A computer cannot generate truly random numbers, but VB .NET's pseudo-random number generator can produce sequences of numbers that meet the requirements of randomness for most situations. Random number operations use the **Random** class, part of the **System** namespace.

The random numbers produced by the **Random** class are based on a seed value that is provided when the class is instantiated. The **Random** class has two constructors. One takes no arguments and seeds the class based on the current time. The second constructor takes a type **Integer** argument and seeds the generator based on that value. Using the same seed value will cause the generator to produce the same sequence of numbers.

The members of the **Random** class are described in Table 14.4.

Table 14.4 Members of the Random class.

Member	Description
Next()	Returns a random integer between 0 and the maximum value of type **Integer**, 2,147,483,647.
Next(*x*)	Returns a random integer between 0 and ***x***. The value of ***x*** must be greater than 0 and less than the maximum value of type **Integer**, 2,147,483,647.
Next(*x*, *y*)	Returns a random integer between ***x*** and ***y***. The value of **x** must be greater than 0, and the value of ***y*** must be greater than ***x*** and less than the maximum value of type **Integer**, 2,147,483,647.
NextDouble()	Returns a random type **Double** greater than or equal to 0 and less than 1.

The following code generates, and displays in the Output window, a sequence of random numbers in the range 0 to 100:

```
Dim r As New System.Random()
Dim I As Integer
For I = 0 To 100
    Debug.Write(r.Next(0, 100))
Next
```

Summary

Visual Basic .NET provides powerful capabilities for manipulating string and number data. String manipulations are accomplished by using the members of the **String** class, and mathematical operations are carried out by members of the **Math** class. If your program needs random numbers, the .NET framework has that covered, too, with the **Random** class.

Chapter 15
Working with Dates and Times

When your program needs to work with dates and times, you'll find that Visual Basic .NET has a rich set of tools that can perform just about any date/time–related task you might require. Capabilities for working with specific times and/or dates are encapsulated in the **DateTime** structure. When you are dealing with time durations, you will use the **TimeSpan** structure. VB .NET also provides a variety of different calendars that are used in different parts of the world—for example, the Hebrew calendar and the Thai Buddhist calendar.

The DateTime Structure

In VB .NET, dates and times are represented by the **DateTime** structure, part of the **System** namespace. The range that can be represented by this structure is from 12:00 A.M. on January 1, 0001, C.E. (Common Era, previously referred to as A.D.) to 11:59:59 P.M., December 31, 9999, C.E. A **DateTime** value represents an instant in time. This is different from a **TimeSpan** value (covered elsewhere in the chapter) that represents a time interval. The accuracy of a **DateTime** value is 100 nanoseconds (0.0000001 second), a unit that is called a *tick*. A specific date and time is stored as the number of ticks since 12:00 A.M. on January 1, 0001.

Although the **DateTime** structure stores its data in 100-nanosecond intervals, this does not mean that you can always work to that accuracy. The system clock is limited in its accuracy to a few tens of milliseconds (0.001 second), with the exact accuracy depending on your operating system as follows:

- Windows NT 3.5 and later, Windows 2000, and Windows XP: 10 milliseconds
- Windows NT 3.1: 16 milliseconds
- Windows 95/98/ME: 55 milliseconds

A **DateTime** value is always expressed in terms of a calendar, which can be a default system calendar or one that is explicitly specified. Calendars are covered later in the chapter. A **DateTime** value makes no assumptions about time zones, and comparisons between two **DateTime** values are meaningful only if they refer to the same zone. It is the programmer's responsibility to maintain time zone information when and if needed. A common programming practice is to express all **DateTime** values in relation to the coordinated universal time (UTC) standard. This time zone was formerly called Greenwich Mean Time, or GMT.

The **DateTime** structure has a wide range of members, both static members and instance members, to perform just about any conceivable date- or time-related task. To refresh your memory about the distinction between static and instance members, a static member is called directly from the class definition without the need to create an instance of the class first. In contrast, an instance member can only be called on an instance of the class, and typically performs some operation involving the date/time value stored in the instance. For example, **Now** is a static property that returns the date and time set on the system clock. You would call it like this:

```
Dim d As DateTime
d = DateTime.Now
```

However, **Day** is an instance property, returning an integer corresponding to the day of the month of a specific date (the date stored in the instance):

```
Dim d As DateTime
Dim dayOfMonth As Integer
d = DateTime.Now
dayOfMonth = d.Day
```

The following sections provide reference material on the **DateTime** structure. Code examples will be presented toward the end of the chapter.

DateTime Constructors

The **DateTime** structure has several overloaded constructors, permitting you to initialize the date/time value in a number of ways. If you instantiate the structure with no arguments, it is initialized to 12:00 A.M., January 1, 0001. The overloaded constructors are shown here, and the arguments will make it clear how each constructor works. Those constructors that take a ***calendar*** argument are initialized with respect to the specified calendar. The **Calendar** class is described later in the chapter.

```
New(ticks)
New(year, month, day)
New(year, month, day, calendar)
New(year, month, day, hour, minute, second)
New(year, month, day, hour, minute, second, calendar)
New(year, month, day, hour, minute, second, millisecond)
New(year, month, day, hour, minute, second, millisecond, calendar)
```

These constructors will throw an **ArgumentOutOfRange** exception if any of the arguments are outside the permitted ranges, as detailed in the documentation. Other exceptions can occur as well. Let's look at some examples. The following code initializes a **DateTime** structure for Christmas Day, 2001:

```
Dim d As New DateTime(2001, 12, 25)
```

This code initializes a **DateTime** structure for one second before midnight on New Year's Eve:

```
Dim d As New DateTime(2001, 12, 31, 23, 59, 59)
```

Getting Date/Time Information

The **DateTime** members that are described in this section all deal with getting date and time information. This includes such tasks as determining the current date/time (as set on the system clock), determining the day of the week that a particular date falls on, and determining whether a specified year is a leap year. Table 15.1 describes these members.

Table 15.1 DateTime structure members for getting date and time information.

Member	Instance or Static	Description
Date	I	Returns a **DateTime** for the date component of this instance (time information set to 0).
Day	I	Returns an **Integer** value 1–31 specifying the day of the month of this instance.
DayOfWeek	I	Returns an **Integer** specifying the day of the week of this instance (Sunday = 0, Saturday = 6).
DayOfYear	I	Returns an **Integer** 1–366 specifying the day of the year of this instance.
DaysInMonth (*year, month*)	S	Returns an **Integer** giving the number of days in the specified month of the specified year. ***month*** is an **Integer** value 1–12 giving the month, and ***year*** is an **Integer** value giving the year.

(continued)

Table 15.1 DateTime structure members for getting date and time information *(continued)*.

Member	Instance or Static	Description
Hour	I	Returns an **Integer** value 0–23 specifying the hour of this instance.
IsLeapYear(*year*)	S	Returns **True** if the specified year is a leap year, **False** if not.
Millisecond	I	Returns an **Integer** value 0–999 specifying the millisecond of this instance.
Minute	I	Returns an **Integer** value 0–59 specifying the minute of this instance.
Month	I	Returns an **Integer** value 1–12 specifying the month of this instance.
Now	S	Returns a **DateTime** corresponding to the current local date and time, as set on the system clock.
Second	I	Returns an **Integer** value 0–59 specifying the second of this instance.
Ticks	I	Returns a **Long** specifying the number of ticks for this instance.
TimeOfDay	I	Returns a **TimeSpan** representing the time elapsed since midnight for this instance.
Today	S	Returns a **DateTime** corresponding to the current local date, with the time part set to 0, as set on the system clock.
ToLocalTime()	I	Returns a **DateTime** corresponding to the current UTC time, adjusted for the local time zone and daylight saving time.
ToUniversalTime()	I	Returns a **DateTime** corresponding to the current local time converted to UTC time.
UtcNow	S	Returns a **DateTime** corresponding to the current UTC date and time, as set on the system clock.
Year	I	Returns an **Integer** value 1–9999 specifying the year of this instance.

Comparing Dates/Times

It is often necessary to compare **DateTime** values, to determine which of two values is earlier. Table 15.2 describes the members for date and time comparisons.

Table 15.2 Date and time comparison members.

Member	Instance or Static	Description
Compare(*d1*, *d2*)	S	**Compares** two **DateTime** values. Returns **–1** if ***d1*** is less than ***d2***, **0** if ***d1*** and ***d2*** are equal, and **1** if ***d1*** is greater than ***d2***.
Equals(*d1*, *d2*)	S	Compares two **DateTime** values and returns **True** if they are equal.
Equals(*obj*)	I	Returns **True** if ***obj*** is a **DateTime** that is equal to this instance, **False** otherwise.

Date/Time Calculations

The **DateTime** structure members described in this section have to do with performing calculations with dates and times. You can perform tasks such as creating a date two months from today or a date exactly four years ago. These members are described in Table 15.3.

Converting and Formatting Dates/Times

The members discussed in this section deal with converting between standard text representations of dates, such as "Feb 3, 2001," and the **DateTime** structure representation. You can work in both directions: from text to **DateTime** and from **DateTime** to text. These members of the **DateTime** structure are described in Table 15.4.

Table 15.3 DateTime members for performing date/time calculations.

Member	Static or Instance	Description
Add(*ts*)	I	Returns a **DateTime** representing the **TimeSpan *ts*** added to the current instance.
AddDays(*n*) **AddHours(*n*)** **AddMilliseconds(*n*)** **AddMinutes(*n*)** **AddMonths(*n*)** **AddSeconds(*n*)** **AddTicks(*n*)** **AddYears(*n*)**	I	Returns a **DateTime** that results from adding ***n*** of the specified interval to the current instance. Passes a negative value for ***n*** to subtract.
Subtract(*ts*)	I	Returns a **DateTime** representing the **TimeSpan *ts*** subtracted from the current instance.
Subtract(*d*)	I	Returns a **TimeSpan** representing the **DateTime *d*** subtracted from the current instance.

Table 15.4 DateTime members for converting and formatting dates and times.

Member	Static or Instance	Description
Parse(s)	S	Parses the string **s** and returns a **DateTime** corresponding to the date and/or time in **s**. The string can be a string representation of a date and/or time in any of the common formats. If **s** does not contain a valid representation of a date/time, an exception of type **FormatException** occurs.
ToLongDateString	I	Returns a string representing the current instance's date in "long" format (for example, **Monday, July 09, 2001**).
ToLongTimeString	I	Returns a string representing the current instance's time in "long" format (for example, **12:41:40 PM**).
ToShortDateString	I	Returns a string representing the current instance's date in "short" format (for example, **7/9/2001**).

(continued)

Table 15.4 DateTime members for converting and formatting dates and times *(continued)*.

Member	Static or Instance	Description
ToShortTimeString	I	Returns a string representing the current instance's time in "short" format (for example, **12:42 PM**).
ToString	I	Returns a string representing the current instance's date and time (for example, **7/9/2001 12:41:40 PM**).

TimeSpan

The **TimeSpan** structure represents a time interval, or duration. This is different from the **DateTime** structure, which represents a fixed instant in time. The interval is stored internally as the number of "ticks," with a single tick being the same duration, 100 nanoseconds, as it is for the **DateTime** structure.

TimeSpan Constructors

The **TimeSpan** structure has several overloaded constructors, letting you initialize the structure as needed. The default parameterless constructor initializes the structure to an interval of 0 ticks. The other constructors are as follows:

```
New(numberOfTicks)
New(hours, minutes, seconds)
New(days, hours, minutes, seconds)
New(days, hours, minutes, seconds, milliseconds)
```

TimeSpan Members

The members of the **TimeSpan** structure that you will need most often are described in Table 15.5. Like the **DateTime** structure, the **TimeSpan** structure has both static and instance members, as indicated in the table.

Table 15.5 Members of the TimeSpan structure.

Member	Static or Instance	Description
TicksPerDay **TicksPerHour** **TicksPerMillisecond** **TicksPerMinute** **TicksPerSecond**	S	These properties return constant values giving the number of ticks in the specified time interval.
Zero	S	Returns a **TimeSpan** instance with a zero interval.

(continued)

Table 15.5 Members of the TimeSpan structure *(continued)*.

Member	Static or Instance	Description
Compare(*t1*, *t2*)	S	Compares two **TimeSpan** values and returns **–1** if ***t1*** is less than ***t2***, **0** if ***t1*** and ***t2*** are equal, and **1** if ***t1*** is greater than ***t2***.
Equals(*obj*)	I	Returns **True** if ***obj*** is a **TimeSpan** and is equal to the current instance, **False** otherwise.
Equals(*t1*, *t2*)	S	Returns **True** if the two **TimeSpans** are equal, **False** if not.
FromDays(*n*) **FromHours(*n*)** **FromMilliseconds(*n*)** **FromMinutes(*n*)** **FromSeconds(*n*)**	S	Returns a **TimeSpan** with an interval equal to ***n*** of the specified unit.
Days **Hours** **Milliseconds** **Minutes** **Seconds**	I	Returns the number of whole units represented by this instance. For example, if the **TimeSpan** contains an interval of 2 days, 6.5 hours, then **Days** will return **2**, **Hours** will return **6**, and **Minutes** will return **30**.
TotalDays **TotalHours** **TotalMilliseconds** **TotalMinutes** **TotalSeconds**	I	Returns the number of whole and fractional units represented by this instance. For example, if the **TimeSpan** contains an interval of 2 days, 6-and-a-half hours, then **TotalDays** will return **2.278033333**, **TotalHours** will return **54.5**, and **TotalMinutes** will return **3270**.
Add(*ts*)	I	Returns a **TimeSpan** with an interval equal to the interval of the **TimeSpan *ts*** plus the interval of the current instance.
CompareTo(*ts*)	I	Compares the **TimeSpan *ts*** to the current instance and returns **–1** if the current instance is less than ***ts***, **0** if they are equal, and **1** if the current instance is greater than ***ts***.
Subtract(*ts*)	I	Returns a **TimeSpan** with an interval equal to the interval of the current instance minus the interval of the **TimeSpan ts**.
ToString()	I	Returns a string representation of the interval of the current instance.

Code Examples

This section provides some examples of using the **DateTime** structure to work with dates and times.

Determining Day of the Week

The function shown in Listing 15.1 shows how to determine the day of the week that New Year's Day falls on for a given year.

Listing 15.1 Determining the day of the week that New Year's Day falls on.

```
Public Function DayOfNewYears(ByVal year As Integer) As String

    Dim d As New DateTime(year, 1, 1)
    Dim day As String

    Select Case d.DayOfWeek
        Case 0
            day = "Sunday"
        Case 1
            day = "Monday"
        Case 2
            day = "Tuesday"
        Case 3
            day = "Wednesday"
        Case 4
            day = "Thursday"
        Case 5
            day = "Friday"
        Case 6
            day = "Saturday"
    End Select

    Return day

End Function
```

Determining the First Monday of the Month

The function shown in Listing 15.2 is passed a month (as a value 1 through 12) and a year. It returns a **DateTime** corresponding to the first Monday in that month. The technique used is to create a **DateTime** corresponding to the first day of the specified month. Then the **DayOfWeek** property is checked. If it returns **1** (Monday), then the first Monday is the first of the month, so that **DateTime** is returned. If it returns another value, then the **AddDays()** method is used to create a **DateTime** that corresponds to the first Monday, as explained in Table 15.6.

Table 15.6 Calculating the first Monday of a month.

If first of month falls on this day of week	This many days must be added to find first Monday
Sunday	1
Tuesday	6
Wednesday	5
Thursday	4
Friday	3
Saturday	2

Listing 15.2 Finding the first Monday of a specified month.

```
Public Function FirstMonday(ByVal month As Integer, _
        ByVal year As Integer) As DateTime

    Dim day As Integer
    ' Create a DateTime corresponding to the first of the month.
    Dim d As New DateTime(year, month, 1)

    ' What day of the week is this?
    day = d.DayOfWeek

    ' If it's a Monday, return it.
    If day = 1 Then
        Return d
    Else
        ' If not a Monday, add the proper number of days
        ' to reach the first Monday.
        Dim d2 As DateTime
        Dim daystoadd As Integer
        If day = 0 Then
            daystoadd = 1
        Else
            daystoadd = 8 - day
        End If
        d2 = d.AddDays(daystoadd)
        Return d2
    End If

End Function
```

Finding the Next Leap Year

The function shown in Listing 15.3 returns an integer specifying the next leap year. If the current year is a leap year, it is ignored. The procedure used is to create a **DateTime** corresponding to the current date, and then repeatedly add 1 year and check if the new **DateTime** is a leap year. If so, its year value is returned.

Listing 15.3 Finding the next leap year.

```
Public Function nextLeapYear() As Integer

    Dim d As DateTime = DateTime.Now
    Dim d2 As DateTime
    Dim i As Integer
    Dim year As Integer

    ' The next leap year is a maximum of 8 years in the future.
    For i = 1 To 8
```

```
        d2 = d.AddYears(i)
        year = d2.Year
        If DateTime.IsLeapYear(year) Then Exit For
    Next

    Return year

End Function
```

Calculating the Number of Minutes Between Two Times

The function presented in Listing 15.4 is passed to **DateTime** values, one representing the start of some process and the other representing the finish. It returns the number of minutes between the two times.

Listing 15.4 Function that returns the number of minutes between two DateTime values.

```
Public Function NumberOfMinutes(ByVal start As DateTime, _
        ByVal finish As DateTime) As Long

    Dim t As TimeSpan

    t = finish.Subtract(start)
    Return t.TotalMinutes

End Function
```

Calendar

A calendar divides time into measures such as weeks, months, and years. Several different calendars are in use around the world, and they differ in the way they divide time. For example, with the Gregorian calendar (the one that is in common use in the United States and Europe), a year has 365 or 366 days and is divided into 12 months, each containing between 28 and 31 days. In a leap year, an extra day is added to one month (February). In contrast, the Hebrew calendar has years ranging from 353 to 355 days (for common years) and from 383 to 385 days (for leap years). A common year is divided into 12 months, while a leap year has 13 months. VB .NET provides the following calendars:

- Gregorian
- Hebrew
- Hijri
- Japanese
- Julian

- Korean
- Taiwan
- ThaiBuddhist

All calendars are derived from the **Calendar** class and therefore share the same methods. All calendars are part of the **System.Globalization** namespace. The **Calendar** class methods perform tasks such as getting information about specific dates and performing calculations. For example, the following code determines the year in the Hebrew calendar in which the Gregorian date January 1, 2002, falls:

```
Dim year As Integer
Dim d As New DateTime(2002, 1, 1)
Dim hc As New System.Globalization.HebrewCalendar()
Year = hc.GetYear(d)
```

Please refer to the VB .NET online help for information on other methods of the **Calendar** class.

Any particular system has a default calendar that is appropriate for its locale, and date/time calculations using the **DateTime** structure automatically use that calendar. As I described previously in this chapter, you can instantiate a **DateTime** structure using a different calendar. For example, someone working in the United States might need to perform date calculations using the Hebrew calendar. Here's how that person would create a **DateTime** structure initialized to the fifteenth day in the fifth month of year 5760 of the Hebrew calendar:

```
Dim hc As New System.Globalization.HebrewCalendar()
Dim hdt As New DateTime(5760, 5, 15, hc)
```

When you create a **DateTime** based on a nondefault calendar, it will be initialized according to that calendar but it will still operate using the system default calendar. Thus, on a system that uses the Gregorian calendar, the **ToLongDateString()** method of the above **DateTime** structure will return **"Saturday, January 22, 2000"**, which is the Gregorian equivalent of the Hebrew calendar date that the structure was initialized with.

Summary

Dates and times are likely to be important for some of the applications you write. Visual Basic .NET provides two structures that provide any capability you are likely to need. The **DateTime** structure is used when dealing with specific instants of time, such as "noon on July 4, 2001". The **TimeSpan** structure is used to work with intervals, or durations, of time. Between these two structures and their many methods, you should be able to perform any date/time–related tasks that your application requires.

Chapter 16
File Access and Management

Working with files is an important part of many of the applications that you will create with Visual Basic .NET. File operations can be divided into two areas. File access deals with writing data to, and reading data from, files. File management involves moving, creating, renaming, and deleting files and folders. I'll cover both in this chapter. There is unavoidably a lot of reference material in this chapter, even though I have trimmed it down to the information that Visual Basic. NET programmers will need most often. However, I also provide sample code for many file access and management tasks so you can see exactly how things work.

File Fundamentals

As with just about everything else in Visual Basic .NET, file access and management is based on classes that exist in the .NET framework. Most of this chapter is devoted to explaining how to use these classes. Before getting to the details, it's a good idea to have an overview of the whole picture. Table 16.1 lists the file-related .NET framework classes that are most important to the Visual Basic .NET developer. All of these classes are in the **System.IO** namespace.

Table 16.1 File-related classes in the .NET framework.

Class	Namespace	Description
BinaryReader BinaryWriter	System.IO	Read and write binary (non-text) data from/to files. Also used with specially encoded text.
Directory	System.IO	Provides static methods for creating, moving, and listing directories (folders).

(continued)

Table 16.1 File-related classes in the .NET framework *(continued)*.

Class	Namespace	Description
DirectoryInfo	**System.IO**	Provides instance methods for creating, moving, and listing directories (folders).
File	**System.IO**	Provides static methods for file operations such as creating, opening, moving, and deleting. Also assists in creating **FileStream** objects.
FileInfo	**System.IO**	Provides instance methods for file operations such as creating, opening, moving, and deleting. Also assists in creating **FileStream** objects.
FileStream	**System.IO**	Represents a stream that is connected to a file, permitting random access to the file.
Path	**System.IO**	Performs operations on directory strings.
StreamReader **StreamWriter**	**System.IO**	Used for reading and writing standard text files.

Exceptions in File Access

By their very nature, file operations are more prone to errors than almost any other area of programming. This is primarily because files are something outside your program over which you usually do not have complete control. If someone else deletes or renames a file, changes security settings for a folder, or renames a network share, that action has the potential to cause problems for any program that accesses files. It's easy to say that such things *should* not happen on a properly maintained system, but the fact is that they *do* happen, and a well-written program will be able to deal with them.

A general rule to follow is that all file-manipulation code should be protected—that is, should be contained within a **Try** block (you learned about **Try** blocks and exception handling in Chapter 5). For file operations, the exceptions you need to be concerned with are listed in Table 16.2.

Note that **DirectoryNotFoundException**, **EndOfStreamException**, **FileLoadException**, and **FileNotFoundException** are all derived from **IOException**, so you can have the choice of

Table 16.2 File operation-related exceptions.

Exception	Description
DirectoryNotFoundException	The program tries to access a directory that does not exist.
EndOfStreamException	The program tries to read past the end of a file.
FileLoadException	The file was found but could not be loaded.
FileNotFoundException	The file is not found.
IOException	A general IO error occurs.
SecurityException	The user does not have the required permission for the operation being attempted.
UnauthorizedAccessException	The program attempts to open a directory as if it were a file, or tries to open a read-only file for writing.

catching these exceptions individually if needed, or catching them all together by catching **IOException**.

Many of the examples in this chapter omit the **Try...Catch** block for the sake of clarity, so the exception-handling code does not obscure the file access code that is, after all, the topic of this chapter. You should not do this in your own code, however.

File Access

File access in Visual Basic .NET is based on the concept of *streams*. A stream is an abstraction of a sequence of bytes that your program is receiving from or sending to some location. This location can be any one of a variety of devices, such as a modem or an Internet connection, but for the purposes of this chapter it is a file on a storage device such as a hard disk. You can think of a stream as a pipe that carries bytes—data—between your program and a file. Accessing a file always involves the creation of a stream object associated with that file. A stream is represented by the **FileStream** class.

Creating a stream is not enough, however. Although the stream provides the connection between your program and the file, it cannot control the flow of information to or from the file. For this, you use either a reader object (when reading from a file) or a writer object (when writing to a file). Thus, the overall arrangement for file access is as shown in Figure 16.1.

Any file is simply a sequence of bytes, but the way those bytes are treated is different depending on the type of data stored in the file. Visual Basic .NET distinguishes between two types of files: text files, which contain character data, and binary files, which contain noncharacter data such as a graphics image or an array of numbers. For most text files, you use the **StreamReader** and **StreamWriter** classes. For binary files and certain encoded text files, you use the **BinaryReader** and **BinaryWriter** classes. The general sequence of steps for reading from a file is as follows:

1. Verify that the file exists.
2. Open the file by creating a stream associated with it.

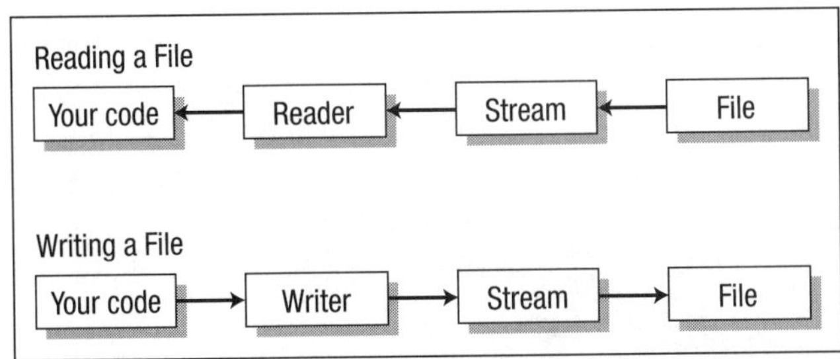

Figure 16.1
File access in Visual Basic .NET involves a reader or writer object and a stream object.

3. Create a **BinaryReader** or **StreamReader** object that is linked to the stream created in Step 2.

4. Use the reader's methods to read data from the file.

5. Close the file.

For writing to a file, follow these steps:

1. Open the file by creating a stream associated with it. If the file already exists, you will specify if it is to be replaced or if new data will be appended to the end of the existing data in the file.

2. Create a **BinaryWriter** or **StreamWriter** object that is linked to the stream created in Step 1.

3. Use the writer's methods to write data to the file.

4. Close the file.

Remember that file access code should always be placed in a **Try** block to guard against exceptions.

The File Class

File is an abstract class that provides a set of static members for working with files. Some of these members deal with file management and are covered later in the chapter. This section covers those **File** methods that are relevant to file access. For the most part, these methods deal with opening files. There are several methods for opening files, and the one you will use depends on the following choices:

- Whether you are opening an existing file or creating a new file
- Whether you are opening a text or a binary file
- Whether you want the method to return a **StreamReader** or **StreamWriter** object or a **FileStream** object

Some of these methods will open a file if it exists and, if not, create a new file. Other methods expect to find an existing file and, if it is not found, will throw an exception. You should carefully choose the method you will use based on exactly what you need to accomplish. In any case, statements that work with files should always be in a **Try...Catch** block because of the many potential exceptions that can occur with file access. Table 16.3 describes members of the **File** class that are related to file access. Table 16.4 describes enumeration members used by the **File** class's **Open()** method.

The **Open()** method is the most flexible member of the **File** class. The entry in Table 16.2 explains its most simple use, but this method is overloaded and can provide different

Table 16.3 Members of the File class that are related to file access.

Method	Description
AppendText(*path*)	Returns a **StreamWriter** for appending text to the file specified by ***path***. If the file does not exist, it is created.
Create(*path*)	Creates a new file specified by ***path*** and returns a **FileStream** associated with the file. If the file already exists, it is replaced.
CreateText(*path*)	Creates a new text file specified by ***path*** and returns a **StreamWriter** associated with the file. If the file already exists, it is replaced.
Exists(*path*)	Returns True if the file specified by ***path*** exists, False if not.
Open(*path, filemode*)	Opens the file specified by ***path*** in the specified mode, and returns a **FileStream** associated with the file. ***Mode*** can be one of the **FileMode** enumeration members (see Table 16.4). See the main text for more details on the **Open()** method.
OpenRead(*path*)	Opens the existing file specified by ***path*** for reading and returns a **FileStream** associated with the file. If the file does not exist, a **FileNotFoundException** is thrown.
OpenText(*path*)	Opens the existing text file specified by ***path*** for reading and returns a **StreamReader** associated with the file. If the file does not exist, a **FileNotFoundException** is thrown.
OpenWrite(*path*)	Opens the existing file specified by ***path*** for reading and writing and returns a **FileStream** associated with the file. If the file does not exist, a **FileNotFoundException** is thrown.

Table 16.4 FileMode enumeration members used by the File class's Open() method.

Constant	Description
Append	Opens the file for writing and appends new data to the end of the file. If the file does not exist, a new one is created.
Create	Creates a new file, overwriting any existing file.
CreateNew	Creates a new file. If the file already exists, an **IOException** is thrown.
Open	Opens an existing file for reading. If the file does not exist, a **FileNotFoundException** is thrown.
OpenOrCreate	Opens an existing file for reading. If the file does not exist, a new file is created.
Truncate	Opens an existing file and truncates its length to zero (erases existing data in the file). If the file does not exist, a **FileNotFoundException** is thrown.

capabilities as needed. Specifically, you can indicate the type of read/write access to the file that your program will have, and the type of read/write access that other processes will have while your program has the file open. The overloaded syntax for the **Open()** method is as follows:

```
Open(path, FileMode, FileAccess)
Open(path, FileMode, FileAccess, FileShare)
```

A Note about Paths

When you specify a path, you can use a relative path, an absolute path, or a UNC (Universal Naming Convention) path (for servers and shares). A relative path is relative to the application directory. For example, data.txt refers to the file data.txt in the application directory, and *"user\data.txt"* refers to the file data.txt in the directory user off the application directory. An absolute path specifies a non-relative location; for example, *"c:\my documents\data.txt"*. A UNC path specifies a location in terms of server and share names; for example, *"\\BigServer\PublicShare"*.

The ***FileAccess*** argument specifies the access to the file. It can be one of the following **FileAccess** enumeration members: **Read**, **Write**, or **ReadWrite**. The ***FileShare*** argument specifies the access that other process have to the file while it is open. It can be one of the following **FileShare** enumeration members: **None**, **Read**, **Write**, **ReadWrite**.

Let's look at some examples of using the **File** class's members. There will be many more examples later in the chapter, so I will present only a few here. This code creates a new file named data.txt:

```
Dim fs As FileStream
fs = File.Create("data.txt")
```

This code checks to see if a file exists. If so, it is opened for reading as a text file. If it does not exist, a message is displayed to the user:

```
Dim r As StreamReader
Const FILENAME = "mydata.txt"
If File.Exists(FILENAME) Then
    r = File.OpenText(FILENAME)
Else
    MsgBox("The file " & FILENAME & " Does not exist.")
End If
```

The following code opens a file for reading. Other processes are prevented from accessing the file while it is open. If the file does not exist, the exception is caught and a message displayed to the user:

```
Dim fs As FileStream
Try
    fs = File.Open("private.dat", FileMode.Open, _
        FileAccess.Read, FileShare.None)
Catch ex As FileNotFoundException
    MsgBox("The file was not found")
End Try
```

The FileStream Class

The **FileStream** class represents a stream that is connected to a file. Although a **FileStream** object is involved in reading and writing file data, it does not do this alone—rather, it must be associated with a reader or writer class (these classes have been mentioned earlier, and will be covered in detail later in the chapter). The **FileStream** class provides several overloaded constructors that can be used to create a **FileStream** object associated with a specific file. Also, you can obtain a **FileStream** reference from some of the **File** class's methods, as was covered in the previous section. After you have a reference to a **FileStream** object, you can use its members to get information about the underlying stream and perform certain manipulations on it.

The **FileStream** class has numerous constructors. The ones you will need most often are as follows:

```
New(path, filemode)
New(path, filemode, fileaccess)
New(path, filemode, fileaccess, fileshare)
```

Path is a string specifying the absolute or relative path of the file.

Filemode is a member of the **FileMode** enumeration, as listed in Table 16.4, that specifies how the file is to be opened.

Fileaccess is a member of the **FileAccess** enumeration specifying the file's access: **Read**, **Write**, or **ReadWrite**.

Fileshare is a member of the **FileShare** enumeration specifying the access other processes will have to the file: **None**, **Read**, **Write**, or **ReadWrite**.

A stream that is associated with a file has both a position and a length. The length is, of course, the length of the file in bytes, which for text files is the number of characters it contains. The position can be thought of as a pointer that indicates where in the file the next read or write operation will occur. When an existing file is opened, the pointer is typically at the start of the file, position 0. One exception is when the file is opened using the **AppendText()** method, in which case the pointer is at the end of the file (where position = length). The **FileStream** class has methods that let you manipulate the position of the pointer, but for many read and write operations this is handled automatically. **FileStream** class members, including those related to the file pointer, are described in Table 16.5.

The following example shows how to create a **FileStream** associated with the file data.txt, opening the file if it exists, or creating it if it doesn't exist. The file pointer is then set to the end of the file:

```
Dim fs As New FileStream("data.txt", FileMode.OpenOrCreate)
fs.Position = fs.Length
```

Table 16.5 Members of the FileStream class.

Member	Description
Lock(position, length)	Prevents other processes from accessing all or part of the file. The arguments are type **Long** values specifying the starting position and length of the file range to lock.
Name	Returns the name of the stream (that was used to open it).
Unlock(*position, length*)	Permits other processes to access all or part of the file that was previously locked. The arguments are type **Long** values specifying the starting position and length of the file range to unlock.
Seek(*offset, origin*)	Sets the stream pointer to the specified position. ***Offset*** is the distance to move the pointer, and ***origin*** specifies whether ***offset*** is to be calculated from the beginning of the file, the end of the file, or the current pointer position. Possible values for this argument are the following members of the **SeekOrigin** enumeration: **Begin**, **Current**, and **End**.
Length	Returns the length of the file.
Position	Gets or sets the current file position.

Note that another way of setting the file position to the end of the file is as follows:

```
fs.Seek(0, SeekOrigin.End)
```

Remember that, by itself, a **FileStream** object does not let you access the contents of a file. To do so, you need one of the writer or reader classes, covered in the following sections.

The BinaryReader Class

You use the **BinaryReader** class to read data from files that contain binary data or text data with certain encodings. The class must be associated with a stream that is connected to the file. You learned how to create a stream earlier in this chapter. After you have the stream, you create a **BinaryReader** object and associate it with the stream by using one of the class's two constructors:

```
New(input)
New(input, encoding)
```

Input is a reference to the stream. ***Encoding*** specifies the character encoding and can be one of the following members of the **Encoding** enumeration: **ASCIIEncoding, UnicodeEncoding, UTF7Encoding, UTF8Encoding**. Please see the sidebar "Character Encoding" for more information. For most applications, where you are reading binary data such as numbers rather than encoded text, you will use the first of these two constructors.

Here is an example that creates a stream associated with a file, then connects that stream to a **BinaryReader** object:

```
Dim fs As FileStream
Dim br As BinaryReader

fs = New FileStream("data.txt", _
    FileMode.OpenOrCreate, FileAccess.ReadWrite)
br = New BinaryReader(fs)
```

The **BinaryReader** class has numerous methods for reading data from the file. These methods fall into two general categories:

- Data-type specific methods read a single "unit" of data from the file and return the result. A unit corresponds to any of Visual Basic's data types. For example, the **ReadInt16()** method reads a type **Short** from the file. The return type of each of the data-specific methods is the same as the data type they read.
- Non-specific methods read a specified number of bytes or characters from the file and return an array containing the data.

These methods are explained in Table 16.6 with additional details given in the main text.

All of these methods (with the single exception of the **PeekChar()** method) advance the file pointer as needed. This means that you can call these methods repeatedly to read the entire contents of a file in sequence. Whichever method you are using, your code needs some means to avoid trying to read beyond the end of the file, which would cause an **EndOfStreamException**. There are several techniques you can use to deal with the end of file:

- You may know how many data items are in the file. This may be the case if your program created the file and now needs to read from it. If you stored, say, 100 type **Integer** data items in the file, then you know that you can read 100 type **Integer** data items back from the file without an end of file exception.

Table 16.6 Data reading methods of the BinaryReader class.

Method	Action
PeekChar()	Returns the next character (byte) from the file but does not advance the file pointer.
ReadBoolean()	Reads a type **Boolean** from the file.
ReadByte()	Reads a type **Byte** from the file.
ReadBytes(*n*)	Reads *n* bytes from the file and returns them in a byte array.
ReadChar()	Reads a type **Char** from the file.
ReadChars(*n*)	Reads *n* characters from the file and returns them in a character array.
ReadDecimal()	Reads a type **Decimal** from the file.
ReadDouble()	Reads a type **Double** from the file.
ReadInt16()	Reads a type **Short** from the file.
ReadInt32()	Reads a type **Integer** from the file.
ReadInt64()	Reads a type **Long** from the file.
ReadSingle()	Reads a type **Single** from the file.

Character Encoding

Characters (letters, numbers, punctuation marks, and so on) are represented by numbers. A character encoding provides the mapping between the numbers and the characters they represent. The Windows operating system uses the Unicode character encoding, but several different character encodings are also in use by other systems, and the .NET framework provides the tools to read and write files in these non-Unicode encodings. Specifically, the ASCII, UTF7, and UTF8 encodings are supported. You can refer to the online help for full information on working with different character encodings.

- Obtain the file length from the **FileStream** object's **Length** property and divide by the length of the data item that the file holds. For example, suppose that the file length is 1000 and the data it holds is type **Short**. Because a type **Short** is 2 bytes long, you know that the file contains 1000/2, or 500, data items. To get information on the length of Visual Basic's data types, view the data type summary in the Help information.
- Call the **PeekChar()** method repeatedly, before each read operation. As long as **PeekChar()** does not return -1, you know that end of file has not been reached. For example, if bw is a reference to the **BinaryWriter** object, you would write the following:

```
While bw.PeekChar <> -1
...
' Read data here.
...
End While
```

When you're reading data from a binary file, it is essential to remember that the **BinaryReader** class and its methods have no way of knowing what data is stored in the file. This means that, for example, you can call the **ReadDouble()** method on any file and it will read the proper number of bytes from the file (8, in this case), interpret these bytes as a type **Double**, and return the result to the program. This will work regardless of what was originally stored in the file. If, for example, the file has text stored in it, **ReadDouble()** will still work in the sense that no exception occurs, but the data it returns will be garbage. The bottom line is that you must be aware of what data is stored in a file and then use the appropriate **BinaryReader** methods to read the data into your program.

Closing Streams

When you are done using a **BinaryWriter** object, you should close the stream it is associated with, which results in the file being closed. To do so, call the **Close()** method of the **BinaryWriter** object.

Accessing the Underlying Stream

For most operations, the **BinaryReader** object manages the underlying **FileStream** object without the need for any intervention on the part of the programmer. This refers specifically to managing the file position pointer, which is adjusted automatically by any read operation. At times, however, you may need to access the underlying **FileStream** directly, to manipulate the pointer when you are not performing a straight start-to-end reading of the file data. You can access a **BinaryWriter** object's base stream using its **BaseStream** property. For example, this code moves the file pointer of the stream associated with the **BinaryWriter** object bw to the start of the file:

```
bw.BaseStream.Seek(0, SeekOrigin.Begin)
```

Likewise, you need to access the underlying stream to determine the length of the file:

```
Filelen = bw.BaseStream.Length
```

I will present a demonstration of using the **BinaryReader** class later, combined with the **BinaryWriter** demonstration.

The BinaryWriter Class

The **BinaryWriter** class is used to write binary data to a file. Like its partner, the **BinaryReader** class, this class must be associated with a **FileStream** object that is connected to the file. You learned earlier in the chapter how to create a **FileStream** object that is associated with a file. To create the **BinaryWriter** and associate it with the stream, you use this syntax (assuming that fs is a reference to the **FileStream** object):

```
Dim bw As BinaryWriter
bw = New BinaryWriter(fs)
```

To write a single item of data to a file, you use the **Write()** method. This method is overloaded and can accept any of Visual Basic .NET's simple data types (**Char**, **Byte**, **Integer**, and so on). The data is written to the file at the current pointer position, and the point is advanced automatically.

The **Write()** method is also overloaded for writing arrays of type **Byte** and type **Char**. The syntax is as follows:

```
Write(buf(), index, count)
```

Buf() is an array of type **Byte** or type **Char**. ***Index*** is the position in the array to start at, with the first element being at position 0. ***Count*** is the number of array elements to write to the file. If the length of ***buf()*** is less than ***index*** plus ***count***, an **ArgumentException** is thrown. If ***index*** or ***count*** is negative, an **ArgumentOutOfRangeException** is thrown. Only type **Byte** and type **Char** arrays can be written in a single operation. For other types of arrays, you must write the array elements one at a time. Other members of the **BinaryWriter** class are explained in Table 16.7.

Table 16.7 Additional members of the BinaryWriter class.

Member	Description
Close()	Closes the **BinaryWriter** and its underlying stream.
Flush()	Flushes all data from memory buffers to the file.
Seek(*offset*, *origin*)	Sets the stream pointer to the specified position. ***Offset*** is the distance to move the pointer, and ***origin*** specifies whether ***offset*** is to be calculated from the beginning of the file, the end of the file, or the current pointer position. Possible values for this argument are the following members of the **SeekOrigin** enumeration: **Begin**, **Current**, and **End**.
BaseStream	Returns a reference to the underlying stream object.

A Binary File Demonstration

Listing 16.1 presents a demonstration of using the **BinaryWriter** class to write data to a file, and then using the **BinaryReader** class to read the data back into the program for display. The code is meant to run in a Windows application, which you create as follows:

1. Create a new Windows application.
2. Add a Button control to the form. Change its Caption property to “Go”.
3. Add a TextBox control to the form. Change its **MultiLine** property to True, and increase the height of the control so it can display several lines of text.
4. Add code to the Button control’s **Click()** event procedure, as shown in Listing 16.1.

When you run the project, the form displays with an empty text box. Clicking the button causes the integers 1 through 20 to be written to the file data.dat. Then the data is read in from the file and displayed in the text box, as shown in Figure 16.2.

Listing 16.1 A demonstration of writing and reading a binary file.

```
Private Sub Button1_Click(ByVal sender As System.Object, _
      ByVal e As System.EventArgs) Handles Button1.Click
    Dim fs As FileStream
    Dim br As BinaryReader
    Dim bw As BinaryWriter
    Dim i As Integer

    Try
        ' Open the file, overwriting any existing file,
        ' in write mode.
        fs = New FileStream("data.dat", FileMode.Create, _
                 FileAccess.Write)
        ' Connect a BinaryWriter to the stream.
        bw = New BinaryWriter(fs)
        ' Write 20 integer values to the file.
```

```
        For i = 1 To 20
            bw.Write(i)
        Next
        ' Close the file.
        bw.Close()
    Catch ex As Exception
        MsgBox(ex.Message)
    End Try
    Try
        ' Open the same file in read mode.
        fs = New FileStream("data.dat", FileMode.Open, _
              FileAccess.Read)
        ' Associate a BinaryReader with the stream.
        br = New BinaryReader(fs)
        ' Read integers in until end of file is reached.
        While br.PeekChar <> -1
            ' Convert this value to text and
            ' add it to the text box.
            TextBox1.Text &= CStr(br.ReadInt32) & vbCrLf
        End While
        ' Close the file.
        br.Close()
    Catch ex As Exception
        MsgBox(ex.Message)
    End Try
End Sub
```

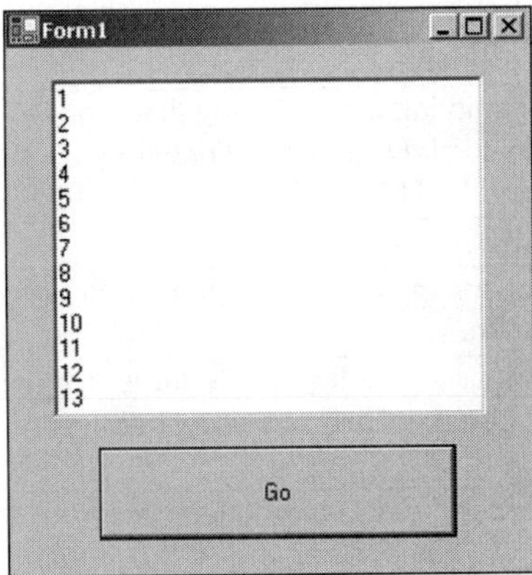

Figure 16.2
The binary file demo displays the integer values read in from the file.

The StreamReader Class

The **StreamReader** class is specialized for reading text from files. This class has a variety of constructors for various specialized uses, but the two you will use most often are as follows:

```
New(input)
New(input, encoding)
```

Input is a reference to the stream. ***Encoding*** specifies the character encoding and can be one of the following members of the **Encoding** enumeration: **ASCIIEncoding**, **UnicodeEncoding**, **UTF7Encoding**, **UTF8Encoding**. Please see the sidebar "Character Encoding" for more information. If you use the first of these two constructors, the class is instantiated to use the default UTF8 encoding.

This class has another constructor that accepts the name of a file directly, and then creates its own stream. The syntax is as follows:

```
New(filename)
```

Use of the **StreamReader** class is quite straightforward (see Table 16.8). It has methods that let you read a single character, an arbitrary number of characters, entire lines of text, or the entire file. The position of the file pointer is maintained automatically, but for special situations you can change it using the **Seek** method of the underlying stream (accessed with the **BaseStream** property).

Table 16.8 Members of the StreamReader class.

Member	Description
BaseStream	Returns a reference to the underlying stream.
CurrentEncoding	Returns **CurrentEncoding** constant specifying the encoding that the **StreamReader** is using. Possible returns values are **ASCIIEncoding**, **UnicodeEncoding**, **UTF7Encoding**, and **UTF8Encoding**.
Close()	Closes the **StreamReader** and its underlying stream.
Peek()	Returns the next character without advancing the stream pointer. Returns -1 if the position is at the end of the stream.
Read()	Reads the next character and returns it as a type **Integer**. Returns -1 if the end of the stream has been reached. Use the **Chr()** function to convert the return value to a character.
ReadBlock(*buf(), index, count*)	*Buf()* is an array of type **Char**. The method reads ***count*** characters from the file and places them in ***buf()*** starting at array position ***index***. If ***count*** is greater than the length of ***buf()*** minus ***index***, an **ArgumentException** is thrown.
ReadLine()	Reads a line of text from the file and returns it as a type **String**.
ReadToEnd()	Reads to the end of the file and returns the result as a type **String**.

Let's look at some examples of using the **StreamReader** class. The following code opens the file test.txt and reads its entire contents into the specified TextBox:

```
Dim sr As StreamReader
sr = File.OpenText("test.txt")
TextBox1.Text = sr.ReadToEnd()
sr.Close()
```

The following is an alternate way to write the above code, using a different **StreamReader** constructor:

```
Dim sr As StreamReader("test.txt")
TextBox1.Text = sr.ReadToEnd()
sr.Close()
```

This code opens the same file and reads characters up to and including the first exclamation point (or end of file, whichever comes first). The resulting string is stored in the variable **buf**:

```
Dim sr As StreamReader
Dim buf As String
Dim input As Integer

sr = File.OpenText("test.txt")
Do
    input = sr.Read()
    If input = -1 Then Exit Do
    buf &= Chr(input)
    If input = Asc("!") Then Exit Do
Loop While True
sr.Close()
```

The following code opens the file and reads its entire contents into an array of type **Char**. Then it goes through the array and counts the number of occurrences of the character "x," and displays the count in a message box:

```
Dim sr As StreamReader
Dim c As Char
Dim total As Long = 0

sr = File.OpenText("test.txt")
Dim buf(sr.BaseStream.Length) As Char
sr.ReadBlock(buf, 0, sr.BaseStream.Length)
sr.Close()
```

```
For Each c In buf
    If c = "x" Then total += 1
Next
MsgBox(total.ToString)
```

The StreamWriter Class

The **StreamWriter** class is used for writing text data to a stream. By default it uses UTF8 encoding, but other character encodings are supported as well. Two of the class constructors associate the **StreamWriter** with an existing **FileStream**:

```
New(output)
New(output, encoding)
```

Output is a reference to the stream that is connected to the output file. ***Encoding*** specifies the character encoding and can be one of the following members of the **Encoding** enumeration: **ASCIIEncoding**, **UnicodeEncoding**, **UTF7Encoding**, and **UTF8Encoding**.

Another **StreamWriter** constructor accepts the name of a file and creates its own stream:

```
New(filename)
```

Text files are usually organized by lines, consisting of some text followed by a line termination character. You have seen how the **StreamReader** class can read text in on a line-by-line basis. The **StreamWriter** class mirrors this capability with the Ability to write text out a line at a time. You can also write partial lines and blank lines. The members of the **StreamWriter** class are described in Table 16.9.

Table 16.9 Members of the StreamWriter class.

Member	Description
BaseStream	Returns a reference to the underlying stream.
CurrentEncoding	Returns **CurrentEncoding** constant specifying the encoding that the **StreamWriter** is using. Possible returns values are **ASCIIEncoding**, **UnicodeEncoding**, **UTF7Encoding**, and **UTF8Encoding**.
Close()	Closes the **StreamWriter** and its underlying stream.
Newline	Specifies the line termination character(s). The default is a carriage return line feed combination ("\r\n") . For output text to be readable by **StreamReader**, use only "\n" or "\r\n".
Write(*item*), **WriteLine(*item*)**	Writes ***item*** to the file. Item can be any of Visual Basic's simple data types, such as **Char**, **Integer**, or **Double**. It can also be an array of type **Char**. For non-text types, the data is converted to a string before being written. If ***item*** is an object reference, the object's **ToString()** method is called and the result is written. **WriteLine()** appends a newline character to the output, whereas **Write()** does not. Call **WriteLine()** with no arguments to write a blank line to the file.

(continued)

Table 16.9 Members of the StreamWriter class *(continued)*.

Member	Description
Write(*buf()*, *index*, *count*) and **WriteLine(*buf()*, *index*, *count*)**	Writes ***count*** characters from type **Char** array ***buf()*** to the file, starting at array position ***index***. If ***index*** plus ***count*** is greater than the length of ***buf()***, an **ArgumentException** is thrown. **WriteLine()** appends a newline character to the output, whereas **Write()** does not.

A Text File Demonstration

The program presented in this section demonstrates both text file input and text file output. It is a console application, to be run from the command line. Written as a complete application, it includes the exception handling and other features that a real-world application should have. For example, it does not assume the input file exists but checks for it and displays a message to the user if it is not found.

The program's function is to read an entire text file and check for lines that are more than 40 characters long. All lines that are 40 characters or fewer are written to the output file unchanged. Lines longer than 40 characters are split into two or more lines of 40 or fewer characters, and these lines are written to the output file. The code is well commented, and you should be able to figure out its operation by looking at the source code in Listing 16.2.

Here's how to create and run this project:

1. Create a new console application, assigning it a name like TextFileDemo.
2. Delete all the code from the application's module, then paste the code from Listing 16.2 into the module.
3. Press Ctrl+Shift+B to build the application.
4. Use a text editor to create an input file, and save it in the \bin directory off the project directory. Or you can copy an existing text file to that directory. Tip: If you are not sure where the project directory is, select the Save Module1.vb As command from the Visual Studio File menu. The Save File As dialog box will point at the project directory.
5. From the Windows Start menu, open a Command Prompt window (sometimes called an MS-DOS window). In this window, navigate to the bin directory off the project directory. Verify that this directory contains a file named *xxxx*.exe, where *xxxx* is the name you assigned to the project.
6. Enter the command "*xxxx*.exe *infile outfile*", where *infile* is the name of the text file you created or copied to the folder, and *outfile* is the name of the file where you want the program's output placed.

After the program runs, assuming there were no errors, you can use a text editor to open the output file and verify that all lines longer than 40 characters have been split into shorter lines.

Listing 16.2 A console application that demonstrates text file input and output.

```
Imports System.IO
Module Module1
    Private Const MAXLINELENGTH = 40
    Sub Main()
        Dim s As String
        ' Check the command line arguments.
        Dim args() As String
        args = GetCommandLineArgs()
        ' Ensure 2 arguments. If not display usage info and quit.
        If args.GetLength(0) <> 2 Then
            s = "Usage: TextFileDemo inputfilename outputfilename"
            Console.WriteLine(s)
            Exit Sub
        End If
        ' Get the input and output file names.
        Dim infile As String = args(0)
        Dim outfile As String = args(1)

        ' Make sure the input file exists.
        If Not File.Exists(infile) Then
            s = infile & " cannot be found."
            Console.WriteLine(s)
            Exit Sub
        End If

        ' If the output file exists, check to see
        ' if overwriting it is OK.
        If File.Exists(outfile) Then
            s = outfile & "alread exists. Overwrite (y or n)?"
            Console.WriteLine(s)
            Dim reply As Integer = Console.Read()
            If reply <> Asc("y") Then Exit Sub
        End If
        ' StreamReader and StreamWriter objects.
        Dim input As StreamReader
        Dim output As StreamWriter

        Try
            input = New StreamReader(infile)
            output = New StreamWriter(outfile)

            Do While True
                s = input.ReadLine
                ' End of file?
                If s = Nothing Then Exit Do
                ' If line is within permitted length, write it
```

```
                ' to the output file.
                If s.Length <= MAXLINELENGTH Then
                    output.WriteLine(s)
                    ' Otherwise break it into MAXLINELENGTH character
                    ' sections and write each one.
                Else
                    Do While Len(s) > MAXLINELENGTH
                        output.WriteLine(Left(s, MAXLINELENGTH))
                        s = Right(s, Len(s) - MAXLINELENGTH)
                    Loop
                    output.WriteLine(s)
                End If
            Loop
        Catch ex As IOException
            Console.WriteLine(ex.Message)
        Finally
            input.Close()
            output.Close()
        End Try
    End Sub
    Function GetCommandLineArgs() As String()
        ' This function retrieves the command line arguments
        ' and returns them in a string array.
        Dim seps As String = " "
        Dim cmds As String = Command()
        Dim a() As String = cmds.Split(seps.ToCharArray)
        Return a
    End Function
End Module
```

File Management

Distinct from file access, *file management* refers to the tasks of creating and deleting directories, copying, deleting and moving files, and obtaining information about drives, directories, and files. .NET's object-oriented approach to this area is clear and easy to use. There are two classes for working with files, and two classes for working with drives and directories.

Working with Files

There are two .NET classes for working with files—**File** and **FileInfo** classes. The differences between these two classes are described in the following list:

- The **FileInfo** class requires that you create an instance of the class associated with a particular file, and its members (for the most part) operate on that file. In contrast, the **File** class doesn't require (or permit) an instance to be created. You call its members and pass as a parameter the name of the file on which to operate.

- The **File** class methods all perform a security check when called, whereas **FileInfo** methods do not always require a security check. If you need to perform multiple operations on the same file, it is usually more efficient to use the **FileInfo** class.

For example, suppose you want to determine the date and time that a file was created. This is how you would do it with the **File** class:

```
Dim d As DateTime
d = File.GetCreationTime("c:\SomeFile.txt")
```

In contrast, here's the code needed to perform the same task using the **FileInfo** class. This example shows the **FileInfo** constructor, which takes the name of the file, including path, as its one argument:

```
Dim d As DateTime
Dim f As New FileInfo("c:\SomeFile.txt")
d = f.CreationTime
```

Table 16.10 shows the members of the **File** and **FileInfo** classes that perform commonly needed file-management tasks. As you may expect, these file-management members provide many opportunities for exceptions to be thrown. Trying to copy a nonexistent file, passing a file name/path that is too long, or trying to delete a file when you lack the required permissions are just a few examples. I advise that you protect all file-management code to ensure that unhandled exceptions cannot occur. You can find the details of these exceptions in the Visual Basic .NET documentation.

Table 16.10 Members of the File and FileInfo classes.

To	With the FileInfo Class	With the File class
Get a type **DateTime** for when the file was created.	**CreationTime**	**GetCreationTime(*filename*)**
Get a type **DateTime** for when the file was last accessed.	**LastAccessTime**	**GetLastAccessTime(*filename*)**
Get a type **DateTime** for when the file was last written to.	**LastWriteTime**	**GetLastWriteTime(*filename*)**
Get the length of the file.	**Length**	Not available
Copy the file to a new location.	**CopyTo(*dest*, *overwrite*)** ***Dest*** is a type String specifying the new name and path for the file. ***Overwrite*** is a type Boolean specifying whether an existing file of the same name will be overwritten.	**Copy(*src*, *dest*, *overwrite*)** Copies the file ***src*** to ***dest***. ***Overwrite*** is a type Boolean specifying whether an existing file of the same name will be overwritten.
Move the file to a new location.	**MoveTo(*dest*)** ***Dest*** is a type String specifying the new name and path for the file.	**Move(*src*, *dest*)** Moves the file ***src*** to ***dest***).
Delete a file.	**Delete()**	**Delete(*filename*)**

Here are some examples of using the **File** and **FileInfo** members. To move the file c:\data\sales.xls to the folder c:\mydocs under the same name, here's the code using the **FileInfo** class:

```
Dim f As New FileInfo("c:\data\sales.xls")
f.Move("c:\mydocs\sales.xls")
```

To perform the same task using the **File** class:

```
File.Move("c:\data\sales.xls", "c:\mydocs\sales.xls")
```

To delete the file c:\docs\lastmonth.dat, you can use this code:

```
File.Delete("c:\docs\lastmonth.dat")
```

You could also use the following code:

```
Dim f As New FileInfo("c:\docs\lastmonth.dat")
f.Delete
```

Working with Directories and Drives

On a Windows computer, permanent storage—in other words, disk drives—are organized into directories (also called folders). Each drive has a single root directory. The root directory may have one or more subdirectories. Those subdirectories may in turn have their own subdirectories, and so on. Network sharing introduces additional complexity. You can refer to shared network drives and directories using their share name (e.g., \\BigServer\MyFolder) or a mapped drive letter. Tasks that you may need to perform in your Visual Basic. NET programs include the following:

- Determining what drives exist.
- Determining if a specific directory exists.
- Creating, moving, and deleting directories.
- Setting the current directory.

The .NET framework provides two classes for performing these tasks. The **Directory** class exposes static (shared) methods for working with directories, whereas the **DirectoryInfo** class provides instance methods. Both classes are part of the **System.IO** namespace. In many ways, these classes parallel the **File** and **FileInfo** classes covered in the preceding section. Because the file system treats a directory as a special kind of file, many class members that are available in the **File** and **FileInfo** classes are also present in the **Directory** and **DirectoryInfo** classes. Specifically, **FileInfo** members also present in **DirectoryInfo** are as follows:

- CreationTime
- Delete
- LastAccessTime
- LastWriteTime
- MoveTo

The **DirectoryInfo** class constructor takes as its one argument a string that specifies the directory with which it is to be associated. The syntax is as follows:

```
New(path)
```

where ***path*** is a string giving the path of the directory. An exception will be thrown if the directory does not exist, if the path string is not properly formed, if the user does not have the required permission, or of the path is longer than 256 characters. Here's an example of creating an instance of this class:

```
Dim d As New DirectoryInfo("c:\my documents")
```

File class members present in the **Directory** class are as follows:

- Delete
- GetCreationTime
- GetLastAccessTime
- GetLastWriteTime
- Move

Additional members of the **Directory** and **DirectoryInfo** classes are described in Tables 16.11 and 16.12.

Table 16.11 Additional members of the Directory class.

Class member	Description
CreateDirectory(*path*)	Creates the specified directory and, if necessary, the path to it. Returns a type **DirectoryInfo** for the new directory.
GetCurrentDirectory()	Returns a type **String** containing the path of the current working directory.
GetDirectories(*path*)	Returns, in an array of type **String**, the names of all subdirectories in the directory specified by ***path***.
GetDirectoryRoot(*path*)	Returns the volume and root information for the specified directory (for example, "c:\").
GetFiles(*path*)	Returns, in an array of type **String**, the names of all files in the specified directory.

(continued)

Table 16.11 Additional members of the Directory class *(continued)*.

Class member	Description
GetFileSystemEntries(*path*)	Returns, in an array of type **String**, the names of all files and subdirectories in the specified directory.
GetLogicalDrives()	Returns, in an array of type **String**, all the logical drives on the system in the form "<drive letter>:\".
GetParent(*path*)	Returns a type **DirectoryInfo** referencing the parent of the specified directory.
SetCurrentDirectory(*path*)	Sets the application's working directory to the specified directory.

Table 16.12 Additional members of the DirectoryInfo class.

Class member	Description
Parent	Returns a type **DirectoryInfo** referring to the parent directory of the instance directory.
Root	Returns a type **DirectoryInfo** referring to the root directory.
CreateSubdirectory(*path*)	Creates the subdirectory specified by ***path*** and returns a type **DirectoryInfo** referring to the new directory.
GetDirectories()	Returns an array of type **DirectoryInfo** containing references to all of the subdirectories in the instance directory.
GetFiles()	Returns an array of type **FileInfo** containing references to all of the files in the instance directory.

The remainder of this section provides some examples of using the **Directory** and **DirectoryInfo** classes. These samples omit exception handling, which in a real program is an important part of essentially all file-management operations you will perform. This code uses the **Directory** class to display, in the immediate window, a list of all subdirectories in the c:\my documents directory:

```
Dim sa() As String
Dim s As String
sa = Directory.GetDirectories("c:\my documents")
For Each s In sa
    Debug.WriteLine(s)
Next
```

The Working Directory

Any running application has a *working directory*. This is where the application's file operations will occur if a path isn't specified for the operation; for example, when opening a file. It's also the location from which relative path specifications are determined. During program development in Visual Studio, this is by default the \bin directory within the project directory. After deployment, it is the directory where the application's .exe file is located. It's rarely a good idea to rely on the default working directory, so your code should either change the working directory or always specify the complete path for file operations.

The following code performs the same task, but this time using the **DirectoryInfo** class:

```
Dim d As New DirectoryInfo("c:\my documents")
Dim da() As DirectoryInfo
Dim x As DirectoryInfo
da = d.GetDirectories
For Each x In da
    Debug.WriteLine(x.FullName)
Next
```

The following code snippet checks to see if a directory already exists. If so, a message to that effect is displayed. If not, it is created:

```
Const DIR_PATH = "c:\my new documents"
If Directory.Exists(DIR_PATH) Then
    MsgBox(DIR_PATH & " already exists.")
Else
    Directory.CreateDirectory(DIR_PATH)
    MsgBox(DIR_PATH & " created successfully.")
End If
```

The final demonstration makes use of the .NET file-management tools to determine the total number of files in a directory, and its subdirectories and their total size. This program uses a powerful technique known as *recursion*, whereby a function calls itself repeatedly to carry out a repetitive task. Here's how recursion works. The function, called **FilesInDirectory()**, is passed a type **DirectoryInfo** referencing the directory of interest. Code in the function obtains a list of all files in that directory and gets the count and total size of these files, adding them to a summary (maintained in a structure defined in the code). Then the code gets a list of all subdirectories that the current directory contains and calls itself for each one. As a result, the code "worms" its way down through all levels of subdirectories and gets the file information for each one. Recursion is not used very often, but in situations where it is appropriate, it's a powerful technique.

The code for this program—a Windows application—is shown in Listing 16.3. In this program, the action is triggered by a button named Button1. Figure 16.3 shows the output of the program.

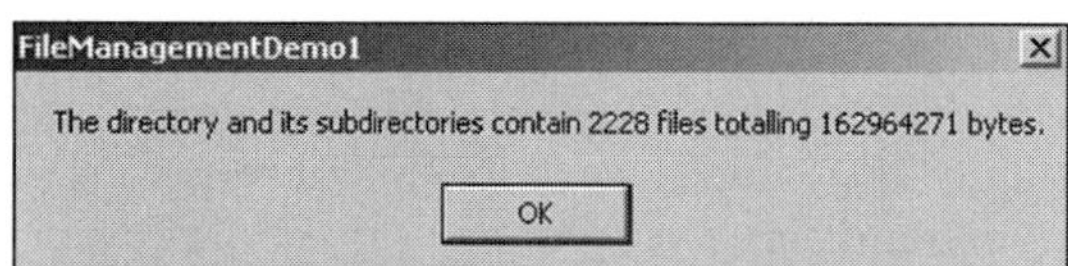

Figure 16.3
File totals displayed by the code in Listing 16.3.

Listing 16.3 Getting total file count and size in a directory.

```
Private Sub Button1_Click(ByVal sender As System.Object, ByVal e As _
  System.EventArgs) Handles Button1.Click
    Dim result As FileSummary
    Dim msg As String
    result = FilesInDirectory(New DirectoryInfo("c:\my documents"))
    msg = "The directory and its subdirectories contain "
    msg &= result.Count.ToString & " files totaling "
    msg &= result.TotalSize.ToString & " bytes."
    MsgBox(msg)
End Sub
Private Function FilesInDirectory(ByVal d As DirectoryInfo) As FileSummary
    ' returns the total number and total size of files in d
    ' and all of its subdirectories.
    Dim fs1 As New FileSummary()
    Dim fs2 As New FileSummary()
    Dim fa() As FileInfo
    Dim f As FileInfo

    ' Get the files in this directory.
    fa = d.GetFiles
    ' Add their info to the summary.
    For Each f In fa
        fs1.Count += 1
        fs1.TotalSize += f.Length
    Next
    ' Now do the same for all the subdirectories.
    Dim da() As DirectoryInfo
    Dim d1 As DirectoryInfo
    da = d.GetDirectories
    For Each d1 In da
        fs2 = FilesInDirectory(d1)
        fs1.Count += fs2.Count
        fs1.TotalSize += fs2.TotalSize
    Next
    ' Return the current totals.
    Return fs1
End Function
Structure FileSummary
    Public TotalSize As Long
    Public Count As Integer
End Structure
```

The File-Related Controls

The .NET framework provides two controls that can be very useful when your program works with files. The OpenFileDialog control provides the functionality of a File Open dialog box, and is in fact the same dialog control that is used by many Windows applications. The SaveFileDialog control provides the functionality of a File Save dialog box. These controls both inherit from the **FileDialog** class.

Readers who are familiar with Visual Basic version 6 may be wondering about its file-related controls, such as the FileListBox and DirectoryListBox controls. These controls are no longer directly supported in Visual Basic .NET; their functionality is replaced with the OpenFileDialog and SaveFileDialog controls. You can still use these controls in your project, however, by utilizing the Visual Basic 6 Compatibility library.

The OpenFileDialog Control

An example of the OpenFileDialog is shown in Figure 16.4. You can see that it offers all the features of the standard Windows Open File dialog box, including access to special folders, such as My Documents, and buttons for creating a new folder, changing the file view, and moving up one level in the directory tree.

You do not place an OpenFileDialog control on a form, as with other controls. Rather, you create it in code. The basic procedure is as follows:

1. Create an instance of the control.
2. Set its properties as needed. These properties control what directory the dialog box displays, what file types it displays, and other aspects of its operation.
3. Display the dialog box. When the user closes the dialog box, use its return value and properties to determine the user's selection.

An important property of this control is the **Filters** property. A filter limits the display of files to those whose names meet the filter criteria. For example, the filter "*.doc" displays only files with the .doc extension. A filter can use regular characters as well as the * and ? wildcards. * matches any sequence of 0 or more characters, whereas ? matches any single character.

An OpenFileDialog filter has two parts: the text that is displayed in the Files Of Type box and the actual filter criteria. The two parts are separated by the pipe (vertical bar) character. Here's an example:

```
Text Files (*.txt)|*.txt
```

The result is that the text "Text Files (*.txt)" displays in the Files Of Type box, and the OpenFileDialog displays only files with the .txt extension. You can assign multiple filters to

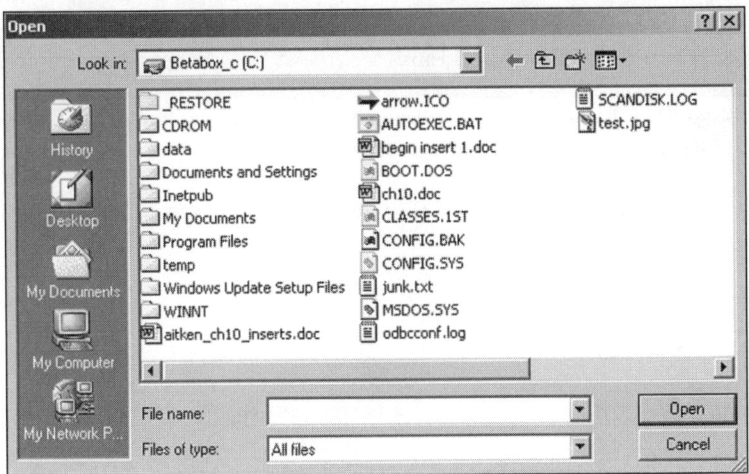

Figure 16.4
The OpenFileDialog control lets the user navigate directories and select a file.

an OpenFileDialog control, permitting the user to select a filter when the dialog box is open. To do so, separate the individual filters with the pipe character:

```
Text Files (*.txt)|*.txt|All Files|*.*
```

When you specify multiple filters, the default is for the first one to be in effect when the dialog box opens. To make another filter the default, set the **FilterIndex** property. Here's an example that creates an OpenFileDialog, sets its **Filter** property, and specifies that the second filter will be the default one:

```
Dim ofd As New OpenFileDialog()
ofd.Filter = " Text Files (*.txt)|*.txt|All Files|*.*"
ofd.FilterIndex = 2
```

Another important property of this class is **InitialDirectory**, which specifies the directory first displayed by the control. If you do not set this property, it defaults to the application directory.

After you have set the control's properties as needed, call its **ShowDialog()** method to display the dialog box. This method shows the dialog box and returns the following:

- The value **DialogResult.OK** if the user selected a file and clicked OK.
- The value **DialogResult.Cancel** if the user canceled the dialog box.

When the dialog box is closed, the program should check the return value to ensure that the user selected OK. Then there are two options:

- To open the selected file for reading and return a **Stream** object associated with the file, call the OpenFileDialog control's **OpenFile()** method.
- To retrieve the name and path of the selected file, use the **FileName** property.

The following shows an example of the first method:

```
Dim fs As filestream
Dim ofd As New OpenFileDialog()

ofd.InitialDirectory = "c:\"
ofd.Filter = "All files|*.*|Text Files (*.txt)|*.txt"

If ofd.ShowDialog = DialogResult.OK Then
    fs = ofd.OpenFile
    ' Code to read from fs goes here.
End If
```

The same result would be obtained with the following code:

```
Dim fs As filestream
Dim ofd As New OpenFileDialog()
ofd.InitialDirectory = "c:\"
ofd.Filter = "All files|*.*|Text Files (*.txt)|*.txt"

If ofd.ShowDialog = DialogResult.OK Then
    fs = New FileStream(ofd.FileName, IO.FileMode.Open)
    ' Code to read from fs goes here.
End If
```

As you can see, using the OpenFileDialog control is fairly simple and saves a lot of effort when compared with creating your own dialog class for the same purpose. Table 16.13 lists additional members of the OpenFileDialog control.

Table 16.13 Additional members of the OpenFileDialog control.

Member	Description
CheckFileExists	If this property is True (the default), the dialog box displays a warning if the user enters the name of a file that does not exist.
CheckPathExists	If this property is True (the default), the dialog box displays a warning if the user enters a pathname that does not exist.

(continued)

Table 16.13 Additional members of the OpenFileDialog control *(continued)*.

Member	Description
DereferenceLinks	If this property is True (the default), then when the user selects a shortcut the dialog box returns the name of the file referenced by the shortcut. If False, it returns the name of the shortcut file.
FileNames	Returns an array of type **String** containing the names of all selected files. Applicable only when **MultiSelect** is True.
MultiSelect	If True, the user can select multiple files in the dialog box. The default is False.
Reset()	Resets all dialog box properties to their default values.
RestoreDirectory	If True, the current directory is restored to its original value when the dialog box is closed. The default is False.
Title	The title of the dialog box.

The SaveFileDialog Control

The SaveFileDialog control is shown in Figure 16.5. It is identical to the standard Windows Save As dialog box, and offers the user access to special folders, network locations, and so on. Its operation is similar in many respects to the OpenFileDialog control that was covered in the preceding section. In broad outline, these are the steps involved in using the SaveFileDialog control:

1. Create an instance of the control.
2. Set the **Filter** property to control which file types will be displayed. By default, all files are displayed.

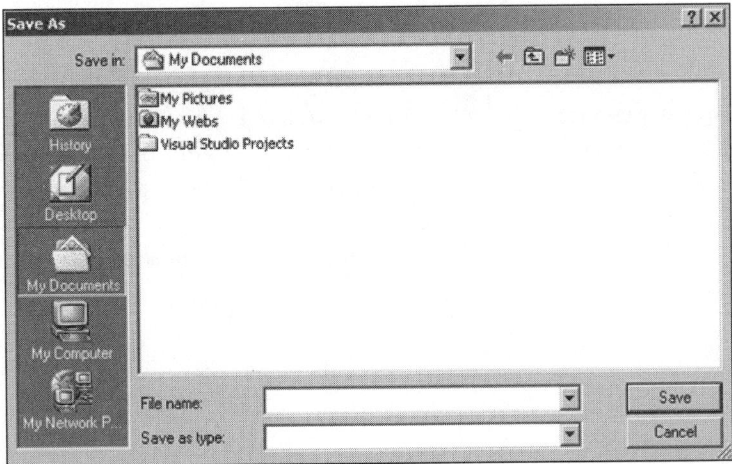

Figure 16.5
The SaveFileDialog control lets the user navigate directories and either enter or select a file name.

3. Set the **FileName** property to set the initial file name.
4. Display the control with the **ShowDialog()** method.
5. Examine the method's return value and the control properties to determine the user's selection.

Let's look at a typical example of using the SaveFileDialog. Suppose that your application saves its data in files with the .xyz extension, and that you want to offer the user a default name in the form data1.xyz, data2.xyz, and so on. Suppose also that your program's default data directory is c:\data. The following code would display the SaveFileDialog as needed:

```
Dim sfd As New SaveFileDialog()
sfd.Filter = "XYZ files|*.xyz"
sfd.FileName = "data1.xyz"
sfd.InitialDirectory = "c:\data"

If sfd.ShowDialog() = DialogResult.OK Then
    ' Code to save file goes here.
    ' Full path of selected filename is retrieved
   '  from the FileName property.
End If
```

Because the operation of the SaveFileDialog control is similar to the OpenFileDialog control, they share many members, including **Filter**, **FilterIndex**, **InitialDirectory**, **FileName**, and **Title**. Please refer to "The OpenFileDialog Control" section for details on these members.

Summary

The .NET framework provides a rich set of classes for file-related operations. Both text and non-text files can be written to and read from with complete flexibility. The way in which .NET treats files as streams makes many input and output operations easy to implement and simple to adapt for different situations. File management is also well covered. Creating, moving, deleting, and copying both files and directories can be accomplished with minimal effort on the part of the programmer.

Chapter 17
Graphics and Printing

The term *graphics* encompasses a wide range of capabilities for the Visual Basic .NET programmer. It might be something as simple as displaying an image on a Windows form, or it could be as complex as creating a sophisticated chart that can be displayed on-screen as well as printed. The .NET framework provides a rich set of classes for just about any graphics need you could imagine. This includes printing and displaying text. This chapter covers the most important parts of .NET's graphics capabilities, starting with using the PictureBox control to display images on a form. Next, I explain how to use the **Graphics** and related classes to perform drawing and text output, and how the **Bitmap** class is used to encapsulate existing images. Finally, the chapter shows you how to send graphical output to the printer.

The PictureBox Control

The PictureBox control is used to display a graphics image. Most often the image originates in a file such as a bitmap, JPEG, icon, Windows metafile, and so on. You can specify the image to display at design time or in code at runtime. The control provides members for controlling the size, position, and clipping of the image. To select an image at design time, use the control's **Image** property. When you set this property, Visual Studio displays a dialog box from which you can select an image file to use. The image becomes a part of your project that is no longer dependent on the image file. The original image file can be changed or deleted without affecting the image displayed in the control.

Changes from VB 6

The PictureBox control has undergone major changes from the Visual Basic 6 version. In .NET, the control is a lot simpler in that it cannot serve as a container for other controls (use the Panel control instead) and it does not provide its own drawing methods. In essence, the new PictureBox control is for displaying images and that's all.

To specify the image at runtime, set the control's **Image** property to an **Image** object representing the file. There are two types of **Image** objects—**Bitmap** and **Metafile**—and they will be explained in more detail later in this chapter. For now, all you need to know is the syntax:

```
PictureBox1.Image = New Bitmap(filename)
PictureBox1.Image = New Metafile(filename)
```

The same PictureBox control can host multiple images during program execution, with each newly loaded image replacing the previous one.

Image display is controlled by the **SizeMode** property. Settings for this property are members of the **PictureBoxSizeMode** enumeration, as described in Table 17.1.

By default, a PictureBox control has no border, but you can display one by setting its **BorderStyle** property to either **BorderStyle.Fixed3D** or **BorderStyle.FixedSingle**.

Graphics

The **System.Drawing** namespace encompasses a wide array of classes, structures, and enumerations that provide a powerful set of graphics tools. In this context, the term *graphics* includes the display of text as well as shapes and images. The support for graphics operations is truly impressive. In addition to the basic graphics functionality in the **System.Drawing** namespace, there are specialized tools for two-dimensional graphics (in **System.Drawing.Drawing2D**), for working with bitmap and metafile images (in **System.Drawing.Imaging**), and for working with text (in **System.Drawing.Text**). The many highly specialized components in these various namespaces are for the most part beyond the scope of this book. This

Table 17.1 Settings for the PictureBox control's SizeMode property.

Constant	Description
AutoSize	The PictureBox's size changes to fit the image's native size.
CenterImage	The image is centered in the PictureBox. If the image is smaller than the control, a blank space is displayed between the edges of the image and the edges of the control. If the image is larger than the control, it is clipped on all four edges.
Normal	The image is displayed in the top-left corner of the PictureBox; neither the image's nor the control's size is changed. This is the default setting.
StretchImage	The image is expanded or shrunk to fit the PictureBox.

section will concentrate on the graphics fundamentals that you need to display text, images, and basic shapes in your Visual Basic programs.

.NET graphics are based on the abstract concept of a *drawing surface*, which can be thought of as a sheet of paper where you draw shapes, display text, and so on. A drawing surface is sometimes connected to a specific *device context* that represents the physical device where the graphics are being created. A drawing surface can also be associated with an image that is in memory (but is not displayed), permitting modifications and additions to the image. If you are going to create graphics in a Windows Form, for example, you will use a device context that is associated with that window. If you are sending graphics to the printer, you will use a device context for the printer. This approach has the advantages that the code for creating graphics is essentially the same regardless of whether the graphics are going to the screen or to a printer. Special considerations for printing will be covered later in this chapter. A device context can also represent an existing image, permitting the use of graphics operations to modify the image.

Introduction to the Graphics Class

The **Graphics** class encapsulates a Graphics Device Interface (GDI+, with the "+" indicating the newest version) drawing surface, and as such it will be involved in just about any graphics operations you do. To instantiate a **Graphics** object for a Windows Form, use the **CreateGraphics()** method. For example, look at this code snippet:

```
Dim MyGraphics As Graphics
MyGraphics = Me.CreateGraphics
```

Here, the **Me** keyword refers to the form that the code is in, so the resulting **Graphics** object is associated with the device context for the form. At this point, the **Graphics** object is ready to be used for drawing. Listing 17.1 shows a simple example of drawing code, with the output shown in Figure 17.1. To create this project, start a new Windows application project,

Figure 17.1
Demonstrating some simple drawing tasks.

place a single Button control on the form, and place the code from the listing in the **Click()** event procedure for the button.

Listing 17.1 Code to draw some text and shapes on a form.

```
Private Sub Button1_Click(ByVal sender As System.Object, _
        ByVal e As System.EventArgs) Handles Button1.Click

    Dim g As Graphics
    g = Me.CreateGraphics

    Dim p As New Pen(System.Drawing.Color.Red)
    g.DrawEllipse(p, 50, 50, 75, 45)

    Dim b As New SolidBrush(System.Drawing.Color.Black)
    g.FillRectangle(b, 170, 50, 65, 85)

    Dim f As New Font("Times", 25)
    g.DrawString("Hello, world.", f, b, 25, 150)

End Sub
```

You should note a few things about this code that provide some insight into how the **Graphics** class works. There is a separate method for each type of drawing operation: in this case, to create an ellipse, a rectangle, and text, but there are lots more. Also, drawing operations are done with an "instrument," such as a pen (for lines, such as required by the ellipse) or a brush (for solid areas, such as the rectangle and text). Finally, text is always displayed in a specific font. I'll present more details on these topics soon.

When you run the program and click the button, the shapes are drawn. If, however, you cover the window—with another form, for example—and then uncover it, you'll see that the graphics have vanished. You must click the button again to see them. This is because of the way Windows graphics work—screen images are not persisted. It would require a lot of memory and overhead to maintain a copy of every covered or partially covered screen element. Rather, these items are redrawn as needed. When you uncover the demonstration program, the form itself and the button are automatically redrawn, but the graphics shapes are not because that code is executed only when the user clicks the button. To have code executed every time the form is displayed, you must place the code in theform's **Paint()** event procedure, which is triggered automatically each time the form and its contents need to be redrawn (such as when the form is restored after being minimized). To see this for yourself, modify the program by cutting the code from the **Click()** event procedure and pasting it into the **Form1_Paint()** event procedure. Now when you run the program, you'll see that the shapes are drawn immediately when the program starts, and they remain visible when the form is hidden, then uncovered.

The **Paint()** event provides an instance of the **Graphics** class all ready for you to use, associated with the screen window that is being repainted. You access this object as follows:

```
Private Sub Form1_Paint(ByVal sender As Object, _
        ByVal e As System.Windows.Forms.PaintEventArgs)_
        Handles MyBase.Paint

    Dim g As Graphics
    g = e.Graphics

    ' Drawing code goes here

End Sub
```

There is a lot more to learn about the **Graphics** class, but first it is necessary to understand some related topics.

Measurement Units and Coordinates

In any graphics operation, you will be using coordinates to specify the location and size of the object being drawn. GDI+, and hence .NET, uses three coordinate systems:

- Device coordinates represent the capabilities of the output device. This will be pixels for screen display and printer "dots" for printer output.
- Page coordinates represent the coordinates used on the drawing surface. They may be the same as device coordinates (pixels), but can also be set to other units, such as inches and millimeters.
- World coordinates are the coordinates your program is using, based on the needs of the program. They can be essentially any arbitrary coordinate system that you define, based on your program's needs.

All three coordinate systems are alike in that the horizontal coordinate, typically referred to as X, increases as you move to the right, and the vertical coordinate (Y) increases as you move down. The device and page coordinate systems are also alike in that the origin, where both X and Y are zero, is always located at the top-left corner of the drawing surface. In world coordinates, however, the origin can be shifted to another location when required by the program.

Code to perform drawing operations always uses world coordinates. During the drawing process, these coordinates must first be translated into page coordinates, which then must be translated into device coordinates. There will be times when all three coordinate systems are the same, and also times when two are the same and only one is different. The **Graphics** class provides members for working with the coordinate systems, as will be explained later in this section.

The Point and PointF Structures

The **Point** and **PointF** structures locate a position, or point, on a two-dimensional surface. No assumptions are made about the units of measurement—these structures simply contain an X coordinate and a Y coordinate, both of type **Integer** in **Point** and type **Single** in **PointF**. The constructor is as follows:

```
New(X, Y)
```

Use the **IsEmpty** property to determine if the **Point** or **PointF** is empty (both X and Y are 0). Use the **Equals()** method to determine if a given **Point** or **PointF** is equal (has the same *X* and *Y* values) to another **Point** or **PointF** structure. The syntax is as follows:

```
p1.Equals(p2)
```

The method returns True only if *p1* and *p2* are both type **Point** or type **PointF** and they contains the same X and Y values.

The Size and SizeF Structures

The **Size** structure represents the size of a rectangular region as a width and a height. Its *Width* and *Height* properties are type **Integer** values. No assumptions are made about the measurement units. There are two constructors, as follows:

```
New(width, height)
New(p)
```

In the first syntax, the **Size** structure is initialized with the supplied width and height values. In the second syntax, the structure is initialized with the values of the type **Point** *p*, with width equal to p.X and height equal to p.Y.

The **SizeF** structure is identical to the **Size** structure except that its **X** and **Y** properties are type **Single**.

The Rectangle and RectangleF Structures

The **Rectangle** structure defines a rectangular area in terms of the location of its top-left corner and its size. It has two constructors:

```
New(p, s)
New(x, y, width, height)
```

In the first syntax, *p* is a type **Point** specifying the location of the rectangle's top-left corner, and *s* is a type **Size** specifying the rectangle's size. In the second syntax, *x* and *y* give the coordinates of the top-left corner, and *width* and *height* specify the size. The **RectangleF** structure is identical to **Rectangle** except that its measurements are kept as type **Single** rather than type **Integer**. Additional **Rectangle** members are described in Table 17.2.

Table 17.2 Members of the Rectangle structure.

Member	Description
Bottom	Specifies the Y coordinate of the rectangle's bottom edge.
Contains(*p*) **Contains(*r*)**	Returns True if the type **Point** *p* or the type **Rectangle** *r* is contained within the current rectangle.
Equals(*r*)	Returns true if the type **Rectangle** *r* is equal in location and size to the current rectangle.
Height	Specifies the height of the rectangle.
Inflate(*s*)	Returns a copy of the **Rectangle** inflated by the type **Size** *s*. The original is unchanged.
IntersectsWith(*r*)	Returns true if type **Rectangle** *r* intersects (overlaps) with the current rectangle.
IsEmpty	Returns True if all measurement properties are equal to zero.
Left	Specifies the X coordinate of the rectangle's left edge.
Location	Specifies, as a type **Point**, the coordinates of the rectangle's top-left corner.
Offset(*x*, *y*)	Offsets (moves) the rectangle by the specified *x* and *y* values.
Right	Specifies the X coordinate of the rectangle's right edge.
Size	Specifies, as a type **Size**, the rectangle's size.
Top	Specifies the Y coordinate of the rectangle's top edge.
Width	Specifies the width of the rectangle.
X	Specifies the X coordinate of the rectangle's upper-left corner.
Y	Specifies the Y coordinate of the rectangle's upper-left corner.

The Region and GraphicsPath Classes

The **Region** class represents the interior of a graphics shape, defined as a set of rectangles and paths. The **GraphicsPath** class represents a series of connected lines and curves. As you'll soon see, these two classes are related.

A **Region** can represent something as simple as a single rectangle, but it is more commonly used to represent irregular shapes. To create a rectangular **Region** use the following constructor:

```
New(r)
```

Where *r* is an instance of either the **Rectangle** or **RectangleF** class specifying the bounds of the **Region**. To create an irregularly shaped **Region** you use this constructor:

```
New(p)
```

Where *p* is a **GraphicsPath** object defining the **Region**. The next two sections show how to create **GraphicsPath** objects for the shapes you need and how to create and use **Region** objects in your programs.

Creating a ***GraphicsPath*** *Object*

The **GraphicsPath** class is quite complex, and has uses besides defining **Region** objects. The class cannot be covered in detail. Rather, my goal is to show you the fundamentals of defining **GraphicsPath** objects for use in defining **Region** objects. You can obtain additional information from the Visual Basic .NET documentation.

To create a **GraphicsPath** object, use its parameterless constructor:

```
Dim gp As New GraphicsPath()
```

This code creates an undefined or "blank" **GraphicsPath** object. To define the path represented by the object, you use its various **Add*xxxx*()** methods where *xxxx* specifies the type of element you are adding to the path. For example, **AddArc()** adds an arc to the path, **AddLine()** adds a straight line to the path, and so on. The resulting path is the collection of all of the individual items you have added to it. The **Add*xxxx*()** methods are listed in Table 17.3.

Note that you can add both open lines and closed shapes (such as a rectangle) to a path. These two types of objects are handled differently. When you add open lines, the lines are automatically connected to each other. For example, if you add an arc to a **GraphicsPath** object and then add a straight line, a line segment will be added to connect the end of the arc and the start of the straight line (unless they happen to coincide). Here's code fragment that does just this, then draws the resulting **GraphicsPath** on the screen:

```
Dim gp As New GraphicsPath()
gp.AddArc(New Rectangle(20, 20, 350, 365), 180, 90)
gp.AddLine(150, 165, 200, 215)
g.DrawPath(Pens.Black, gp)
```

Table 17.3 Methods for adding elements to a GraphicsPath object.

Method	Description
AddArc(*r*, *startAngle*, *sweepAngle*)	Adds an arc bounded by type **Rectangle *r*** with the specified starting and sweep angles.
AddBezier(*p1*, *p2*, ,*p3*, *p4*)	Adds a Bézier curve defined by the four type **Point** arguments.
AddClosedCurve(*p()*)	Adds a closed cardinal spline curve where *p()* is an array of type **Point** defining the curve's points.
AddCurve(*p()*)	Adds a non-closed cardinal spline curve where *p()* is an array of type **Point** defining the curve's points.
AddEllipse(*r*)	Adds an ellipse defined by the specified type **Rectangle**.
AddLine(*p1*, *p2*)	Adds a straight line defined by the two type **Point** arguments.
AddPath(*p*, *connect*)	Adds the type GraphicsPath specified by *p*. If *connect* is true, the new path is connected to the exiting path (if possible).

(continued)

Table 17.3 Methods for adding elements to a GraphicsPath object *(continued)*.

Method	Description
AddPie(*r, startAngle, sweepAngle*)	Adds a pie wedge defined by the type **Rectangle** *r* and the specified start and sweep angles.
AddPolygon(*p()*)	Adds a closed polygon defined by the specified array of type **Point**.
AddRectangle(*r*)	Adds a rectangle defined by the type **Rectangle** *r*).

In this code, **g** is an instance of the **Graphics** object for the window. Figure 17.2 shows the output. The arc and the shorter line segment were created by the program, while the longer line segment was added automatically to create a continuous path.

When you add a closed shape, it is handled differently. It is simply superimposed on the path without being connected to elements that are added before or after it. To illustrate, add the following line of code to the preceding snippet (as the second-to-last line) to add a rectangle to the path along with the arc and line. The resulting output is shown in Figure 17.3.

```
gp.AddRectangle(New Rectangle(75, 75, 80, 55))
```

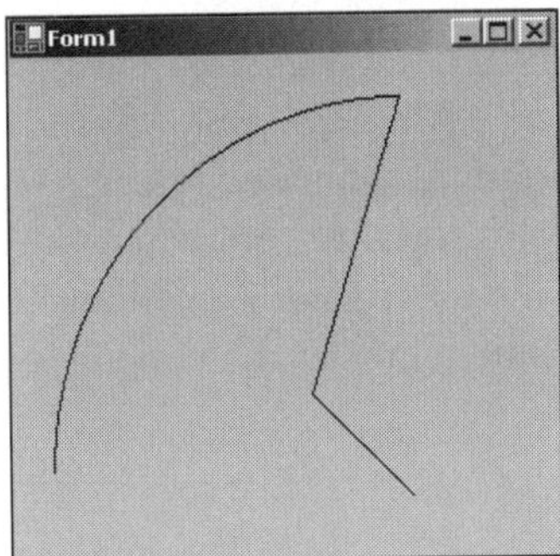

Figure 17.2
The path created by the code snippet in the text.

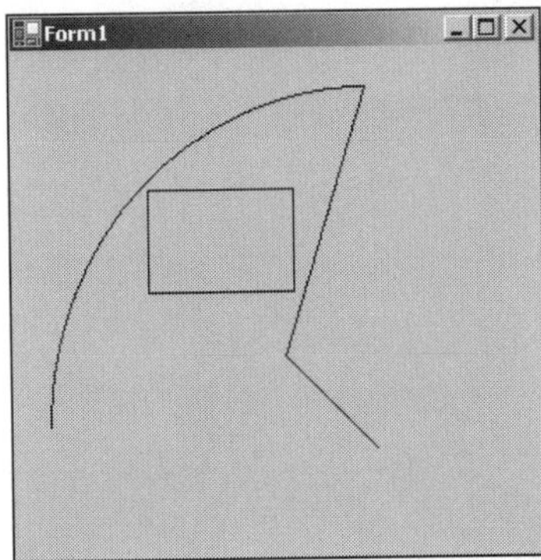

Figure 17.3
The result of adding a rectangle to the path.

Working with Regions

After you define a **GraphicsPath** object, you can use it to instantiate a **Region** object, employing the constructor that was shown in the preceding section. To review, if **gp** is your **GraphicsPath** object, you would create a **Region**, as follows:

```
Dim r As New Region(gp)
```

The way in which the region is defined depends on the nature of the path. If the path defines a single closed area, the region will correspond to that area. Several other possibilities exist:

- If the path defines an open area (as, for example, shown previously in Figure 17.2), the ends of the path are connected to create a closed region.
- If the path completely contains a closed shape (as, for example, shown previously in Figure 17.3), the area inside the closed shape will not be part of the region. This is shown in Figure 17.4, which shows the region created from the path from Figure 17.3.
- If the path partially overlaps but doesn't completely contain a closed shape, part of the shape will be in the region and part will not. This is illustrated in Figure 17.5.

Members of the **Region** class are described in Table 17.4.

One use for regions is for *hit testing*—in other words, to determine whether a specific screen location, such as the coordinates of a mouse click, falls within the region, which is easily accomplished by using the **IsVisible()** method. Another use for regions is to define a clipping area for a drawing surface. This use will be demonstrated later in the chapter, in the section on the **Graphics** object.

Figure 17.4
A region created from a path that contains a closed shape.

Figure 17.5
A region created from a path that overlaps a closed shape.

Table 17.4 Members of the Region class.

Member	Description
GetBounds()	Returns a type **RectangleF** for the region's bounding rectangle (the smallest rectangle that contains the entire region).
Intersect(*where*)	Updates the **Region** object to the intersection (area of overlap) between it and the type **Rectangle**, **RectangleF**, **GraphicsPath**, or **Region** specified by *where*.
IsEmpty(*g*)	Returns True if the region is empty on the drawing surface specified by the type **Graphics** *g*.
IsVisible(*p*, *g*) **IsVisible(*r*, *g*)**	Returns true if the type **Point *p*** or any part of the type **Rectangle *r*** is contained within the region when drawn on the surface represented by the type **Graphics** *g*.
Translate(*x*, *y*)	Translates (offsets) the region by the specified *x* and *y* values. The arguments can both be type **Integer** or type **Single**.
Union(*where*)	Updates the **Region** object to the union (total combined area) between it and the type **Rectangle**, **RectangleF**, **GraphicsPath**, or **Region** specified by *where*.

Pens

A pen is used to draw lines, curves, and the outlines of shapes. It is represented by an instance of the **Pen** class. At its most basic, a pen has a color and a width. The class has several overloaded constructors. You can specify the color explicitly with these two constructors:

```
New(color)
New(color, width)
```

Color is a **Color** structure that specifies the pen color (the **Color** structure was covered in Chapter 8). The first syntax creates a pen with a width of 1. The second syntax creates a pen with the specified width, a type **Single**. The other two constructors create a pen based on an existing brush (covered soon):

```
New(brush)
New(brush, width)
```

A **Pen** object has a variety of properties that control the appearance of the lines it draws. The most important of these properties are summarized in Table 17.5. Please refer to the Visual Basic .NET documentation for details on how these properties work.

You can also obtain colored pens of width 1 from the **Pens** class. This class provides a set of static (shared) properties of the form **Pens.*XXXX***, where *XXXX* identifies the color of the pen. Therefore, **Pens.Black** returns a black pen. You'll find a complete list of the available pens in the Visual Basic .NET documentation in the section on the **Pens** class.

Brushes

A brush is used to fill the interior of shapes and text. The .NET framework provides several brushes for different tasks, all derived from the abstract base class **Brush**. They are as follows:

- HatchBrush
- LinearGradientBrush
- PathGradientBrush
- SolidBrush
- TextureBrush

Table 17.5 Properties of the Pen class.

Property	Description
Color	Specifies, as a type **Color**, the color of the pen.
CompoundArray	Lets you define a pen that draws two or more parallel lines.
CustomEndCap **CustomStartCap**	Lets you define custom caps for the starting and ending of lines.
DashCap	Specifies the style of line cap to use with dashed lines.
DashPattern	Lets you define a custom pattern of dots and dashes.
DashStyle	Lets you draw a line in one of several predefined dot/dash styles.
EndCap **StartCap**	Specifies the type of cap to be used with solid lines.
PenType	Specifies the style of lines (hatched, gradients, etc.)
Width	The width of the line drawn.

The function of each brush is obvious from its name. For the present purposes, I will limit explanation to the **SolidBrush**, which is used to fill areas with a solid color. You can explore the other brush types when and if the need arises.

A brush has a color, but unlike a pen it has no width because the extent of the area "painted" depends on the shape being drawn. The constructor for the **SolidBrush** class is as follows:

```
New(color)
```

Color is a **Color** structure specifying the brush's color. After you have created a brush of the desired color, you use it in various drawing operations as described later in this section.

Another way to obtain specific brushes is to use the various shared properties of the **Brushes** class. These properties have the syntax **Brushes.*XXXX***, where *XXXX* identifies the color of the brush. Thus, **Brushes.Beige** returns a reference to a beige brush. You'll find a complete list of these predefined system brushes in the Visual Basic .NET documentation.

Fonts

Whenever you want to draw text, you must specify the font to be used. A font is encapsulated in a **Font** object, which controls all aspects of the font's appearance, including its typeface, size, and style. The **Font** class has more than a dozen overloaded constructors. The two constructors used most often are as follows:

```
New(fontname, size)
New(fontname, size, style)
```

Fontname is a string specifying the name of a typeface, such as Arial, Times, Courier, or Coronet. *Size* is the size of the font, in points (1/72 inch). The optional *style* argument is a member of the **FontStyle** enumeration, as follows:

- Bold
- Italic
- Regular
- Strikeout
- Underline

For example, this line creates a **Font** instance in the Arial typeface, 16 points in size, regular style:

```
Dim f1 As New Font("Arial", 16)
```

The following example creates a Times typeface font in 24 point size, boldface:

```
Dim f2 As New Font("Times", 24, FontStyle.Bold)
```

After you have created a **Font** instance, you will pass it to the various text-drawing methods, as described in the next section.

The Graphics Class, Continued

You were introduced to the **Graphics** class earlier in this chapter, and you learned how to instantiate the class and also saw a brief demonstration program. **Graphics** is an extremely complicated class, but also very powerful. The members of the **Graphics** class can be divided into two categories:

- Methods and properties that provide information and control the way drawing is done, but do not actually draw anything.
- Methods that perform actual drawing operations.

In this section, I cover the informational and control members first. Next, I present some details and examples on working with coordinate systems.

*Information and Control Members of the **Graphics** Class*

By default, a **Graphics** object uses device coordinates (pixels) for both page and world coordinates. The rendering origin (0,0) is at the top-left corner of the drawing surface, and no clipping is applied. By using the members described in Table 17.6, you can modify the **Graphics** object's units and scale as required for the needs of your program. Directly related to the **Graphics** object is the **GraphicsUnit** enumeration, which is detailed in Table 17.7.

Table 17.6 Informational and control members of the Graphics class.

Member	Description
Clip	Specifies a **Region** object that defines the clipping area of the drawing surface. Only drawing operations within this region will be displayed.
DpiX **DpiY**	Returns the horizontal and vertical resolution, in dots per inch, of the device context.
PageScale	Specifies the scaling factor between world units and page units.
PageUnit	Specifies the unit of measurement for page coordinates. Can be any member of the **GraphicsUnit** enumeration (see Table 17.7).
RenderingOrigin	A type **Point** that specifies the drawing origin relative to the origin of the page.
TranslateTransform(*x*, *y*)	Translates the rendering origin by *x* units horizontally and *y* units vertically.

Table 17.7 **Members of the GraphicsUnit enumeration.**

Constant	Unit of measurement
Display	1/75 inch
Document	1/300 inch
Inch	Inch
Millimeter	Millimeter
Pixel	1 device pixel
Point	Printer's point (1/72 inch)

The **DpiX** and **DpiY** properties are read-only, and are useful when you have changes to another measurement unit but still want to specify some measurement units in pixels. For example, suppose you want to use a PageUnit of inches and then draw a line. Here is code that you might write (assuming that g is a reference to the **Graphics** object):

```
g.PageUnit = GraphicsUnit.Inch
Dim p As New Pen(System.Drawing.Color.Black)
g.DrawLine(p, 0, 0, 5, 10)
```

The resulting line will be one inch thick because the page unit in inches and the default pen thickness is one unit. If you want to draw the thinnest possible line, one pixel, you would accomplish it as follows:

```
Dim p As New Pen(System.Drawing.Color.Black, 1 / g.DpiX)
```

The expression **1/g.DpiX** evaluates to the inch equivalent of one pixel—just what you want.

Working with Coordinates and Scaling

Perhaps the most confusing aspect of the **Graphics** object is the relationships between the three coordinate systems and the way your program can use these systems to obtain the desired results. The best way to understand this is to look at some examples. Suppose that you draw a line from coordinate 0,0 to coordinate 50,50 with the following code (in this and other examples, g is a reference to a **Graphics** object for the screen window):

```
Dim p As New Pen(System.Drawing.Color.Black)
g.DrawLine(p, 0, 0, 50, 50)
```

Because you have changed no coordinate-related properties, all three coordinate systems are the same, and use pixels. As a result, the line, shown in Figure 17.6, is 70 pixels long (the diagonal of a box that is 50 pixels on a side) and one pixel wide (the default pen width is one unit).

Figure 17.6
Drawing a line with the default coordinate system.

Next, modify the code so the **Graphics** object uses millimeters as the unit of page measure. The code now looks like this:

```
g.PageUnit = GraphicsUnit.Millimeter
Dim p As New Pen(System.Drawing.Color.Black)
g.DrawLine(p, 0, 0, 50, 50)
```

The output is shown in Figure 17.7. The line is 70 millimeters long (the diagonal of a 50mm square) and it is 1mm wide. In this example, world and page coordinates are the same (millimeters) and device coordinates, always pixels, are different. The **Graphics** object has translated your world/page coordinates to device coordinates.

The next modification involves translating the rendering origin, which has the effect of moving the origin (the 0,0 coordinate) away from the top-left corner of the drawing surface. Here's the code:

```
g.PageUnit = GraphicsUnit.Millimeter
g.TranslateTransform(25, 10)
Dim p As New Pen(System.Drawing.Color.Black)
g.DrawLine(p, 0, 0, 50, 50)
```

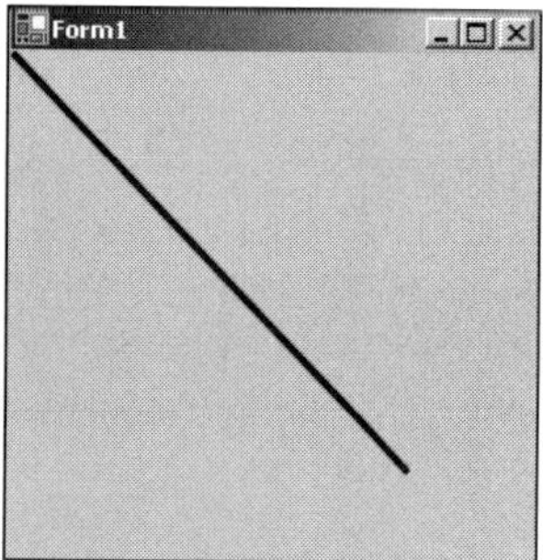

Figure 17.7
Drawing the same line with the PageUnit set to Millimeters.

You can see from Figure 17.8 that the line is the same width and length as previously, but now it starts at a different location. In this example, the origin has been moved to page coordinates 25, 10. In this situation, all three coordinate systems are different. In world coordinates, the line is drawn at (0,0)-(50,50). In page coordinates, it is drawn from (25,10)-(75,65). In device coordinates (pixels), the values will be different again.

The final demonstration will illustrate the use of the **PageScale** property. Modify your code as shown here, setting **PageScale** to 0.5:

```
g.PageUnit = GraphicsUnit.Millimeter
g.TranslateTransform(25, 10)
g.PageScale = 0.5
Dim p As New Pen(System.Drawing.Color.Black)
g.DrawLine(p, 0, 0, 50, 50)
```

The new output is shown in Figure 17.9. You can see that all aspects of the output—the line length, its thickness, and the location of the origin—have been affected by the **PageScale** setting. In effect, the world coordinates that you pass to various **Graphics** members are all

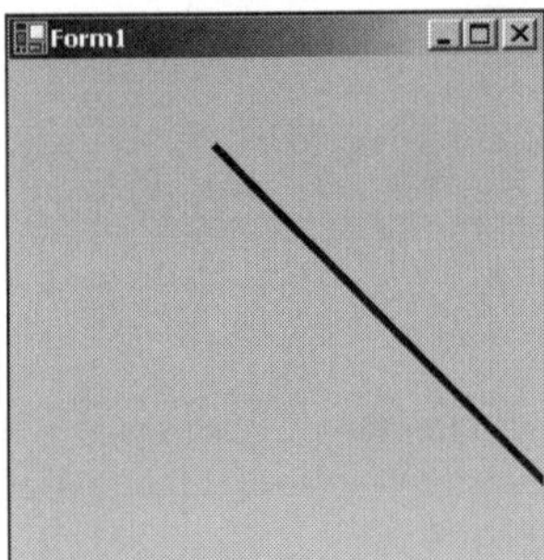

Figure 17.8
The output after translating the rendering origin.

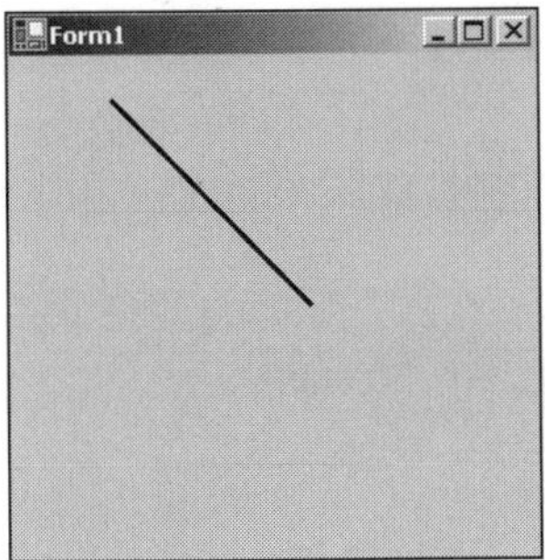

Figure 17.9
The output after changing the **PageScale** property.

multiplied by the **PageScale** factor before being implemented. This property provides a quick way to scale your graphics output.

*Drawing Members of the **Graphics** Class*

The **Graphics** class provides a wide range of methods for drawing different items, including text. Almost all of these methods are overloaded, with several versions of how you provide the information to the method. For example, the **DrawRectangle()** method lets you specify the coordinates of the rectangle as a type **Rectangle**, as four type **Integer** values, or as four type **Single** values. In Table 17.8, I explain only one version of each method, and you can explore the other overloads in the Visual Basic .NET documentation. In addition, I am omitting some specialized drawing methods such as those for creating Bézier curves.

Many of the shape-drawing methods come in two versions. A **Draw*xxxx*()** method creates an outline of the shape using a specified pen, while a **Fill*xxxx*()** method creates a filled shape using the specified brush.

The code presented in Listing 17.2 demonstrates the use of some of these drawing methods. Create a new Windows application, place this code in the **Paint()** event procedure, and run the program. The output is shown in Figure 17.10. You can use this program as a model for your own experimentation.

Table 17.8 Drawing members of the Graphics class.

Method	Description
Clear(*color*)	Erases the entire drawing surface and fills it with the specified color (as a type **Color**).
DrawArc(*pen, r, start, sweep*)	Draws an arc bounded by the type **Rectangle** *r* with the specified starting angle and sweep angle. The starting angle is measured from the 9 o'clock position.
DrawCurve(*pen, p()*)	Draws a cardinal spline through the coordinates specified by an array of type **Point**. A cardinal spline connects a series of points with a smooth, curved line.
DrawPolygon(*pen, p()*) **FillPolygon(*brush, p()*)**	Draws a polygon whose vertices are specified by an array of type **Point**.
DrawEllipse(*pen, r*) **FillEllipse(*brush, r*)**	Draws an ellipse bounded by the type **Rectangle** *r*.
DrawImage(*image, r*)	Draws the specified image (as a type **Image**) at the location and size specified by type **Rectangle *r***.
DrawLine(*pen, p1, p2*)	Draws a line between *p1* and *p2*, both type **Point** arguments.
DrawRectangle(*pen, r*) **FillRectangle(*brush, r*)**	Draws the rectangle specified by type **Rectangle** *r*.
DrawString(*s, f, brush, p*)	Draws the string *s* using the type **Font *f*** at the location specified by the type **Point** *p*. The position specifies the upper left corner of the text.

Listing 17.2 Demonstrating some of the Graphics class drawing methods.

```
Private Sub Form1_Paint(ByVal sender As Object, _
       ByVal e As System.Windows.Forms.PaintEventArgs) _
       Handles MyBase.Paint

    Dim g As Graphics

    g = e.Graphics

    ' Draw a filled black triangle.
    Dim triangle(2) As Point
    triangle(0) = New Point(50, 10)
    triangle(1) = New Point(10, 70)
    triangle(2) = New Point(90, 70)
    g.FillPolygon(New SolidBrush(System.Drawing.Color.Black), _
        triangle)

    ' Note that the above line could also have been written:
    ' g.FillPolygon(Brushes.Black, triangle)

    ' Put a white "!" in the triangle.
    Dim f As New Font("Ariel", 24)
    g.DrawString("!", f, Brushes.White, 40, 30)

    ' Draw a cardinal spline.
    Dim spline(5) As Point
    spline(0) = New Point(50, 10)
    spline(1) = New Point(200, 40)
    spline(2) = New Point(60, 210)
    spline(3) = New Point(5, 150)
    spline(4) = New Point(45, 90)
    spline(5) = New Point(150, 100)

    g.DrawCurve(New Pen(System.Drawing.Color.Red, 2), spline)

    ' Draw an arc.
    g.DrawArc(New Pen(System.Drawing.Color.Black, 3), _
        New Rectangle(35, 210, 220, 50), 0, 180)

    'Draw a "chain" of ellipses.
    Dim r As New Rectangle(230, 15, 20, 50)
    Dim i As Integer
    For i = 0 To 3
        g.FillEllipse(New SolidBrush(System.Drawing.Color.Green), r)
        ' Move the rectangle down 50 units.
        r.Offset(0, 50)
    Next

End Sub
```

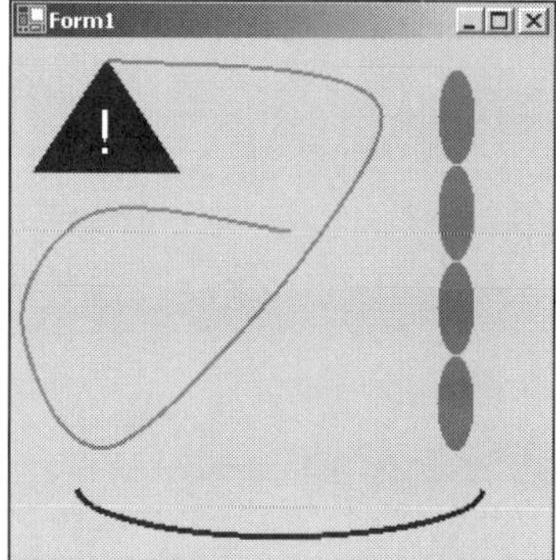

Figure 17.10
The output of the graphics drawing demonstration.

Defining a Clipping Region

By using the **Region** class, described previously in this chapter, you can create a clipping region for a graphics-drawing surface. Only output within the region will display; everything else will be clipped. This technique is illustrated by the code in Listing 17.3. It defines a triangular region and assigns that region as the **Graphics** object's **Clip** property. Some text is then displayed. The resulting output is shown in Figure 17.11.

Listing 17.3 Defining a clipping region for graphics output.

```
Private Sub Form1_Paint(ByVal sender As Object, _
    ByVal e As System.Windows.Forms.PaintEventArgs) _
    Handles MyBase.Paint

    Dim g As Graphics = e.Graphics
    Dim gp As New GraphicsPath()
    Dim p(2) As Point
    p(0).X = 130
    p(0).Y = 10
    p(1).X = 20
    p(1).Y - 190
    p(2).X = 240
    p(2).Y = 190

    gp.AddPolygon(p)
    Dim r As New Region(gp)
    g.Clip = r
    Dim f As New Font("Arial", 30)
    Dim y As Integer

    For y = 0 To 120 Step 40
        g.DrawString("Clipped text", f, Brushes.Black, 40, y)
    Next y

End Sub
```

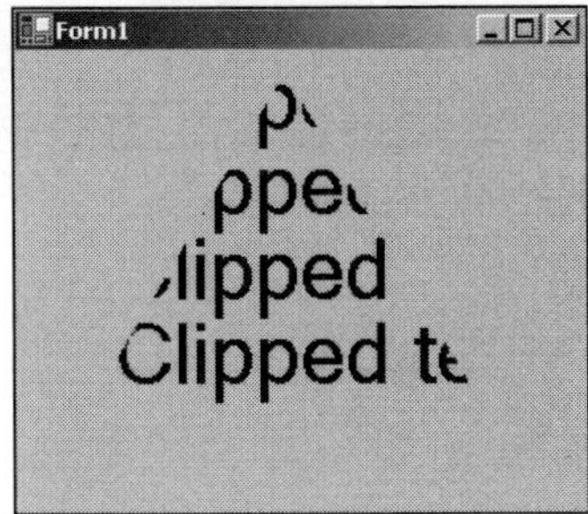

Figure 17.11
Using a clipping region to restrict output.

The Image Class

Image is an abstract class that serves as the base class for three classes that are important for graphics programming: **Bitmap**, **Metafile**, and **Icon**. These three classes all represent images, with the following distinctions:

- The **Bitmap** class represents an object as a collection of pixels. Each pixel is represented by a number that specifies its color.
- The **Metafile** class represents an image as a series of drawing instructions. When the instructions are carried out, the image is reproduced.
- The **Icon** class is a special type of bitmap that is used for icons, the small graphical images used to represent objects in Windows and Windows programs.

Most of the images that Windows programs work with are bitmaps. This includes images stored in files with the .jpg, gif, .tiff, .pcx, and .bmp extensions, among others. For this reason, the information in this section will be limited to the **Bitmap** class. When you know how to use this class, the procedures are easily extended to the **Icon** and **Metafile** classes.

Creating a Bitmap Object

You can create a **Bitmap** object from an existing image file, or you can create an empty **Bitmap** object of a specified size to work with. The constructors are as follows:

```
New(filename)
New(width, height)
```

In the first syntax, the **Bitmap** object created has a size and pixel format as determined by the image file. In the second syntax, an empty bitmap is created with the specified size and using the 32 bit-per-pixel format. This format assigns 32 bits for each pixel, with 8 bits for each of the three primary colors (red, green, blue) and 8 bits for alpha information (which remains unused in most applications). The **Bitmap** class has additional overloaded constructors for creating bitmaps from other sources and in other pixel formats. You can find the details in the Visual Basic .NET documentation.

Modifying a Bitmap

After you create a **Bitmap** object, you can modify it in many different ways. One type of modification relies on the fact that a bitmap image can be treated as a drawing surface. You can create a **Graphics** object that is associated with the bitmap, and then use any of the **Graphics** methods to draw on the image, adding text, lines, and shapes as needed. You can also use the **Graphics.DrawImage()** method to superimpose one bitmap image on another. To create a **Graphics** object associated with a bitmap, use the static **Graphics.FromImage()** method, as follows:

```
Dim g As Graphics
g = Graphics.FromImage(image)
```

Image is a reference to the type **Bitmap**. The code in Listing 17.4 demonstrates this technique. It creates a **Bitmap** object based on a disk file, then draws some text on the image. Finally the modified image is displayed on the form. The output is shown in Figure 17.12.

Listing 17.4 Displaying text on a bitmap image.

```
Private Sub Form1_Paint(ByVal sender As Object, _
        ByVal e As System.Windows.Forms.PaintEventArgs) _
        Handles MyBase.Paint

    Dim g As Graphics
    g = e.Graphics
    Dim im As New Bitmap("c:\images\bmw1.jpg")
    Dim g2 As Graphics = Graphics.FromImage(im)
    Dim f As New Font("Arial", 16, FontStyle.Bold)
    Dim b As New SolidBrush(System.Drawing.Color.White)

    ' Draw the text on the bitmap.
    g2.DrawString("My New BMW", f, b, 10, 10)

    ' Display the bitmap on the form.
    g.DrawImage(im, New Point(0, 0))

End Sub
```

Another way you can modify a bitmap image is by rotating and flipping it. You use the **RotateFlip()** method for this task. The syntax is as follows:

```
RotateFlip(type)
```

The *type* argument specifies how the image should be rotated and/or flipped. You use members of the **RotateFlipType** enumeration. The constants in this enumeration have the following form:

```
RotateRFlipF
```

Figure 17.12
Drawing text on a bitmap image.

R specifies how many degrees the image should be rotated; it can be **90**, **180**, **270**, or **None**. *F* specifies how the image should be flipped; it can be **X** (flip horizontally), **Y** (flip vertically), **XY** (flip both ways), or **None**. Here are some examples:

- **RotateNoneFlipX**—Flip horizontally; do not rotate.
- **Rotate180FlipNone**—Rotate 180 degrees; do not flip.
- **Rotate90FlipY**—Rotate 90 degrees; flip vertically.

Saving a Bitmap

After modifying a bitmap image, you may want to save it. To save it with the original format, use the **Save()** method:

```
Save(filename)
```

You can also specify the file format by using this overload of the **Save()** method:

```
Save(filename, format)
```

Format is a member of the **ImageFormat** enumeration, as detailed in Table 17.9. For example, the following line saves the image as a TIFF file:

```
MyBitmap.Save("c:\images\car.tif", ImageFormat.Tiff)
```

Table 17.9 Members of the ImageFormat enumeration.

Constant	Format
Bmp	Bitmap
Emf	Windows enhanced metafile
Exif	Exchangeable image
Gif	Graphics interchange

(continued)

Table 17.9 Members of the ImageFormat enumeration *(continued)*.

Constant	Format
Icon	Windows icon
Jpeg	Joint Photographic Experts Group
Png	Portable network graphics
Tiff	Tagged image file
Wmf	Windows metafile

Printing

Printing from a Windows application is based on the **PrintDocument** class. This class has properties that control various aspects of a print job, such as which printer to use, the paper source, and the page orientation. It is part of the **System.Drawing.Printing** namespace. The general procedure for printing is as follows:

1. Create an instance of the **PrintDocument** class.
2. Write code to create the actual print output, whether it is graphics, text, or a combination of the two. This code is placed in the **PrintDocument.PrintPage()** event handler.
3. Call the **PrintDocument.Print()** method.
4. Each time a new page is about to be printed, the **PrintDocument.PrintPage()** event handler is triggered, and the code that you wrote sends that page's output to the printer.

How do you send output to the printer? This is done using one of the arguments to the **PrintDocument.PrintPage()** event handler, which is of type **PrintPageEventArgs**. Specifically, this class has a **Graphics** property that exposes a **Graphics** object that you use to create the print output. You learned about the **Graphics** class earlier in this chapter, and that information will not be repeated in this section.

Here is an example of a **PrintDocument.PrintPage()** event handler that will print a filled blue rectangle:

```
Private Sub MyPrintDoc_PrintPage(ByVal sender As Object, _
    ByVal e As System.Drawing.Printing.PrintPageEventArgs) _
    Handles MyPrintDoc.PrintPage

    e.Graphics.FillRectangle(Brushes.Blue, _
        new Rectangle(100,100,200,200))

End Sub
```

This handler must be connected to the event using the standard Visual Basic **AddHandler** syntax. For example, if your **PrintDocument** object is called **MyPrintDoc**, you would use the following code:

```
AddHandler MyPrintDoc.PrintPage, AddressOf Me.MyPrintDoc_PrintPage
```

The **PrintPageEventArgs** that is passed to this procedure is central to the printing process, and will be covered in detail later in this chapter.

Printer Settings and the PrintDialog Class

Printer settings are those aspects of a print job that are directly related to the printer. This includes which printer to use (if more than one is available), the paper source, the number of copies, and whether output should go to a file rather than to a printer. The .NET framework provides the **PrinterSettings** class to encapsulate all these settings, and also provides the **PrintDialog** class to permit users to make changes to the printer settings. This dialog box is shown in Figure 17.13.

To allow the user to select printer settings, follow these steps:

1. Create an instance of the **PrintDialog** class.
2. Set the **PrintDialog** object's **Document** property to the **PrintDocument** object you will be using for the print job.
3. Set the **PrintDialog** object's properties as needed (more on this soon).
4. Display the **PrintDialog** using its **ShowDialog()** method.
5. Check the **ShowDialog()** method's return value to determine if the user closed the dialog box by selecting OK or Cancel. If the former, call the **PrintDocument** object's **Print()** method to start printing.

Connecting the **PrintDialog** with a specific instance of the **PrintDocument** class (Step 2 in the preceding list) ensures that the user's settings are transferred automatically and that you do not have to work with an instance of **PrinterSettings**.

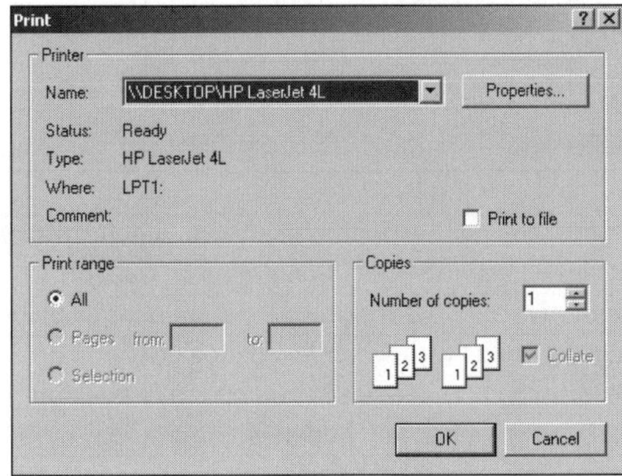

Figure 17.13
The PrintDialog dialog box lets the user select printer settings.

The **PrintDialog** class has several properties that control the options that are available to the user when the dialog box is displayed. These properties and some class methods are described in Table 17.10.

The code in Listing 17.5 shows code that prints the message, "Visual Basic is great!" using the printer settings specified by the user. The code assumes that the program has a Button control named Button1 that the end user can click on to initiate printing.

Listing 17.5 Printing a short text message with user-specified printer settings.

```
Private Sub Button1_Click(ByVal sender As System.Object, _
     ByVal e As System.EventArgs) Handles Button1.Click

   Dim pd As New PrintDocument()
   Dim prDialog As New PrintDialog()

   prDialog.Document = pd

   If prDialog.ShowDialog() = DialogResult.OK Then
     AddHandler pd.PrintPage, AddressOf Me.pd_PrintPage
     pd.Print()
   End If

End Sub

Private Sub pd_PrintPage(ByVal sender As Object, _
    ByVal e As System.Drawing.Printing.PrintPageEventArgs)

   Dim msg As String = "Visual Basic is great!"
   Dim printFont As New Font("Arial", 24)
   e.Graphics.DrawString(msg, printFont, Brushes.Black, 100, 100)

End Sub
```

Table 17.10 Members of the PrintDialog class.

Member	Description
AllowPrintToFile	Boolean value that specifies whether the print to file option will be available.
AllowSelection	Boolean value that specifies whether the Selection option is available.
AllowSomePages	Boolean value that specifies whether the From...To Page option is available.
Document	Specifies the **PrintDocument** object with which the dialog box is associated.
PrintToFile	Boolean value that specifies whether the Print To File option is available.
ShowHelp	Boolean value that specifies whether a Help button is displayed.
Reset()	Resets all settings in the dialog box to their default values.
ShowDialog()	Shows the dialog box and returns either **DialogResult.OK** or **Dialogresult.Cancel**, depending on how the user dismissed the dialog box.

You do not have to use the **PrintDialog** dialog box for changing printer settings, but can do so directly in code by means of the **PrintDocument** class's **PrinterSettings** property. For example, the following code sets the **PrintDocument** to print three uncollated copies:

```
pd.PrinterSettings.Copies = 3
pd.PrinterSettings.Collate = False
```

Page Settings and the PageSetupDialog Class

Page settings control aspects of a print job that are related to output pages, such as margins and paper orientation. The .NET framework provides the **PageSetupDialog** class to permit the user to make changes to the default page settings. This dialog box is shown in Figure 17.14. You can see that this dialog box has a button labeled "Printer." This button lets the user both access and change some printer settings.

The way you use the **PageSetupDialog** class is similar to the technique for the **PrintDialog** class covered in the previous section. To review briefly:

1. Associate the **PageSetupDialog** with a **PrintDocument** object by setting its **Document** property.
2. Display the dialog box by calling the **PageSetupDialog.ShowDialog()** method.
3. Check the method's return value.

The **PageSetupDialog** class has a number of properties that determine the options available to the user when the dialog box is displayed. These properties and some other class members are described in Table 17.11.

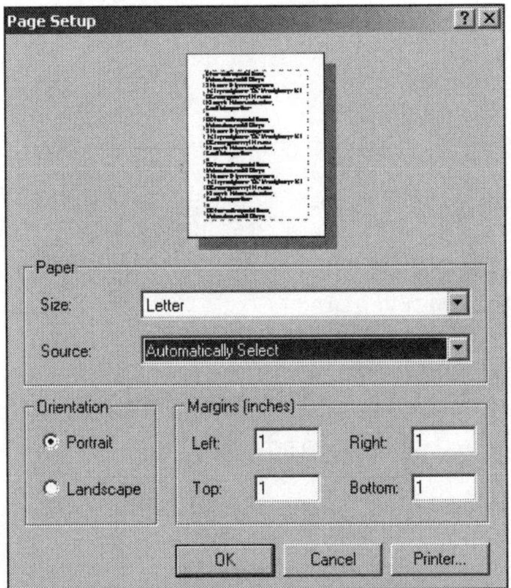

Figure 17.14
The Page Setup dialog box.

Table 17.11 Members of the PageSetupDialog class.

Members	Description
AllowMargins	Boolean value specifying whether the margins section of the dialog box is displayed.
AllowOrientation	Boolean value specifying whether the orientation (portrait/landscape) section of the dialog box is displayed.
AllowPaper	Boolean value specifying whether the paper size and paper source sections of the dialog box are displayed.
AllowPrinter	Boolean value specifying whether the Printer button is enabled.
Document	Specifies the **PrintDocument** object the dialog box is associated with.
MinMargins	Specifies the smallest margins the user can set, in 1/100 of an inch.
Reset()	Resets all dialog box settings to their default values.
ShowDialog()	Shows the dialog box and returns either **DialogResult.OK** or **Dialogresult.Cancel** depending on how the user dismissed the dialog box.

The code in Listing 17.6 shows how to use the **PageSetupDialog** class in a program. Note that this listing is almost identical to the previous listing, differing only in that a **PageSetupDialog** is displayed instead of a **PrintSetup** dialog box.

Listing 17.6 Using the PageSetupDialog class to specify page settings.

```
Private Sub Button1_Click(ByVal sender As System.Object, _
      ByVal e As System.EventArgs) Handles Button1.Click

  Dim pd As New PrintDocument()
  Dim psDialog As New PageSetupDialog()

  psDialog.Document = pd
  If psDialog.ShowDialog() = DialogResult.OK Then
    AddHandler pd.PrintPage, AddressOf Me.pd_PrintPage
    pd.Print()
  End If

End Sub

Private Sub pd_PrintPage(ByVal sender As Object, _
    ByVal e As System.Drawing.Printing.PrintPageEventArgs)

  Dim msg As String = "Visual Basic is great!"
  Dim printFont As New Font("Arial", 24)
  e.Graphics.DrawString(msg, printFont, Brushes.Black, 100, 100)

End Sub
```

It is important to note that some page settings take effect automatically, whereas others do not. For example, if the user selects Landscape mode in the Page Setup dialog box, the document will be printed in landscape orientation (assuming the printer supports it) with no further effort on the part of the programmer. On the other hand, margin settings do not take effect automatically. Your code, in the **PrintPage()** procedure, must take the margin settings into account and locate output on the page accordingly. You'll see how to do this shortly.

Using the PrintPage() Event Procedure

The real work of sending output to the printer occurs in the **PrintPage()** procedure. This procedure is passed an argument of type **PrintPageEventArgs**, which serves two purposes. First, it provides information about the print job, such as the margin settings. Your code will use this information to position output on the page appropriately. Second, it provides members that your code uses to control the print job, such as specifying whether there are more pages to print after the current one. Table 17.12 explains the members of this class, after which I provide some examples.

The **PageBounds** and **MarginBounds** properties each return a type **Rectangle** that describes the rectangle representing the entire page or the area inside the margins, respectively. This is illustrated in Figure 17.15. The measurements are always expressed in 1/100 of an inch. You use the **Rectangle** members **Top**, **Left**, **Width**, and **Height** to obtain specific information. Of course, **PageBounds.Top** and **PageBounds.Left** are always 0 because they refer to the top-left corner of the page.

In the **PrintPage()** procedure, your code makes use of the margin measurements to position print output within the user-specified margins. For example, the following line of code, in the **PrintPage()** procedure, prints the image referenced by **MyImage** at the top-left margins of the page:

```
Private Sub pd_PrintPage(ByVal sender As Object, _
        ByVal ev As PrintPageEventArgs)

    ev.Graphics.DrawImage(MyImage, ev.MarginBounds.Left, _
      ev.MarginBounds.Top)

End Sub
```

Table 17.12 Members of the PrintPageEventArgs class.

Member	Description
Cancel	If code in the **PrintPage()** procedure sets this property to True, the print job is canceled.
Graphics	References the **Graphics** object used to paint the page.
HasMorePages	If there are more pages to print after the current one, code in the **PrintPage()** procedure should set this property to True.
MarginBounds	Returns, as a type **Rectangle**, the area of the page inside the margins.
PageBounds	Returns, as a type **Rectangle**, the area of the entire page.
PageSettings	Returns a type **PageSettings** for the current page.

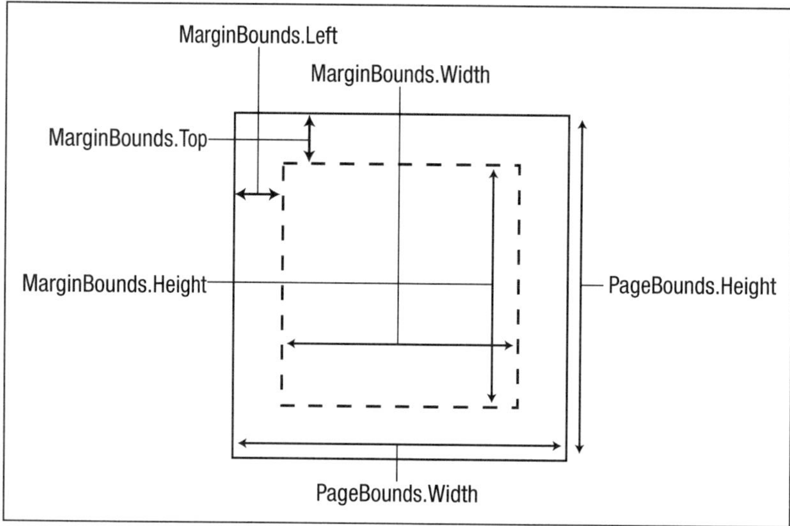

Figure 17.15
Measurements provided by the **PageBounds** and **MarginBounds** properties.

You can also use this margin information to make sure the print output is not larger than the page. The following code checks to see if the image being printed will fit within the page margins; if so, the image is printed centered on the page:

```
Private Sub pd_PrintPage(ByVal sender As Object, _
        ByVal ev As PrintPageEventArgs)

  If MyImage.Width > ev.MarginBounds.Width Or _
        MyImage.Height > ev.MarginBounds.Height Then
    MsgBox("The image is too big for the page.")
    Exit Sub
  End If

  Dim Xpos As Integer
  Dim YPos As Integer

  Xpos = ev.MarginBounds.Left + ((ev.MarginBounds.Width - _
    MyImage.Width) / 2)
  YPos = ev.MarginBounds.Top + ((ev.MarginBounds.Height - _
    MyImage.Height) / 2)
  ev.Graphics.DrawImage(MyImage, Xpos, YPos)

End Sub
```

When you're printing text, the question arises of how many lines will fit on a page. Given that you know the vertical extent of the area in the margins, the other piece of information that you need is the height of a single line of text. This information is available from the **Font** object's **GetHeight** method, as follows:

```
Font.GetHeight(Graphics)
```

Font is a reference to the **Font** object that will be used for print output, and *Graphics* is a reference to the graphics object being used for printing. Then, by dividing the line height into **MarginBounds.Height** you obtain the number of lines that can be printed on a page. Code in your **PrintPage()** procedure can output that number of lines before moving to the next page. The program presented in Listing 17.7 demonstrates how to do this. The program's form contains only a single Button control; when the user clicks it, the file c:\data.txt is printed on as many pages as required. In this example, the name of the file and the print font are hard-coded, but it would be an easy matter (and good practice for you) to improve the program to permit the user to select the file to print, the page setup, and the font.

Listing 17.7 Printing a multipage text document.

```
Imports System.Drawing.Printing
Imports System.IO

Public Class Form1
  Inherits System.Windows.Forms.Form

  Dim InputStream As StreamReader


  Private Sub btnPrint_Click(ByVal sender As System.Object, _
          ByVal e As System.EventArgs) Handles btnPrint.Click

    Dim pd As New PrintDocument()
    Try
      ' Create the StreamReader for the file to be printed.
      InputStream = New StreamReader("c:\data.txt")
      ' Set up for printing.
      AddHandler pd.PrintPage, AddressOf Me.pd_PrintPage
      pd.Print()
    Catch ex As Exception
      MsgBox("Error: " & ex.Message)
    Finally
      InputStream.Close()
    End Try
  End Sub
```

```
  Private Sub pd_PrintPage(ByVal sender As Object, _
          ByVal ev As PrintPageEventArgs)

    Dim YPos As Integer = ev.MarginBounds.Top
    Dim count As Integer
    Dim currentLine As String
    Dim XPos As Integer = ev.MarginBounds.Left
    Dim f As New Font("Times", 11)
    Dim lineHeight As Integer = f.GetHeight(ev.Graphics)
    Dim numOfLines As Integer = ev.MarginBounds.Height / lineHeight

    Do Until count = numOfLines
      ' Get the next line.
      currentLine = InputStream.ReadLine
      ' If no next line we are done.
      If currentLine Is Nothing Then Exit Do
      ev.Graphics.DrawString(currentLine, f, Brushes.Black, XPos, YPos)
      YPos += lineHeight
      count += 1

      ' If there are more lines, print another page.
      If Not (currentLine Is Nothing) Then
        ev.HasMorePages = True
      Else
        ev.HasMorePages = False
      End If
    Loop

  End Sub
End Class
```

Summary

The .NET framework provides a full set of tools for creating graphical output. You can create graphical shapes, work with existing images, and create text for any imaginable programming need. Much of .NET's graphics functionality is encapsulated in the **Graphics** class, which provides members for outputting shapes, images, and text. The output can be sent to the screen or to the printer with equal ease. When you're sending graphics to the printer, the **PrintDocument** class gives your program access to a variety of printing-specific items, such as page margins. The graphics tools provided by .NET should meet any programming challenge that you encounter.

Chapter 18
Processing XML

XML (Extensible Markup Language) is attaining greater and greater importance in the world of computing. Microsoft recognized this importance when the .NET framework was developed, and Visual Basic .NET programmers have a rich and powerful set of XML tools available to them. This chapter shows you how to use some of these tools. Note the .NET framework's support for XML is extensive and goes way beyond what I can cover in a single chapter. This chapter gets you started with some of the more valuable XML tools; then—at the end—I provide a few pointers for further explorations on your own.

In this chapter, I assume that you are familiar with XML. Beyond a brief introductory overview, I make no attempt to explain how XML works or to describe its syntax rules. That's a large subject and has been the topic of entire books; there is no way I could do it justice in a single chapter. You can find detailed information on most aspects of XML and related technologies on the World Wide Web Consortium's (the standards body for XML and related technologies) Web site at **www.w3.org**.

XML Overview

XML is a *markup language* that is used to provide organization and structure for data. XML files are plain text, containing the data as well as the XML markup that structures the data. Let's look at a simple XML file:

```
<?xml version="1.0" encoding="UTF-8" ?>
<people>
```

```
  <person type="friend">
    <name>Ann Smith</name>
    <address>35 Oak Street</address>
    <city>Albany</city>
    <state>NY</state>
    <zipcode>12345</zipcode>
  </person>
  <person type="family">
     <name>Jose Gomez</name>
     <address>12A Western Boulevard</address>
     <city>Sacramento</city>
     <state>CA</state>
     <zipcode>98765</zipcode>
  </person>
</people>
```

Let's take a close look at this file:

- The first line is an XML processing instruction. It identifies the file as a version 1 XML file that uses UTF-8 (standard text) encoding.
- The second line is the opening tag of the file's root, or top-level, element. XML tags are enclosed in angle brackets and usually come in pairs, with the start tag and end tag identical except for a slash in the end element. The last line of the file is the end tag for the **<people>** element.
- The root element contains two **<person>** elements. Each **<person>** element has an attribute called "type". This is one way an XML file stores data—as attributes.
- Each **<person>** element contains child elements: **<name>**, **<address>**, and so on. Each of these child elements contains data between the start and end tags. Note that each **<person>** element is itself a child of the **<people>** element.

In XML, the names of the tags, or elements, is completely open (note that XML is case sensitive). In addition, the structure of the file—what elements and attributes are present, and their relationship to one another—is essentially unrestricted. This means that you can design an XML file to precisely match the specific needs of your data. Despite this flexibility, an XML document must follow the rules of XML syntax. An XML document that contains no syntax violations is said to be *well formed.*

Sometimes, it is desirable to place restrictions on XML files. For a particular application, you would want to ensure that all the XML files follow a certain structure. Using the address list example from above, you could require the following:

- The root element is named **<people>**.
- The root element can contain only **<person>** child elements.

- The **<person>** element has an attribute called "type".
- Each **<person>** element must contain the child elements **<name>**, **<address>**, and so on.

There are two ways to define a structure for an XML document, sometimes called a *vocabulary*: Document Type Definitions (DTDs) and XML Schemas. XML Schemas is a newer and somewhat more flexible technique than DTDs, but both approaches are in common use. A DTD or Schema may be embedded within an XML file, but more often it will be contained in a separate file. An XML processing program, called a *parser*, can check an XML document against its DTD or Schema to see if it follows the rules; this process is called *validation*. An XML file that follows all the rules in its DTD or Schema is said to be *valid*.

An XML document says nothing about how its data is to be displayed. In fact, this is one of XML's strengths—keeping the storage of data completely separate from the display of data. An XML file's data can be processed for display in many different ways: for display on-screen, for printed output, for voice synthesis, for a cell phone, and so on. The prevailing technology for formatting XML for screen display is Cascading Style Sheets (CSS). Originally developed for formatting HTML (Web pages), CSS has been extended for XML, and it provides the capability to specify fonts, colors, borders, placement, and other display parameters. The same XML data can be displayed in different ways simply by using different style sheets.

The last area of XML that I will cover is called *transformations*. A transformation consists of taking an XML file as input and, based on a set of rules, producing the desired output. Transforms are defined using the Extensible Stylesheet Language Transformations (XSLT) language, which is itself an XML vocabulary that provides essentially unlimited flexibility in defining transformation rules. Some of the more common uses of transformations include:

- Converting XML data to HTML for display in a browser
- Modifying the structure of an XML document
- Extracting a subset of the data from an XML document
- Outputting XML data with typesetting codes for printing

Schema naming confusion

You'll see at least three different names used for schemas, and it's easy to get confused. XML Schema, as I refer to in this chapter, is a schema specification developed by the World Wide Web Consortium. Sometimes, these same schemas are called XSD Schemas, for XML Schema Definition Language. For this reason, the .xds extension is usually used for files that contain XML (or XSD) Schemas. A second type of schema, XDR (for XML Data Reduced) is a Microsoft schema vocabulary used only by a few Microsoft products.

XML Standards and the W3C

One of the main reasons for the importance and popularity of XML is that it is a public, nonproprietary standard that is not controlled by any commercial interests. The standards, or specifications, for XML and most of the related technologies are developed by the World Wide Web Consortium (W3C), whose membership is open to essentially any interested party—corporations, universities, and government agencies, among others. Through a consensual public process, the W3C has developed standards for XML, XML Schemas, and the XSLT vocabulary (along with many other technologies, including non-XML related areas). A W3C standard, called a Recommendation, is freely available to one and all. The W3C has no enforcement powers, but because of the many advantages of standardization, the W3C Recommendations are widely, if not quite universally, followed.

.NET Tools for XML

Most of the .NET classes that are used for working with XML are located in the **System.Xml** namespace. They are described briefly here; detailed information and examples are provided for most of the classes in the remainder of the chapter.

One of the two classes that .NET provides for reading XML is the **XmlTextReader** class. This class performs forward-only, non-cached reading of an XML document. *Forward-only* means that the class reads the document from start to end, one node (element) at a time, and cannot "back up" to read a node after it has been passed. *Non-cached* means that the document is not maintained, or cached, in memory. Your code can access the current node as it is read, but it cannot randomly access other parts of the document. The **XmlTextReader** class checks a document for well-formedness, but it does not perform validation. Use this class for reading XML data in most situations. It is not suited for modifying XML data.

The other .NET class for reading XML is **XmlDocument**. This class implements the W3C Document Object Model (DOM) levels 1 and 2. It provides random cached access to the XML document. The entire document is maintained (cached) in memory as a node tree, and your program has random access to any part of the document. The **XmlDocument** class checks a document for well-formedness, but it does not perform validation. Use this class when you need to modify the data or structure of an XML document, and for reading a document when random access is required (for example, when the user is interacting with the data). The **XmlDocument** class is much slower than **XmlTextReader** and places higher demands on the system resources (memory).

The **XmlValidatingReader** class performs XML document validation. This class does not operate on its own, but works in conjunction with an **XmlTextReader** or **XmlDocument** instance. You can use this class to validate against either a DTD or an XML Schema.

Although I will be limiting coverage of XML to these three classes, it is important for you to realize that the .NET framework's support of XML goes well beyond what can be covered in a single chapter. I'll explain the basics here, and then you can delve into the .NET documentation as needed to learn more.

Reading XML with the XmlTextReader Class

The **XMLTextReader** class is designed for fast, forward-only access to the contents of an XML file. It is not suited for making modifications to the file's contents or structure (for that you will use the **XmlDocument** class). The **XmlTextReader** class works by starting at the beginning of the file and reading one node at a time. As each node is read, your program can either ignore it or access the node information as dictated by the needs of the application.

The steps for using the **XmlTextReader** class are as follows:

1. Create an instance of the class, passing to the constructor the name of the XML file to be read.
2. Set up a loop that calls the **Read()** method repeatedly. This method starts with the first node in the file and then reads all remaining nodes, one at a time, as it is called. It returns True if there is a node to read, False when the end of the file has been reached.
3. In the loop, examine the properties of the **XmlTextReader** object to obtain information about the current node (its type, name, data, and so on).
4. Loop back until **Read()** returns False.

The **XmlTextReader** class has a large number of public properties and methods. The ones you will need most often are explained in Tables 18.1 and 18.2.

As I state in Table 18.1, the **NodeType** property returns an **XmlNodeType** identifying the current node's type. Table 18.3 defines the meaning of the values of the **XmlNodeType**.

XML and SAX

The **XmlTextReader** class is somewhat similar to the popular SAX (Simple API for XML) model that you may be familiar with. There is one major difference between **XmlTextReader** and SAX: SAX uses a *push* model in which the XML processor informs the host program that node data is available by means of an event. In other words, the data is pushed from the XML processor to the host, and can be accepted or ignored. In contrast, **XmlTextReader** uses a *pull* model in which the parent program explicitly requests that the XML processor read a node, and then uses data from that node as needed. The parent program pulls the data from the processor as it is needed. Both models work perfectly well, although the host program coding is quite different. The .NET framework does not provide SAX support. In a situation where SAX would be appropriate, you can use the **XmlTextReader** class or you can use one of the external SAX tools that are available, such as the MSXML parser. This technique, however, is not covered here.

Table 18.1 Commonly needed properties of the XmlTextReader class.

Property	Description
AttributeCount	Returns the number of attributes that the current node has.
Depth	Returns the current node's depth (nesting level).
EOF	Returns True if the **XmlTextReader** is at the end of the file, False otherwise.
HasAttributes	Returns True if the current node has attributes.
HasValue	Returns True if the current node can have a value. A value of true does not necessarily mean that the node does have a value, only that it can.
IsEmptyElement	Returns True if the current node is an empty element (for example, **<ElementName/>**).
Item	Returns the value of an attribute.
LocalName	Returns the current node's name without any namespace prefix.
Name	Returns the current node's name with any namespace prefix.
NodeType	Returns an **XmlNodeType** identifying the current node's type (see Table 18.3).
Value	Returns the current node's value.

Table 18.2 Commonly needed methods of the XmlTextReader class.

Method	Description
Close()	Closes the XML file and reinitializes the reader.
GetAttribute(*att*)	Gets the value of an attribute. *Att* is a number specifying the position of the attribute, with the first attribute being 0, or a string specifying the name of the attribute.
IsStartElement()	Returns True if the current node is a start element or an empty element.
MoveToAttribute(*Att*)	Moves to a specific attribute. *Att* is a number specifying the position of the attribute, with the first attribute being 0, or a string specifying the name of the attribute. If you specify an attribute name, the method returns False if the attribute is not found, True otherwise.
MoveToElement()	Moves to the element that contains the current attribute.
MoveToFirstAttribute()	Moves to the first attribute.
MoveToNextAttribute()	Moves to the next attribute.
Read()	Reads the next node from the XML file. Returns True on success, False if there are no more nodes to read.

Table 18.3 XmlNodeType values returned by the NodeType property.

Value	Meaning
Attribute	An attribute
CDATA	A CDATA section
Comment	A comment
Document	The document node (root element)
DocumentType	A DOCTYPE element
Element	The start of an element (the opening tag)
EndElement	The end of an element (the closing tag)
EntityReference	An entity reference
ProcessingInstruction	An XML processing instruction
Text	The text content of an element
XmlDeclaration	The XML declaration element

Working with Nodes

It is important to realize that a "node" read by the **Read()** method does not correspond to an entire XML element. For example, look at this XML element:

```
<name>Harry</name>
```

From the perspective of the **XmlTextReader**, the three nodes will be read in the following order:

1. A node corresponding to the opening tag. This node has type **Element** and value "name".
2. A node corresponding to the data. This node has type **Text** and value "Harry".
3. A node corresponding to the closing tag. This node has type **EndElement** and value "name".

Here's a more complex example:

```
<checkbook>
  <check number="1000" date="09/01/2001">
    <payee>Amnesty International</payee>
    <amount>250.00</amount>
    <category>charity</category>
  </check>
```

When reading this XML, the **XmlTextReader** will read nodes as follows:

1. Type **Element**, name "checkbook"
2. Type **Element**, name "check"
3. Type **Element**, name "payee"
4. Type **Text**, value "Amnesty International"
5. Type **EndElement**, name "payee"
6. Type **Element**, name "amount"
7. Type **Text**, value "250.00"
8. Type **EndElement**, name "amount"

The process continues until all nodes have been read. You should note two things about the way nodes are read. First, attributes are not treated as nodes (as they are in some other XML reading technologies). When the current node is type **Element**, you can access its attributes (if any) by means of the **XmlTextReader** members. Second, the fact that an element's start tag and its data are separate nodes means that your code must perform one read operation to determine the name of an element and a second read operation to determine the element's data. This is illustrated in the second example in the following section.

Dealing with XML Exceptions

When the **XmlTextReader** class processes an XML file, it checks it for syntax (well-formedness) and also resolves external references (if any). Problems can crop up in many places, aside from the obvious one where the specified file is not found or cannot be opened. Any XML syntax error will raise an exception of type **System.Xml.XmlException**. The **Message** property of this class returns a descriptive message about the error (as is the case with all **Exception** classes). This message will, if possible, include the line number and position where the error was found. Figure 18.1 shows an example of such a message. In this case, the error was caused by using the ampersand character in XML data instead of the **&** entity (the ampersand is an XML reserved character).

The **System.Xml.XmlException** class has two additional properties, **LineNumber** and **LinePosition**, that return the line number and character position of the error. You can use this information as needed. For example, your program could open and display the offending XML file with a pointer indicating where the error occurred.

Exception handling in programs that use the **XmlTextReader** class (and other XML-related classes) follows this general scheme:

1. Catch exceptions of type **System.Xml.XmlException** to deal with XML parsing errors.
2. Catch other exceptions to deal with other types of errors.

You'll see this demonstrated in the examples that follow.

XmlTextReader Examples

Let's look at some examples of using the **XmlTextReader** class. These and other examples will make use of the XML data file in Listing 18.1. These examples consist of code fragments that you could adapt for use in your programs.

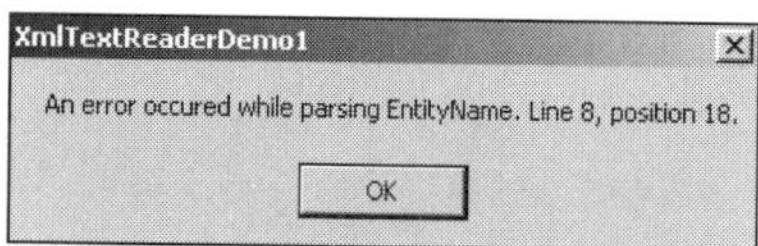

Figure 18.1
An error message provided by the **System.Xml.XmlException** class.

Listing 18.1 Checkbook.xml, an XML data file used by some of this chapter's examples.

```
<?xml version="1.0"?>
<checkbook>
  <check number="1000" date="2001-09-04">
    <payee>Amnesty International</payee>
    <amount>250.00</amount>
    <category>charity</category>
  </check>
  <check number="1001" date="2001-09-05">
    <payee>Acme Plumbing</payee>
    <amount>98.45</amount>
    <category>household</category>
  </check>
  <check number="1002" date="2001-09-12">
    <payee>Wilson Groceries</payee>
    <amount>125.12</amount>
    <category>food</category>
  </check>
  <check number="1003" date="2001-09-12">
    <payee>Western BMW</payee>
    <amount>455.00</amount>
    <category>auto repair</category>
  </check>
  <check number="1004" date="2001-09-14">
    <payee>Northern Mortgage Co.</payee>
    <amount>1225.50</amount>
    <category>mortgage</category>
  </check>
  <check number="1005" date="2001-09-18">
    <payee>Nature Conservancy</payee>
    <amount>100.00</amount>
    <category>charity</category>
  </check>
</checkbook>
```

The following code fragment creates an **XmlTextReader** for the file Checkbook.xml. It reads the file and looks for **<check>** elements. For each **<check>** element, it reads the value of the date attribute. All of the date values are concatenated together in a type **StringBuilder** (a useful class for certain string manipulations—please refer to the Visual Basic .NET documentation for details). Here it is:

```
Dim rdr As XmlTextReader
Dim buf As New StringBuilder()
```

```
Try
  rdr = New XmlTextReader("checkbook.xml")
  While rdr.Read()
    ' Look for the start node.
    If rdr.NodeType = XmlNodeType.Element Then
      ' Is it a "check" element?
      If rdr.Name = "check" Then
          buf.Append(rdr.GetAttribute("date") _
              & vbCrLf)
      End If
    End If
  End While
Catch ex As System.Xml.XmlException
  MsgBox("Xml error " & ex.Message)
Catch ex As Exception
  MsgBox("General error " & ex.Message)
Finally
  If Not rdr Is Nothing Then rdr.Close()
End Try
```

The following code counts the number of checks written to the category "charity" and totals the amount of the checks. Note how the code makes use of flags to keep track of the name of the element that was just read. The results are displayed in a message box. The code is as follows:

```
Dim rdr As XmlTextReader
Dim amount As String
Dim total As Single = 0
Dim count As Integer = 0
Dim isAmountElement As Boolean
Dim isCategoryElement As Boolean

Try
  rdr = New XmlTextReader("checkbook.xml")
  While rdr.Read()
    ' Look for a start node.
    If rdr.NodeType = XmlNodeType.Element Then
      ' Is it an "amount" or "category" element?
      ' If so, set the corresponding flag.
      If rdr.Name = "amount" Then
        isAmountElement = True
      Else
        isAmountElement = False
      End If
      If rdr.Name = "category" Then
        isCategoryElement = True
```

```
      Else
        isCategoryElement = False
      End If
    End If
    If rdr.NodeType = XmlNodeType.Text Then
      ' Is it a "category" element with the
      ' value "charity"? If so, increment
      ' the count and add the amount to the total.
      If isCategoryElement And rdr.Value = "charity" Then
        count += 1
        total += amount
      End If
      ' If it is an "amount" element, save the
      ' value for possible future use.
      If isAmountElement Then
        amount = rdr.Value
      End If
    End If
  End While
Catch ex As Exception
  MsgBox("Error " & ex.Message)
Finally
  If Not rdr Is Nothing Then rdr.Close()
End Try
MsgBox("You wrote " & count.ToString & _
    " checks to charity totaling " & Format(total, "C"))
```

Validating XML with the XmlValidatingReader Class

To validate an XML file against a DTD or a Schema, you use the **XmlValidatingReader** class. This class does not work alone, but is used in conjunction with an instance of the **XmlTextReader** class. The result is that you get validation along with the same access to the document contents that **XmlTextReader** provides. The properties and methods of these two classes are almost identical, with the differences being in three properties of the **XmlValidatingReader** class that are related to validation.

The first of these properties is **ValidationType**, which specifies the type of validation to be performed. The possible settings for this property are the **ValidationType** constants that are described in Table 18.4.

The second property is **Schemas**, which references an **XmlSchemaCollection** that contains the schema(s) that will be used for validation. You use this property when the **ValidationType** property is set to **Schema** or **XDR**.

Table 18.4 ValidationType constants for the ValidationType property.

Constant	Description
Auto	Validates using information embedded in the XML document. This can be a DTD defined in a **DOCTYPE** element, a "schemalocation" attribute, or an inline schema. If no validation information is found, no error occurs and the class acts as a nonvalidating parser.
DTD	Validates against a DTD. The DTD can be embedded within the XML or located in an external file that is referenced in the XML file.
None	Performs no validation.
Schema	Validates against an XML Schema identified by the **Schemas** property.
XDR	Validates against an XDR Schema (a proprietary Microsoft schema vocabulary) identified by the **Schemas** property.

The final property is **ValidationEventHandler**, used to inform the XML reader of the event procedure that will handle validation errors. This event procedure, which you have to create, must have the following form:

```
Sub CallBackName(sender As Object, args As ValidationEventArgs)
' Code to handle error goes here.
End Sub
```

The name of the procedure can be anything you like within Visual Basic's naming rules. When a validation error occurs, the XML reader calls the procedure, with information about the error contained in the *args* argument. Code in this procedure can display messages to the user, set flags, or perform other actions as required by the program. Use **args.ErrorCode** to obtain the error's numerical code and **args.Message** to obtain the error's text description. You can also use the **LineNumber** and **LinePosition** properties of the **XMLValidatingReader** instance to get information about the location of the error in the XML file.

To inform the **XmlValidatingReader** object of your event handler, use the following syntax (vrdr is an instance of the **XmlValidatingreader** class). Note that this is a different syntax than is usually used to set a property, requiring the **AddHandler** statement and the **AddressOf** operator:

```
AddHandler vrdr.ValidationEventHandler, AddressOf Me.CallBackName
```

You do not have to specify a handler for validation errors. In this case, the reader will throw an exception when a validation error occurs. The advantage of using a validation error handler is that multiple validation errors can be detected and reported during a single pass over the XML file. Without an error handler, the reader reports and stops when the first error is encountered.

Note that the validation event handler is called *only* for validation errors. If another kind of error occurs, such as a syntax error in your XML or DTD file, an exception is thrown and must be caught in the usual manner.

To use the **XmlValidatingReader** class to validate an XML document and read its data, follow these general steps. This assumes that the XML file contains the DTD/Schema to be used for validation, either inline or as a reference. Here are the steps:

1. Create an instance of the **XmlTextReader** class connected to the XML file.

2. Create an instance of the **XmlValidatingReader** class and pass it a reference to the **XmlTextReader** class that was created in Step 1.

3. Create an event handler procedure to handle validation errors.

4. Set the **XmlValidatingReader** object's **ValidationType** and **ValidationEventHandler** properties.

5. If you are validating against an external XML or XDR Schema, set the **Schemas** property to identify the Schema file.

6. Call the **XmlValidatingReader** object's **Read()** method repeatedly until the end of the XML file is reached.

Validating Against a DTD

To demonstrate validating an XML file against a DTD, I have created a DTD for the checkbook.xml file that was presented in Listing 18.1. This DTD, checkbook.dtd, is shown in Listing 18.2. This is an admittedly simple DTD, but it will serve perfectly well for the demonstration. The DTD specifies that the XML file must be structured as follows:

- The **<checkbook>** element can contain one or more **<check>** elements.

- Each **<check>** element must contain exactly one each of the **<payee>**, **<amount>**, and **<category>** elements.

- The **<payee>**, **<amount>**, and **<category>** elements each contain text data.

- Each **<check>** element must have attributes named number and date.

The XML file to be validated is the one shown previously in Listing 18.1. It needs one minor modification—the addition of a **DOCTYPE** element to reference the DTD file. Add the following line to Listing 18.1, just before the opening **<checkbook>** tag:

```
<!DOCTYPE checkbook SYSTEM "checkbook.dtd">
```

This is the tag that tells the **XmlValidatingReader** what DTD to use when validating the file. Of course, both the XML file and the DTD file must be in the project's bin directory for the program to be able to access them.

Listing 18.2 Checkbook.dtd provides a DTD for the Checkbook.xml file.

```
<!ELEMENT checkbook (check)+>
<!ELEMENT check (payee, amount, category)>
<!ELEMENT payee (#PCDATA)>
<!ELEMENT amount (#PCDATA)>
<!ELEMENT category (#PCDATA)>
<!ATTLIST check number CDATA #REQUIRED>
<!ATTLIST check date CDATA #REQUIRED>
```

The demonstration project is a Windows console application. Run from the command line, it opens the file checkbook.xml and validates it against the DTD checkbook.dtd. The source code for this project is shown in Listing 18.3.

Listing 18.3 Source code for the project ValidateDTDDemo.

```
Imports System
Imports System.IO
Imports System.Xml
Imports System.Xml.Schema

Module Module1

  Public Class ValidateXML
    Private vrdr As XmlValidatingReader
    Private rdr As XmlTextReader
    Private Succeeded As Boolean = True

    Public Sub DoValidation(ByVal filename As String)

      ' This method does the validation.
      Try
        ' Create the XmlTextReader
        rdr = New XmlTextReader(filename)
        ' Create the validating reader.
        vrdr = New XmlValidatingReader(rdr)
        ' Validation type is DTD.
        vrdr.ValidationType = ValidationType.DTD
        ' Register the callback procedure.
        AddHandler vrdr.ValidationEventHandler, AddressOf Me.MyCallBack
        ' Read the document.
        While vrdr.Read()
          ' You could access the contents of the XML file in this loop
          ' if desired.
        End While
```

```
    Catch ex As System.Xml.XmlException
      Console.WriteLine("Xml Exception: " & ex.Message)
      Exit Sub
    Catch ex As Exception
      Console.WriteLine("General Exception: " & ex.Message)
      Exit Sub
    Finally
      If Not vrdr Is Nothing Then
        vrdr.Close()
      End If
    End Try
    ' Display a success or failure message.
    If Succeeded Then
      Console.WriteLine("Validation was successful.")
    Else
      Console.WriteLine("Validation failed.")
    End If
    ' The following line makes the program wait until the
    ' user presses Enter.
    Console.ReadLine()

  End Sub

  Private Sub MyCallBack(ByVal sender As Object, _
      ByVal args As ValidationEventArgs)

    ' This method is called when a validation error occurs.
    Succeeded = False
    ' Display error information to the user.
    Console.WriteLine("Validation error: " & args.Message)
    If rdr.LineNumber > 0 Then
      Console.WriteLine("Line: " & rdr.LineNumber & " Position: " _
          & rdr.LinePosition)
    End If

  End Sub

End Class

Sub Main()

  ' Create an instance of the validation class.
  Dim vc As New ValidateXML()
  ' Call the validation method.
  vc.DoValidation("checkbook.xml")

End Sub

End Module
```

Validation errors are displayed at the command prompt with the line number and position identified. An example of this is shown in Figure 18.2. Messages for other errors (nonvalidation) are displayed as well. If there are no errors and the validation succeeds, the message "Validation was successful" is displayed. I suggest that you experiment by modifying the file checkbook.xml so that it will fail validation. For example, you could change the name of an element or delete one of the attributes.

Validating Against a Schema

Validating an XML file against an XML Schema is similar in principle to validating against a DTD, but different in the details. The XML Schema file is not referenced in the XML file, but rather must be specified separately. This is done using the **XmlSchemaCollection** class, part of the **System.Xml.Schema** namespace. This class can hold one or more schemas, each with an optional associated namespace. To create an instance of this class and add a schema to it, use this syntax:

```
Dim xsc As New XmlSchemaCollection()
xsc.Add(namespace, schemaFileName)
```

If you do not want a namespace associated with this schema, pass an empty string for the first argument. The **XmlSchemaCollection** class has several other constructors that let you add a schema that is specified by an **XmlSchema** object or a schema that is connected to an **XmlReader** object (**XmlReader** is the base class for **XmlTextReader** and **XmlValidatingReader**). You can refer to the Visual Basic .NET documentation for information on these other constructors.

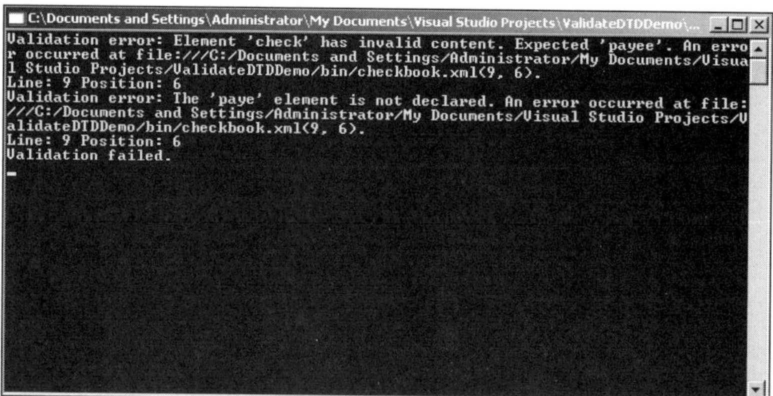

Figure 18.2
A validation error message displayed by the ValidateDTDDemo program.

After you have added the required schema(s) to the **XmlSchemasCollection** object, you associate the schemas with your **XmlValidatingReader** object by means of its **Schemas** property. If vrdr is a reference to the **XmlValidatingreader** object, and xsc is a reference to the **XmlSchemaCollection** object, the syntax is as follows:

```
vrdr.Schemas.Add(xsc)
```

You may have noticed that this arrangement makes it possible to load more than one schema into an **XmlSchemaCollection** object, and then associate more than one **XmlSchemaCollection** object with an **XmlValidatingReader**. How, then, does the reader know which schema or schemas to use when validating a particular XML file? The answer lies in namespaces, a central part of XML. The details are beyond the scope of this book, but by proper use of namespaces, you can ensure that the proper schema is used.

When you use the **XmlValidatingReader** to validate an XML file against a schema, validation errors will be caught by a callback procedure that you create (as described earlier in this chapter in the section on validating against DTDs). Other exceptions can occur, and these must be caught using a **Try...Catch** block in the usual manner. Specifically:

- If the XML file contains a syntax error or nonresolvable reference, an **XmlException** is thrown.
- If the XML Schema file contains an error, such as referencing a nonexisting data type, an **XmlSchemaException** is thrown.

To demonstrate how to validate an XML file against an XML Schema, I have created the XML Schema shown in Listing 18.4. The XML file is checkbook.xml from Listing 18.1. This schema imposes essentially the same constraints on the XML as the DTD presented previously in the chapter. It goes further than the DTD in that the specific data type of some elements is specified—for example, that the date attribute must be type **date** rather than any string.

Listing 18.4 Checkbook.xsd is a schema for the checkbook XML data file.

```
<xsd:schema xmlns:xsd="http://www.w3.org/2001/XMLSchema"
    xmlns="urn:checkbook-schema"
    elementFormDefault="qualified"
    targetNamespace="urn:checkbook-schema">

<xsd:complexType name="onecheck">
  <xsd:sequence>
    <xsd:element name="payee" type="xsd:string"/>
    <xsd:element name="amount" type="xsd:float"/>
    <xsd:element name="category" type="xsd:string"/>
  </xsd:sequence>
```

```
  <xsd:attribute name="number" type="xsd:integer" use="required"/>
  <xsd:attribute name="date" type="xsd:date" use="required"/>
</xsd:complexType>

<xsd:complexType name="checklist">
  <xsd:sequence>
    <xsd:element name="check" type="onecheck" minOccurs="0"
     maxOccurs="unbounded"/>
  </xsd:sequence>
</xsd:complexType>

<xsd:element name ="checkbook" type="checklist"/>

</xsd:schema>
```

To create the demonstration program, follow these steps:

1. Create a new Windows Form application named ValidateSchemaDemo. Change the **Text** property of the form to XML Validation.
2. Place a TextBox control on the form. Set its properties as follows, and then increase the height of the TextBox control so it can display multiple lines:
   - **Name**: txtOutput
   - **MultiLine**: True
   - **Locked**: True
   - **Scrollbars**: Vertical
   - **Text**: (a blank string)
3. Place a Button control on the form. Change its properties as follows:
   - **Name**: btnStart
   - **Text**: Start
4. Place another Button control on the form, as follows:
   - **Name**: btnQuit
   - **Text**: Quit
5. Add the code from Listing 18.5 to the project's form. This listing does not show the Windows Form Designer–generated code.

Listing 18.5 Code in the Schema validation demo.

```
Imports System.Xml
Imports System.Xml.Schema
Imports System.text

Public Class Form1
  Inherits System.Windows.Forms.Form

  ' These variables must be global so
  ' declare them here.
  Dim Succeeded As Boolean = True
  Dim rdr As XmlTextReader
  Dim vrdr As XmlValidatingReader

  Private Sub btnStart_Click(ByVal sender As System.Object, _
        ByVal e As System.EventArgs) Handles btnStart.Click

    Dim ofd As New OpenFileDialog()
    Dim xmlFileName As String
    Dim xsdFileName As String

    ' Set up the dialog to open an XML file.
    ofd.Filter = "XML Files (*.xml)|*.xml"
    If ofd.ShowDialog = DialogResult.OK Then
      xmlFileName = ofd.FileName
    Else
      ' If no file selected, exit.
      Exit Sub
    End If

    ' Set up the dialog to open an XSD file.
    ofd.Filter = "XSD Files (*.xsd)|*.xsd"
    If ofd.ShowDialog = DialogResult.OK Then
      xsdFileName = ofd.FileName
    Else
      ' If no file selected, exit sub.
      Exit Sub
    End If

    ProcessXML(xmlFileName, xsdFileName)

  End Sub
```

```
Private Sub ProcessXML(ByVal xmlFileName As String, _
        ByVal xsdFileName As String)

    ' This method does the actual processing.
    Dim xsc As New XmlSchemaCollection()
    Try
      ' Set up the reader and the validating reader.
      rdr = New XmlTextReader(xmlFileName)
      vrdr = New XmlValidatingReader(rdr)
      ' Add the selected Schema file to the collection.
      xsc.Add("urn:checkbook-schema", xsdFileName)
      ' Set the validating reader's validation properties.
      vrdr.ValidationType = ValidationType.Schema
      vrdr.Schemas.Add(xsc)
      ' Specify the callback handler for validation errors.
      AddHandler vrdr.ValidationEventHandler, AddressOf ValidationCallBack
      ' Read the entire file.
      While vrdr.Read()
      End While
    Catch ex As XmlException
      MsgBox("XML exception: " & ex.message)
      Exit Sub
    Catch ex As XmlSchemaException
      MsgBox("Schema exception: " & ex.message)
      Exit Sub
    Catch ex As Exception
      MsgBox("General exception: " & ex.message)
      Exit Sub
    Finally
      If Not vrdr Is Nothing Then vrdr.Close()
      ' Display result message.
      If Succeeded Then
        MsgBox("Validation OK")
      Else
        MsgBox("Validation failed")
      End If
    End Try

End Sub

Private Sub btnQuit_Click(ByVal sender As System.Object, _
        ByVal e As System.EventArgs) Handles btnQuit.Click
    End
End Sub
```

```
  Private Sub ValidationCallBack(ByVal sender As Object, _
          ByVal args As ValidationEventArgs)
    ' This is the callback for validation errors.
    Dim buf As New StringBuilder()
    Succeeded = False
    ' Add any text currently in the TextBox to buf.
    buf.Append(txtOutput.Text)
    ' Append the latest validation error information.
    buf.Append("Validation error: ")
    buf.Append(args.Message & vbCrLf)
    ' If available, append line number info.
    If rdr.LineNumber > 0 Then
      buf.Append("line " & rdr.LineNumber)
      buf.Append("  Position: " & rdr.LinePosition)
    End If
    ' Add two blank lines.
    buf.Append(vbCrLf & vbCrLf)
    ' Put text back in TextBox.
    txtOutput.Text = buf.ToString
  End Sub

End Class
```

When the program runs, click on the Start button. You next select an XML file and an XSD file (containing the XML Schema) to process. If the validation is successful, a message box pops up with a message to that effect. If the validation fails, the validation error messages are displayed in the program's text box, and a "failure" message is displayed. Figure 18.3 shows an example of such a validation error message. This error was caused by the "date" attribute being omitted from one of the **<check>** elements in the checkbook.xml file. Because the checkbook.xsd schema defines this as a required attribute, this omission triggers a validation error.

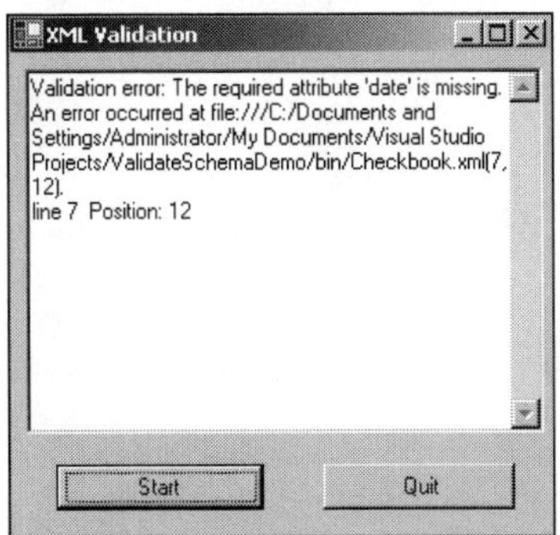

Figure 18.3
The XML Schema Validator demonstration displaying a validation error message.

Using the XmlDocument Class

The **XmlDocument** class provides a Visual Basic .NET program with access to the contents and structure of an XML document. This class implements the W3C DOM levels 1 and 2 (**www.w3.org/DOM/**). It can be used to read data from the document as well as to modify the document's data and structure. The **XmlDocument** class reads the entire XML document and stores it in memory as a *node tree*. Everything in the document—elements, attributes, processing instructions, comments, and so on—is a node. There is a root node representing the document itself, with all other nodes branching off from it. Here are some terms that are used when discussing node trees:

- *Parent*—The node one step above a given node. Every node except the root node has a parent.
- *Child*—A node one step below a given node. A node can have zero or more children.
- *Descendant*—Any node below a given node on the same branch.
- *Ancestor*—Any node above a given node on the same branch.
- *Sibling*—A node with the same parent as a given node.
- *Leaf*—A node with no children.

The concept of *walking the tree* is important when you're working with the **XmlDocument** class. Starting at any location on the tree, often at the root, you can traverse or *walk* the nodes and branches to reach any node in the tree. The notion of walking the tree is evident in many of the members of the **XmlDocument** class. For example, given any node in the tree, the **FirstChild** property returns that node's first child (if any), and the **PreviousSibling** property returns the preceding node.

Overview of Working with the XmlDocument Class

Before looking at the details of the **XmlDocument** class, it will be useful to have an overview of the process, in very simple form, as shown here:

1. Create an instance of the **XmlDocument** object.
2. Load the XML into the **XmlDocument** object. An XML file can be loaded from a disk file or from a URL.
3. Use the members of the **XmlDocument** object to read the document's content and structure and to modify its content and structure.
4. If the document was modified, save it.

When you're working with the **XmlDocument** class and the DOM, numerous additional classes will be involved. Table 18.5 lists and briefly describes these classes. Covering the details of all these classes is beyond the scope of this chapter, but by knowing these classes exist, you can look up the required details in the online help when and if you need to use them.

Loading and Saving XML Documents

The first step in using the **XmlDocument** class is to load your XML into it. You can load XML directly from a file or URL as follows. The following examples assume that xmlDoc is a reference to an instance of the **XmlDocument** class.

```
XmlDoc.Load(source)
```

Source is the name of the XML file, including the path, or a URL. Parse errors (XML syntax errors) are reported by means of throwing a **System.Xml.XmlException**. Another way to

Table 18.5 Other classes that are used when you work with the XmlDocument class.

Class	Description
XPathNavigator	Use to navigate a DOM node tree and to select subsets of nodes based on XPath expressions (XPath is a language for identifying sections of XML documents; it is not covered here.).
XmlAttribute*	Represents an attribute node.
XmlAttributeCollection	Represents a collection of attributes.
XmlCDataSection*	Represents a CDATA node.
XmlComment*	Represents an XML comment node.
XmlDeclaration*	Represents the XML declaration node.
XmlDocumentFragment*	Represents a fragment of an XML document.
XmlDocumentType*	Represents an XML document type declaration node.
XmlElement*	Represents an XML element node. Note that all elements are nodes, but all nodes are not elements.
XmlEntity*	Represents an XML entity declaration node.
XmlEntityReference*	Represents an entity reference node.
XmlNamedNodeMap	Represents a collection of nodes.
XmlNode	Represents a single document node. This is an abstract class that is inherited by many of the other classes listed in this table (as marked by an asterisk). Note that the **XmlDocument** class is itself based on the **XmlNode** class, underscoring the fact that the DOM sees the entire document as a node.
XmlNodeList	Represents an ordered collection of nodes.
XmlNotation*	Represents an XML notation declaration.
XmlProcessingInstruction*	Represents a processing instruction node.
XmlText*	Represents the text contents of an element or attribute.

** Classes that inherit from **XmlNode**.*

load XML is to first associate the XML file with a type **XmlTextReader** and then call the **Load()** method to associate the **XmlTextReader** with the **XmlDocument** object:

```
Dim rdr As New XmlTextReader(source)
Dim xmlDoc As New XmlDocument
xmlDoc.Load(rdr)
```

In this case, parse errors will be reported by the **XmlTextReader** object, not the **XmlDocument** object. By using this technique, you can validate the XML against a DTD or a schema, something that the **XmlDocument** class cannot do on its own. All you need to do is use the **XmlValidatingReader** to validate the XML as described earlier in this chapter, then load it into the **XmlDocument** object. This code fragment shows how:

```
Dim xmlDoc As New XmlDocument
Dim rdr As New XmlTextReader(source)
Dim vrdr As New XmlValidatingReader(rdr)
' Set validation options and perform validation here.
xmlDoc.Load(vrdr)
```

You can also load an XML document or fragment that exists as a string in a program variable with the **LoadXML()** method. The syntax is as follows:

```
xmlDoc.loadXML(s)
```

Here, ***s*** is a string containing the XML. The result of this method is the same as if the XML had been in a file and loaded with the **Load()** method.

If your program has modified the XML, you will probably want to save it. This is done with the **Save()** method with the following syntax:

```
xmlDoc.save(s)
```

S can be a file name or a reference to an **XmlTextWriter** object (covered later in the chapter).

Walking the Tree

After loading an XML document into an **XmlDocument** object, you are ready to access the XML tree created by the parser. Generally you will do this by means of the **DocumentElement** property, which returns a reference to the root element of the XML tree (or **Null** if no root exists, which would happen only if a document has not been loaded). The reference returned by this property is to a type **XmlElement** object. This class is one of the classes, listed in Table 18.5, that is used by the DOM to represent various parts, or nodes, of the XML document tree. Note that many of the members discussed here return a type **XmlNode**, which is, you may recall, an abstract type. The model is designed this way because you usually do not know the exact type of node that will be returned by a method or property. For example, if you call **FirstChild** the return will be a type **XmlElement** if the first child is an element, a type **XmlComment** if the first child is a comment, and so on. Because all these specific types inherit from **XmlNode** (as detailed in Table 18.5), you have the flexibility needed to deal with the various return types.

When you have a reference to the root element (or any other element), you can "walk" the tree to any desired location using the following properties:

- **FirstChild**—A reference to the first child element (in document order).
- **LastChild**—A reference to the last child element (in document order).
- **ChildNodes**—An **XmlNodeList** of all the child elements. The list will have length 0 if there are no children.
- **NextSibling**—A reference to the next sibling element (as determined by the parent node's child list).
- **PreviousSibling**—A reference to the previous sibling element (as determined by the parent node's child list).
- **ParentNode**—A reference to the parent node.
- **HasChildNodes**—Returns True if the current node has children, False if not.

Using these properties, you can start anywhere in the document tree and move to any element in the tree, as well as perform other tasks related to the document tree. These properties return the special value **Nothing** if the referenced node does not exist. Some examples are presented in Table 18.6.

Although you will almost always start at the root element, you do not have to continue using the root as your reference point. Doing so can lead to some cumbersome code if you need to reference nodes at some distance from the root. Instead, you can create a separate reference to a specific node and then use that as your reference. Suppose, for example, that

Table 18.6 Some tree-walking examples.

To	Do This
Reference the second child of element N	**N.FirstChild.NextSibling**
Reference the last sibling of element N	**N.ParentNode.LastChild**
Determine if element N has any children	If **N.HasChildNodes** is True
Reference the first child element of node N's grandparent element	**N.ParentNode.ParentNode.FirstChild**

you want to work with the second **<check>** element from the XML file in Listing 18.1. Here's how you would do it (assuming that the XML file has already been loaded into xmlDoc):

```
Dim n As XmlNode
n = xmlDoc.DocumentElement.FirstChild.NextSibling
```

Reading Element and Attribute Data

Many of the tasks that you'll use the **XmlDocument** class for involve accessing the data in elements and in attributes. For this present discussion, this refers to the names of the elements and attributes as well as to the text stored in them. Some of the properties you will use for this purpose are described in Table 18.7. Note that some of these properties can be used to change the XML data, as will be covered later in this chapter.

The first examples will deal with retrieving element data (as opposed to attribute data, which will be covered later). To illustrate some of these properties, I will use the following XML fragment:

```
<person category="friend">
  <name>John Doe</name>
  <yearofbirth>1955</yearofbirth>
  <phone>555-555-1212</phone>
</person>
```

Assume that you have walked the tree and that the variable **MyNode** is a reference to this element (the **<person>** element). The return of the properties from Table 18.7 is shown in Table 18.8.

Data in this form is useful for some situations, but not for others. Let's take the example a step further and see how things work if you are working with a simple element—one that contains no child elements but only text. In this case, I will use the **<name>** element from the above XML fragment, referenced as **MyNode.FirstChild**. The results are shown in Table 18.9.

Table 18.7 Properties for reading element information.

Property	Description
InnerText	Gets or sets the text contained in the node and all its children, concatenated into a single string.
InnerXml	Gets or sets the XML markup representing the children of the current node.
LocalName	Gets the name of the node without any namespace prefix.
Name	Gets the name of the node with any namespace prefix.
OuterXml	Gets or sets the XML markup representing the node and its child nodes.
Value	Gets or sets the value of the node. The data returned depends on the type of node.

Table 18.8 Examples of retrieving data from XML.

Example	Return value
MyNode.InnerText	John Doe1955555-555-1212
MyNode.InnerXml	<name>John Doe</name><yearofbirth>1955</yearofbirth> <phone>555-555-1212</phone>
MyNode.OuterXml	<person category="friend"> <name>John Doe</name> <yearofbirth>1955</yearofbirth> <phone>555-555-1212</phone></person>
MyNode.Name **MyNode.LocalName**	person
MyNode.Value	Nothing (a blank string)

Table 18.9 More examples of retrieving data from XML.

Example	Return value
MyNode.FirstChild.InnerText	John Doe
MyNode.FirstChild.InnerXml	John Doe
MyNode.FirstChild.OuterXml	<name>John Doe</name>
MyNode.FirstChild.Name MyNode.FirstChild.LocalName	name
MyNode.FirstChild.Value	Nothing (a blank string)

You may be wondering why, in both of these examples, the **Value** property returns an empty string. This has to do with the way nodes in the tree are arranged. Suppose you navigate to a simple node such as this one:

```
<name>John Doe</name>
```

You may think that you are at a leaf (a node with no children) but in fact you are not. The node that represents this element, a type **XmlElement** node representing the entire **<name>** element, itself has a child: a type **XmlText** node representing the text data in the element. The **Value** property always returns a blank string for type **XmlElement** nodes (and also for several other node types, as detailed in the .NET online reference material). If, however, you navigate to the element's child—in other words, from the **XmlElement** node to the **XmlText** node—the **Value** property returns the text in the element. This means that you have two ways to retrieve the text data in an element: navigate to the element and use its **InnerText** property, or navigate to the element's child and use the **Value** property.

To access an element's attributes, use the **Attributes** property. If the current node is an element node, this property returns a type **XmlAttributeCollection**, even if the node has no attributes. If the node is of another type, this property returns **Nothing**. The **XmlAttributeCollection** class has members that you use to work with the attributes. The most commonly needed ones are as follows:

- **Count** returns the number of attributes, zero if the element has no attributes.
- **ItemOf(*sel*)** returns a reference to an attribute as a type **XmlAttribute**. *Sel* can be an integer giving the attribute position (0 through **Count-1**) or a string specifying the attribute's name.

After you have a reference to an attribute, use the **Name** and **Value** properties to get the attribute's name and value, respectively. For example, the following code fragment displays all of an element's attribute names and values in the Visual Studio Output window. Assume that **n** is a reference to a node of type **XmlElement**:

```
Dim i As Integer
With n.Attributes
  If .Count > 0 Then
    For i = 0 To .Count - 1
     Debug.Writeline(.Item(i).Name & ": " & .Item(i).Value)
    Next
  End If
End With
```

Demonstrating the XmlDocument Class

The program developed in this section demonstrates how to use the **XmlDocument** class to access element and attribute data in an XML file. It makes use of the checkbook.xml file that was presented earlier in this chapter. Note that the program performs no error checking, something that should always be present in any production application. The code "walks" through the XML file and extracts the names and values of the attributes and elements, and concatenates them together for display in a text box. Follow these steps to create the demo program:

1. Start a new Windows Application project. Change the form's **Text** property to "XmlDocument Demo".
2. Place a TextBox control on the form. Set its properties as follows:
   - **Name**: txtOutput
   - **MultiLine**: True
   - **Text**: (a blank string)
   - **ScrollBars**: Vertical
3. Resize the TextBox control to fill the width of the form and about two-thirds of its height.

4. Add a Button control beneath the TextBox control. Set its properties as follows:

   - **Name**: btnProcess
   - **Text**: Process

5. Place the code from Listing 18.6 into the **Click()** event procedure for the button. If necessary, edit the first line so it points to the location of the checkbook.xml file. Figure 18.4 shows the XmlDocument demo's display.

Listing 18.6 Demonstrating the XmlDocument class.

```
Private Sub BtnProcess_Click(ByVal sender As System.Object, _
          ByVal e As System.EventArgs) Handles btnProcess.Click

  Dim rdr As New XmlTextReader("checkbook.xml")
  Dim xmlDoc As New XmlDocument()
  xmlDoc.Load(rdr)
  Dim n As XmlNode
  Dim n1 As XmlNode
  Dim i As Integer
  Dim s As String

  ' Set n to the first <check> node.
  n = xmlDoc.DocumentElement.FirstChild
  Do While True
    ' Write out this element's attributes.
    With n.Attributes
      If .Count > 0 Then
        For i = 0 To .Count - 1
          s &= .Item(i).Name & ": " & .ItemOf(i).Value & vbCrLf
        Next
      End If
    End With
    ' Set n1 to the first child node (a <payee> node).
    n1 = n.FirstChild
    Do While Not n1 Is Nothing
      s &= n1.Name & ": " & n1.InnerText & vbCrLf
      n1 = n1.NextSibling()
    Loop
    n = n.NextSibling()
    If n Is Nothing Then Exit Do
    ' A blank line.
    s &= vbCrLf
  Loop

  txtOutput.Text = s

End Sub
```

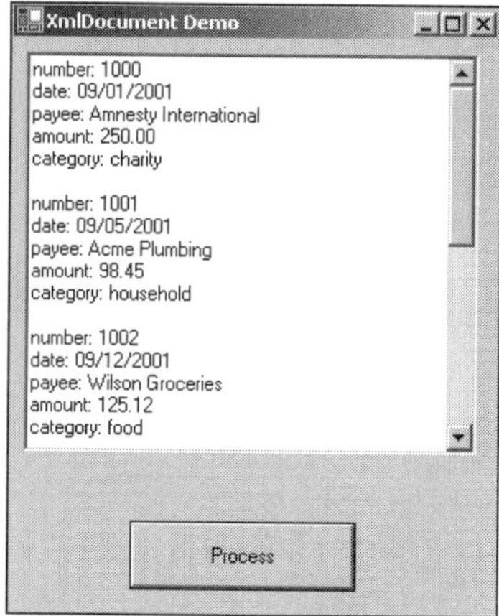

Figure 18.4
The XmlDocument demo program displaying data from checkbook.xml.

Other XML Tools

This chapter has covered only a few of the most important .NET classes for working with XML. The .NET framework includes many more XML-related components, and covering all or even most of them would require an entire book. With the start provided in this chapter, you can explore .NET's XML capabilities in more detail when and if the need arises. Here's a quick overview of some of the goodies you will find:

- The **XmlDocument** class, in addition to its capabilities covered in this chapter, provides for modification of XML document data and structure.
- The **XmlTextWriter** class writes XML to a stream or file. The XML produced by this class conforms to the W3C XML 1.0 Recommendation.
- The **XmlDataDocument** class provides access to XML data using more traditional database techniques.
- The **XmlNamedNodeMap** class provides access to members of a node map by name or index.
- The **XPathNavigator** class navigates through XML data using XPath expression.
- The **XslTransform** class performs XSLT transformations on XML data.

Summary

Extensible Markup Language is an important technology in many areas of computing. Visual Basic .NET programmers will be happy to know that they have an extremely powerful set of XML tools to work with. This chapter shows you how to use some of the more important XML tools that the .NET framework offers: **XmlTextReader** for fast reading of XML data, **XmlValidatingReader** for validation of XML data, and **XmlDocument** for access to XML data using the Document Object Model. With this start, you should be able to fully explore Visual Basic .NET's XML tools to meet any XML programming challenge that you might face.

Chapter 19
Database Access with ADO.NET

If you surveyed all the computers in the world, what kind of program would be running most often? Not games, not word processors, but database programs. When a long-distance company calls to pitch its service, the agent uses a database program. When someone sends an order for elk-lined pajamas to L. L. Bean, the order goes into a database program. When the clerk at the auto parts store checks to see whether a left-handed cam inverter for your 1971 Ford Falcon is in stock, he or she uses a database program. Wherever information needs to be managed, you usually find a database program at work.

From its beginnings, Visual Basic has provided excellent support for database programming, and this tradition continues with Visual Basic .NET. With the powerful database tools at your disposal, you'll be able to create sophisticated user interfaces and access a variety of standard database file formats, all with relatively little programming.

The first part of this chapter covers some necessary fundamentals by providing a brief introduction to database concepts such as tables, records, fields, relational databases, and primary keys. I do not attempt anything approaching complete coverage of database principles and fundamentals; this subject could occupy its own book. If you already have a good familiarity with this material, you can skip ahead to the section "ADO.NET." The remainder of the chapter provides an introduction and some examples of using ADO.NET in your Windows applications.

So, What's a Database?

A *database* is a collection of information, or data, arranged in a specific manner. The basic unit of information in a database is called a *record*. Each record in a database contains two or more *fields* that hold specific types of information. Perhaps the most common example of a database is an address list. Each entry in the database constitutes one record: an individual's name and address information. Each record in the database contains fields that hold separate items of information: first name, last name, address, city, and so on. These fields are the same for every record in the database, and they are assigned names identifying the data they contain.

A database is sometimes displayed in row and column format. Each row contains one record, and each column contains one field, as illustrated in Figure 19.1. In this case, a single record can be referred to as a *row* and an individual field as a *column*. The entire collection of records is called a *table*. Some databases contain more than one table, with the records in each table having a different field structure. We will deal with multiple-table databases soon.

A database program is designed to let you work with the information in a database. Some capabilities are common to any database program—adding, finding, and deleting records, for example. Many other capabilities are customized to fit a specific program. In an address list database, for example, you might want the ability to print envelopes and sort the records by ZIP code. A graphics database might need the capability to input and store images from a scanner. The possibilities are endless. If you write database programs as part of your job, you never know what someone might ask you to do next. Here's one of the advantages of Visual Basic: As a full-featured programming language, it offers the flexibility to build many capabilities right into the database program. Thanks to its database tools, most of the fundamental database tasks are simple to accomplish.

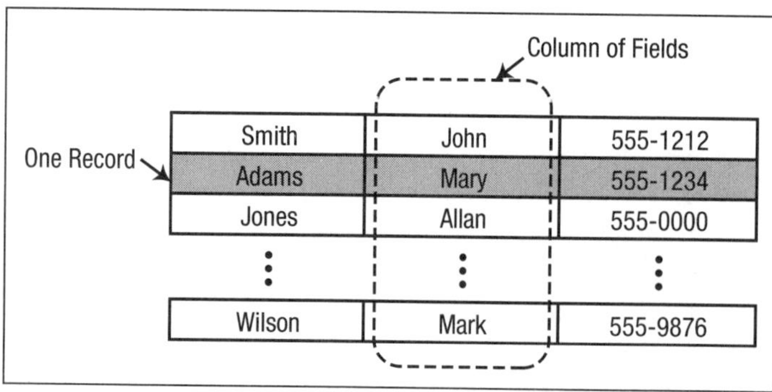

Figure 19.1
A database table has one row per record and one column per field.

Relational Databases

With rare exceptions, all modern database development involves *relational* databases rather than *flat-file* databases. A flat-file database contains only a single table—thus, it is two-dimensional, or *flat*. One dimension is represented by the *fields*, or *columns*, and the other dimension is represented by the *records*, or *rows*. Flat-file databases are perfectly suitable for tasks such as the address list example mentioned earlier, but as users' demands grow more complex, the flat-file structure soon reveals its weaknesses.

The contrast between flat-file and relational databases can be shown best through an example. I'll use a database that is intended to keep track of inventory for an electronics store. Each record in the database table contains the following fields, which are necessary to hold the information about a single stock item:

- Stock Number
- Description
- Type
- Wholesale Cost
- Retail Price
- Quantity On Hand
- Manufacturer Name
- Manufacturer Order Number
- Manufacturer Street Address
- Manufacturer City
- Manufacturer State
- Manufacturer Postal Code
- Manufacturer Telephone

This list may seem adequate at first glance, but imagine what happens if the store has many stock items from one manufacturer. For each stock item, the manufacturer's name, address, and other information have to be entered in a separate record, even though this data is the same in each case. This approach is highly inefficient, not only because it wastes operator time and increases the chance of errors, but also because it consumes valuable disk space by storing all the duplicate information. The solution? A *relational* database. Instead of a single table that contains all the necessary information, the relational database contains multiple tables, with the information spread among them. For this example, the relational database structure might consist of two tables.

First, the Stock Items table:

- Stock Number
- Description
- Type
- Wholesale Cost
- Retail Price
- Quantity On Hand
- Manufacturer Name

And the Manufacturers table:

- Manufacturer Name
- Street Address
- City
- State
- Postal Code
- Telephone

The information is not duplicated unnecessarily within this structure. One record exists in the Manufacturers table for each manufacturer, and one record exists in the Stock Item table for each stock item. The two tables are linked by the one field they have in common, the manufacturer name. A relational database manager—the application program—has the capability to relate or *join* the tables in various ways, as required by the user. For example, in this application, the user probably wants (among other things) the following:

- An automatic prompt for the manufacturer's address information (if the manufacturer isn't already entered in the Manufacturers table) when a new entry is created in the Stock Items table
- The capability to print out or display the manufacturer's address for a particular stock item
- The capability to list all stock items that come from a specific manufacturer

With two or more tables, the database is no longer flat—the multiple tables add a third dimension. The tables are designed to hold all the needed information. The relational database program can *relate* information in one table to information in other tables in a variety of ways, such as those just listed. The term *relational* derives from this capability.

An individual table in a relational database is really no different than a table in a flat-file database. Each column, or field, holds an individual piece of information, while each record, or row, holds all the information about an individual item. Note that in almost all cases, each table in a database represents something that exists in the real world—people, invoices, parts, orders, and so on.

Database programming uses some additional terminology. A table is sometimes referred to as an *entity* or an *entity class*. Rows (records) are sometimes called *tuples* or *entity occurrences*. Columns (fields) may be called *attribute classes*. An attribute class or field represents the most granular level of data—the smallest unit of information. The intersection of a row and column—a single field in a specific record—is an *attribute*. An attribute represents one unit of information about a real-world object, such as a specific individual's last name or a specific company's postal code.

Tables in a relational database have one requirement that is not necessary for flat-file databases. Each table must have a *primary key*, a field that uniquely identifies each record in the table. In other words, the data in the primary key field must be unique for each record in the table. In the example database, Stock Number is the primary key field for the Stock Items table, and Manufacturer Name is the primary key field for the Manufacturers table. Most relational database applications support *compound* primary keys, which are primary keys that consist of data from more than one field. Compound primary keys can be used when the combined data from two or more fields uniquely identifies each record, as opposed to data from a single field.

You must be alert for situations in which the data being placed in the table does not include a primary key. In a table that contains name and address information, for example, you can't be sure that the first name, last name, or even telephone number won't be duplicated between two or more records. Granted, duplication in some situations is extremely unlikely. For example, if Social Security Number is one of the table's fields, it may be used as the primary key—because it is unique for each individual. Lacking such a unique field, however, you can create your own primary key by adding a field to the table that will contain data that you know is unique, such as a sequential number that is incremented for each new record that is added. Note that the primary key field doesn't have to contain meaningful data (although this is preferred)—just *unique* data.

A *foreign key* is a field whose data serves to link the records in the table with the primary key in another table. The data in a foreign key field doesn't have to be unique for each record—in fact, it rarely is unique. In the Stock Items table, Manufacturer Name is the foreign key. The Manufacturers table doesn't have a foreign key.

In database terminology, tables are sometimes referred to as primary and dependent. A *dependent* table is one in which the records depend on information in another table for completion. The records in a *primary* table have no such dependency, being complete in and of themselves. In the example, the Stock Items table is dependent, requiring information from the Manufacturers table to provide complete data for one stock item. The

Manufacturers table is a primary table, because it doesn't depend on another table to provide complete information about a manufacturer (address, telephone, and so on). Generally, primary tables are created to avoid duplicate information being placed in another table.

ADO.NET

The database technologies available to the Visual Basic .NET programmer are subsumed under the ADO.NET umbrella. ADO stands for *ActiveX Data Objects*, and it has been central to Microsoft's data access strategy for several years. ADO.NET is the latest version of ADO, with significant improvements in interoperability, ease of programming and maintenance, and performance. If you have used earlier versions of ADO, you will note some significant changes in the new one.

ADO.NET is designed to create what are called *n-tier* applications. This means that the logical components of the program are divided into a number, typically three, of self-contained and largely independent units. These are as follows:

- The data tier, where the actual database files, or data source, are located.
- The business tier, where business rules are enforced. This will include things such as, in an online ordering database, calculating shipping costs and applying discounts.
- The presentation tier, where the users see and interact with the program.

This logical arrangement is shown schematically in Figure 19.2. Remember that this is a logical structure that may or may not correspond to an application's physical structure.

This n-tier approach offers several advantages. One major advantage is that one part of the application can be changed without the need to fiddle with the other parts. For example, a

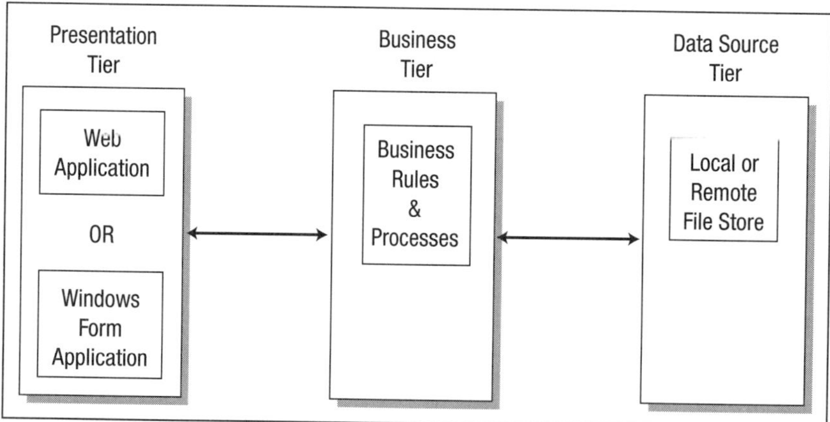

Figure 19.2
ADO.NET supports multiple-tier database applications.

new set of business rules could be put into effect without having to reprogram the presentation components. Another advantage is that the various tiers can be spread out over multiple computers for improved performance. Note, however, that the various tiers of a database application do not have to be split across separate components and/or computers. For example, it is not uncommon to design an application in which the presentation and business tiers are combined in one component.

ADO.NET is based on a disconnected architecture. This means that an open connection between the tiers is not maintained continuously for the duration of a session. Maintaining such connections can result in major performance problems particularly when a large number of users are connected to the data source. ADO.NET works by connecting to the data source and extracting the data the client needs to work with, then closing the connection. The extracted data is represented by a **DataSet** object, which provides an in-memory cache that the client application can work with. If the user adds to or modifies the data, the changed data in the **DataSet** is eventually written back to the data source. The point is that the client program is working with a local **DataSet** object and not with the data source, which is likely to be remote. Note that for some specialized applications a continuous connection to the data source is desirable, and ADO.NET can do this, but it is not the default model.

ADO.NET Classes for Data Access

You have already been introduced to the **DataSet** class, which is central to many of the things you will do with ADO.NET. It does not work alone, however. In this section, I will explain some of the classes, including the **DataSet** class, that provide the foundation of ADO.NET's capabilities. Most of Visual Basic .NET's data-related classes are in the **System.Data** namespace.

The SqlConnection and OleDbConnection Classes

Before you can do anything with a data source, you must establish a connection to it. This is the job of the **SqlConnection** and **OleDbConnection** classes. These two classes perform the same task and differ as follows:

- The **SqlConnection** class is used to create a connection to Microsoft SQL Server databases (version 7 and later). This class (and most other SQL-specific classes) is in the **System.Data.SqlClient** namespace.

- The **OleDbConnection** class is used to create a connection to databases supported by the OLE DB technology. This includes Microsoft Access databases, Oracle, third-party SQL products, and SQL Server version 6.5 and earlier. This class and other OLE DB–related classes are in the **System.Data.OleDb** namespace.

In many cases, the data source you are using will dictate the choice between **SqlConnection** and **OleDbConnection**. In some instances, a data source will be supported by both classes, and your choice of which to use will depend on various factors that are beyond the scope of this discussion. You can find related information in the .NET documentation under the topic ".NET Data Providers."

At the heart of using either type of connection is the *connection string*, a text property that specifies all the aspects of the connection, including the data source name and other details, such as security information, password (if required), and server name. The connection string is often passed to the constructor, as shown here:

```
Dim sqlCon As New SqlConnection(ConString)
```

Alternately, the instance can be created separately and the connection string passed to the **ConnectionString** property:

```
Dim sqlCon As New SqlConnection()
...
sqlCon.ConnectionString = ConString
```

The syntax is the same for the **OleDbConnection** class. After the connection string has been set, the next step is to call the **Open()** method, which opens the connection. There is no return value for this method. Any problem that occurs opening the connection is signaled by throwing either an **InvalidOperationException** or an **SqlException** (or **OleDbException** for the **OleDbConnection** class). After the **Open()** method has executed successfully, the connection exists and is ready to be used (as will be explained soon).

When you have finished using the connection, it must be closed using the **Close()** method. This is important to take advantage of ADO.NET's disconnected architecture. Just because the reference to the connection goes out of scope does not mean it will be closed automatically—you *must* do it in code. Here's a real example of creating, opening, then closing a connection:

```
Dim conStr As String
ConStr = "data source=BETA-BOX;initial catalog=Northwind;"
ConStr &= "user id=sa;password=redwine;"
Dim sqlCon As New SqlConnection(ConStr)
sqlCon.Open()
'
' Code to use the connection goes here.
'
sqlCon.Close()
```

Creating Connection Strings

So far, creating a connection seems pretty easy. The difficult part is creating the proper connection string for your exact situation. Unfortunately, there is no way to explain all the details of connection strings because there are so many possible variants depending on the capabilities of the data source in use and the security and other needs of your application. The connection string used in the previous example is actually a fairly simple one. It has four parts, as follows:

```
data source=BETA-BOX;
```

This part of the connection string identifies the SQL Server that the program will be connected to. In this case, the SQL server is identified by the name of the computer on which it is running, BETA-BOX.

```
initial catalog=Northwind;
```

This section identifies the specific database that is to be used. Because SQL Server can have multiple data sources active at one time, it is necessary to specify which one to make the connection to.

```
user id=sa;
```

This part of the connection string identifies the user whose credentials are being used to log on to SQL Server.

```
password=redwine;
```

This specifies the password for the user sa. Depending on how the SQL Server is set up, a password might not be required or it might be specified elsewhere (not in the connection string).

There are essentially three approaches you can take when it comes to creating a connection string for your application:

- If the data source is one that you have been working with, or are involved in administering, then you probably already have the information and knowledge needed to create the connection string.
- If you are not involved in administering the data source, someone else should be. You need to locate that person and ask him or her to assist you.
- You can turn to Visual Studio's tools for creating database connections, as described later in the chapter.

The SqlAdapter and OleDbAdapter Classes

After you have created a connection to your data source, then what? In order to populate a **DataSet** with the required data, you use a *data adapter*. There are two related classes: **SqlDataAdapter** for use with **SqlConnection** objects, and **OleDbDataAdapter** for use with

OleDbConnection objects. You can think of a data adapter as serving as the bridge between the data source (connection) and your **DataSet**. This is shown in a diagram in Figure 19.3.

In order to use a data adapter, you just create a Structured Query Language (SQL) statement that describes the data that you want. (SQL is explained in more detail later in the chapter.) After you have instantiated the data adapter, you pass it a command that identifies the data connection to use as well as the SQL statement to be applied. This command is encapsulated in an **SqlCommand** object, as shown here:

```
Dim myCmd As New SqlCommand(sql, connection)
```

Sql is the SQL statement, and *connection* is a reference to the connection object to be used. The **SqlCommand** object is associated with the data adapter by assigning it to the **SelectCommand** property as follows:

```
Dim adap As New SqlDataAdapter()
adap.SelectCommand = myCmd
```

The syntax is the same for the **OleDbDataAdapter** class. Usually the two steps are combined as follows:

```
adap.SelectCommand = New SqlCommand(sql, connection)
```

Then, call the data adapter's **Fill()** method, passing it a reference to the **DataSet** object where you want the data placed. The **Fill()** method also takes an optional string argument specifying the name that will be assigned to the new table in the **DataSet**. If this argument is omitted, a default name such as "Table" will be assigned. The following code fragment shows all the steps involved; it assumes that **sqlCon** is a reference to an already-open **SqlConnection** object:

```
sqlAdapter = New SqlDataAdapter()
sqlAdapter.SelectCommand = _
    New SqlCommand("select * from customers", sqlCon)
' Create a dataset called Customers.
ds = New DataSet("Customers")
' Fill the dataset, assigning the name
' My Customers to the new table.
sqlAdapter.Fill(ds, "My Customers")
```

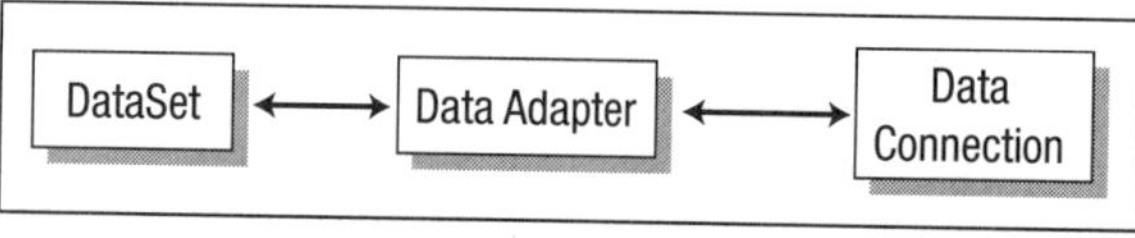

Figure 19.3
A data adapter serves as the bridge between a data connection and a **DataSet** object.

After this code executes, the **DataSet** ds will contain the data from the data source that is connected to **sqlCon**, matching the SQL statement "select * from customers". You could repeat this process, adding data to the **DataSet** object. Each fill operation creates another table in the **DataSet**. You can also define relationships between the tables, as will be covered later in the chapter.

The DataSet Class

A **DataSet** object provides an in-memory cache, or copy, of data that has been extracted from a data source. In the simplest case, as in the examples presented so far, a **DataSet** contains a single table. The **DataSet** class is a lot more capable than this, however, and can hold multiple data tables as well as definitions of the relationships between them. In any case, after you have created the **DataSet** containing the data your program needs, how do you work with that data?

The tables in the **DataSet** are contained in a collection that you access by the **Tables** property. Use the **Tables.Count** property to determine how many tables the **DataSet** contains. Then, use the **Tables.Item()** method to obtain a reference to a specific table:

```
ds.Tables.Item(table)
```

Table is either an integer value giving the 0-based position of the table in the collection, or a string specifying the table's name. The method returns a null value if the requested table does not exist. You can also loop through all the tables in the collection using a **For Each...Next** loop. Each table in a **DataSet** is represented by a **DataTable** object. This code shows how to get a reference to the table named Sales in the **DataSet** ds:

```
Dim dt As DataTable
dt = ds.Tables.Item("Sales")
```

The Item Property as Indexer

Many of the ADO classes have an **Item** property that retrieves a specific item from a collection based on its index position or, in some cases, its name. **Tables.Item()** is one example. In almost all cases, the **Item** property is the *indexer* for the collection. This means that the property name can be omitted. Thus, this line of code:

```
ds.Tables.Item("Sales")
```

is exactly equivalent to the following:

```
ds.Tables("Sales")
```

This is similar to the way default properties work in earlier versions of Visual Basic. For sample code in this chapter, I will always explicitly spell out the property name for the sake of clarity, but if you see code that does not do so, you will know what is going on.

Constraints and Relations

In addition to rows and columns, a **DataSet** can contain constraints and relationships. A *constraint* is associated with a specific table and defines a rule or restriction on the data in a particular column, such as requiring that the Price column contain a value greater than 0 or that the ZipCode column contain an entry exactly five characters long. A *relationship* defines the relationship between two tables in the **DataSet**, such as specifying that the Stock Items table and the Manufacturers table are linked by the Manufacturer Name field. Both parent and child relationships are supported.

This code loops through all the tables in the **DataSet** ds:

```
Dim dt As DataTable
For Each dt In ds.Tables
' Do something with each table here.
Next
```

Each table consists of rows (the records in the table) and columns (the fields in the table). For a given table, these are accessed by means of the **Columns** and **Rows** collections:

- The **Columns** property returns a type **DataColumnCollection**, which in turn contains one type **DataColumn** for each column in the table.
- The **Rows** property returns a type **DataRowCollection**, which in turn contains one type **DataRow** for each column in the table.

The structure of a **DataSet** object is diagrammed in Figure 19.4. Table 19.1 shows some aspects of how to use these references to work with rows and columns. In this table, dt is assumed to be a reference to a **DataTable** object.

The **DataSet** class and its related classes **DataColumn** and **DataRow** are very flexible and powerful. Unavoidably, they are also rather complex, with long lists of properties and methods. Rather than filling the chapter with reference tables, I have instead taken a task-based approach. Thus, I have made no effort to explain all the members of these classes, but I show you how to perform a variety of commonly needed tasks with a **DataSet** object.

Reading Field Data

An individual piece of data in a table, such as a person's phone number in a Personal Contacts database, belongs to a specific row (record) and a specific field (column). To get at the data, therefore, you must identify its row and its column. This is done by first getting a reference to the row, and then specifying the column. You use the **DataRow** object's **Item()** property for this. There are several overloads for this property (dr is a reference to the row):

```
dr.Item(name)        ' name is the column name.
dr.Item(index)       ' index is the 0-based column position.
dr.Item(DC)          ' DC is a type DataColumn referencing the column.
```

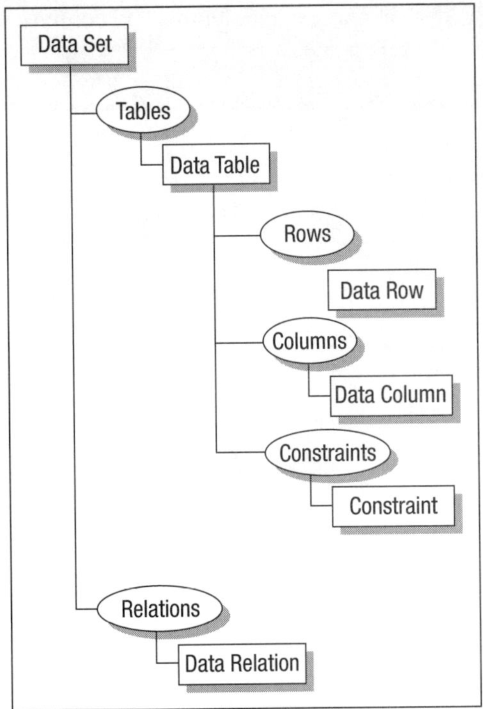

Figure 19.4
Structure of a **DataSet** object. In this diagram, ovals are collections and rectangles are objects.

Table 19.1 Using the DataTable object's Columns and Rows collections.

Syntax	Description
dt.Columns.Count **dt.Rows.Count**	Returns the number of columns or rows in the table.
dt.Columns.Item(*col*)	Returns a type **DataColumn** for the specified column. *Col* is an integer specifying the 0-based position of the column, or a string specifying the column name. The method returns a null value if the column does not exist.
dt.Rows.Item(*row*)	Returns a type **DataRow** for the specified row. *Row* is an integer specifying the 0-based position of the row. The method returns a null value if the row does not exist.
dt.Rows.Contains(*val*)	Returns True if a row in the table contains the value *val* in the primary key field.
dt.Rows.Find(*val*)	Returns a reference to a **DataRow** that contains the primary key value *val*, or a null reference (**Nothing**) if no matching row is found.

The return type of this property is **Object**, permitting it to handle any type of data that may be stored in the table. Here are some examples. For the first code snippet, assume that ds is a reference to a **DataSet** object that contains a table named My Clients. Assume also that this table contains columns named CompanyName and ContactName. This code goes through all the rows in the table, extracts the data in these two columns, and combines the data in a string, which is finally displayed in a TextBox control:

```
Dim dr As DataRow
Dim buf As String
For Each dr In ds.Tables("My Clients").Rows
   buf &= dr.Item("CompanyName") & ": " & dr.Item("ContactName") _
          & ControlChars.CrLf
Next
TextBox1.Text = buf
```

The next example shows how to loop through all the rows and all the columns in a table:

```
Dim dr As DataRow
Dim dc As DataColumn
For Each dr In ds.Tables("My Clients").Rows
    For Each dc In ds.Tables("My Clients").Columns
       ' Each time this loop repeats, dr.Item(dc) will
       ' return the data in the current column of the current row.
    Next
Next
```

Modifying Field Data

Modifying field data is essentially the reverse of the process of reading data. You must locate the row and the column whose data you want to modify and then set the value. When you change the data in a **DataSet**, your changes become part of the **DataSet** but are not automatically transferred to the data source. To permanently save your changes, you must follow the steps outlined in the section "Saving Changes" later in this chapter.

I'll present a code example for modifying data in the next section.

Finding Records

Many of the things you will do with databases involve selecting, or locating, specific records in the database. From a mailing list database, for example, you might want to extract all addresses in California for a specialized mailing. In a product catalog database, you might need to update the price on a specific item. In an employee database, you might need to change an employee's address. All of these tasks require that you find the record or records of interest before taking action on them.

Often the process of finding specific records will be done at an earlier step, when creating the **DataSet**. When you define your data adapter, which serves to transfer data from the data source to the **DataSet**, you can design your SQL statement to extract only those records that you need.

At other times, however, your **DataSet** will not contain only the data of interest—you'll have to find those records yourself. If you are looking for a record based on the value in its primary key field, you can use the **Rows** collection's **Find()** method. The syntax is as follows (assuming that dt is a reference to the **DataTable** you are searching):

```
dt.Rows.Find(val)
```

Val is the value you are looking for. This method returns a reference to the matching row, or **Nothing** if no match is found. Because this method searches the primary key, you can be sure that there will be at most a single match. If the table you are searching does not have a primary key defined, a **System.Data.MissingPrimaryKeyException** is thrown.

The following code shows how to look for a record in the table My Customers that has the primary key BERGS. If the record is found, the data in the ComanyName field is displayed. If a matching record is not found, a message to that effect is displayed. Here is the code:

```
Dim dr As DataRow
dr = ds.Tables("My Customers").Rows.Find("BERGS")
If dr Is Nothing Then
  MsgBox("The requested record was not found")
Else
  MsgBox("The company name is " & dr.Item("CompanyName"))
End If
```

In other situations, you will be looking for data that is not in a primary key field. Then you must loop through all the records in the table, examining each one for a match. This next code looks for a record in the table where CompanyName is Consolidated Holdings. If the record is found, the value of the ContactName field for that record is changed to Mary Anderson:

```
Dim dr As DataRow
Dim ToBeFound As String
Dim Found As Boolean = False

ToBeFound = "Consolidated Holdings"
For Each dr In ds.Tables("My Customers").Rows
  If dr.Item("CompanyName") = ToBeFound Then
    Found = True
    dr.Item("ContactName") = "Mary Anderson"
    Exit For
  End If
Next

If Found Then
  MsgBox("The contact person at " & ToBeFound & " has been updated."
```

```
Else
  MsgBox("The company " & ToBeFound & " was not found")
End If
```

When you are searching for data in fields that are not primary keys, you might have to deal with the possibility of duplicate data. Depending on the design of the database, such a field might permit duplicate data. In the previous example, it is possible that the table will contain two or more records where the field CompanyName is equal to Consolidated Holdings.

Deleting Rows

To delete an entire row from a table, obtain a reference to the row and then call the **Delete()** method. The following code looks through the table My Customers and deletes the record where the CompanyName field is equal to Ajax Widgets:

```
Dim dr As DataRow
Dim ToBeFound As String
Dim Found As Boolean = False

ToBeFound = "Ajax Widgets"
For Each dr In ds.Tables("My Customers").Rows
  If dr.Item("CompanyName") = ToBeFound Then
    dr.Delete()
    Exit For
  End If
Next
```

Adding Rows

To create a new row that has the same schema (fields) as an existing table, call the table's **NewRow()** method. This method creates a new row with the same fields as the other table rows, and returns a reference to it. If dt is a reference to the table, here is the syntax:

```
Dim NewRow As DataRow
NewRow = dt.NewRow()
```

At this point, you have a new, empty row. It is not yet part of any table but exists independently. The next steps are to place data in the row and then add it to the table using the **Rows** collection's **Add()** method. Suppose, for example, that the **DataSet** ds contains a table named My Friends. This table contains three fields: Name, Phone, and Email. The following code creates a new row with the same three fields, places data in the row, and then adds it to the table:

```
Dim dt As DataTable
Dim NewRow As DataRow
```

```
dt = ds.Tables("My Friends")
NewRow = dt.NewRow()
NewRow.Item("Name") = "Al Capone"
NewRow.Item("Phone") = "222-333-4444"
NewRow.Item("Email") = "al@alcatraz.gov"
dt.Rows.Add(NewRow)
```

When you call the **Add()** method, several things can go wrong. These are listed, along with the corresponding exceptions, in Table 19.2. Clearly code that adds new rows to a table must be protected inside a **Try...Catch** block.

Saving Changes

When you make changes to a table—changing existing data, deleting rows, or adding rows—the changes are temporary until you take steps to make them permanent. There are two levels to saving changes. The first has to do with the specific table you are working with. When you modify a table, changes are recorded but not made permanent. You can deal with these changes with the methods shown in Table 19.3.

The ability to accept or reject changes is important when you are dealing with changes that must be made as a group. Suppose that a user is making changes to a company's parts inventory, and before the table is used for other purposes, it is important that all the changes be made—a table with only partial changes would cause problems down the line. To guard against power outages or operator interruptions, the program would not call **AcceptChanges()** until it was sure that all the required changes had been entered.

Table 19.2 Exceptions that can be thrown by the Add() method.

Exception	Occurs...
ArgumentNullException	If the row you are adding is Null.
ArgumentException	If the row already belongs to this or another table.
ConstraintException	If data in the new row violates a table constraint.
NoNullAllowedException	If the new row contains Null in a field where **AllowDBNull** is False.

Table 19.3 Methods to work with changes to a table.

Method	Description
AcceptChanges()	Commits all changes made to the table since it was created or since the last time **AcceptChanges()** was called.
GetChanges()	Gets a copy of the table containing all changes that were made since it was created or since the last time **AcceptChanges()** was called.
RejectChanges()	Rejects all changes made to the table since it was created or since the last time **AcceptChanges()** was called.

The second level to saving changes has to do with persisting the changes back to the data source. Remember that a **DataSet** is an in-memory copy of data that originated in a data source, and was copied from the data source to the **DataSet** by a data adapter. To copy changes from your **DataSet** back to the data source—to persist the changes—you call the data adapter's **Update()** method. This *must* be done before you either accept or reject the **DataSet** changes as described earlier in this section. This method applies to both types of data adapter, the **SqlDataAdapter** class and the **OleDbAdapter** class. You can call this method to persist all the changes in the **DataSet** as follows:

```
adap.Update(ds)
```

Adap is a reference to the data adapter, and *ds* is a reference to the **DataSet**. Or, you can persist just the changes in a specific table referenced by *dt*:

```
adap.Update(dt)
```

In both cases, the method's return value is the number of rows successfully updated. When passing a **DataTable** to the **Update()** method, you can pass the original table in which you made the changes, or you can create a new **DataTable** containing only the changes by calling the original table's **GetChanges()** method. This is demonstrated in the sample code following the next paragraph.

In order for the **Update()** method to work properly, the data adapter must be provided with the appropriate SQL update command. This can be done manually, but it is a lot easier to use a command builder that you associate with the data adapter. There are two types of command builders: **SqlCommandBuilder**, for use with **SqlDataAdapter**, and **OleDbCommandBuilder**, for use with **OleDbDataAdapter**. By creating a command builder and associating it with your data adapter, you enable the required SQL command to be generated automatically. Thus, if **sqlAdap** is a reference to your instance of **SqlDataAdapter**, you would write the following:

```
Dim custCB As SqlCommandBuilder = New SqlCommandBuilder(sqlAdap)
```

The code in Listing 19.1 demonstrates how to locate a specific row in a table, change some data in the row, and persist the data back to the data source. This example uses SQL Server and the Northwind sample database that is provided with it.

Listing 19.1 Updating the data source from a modified data table.

```
Public Sub UpdateDatabase()

  Dim dr As DataRow
  Dim ToBeFound As String = "Consolidated Holdings"
  Dim Found As Boolean = False
  Dim conString As String
```

```
    conString = "data source=BETA-BOX;initial catalog=Northwind;"
    conString &= "user id=sa;password=victoria;"
    sqlCon = New SqlConnection(conString)
    Try
      sqlCon.Open()
      sqlAdapter = New SqlDataAdapter()
      sqlAdapter.SelectCommand = New SqlCommand("select * from customers", _
          sqlCon)
      ' Create the command builder and associate it with the sqlAdapter.
      Dim custCB As SqlCommandBuilder = New SqlCommandBuilder(sqlAdapter)
      ds = New DataSet("Customers")
      sqlAdapter.Fill(ds, "My Customers")
      Dim dt As DataTable = ds.Tables("My Customers")
      For Each dr In dt.Rows
        If dr.Item("CompanyName") = ToBeFound Then
          Dim newName As String = InputBox("Enter the new contact person's
              name.")
          dr.Item("ContactName") = newName
          Found = True
          Exit For
        End If
      Next

      If Found Then
        sqlAdapter.Update(dt)
        ' The following 2 lines are an alternative to the previous one.
        'Dim dtNew As DataTable = dt.GetChanges()
        'sqlAdapter.Update(dtNew)
        MsgBox("The database was updated successfully.")
      Else
        MsgBox("The database could not be updated.")
      End If

    Catch ex As SqlException
      MsgBox("SQL exception: " & ex.Message)
    Catch ex As Exception
      MsgBox("General exception: " & ex.Message)
    Finally
      sqlCon.Close()
    End Try

  End Sub
```

SQL

Structured Query Language is almost always referred to as SQL (pronounced "S-Q-L," not "sequel," as it is more commonly but incorrectly pronounced). SQL is designed specifically for accessing and manipulating databases, and it has become the *de facto* standard for database programming. I am not aware of any relational database back end that doesn't support SQL (although they often support other proprietary languages, as well).

SQL originated in 1974 at an IBM research lab as the *Structured English Query Language*, or SEQUEL. Since then, the language has evolved into today's SQL. Unfortunately, the plural—SQLs—should probably be used, because no single accepted SQL standard exists. Not only do several SQL "standards" exist, but many vendors have added product-specific extensions (extra features) to SQL for their database programs. Access SQL, supported by the Access database engine, is a good example. Although the bulk of the language is common to all the different implementations, differences do exist.

Unlike Visual Basic and most other programming languages, SQL is a *nonprocedural* language, which means that SQL contains no statements or constructs to control the sequence, or order, of program execution. Thus, SQL does not have the equivalent of Visual Basic's **If...Then...Else** or **Select Case** statements, nor does SQL support named procedures. SQL statements are limited to expressing *what* you want to do; the program that carries out the SQL instructions interprets the statement and returns the result.

Before going any further, take a look at a couple of example SQL statements to become familiar with its structure. These examples work with a table named Clients that has fields named FirstName, LastName, Address, City, State, ZIP, and Telephone. To obtain a list of all the records for individuals in New York, the following SQL statement is used:

```
SELECT * FROM Clients WHERE State = 'NY'
```

Can you see why SQL is described as "English-like"? The meaning of this command is clear: Select all fields from the table named Clients where the State field contains NY. What if you don't need all the fields in the result? The following SQL statement selects only the FirstName, LastName, and Telephone fields from those records where the State field contains NY:

```
SELECT FirstName, LastName, Telephone FROM Clients WHERE State = 'NY'
```

The following statement goes one step further and sorts the result list by LastName:

```
SELECT FirstName, LastName, Telephone FROM Clients WHERE_
       State = 'NY'   ORDER BY LastName
```

SQL can go well beyond this sort of simple selection statement. One important capability has to do with defining joins between tables in a relational database. The SQL language is a complex topic, and detailed coverage of it is beyond the scope of this chapter. Numerous SQL tutorials have been published on the Web, and you can find one by doing a search on

Yahoo!, Google, or another Web search site. Books are also available on the subject. For your own database projects, if you are not sure about creating SQL statements, you can use the Query Builder tool that is part of the Data Adapter Configuration Wizard. This is covered later in this chapter in the section "Visual Studio Tools for Database Applications."

The DataView Class

The **DataView** class is designed to provide a customized view of the data in a **DataTable**. Specifically, a **DataView** can apply sorting and/or filtering to a table. The name **DataView** is somewhat misleading, because this class does not actually display the data and in fact has no visual representation at all. Rather, the class provides a way to organize and select data from a table and make it available for various uses. One important use of the **DataView** class is to provide a source for data binding, a topic that will be covered later in the chapter. Another use is to provide multiple views of the same data by connecting two or more differently configured **DataViews** to the same data table.

The first step in using a **DataView** is to associate it with a table. You can do this with the class constructor, as shown here:

```
Dim MyView As New DataView(table)
```

Table is a reference to the **DataTable** object whose data will be contained in the **DataView**. You can also create an empty **DataView** and then associate it with a data table later by means of its **Table** property:

```
Dim MyView As New DataView()
...
MyView.Table = table
```

Filtering a DataView

By default, a **DataView** "displays" all the data in the **DataTable**, in its original order. You can filter the data rows based on the row state of each row. The *row state* has to do with rows in the table that were modified, added, and/or deleted (as was covered earlier in this chapter). Filtering rows based on row state is controlled by the **DataView's RowStateFilter** property. The possible settings for this property are from the **DataViewRowState** enumeration, as detailed in Table 19.4. Note that these filters work only if the underlying table had not has its **AcceptChanges()** or **RejectChanges()** method called.

You can create custom row state filters by adding the appropriate constants together. For example, this line sets the **DataView** to display only new and deleted rows:

```
MyDataView.RowStateFilter = DataViewRowState.Added + _
  DataViewRowState.Deleted
```

Table 19.4 Members of the DataViewRowState enumeration used for the RowStateFilter property.

DataViewRowState member	The DataView shows...
Added	Rows that have been added to the table.
CurrentRows	All current (non-deleted) rows, including original, new, and modified rows.
Deleted	All deleted rows.
ModifiedCurrent	All current modified rows.
ModifiedOriginal	The original versions of modified rows.
None	No rows.
OriginalRows	All original rows including deleted and unmodified ones.
Unchanged	All original unmodified rows.

Another way to filter the data in a **DataView** is based on the data in the rows. This is accomplished by setting the **DataView**'s **RowFilter** property. This property is a string that identifies a column name, an operator, and a filter value in a specific format. For example, the string

```
City = 'Albany'
```

creates a filter that will display only those rows where the City field contains the data Albany. Note that the filter value must be in single quotes if it is a text value. You can use Visual Basic's comparison and logical operators in creating filters. Here are some examples. To show only those records where the City field contains Madrid or London:

```
MyDataView.RowFilter = "city='Madrid' Or city='London'"
```

To show records where the City field contains Paris and the OrderDate field contains a date since January 1, 2001 use the following:

```
MyDataView.RowFilter = "city='Paris' And OrderDate>#1/1/2001#"
```

You can combine the **RowStateFilter** and **RowFilter** properties to create specialized views. This example shows those records that were added and have the Name field equal to Smith:

```
MyDataView.RowFilter = "Name='Smith'"
MyDataView.RowStateFilter = DataViewRowState.Added
```

Sorting a DataView

Use the **DataView** object's **Sort** property to specify how the rows in the **DataView** will be sorted. You can sort on one or more columns (fields) in either ascending or descending order. The **Sort** property is set to a string that lists the field name or names to sort on plus the option's DESC modifier for a descending sort (the default is ascending). This example sorts the view on the City field in ascending order:

```
MyDataView.Sort = "City"
```

This example sorts the view on the City field in descending order:

```
MyDataView.Sort = "City DESC"
```

This example sorts the view by the City field and then by the Name field, both in ascending order. This means that fields where City contains the same value are sorted by Name:

```
MyDataView.Sort = "City, Name"
```

Additional DataView Members

A **DataView** has additional capabilities, such as adding and deleting rows. The class members for these additional tasks are described in Table 19.5.

As was mentioned previously, **DataView**s are usually created to be used with data binding, covered in the following section.

Binding Controls to Data

An extremely powerful technique provided by Visual Basic .NET is called *data binding*. With binding, a Windows Form control is linked to a source of data, typically a **DataView** object, as explained in the previous section of this chapter. The control automatically displays the linked data, and changes to the data made in the control are automatically passed back to the data source. By using data binding, a program can easily implement complex and sophisticated user interfaces without all of the complex programming that would otherwise be required. Several types of binding are available, depending on the nature of the control that is being used.

Simple Binding

Simple binding lets you bind a single value in a data source to any property of a control. For example, the **Text** property of a TextBox control can be bound to the Name field in a

Table 19.5 Additional members of the DataView class.

Member	Description
AddNew()	Adds a new row to the view and returns a reference to a type **DataRowView** for the new row.
AllowDelete	True/False value specifying whether the **DataView** allows rows to be deleted.
AllowEdit	True/False value specifying whether the **DataView** allows rows to be edited.
AllowNew	True/False value specifying whether the **DataView** allows rows to be added.
Count	Returns the number of rows in the **DataView**.
Delete(*i*)	Deletes the row at position *i*.
Item(*i*)	Returns a type **DataRowView** referencing the row at position ***i*** in the **DataView**.

Contacts database, and will automatically display the data. To create a simple binding, the first step is to create an instance of the **Binding** class that contains the details of the binding. The constructor for this class has the following syntax:

```
New(property, source, member)
```

Property specifies the control property that is to be bound to the data source. *Source* identifies the data source, which can be a **DataSet**, **DataTable**, or **DataView**. *Member* identifies the specific column and, if necessary, table in the source to bind to.

After you create the **Binding** object, the next step is to add it to the control's **DataBindings** collection. Typically, the steps of creating the **Binding** object and adding it to the collection are done at the same time. For example, assuming that dv is a reference to a **DataView** object, the following code binds the **Text** property of TextBox1 to the ContactName column in the **DataView**:

```
TextBox1.DataBindings.Add(New Binding("Text", dv, "ContactName")
```

If ds is a **DataSet**, the following code binds the **Text** property of the control Label1 to the CompanyName column in the My Customers table. Note that because a **DataSet** may contain multiple tables, it can be necessary to specify a table name as in this example:

```
Label1.DataBindings.Add(New Binding("Text", ds, _
    "My Customers.CompanyName")
```

After you have bound one or more controls to a data source, how do you control which row in the data source is displayed? This is not as simple as you might think because the objects that serve as data sources for binding, such as a **DataTable** or a **DataView**, do not include the concept of a "current row." Instead, you use a class called **BindingManagerBase** to keep track of and change the "current position" in a data source and synchronize the display of all the bound controls. You get a reference to this class from the **BindingContext** property of the form that the bound controls are located on. When you obtain this reference you pass information that identifies the bindings that this **BindingManagerBase** instance is to keep track of. This information identifies the data source object and, if necessary, the table. This will be clearer with a couple of examples.

For the first example, I will use a situation where some controls are bound to a **DataView**. Here, assume that dv is a reference to the **DataView**. The bindings would be set up as follows:

```
TextBox1.DataBindings.Add(New Binding("Text", dv, "ContactName"))
TextBox2.DataBindings.Add(New Binding("Text", dv, "CompanyName"))
```

Then, you would get the **BindingManagerBase** instance as follows:

```
Dim myBMBase As BindingManagerBase
...
myBMBase = Me.BindingContext(dv, "")
```

The **Me** keyword is used to reference the form. Note that this line of code identifies the data source, namely the **DataView** dv. Because the **DataView** contains only a single table, no table identification is needed, hence the second argument is a blank string.

The next example shows how to deal with a case where the controls are bound to a specific table My Customers in a **DataSet**. This code assumes that ds is a reference to the **DataSet**:

```
TextBox1.DataBindings.Add(New Binding("Text", ds, _
    "My Customers.ContactName"))
TextBox2.DataBindings.Add(New Binding("Text", ds, _
    "My Customers.CompanyName"))
```

Then, the **BindingManagerBase** instance is obtained as follows:

```
Dim myBMBase As BindingManagerBase
...
myBMBase = Me.BindingContext(ds, "My Customers")
```

After you have created the **BindingManagerBase** instance, you can use it to move from record to record by using its **Count** and **Position** properties as follows:

- To view the first row, set **Position** to 0.
- To view the last row, set **Position** to **Count-1**.
- To view the previous record, decrement **Position** by 1 (but not to a value less than 0).
- To view the next record, increment **Position** by 1 (but not to a value greater than **Count-1**).

A Simple Binding Demo

The program presented in this section shows you how to implement a program that uses data binding to display and navigate among records in a database. It uses the Customers table from the Northwind sample database, but you could adapt it to work with any database you like. The program displays three fields from the database, and provides buttons to move through the records: first record, previous record, next record, and last record.

1. Create a new Windows Application project with the name SimpleBindingDemo.
2. Change the form's **Text** property to Simple Binding Demo.

3. Place three TextBox controls on the form, one above the other. Change the **Name** property of the top TextBox to txtCompanyName, of the next TextBox to txtContactName, and of the bottom TextBox to txtPhone.

4. Place a Label control to the left of each TextBox and change the **Text** property of each so it identifies the adjacent TextBox.

5. Place four Button controls in a row across the bottom of the form. Change their properties as follows, working from left to right:

   - **Name**: txtFirst; **Text**: First
   - **Name**: txtPrevious; **Text**: Previous
   - **Name**: txtNext; **Text**: Next
   - **Name**: txtLast; **Text**: Last

6. Open the form's code window and add a declaration of a variable to refer to the BindingManagerBase. This variable must be global throughout the module, so its declaration must be placed in the class right after the **Inherits** statement:

   ```
   Dim myBMBase As BindingManagerBase
   ```

7. At the very beginning of the module, before the **Class** statement, place the following **Imports** statements to provide references to the ADO classes that the project uses:

   ```
   Imports System.Data
   Imports System.Data.SqlClient
   ```

8. Create a **Load()** event procedure for the form and add the code shown in Listing 19.2. Be sure to modify the connection string as needed to work on your system.

9. Create **Click()** event procedures for the four Button controls. Add the code as shown in Listing 19.3.

When you run the program, it displays data from the first record. You can use the buttons to move through the records as desired. Figure 19.5 shows the program in operation.

Listing 19.2 The code in the Form_Load() procedure creates the data source and defines the bindings.

```
Private Sub Form1_Load(ByVal sender As System.Object, _
      ByVal e As System.EventArgs) Handles MyBase.Load

    Dim sqlCon As New SqlConnection()
    Dim sqlAdapter As SqlDataAdapter
    Dim conString As String
    Dim ds As DataSet
```

```
' Set up the connection string.
conString = "data source=BETA-BOX;initial catalog=Northwind;"
conString &= "user id=sa;password=victoria;"
sqlCon.ConnectionString = conString

Try
  sqlCon.Open()
  sqlAdapter = New SqlDataAdapter()
  sqlAdapter.SelectCommand = New SqlCommand _
      ("select * from customers", sqlCon)
  ds = New DataSet("Customers")
  sqlAdapter.Fill(ds, "My Customers")
  sqlCon.Close()
  ' Set up a DataView sorted by CompanyName.
  Dim dv As New DataView(ds.Tables("My Customers"))
  dv.Sort = "CompanyName"

  ' Establish the data bindings.
  txtCompanyName.DataBindings.Add(New Binding("Text", _
    dv, "CompanyName"))
  txtContactName.DataBindings.Add(New Binding("Text", _
    dv, "ContactName"))
  txtPhone.DataBindings.Add(New Binding("Text", dv, "Phone"))

  ' Create the BindingManagerBase.
  myBMBase = Me.BindingContext(dv, "")

Catch ex As SqlException
  MsgBox("SQL Exception: " & ex.Message)
Catch ex As Exception
  MsgBox("General Exception: " & ex.Message)
End Try

End Sub
```

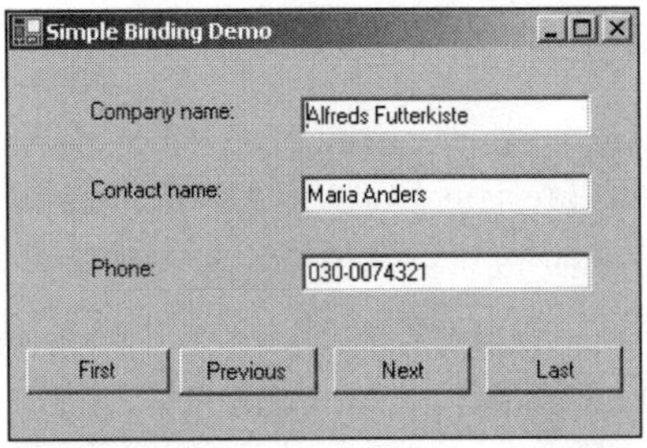

Figure 19.5
The Simple Binding Demo program.

Listing 19.3 The Click() event procedures for moving through the records.

```
Private Sub btnFirst_Click(ByVal sender As System.Object, _
    ByVal e As System.EventArgs) Handles btnFirst.Click

  myBMBase.Position = 0

End Sub

Private Sub btnPrevious_Click(ByVal sender As System.Object, _
    ByVal e As System.EventArgs) Handles btnPrevious.Click

  If myBMBase.Position > 0 Then
    myBMBase.Position -= 1
  End If
End Sub

Private Sub btnNext_Click(ByVal sender As System.Object, _
    ByVal e As System.EventArgs) Handles btnNext.Click

  With myBMBase
    If .Position < .Count - 1 Then
      .Position += 1
    End If
  End With

End Sub

Private Sub btnLast_Click(ByVal sender As System.Object, _
    ByVal e As System.EventArgs) Handles btnLast.Click

  myBMBase.Position = myBMBase.Count - 1

End Sub
```

Complex Binding

Complex binding refers to data binding with controls that can bind to more than one element in a database. For Windows forms, these are the DataGrid control and the ComboBox control. Complex data binding is, well, a complex topic, and I will cover only the basics here.

The ComboBox can display a list of values, and when bound to a column in a table it will automatically display the values from that column, for all rows in the table. To bind a

ComboBox, set its **DataSource** property to the source, which can be a **DataSet**, **DataTable**, or **DataView**. The,n set its **DisplayMember** property to specify which column from the data source is to be displayed in the control. This code binds the ComboBox to the columns CompanyName in the table My Customers in the **DataSet** ds:

```
ComboBox1.DataSource = ds
ComboBox1.DisplayMember = "My Customers.CompanyName"
```

If you are binding to a **DataView** or a **DataTable**, there is no need to specify a table:

```
ComboBox1.DataSource = dv
ComboBox1.DisplayMember = "CompanyName"
```

A DataGrid control can display entire tables in row and column format. It can also contain multiple related tables and let the user select which table to display. An example of the DataGrid control in use is shown in Figure 19.6. On the surface, the DataGrid control is simple to use. All you need to do is set its **DataSource** property to point to a **DataSet** or **DataView** and everything else happens automatically—column names are assigned, the user can select rows, change the sort order, and so on. Under the hood, however, this is an extremely complicated and powerful control. Many seemingly difficult database-programming tasks are greatly simplified by the use of a DataGrid control.

DataGrid Demo

CustomerID	Company	ContactName	ContactTitle	Address	City	Region	PostalCode
ALFKI	Alfreds Futter	Maria Anders	Sales Repres	Obere Str. 57	Berlin	(null)	12209
ANATR	Ana Trujillo E	Ana Trujillo	Owner	Avda. de la C	México D.F.	(null)	05021
ANTON	Antonio More	Antonio More	Owner	Mataderos 2	México D.F.	(null)	05023
AROUT	Around the H	Thomas Hard	Sales Repres	120 Hanover	London	(null)	WA1 1DP
BERGS	Berglunds sn	Christina Ber	Order Admini	Berguvsväge	Luleå	(null)	S-958 22
BLAUS	Blauer See D	Hanna Moos	Sales Repres	Forsterstr. 57	Mannheim	(null)	68306
BLONP	Blondesddsl	Frédérique Ci	Marketing Ma	24, place Klé	Strasbourg	(null)	67000
BOLID	Bólido Comid	Martín Somm	Owner	C/ Araquil, 67	Madrid	(null)	28023
BONAP	Bon app'	Laurence Leb	Owner	12, rue des B	Marseille	(null)	13008
BOTTM	Bottom-Dollar	Elizabeth Lin	Accounting M	23 Tsawasse	Tsawassen	BC	T2F 8M4
BSBEV	B's Beverage	Victoria Ashw	Sales Repres	Fauntleroy Ci	London	(null)	EC2 5NT
CACTU	Cactus Comi	Patricio Simp	Sales Agent	Cerrito 333	Buenos Aires	(null)	1010
CENTC	Centro comer	Francisco Ch	Marketing Ma	Sierras de Gr	México D.F.	(null)	05022
CHOPS	Chop-suey C	Yang Wang	Owner	Hauptstr. 29	Bern	(null)	3012
COMMI	Comércio Min	Pedro Afonso	Sales Associ	Av. dos Lusía	Sao Paulo	SP	05432-043
CONSH	Consolidated	Holly Holly	Sales Repres	Berkeley Gar	London	(null)	WX1 6LT
WANDK	Die Wandern	Rita Müller	Sales Repres	Adenaueralle	Stuttgart	(null)	70563
DRACD	Drachenblut	Sven Ottlieb	Order Admini	Walserweg 2	Aachen	(null)	52066
DUMON	Du monde en	Janine Labru	Owner	67, rue des Ci	Nantes	(null)	44000
EASTC	Eastern Conn	Ann Devon	Sales Agent	35 King Geor	London	(null)	WX3 6FW
ERNSH	Ernst Handel	Roland Mend	Sales Manag	Kirchgasse 6	Graz	(null)	8010
FAMIA	Familia Arqui	Aria Cruz	Marketing As	Rua Orós, 92	Sao Paulo	SP	05442-030
FISSA	FISSA Fabric	Diego Roel	Accounting M	C/ Moralzarz	Madrid	(null)	28034

Figure 19.6
The DataGrid control can display entire data tables.

Visual Studio Tools for Database Applications

Visual Studio provides several tools that can assist you in developing your database applications. These tools are described here briefly. You can explore the details of using these tools on your own.

The Server Explorer

The Server Explorer is located on a tab that shares space with the Visual Studio Toolbox. Its Data Connections node lists database connections on the local system, and its Servers node lists connections to available servers, including the local system. Each database connection under the Data Connections node can be expanded to view its tables, views, and stored procedures. For example, Figure 19.7 shows the tables and stored procedures provided by the SQL Server connection to the Northwind database.

You can use the Server Explorer to add database components to your project as follows:

- To create a program connection to the entire data source, drag the source from the Server Explorer and drop it on your form. Visual Studio adds to your form an **SqlConnection** object that is connected to the data source.

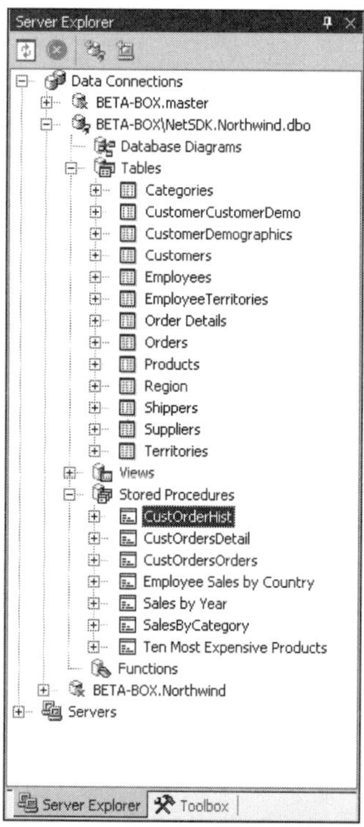

Figure 19.7
The Server Explorer makes tables, views, and stored procedures available to your program.

- To connect to a specific table or view in the data source, drag the table name or the view name from the Server Explorer to your form. Visual Studio adds an **SqlConnection** and an **SqlDataAdapter** to your project, configured to connect to the specified table or view.

- To use a stored procedure in your project, drag a stored procedure name onto your form. Visual Studio creates an **SqlCommand** object for the specified stored procedure.

These examples are given for SQL Server data sources, but the Server Explorer works the same way for OLE DB data sources. The difference is that Visual Studio will add **OleDbConnection**, **OleDbDataAdapter**, and **OleDbCommand** objects to your project.

The Data Connections node in Server Explorer initially lists the SQL Server connections on the local system. To add or create a new connection, right-click the Data Connections node and then:

- To add an OLE DB connection, click Add Connection then follow the prompts in the Data Link Properties dialog box.

- To create a new SQL server database, click Create New SQL Server Database and enter the requested information in the Create Database dialog box.

To connect to another server (computer), right-click the Servers node and select Add Server. Enter the server name in the dialog box, then click OK. Assuming the connection is successful, the new server will be listed under the Servers node, and any SQL Servers it provides will be available to your project.

The Data Toolbox

One of the sections of the Visual Studio Toolbox is called Data. This section of the toolbox contains those classes that are used most often in ADO.NET data projects: **DataSet**, **DataView**, **OleDbDataAdapter**, **SqlDataAdapter**, **SqlConnection**, **OleDbConnection**, **SqlCommand**, and **OleDbCommand**. You can add any of these classes to your project by dragging from the Toolbox to your form. As with all classes that do not have a visual interface, these classes are displayed in the tray beneath your form.

The Data Adapter Configuration Wizard

If you add a "blank" data adapter to your project, by dragging it from the Toolbox, Visual Studio will start the Data Adapter Configuration Wizard. This wizard walks you through the steps of configuring the data adapter, which means selecting a data connection and defining the query that the data adapter will use to retrieve data from the connection. This wizard can be helpful, particularly when your data adapter needs to execute a complex query and you do not want to write the SQL statements yourself.

After its opening screen, the wizard first lets you select the data connection to use (Figure 19.8). You can select an existing data connection from the drop-down list, or

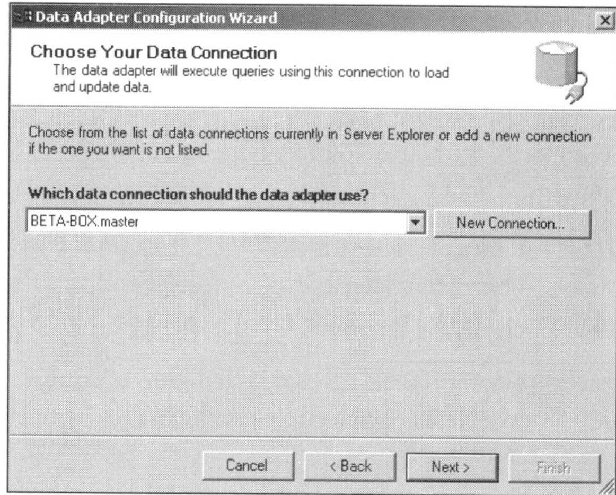

Figure 19.8
The first step in the Data Adapter Configuration Wizard is selecting a data connection to use.

click the New Connection button to set up a new data connection. For an existing connection, you may be asked to log in if the database requires it.

The next step is the type of query that the data adapter will use. You have a choice of creating SQL statements, creating stored procedures, or using existing stored procedures. The remainder of this section will focus on creating SQL statements. If you select the Use SQL Statements option and click Next, the wizard displays the dialog box shown in Figure 19.9.

If you are skilled at writing SQL, you can type the statement directly into the box. However, this dialog box provides access to one of Visual Studio's most useful tools: the Query Builder. Click the Query Builder button to open the Query Builder.

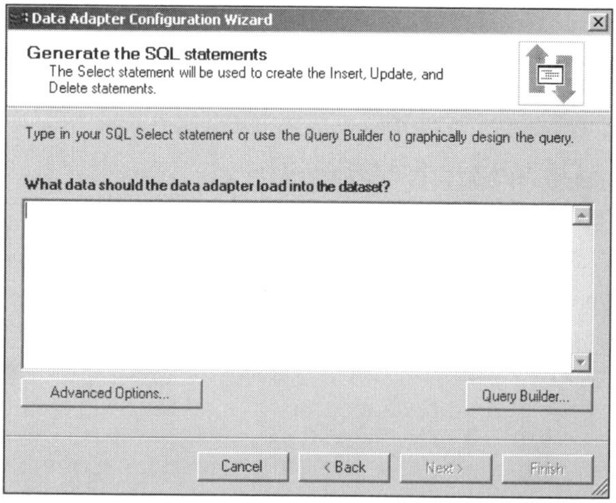

Figure 19.9
This wizard dialog box lets you generate SQL statements for the data adapter to use.

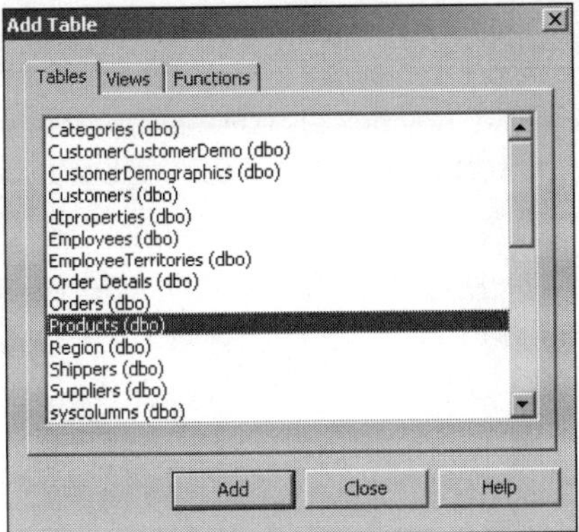

Figure 19.10
Adding tables and views to your query.

The first Query Builder dialog box lets you add one or more tables and/or views to the Query (Figure 19.10). Select a table or view and click the Add button, repeating until all the needed tables and views have been added, then click the Close button.

The next wizard dialog box, shown in Figure 19.11, is the heart of the Query Builder. At the top it displays the tables and views that you added to the query in the previous step. In the figure, the Products table and the Categories table are present. Each table lists its fields with

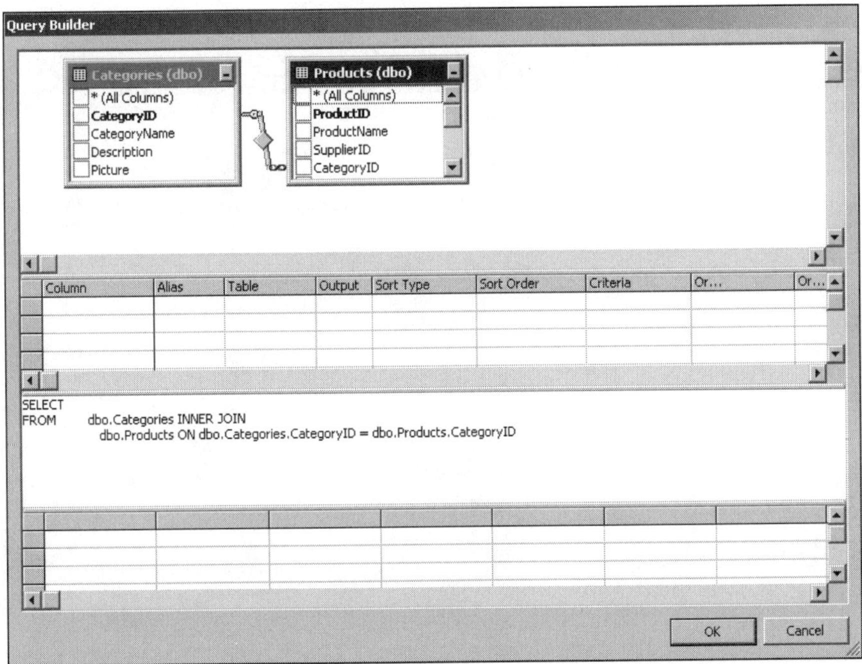

Figure 19.11
Designing your query.

a checkbox next to each field name. A table's primary key is in bold (CategoryID and ProductID in the figure), and relationships between the tables are indicated by a link between the field names (CategoryID in the figure). The dialog box also displays a list of fields that have been added to the query (which is empty in the figure) and the SQL statement that has been generated so far. To design your query:

- *Add a field to the query*—Click its name to place a checkmark in the adjacent box. The field name will be added to the field list. For a field to be included in the data adapter output, its Output column must be checked.
- *Specify a selection criterion for a field*—Enter the criterion value in the Criteria column in the field list. If needed, enter additional criteria in the Or columns.
- *Specify a sort order*—Enter a value in a field's Sort Order column. A value of 1 means that the field is the primary sort key, a value of 2 means that the field is the secondary sort key, and so on.
- *Assign an alias to a field*—Enter the new name in the Alias column. An alias is the name by which a field will be referred to in your program.

Continue designing your query as described previously until you are done. Figure 19.12 shows what the dialog box will look like for a query that includes the Description and CategoryName fields from the Categories table and the UnitsInStock field from the Products table. The query includes only records where CategoryName is Beverages or Produce and is sorted on Description.

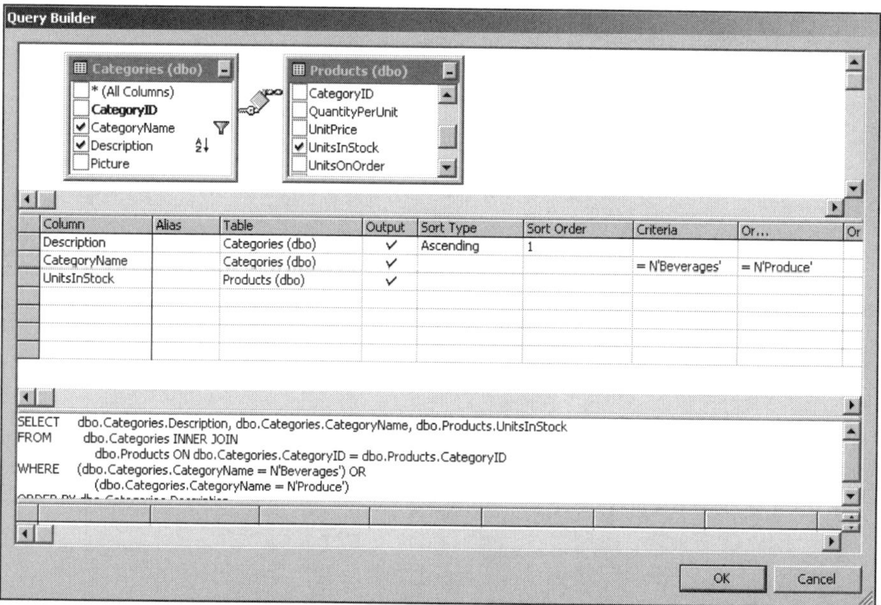

Figure 19.12
A completed query.

When you have finished, click the OK button. You will be returned to the previous Data Adapter Configuration Wizard dialog box with the generated SQL statement entered in the box. Click Finish to complete the wizard. The final dialog box will display any errors or warnings that occurred. Your project will now contain a data adapter that is configured according to the entries you made in the wizard.

Summary

ADO.NET represents an essentially complete redesign of Microsoft's ActiveX Data Objects. It provides the programmer with a powerful and complete set of classes for accessing and manipulating databases of almost any kind. By design, ADO.NET simplified many of the tasks that used to give programmers gray hairs, such as working with remote data sources, using a disconnected model, and defining links between controls and data. ADO.NET is a rich and complex topic, and I have been able to only scratch the surface in this chapter. As your database programming needs grow, you can turn to one of the specialized books on ADO.NET.

Chapter 20

Creating Web Applications with ASP.NET

One of the most exciting features of Visual Basic .NET is the ability to create Web applications. Unlike Windows applications, which are restricted to running on a local computer or at best a local area network, Web applications open up the entire Internet as a platform for your programs. The possibilities are almost endless—if you have ever used the Web to order merchandise, check your investment account, or search for information, you have used a Web application. With .NET's tools, creating such applications is faster and easier than ever before. This chapter gets you started with the fundamentals of Web applications; subsequent chapters go into the details.

Creating Web applications involves many aspects, particularly in regard to the use of the Visual Studio environment, that are similar or identical to creating Windows applications. Throughout this chapter, I will assume that you are familiar with the material presented earlier in the book, particularly in Chapters 2 ("Working with Visual Studio") and 7 ("Creating Windows Applications").

What Is a Web Application?

A Web application, also called an ASP.NET application, is similar to a regular Windows application in some ways, particularly from the point of view of the user. The application consists of one or more windows, or forms, that the user views on-screen. Each form contains controls that make up the visual interface of the program. The application has code that executes to carry out the various program tasks. So far, the two types of applications seem pretty much the same, but the similarities stop here.

A Web application is designed to run on the Internet. This means that the application is located on a Web server and is accessed remotely by a client using a standard Web browser. The user views the application in the browser, but the application is actually running on the server. A two-way communication takes place between the client (browser) and the server, permitting the application to respond to user actions and to send updated information to the client.

Web applications are certainly not new with the .NET framework. Various other approaches to creating Web-based application existed previously, including Microsoft's own Active Server Pages (ASP) technology. ASP.NET is based on the older ASP in many ways, and conceptually the two technologies have a lot in common. ASP.NET offers significant improvements over ASP in various areas, including performance, security, deployment, and state management. ASP applications can be migrated to ASP.NET, and ASP applications can also coexist with ASP.NET applications, so any investment you might have in ASP applications is certainly not lost.

How Web Applications Work

When you use a Web browser to navigate to a Web page, the request, or URL (Uniform Resource Locator) will look something like this:

```
http://www.microsoft.com/index.htm
```

There are three parts to this:

- *http://*—This part of the URL identifies the protocol, which is the set of rules that the computers use to transmit information over the Internet. HTTP stands for Hypertext Transfer Protocol, a widely accepted protocol for transmitting text data.
- *www.microsoft.com*—This part of the URL identifies the specific computer to which the request is directed. Specialized computers on the Internet, called Domain Name Servers, have the information concerning the exact location of this computer on the Internet and can route the request to it.
- *index.htm*—This is the name of the specific resource, or file, that is being requested. In cases where the URL does not specify a file name, the Web server returns a designated default file.

When the Web server receives a request such as this, it examines the extension of the file being requested—in this case, .htm. For files that end with the .htm or .html extension, the Web server is programmed to simply read the content of the file and send it, unmodified, back to the computer that made the request.

Now let's look at what happens when someone navigates to an ASP.NET application. Such applications are located in files with the .aspx extension, so the request might look something like this:

```
http://www.microsoft.com/myapp.aspx
```

When the server gets this request, it "knows" based on the file extension that the file is an ASP.NET application. The server will then hand off the file to the ASP.NET process running on the server. ASP.NET will process the page, executing any code it contains. The result of this code processing is an HTML page, which is then returned to the client that made the original request.

Things don't stop here, however. After a page is loaded (displayed in the browser), it can continue to interact with the program on the server. In fact, such interactions are at the heart of ASP.NET. For example, a search page might display a field where the user enters the search term and a button to click in order to initiate the search. When the user clicks the button, the page sends a message called a *postback* to the server. The program on the server will detect this postback, extract the search request that the user entered, and open the relevant database file to perform the search. When done, the server program will send an update to the page and the user will see the results displayed in his or her browser.

Web applications are not limited to using the special server-side ASP.NET controls. You can place the standard HTML controls on a Web page, and in fact the Visual Studio Toolbox has a panel labeled HTML from which you can select these controls and add them to the page. These controls do not run at the server, but can exist alongside ASP.NET controls and interact with client-side scripts (a script that runs on the client computer rather than on the server) on the page.

What You Need

To develop Web applications, you must ensure that your computer meets some special requirements. First, you must be running one of the following operating systems: Windows NT 4 Workstation or Server, Windows 2000 Professional or Server, Windows XP, or a higher Windows operating system such as Advanced Server or Datacenter Server. To my knowledge there is, at least at present, no way to develop .NET Web applications using Windows 95, 98, or ME. Second, the computer must be running an Internet server that supports ASP.NET. Usually, this means Microsoft Internet Information Server version 4 or later, although you can also use the Microsoft Personal Web Server running on Windows NT 4 Workstation. Finally, the system must have Visual Studio .NET installed.

Parts of a Web Application

At the heart of every Web application is a Web form. A Web application can actually contain multiple Web forms, but it always has at least one. A Web form represents one page or window in the application. It contains HTML elements that define the page's appearance, and it also contains Visual Basic code that defines the page's behavior. Visual Studio keeps a Web form's HTML and its code in separate files: for a form named WebForm1, the HTML is in a file named WebForm1.aspx and the code is in a file named WebForm1.aspx.vb. This technique of keeping the code separate from the HTML is called *code behind*, and it serves to reduce the confusion that sometimes resulted when code and HTML were in the same file (as was the case with the old ASP). An ASP.NET page can have code and HTML

Your Local Web Server

As I mentioned earlier, you must have a Web server installed and running on the computer that you will be using for ASP.NET development. During development, you will be accessing the server locally. If you are using Microsoft IIS, the default configuration makes the service available locally as either the name localhost or as the IP address 127.0.0.1. Thus, if you open your browser and navigate to either of these URLs:

http://localhost/mywebapp/webform1.aspx

http://127.0.0.1/mywebapp/webform1.aspx

your browser will load the page Webform1.aspx (assuming that it is present in the specified directory).

in the same file, with the code marked off by special tags, and programmers who program ASP.NET without using Visual Studio can choose to do that. In this chapter, however, I will be limiting discussion to programming with Visual Studio, so code and HTML will always be separate.

When you create a Web application in Visual Studio, you'll see that several other files are created, with names such as Styles.css, Web.config, and AssemblyInfo.vb. My advice to you is, at least for now, to ignore these files. Visual Studio will manage these files automatically, and a programmer rarely needs to modify them. In fact, you should make it a point *not* to modify these files, because unless you know exactly what you are doing it will almost surely cause problems.

Visual Studio maintains two directories for each Web application that you create. Both are assigned the name that you gave to your application when it was first created. The first directory is located in the assigned location for Visual Studio projects—for example, My Documents\Visual Studio Projects. This directory contains certain information about the project, but not the project files themselves. These files are placed in the second folder, located off the local Web server's virtual root. For example, in many IIS installations the virtual root is mapped to the physical directory C:\Inetpub\wwwroot. Then, a Web application named MyWebApp would be placed in the directory C:\Inetpub\wwwroot\MyWebApp.

A First Web Application

Before we get into the details of creating Web applications, it will be helpful to walk through the process of creating a simple project in order to give you a feel for the steps involved and the way in which the Visual Studio tools are used. This will be a simple project to calculate loan payments, and it will use only a few of ASP.NET's many capabilities.

To get started, fire up Visual Studio and create a new Visual Basic ASP.NET Web Application project named MyFirstWebApp. Your Visual Studio window will look like Figure 20.1, and in this window you'll note the following:

- The large blank area in the center is the Page Designer, where you will design the application's page layout. At the bottom of the Designer are two tabs, one for viewing the page's visual appearance and the other for viewing the underlying HTML. As you add elements to the page, Visual Studio automatically generates the associated HTML and adds it to the page.
- On the left is the Toolbox displaying the assortment of Web Forms controls that can be used on your pages.
- At the upper right is the Solution Explorer, which provides a summary view of all your project's elements (files). You can click the Class View tab to view your project organized by classes.
- At the lower right is the Properties window, where you set object properties. At present, it is displaying the properties for the project. As you work, the Properties window will display properties for the active component, such as a control or a form.

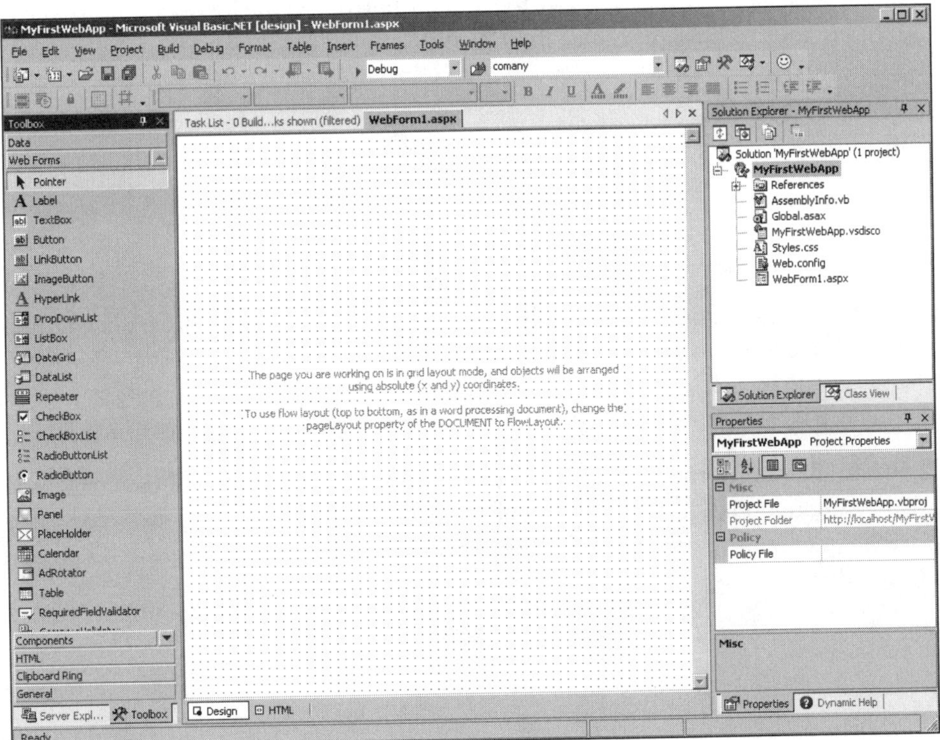

Figure 20.1
The Visual Studio screen after starting a new ASP.NET project.

Designing the Visual Interface

The first step is to change the name of the project's one page. In the Solution Explorer, right-click WebForm1.aspx, then from the context menu select Rename. Edit the name to Loan.aspx, then click back in the Designer to accept the change.

Start designing the page by adding a Label control to the page and setting its properties so that it serves as a page heading. Here are the steps required:

1. Double-click the Label control in the Toolbox to add a label to the page. You can also single-click the control in the Toolbox and then drag on the page to place the control.
2. Use the Properties window to change the Label control's **Text** property to Loan Calculator and its **Font Size** property to X-Large.
3. With your mouse, drag the Label control to the desired position and size.

The form next needs four more Label controls that will serve to identify the data entry control that will be added next. Place four Label controls on the form, one above the other, and working top to bottom change their **Text** properties as follows:

- Loan amount
- Interest rate
- Term in years
- Monthly payment

The first three Label controls need only be wide enough to display their text. The "Monthly payment" label should be stretched out to almost fill the width of the form—this is because this label will be used to display the program output. To enable the program to clearly identify the label that will be used for output, change its **Name** property to lblOut.

The next addition to the form is three TextBox controls. The user will employ these controls to enter information about the load. Place a TextBox to the right of the "Loan amount," "Interest rate," and "Term in years" labels. From top to bottom, change the **ID** property of the TextBox controls as follows:

- txtAmount
- txtRate
- txtTerm

Finally, add a Button control to the form, below the "Monthly payment" label. Change its **Text** property to Calculate and its **ID** property to btnCalculate. At this point, the page design is complete and your Designer should look more or less like Figure 20.2.

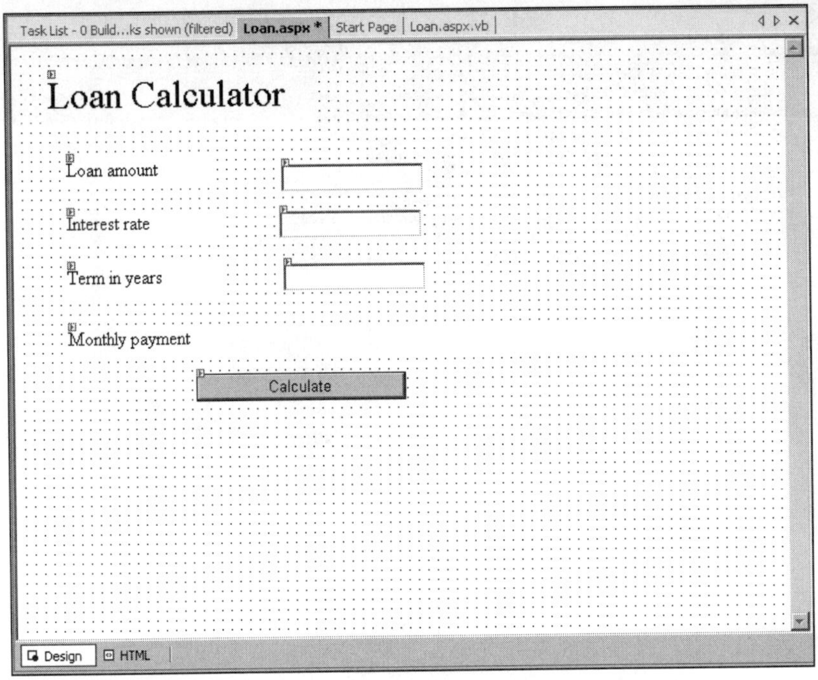

Figure 20.2
The completed page viewed in the Designer.

You can run your project now by pressing F5. Visual Studio will process your files and then start your browser (most likely Internet Explorer) and load the Loan.aspx page that you just created. The page will look lovely, and you'll even be able to enter data into the TextBox controls and click the button. However, nothing happens because you have not written the page's code yet. Close the browser by selecting Close from its File menu.

Writing the Code

To work on the form's code, select Loan.aspx in the Solution Explorer, then click the View Code button at the top of the Solution Explorer. Visual Studio opens Loan.aspx.vb, the page's code behind page. As shown in Figure 20.3, this file already contains some code. It will be instructive to take a look at this code before starting to add the project's own code. You should note the following:

- The entire page, or form, is defined as a class that inherits from **System.Web.UI.Page**. This base class provides much of the capability that you have available in your Web forms. I will present more information about this class later in the chapter. The class has the original default name WebForm1, even though you changed the file name to Load.aspx. You can change the class name by editing the **Public Class** statement, but for this project there is no reason to do so.

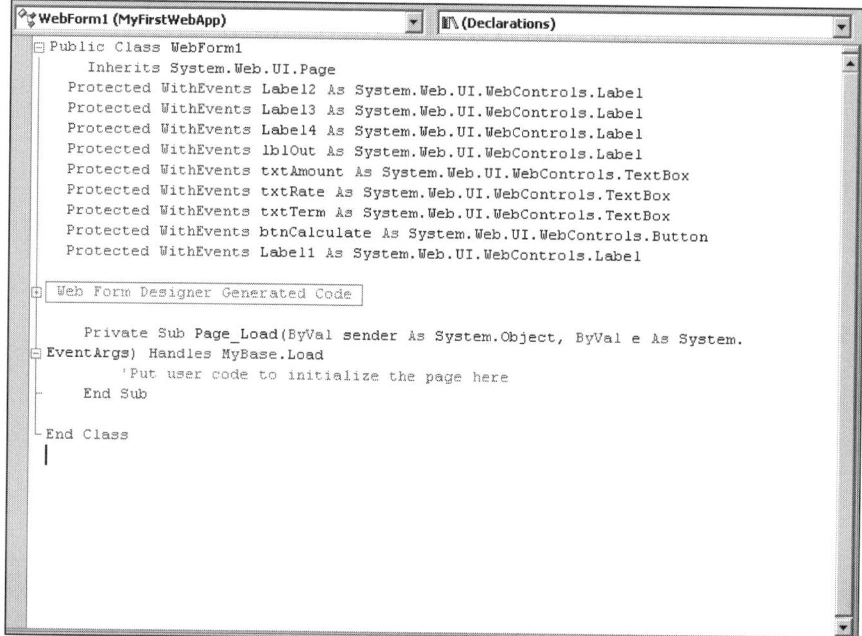
```
Public Class WebForm1
    Inherits System.Web.UI.Page
    Protected WithEvents Label2 As System.Web.UI.WebControls.Label
    Protected WithEvents Label3 As System.Web.UI.WebControls.Label
    Protected WithEvents Label4 As System.Web.UI.WebControls.Label
    Protected WithEvents lblOut As System.Web.UI.WebControls.Label
    Protected WithEvents txtAmount As System.Web.UI.WebControls.TextBox
    Protected WithEvents txtRate As System.Web.UI.WebControls.TextBox
    Protected WithEvents txtTerm As System.Web.UI.WebControls.TextBox
    Protected WithEvents btnCalculate As System.Web.UI.WebControls.Button
    Protected WithEvents Label1 As System.Web.UI.WebControls.Label

 Web Form Designer Generated Code

    Private Sub Page_Load(ByVal sender As System.Object, ByVal e As System.
EventArgs) Handles MyBase.Load
        'Put user code to initialize the page here
    End Sub

End Class
```


Figure 20.3
The default code in Loan.aspx.vb.

- The class includes declarations for all the controls that you placed on the form. You can see that each control is an instance of a specific class and that they are all declared using the **WithEvents** keyword. These declarations make the controls available to code, and the **WithEvents** keyword specifies that the control can raise events.
- At the top of the code-editing window are two drop-down lists that work just the same as in the code-editing window for Windows applications. You use the left list to select a component in the class and the right list to select an event for the selected component. Visual Studio automatically takes you to the corresponding event procedure if it exists or creates the procedure if it does not exist.
- Visual Studio has inserted the blank skeleton of the **Page_Load()** method. This method is called automatically when the page is loaded into a browser, and it is very important in Web applications that need to perform various kinds of initialization on a page. For this project, however, it will not be used and could be erased—but don't do so now because you will use this procedure later in the chapter.

Before you start writing code, it is always a good idea to do some planning. What will this code need to do, and when will it be executed? The first question is easy—it will be executed when the user clicks the Calculate button. The second question requires a bit more thought. At a minimum, the code will need to do the following:

1. Get the data the user entered from the three TextBox controls.

2. Use this data to calculate the monthly payment.
3. Display the result in the Label control.

A well-designed application, however, will do more than this. Specifically, it will try to avoid problems that could arise if the user enters inappropriate data or omits some data altogether. For this application, the requirements are as follows:

- The amount of the loan must be greater than zero.
- The interest rate must be between 1 percent (0.01) and 20 percent (0.20).
- The term in years must be 1 or greater.

Thus, the task is to write code that first checks the data entered by the user and, if any of the above conditions are not met, displays a message to the user. If the data is okay, the code will perform the calculation and display the monthly payment. The calculation itself is easy, making use of Visual Basic's **Pmt()** function.

The code will be placed in the **Click()** event procedure for the form's one button. To create this procedure, select btnCalculate in the list at the top left of the code-editing window, and then select Click in the list at the top right. Visual Studio enters the blank skeleton of the event procedure, ready for you to enter your code. The code for the procedure is shown in Listing 20.1. After you enter this code, the program is ready for a tryout. Press F5 to run the program; it is shown executing in Internet Explorer in Figure 20.4.

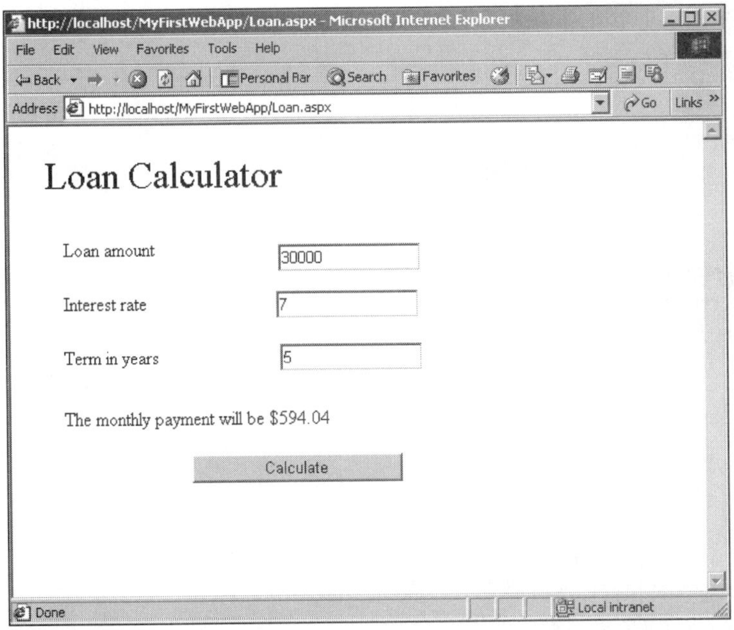

Figure 20.4
The Loan Calculator ASP.NET program executing.

This example program uses form-level validation with custom code. Another approach to validating user input is to use the validation controls provided by ASP.NET. These controls are covered in Chapter 21.

Listing 20.1 The code for the loan calculator program's btnCalculate_Click() event procedure.

```
Private Sub btnCalculate_Click(ByVal sender As Object, _
    ByVal e As System.EventArgs) Handles btnCalculate.Click

  Dim amt As Single
  Dim rate As Single
  Dim term As Integer
  Dim payment As Single

  ' Make sure the loan amount is > 0.
  amt = Val(txtAmount.Text)
  If amt <= 0 Then
    lblOut.Text = "You must enter an amount."
    Exit Sub
  End If

  ' Get the rate and ensure the proper
  ' form - e.g., if the user enters 8 convert to 0.08
  rate = Val(txtRate.Text)
  If rate > 1 Then rate /= 100
  If rate < 0.01 Or rate > 0.2 Then
    lblOut.Text = "That is an invalid interest rate."
    Exit Sub
  End If
  ' Convert to annual rate to a monthly rate,
  ' as required by the Pmt() function.
  rate /= 12

  ' Get the term and validate.
  term = Val(txtTerm.Text)
  If term < 1 Then
    lblOut.Text = "That is an invalid loan term."
    Exit Sub
  End If
  ' Convert the term from years to months.
  term *= 12

  ' Calculate the monthly payment. Note that the sign is
  ' inverted because the Pmt() function returns negative
  ' values for payments to be made.
```

```
  payment = -Pmt(rate, term, amt)
  lblOut.Text = "The monthly payment will be " & _
     FormatCurrency(payment)

End Sub
```

Examining the HTML

When you created the visual interface for this application, Visual Studio was converting your design steps into HTML in the Loan.aspx page. It will be instructive to look at this HTML, even though you may not need to do so during development. It will help you to understand the way that ASP.NET works. The HTML for Loan.aspx is shown in Listing 20.2. The lines are numbered for easy reference in the explanation that follows.

Listing 20.2 The HTML in Loan.aspx.

```
1: <%@ Page Language="vb" AutoEventWireup="false"
2:   Codebehind="Loan.aspx.vb" Inherits="MyFirstWebApp.WebForm1"%>
3: <!DOCTYPE HTML PUBLIC "-//W3C//DTD HTML 4.0 Transitional//EN">
4: <HTML>
5: <HEAD>
6:   <title></title>
7:   <meta content="Microsoft Visual Studio.NET 7.0" name="GENERATOR">
8:   <meta content="Visual Basic 7.0" name="CODE_LANGUAGE">
9:   <meta content="JavaScript" name="vs_defaultClientScript">
10:   <meta content="http://schemas.microsoft.com/intellisense/ie5"
      name="vs_targetSchema">
11: </HEAD>
12: <body MS_POSITIONING="GridLayout">
13:   <form id="Form1" method="post" runat="server">
14:     <asp:label id="Label1" style="Z-INDEX: 101; LEFT: 31px;
15:         POSITION: absolute; TOP: 24px" runat="server"
16:         Width="232px" Height="46px"
17:         Font-Size="X-Large">Loan Calculator</asp:label>
18:     <asp:label id="Label2" style="Z-INDEX: 102; LEFT: 46px;
19:         POSITION: absolute; TOP: 94px" runat="server"
20:         Width="123px" Height="26px">Loan amount</asp:label>
21:     <asp:label id="Label3" style="Z-INDEX: 103; LEFT: 46px;
22:         POSITION: absolute; TOP: 139px" runat="server"
23:         Width="135px" Height="23px">Interest rate</asp:label>
24:     <asp:label id="Label4" style="Z-INDEX: 104; LEFT: 46px;
25:         POSITION: absolute; TOP: 184px" runat="server"
26:         Width="132px" Height="26px">Term in years</asp:label>
27:     <asp:label id="lblOut" style="Z-INDEX: 105; LEFT: 46px;
28:         POSITION: absolute; TOP: 235px" runat="server"
29:         Width="536px" Height="28px">Monthly payment</asp:label>
30:     <asp:TextBox id="txtAmount" style="Z-INDEX: 106; LEFT: 231px;
```

```
31:             POSITION: absolute; TOP: 100px" runat="server"
32:             Width="121px" Height="23px"></asp:TextBox>
33:         <asp:TextBox id="txtRate" style="Z-INDEX: 107; LEFT: 229px;
34:             POSITION: absolute; TOP: 139px" runat="server"
35:             Width="121px" Height="23px"></asp:TextBox>
36:         <asp:TextBox id="txtTerm" style="Z-INDEX: 108; LEFT: 232px;
37:             POSITION: absolute; TOP: 183px" runat="server"
38:             Width="121" Height="23"></asp:TextBox>
39:         <asp:Button id="btnCalculate" style="Z-INDEX: 109; LEFT: 156px;
40:             POSITION: absolute; TOP: 275px" runat="server"
41:             Width="179px" Height="23px" Text="Calculate"></asp:Button>
42:     </form>
43: </body>
44: </HTML>
```

Lines 1 and 2 (actually a single line, but split into two to fit on the page) provide attributes for the page. These attributes identify the language that is used (vb), the name of the page's code behind module (Loan.aspx.vb), and the form from which the page gets its layout (MyFirstWebApp.WebForm1).

Lines 5 through 11 comprise the traditional HTML **<head>** section. The **<meta>** tags in this section provide information about various things, including the application that generated the page.

Line 13 marks the start of an HTML form. All of the page content is inside the form, the end of which is marked by line 42. Note that the opening **<form>** tag has the **runat="server"** attribute, indicating that this form is to be processed at the server rather than the client.

Lines 14 through 41 contain the tags defining the form's controls—the labels, text boxes, and button that you added to the form when you designed it. Each control is identified with a tag whose name starts with "asp:", identifying it as an ASP.NET control rather than a standard HTML control. The properties of each control, such as its size and position, are specified by attributes within its tag. Note that, like the **<form>** tag, each control tag specifies **runat="server"** to identify it as a server control.

Page Layout Modes

The Visual Studio Page Designer has two layout modes. The default, and the one that you used for the sample project, is called Grid Layout. This mode positions controls at a precise location with respect to the page surface. Each control's HTML tag contains information about the location of the control, as you saw in Listing 20.2. This is similar to the way in which Windows forms are designed, and permits precise page design and sophisticated layouts. However, it does not permit plain text to be interspersed among the controls on a form—at least not directly. Using the Panel Control, covered in the next chapter, you can add static HTML text to a page that is in Grid Layout mode.

The other layout mode is called Flow Layout. In this mode, elements that are placed on the page are inserted starting at the top left and then working across and down. This is sort of like the way a word processor works. There is a vertical insertion cursor on the page, which can be moved with the mouse or arrow keys. Any control that you add (by double-clicking the control in the Toolbox) is inserted at a default size at the cursor location. Likewise, text that you type is inserted at the cursor location, permitting you to intersperse plain text with your form's controls. When a page is designed in Flow Layout mode, tags for controls do not include position information because a control's position depends only on its location with respect to other page elements in the HTML.

From the end user's point of view, the difference between Grid Layout and Flow Layout becomes important when the browser is made narrow. With Flow Layout, the page elements are "wrapped" from one line to the next and always remain visible. With Grid Layout, page elements on the right side of the page are hidden as the browser is made narrower than the page, and the user must use the horizontal scrollbar to bring them back into view.

The layout mode is determined by the **PageLayout** property of the **Document** object, which represents the aspx page. You can change this property in one of two ways:

- Select DOCUMENT in the drop-down list at the top of the Property window, then scroll down to the **PageLayout** property and select the desired setting.
- With the page displayed in the Designer, right-click anywhere on the page background and then select Properties from the context menu. In the Document Property Pages dialog box that appears, open the Page Layout list on the General tab and select the desired layout mode.

Controls for Web Applications

A quick glance at the Web Forms Toolbox should be enough to convince you that Microsoft has provided a rich set of controls for use in Web applications. Some of the Web Forms controls seem to be identical to the equivalent Windows Forms controls—for example, the TextBox and Label controls. Although these controls might seem similar, they are actually quite different. The Web Forms controls are designed specifically for use in Web applications, and under the hood they are very different from the corresponding Windows Forms controls. From the perspective of the programmer, these differences are, for the most part, hidden and you need not be concerned with them.

Other Web Forms controls do not have any counterparts in the Windows Forms controls Toolbox, but are unique to Web applications. The AdRotator and Repeater controls are two such examples.

The System.Web.UI.Page Class and the Page_Load() Event

Every Web form that you create is based on the **System.Web.UI.Page** class (referred to simply as the **Page** class from now on). This class provides an event, **Page_Load()**, that is fired every time the page receives a "hit," or request. This includes the first time a user navigates to the page as well as every time the page receives a postback. Code in this event procedure can be used to perform a variety of tasks, such as initializing control values and opening database connections, depending on the needs of the program. A potential problem with this event is that sometimes your program needs to do one thing when it is first hit, and something else for subsequent postback hits. Here's where the **IsPostBack** property comes into play. The first time a page is loaded, this property is False, but for each subsequent postback it is True. Code in the **Page_Load()** event procedure can examine this property and take action as needed.

To demonstrate, make a modification to the Loan Calculator project that you created earlier in the chapter. Locate or create the **Page_Load()** event procedure, and add the code from Listing 20.3 to it. This code examines the **IsPostBack** property. If it is False, indicating that the page is being loaded for the first time, the code initializes the form's three TextBox controls to 0 and the lblOut Label control to a blank string. On subsequent hits, when **IsPostBack** will be True, the code is not executed so the controls are not modified. In this code, note that the **IsPostBack** property can be referenced directly without a qualifier, because the code is running inside the class.

Listing 20.3 Using the IsPostBack property in the Page_Load() event procedure to initialize the form.

```
Private Sub Page_Load(ByVal sender As Object, _
    ByVal e As System.EventArgs) Handles MyBase.Load

  If Not IsPostBack Then
    txtAmount.Text = 0
    txtRate.Text = 0
    txtTerm.Text = 0
    lblOut.Text = ""
  End If

End Sub
```

Managing State in Web Applications

Many Web applications need to keep track of what an individual user has done during a session. An online catalog will need to remember what items a user has already ordered, for example. A search page might want to maintain a list of a user's previous searches. This is what the term *state management* refers to—remembering what a user has done previously.

State management becomes problematic in Web applications because HTTP is by its very nature a stateless protocol. Thus, each HTTP request is independent of any previous requests from the same user, and the server has no way of knowing if a sequence of requests is from the same user or different users, or whether a particular user is still viewing the page that he or she requested. Web programmers have had to come up with some clever ways to maintain user information between hits. One approach is the use of *cookies*, which are small bits of information stored in text files on the client computer. One shortcoming of cookies is that they are limited in size. A more serious problem is that users can disable cookies altogether or delete all cookies on a regular basis. This means that while cookies can be useful in certain noncritical situations, you cannot rely on them.

Another approach to state management involves the use of hidden fields. When an HTML form is submitted to the server, the data in the form elements is sent as part of the submission. The programmer could store state information in one or more hidden fields on the form, which would then be sent to the server, in effect "saving" the state information between page hits. While workable, this method of managing state is rather clunky and difficult to use for large amounts of information.

One of the design goals for ASP.NET was to improve state management. Perhaps the most important way this was done was in the creation of the ASP.NET controls. Unlike standard HTML controls, ASP.NET controls run on the server (remember the **runat="server"** attribute in the control tags?). This means that the state, or data, of every ASP.NET control is maintained automatically, without any special programming needed on your part. The state of server-side controls is actually maintained as an encoded string that is stored as a "viewstate" in a hidden text field on the Web form. If you are viewing an ASP.NET application, you can see this by selecting Source from the View menu to open the page's underlying HTML in Notepad. You'll see something like the following in the HTML:

```
<input type="hidden" name="__VIEWSTATE"
value="dDwtNjI3MTUONjQy03Q802w8aTwxPjs+02w8dDw7bDxpPDM+0z47bDxOPHA8cDxsP
FRleHQ7PjtsPFRoaXMgYXBwIGhhcyBoYWQgMSBoaXRzLjs+Pjs+Ozs+Oz4+Oz4+Oz4=" />
```

This is all taken care of automatically by ASP.NET, so don't be concerned with it. Additional state management capabilities are provided by the **Session** and **Application** objects. They are not new to ASP.NET, having been carried over, with improvements, from the previous ASP implementation.

The Session Object

Every time a new client hits your ASP.NET application, a **Session** object is created for that user. The object is maintained as long as the same client continues to hit the application, and your application can use the **Session** object to store state information relevant to the specific user. You access the **Session** object via the **Session** keyword.

To store information in the **Session** object, use the following syntax:

```
Session(ItemName) = ItemValue
```

ItemName is the name of the item being stored, and can be thought of as being analogous to a variable name. *ItemValue* is the data being stored. All items stored in **Session** are of type **Object**, so there are essentially no limitations to what you can store there. Here's an example of storing an item of data. Assume that the user has logged on as a registered user, which has given the user more access than an unregistered user. You might store the user's status in **Session** as follows:

```
Session("RegisteredUser") = True
```

To retrieve data from the **Session** object, simply use **Session(*ItemName*)** as an expression. For example, in another of your application's pages you can retrieve the user's status as follows:

```
Dim RegisteredUser As Boolean
RegisteredUser = Session("RegisteredUser")
```

If the **Session** object does not contain a stored item of the specified name, it returns the value **Nothing**.

Although you can store essentially anything in the **Session** object, this does not mean that you should. In particular, large amounts of data should not be stored in the **Session** object because of the demands this can place on the server. A busy site may have dozens if not hundreds of users at the same time, and with each user assigned a separate **Session** object, the total storage demands on the Web server can mount up pretty quickly. For large quantities of data, it is preferable to use database technologies (as will be covered in Chapter 22).

Removing Session Items

Because a session will automatically time out, you rarely need to explicitly remove items from it. You can, however, using the **Remove()** method:

```
Session.Remove(name)
```

Name is the name of the item to remove. If the specified item does not exist in the session, no action is taken and no error occurs. To remove all items from the session, call the **RemoveAll()** method or the **Clear()** method, which do the same thing. Note that removing all items from a session does not destroy the session itself.

Identifying Users

You may be asking how ASP.NET knows that subsequent hits from a user belong to the same **Session**. No magic is involved! Each session is identified by a unique 120-bit session identifier that is generated using an algorithm that guarantees sessions will not collide (two users being assigned the same session ID) and that makes it essentially impossible for hackers to break into existing sessions. By default, ASP.NET uses a cookie to store the session ID. In other words, when a user first hits an ASP.NET application, a session ID is generated and stored on the client computer. With subsequent hits, this information lets the ASP.NET server determine that the user "belongs" to an existing session. In the event that a user has cookies disabled, ASP.NET has an alternate way to associate a session ID with a particular user, involving a modified URL.

Session Lifetime

How long does the server maintain a **Session** object? Clearly, after a user leaves the application you do not want his or her session information maintained indefinitely. On the other hand, you do not want a user's session information deleted if he or she simply takes a coffee break! By default, **Session** objects are deleted after 20 minutes with no hits from the user. You can determine or change the timeout value from the **Session** object's **TimeOut** property.

Session Members

The **Session** object has some additional members that you can use in your applications. The **Session** object is actually an instance of the **HttpSessionState** class, so that's what you need to look up if you want to obtain more information from the .NET documentation. These members are detailed in Table 20.1.

Table 20.1 Members of the HttpSessionState class.

Member	Description
Abandon()	Cancels the current session. If the user hits the application again, he or she will be treated as a new user.
Add(*name, value*)	Adds a new item to the session. Equivalent to using the **Session(*name*)** = *value* syntax.
Clear()	Deletes all items from the session.
Count	Returns the number of items stored in the session.
IsCookieless	Returns True if the session is being managed without cookies, False otherwise.
IsNewSession	Returns True if the session is new—in other words, if the session was created with the current request.
Remove(*name*)	Removes the specified item from the session.
RemoveAll()	Deletes all items from the session. Equivalent to **Clear()**.
SessionID	Returns the unique session ID.
TimeOut	Gets or sets the session timeout period, in minutes.

The Application Object

The ASP.NET server maintains an **Application** object for each ASP.NET application. This object can be used to store state information that is global to the entire application, as opposed to session-specific information that is stored in the **Session** object. For instance, suppose that 10 users are using your ASP.NET application. Each of those users will have his or her own **Session** object, but all will share the same **Application** object.

Adding data to the **Application** object, and retrieving the data, is done in the same way as you would for the **Session** object. For example:

```
Application(name) = value
myVar = Application(name)
```

Because the **Application** object is used by all sessions for a given application, there is the possibility that two or more sessions will try to write the same item at the same time. To avoid the potential for data corruption, it is necessary to lock the **Application** object before writing to it, then unlock it after the write is complete:

```
Application.Lock()
Application(name) = value
Application.UnLock()
```

Locking the **Application** object can slow things down, because any other instance of your application that tries to write to it will be paused while the lock is in place. The Web site may be unresponsive to other users, something that is best to avoid. In general, the **Application** object is best used for data that does not need to be updated frequently.

To remove a single item from the **Application** object, use this syntax:

```
Application.Remove(name)
```

To remove all items, call the **RemoveAll()** method. The **Application** object has additional members that are very similar to the members presented for the **Session** object in Table 20.1. The **Application** object does not, however, have the **Abandon()** method. For further details, look for the **HttpApplicationState** class in the .NET documentation.

The **Application** object is created when the first user makes the first hit on your application. It remains in existence until the Web server is shut down or until the web.config file is changed (a topic that is beyond the scope of this chapter). When you are running a Web application from within Visual Studio, a new **Application** object is created each time you run the application.

To demonstrate one common use for the **Application** object, Listing 20.4 shows how it can be used to maintain a "hit counter" for an application. By placing this code in an application's

Page_Load() event procedure (if the application has multiple pages, place it in the page that users tend to visit first), a count of total hits on the application will be maintained and can be used as you wish. Note how the code avoids counting hits that are postbacks by examining the **IsPostBack** property of the **Page** object. The code also avoids counting multiple hits from the same user during the same session by examining the **Session** object's **IsNewSession** property.

Listing 20.4 Using the Application object to count hits.

```
Private Sub Page_Load(ByVal sender As System.Object, _
    ByVal e As System.EventArgs) Handles MyBase.Load

' If the Application(Hits) item does not exist,
' this is the very first hit to this application.
If Application("Hits") Is Nothing Then
  Application.Lock()
  Application("Hits") = 1
  Application.UnLock()
Else
  ' If this is a new session and not a postback,
  ' increment the hit counter.
  If Session.IsNewSession And Not IsPostBack Then
    Application.Lock()
    Application("Hits") += 1
    Application.UnLock()
  End If
End If

End Sub
```

Events in a Web Application

You have already met one of the most important ASP.NET events, **Page_Load()**. There are many other events that you can use in your Web applications, some associated with the **Page** object, others with controls, and yet others with the **Application** and **Session** objects.

The **Page** object has several events in addition to **Load()**. The only one that you need to know about is the **Unload()** event. As the name indicates, this event is fired when the page is about to be unloaded—when, for example, the user navigates to another page. You can use this event procedure to perform any cleanup tasks that the page requires, such as closing database connections.

Most of the events that you will be working with are related to Web controls. The Web Forms event model is similar in some ways to the event model for Windows applications, but differs in one important respect. With a Web application, the form is being viewed on the client computer but event procedures are executed on the server. This means that every time an event occurs, such as the user clicking on a Button control, the client must notify the server of the event and the server will (at least usually) send a response. This is a postback, sometimes called a *round trip*, and even with today's fast Internet connections it does consume some time.

One way in which the Web Forms event model deals with the necessity of round trips is to limit the number of events that are available. In particular, Windows Forms events that can fire many times in quick succession, such as **MouseMove()**, are absent from the Web Forms event model. Such events are still available in the browser and can be handled by a client-side script, but they are not supported by ASP.NET.

Another technique used by ASP.NET is to design some events so they do not require a postback, at least not immediately. For example, the TextBox control has a **TextChanged()** event that is fired when the user modifies the text in the control. This event does not cause an immediate postback, however, but is sent along the next time a postback occurs for other reasons.

Control events will be covered in detail in the next chapter.

Security and Web Applications

The Internet was designed to be open and accessible, and that's one reason why it has been so successful. This openness, however, poses significant problems for anyone trying to implement security for a Web application. With the Web being used more and more for security-sensitive tasks such as banking and retail sales, security has become a primary concern for many Web developers. This section provides an introduction to security implementation for ASP.NET applications. As you might imagine, security is a wide and complex topic and I strongly recommend that you seek out additional, specialized sources of information if you are given the task of securing a critical Web application.

User Authentication

Authentication is the process of verifying that users are in fact who they claim to be. Assigning a username and a password is perhaps the commonest form of authentication. You can create your own authentication scheme or use one of several existing schemes that are available: Windows, Forms, or Passport. You set an application's authentication method by a tag in the web.config file that looks like this:

```
<authentication mode="mode" />
```

Mode can be Windows (the default), Passport, Forms, or None. Use the None setting if you are going to implement a custom authentication scheme.

Windows Authentication

Windows authentication makes use of the authentication services provided by the Windows operating system (NT/2000/XP). You create an account for each authorized user on the server computer, and the Web server software (IIS) takes care of performing the authentication.

There are three distinct types of Windows authentication that IIS can use: Basic, Digest, and Integrated. Digest and Integrated authentication require that all users run Internet Explorer, which of course limits the availability of your Web site. These two options will not be covered further, but you can find more information on Integrated and Digest authentication at **http://msdn.microsoft.com**.

Basic authentication works on both Internet Explorer and Netscape browsers, including older and newer versions. You set up Windows authentication on a directory basis. Because each ASP.NET application will reside in its own directory, you can set up Basic authentication for any or all of the Web applications on your server. Here are the steps to follow; these steps assume you are using IIS on Windows 2000:

1. Open up the Internet Information Services Manager. (Open Control Panel, open Administrative Tools, and then open Internet Services Manager).
2. One the left side of the IIS dialog box, open the tree and locate the virtual directory for the Web service whose authentication you are setting. Right-click on the virtual directory and select Properties from the context menu. A property page will appear.
3. On the property page, select the Directory Security tab, then click the Edit button at the top in the section Anonymous Access And Authentication Control. The Authentication Methods dialog box will be displayed, as shown in Figure 20.5.
4. Clear the Anonymous Access checkbox. This prevents people from browsing to the Web application without authenticating themselves.

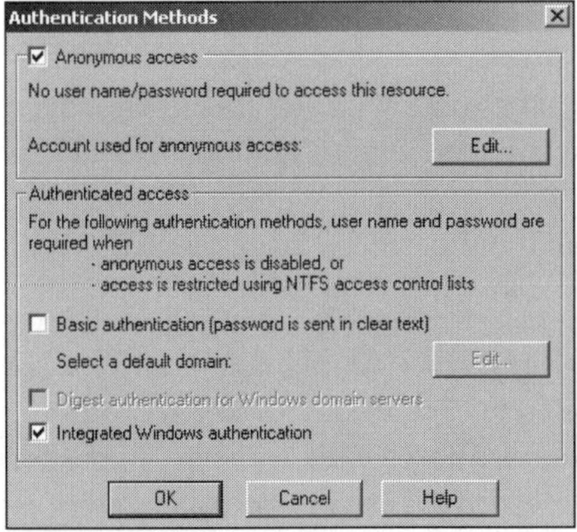

Figure 20.5
Setting basic user authentication for a Web application.

HTTPS and Security

The standard HTTP protocol sends information as plain text that, in theory, could be intercepted by a third party. HTTPS provides greater security by encrypting the information. There are three parts to using HTTPS. First, the Web server must support HTTPS, and secure communications must be enabled for the Web site in question. With Microsoft IIS, this requires obtaining a security certificate and making some changes to the IIS configuration. These topics are beyond the scope of this book, but they are explained in the IIS online documentation.

Second, the user's Web browser must support a session key strength of at least 40 bits. All current and recent versions of Internet Explorer meet this requirement.

Finally, navigation must be performed specifying the https:// protocol rather than http://. For example, you would navigate to **https//www.yoursite.com/YourApplication.aspx**.

5. Select the Basic Authentication checkbox. When a warning dialog box appears; click the Yes button. This turns on Basic authentication.
6. Clear the Integrated Windows Authentication and Digest Authentication For Windows Domain Servers checkboxes if they are checked.
7. Close the dialog box, then close the property page.

After this procedure has been followed, anyone trying to browse to the Web application will have to enter his or her username and password before proceeding. This information must match a valid Windows account. Basic Windows authentication is fine for a limited number of users, but clearly it is not suited for sites with large numbers of authorized users.

Basic authentication involves sending usernames and passwords directly over the Internet, without encryption, which opens the possibility that they could be intercepted. By combining Basic authentication with secure HTTP (HTTPS, explained in the "HTTPS and Security" sidebar), you can achieve a highly secure authentication process.

Passport Authentication

Passport authentication makes use of Microsoft's Passport Web site to authenticate users. Microsoft created Passport as an authentication infrastructure that allows anyone with an email account to create his or her own Passport account. If your Web application uses Passport authentication, users who try to log on are authenticated by checking their credentials with their Passport account.

Passport authentication has many desirable features. For example, users can (but are not required to) enter personal information and preferences in their Passport account, permitting Passport-enabled sites to gather statistics on visitors to your Web site. Implementing Passport authentication requires that you download the Passport Software Development Kit from **www.passport.com/business**, which requires that you register and pay a fee. You then use the SDK to implement the authentication for your Web applications.

Forms Authentication

Forms authentication is similar to basic authentication in that it requires users to log in with a username and a password. It differs in that the users are independent of Windows user accounts; rather, user accounts are set up separately. You can use forms authentication with ASP.NET Web applications but not with ASP.NET Web services (a topic covered in Chapter 23).

Forms authentication relies on usernames and passwords that are stored in the web.config file. If a user tries to browse to any page in your Web application, ASP.NET automatically redirects the user to a login page that you create. It is advisable to use HTTPS for the login page to prevent usernames and passwords from being sent without encryption.

To establish one or more user accounts to be used with forms authentication, add the information to your application's web.config file. The format to use is shown in Listing 20.5, which shows a web.config file that defines two users, one with the username "Maxwell" and the password "silverhammer," the other with the username "Alice" and the password "wonderland."

Listing 20.5 Defining user accounts for forms authentication.

```
<configuration>
  <system.web>
    <authentication mode="Forms">
      <forms name="MyFormsAuthentication" loginUrl="login.aspx">
        <credentials passwordFormat="Clear">
          <user name="Maxwell" password="silverhammer" />
          <user name="Alice" password="wonderland" />
        </credentials>
      </forms>
    </authentication>
    <authorization>
      <deny users="?" />
    </authorization>
  </system.web>
</configuration>
```

This web.config file specifies forms authentication method for the current virtual, using the **<authentication>** tag and mode attribute. The next line identifies the login page to be used (which you must create). The user information is added within the **<credentials>** element, with each user defined in a separate **<user>** element. The **passwordFormat="clear"** attribute specifies that the passwords in the file are stored "in the clear." Passwords can also be stored in encrypted format, which guards against the possibility of someone getting hold of your web.config file. Usernames and passwords can also be stored in another file or in a database, but I will not go into these techniques. You can find details about these techniques in the Visual Basic .NET documentation.

Note the **<authorization>** section near the end of the file. This entry denies access to anonymous users. Notice that the listing uses a question mark (the **<deny users="?" />** line) to single out anonymous users.

I have mentioned that you must create the login page to be used with forms authentication. This page must use the **FormsAuthentication** class (in the **System.Web.Security** namespace) to check usernames and passwords and then, if login is successful, to redirect the user to the page that he or she originally requested.

A login page can be quite simple, requiring at a minimum a TextBox for the username, another for the password, and a Button control to submit the form. Also, some way of displaying a message is advisable, to inform users if their login was not successful. The code is simple, too. Listing 20.6 shows the code behind for a simple login page that can be used with the web.config file from Listing 20.5. Note that this listing shows only the **Click()** event procedure for the button, and not the remainder of the page's code. When the user clicks the LogIn button, the username and password that were entered are passed to the **FormsAuthentication.Authenticate()** method, which returns True only if the user is found in the web.config file, and the password is correct.

Listing 20.6 A simple login page for forms authentication.

```
Private Sub btnLogIn_Click(ByVal sender As Object, _
        ByVal e As System.EventArgs) Handles btnLogIn.Click

  Dim username As String = txtUserName.Text
  Dim password As String = txtPassword.Text
  If FormsAuthentication.Authenticate(username, password) Then
    ' Login was successful.
    FormsAuthentication.RedirectFromLoginPage(username, False)
  Else
    ' Login failed.
    lblMessage.Text = "Username and password not found."
  End If

End Sub
```

Custom Authentication

It seems that ASP.NET's built-in options for user authentication cover just about every possible need. If not, however, you can always implement your own custom scheme. There are essentially no limitations on how you might do this. For example, you could store usernames and passwords in a database, and retrieve them when a user tries to log in. Of course, the database itself must be secure. This can involve keeping the database on a separate computer that is behind a security firewall.

Summary

In today's ever more connected world, it is becoming increasingly important for developers to have the ability to create distributed applications with remote data access. Such applications must be robust, easy to maintain, and secure. With Web applications, Visual Basic .NET provides the programmer with a powerful set of Web-related components and tools. Although they may seem complex at first glance, Web applications actually set new standards for simplicity and ease of use.

This chapter showed the basics of creating and using Web applications. The next chapter covers the various Web controls that you can use to create your Web application's user interface.

Chapter 21
Controls for Web Applications

In the previous chapter, you learned the fundamentals of creating Web applications with ASP.NET and Visual Basic. A Web application is built around a form, or page, that displays in the client's browser. The visual interface of the page is composed of ASP.NET server-side controls as well as other optional items, such as HTML elements. Now it's time to learn about the ASP.NET controls that are available and how to use them in your Web applications.

Web Control Overview

The design and implementation of the .NET framework's Web controls presented some special challenges. Here is a component whose code will run on a server, while its visual representation will be rendered, and its user interactions will occur on a client system. From the perspective of the user, a Web control usually acts like a standard Windows form controls, and the fact that they are executing on a server that may be a thousand miles away usually does not come into play (barring a slow Web connection!). From the programmer's point of view, a Web control can be placed on a page and manipulated in pretty much the same way as a Windows form control.

All of the Web controls derive from the **WebControl** class, which in turn derives from the **Control** class. Specifically, controls that have a visual interface derive from **WebControl**, while those Web controls that do not have a user interface derive directly from **Control**. Note that this **Control** class is distinct from the **Control** class that is the base for Windows form controls. The latter is in the **System.Windows.Forms** namespace, while the Web controls are all in the **System.Web.UI** namespace. Note that not only do Web controls derive from the **System.Web.UI.Control** class, but the **Page** class does also.

The Web controls are cleverly designed so that they do not require special browser capabilities (although some features are supported only by recent versions of Internet Explorer). When a user browses to a Web application page, the ASP.NET controls that the programmer placed on the page are rendered as standard HTML controls. You can see this if you view the source HTML when viewing a Web application in your browser. Thus, a Web control can be thought of as a standard HTML control with special capabilities provided by server code and links between the client page and the server.

Common Web Control Members

This section covers those members that all or most server controls have in common. They are primarily the members that are inherited from the **Control** or **WebControl** classes. Some of the members covered here, such as those for control appearance, apply only to those controls with a visual representation.

Control Appearance

Perhaps the most fundamental aspect of a control's appearance is whether it is visible. This is determined by the **Visible** property, which can be set to True or False.

The size of a control is specified by its **Height** and **Width** properties. Usually, you will set a control's size visually using the Page Designer, which will enter the appropriate property values for you. You can also set these properties directly, in the Properties window or in code. The measurements are in pixels by default, but you can use other units of measurement by suffixing the property value with the desired unit abbreviation: "in" for inches, "mm" for millimeters, "cm" for centimeters, and "pt" for points.

You specify a control's colors with the **ForeColor** and **BackColor** properties. If the control has a border, you can also specify its **BorderColor** property. Colors are specified using the **Color** structure, which is a member of the **System.Drawing** namespace. You learned the details of this structure in Chapter 8.

You can place a border around a control with the **BorderStyle** property, using one of the **BorderStyle** enumerations. Table 21.1 describes the members of this enumeration. The width of the border is specified by the **BorderWidth** property and the color of the border by the **BorderColor** property.

The font used for the control's text is determined by the **Font** property. In the Designer, you can set individual aspects of the font appearance in the Properties window, including its size, typeface, and whether it is bold, italic, and/or underlined. In code, you set this property using a **FontInfo** object, referenced by the **Font** property. The **FontInfo** object has properties as described in Table 21.2.

Table 21.1 Members of the BorderStyle enumeration.

BorderStyle Member	Description
Dashed	A dashed line border
Dotted	A dotted line border
Double	A double solid line border
Groove	A grooved border for a sunken border appearance
Inset	An inset border for a sunken control appearance
None	No border
NotSet	No set border style
Outset	An outset border for a raised control appearance
Ridge	A ridged border for a raised border appearance
Solid	A solid line border

Table 21.2 Members of the FontInfo class.

Property	Description
Bold	Boolean value specifying whether the font is boldface
Italic	Boolean value specifying whether the font is italicized
Name	String identifying the name of the font's typeface, such as "Times" or "Arial"
Size	Specifies the size of the font as a **FontUnit** member (explained in the main text)
Strikeout	Boolean value specifying whether the font is struck out
Underline	Boolean value specifying whether the font is underlined

When specifying font size for a Web page font, you do so using the **FontUnit** class. You have two choices. One is to use the class's built-in fields that specify relative font sizes such as Large or Small. The permitted settings are as follows:

```
XXSmall
XSmall
Smaller
Small
Medium
Large
Larger
XLarge
XXLarge
```

This code, for example, sets the font size of the TextBox to XLarge:

```
TextBox1.Font.Size = FontUnit.Xlarge
```

The alternative is to use the **FontUnit** constructor to specify a font of a specific size. Here are some examples:

```
TextBox1.Font.Size = New FontUnit("20pt") ' 20 point size
TextBox1.Font.Size = New FontUnit("0.5in") ' 1/2 inch size
```

Control Events

Relatively few events are common to all Web controls. In most programs, you will not need to use any of these events (although you will use the specific events possessed by each individual control, as detailed later in this chapter). Table 21.3 describes the common Web control events.

Other Control Members

Table 21.4 describes some additional control members that you may need to use in your programs.

The Web Form Controls

This part of the chapter provides details on the individual Web form controls. As you read this section, remember that all these controls share the various common members that were described in the first section of this chapter.

Table 21.3 Common Web control events.

Event	Description
Init()	Fires when the control is first initialized. This is the first event in a control's life cycle.
Load()	Fires when the control is loaded into the **Page** object.
Render()	Fires just before the control is rendered onto the page (just before the control's HTML is sent to the client).
Unload()	Fires just before the control is unloaded (destroyed).

Table 21.4 Other members of Web controls.

Member	Description
AccessKey	Sets the access key that is used to move the focus to the control. Works only in Internet Explorer version 4 and later. Alt+ is the specified access key. For example, if the **AccessKey** property is set to "F", then the user presses Alt+F to move to the control.
Enabled	A Boolean value specifying whether the control is enabled. A disabled control cannot accept user input, does not fire events, and in Internet Explorer 4 and later displays as grayed out.
EnableViewState	A Boolean value specifying whether the control's view state is saved. When this property is True (the default), the control's state (its properties) is saved across HTTP requests. If your program doesn't require its state to be preserved, set this property to False to improve performance.
ID	The name of the control, used to refer to it in code.
Page	Returns a reference to the **Page** object that contains the control.
TabIndex	Gets or sets the control's tab index.
ToolTip	Gets the ToolTip text that is displayed when the mouse cursor hovers over the control.

The Label Control

The Label control is used to place static text on a page—text that cannot be changed by the user, although it can be changed by program code. If you want to insert text that will not be changed at all, you can simply type in the text (in Flow Layout mode) or use a Panel control (in Grid Layout mode). The main reason to use a Label control is when you will need to change the text programmatically. For example, a Label control can be used to display status messages to the user based on program operation.

The text displayed in a Label control is determined by its **Text** property. All of its other properties are inherited from the **Control** or **WebControl** class.

The TextBox Control

The TextBox control provides for display of text that can be entered and edited by the user. It is perhaps the most frequently used of all the Web controls, and you should have a good understanding of how it works. The most important control property is **Text**, which gets or sets the text displayed in the control. The control can operate in one of three basic modes, as set by its **TextMode** property. They are as follows:

- *Single line*—If **TextMode** is set to **SingleLine** (the default), the TextBox displays a single line of text. If the text length exceeds the width of the control, it scrolls to the left as needed. If the user presses Enter in a single-line TextBox, it is either ignored or, depending on the design of the page, it may activate a Button control.
- *Multiple line*—If **TextMode** is set to **MultiLine**, the TextBox can display multiple lines of text. If the user presses Enter, it starts a new line. A vertical scrollbar is displayed to enable scrolling of text if needed. Set the **Wrap** property to True if you want text to wrap automatically when it reaches the right edge of a multiline TextBox.
- *Password*—If **TextMode** is set to **Password**, the TextBox displays all characters as asterisks.

You can set the size of a TextBox control by using the **Width** and **Height** properties. Sometimes, however, it's more useful to size the control in terms of columns and rows of text rather than the screen coordinate units used by the **Width** and **Height** properties. To do this, set the **Columns** and **Rows** properties (the **Rows** property is relevant only for a multiline text box). The text box will be sized to the specified number of columns and/or rows in the selected font. Setting **Columns** and **Rows** to 0 (their default value) results in the control being sized according to the **Width** and **Height** properties.

You can limit the number of characters in a TextBox by setting the **MaxLength** property. The default setting is 0, which places no restriction on length. This property doesn't apply when **TextMode** is **MultiLine**.

To create a read-only text box, one the user cannot edit, set the **ReadOnly** property to True.

The one important event for the TextBox control is **TextChanged()**. This is a "deferred postback" event, discussed in Chapter 20. When the user changes the text in a TextBox, the **TextChanged()** event is noted, but a postback doesn't occur immediately. When a postback is generated from some other cause, such as the user clicking a Button control, then the **TextChanged()** event is included in the postback. This delayed event posting reduces unnecessary roundtrips to the server. There may be specialized situations, however, when you want **TextChanged()** events to be posted to the server immediately. To enable this, set the control's **AutoPostBack** property to True.

The Button Controls

A Button control is a screen element that the user clicks in order to make something happen. ASP.NET provides three varieties of Button controls:

- *Button*—The basic Button control displays a text caption and can be used to trigger any code as required by the program.
- *LinkButton*—Displays a hyperlink. A LinkButton has the appearance of a HyperLink control and the functionality of a Button control.
- *ImageButton*—Displays an image that responds to mouse clicks.

Examples of the three buttons are shown in Figure 21.1.

The **Text** property controls the caption that is displayed on Button and LinkButton controls. When you add a Button control to a page, it is assigned a default **ID** property of the

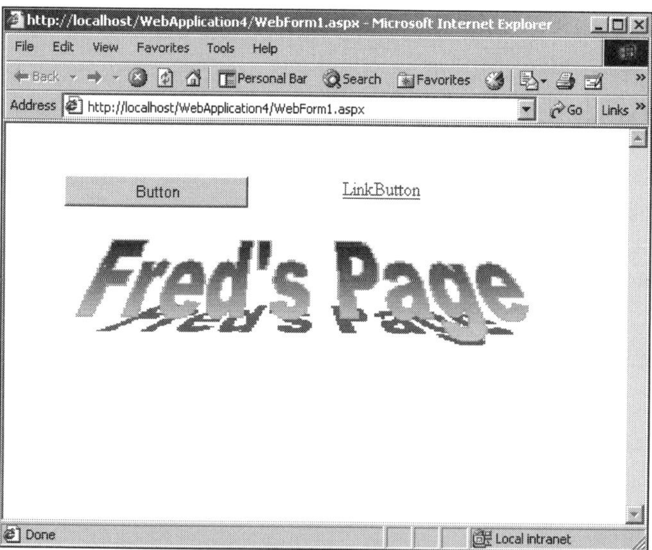

Figure 21.1
ASP.NET's three types of Button controls.

form Button1, Button2, and so on. You should change this property to provide some indication of the function of the button. Then, in the page's code behind module, create an event handler for the button's **Click()** event and place the code that you want executed in that procedure. Remember, in the code editor, you can select the component and the event from the lists at the top of the code-editing window, and Visual Studio will enter the skeleton of the event procedure for you to edit.

The LinkButton control works exactly like the Button control except that its caption is displayed as a link. By default, this means the text is in blue and underlined. Also, in the browser, the mouse cursor changes when over a LinkButton. Note, however, that clicking a LinkButton does not automatically cause any navigation to occur. Therefore, to provide a working hyperlink, you use the HyperLink control (which is covered later in this chapter), and you would use the LinkButton control only when you want the functionality of a Button control with the appearance of a HyperLink control.

The ImageButton control is more closely related to the Image control than to the Button control. You can think of an ImageButton as an Image control that responds to clicks. Use the **ImageURL** property to specify the image to be displayed. See the section on the Image control for more information.

Demonstration 1

The program presented here demonstrates the use of the Label, TextBox, and Button controls. It also lets you see the relationship between the **Click()** and **TextChanged()** events. Follow these steps to create the project:

1. Start a new ASP.NET Web application.
2. Add two TextBox controls to the page. Leave all their properties at the default values.
3. Add a Button control to the page and change its **Text** property to "Button 1".
4. Add another Button control to the page and change its **Text** property to "Button 2".
5. Add a Label control to the page, and change its **Text** property to a blank string.

At this point, your page will look more or less like Figure 21.2. Now it is time to add the code.

The demonstration program needs five event procedures: one for the **Click()** event of each Button control and one for the **TextChanged()** event of each TextBox control. The fifth required event procedure is **Page_Load()**, which will be used to clear the Label control with each postback. Code in these event procedures will write text to the Label control, which you can use to view the events that happened and the order in which they occurred. Open the code behind file for the page, insert these four event procedures, and then add the code as shown in Listing 21.1.

When you run the program, try different combinations of editing the TextBox controls and clicking the Button controls. You'll see that the Label control displays a message identifying

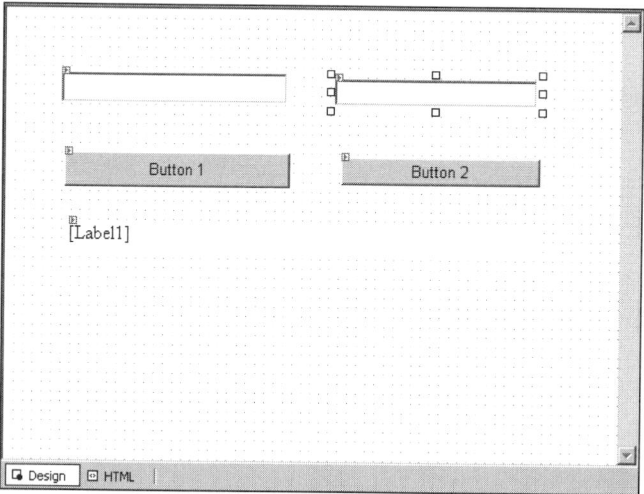

Figure 21.2
Designing the page for the demonstration program.

the events that happened, and in what order. For example, Figure 21.3 shows the program after we entered some text in both TextBox controls and then clicked Button 1.

You can use this program to see the effect of changing the **AutoPostback** property to True. Do so for the first TextBox, then run the program. Now, if you edit the text in that TextBox and move the focus to another control (by pressing Tab, for example), the **TextChanged()** event is fired even though a button was not clicked.

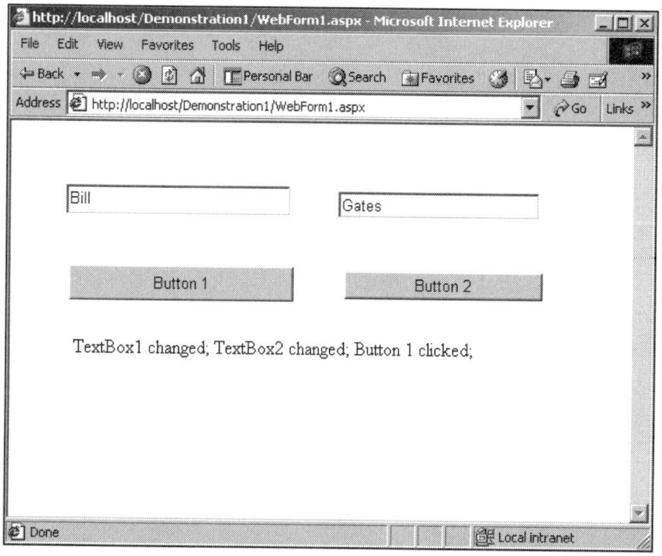

Figure 21.3
The demonstration program identifies the events that happened.

Listing 21.1 Event procedures in the demonstration program.

```
Private Sub Page_Load(ByVal sender As System.Object, _
    ByVal e As System.EventArgs) Handles MyBase.Load

  Label1.Text = ""

End Sub

Private Sub Button1_Click(ByVal sender As Object, _
    ByVal e As System.EventArgs) Handles Button1.Click

  Label1.Text &= "Button 1 clicked; "

End Sub

Private Sub Button2_Click(ByVal sender As Object, _
    ByVal e As System.EventArgs) Handles Button2.Click

  Label1.Text &= "Button 2 clicked; "

End Sub

Private Sub TextBox1_TextChanged(ByVal sender As Object, _
    ByVal e As System.EventArgs) Handles TextBox1.TextChanged

  Label1.Text &= "TextBox1 changed; "

End Sub

Private Sub TextBox2_TextChanged(ByVal sender As Object, _
    ByVal e As System.EventArgs) Handles TextBox2.TextChanged

  Label1.Text &= "TextBox2 changed; "

End Sub
```

The HyperLink Control

The HyperLink control displays a hyperlink on a page and automatically navigates to the specified URL when clicked. It can display text or an image. The members of the HyperLink control are listed in Table 21.5. Use this control when you want navigation to be automatic rather than under program control.

Table 21.5 Members of the HyperLink control.

Member	Description
ImageURL	The URL of the image to display for the link. If both the text and **ImageURL** properties are set, the latter takes precedence.
NavigateURL	The URL to navigate to.
Target	Specifies the target window or frame to use for the linked content. The default setting displays the linked page in the current window. Other settings are **_blank** (display in a new window with no frames), **_parent** (display in the current frameset's immediate parent), **_self** (display in the current frame, with focus), and **_top** (displays in the full window without frames).
Text	The hyperlink's caption. Can be superceded by the **ImageURL** property.

The List Controls

The .NET framework provides two Web server controls for displaying lists of information. The ListBox control presents a list of items from which the user can select one or more items. The DropDownList control presents a drop-down list of items from which the user can select one item.

ListBox

Items can be added to a ListBox during program design by means of its **Items** property. Each item in a ListBox is represented by a **ListItem** object, with the following three properties:

- **Text**—The text displayed in the list.
- **Value**—The value returned by the item when selected. By default, this is the same as the **Text** property.
- **Selected**—True if the item is selected (highlighted), False otherwise.

When you select the **Items** property in the Properties window, the ListItem Collection editor is displayed, as shown in Figure 21.4. This figure shows the collection with two items already added and a third new one open for editing. To add and modify items in the collection, follow these steps:

- To add a new item, click Add, then edit the item's properties in the right pane.
- To edit an existing item, click it in the left pane, then edit its properties in the right pane.
- To delete an existing item, click it in the left pane, then click Remove.
- To change the position of an item in the list, click it and then click the up and down arrows to move it to the desired position.
- When finished, click OK.

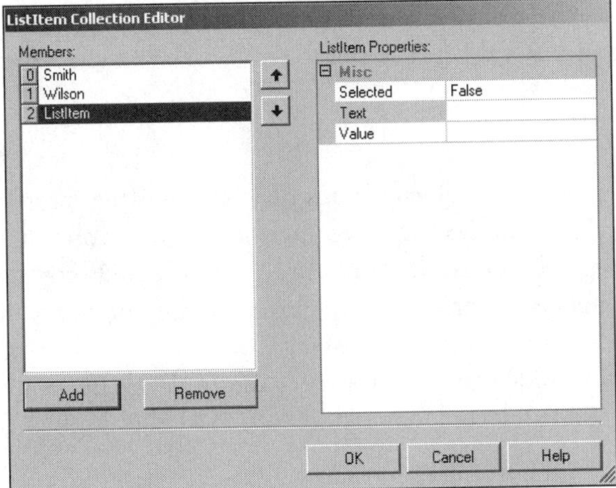

Figure 21.4
You use the ListItem Collection editor to add items to a ListBox at design time.

To add items to a ListBox programmatically, use the **Items.Add()** method. You can use this method to add a string to the end of the list, in which case the item's **Value** property will be the same as its text property, and its **Selected** property will be False. Here's an example:

```
MyListBox.Items.Add("Strawberry")
MyListBox.Items.Add("Banana")
MyListBox.Items.Add("Tangerine")
```

You can also use the **Add()** method to add a type **ListItem** to the list, permitting the item's **Text** and **Value** properties to be different:

```
MyListBox.Items.Add(New ListItem(text, value))
```

To remove an item from the list, use the **Remove()** method:

```
MyListBox.Items.Remove("Strawberry")
```

If the specified item does not exist, no action is taken. To clear the entire list, call the **Clear()** method.

A ListBox's default is to permit the user to select a single item. To permit multiple items to be selected, change the **SelectionMode** property to **Multiple**. In this mode, the user can select multiple contiguous items by holding down Shift while clicking, or multiple non-contiguous items by holding down Ctrl while clicking.

When your program is running, you use the **SelectedIndex** and **SelectedItem** properties to determine what, if anything, is selected in the ListBox. The **SelectedIndex** property returns the 0-based index of the selected item, or -1 if no item is selected. The **SelectedItem** property returns a type **ListItem** for the selected item, or the value Nothing if no item is selected. You then use the **ListItem** object's **Text** and/or **Value** properties to retrieve the selected item:

```
SelectedItem = ListBox1.SelectedItem.Text
```

If the ListBox is in multiple select mode, the **SelectedIndex** and **SelectedItem** properties return information about the first (lowest index) selected item in the list. To obtain all selected items, you must loop through the entire list and check the **Selected** property of each item. You do this using the **Items.Count** property, which returns the number of items in the list. By starting at **SelectedIndex** and looping up to **Items.Count-1**, you will examine all the items in the list. The following code snippet shows how to check if a ListBox is in multiple selection mode. If not, the single selected item is displayed in a Label control. If so, all selected items are displayed:

```
Dim s As String
Dim i As Integer
' Make sure something is selected.
If ListBox1.SelectedIndex <> -1 Then
  If ListBox1.SelectionMode = ListSelectionMode.Single Then
    Label1.Text = ListBox1.SelectedItem.Text
  Else
    For i = ListBox1.SelectedIndex To ListBox1.Items.Count - 1
      If ListBox1.Items(i).Selected Then
        s &= ListBox1.Items(i).Text & ";"
      End If
    Next
    Label1.Text = s
  End If
End If
```

The ListBox control has a single event, **SelectedIndexChanged()**, that fires when the user changes the selection in the list. This is a "deferred" event that won't be posted back to the server immediately unless the control's **AutoPostBack** property is set to True.

DropDownList

A DropDownList looks like a TextBox with a down arrow at one end. When the user clicks the arrow, the full list of items is displayed, from which the user can select one item. At both design time and runtime, items are added to a DropDownList in exactly the same way as for a ListBox, as was described in the previous section. By default, the control displays the first item in the list, but this does not mean that the item is selected. If an item is selected, it is displayed in reverse text. You use the **SelectedIndex** property to retrieve the 0-based index of the selected item; this property returns -1 if no item is selected. The **SelectedItem** property returns the selected item itself (as a **ListItem** object). The control has the **SelectedIndexChanged()** event that works just like the ListBox control's event of the same name.

Demonstration 2

This program demonstrates the use of the ListBox and DropDownList controls. It lets the user place an ice cream order, specifying one or more flavors and then an item. The order summary is displayed on the page. Follow these steps to create the project:

1. Create a new ASP.NET Web Application project.
2. Place a ListBox control on the page and change its **ID** property to lbFlavors.
3. Place a DropDownList control on the page and change its **ID** property to ddlType.
4. Place two Label controls on the form to identify the list controls (see Figure 21.5).
5. Place a Button control on the page and change its **ID** property to btnOrder and its **Text** property to Order.
6. Place another Label control on the form, stretching it out beneath the other controls. Change its **ID** property to lblOutput.

All initialization of the list controls is done in code, in the **Page_Load()** event procedure. The remainder of the program's code is in the **Click()** event procedure for the Button control. Both of these procedures are shown in Listing 21.2. When the program runs, the user must select one or more flavors and also a type of item. Pressing the Order button processes the order, which is then displayed in the Label control, as shown in Figure 21.5.

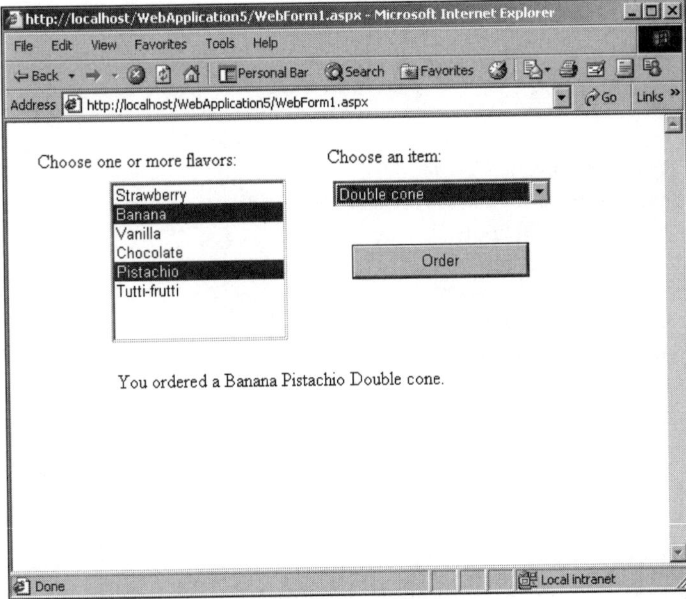

Figure 21.5
Running the list control's demonstration program.

Listing 21.2 Code in the list control demonstration program.

```
Private Sub Page_Load(ByVal sender As System.Object, _
    ByVal e As System.EventArgs) Handles MyBase.Load

  ' Initialize the ListBox and DropDownList.
  If Not IsPostBack Then
    lbFlavors.Items.Add("Strawberry")
    lbFlavors.Items.Add("Banana")
    lbFlavors.Items.Add("Vanilla")
    lbFlavors.Items.Add("Chocolate")
    lbFlavors.Items.Add("Pistachio")
    lbFlavors.Items.Add("Tutti-frutti")
    lbFlavors.SelectionMode = ListSelectionMode.Multiple

    ddlType.Items.Add("Cone")
    ddlType.Items.Add("Sundae")
    ddlType.Items.Add("Double cone")
    ddlType.Items.Add("Dish")
    ' Clear the Label control.
    lblOutput.Text = ""
  End If
End Sub


Private Sub btnOrder_Click(ByVal sender As System.Object, _
    ByVal e As System.EventArgs) Handles btnOrder.Click

  Dim s As String
  Dim i As Integer

  ' Make sure something is selected.
  If lbFlavors.SelectedIndex = -1 Or ddlType.SelectedIndex = -1 Then
    ' Nothing is selected in one or both lists.
    s = "Please select flavors and an item."
  Else
    ' Both lists have something selected. Loop thru the
    ' flavors list to get all selected items.
    s = "You ordered a "
    For i = lbFlavors.SelectedIndex To lbFlavors.Items.Count - 1
      If lbFlavors.Items(i).Selected Then
        s &= lbFlavors.Items(i).Text & " "
      End If
    Next
    ' Get the selection from the type list.
    s &= ddlType.SelectedItem.Text & "."
  End If
  lbloutput.Text = s
End Sub
```

Controls for Making Choices

This section describes the ASP.NET controls that are designed to let the user make choices by turning options on or off. There are two such controls. The CheckBox control is used to turn individual options on or off. The RadioButton control is used when only one option in a group can be on at a time.

CheckBox

The CheckBox control displays a small box with an optional adjacent label. The box can be empty (option off) or have a small checkmark displayed in it (option on), and the user toggles the state of the box by clicking it or by moving the focus to it and pressing the spacebar. The relevant properties are:

- **Text**—The caption displayed next to the box.
- **Checked**—True if the box is checked, False if not. Set this property in code or at design time of you want the box checked initially.

The CheckBox control has the **CheckChanged()** event, which is fired when the state of the control changes. This is a deferred event.

CheckBoxList

The CheckBoxList control provides two or more individual checkboxes within a single control. It does not provide the same layout flexibility as the individual CheckBox control, but it is easier to write code that determines which items are selected.

A CheckBoxList control has an **Items** collection that contains one element for each checkbox in the list. The control starts off with a single checkbox when placed on a page; you then add items using the property window or in code. Beneath the surface, the CheckBoxList is essentially identical to a ListBox control except that each item in the list has a checkbox displayed next to its text. The following code places five items in a CheckBoxList and then selects the first and third items:

```
With CheckBoxList1
   .Items.Add("Stamp collecting")
   .Items.Add("Sky diving")
   .Items.Add("Cooking")
   .Items.Add("Model airplanes")
   .Items.Add("Biking")
   .Items(0).Selected = True
   .Items(2).Selected = True
End With
```

To determine which items in a CheckBoxList are selected, use the same techniques as for detecting multiple selections in a ListBox.

RadioButton

The RadioButton control is like the CheckBox in that it lets the user turn options on or off. It displays a small circle that can contain a dot (option on) or not (option off). It differs in that only one in a group of RadioButton controls can be on at one time; if one is turned on, the one that was on previously is turned off automatically. You define a group of RadioButton controls by assigning the same value to their **GroupName** property. Otherwise, the control works exactly the same as the CheckBox control.

RadioButtonList

The RadioButtonList control provides two or more individual radio buttons within a single control. It is essentially identical to a CheckBoxList control except that it permits only one item to be selected at a time.

The Image Control

You use the Image control to display an image on a page. The control properties identify the image (as an URL) and the alignment of the image with respect to other elements on the page. The control supports several image formats: bitmaps (*.bmp), Windows metafiles (*.wmf), Graphics Interchange Format (*.gif), Portable Network Graphics (*.png), and JPEG (*.jpg). At design time, setting the **ImageURL** property is done using the Select Image dialog box, shown in Figure 21.6. You can select an image on a local drive or at a remote or local URL. In the dialog box, you can specify one of three types of URLs, as set with the URL type drop-down list:

- *Absolute*—The URL specifies the complete path to the image file; for example, **http://localhost/images/bmw1.jpg**.

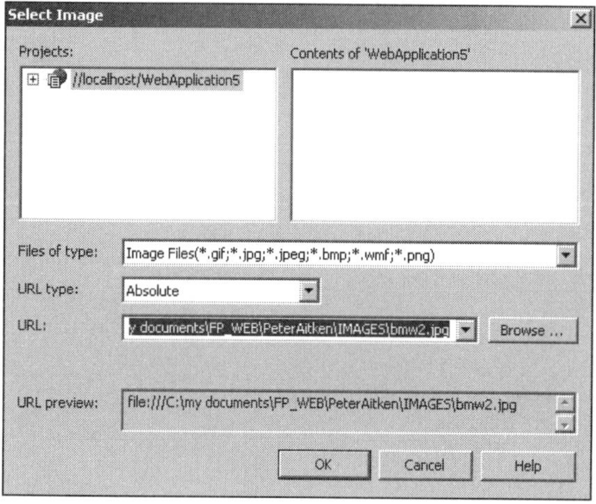

Figure 21.6
Selecting an image to display in an Image control.

- *Document Relative*—The URL specifies the path to the image file relative to the location of the page containing the Image control; for example, bmw1.jpg (assuming the image file is in the same directory as the ASPX page).
- *Root Relative*—The URL specifies the path to the image file relative to the parent directory of the current file; for example, /MyProject/bmw1.jpg.

Like all controls with a visual interface, the Image control has **Width** and **Height** properties. If you leave these properties blank, the control will automatically size to fit the image loaded into it. Otherwise, the image will be shrunk or expanded to fit the size of the control. The properties of the **Image** class are described in Table 21.6.

Table 21.6 Members of the Image class.

Property	Description
AlternateText	Text that is displayed on the page if the image cannot be loaded.
ImageAlign	Specifies how the image is to be aligned with respect to other elements on the page. Relevant in Flow Layout mode only.
ImageURL	The absolute or relative URL of the image to display.

The Panel Control

The Panel control serves as a container for other controls. It can be used for various tasks, including generating controls programmatically or hiding/showing a group of controls as a unit. The Panel control can also display a background image or a different background color than the rest of the page, permitting you greater freedom in designing the visual appearance of your page. When a control such as a TextBox or a Label is contained in a Panel, it is partially independent of other controls on the page. Its position is defined with respect to the Panel control, and its visibility is controlled by the Panel control's **Visible** property.

To add a control to a Panel control in design mode, make sure the Panel is selected, then double-click the desired control in the Toolbox. The new control will appear at the top-left corner of the Panel, and you can size it as needed. Within a Panel control, layout is always in Flow mode, so you cannot freely position controls at arbitrary locations in the Panel. Rather, elements that are placed on the page are inserted starting at the top left and then working across and down. If the Panel already contains one or more controls, any new control is added immediately after the selected control.

You can add plain text to a Panel control as follows. First, activate the control by selecting it and then clicking it again (not a double-click, but two separate clicks). When activated, the Panel control displays with a thick hatched border, and a blinking vertical cursor is shown in the control. You can move this cursor using the arrow keys, then type in the desired text.

The **HorizontalAlign** property determines how child controls are arranged horizontally within the Panel control. Possible settings for this property are as follows:

- **Center**—Child controls are centered within the Panel.
- **Justify**—Child controls are spread out to be aligned at the right and left margins.
- **Left**—Child controls are aligned at the left margin.
- **NotSet**—Horizontal alignment is not set.
- **Right**—Child controls are aligned at the right margin.

To display a background image in a Panel control, set its **BackImageURL** property. If necessary, the image is tiled to fully cover the Panel control.

To add controls to a Panel programmatically, use the **Add()** method of its **Controls** collection. For example, the following code adds a Label control to the Panel control:

```
Dim MyLabel As New Label()
Panel1. Controls. Add(MyLabel)
```

You'll see more details on adding controls in code in the next demonstration.

The Literal Control

The Literal control is designed for inserting HTML text into pages in situations where you cannot add the text directly. For example, if you are adding HTML tags to a Panel control in code, you cannot insert the tags directly into the Panel but must create a Literal control for each HTML tag. When the Literal is rendered, the output is the tag it contains. This text is specified by the control's **Text** property. For example, this code creates a Literal control that will render as an HTML paragraph tag:

```
Dim para As New Literal()
para.text = "<p>"
```

You'll see an example of using this control in the next demonstration program.

Demonstration 3

The program presented in this section demonstrates several of the controls that we have discussed. It shows how to use the RadioButton control to let the user select an option, how to add controls to a Panel control at runtime, and how to use the Literal control to insert HTML text into a Panel control. Here are the steps to follow:

1. Create a new ASP.NET Web application called PanelDemo.
2. Add a Panel control to the page. Change its **BorderStyle** property to **Solid**.
3. Add three RadioButton controls to the page. Set their properties as follows. Note that the **GroupName** property setting does not matter as long as it is the same for all three controls:
   - *First RadioButton—Text*: Labels; **ID**: rdLabels; **GroupName**: g; **Checked**: True
   - *Second RadioButton—Text*: Text Boxes; **ID**: rdTextBoxes; **GroupName**: g
   - *Third RadioButton—Text*: Check Boxes; **ID**: rdCheckBoxes; **GroupName**: g
4. Add a Label control with the **Text** property set to "How Many?".
5. Add a TextBox control with **ID** set to txtHowMany and **Text** set to "4".
6. Add a Button control with **ID** set to btnGo and **Text** set to "Go".

At this point, your Page Designer should look something like Figure 21.7. The next step is to write the code that will add controls to the Panel when the user clicks the Go button. This code, shown in Listing 21.3, is placed in the Button's **Click()** event procedure.

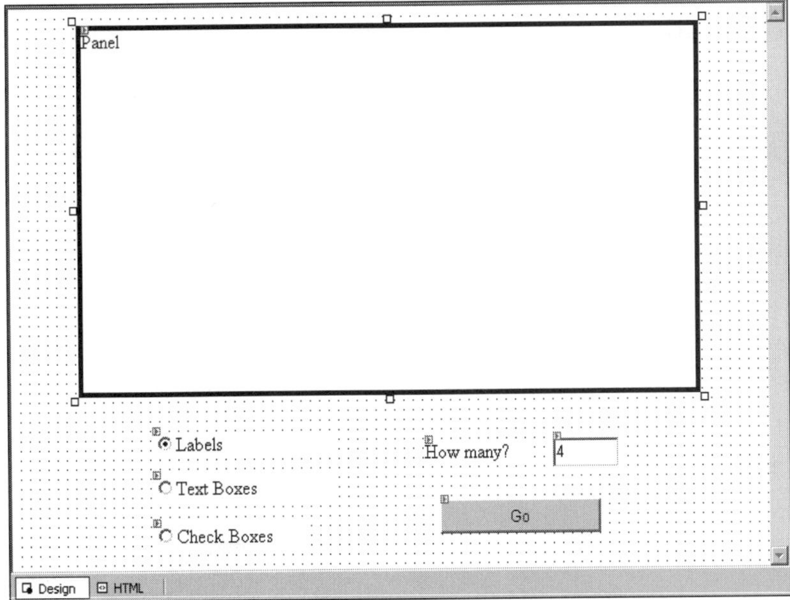

Figure 21.7
Designing the Panel demonstration page.

Listing 21.3 Adding controls to a Panel programmatically.

```
Private Sub btnGo_Click(ByVal sender As System.Object, _
  ByVal e As System.EventArgs) Handles btnGo.Click

  Dim i As Integer

  If rdLabels.Checked Then
    For i = 1 To Val(txtHowMany.Text)
      Dim lb As New Label()
      lb.ID = "Label" & i
      lb.Text = "Label" & i
      Dim l1 As New Literal()
      l1.Text = "<p>"
      Panel1.Controls.Add(l1)
      Panel1.Controls.Add(lb)
      Dim l2 As New Literal()
      l2.Text = "</p>"
      Panel1.Controls.Add(l2)
    Next
  ElseIf rdTextBoxes.Checked Then
    For i = 1 To Val(txtHowMany.Text)
      Dim tb As New TextBox()
      tb.ID = "TextBox" & i
      tb.Text = "TextBox" & i
      Dim l1 As New Literal()
      l1.Text = "<p>"
      Panel1.Controls.Add(l1)
      Panel1.Controls.Add(tb)
      Dim l2 As New Literal()
      l2.Text = "</p>"
      Panel1.Controls.Add(l2)
    Next
  ElseIf rdCheckBoxes.Checked Then
    For i = 1 To Val(txtHowMany.Text)
      Dim cb As New CheckBox()
      cb.ID = "CheckBox" & i
      cb.Text = "CheckBox" & i
      Dim l1 As New Literal()
      l1.Text = "<p>"
      Panel1.Controls.Add(l1)
      Panel1.Controls.Add(cb)
      Dim l2 As New Literal()
      l2.Text = "</p>"
      Panel1.Controls.Add(l2)
    Next

  End If

End Sub
```

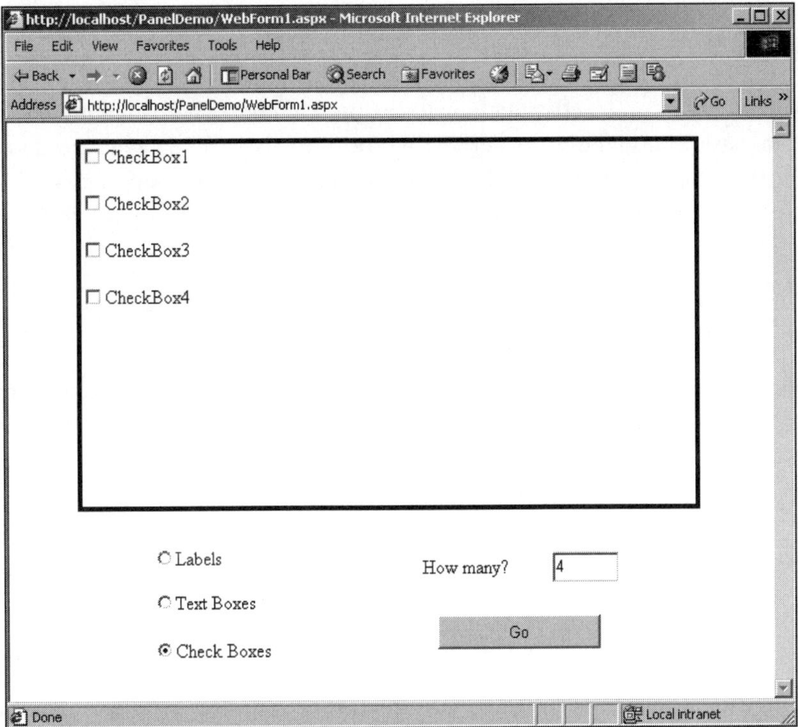

Figure 21.8
The Panel demonstration program in action.

The program is shown in Figure 21.8 after adding four CheckBox controls to the Panel. Note that the added controls are on separate lines because the program uses the Literal control to insert HTML paragraph codes in the Panel.

Suppose that you use the program to add some controls—TextBoxes, for example—to the Panel. Then, you change the options and click Go again, adding a different type of control. You will see that the first batch of controls disappears and is replaced by the second batch. This is because controls that are added programmatically are not part of the page's view state, which means that they are not automatically saved and restored after a roundtrip to the server. If you want to maintain the state of controls added programmatically, you must do so yourself using the techniques for state management that were covered in Chapter 20.

Validation Controls

The ASP.NET validation controls are designed for one task: validation. What exactly does this mean? A common cause of problems in Web applications is when the user does not enter valid data. For example, on a Web-based ordering system the customer may forget to enter the quantity desired for an item being ordered. Or, due to a slip of the finger a six-digit postal code might be entered. Examples of this abound, but the bottom line is that after invalid data gets into a program there is no end to the problems it can cause. Programmers realized long ago that the best approach is to validate the data as soon as it is entered, before it has a chance to cause problems.

Until now, data validation was pretty much up to the programmer, who had to write custom code for each validation task. This was better than nothing, but the people who designed the ASP.NET controls realized that validation was a task for which components could be created, decreasing the load on the programmer and lessening the chance of errors. Thus, ASP.NET's validation controls came into being. There are six controls:

- The RequiredFieldValidator control makes sure that the user has entered text or made a selection in a group of one or more controls.
- The CompareValidator control compares the value of a control with a specific value or with the value of another control.
- The RangeValidator control confirms that the value of a control falls within a specified range.
- The RegularExpressionValidator control compares a control value against a regular expression.
- The CustomValidator control implements custom validation using code that you supply.
- The ValidationSummary control gathers information from multiple validation controls and formats the data for presentation to the user.

You can associate more than one validation control with a given input control. For example, you could use a RequiredFieldValidator to ensure that a TextBox is not left empty, and a RangeValidator to ensure that the value entered is within a specified range.

The first five validation controls have several properties in common. They are as follows:

- **ControlToValidate**—Identifies the control to be validated. At design time, if the control you want to validate has already been added to the page, you can select this property value from a list in the Properties window.
- **ErrorMessage**—Specifies the message to be displayed if the validation fails. You can include HTML tags in this property to format the error message.
- **Display**—Determines how the error message is displayed when validation fails. Settings are **None** (the message is never displayed), **Static** (space for the message is allocated in the page layout), and **Dynamic** (space for the message is added to the page dynamically when and if the message needs to be displayed).
- **IsValid**—Is True if the associated control passes validation, False if not.
- **Type**—Specifies the data type for the validation. The values being compared are cast to this type before the validation is performed. Possible settings are **String** (the default), **Integer**, **Double**, **Date**, and **Currency**.

The Page Object's IsValid Property

The Page object has its own **IsValid** property that is True only if the **IsValid** property of all contained validation controls is True. If a single validation control fails, then **Page.IsValid** will be False.

The way the validation controls work is as follows. The validation is performed when the page is posted to the server. Depending on the settings for each validation control, a failed validation can be handled in one of three ways:

- The control will display an error message on the page.
- A ValidationSummary control will gather validation information from your validation controls and display it.
- Your code will examine the **IsValid** property of the validation control and take appropriate action.

RequiredFieldValidator

The RequiredFieldValidator control is used to ensure that the user has entered data or made a selection in a TextBox, DropDownList, ListBox, or RadioButtonList control. The RequiredFieldValidator can also ensure that a control's value has changed from an initial value. This is done with the **InitialValue** property, where you place the initial value of the control being validated. If the control still has this value at postback, it fails validation. Be careful when using the **InitialValue** property. If you enter a value for this property, the associated control will pass validation if it is blank. Use two RequiredFieldValidator controls to ensure that a TextBox is not left at an initial value.

CompareValidator

The CompareValidator performs a comparison between the value of a control and a value, which can be entered as a control property or in a third control. If the control to be validated is empty, validation always succeeds. The CompareValidator control offers the following validation comparisons, set as the **Operator** property:

- **Equal**
- **NotEqual**
- **GreaterThanEqual**
- **GreaterThan**
- **LessThan**
- **LessThanEqual**
- **DataTypeCheck**

These are all self-explanatory except for the **DataType** comparison. This type of validation determines if the data in the control can be converted to the data type specified by the **Type** property. For example, if **Type** is set to **Date** and the control being validated contains "Peter", then validation fails because "Peter" cannot be converted to a date.

RangeValidator

The RangeValidator control checks that a control's value falls in a specified range. The range can be numeric, alphabetic, or date. Use the **MinimumValue** and **MaximumValue** properties to set the lower and upper limits of the permitted range.

RegularExpressionValidator

The RegularExpressionValidator checks a control's value against a regular expression, a pattern that defines the rules for the data. Validation always succeeds if the control being validated is empty. You specify the regular expression to be used as the control's **ValidationExpression** property. Regular expressions are a complex topic. I present the elements that are needed most often in Table 21.7.

Table 21.7 Summary of regular expression components.

Character(s)	Description	Example
(any)	Matches itself. Use "\(" and "\)" to match parentheses.	xyz matches xyz
\	Marks the next character as a special character or a literal.	\n matches the newline character. \\ matches \
^	Matches the start of text.	^Dear matches Dear only at the beginning of a string
$	Matches the end of text.	.NET$ matches .NET only at the end of a string
*	Matches the preceding character zero or more times.	bo* matches b or bo or boo
+	Matches the preceding character one or more times.	bo+ matches bo or boo
?	Matches the preceding character zero or one times.	bo?b matches bb and bob but not boob
. (period)	Matches any single character except a newline.	t.t matches tat, tbt, tct, etc. but not toot
x|y	Matches either x or y.	(b|h)ead matches bead or head
{*n*}	Matches exactly *n* times, where *n* is an integer greater than 0.	.o{2}d matches food, hood, good, etc.
{*n*,}	Matches at least *n* times, where *n* is an integer greater than 0.	ba(2,}d matches baad, baaad, etc. but does not match bad
{*n*,*m*}	Matches at least *n* times and at most *m* times, where *n* and *m* are integers greater than 0 with *m*>*n*.	bo{1,3}k matches bok, book, and boook
[*chars*]	Matches any one of the enclosed characters.	b[ae]d matches bed or bad

(continued)

Table 21.7 Summary of regular expression components *(continued)*.

Character(s)	Description	Example
[^*chars*]	Matches any single character except those enclosed.	b[^ae]d matches bbd, bcd, etc. but not bad or bed
[a-z]	Matches any character in the specified range.	[d-p] matches any single character from d to p
[^a-z]	Matches any character not in the specified range.	[^a-e] matches f through z
\b	Matches a word boundary.	ed\b matches the ed in fried but not the ed in bedbug
\B	Matches a nonword boundary.	ed\B matches the ed in bedbug but not the ed in fried
\d	Matches any digit character 0-9.	Equivalent to [0-9]
\D	Matches any nondigit character.	Equivalent to [^0-9]

CustomValidator

The CustomValidator control lets you integrate your own validation code with the convenience of a validation control. You must write code to perform the validation and place it in the control's **ServerValidate()** event procedure, which has the following signature:

```
Sub ServerValidate(ByVal source As Object, _
    ByVal args As System.Web.UI.WebControls.ServerValidateEventArgs)

End Sub
```

Within the validation event procedure, the data to be validated—in other words, the value of the associated control—is available as the **Value** property of the **args** parameter. Code in the procedure can validate this data in any way needed. If validation fails, set the **args.IsValid** property to False; if validation succeeds, set this property to True. For example, suppose your CustomValidation control is named CustomValidator1. In your code behind file, place the following event handler:

```
Private Sub CustomValidator1_ServerValidate(ByVal source As Object, _
    ByVal args As System.Web.UI.WebControls.ServerValidateEventArgs) _
    Handles CustomValidator1.ServerValidate

  If Len(args.Value) = 5 Then
    args.IsValid = True
  Else
    args.IsValid = False
  End If

End Sub
```

This code will permit entries in the associated control that are five characters long; all other entries will fail validation.

The CustomValidator can also be used to perform client-side validation. This is when the code to perform the validation exists in the Web page as a client-side script. To use this capability, set the CustomValidator control's **ClientValidationFunction** property to the name of the client-side validation procedure, and set the **EnableClientScript** property to True. Client-side validation is performed before server-side validation, which permits some validation errors to be caught before a roundtrip to the server. Client scripts are beyond the scope of this chapter, however, and you can find more details in the .NET framework documentation.

ValidationSummary

The ValidationSummary control is used to gather the error messages from several validation controls and display them together on the page. The summary of error messages can be displayed as a list, a bulleted list, or a paragraph. A ValidationSummary control automatically links with all the validation controls on your page. For each individual control, set the **Display** property to None so the error message will be displayed only in the ValidationSummary control and not in the individual validation controls. Properties for this control are summarized in Table 21.8

Table 21.8 Properties of the ValidationSummary control.

Property	Description
DisplayMode	Determines how the summary of validation messages are displayed. Set to one of the following members of the **ValidationSummaryDislayMode** enumeration: **BulletedList**, **List**, **SingleParagraph**.
HeaderText	Specifies the text to be displayed at the top of the validation summary.
ShowMessageBox	If True, the validation summary is displayed in a message box rather than on the page. The default is False. Setting this property to True has an effect only if client-side validation is enabled.
ShowSummary	If True (the default), a validation summary is displayed.

Other Web Controls

This chapter has covered the most important Web controls, the ones that you will use most often in your ASP.NET applications. There are some additional controls that were not covered, however, and they are briefly described in Table 21.9. You can obtain information on these controls from the ASP.NET documentation. Note that some of these controls are used primarily with database access, and are covered in Chapter 22.

Table 21.9 Additional ASP.NET Web controls.

Control Name	Description
AdRotator	Displays banner ads on a page. You associate multiple ads with the control, and they are automatically rotated, with a different ad displayed each time the page is refreshed. When users click an ad, they are directed to the associated URL.
Calendar	Provides for the display and user selection of dates.

(continued)

Table 21.9 Additional ASP.NET Web controls *(continued)*.

Control Name	Description
DataGrid	Binds to a data source and displays data in a row and column format.
DataList	Binds to a data source and displays a list of items.
PlaceHolder	Serves as a container for controls that are added to a page programmatically. In this, it's like the Panel control; however, the PlaceHolder has no visual representation. So, unlike a Panel it cannot display a border or background image. Also, you cannot add child controls to a PlaceHolder at design time, but only in code.
Repeater	A container control that permits you to create custom lists based on programmer-defined templates.
Table	User created programmable tables that display information in row and column format. The content of the table can be data or it can be other controls and/or HTML elements. Use this control when you need to perform table manipulations, such as adding rows and columns, in code.
XML	Displays an XML document or the results of an XML transform.

Summary

The assortment of server-side controls available to the Visual Basic .NET programmer is impressive indeed. They cover almost any imaginable need, and with their server-side execution and automatic state management they make the programmer's job easier than ever. In many ways, the ASP.NET controls parallel the traditional HTML controls, and in fact are generally rendered as HTML controls permitting wide browser support. Of particular interest are the validator controls, which simplify the important task of data validation.

Chapter 22

Database Access in Web Applications

As you saw in Chapter 19, database access is one of the most common programming tasks and is used in a wide variety of applications. As the importance of the Web grows, the need for database programming has expanded from the desktop to the Internet. Fortunately for developers, the .NET framework pays as much attention to Web database programming as it does to desktop database tools. In particular, the .NET framework provides several sophisticated controls that you can use to create data-aware Web applications. Most of this chapter is devoted to showing you how to use these controls.

ADO.NET and ASP.NET

Microsoft's data access strategy, ActiveX Data Objects, has been around for a while. With the .NET framework, however, it has undergone significant changes and improvements and is now referred to as ADO.NET. You learned about using ADO.NET with Windows applications in Chapter 19. Web applications also use ADO.NET for database access, and much of the information that was presented in Chapter 19 is relevant here as well. I strongly suggest that you read Chapter 19 before continuing with this chapter.

How is database access in Web applications different from database access in Windows applications? At the level of the server, there are very few differences. Your Web application code, running on the server, connects to a data source and retrieves data; if needed, new or modified data is written back to the data source.

Remember Your Imports

Any ASP.NET program that uses data ADO should import the **System.Data** namespace. Then, depending on whether you are using a SQL Server data source or an OLE DB data source, you should also import the **System.Data.SqlClient** or the **System.Data.OleDb** namespace.

In concept, this is no different from a Windows application running on a local computer and accessing a database. Thus, many of the techniques that were covered in Chapter 19 for Windows applications are equally relevant to data access in Web applications. This includes the following:

- Use of the connection classes (**SqlConnection** and **OleDbConnection**) to connect to a data source
- Use of the data adapter classes (**SqlDataAdapter** and **OleDbDataAdapter**) to extract data from a data source
- Use of the **DataSet** class to maintain an in-memory disconnected data cache
- Use of the **DataView** class to define a filtered and sorted view of a data table

Where data access in Web applications differs is in the controls that are used. ASP.NET controls are totally distinct from the Windows Form controls. Thus, ASP.NET provides both a DataGrid and a DataList control, but they are different from the controls of the same names that are used for Windows applications. The function of these controls is similar, however, although they are used differently. An important goal of this chapter is to show you how to use the ASP.NET data controls.

Reading Data with the DataReader Class

The data reader classes are designed for fast, forward-only reading of data. There are two versions, as is the case with many ADO.NET classes: **SqlDataReader** for working with SQL Server data sources and **OleDbDataReader** for working with OLE DB data sources. These classes do not have a visual interface, but work behind the scenes to make data available in your ASP.NET program. Then, you can make use of that data in whatever way your program needs. The data reader classes cannot be used if you want to modify the data source, but only to read it. The examples in this section will use the **SqlDataReader** class, but the procedures are the same for the **OleDbDataReader** class. As before, I will use the Northwind sample database for the sample programs.

To use the **SqlDataReader** class, you must first create and open a connection to the data source and then create an **SqlCommand** representing the SQL command that will select the desired data from the data source. I covered these steps in detail in Chapter 19. Here's what the code might look like:

```
Dim ConStr As String

ConStr = "data source=BETA-BOX;initial catalog=Northwind;"
ConStr &= "user id=sa;password=victoria;"
Dim sqlCon As New SqlConnection(ConStr)
sqlCon.Open()
Dim cmd As New SqlCommand("select * from customers", sqlCon)
```

Next, execute the **SqlConnection** object's **ExecuteReader()** method to obtain the data reader:

```
Dim rdr As SqlReader = cmd.ExecuteReader()
```

After you have created the data reader, call its **Read()** method to access data. This method returns True until the end of the data records is reached; then it returns False. Be sure to call **Read()** once before accessing data. The most common approach taken is to call **Read()** in a loop until it returns False, which loops through all the records in the data reader. Here's an example:

```
While rdr.Read()

End While
```

Within the loop, you access the data records from the data reader using its **Item** property. The syntax is as follows:

```
rdr.Item(id)
```

The argument *id* can be an integer specifying the 0-based position of the column whose data you are retrieving, or a string specifying the column name. The **Item** property returns the data in its native format, meaning whatever format, or data type, it was stored as. The return type of the property is **Object**. Because the **Item** property is the indexer for the class, you can omit it as follows:

```
rdr(id)
```

Another way to retrieve data from a data reader is with the various **Get*xxxx*()** methods. Each of these methods is designed to return a specific data type, as reflected by the method name. The syntax for these methods is as follows:

```
rdr.Getxxxx(idx)
```

The *idx* argument is the 0-based column position (these methods cannot retrieve data by column name). The return type of each method is the same as the type of data it retrieves. For example, **GetBoolean()** returns type **Boolean**, **GetString()** returns type **String**, and so on. Please refer to the documentation for the **SqlDataReader** or **OleDbDataReader** for details on the full range of **Get*xxxx*()** methods.

Other data reader members you may need to use are the following:

- **FieldCount**—Returns the number of fields (columns).
- **IsClosed**—Returns True if the data reader is closed, False otherwise.
- **Close()**—Closes the data reader. You must call this method before the associated data connection can be used for any other purpose.

To show how to use the **SqlDataReader** class, I have created a short program that uses the class to extract a subset of records from a database and then display them to the user. The program uses the Products table in the Northwind database. The goal is to let the user specify a minimum stock level (units on hand) and then display a list of all products with a stock level below the user-specified value.

To create the demonstration program, start a new ASP.NET Web application and then follow these steps:

1. Place a TextBox control on the page and change its **ID** property to txtStockLevel.
2. Place a Label control next to this TextBox to identify it with the text "Stock level:".
3. Place a Button control on the page with the **ID** property set to btnSearch and the **Text** property set to Search.
4. Place another TextBox control on the page, making it fairly wide and tall (see Figure 22.1). Set its **ID** property to txtOutput, its **ReadOnly** property to True, and its **TextMode** property to MultiLine.
5. Place the code from Listing 22.1 into the **Click()** event procedure for the Button control. Make sure that you change connection string details as needed for the data source connection on your system.

When you run the program, enter the desired minimum stock level in the text box, and then click the Search button. The program will display a list of products and the number on hand for all products below the specified stock level. This is shown in Figure 22.1.

This program demonstrates how simple it is to use the data reader class. Not only is it easy to program, it is fast and efficient, and for many data-related tasks it will be your first choice.

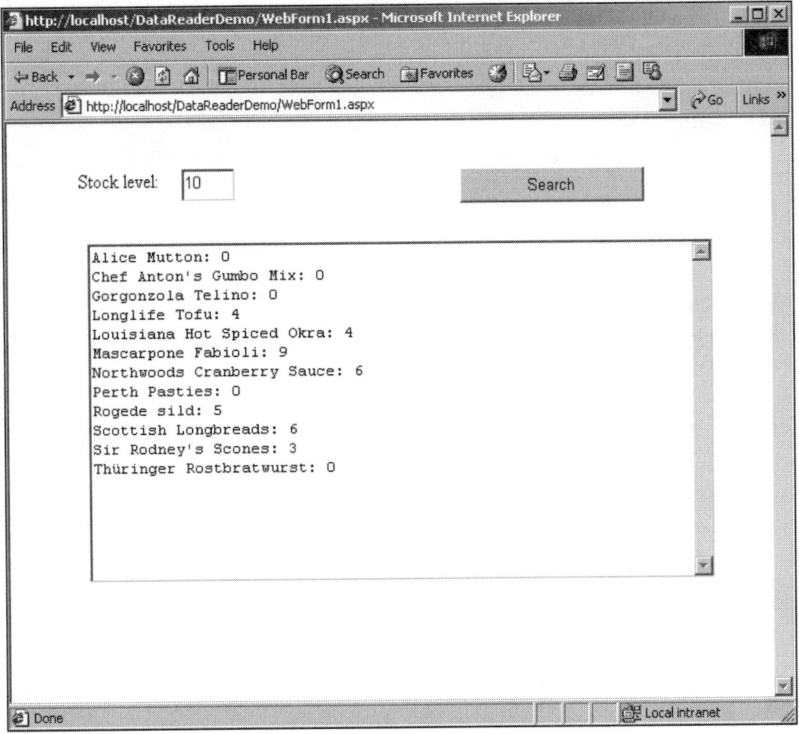

Figure 22.1
The data reader demonstration program in action.

Listing 22.1 Demonstrating the SqlDataReader class.

```
Private Sub btnSearch_Click(ByVal sender As Object, _
    ByVal e As System.EventArgs) Handles btnSearch.Click

  Dim conStr As String
  Dim cmdStr As String
  Dim FoundAny As Boolean = False
  Dim output As String

  If Val(txtStockLevel.Text) < 1 Then
    txtOutput.Text = _
        "Please enter a minimum stock level greater than zero."
    Exit Sub
  End If

  conStr = "data source=BETA-BOX;initial catalog=Northwind;"
  conStr &= "user id=sa;password=redwine;"
  Dim sqlCon As New SqlConnection(conStr)
```

```
    cmdStr = "Select ProductName, UnitsInStock from Products "
    cmdStr &= "where UnitsInStock<" & txtStockLevel.Text
    cmdStr &= " order by ProductName"
    Dim cmd As New SqlCommand(cmdStr, sqlCon)

    Try
      sqlCon.Open()
      Dim rdr As SqlDataReader = cmd.ExecuteReader()
      While rdr.Read()
        FoundAny = True
        output &= rdr("ProductName") & ": " & rdr("UnitsInStock") & _
           ControlChars.CrLf
      End While
      rdr.Close()
      sqlCon.Close()
    Catch ex As SqlException
      txtOutput.Text = "Sql Exception: " & ex.message
    Catch ex As Exception
      txtOutput.Text = "General Exception: " & ex.message
    End Try

    If FoundAny Then
      txtOutput.Text = output
    Else
      txtOutput.Text = "No matching records found."
    End If

  End Sub
```

The Repeater Control

The Repeater control is used to define custom lists, or tables, for the display of data on an ASP.NET page. This is a container control, meaning that it does not have any visual appearance of its own but rather lets the programmer define its appearance by means of templates. You can, for example, create a row-and-column table, a numbered list, a comma-delimited list, or essentially any other type of output. The Repeater control must be bound to a data source, and its templates are organized based on the concept of rows:

- *ItemTemplate*—Defines the appearance and content of each row in the data source.
- *AlternatingItemTemplate*—Defines the appearance and content of alternate rows in the data source. Optional; use to create a table that is easier to read.
- *HeaderTemplate*—Defines the appearance of the table header.

- *FooterTemplate*—Defines the appearance of the table footer.
- *SeparatorTemplate*—Defines elements to render between rows.

Each individual template is defined as HTML elements that are rendered when the page is displayed. The HeaderTemplate is rendered first, then the ItemTemplate (or AlternatingItemTemplate) and the SeparatorTemplate are rendered once for each row in the bound data source. Finally, the FooterTemplate is rendered.

Binding a Repeater Control

The Repeater control can be bound to any data source, such as a DataView or a DataSet. The binding is specified by the Repeater control's **DataSource** property. If the data source contains more than one table, you must identify the specific table to be bound by setting the **DataMember** property. If the data source contains only a single table, you do not need to set the **DataMember** property. At design time, if you have added one or more data sources to your project, you can select one from the drop-down list for the Repeater control's **DataSource** property. Otherwise, you will set the property in code:

```
Repeater1.DataSource = MyDataView
```

Whether the **DataSource** (and, if needed, **DataMember**) properties are set at design time or in code at runtime, the next required step is to call the Repeater control's **DataBind()** method. This method establishes the actual binding connections based on the information provided in the **DataSource** and **DataMember** properties.

Defining Templates

The templates that are used with a Repeater control are entered and edited using the HTML view of the Page Designer (click the HTML tab at the bottom of the Designer window). The tags for the Repeater control will look something like this:

```
<asp:Repeater id="Repeater1" runat="server">
  <HeaderTemplate>
    <!-- Header template contents go here -->
  </HeaderTemplate>
  <ItemTemplate>
    <!-- Item template contents go here -->
  </ItemTemplate>
  <FooterTemplate>
    <!-- Footer template contents go here -->
  </FooterTemplate>
</asp:Repeater>
```

The only template that is required is the ItemTemplate. When you are working on the templates in HTML view, the editor has features to help you enter the various HTML elements that you may want to use.

The HeaderTemplate, SeperatorTemplate, and FooterTemplate are fairly simple to work with because they are not data bound but rather contain only HTML elements to format the display of the Repeater control. For example, if you want to display the data as an HTML table, the HeaderTemplate could contain the HTML tag **<table>** to mark the start of the table, and the FooterTemplate could contain the HTML tag **</table>** to mark the end of the table. You can get more involved and define a table header with column names, a border, and so on. Here's an example of a HeaderTemplate that defines a table with a border and a heading containing two column heads, Name and Country.

```
<HeaderTemplate>
  <table border="1">
  <thead>
  <tr>
    <th>Name</th><th>Country</th>
  </tr>
  </thead>
</HeaderTemplate>
```

Creating the ItemTemplate is a bit more involved because it requires special elements to retrieve items of data from the data source. You do this using the **Eval()** method of the **DataBinder** object. The **DataBinder** object is automatically present in a bound Repeater control, and the **Eval()** method lets you retrieve data from a specified column. The syntax is

```
DataBinder.Eval(Container.DataItem, column)
```

The **Container** keyword references the container, in this case the Repeater control. The **DataItem** qualifier references the current row of data. *Column* is a string that identifies the specific column from which data is to be retrieved. In a simple situation where the Repeater control is bound to a single table, it will be simply the column name:

```
DataBinder.Eval(Container.DataItem, "CustomerName")
```

In more complex situations, you will have to identify a table and/or a view as well as a column name:

```
DataBinder.Eval(Container.DataItem, _
    "Tables(0).DefaultView(1).CustomerName")
```

The **DataBinder.Eval** method takes an optional third argument that specifies the formatting of the output. For example, assuming the data being output is numeric, the following formats it as currency:

```
DataBinder.Eval(Container.DataItem, "ItemPrice", "{0:C}")
```

Table 22.1 lists the available format strings.

In your ItemTemplate, the expression referencing the DataBinder must be placed inside tags, like this:

```
<%# DataBinder.Eval(Container.DataItem, "CustomerName") %>
```

Suppose the data source contains columns named Name and City and you want to display the data from these fields, separated by a comma, in the Repeater control. Here's what the ItemTemplate would look like:

```
<ItemTemplate>
<%# DataBinder.Eval(Container.DataItem, "Name") %>
, 
<%# DataBinder.Eval(Container.DataItem, "City") %>
<br>
</ItemTemplate>
```

Note that ** ** is the HTML code for a space and that **
** is the tag for a line break. To display the data that same way but with alternating lines in boldface, you would use the same ItemTemplate as above but also include the following AlternatingItemTemplate:

```
<AlternatingItemTemplate>
<b><%# DataBinder.Eval(Container.DataItem, "Name") %>
, 
<%# DataBinder.Eval(Container.DataItem, "City") %></b>
<br>
</AlternatingItemTemplate>
```

Note that this template is identical to the ItemTemplate except for the addition of **<b>** and **</b>** tags, which turn boldface on and off.

You might think that the SeparatorTemplate is redundant because you could achieve the same effect by including the desired separator elements at the end of each ItemTemplate. The effect is not quite the same, however. Any elements placed at the end of ItemTemplate

Table 22.1 Format strings that can be used with DataBinder.Eval.

Format String	Output
{0:C}	Currency: $*xx,xxxx.xx*
{0:N}	Number: *xx,xxxx.xx*
{0:D} (with number objects)	Decimal: *xxxxxx*
{0:d} (with datetime objects)	Short Date: *m/d/yyyy*
{0:D} (with datetime objects)	Long Date: Tuesday, August 28, 2001

will be rendered after each and every row, including the last one. In contrast, elements placed in the SeparatorTemplate are placed between rows but *not* after the final row. For example, the following template displays dashed lines between rows:

```
<SeparatorTemplate>
--------------<br>
</SeparatorTemplate>
```

Other Repeater Features

The Repeater control has a great deal of flexibility that has not been touched on here. For example, a row in the control can display, in addition to its data, a Button control. The Repeater can detect when the button is clicked and take various actions. These capabilities are similar to those found in the DataList control, which is covered soon.

A Repeater Demonstration

The program presented here shows how to use the Repeater control to display data in an attractive and easy-to-read format. It uses data from the Customers table in the Northwind database, extracting the contact person's name, title, and company name from each record in the table. The data is displayed in a table with alternating blue and white background for the rows, as shown in Figure 22.2.

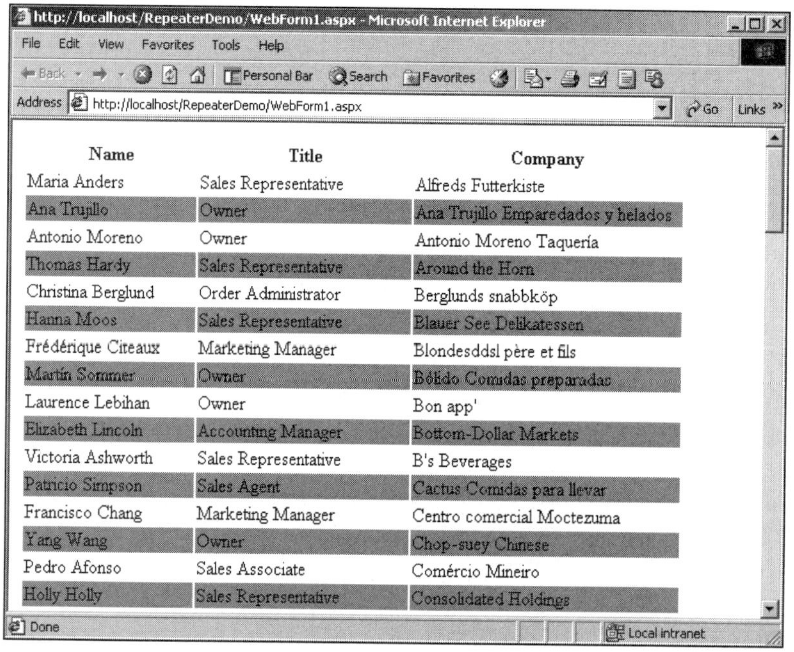
http://localhost/RepeaterDemo/WebForm1.aspx - Microsoft Internet Explorer
File Edit View Favorites Tools Help
Address http://localhost/RepeaterDemo/WebForm1.aspx
Name Title Company
Maria Anders Sales Representative Alfreds Futterkiste
Ana Trujillo Owner Ana Trujillo Emparedados y helados
Antonio Moreno Owner Antonio Moreno Taquería
Thomas Hardy Sales Representative Around the Horn
Christina Berglund Order Administrator Berglunds snabbköp
Hanna Moos Sales Representative Blauer See Delikatessen
Frédérique Citeaux Marketing Manager Blondesddsl père et fils
Martín Sommer Owner Bólido Comidas preparadas
Laurence Lebihan Owner Bon app'
Elizabeth Lincoln Accounting Manager Bottom-Dollar Markets
Victoria Ashworth Sales Representative B's Beverages
Patricio Simpson Sales Agent Cactus Comidas para llevar
Francisco Chang Marketing Manager Centro comercial Moctezuma
Yang Wang Owner Chop-suey Chinese
Pedro Afonso Sales Associate Comércio Mineiro
Holly Holly Sales Representative Consolidated Holdings
Done
Local intranet

Figure 22.2
Data displayed in a Repeater control.

The program is easy to create. Start a new ASP.NET Web application and place a Repeater control on the page. The code in Listing 22.2 shows the **Page_Load()** event procedure, which performs the tasks of creating the database connection, creating a **DataSet** containing the desired data, and binding it to the Repeater control. Listing 22.3 shows the HTML for the Repeater control. As a reminder (assuming you are working in Visual Studio), the code from Listing 22.3 goes in the ASPX page and the code from Listing 22.2 goes in the page's code-behind file.

Listing 22.2 The Page_Load() procedure sets up the data connection and binding.

```
Private Sub Page_Load(ByVal sender As System.Object, _
    ByVal e As System.EventArgs) Handles MyBase.Load

  If Not IsPostBack Then
    Dim sqlCon As New SqlConnection()
    Dim sqlAdapter As SqlDataAdapter
    Dim conString As String
    Dim cmdString As String
    Dim ds As DataSet

    ' Set up the connection string.
    conString = "data source=BETA-BOX;initial catalog=Northwind;"
    conString &= "user id=sa;password=redwine;"
    sqlCon.ConnectionString = conString

    Try
      sqlCon.Open()
      sqlAdapter = New SqlDataAdapter()
      cmdString = "select ContactName, ContactTitle, CompanyName "
      cmdString &= "from customers order by CompanyName"
      sqlAdapter.SelectCommand = New SqlCommand(cmdString, sqlCon)
      ds = New DataSet("Customers")
      sqlAdapter.Fill(ds, "My Customers")
      sqlCon.Close()
      Repeater1.DataSource = ds
      Repeater1.DataMember = "My Customers"
      Repeater1.DataBind()
    Catch
    End Try
  End If

End Sub
```

Listing 22.3 The HTML definition for the Repeater control.

```
<asp:Repeater id="Repeater1" runat="server">
<HeaderTemplate>
  <table>
```

```
        <thead>
          <tr>
            <th>Name</th><th>Title</th><th>Company</th>
          </tr>
        </thead>
    </HeaderTemplate>
    <ItemTemplate>
      <tr><td>
        <%# DataBinder.Eval(Container.DataItem, "ContactName") %>
      </td><td>
        <%# DataBinder.Eval(Container.DataItem, "ContactTitle") %>
      </td><td>
        <%# DataBinder.Eval(Container.DataItem, "CompanyName") %>
      </td></tr>
    </ItemTemplate>
    <AlternatingItemTemplate>
      <tr bgcolor="#6699ff"><td>
        <%# DataBinder.Eval(Container.DataItem, "ContactName") %>
      </td><td>
        <%# DataBinder.Eval(Container.DataItem, "ContactTitle") %>
      </td><td>
        <%# DataBinder.Eval(Container.DataItem, "CompanyName") %>
      </td></tr>
    </AlternatingItemTemplate>
    <FooterTemplate>
      </table>
    </FooterTemplate>
    </asp:Repeater>
```

The DataList Control

The DataList control can be thought of as a Repeater control with additional features included. Like the Repeater, it can display data in rows, but it can also display data in a non-tabular format. It can also be configured to allow users to edit or delete information, to select rows, and to perform other manipulations that are not possible with the Repeater.

If the DataList control is used to modify data—specifically, to edit or delete existing rows—remember that the changes are made in the object, such as a DataSet, that the control is bound to but are not automatically saved in the original database. Your code must take special steps to persist data changes back to the data source. These techniques were covered in Chapter 19.

The DataList control must be bound to data, and it can be bound to any available data source, such as a DataSet, DataView, SqlDataReader, or DataTable. The control's appearance on the page is determined by templates, and it supports the same five templates that the Repeater control does: HeaderTemplate, FooterTemplate, ItemTemplate, AlternatingItemTemplate, and SeparatorTemplate. In addition, it has the following two templates:

- *SelectedItemTemplate*—Defines the elements to render for the row that has been selected by the user.
- *EditItemTemplate*—Defines the elements to render for a row that is being edited.

One of the most common uses for the DataList control is to display one or more Button controls in each row. Clicking the button then carries out some action with that record. For example, a list of products could have an "Add To Shopping Cart" button, which adds the selected item to the user's order.

Displaying a Button in a Row

To display a button in each row in a DataList control, include the control tag in the ItemTemplate (and AlternatingItemTemplate, if used). For example:

```
<asp:Button text="Details" CommandName="select" runat="server" />
```

Note that the **CommandName** attribute must be set; I'll talk about this shortly. You can include multiple buttons in the template. Here is an example of an ItemTemplate that displays a table with the data from the ProductName field in the left column, a Details button in the middle column, and an Edit button in the third column (the output this produces is shown in Figure 22.3):

```
<ItemTemplate>
  <tr>
  <td>
    <%# DataBinder.Eval(Container.DataItem, "ProductName") %>
  </td>
  <td>
    <asp:Button text="Details" CommandName="select" Runat="server"/>
  </td>
  <td>
    <asp:Button text="Edit" CommandName="edit" Runat="server" />
  </td>
  </tr>
</ItemTemplate>
```

Previously, I mentioned that you need to set the **CommandName** attribute when including a button in a template as described previously. This is because the value of a button's **CommandName** attribute determines what happens when the user clicks it. Specifically, when a button is clicked, an event is triggered in the DataList control; when any button is clicked, the **ItemCommand()** event is triggered. The syntax is as follows:

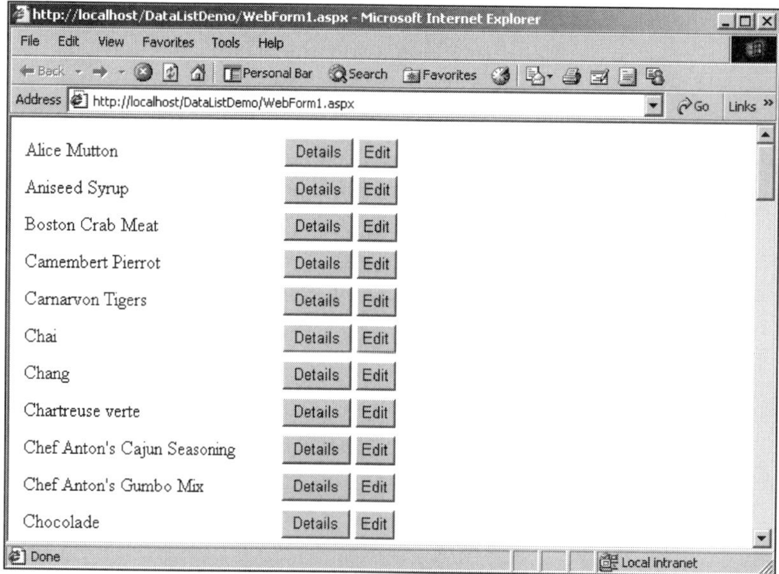

Figure 22.3
Displaying buttons in a DataList control.

```
Private Sub DataListName_ItemCommand(ByVal source As Object, _
  ByVal e As System.Web.UI.WebControls.DataListCommandEventArgs) _
  Handles DataListName.ItemCommand
```

Within the event procedure, you can obtain the identity of the button that was clicked from the **e.CommandName** property. Based on this information, your code can take the appropriate action, such as selecting the row or putting it into edit mode. In addition, special event procedures are automatically called when buttons with specific **CommandName** properties are clicked. These are detailed in Table 22.2.

To summarize, if a button with the **CommandName** property set to any of the values in Table 22.2 is clicked, its special event procedure is called, and then the **ItemCommand()** event procedure is called. If a button with the **CommandName** property set to any other value is clicked, the **ItemCommand()** event procedure is called and the button is identified

Table 22.2 Settings for a button's CommandName attribute.

Value of CommandName	Procedure Called
edit	**EditCommand()**
delete	**DeleteCommand()**
update	**UpdateCommand()**
cancel	**CancelCommand()**

Note that these values are case sensitive.

using the **e.CommandName** property. Therefore, for the edit, delete, update, and cancel actions, you have the option of using the **ItemCommand()** event procedure or the special procedures listed in Table 22.2. I prefer the former approach because it lets you put all your button-handling code in one procedure. In this case, do not use the **CommandName** settings listed in Table 22.2, but something else—"itemedit" rather than "edit", for example.

What would your program do in response to these button clicks? There is really no limitation, but the most common things are selecting, editing, and deleting items. When an item is being edited, updating and canceling are also available. These are explained in the following sections.

Edit

Putting a row in edit mode lets the user edit the record. Your code must put the row in edit mode by setting the DataList control's **EditItemIndex** property to the index of the current item, as shown here:

```
Private Sub DataList1_ItemCommand(ByVal source As Object, _
      ByVal e As System.Web.UI.WebControls.DataListCommandEventArgs) _
      Handles DataList1.ItemCommand

    If e.CommandName = "itemedit" Then
      DataList1.EditItemIndex = e.Item.ItemIndex
    ...
    End If
```

The row will automatically be displayed using the EditItemTemplate. This template should contain Update and Cancel buttons, as described below. Remember that the DataList must be rebound to the data after this operation.

Select

Selecting an item, or row, can be used for various tasks. For example, the selected row might display more details about the item than the normal display. The technique is essentially the same as for editing an item except it is the **SelectedIndex** property that must be set to the item index:

```
Private Sub DataList1_ItemCommand(ByVal source As Object, _
      ByVal e As System.Web.UI.WebControls.DataListCommandEventArgs) _
      Handles DataList1.ItemCommand

    If e.CommandName = "itemselect" Then
      DataList1.SelectedIndex = e.Item.ItemIndex
    ...
    End If
```

Delete

To delete an item in the DataList, you actually delete the item (row) in the underlying data source (DataTable, DataView, and so on) then rebind the DataList control to the source. This is done as follows:

1. Obtain a unique item of data, such as the database's primary key field, from the DataList item that is to be deleted.
2. Use the information obtained in Step 1 to locate the row in the underlying data source and delete it.
3. Rebind the DataList control to the data source.

Update

When in edit mode, one option for the user should be to update the data—in other words, to accept the editing changes that have been made. You can use two general approaches to this task, and both of these work equally well. You can locate the affected row in the underlying data source and make the necessary changes. Alternatively, you can delete the original row, then create a new row with the edited data, and add the new row to the data source. In either case, the DataList must be rebound to the data source.

Cancel

To cancel an editing operation, simply set the DataList control's **EditItemIndex** property to –1, which returns the item to ItemTemplate view and discards any changes.

A DataList Demonstration

The program that is presented here shows how to create a DataList control that is bound to an SQL Server data source. The user can do the following:

- View a condensed form of all items.
- Expand an individual item for a more detailed view.
- Edit an item to allow for changing of information.
- Either accept or reject any editing changes made.

The code for editing an item does not actually save the changes to the data source—this is left as an exercise for the reader, as is the code for deleting an item. To create this project, start a new ASP.NET Web application. Then place a Label control on the form. Set its **ID** property to lblMessage and its **Text** property to a blank string. This control will be used to display error messages.

Next, place a DataList control on the form. Leave its **ID** property at the default setting DataList1. Change its other properties as follows:

- **BorderColor**—Black or any dark color
- **BorderWidth**—1px
- **BorderStyle**—Solid
- **GridLines**—Both

The remainder of the programming of the DataGrid control consists of defining its various templates. As mentioned earlier, this is best done using HTML view in the Designer. Listing 22.4 shows the full HTML code for the DataGrid control, including its templates. The code behind for the page is shown in Listing 22.5.

When you run the program, it connects to the data source and displays the Suppliers data in the view defined by the ItemTemplate. This is shown in Figure 22.4. If you click a Show Details link, that item is displayed as defined by the SelectedItemTemplate (not shown). If you click an Edit link, that item is displayed for editing as defined by the EditItemTemplate, as shown in Figure 22.5.

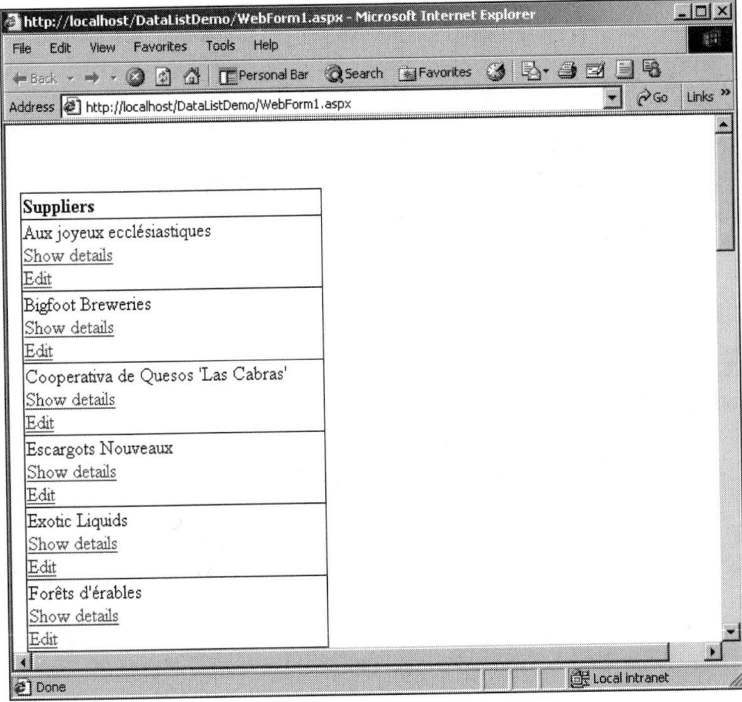

Figure 22.4
Items displayed by the DataList in the default view.

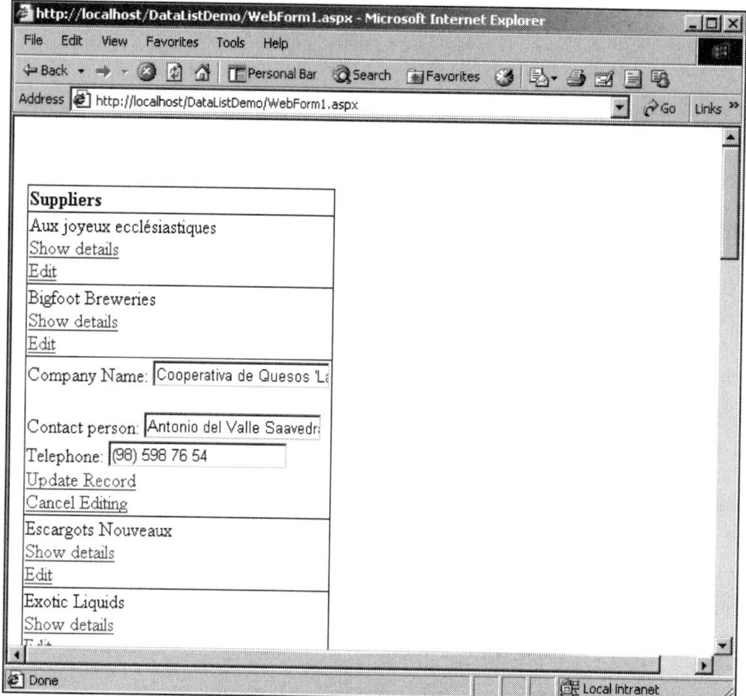

Figure 22.5
One item is displayed for editing.

Listing 22.4 The HTML for the DataList control.

```
<asp:datalist id="DataList1" style="Z-INDEX: 101; LEFT: 12px;
        POSITION: absolute; TOP: 56px" runat="server"
        BorderColor="#400000" BorderWidth="1px" BorderStyle="Solid"
        GridLines="Both">
  <HeaderTemplate>
    <b>Suppliers</b>
  </HeaderTemplate>
  <SelectedItemTemplate>
    Company name:
    <%# DataBinder.Eval(Container.DataItem, "CompanyName") %>
    <br>
    Contact person:
    <%# DataBinder.Eval(Container.DataItem, "ContactName") %>
    <br>
    Telephone:
    <%# DataBinder.Eval(Container.DataItem, "Phone") %>
    <br>
    <asp:LinkButton ID="Linkbutton2" Runat="server"
        CommandName="itemunselect" Text="Close" />
```

```
 </SelectedItemTemplate>
 <ItemTemplate>
   <%# DataBinder.Eval(Container.DataItem, "CompanyName") %>
   <br>
   <asp:LinkButton ID="btnSelect" Runat="server"
       CommandName="itemselect" Text="Show details" />
   <br>
   <asp:LinkButton ID="btnEdit" Runat="server"
       CommandName="itemedit" Text="Edit" />
   <br>
 </ItemTemplate>
 <EditItemTemplate>
   Company Name:
   <asp:TextBox runat="server" Text=
       '<%# DataBinder.Eval(Container.DataItem, "CompanyName") %>'
       ID="Textbox1" NAME="Textbox1" />
   <br>
   Contact person:
   <asp:TextBox runat="server" Text=
       '<%# DataBinder.Eval(Container.DataItem, "ContactName")%>'
       ID="Textbox2" NAME="Textbox2" />
   <br>
   Telephone:
   <asp:TextBox runat="server" Text=
       '<%# DataBinder.Eval(Container.DataItem, "Phone")%>'
       ID="Textbox3" NAME="Textbox3" />
   <br>
   <asp:LinkButton id="btnUpdate" runat="server"
       CommandName="itemupdate" Text="Update Record" />
   <br>
   <asp:LinkButton id="btnCancel" runat="server"
       CommandName="canceledit" Text="Cancel Editing" />
 </EditItemTemplate>
</asp:datalist>
```

Listing 22.5 The code behind for the DataList demonstration.

```
Imports System.Data
Imports System.Data.SqlClient

Public Class WebForm1
  Inherits System.Web.UI.Page
    Protected WithEvents DataList1 As System.Web.UI.WebControls.DataList
    Protected WithEvents lblMessage As System.Web.UI.WebControls.Label
```

```
Private Sub Page_Load(ByVal sender As System.Object, _
    ByVal e As System.EventArgs) Handles MyBase.Load

  ' On the first hit, connect to the
  ' data source and bind the control.
  If Not IsPostBack Then BindList()

End Sub

Private Sub BindList()

  ' This procedure calls GetData() which returns a
  ' DataView containing the data of interest. The DataList is then
  ' bound to that DataView
  DataList1.DataSource = GetData()
  DataList1.DataBind()

End Sub

Private Function GetData() As DataView

  ' Opens the Northwind database and returns a DataView
  ' containing the entire Suppliers table sorted by
  ' CompanyName.
  Dim sqlCon As New SqlConnection()
  Dim sqlAdapter As SqlDataAdapter
  Dim conString As String
  Dim cmdString As String
  Dim ds As DataSet

  ' Set up the connection string.
  conString = "data source=BETA-BOX;initial catalog=Northwind;"
  conString &= "user id=sa;password=victoria;"
  sqlCon.ConnectionString = conString

  Try
    sqlCon.Open()
    sqlAdapter = New SqlDataAdapter()
    cmdString = "select * from Suppliers order by CompanyName"
    sqlAdapter.SelectCommand = New SqlCommand(cmdString, sqlCon)
    ds = New DataSet("Products")
    sqlAdapter.Fill(ds, "Products")
    sqlCon.Close()
    Return ds.Tables("Products").DefaultView
```

```
    Catch ex As SqlException
      lblMessage.Text = "SQL exception: " & ex.Message
    Catch ex As Exception
      lblMessage.text = "General exception: " & ex.Message
    End Try

  End Function

  Private Sub DataList1_ItemCommand(ByVal source As Object, _
      ByVal e As System.Web.UI.WebControls.DataListCommandEventArgs) _
      Handles DataList1.ItemCommand

    ' Called when the user clicks a button in the DataList.
    If e.CommandName = "itemunselect" Then
      DataList1.SelectedIndex = -1
    ElseIf e.CommandName = "itemselect" Then
      DataList1.SelectedIndex = e.Item.ItemIndex
    ElseIf e.CommandName = "itemedit" Then
      DataList1.EditItemIndex = e.Item.ItemIndex
    ElseIf e.CommandName = "itemdelete" Then
      ' Code here to delete the item - omitted.
    ElseIf e.CommandName = "itemupdate" Then
      ' Code here to save editing changes - omitted.
      DataList1.EditItemIndex = -1
    ElseIf e.CommandName = "canceledit" Then
      DataList1.EditItemIndex = -1
    End If

    ' Re-bind the control.
    BindList()

  End Sub

End Class
```

The DataList control is very flexible, and I have only touched on its capabilities in this chapter. As you work with it and learn more of its capabilities, I think that you'll find many places in your ASP.NET database applications where it can be used.

The DataGrid Control

The ASP.NET DataGrid control is designed for tabular display of data. It can be bound to any available data source, either at design time or at runtime, and with its default settings will display all the columns and rows in the data source using the rather plain formatting shown in Figure 22.6.

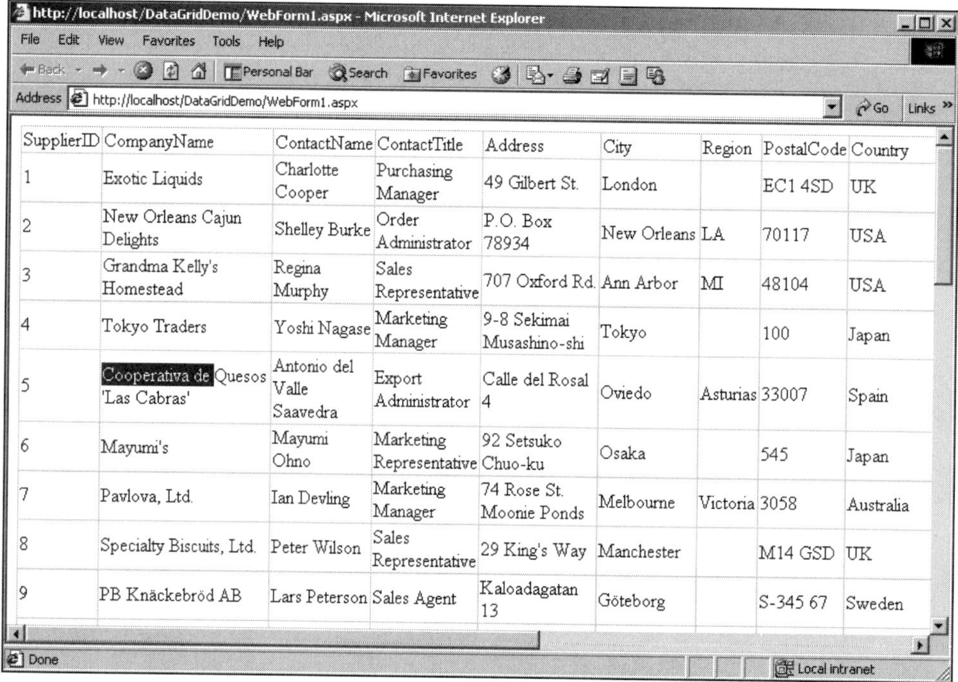

SupplierID	CompanyName	ContactName	ContactTitle	Address	City	Region	PostalCode	Country
1	Exotic Liquids	Charlotte Cooper	Purchasing Manager	49 Gilbert St.	London		EC1 4SD	UK
2	New Orleans Cajun Delights	Shelley Burke	Order Administrator	P.O. Box 78934	New Orleans	LA	70117	USA
3	Grandma Kelly's Homestead	Regina Murphy	Sales Representative	707 Oxford Rd.	Ann Arbor	MI	48104	USA
4	Tokyo Traders	Yoshi Nagase	Marketing Manager	9-8 Sekimai Musashino-shi	Tokyo		100	Japan
5	Cooperativa de Quesos 'Las Cabras'	Antonio del Valle Saavedra	Export Administrator	Calle del Rosal 4	Oviedo	Asturias	33007	Spain
6	Mayumi's	Mayumi Ohno	Marketing Representative	92 Setsuko Chuo-ku	Osaka		545	Japan
7	Pavlova, Ltd.	Ian Devling	Marketing Manager	74 Rose St. Moonie Ponds	Melbourne	Victoria	3058	Australia
8	Specialty Biscuits, Ltd.	Peter Wilson	Sales Representative	29 King's Way	Manchester		M14 GSD	UK
9	PB Knäckebröd AB	Lars Peterson	Sales Agent	Kaloadagatan 13	Göteborg		S-345 67	Sweden

Figure 22.6
The display produced by the DataGrid control's default settings.

As you have seen with other data-bound controls, the most basic steps required are as follows:

1. Set the control's **DataSource** property to the data source (a DataSet, DataView, and so on).
2. If necessary, set the **DataMember** property to the specific table to display. This is required only if the data source is a type that can contain multiple tables, such as a DataSet.
3. Call the **DataBind()** method.

DataGrid Pages

The default behavior of the DataGrid control is to display all of the rows in the data source. The control may "disappear" off the bottom of the browser page and can be brought back into view by scrolling the browser. The control has the option of *paging*, in which a specified maximum number of rows is displayed at one time and, at the bottom of the control, a *pager* is displayed with links to additional pages. In order to use the paging feature, set the **AllowPaging** property to True and set the **PageSize** property to the number of rows to display on each page.

Changing DataGrid Appearance

For the sake of controlling visual appearance, the DataGrid control is divided into sections. Each section has its own style, which in turn is made up of individual properties that determine things such as the background color, font, and border width for that section of the control. The sections are as follows:

- *Item*—Each row of data in the control.
- *Alternating Item*—Alternate rows of data. By default, this is set the same as the Item style.
- *Header*—The control header (column names and so on).
- *Footer*—The control footer.
- *Edit Item*—A row that is being edited.
- *Selected Item*—A row that is selected.
- *Pager*—The control pager (when **AllowPaging** is True).

When you are working with a DataGrid control in the Designer, the property window displays an entry for each of these sections. If you click the + symbol next to one of these entries, it expands to show the individual properties for this section. For example, Figure 22.7 shows the property window with the style properties displayed for the Item style.

To specify the style settings for your DataGrid control, you can set these style properties directly. You can also use the Property Builder or AutoFormat tools, as described in the following sections.

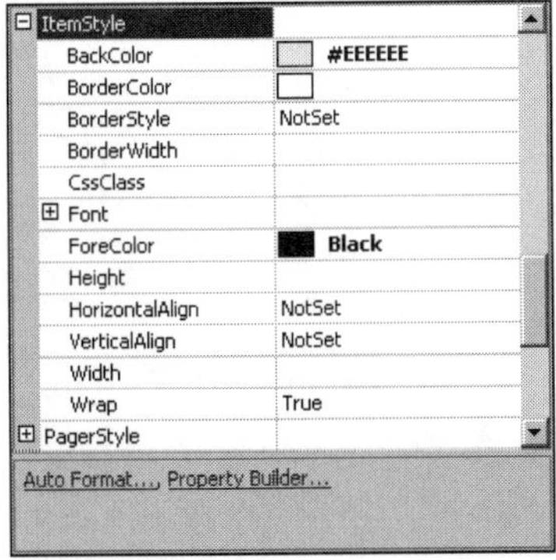

Figure 22.7
Setting the style properties for the Item section of the DataGrid control.

Using AutoFormat Settings

The DataGrid control comes with an assortment of predefined appearances, or schemes, that you can access via the AutoFormat command on the context menu (right-click the DataGrid in the Designer and select AutoFormat). The Auto Format dialog box is shown in Figure 22.8. In this dialog box, the list on the left shows the available schemes and the picture on the right is a preview of what the selected scheme looks like. When you select a scheme, the properties of the control are changed in the property window, where you can examine them and make further changes. This is a useful tool because it lets you select a predefined scheme that is close to what you want and then tweak the individual property settings until it is just right.

Using the Property Builder

An easy way to set the properties of a DataGrid control is by using the Property Builder. This tool works with all of the control's properties, including those that are related to its appearance. To display this tool, right-click the DataGrid in the Designer and then select Property Builder from the context menu. The dialog box is shown in Figure 22.9. You can see that the column on the left side of the dialog box lists categories of properties and that the area on the right side displays the properties for the selected category (Format in the figure). Use the panes of this dialog box to make the property settings needed by your program, and they are automatically entered in the property window.

Working with DataGrid Columns

The easiest way to set up the columns of a DataGrid control is to set the **AutoGenerateColumns** property to True. Then, the control will automatically create a default type column for each field in the data source. This is suitable for some applications,

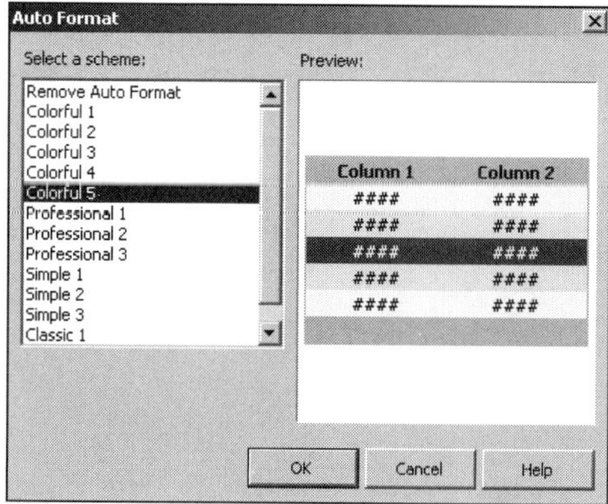

Figure 22.8
Select a predefined DataGrid style using the Auto Format dialog box.

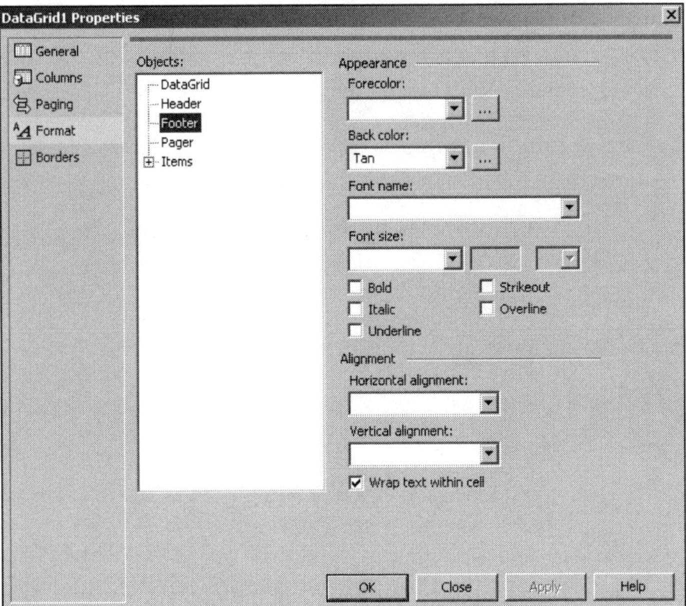

Figure 22.9
Setting DataGrid properties using the Property Builder.

but the DataGrid control offers significantly more flexibility for those situations that call for it. You can specify which data fields are displayed and in what order. Also, you can use the five different types of columns that can be displayed by a DataGrid control, as detailed in Table 22.3.

All column types have the following properties in common:

- **Header Text**—Text displayed at the top of the column. Can include HTML tags. This text becomes the identifier for the column.
- **Footer Text**—Same as Header Text but displayed at the bottom of the column.

Table 22.3 DataGrid column types.

Column Type	Description
BoundColumn	The default. The column is bound to the corresponding field in the data source.
ButtonColumn	Displays a user-defined button.
EditCommandColumn	Displays Edit, Update, and Cancel buttons.
HyperLinkColumn	Displays the contents of the column as a hyperlink.
TemplateColumn	Displays the contents of the column according to a user-defined template.

- **Header Image**—The URL of an image file to display at the head of the column. You can assign both a Header Image and a Header Text property, in which case the image is displayed but the text serves as the column identifier.
- **Sort Expression**—The sorting expression that is passed when the column is selected as the sort key (see the section, "Sorting a DataGrid" later in this chapter).
- **Visible**—Specifies whether the column is visible when the control is first displayed.

In addition to the common properties, a BoundColumn has the following properties:

- **Data Field**—The name of the data field to which the column is bound.
- **Data Formatting Expression**—A formatting expression that controls the way the data is displayed.
- **Read Only**—Specifies whether the field will be editable when the DataGrid row is placed in edit mode.

A ButtonColumn can display either a standard Button control or a LinkButton control. Its properties are as follows:

- **Text**—The text to display on the button (if every row is to have the same text on the button).
- **Command**—The string that is passed to the **ItemCommand()** event procedure when the button is clicked.
- **Text Field**—The data field to which the button is bound (to display data rather than fixed text on the button).
- **Button Type**—Either LinkButton (the default) or PushButton.
- **Text Format String**—A formatting expression that controls how the button's text is displayed.

An EditCommandColumn normally displays an Edit button. When this button is clicked, the row is put into edit mode and the EditCommandColumn then displays Update and Cancel buttons. This type of column has the following properties:

- **Edit Text**—The text to display on the Edit button.
- **Cancel Text**—The text to display on the Cancel button.
- **Update Text**—The text to display on the Update button.
- **Button Type**—Either LinkButton (the default) or PushButton.

A HyperLinkColumn has the following properties:

- **Text**—The text to display on the button (if every row is to have the same text on the button).
- **Text Field**—The data field to which the button is bound (to display data rather than fixed text on the button). Overrides the **Text** property.
- **URL**—The URL associated with the link (if every row is to be linked to the same URL).
- **URL Field**—The data field to which the button's URL is bound (if each button is to be associated with a different link). Overrides the **URL** property.

A TemplateColumn has the common properties listed previously in this section. This type of column can include any HTML text and controls, and is designed in the page's HTML. It supports the following templates: EditItemTemplate, ItemTemplate, HeaderTemplate, FooterTemplate. These templates work the same way as the templates for the DataList control, as described previously in this chapter.

Adding Columns in the Designer

To add custom columns to a DataGrid using the property window, select the **Columns** property and then click the ellipsis. The property window will open, displaying the section for columns definition, as shown in Figure 22.10. The Available Columns list displays the

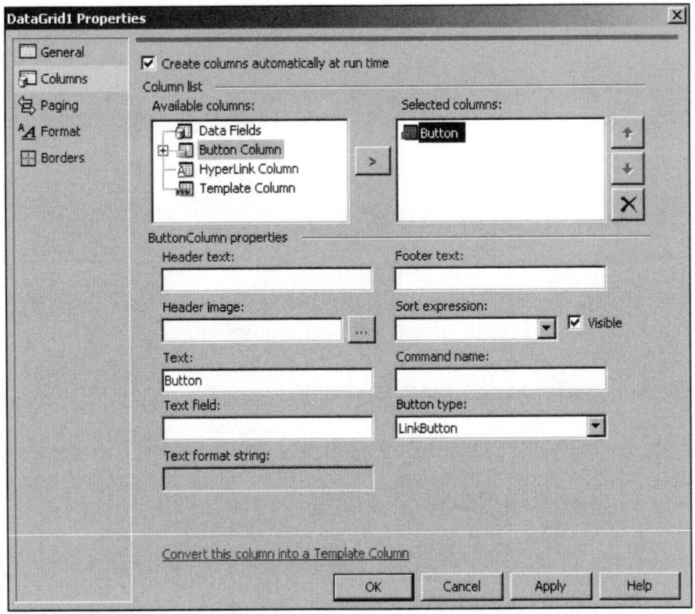

Figure 22.10
Adding custom columns to a DataGrid control.

columns that are available, including data fields if the control is already bound to a populated data source. Then follow these steps:

1. Turn the Create Columns Automatically At Run Time option on or off as desired.
2. Select a column type and click the > button to add it to the control.
3. Select a column in the Selected Columns list and enter its properties in the fields in the property window.
4. Click the up-arrow and down-arrow buttons to change the position of the selected column.
5. Click the X button to remove the selected column.
6. When finished, click OK.

Adding Columns in HTML

When you add columns to a DataGrid using the Designer, as described in the previous section, the corresponding HTML is added to the page. You may prefer to work directly with the HTML rather than using the property window—or to employ a combination of the property window and direct HTML editing. Within the HTML tags for a DataGrid control, you will find a Columns section that contains the definitions of all custom columns:

```
<columns>
...
</columns>
```

For example, Listing 22.6 shows the columns definition HTML for a DataGrid control. From left to right, this control will display:

- An EditCommand column with an Edit LinkButton
- A TemplateColumn that contains a Delete LinkButton
- Five BoundColumns that are each bound to a field in the data source
- A TemplateColumn that contains a CheckBox to display the value of a True/False field

Listing 22.6 An example of HTML that defines columns for a DataGrid control.

```
<Columns>

  <asp:EditCommandColumn
      EditText="Edit"
      CancelText="Cancel"
      UpdateText="Update"
```

```
      ItemStyle-Wrap="false"
      HeaderText="Edit Employee"
      HeaderStyle-Wrap="false"
      />

  <asp:TemplateColumn HeaderText="Delete">
    <ItemTemplate>
      <asp:LinkButton id="Delete" text="Delete"
               CommandName="Delete" runat="server"/>
    </ItemTemplate>
  </asp:TemplateColumn>

  <asp:BoundColumn HeaderText="ID" DataField="Index"
                 ReadOnly="True" />
  <asp:BoundColumn HeaderText="Employee Name" DataField="Name"
                 SortExpression="Name"/>
  <asp:BoundColumn HeaderText="Hire Date" DataField="Hire Date"
                  DataFormatString="{0:d}"
                 SortExpression="Hire Date"/>
  <asp:BoundColumn HeaderText="Salary" DataField="Salary"
                 SortExpression="Salary" />
  <asp:BoundColumn HeaderText="Location" DataField="Location"
                 SortExpression="Location"/>

  <asp:TemplateColumn HeaderText="Benefits?" SortExpression="Has Benefits">
    <ItemTemplate>
      <asp:Checkbox id="HasBenefits" runat="server" Checked=
       <%# DataBinder.Eval(Container.DataItem, "Has Benefits") %>
       Enabled="false" />
    </ItemTemplate>
  </asp:TemplateColumn>

</Columns>
```

Sorting a DataGrid

The default for a DataGrid is to display the rows of data in the same order they have in the data source. It can be useful to permit the user to control the sorting, changing it as needed while the DataGrid is displayed. You can do so using the **SortExpression** property of each column and the **AllowSorting** property of the DataGrid control. **AllowSorting** is by default False, but if it's set to True, the header text of each column that has a **SortExpression** property assigned to it is displayed as a LinkButton. When the user clicks the header of such a column, the **SortCommand()** event procedure is called. Code in this procedure can access the column's **SortExpression** property and then perform the sorting as defined by that expression. Finally, the DataGrid and the newly sorted data source must be rebound. Here's a code snippet showing the basics:

```
Private Sub DataGrid1_SortCommand(ByVal source As Object, _
  ByVal e As System.Web.UI.WebControls.DataGridSortCommandEventArgs) _
  Handles DataGrid1.SortCommand

  Dim SortExp As String = e.SortExpression.ToString()
  ' Perform sorting and rebinding here.

  End Sub
```

A DataGrid Demonstration

The program in this section shows how to use a DataGrid control to display data. It also demonstrates two new techniques that you have not seen so far. One has to do with the source of the data. Rather than binding to a database using SQL Server or OLE DB, the program generates its own data in code and puts the data into a DataTable, which is then linked to the DataGrid. Following the same approach, you can use data from essentially any source and still have the advantages of ASP.NET's data-binding capabilities.

The second technique has to do with the program structure. Previously in this chapter, you have used Visual Studio to create your ASP.NET projects, with a page's HTML and code divided into two separate files. You can also create a page as a single file, using any text editor. In this case, the VB code, rather than being in a separate code behind file, is in the same file as the HTML and is marked off by **<script>** tags. The end result is the same: When a user navigates to the ASPX file, the HTML and code work just as if they were in two separate files. For example, on your local computer, you would do the following:

1. Create a directory for the application.
2. Use Internet Information Services configuration to create a virtual directory that points to the application directory.
3. Use any text editor to create DataGridDemo.aspx with the code from Listing 22.7 and save it in the application directory.
4. To run the program, open Internet Explorer and navigate to **http://localhost/*VirtualDirectoryName*/datagriddemo.aspx**.

The program, whose code is presented in Listing 22.7, illustrates some other powerful techniques available to the Visual Basic.NET programmer. These techniques include the built-in capabilities for editing that the DataGrid control provides, as well as how to store program information in the session state between hits. I will not explain these aspects of the program in detail, but they are well commented in the code, and you should be able to figure out how things work. Figure 22.11 shows the program running.

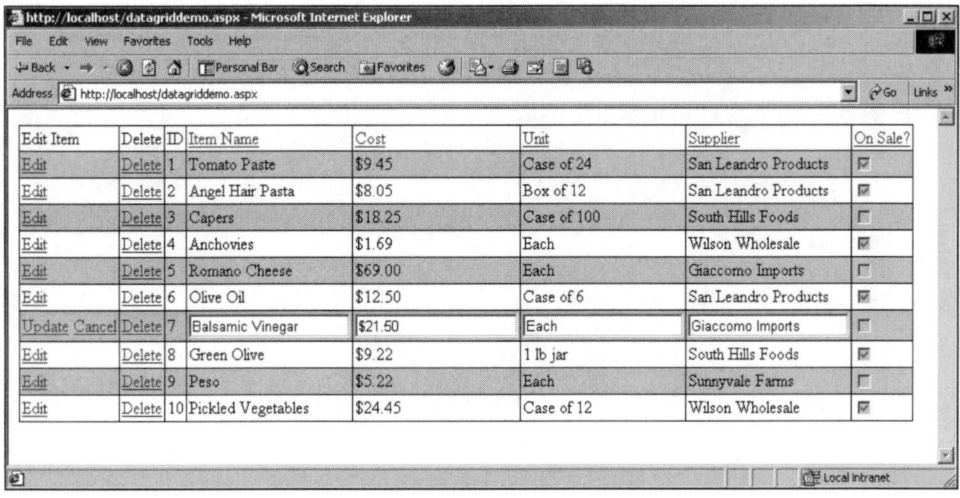

Figure 22.11
Using the DataGrid control's built-in editing capabilities.

Listing 22.7 DataGridDemo.aspx shows how to use a DataGrid control in your ASP.NET programs.

```
<%@ Import NameSpace="System.Data" %>
<%@ Import NameSpace="System " %>
<script language="VB" runat="server">

'Declare our data table and view objects with Page scope.
Dim dt as DataTable
Dim dv as DataView

' This method creates a data table containing program-generated
' data. The data could come from any source and be used
' in the same way.

Sub MakeDataTable()

  ' Create the columns for the data table. The table
  ' dt has been declared globally.
  dt.Columns.Add(new DataColumn("Index", GetType(integer)))
  dt.Columns.Add(new DataColumn("Item", GetType(string)))
  dt.Columns.Add(new DataColumn("Cost", GetType(single)))
  dt.Columns.Add(new DataColumn("Unit", GetType(string)))
  dt.Columns.Add(new DataColumn("Supplier", GetType(string)))
  dt.Columns.Add(new DataColumn("OnSale", GetType(boolean)))
```

```
' Set the primary key for the data table.
Dim primaryKeys(0) As DataColumn
primaryKeys(0) = dt.Columns(0)
dt.PrimaryKey = primaryKeys

'Populate the data table with 10 rows.
  Dim dr as DataRow
  dr = dt.NewRow()
  dr("Index") = 1
  dr("Item") = "Tomato Paste"
  dr("Cost") = 9.45
  dr("Unit") = "Case of 24"
  dr("Supplier") = "San Leandro Products"
  dr("OnSale") = True
  dt.Rows.Add(dr)

  dr = dt.NewRow()
  dr("Index") = 2
  dr("Item") = "Angel Hair Pasta"
  dr("Cost") = 8.05
  dr("Unit") = "Box of 12"
  dr("Supplier") = "San Leandro Products"
  dr("OnSale") = True
  dt.Rows.Add(dr)

  dr = dt.NewRow()
  dr("Index") = 3
  dr("Item") = "Capers"
  dr("Cost") = 18.25
  dr("Unit") = "Case of 100"
  dr("Supplier") = "South Hills Foods"
  dr("OnSale") = False
  dt.Rows.Add(dr)

  dr = dt.NewRow()
  dr("Index") = 4
  dr("Item") = "Anchovies"
  dr("Cost") = 1.69
  dr("Unit") = "Each"
  dr("Supplier") = "Wilson Wholesale"
  dr("OnSale") = True
  dt.Rows.Add(dr)

  dr = dt.NewRow()
  dr("Index") = 5
  dr("Item") = "Romano Cheese"
  dr("Cost") = 69.00
```

```
dr("Unit") = "Each"
dr("Supplier") = "Giaccomo Imports"
dr("OnSale") = False
dt.Rows.Add(dr)

dr = dt.NewRow()
dr("Index") = 6
dr("Item") = "Olive Oil"
dr("Cost") = 12.50
dr("Unit") = "Case of 6"
dr("Supplier") = "San Leandro Products"
dr("OnSale") = True
dt.Rows.Add(dr)

dr = dt.NewRow()
dr("Index") = 7
dr("Item") = "Balsamic Vinegar"
dr("Cost") = 21.50
dr("Unit") = "Each"
dr("Supplier") = "Giaccomo Imports"
dr("OnSale") = False
dt.Rows.Add(dr)

dr = dt.NewRow()
dr("Index") = 8
dr("Item") = "Green Olive"
dr("Cost") = 9.22
dr("Unit") = "1 lb jar"
dr("Supplier") = "South Hills Foods"
dr("OnSale") = True
dt.Rows.Add(dr)

dr = dt.NewRow()
dr("Index") = 9
dr("Item") = "Peso"
dr("Cost") = 5.22
dr("Unit") = "Each"
dr("Supplier") = "Sunnyvale Farms"
dr("OnSale") = False
dt.Rows.Add(dr)

dr = dt.NewRow()
dr("Index") = 10
dr("Item") = "Pickled Vegetables"
dr("Cost") = 24.45
dr("Unit") = "Case of 12"
dr("Supplier") = "Wilson Wholesale"
```

```
    dr("OnSale") = True
    dt.Rows.Add(dr)

End Sub

Sub Page_Load(Sender As Object, e As EventArgs)

  'If the data table isn't in Session, create a new one and add it to Session.
  'We are creating a new DataView object every time the page is hit.

  if Session("datatable") is Nothing then

    'Create the data table object and populate it.
    dt = new DataTable()
    MakeDataTable()

    'Make a view for the data.
    dv = new DataView(dt)

    'Store the entire data set in Session along
    'with sort and edit index info.
    Session("datatable") = dt
    Session("EditIndex") = -1
    Session("SortKey") = "Index"

  'Otherwise retrieve the data table from session store
  else
    dt = CType(Session("datatable"), DataTable)
    dv = new DataView(dt)
    dv.Sort = CStr(Session("SortKey"))
    MyDataGrid.EditItemIndex = CInt(Session("EditIndex"))
  End if

  BindGrid()

End Sub

'This method is called to update the DataGrid after the user has
'made some modifications such as editing or deleting rows.

Sub BindGrid()

  MyDataGrid.DataSource = dv
  MyDataGrid.DataBind()

End Sub
```

```
'This event is triggered when the heading of a sortable column is
'clicked. It updates the sort field name in Session and in
'the data view.

Protected Sub SortGrid(sender as object, e as DataGridSortCommandEventArgs)

  Session("SortIndex") = e.SortExpression
  dv.Sort = e.SortExpression
  BindGrid()

End Sub

'This event is triggered when the Delete link is clicked.
Protected Sub Command(Sender as Object, e as DataGridCommandEventArgs)

  if e.CommandName = "Delete" then

    'Get the item id, which will be the third element of the
    'Cells collection (the third column in the DataGrid)
    Dim strEmpID as String = e.Item.Cells(2).Text

    'Convert ID to an integer
    Dim nEmpID as integer = CInt(strEmpID)

    'Find the data row with this id
    Dim dr as DataRow = dt.Rows.Find(nEmpID)

    'Delete the row
    dt.Rows.Remove(dr)

    BindGrid()
  End If

End Sub

' This event is triggered when the user clicks the update link in
' a row they have been editing.
' The technique used to save the changes is to delete the entire
' old row and add a new one.

Protected Sub Update(sender as Object, e as DataGridCommandEventArgs)

    'Filter the view so that the row to be deleted is
    'the only one that is visible, then delete it.
```

```
        dv.RowFilter = "Index=" & e.Item.Cells(2).Text
        if dv.Count > 0 then
           dv.Delete(0)
        End If
        'Turn off the row filter
        dv.RowFilter = ""

        'Create the new row. The new data the user has entered
        'is the first element of the controls collection of each cell.
        'Each element must be cast to type TextBox before its text
        'can be retrieved.
        Dim dr as DataRow = dt.NewRow()
        dr("Index") = e.Item.Cells(2).Text
        dr("Item") = CType(e.Item.Cells(3).Controls(0), TextBox).Text
        dr("Cost") = CSng(CType(e.Item.Cells(4).Controls(0), TextBox).Text)
        dr("Unit") = CType(e.Item.Cells(5).Controls(0), TextBox).Text
        dr("Supplier") = CType(e.Item.Cells(6).Controls(0), TextBox).Text
        dr("OnSale") = False
        dt.Rows.Add(dr)

        ' Save table in Session.
        Session("datatable") = dt

        ' We need a new view.
        dv = new DataView(dt)
        'dv.Sort = CStr(Session("SortIndex"))
        MyDataGrid.EditItemIndex = -1
        Session("EditIndex") = -1
        'Rebind.
        BindGrid()

    End Sub

    'This event is triggered when the user clicks the cancel link
    ' while editing a row. Set the edit index to -1.

    Protected Sub Cancel(sender As Object, e as DataGridCommandEventArgs)

      MyDataGrid.EditItemIndex = -1
      Session("EditIndex") = -1
      BindGrid()

    End Sub

    'Called when the user clicks a row's Edit button.
    Protected Sub Edit(sender as Object, e as DataGridCommandEventArgs)
```

```
  MyDataGrid.EditItemIndex = CInt(e.Item.ItemIndex)
  BindGrid()
  Session("EditIndex") = MyDataGrid.EditItemIndex

End Sub

</script>
<html>
<body>
  <form runat="server">

  <asp:DataGrid id="MyDataGrid" runat="server" enableviewstate="false"
    BorderColor="black"
    BorderWidth="1"
    GridLines="Both"
    CellPadding="2"
    Font-Name="Times"
    Font-Size="12pt"
    ItemStyle-BackColor="LightGray"
    AlternatingItemStyle-BackColor="White"
    AutoGenerateColumns = "false"
    AllowSorting="true"
    OnSortCommand="SortGrid"
    OnItemCommand="Command"
    OnEditCommand="Edit"
    OnCancelCommand="Cancel"
    OnUpdateCommand="Update"
    AllowPaging="False"
    PageSize="10"
    PagerStyle-Mode="NumericPages"
    PagerStyle-HorizontalAlign="Right"
    PagerStyle-NextPageText="Next"
    PagerStyle-PrevPageText="Prev"
     >

    <Columns>

      <asp:EditCommandColumn
          EditText="Edit"
          CancelText="Cancel"
          UpdateText="Update"
          ItemStyle-Wrap="false"
          HeaderText="Edit Item"
          HeaderStyle-Wrap="false"
          />
```

```
        <asp:TemplateColumn HeaderText="Delete">
          <ItemTemplate>
            <asp:LinkButton id="Delete" text="Delete"
                   CommandName="Delete" runat="server"/>
          </ItemTemplate>
        </asp:TemplateColumn>

        <asp:BoundColumn HeaderText="ID" DataField="Index"
                ReadOnly="True" />
        <asp:BoundColumn HeaderText="Item Name" DataField="Item"
                SortExpression="Item"/>
        <asp:BoundColumn HeaderText="Cost" DataField="Cost"
                 DataFormatString="{0:C}"
                SortExpression="Cost"/>
        <asp:BoundColumn HeaderText="Unit" DataField="Unit"
                SortExpression="Unit" />
        <asp:BoundColumn HeaderText="Supplier" DataField="Supplier"
                SortExpression="Supplier"/>

        <asp:TemplateColumn HeaderText="On Sale?" SortExpression="OnSale">
          <ItemTemplate>
            <asp:Checkbox id="OnSale" runat="server" Checked=
              <%# DataBinder.Eval(Container.DataItem, "OnSale") %> _
                   Enabled="false" />
          </ItemTemplate>
        </asp:TemplateColumn>

      </Columns>
    </asp:DataGrid>

  </form>
</body>
</html>
```

Summary

After you read this chapter, I think you will agree that ASP.NET provides a nice set of controls for data access in your Web applications. For relatively simple data access and presentation needs, the Repeater control can save you a lot of development time. For additional flexibility in designing layouts, and the ability to let the user edit and delete data, turn to the DataList control—it's somewhat complicated, I will be the first to admit, but well worth the effort to learn how to use it. For the ultimate power in presenting data in a grid-like format, use the DataGrid control. These three controls are the "big guns" in ASP.NET's data access arsenal, but they are not all that it has to offer. By exploring the documentation, you can learn about other tools and techniques that you may want to employ.

Chapter 23
Creating and Using Web Services

One of the most exciting parts of Visual Basic .NET is the ability to create and use Web services. Web services are not really new, but they have been gaining in popularity over the past few years. What is special about .NET is how easily you can create and publish Web services and write programs that utilize them. These are the subjects of this chapter.

What Are Web Services?

A Web service is a program that provides methods that can be called over the Internet. Any other program that knows about your Web service and has the proper permissions can call these methods from anywhere on the Web. Let's look at a simple example.

Suppose that you have realized that lots of programs need to add numbers together, and you have decided to create a Web service for this task (this is not something you would actually create a Web service for, but it serves as a good illustration). You create and publish your "Addition" Web service to a Web server, where it becomes available to any other program that needs it.

In another city, Joe Programmer is working on a program that will need to add numbers together. Joe decides not to write the code for adding numbers but rather to use your service. When his program runs, it will "call" your Web service by sending a request that includes the numbers to be added. Your Web service will receive the request, add the numbers together, and send a respond to Joe's program that includes the result.

Web services are not used for performing addition, although they certainly could be! More typical tasks would include things such as credit card authorization, online information retrieval, loan applications—you name it! One important thing to remember about Web services is that they are strictly a computer-to-computer, or more precisely a program-to-program, technology. No user interface or user input is involved.

There is nothing really new about Web services. Technologies such as CORBA and DCOM permitting the development of Web services have been around for a while. Even so, none of these earlier technologies ever gained a critical mass of acceptance, and for the most part they were not all that easy to work with. Web services in .NET are therefore not a new idea, but a new and better implementation of an existing idea.

A First Web Service

To give you a feel for how Web services work, and how they are created, it will be instructive to work through the creation of a simple Web service and a client program that uses it. Keeping with the preceding example, this simple service will add numbers together. First, let's create the service and then create a client to use it.

Creating the Web Service

Start by creating a new Visual Basic.NET project; select ASP.NET Web Service as the type of project. Enter "Adder" in the Name box. Visual Studio will create the project directory Adder off your Web server virtual root. In the Solution Explorer, you will see several files that Visual Studio has created. Of interest at the present moment is the file Service1.asmx, assigned this default name by Visual Studio. The .asmx extension is used for Web service files. Right-click the file name in the Solution Explorer and select View Code. Note that like many other types of Visual Studio files, this file has a code behind component in a separate file called Service1.asmx.vb. Its initial contents are shown in Figure 23.1. You should note the following:

- The file imports the **System.Web.Services** namespace, which contains the classes for creating Web services.
- The code defines a class named Service1; this class inherits from the .NET class **System.Web.Services.WebService**.
- In the comments, you will see an example of implementing a simple "Hello World" Web service.

To create the sample Web service, make the following two additions to the code. First, add this namespace declaration just before the **Public Class Service1** line:

```
<WebService(Namespace:="http://tempuri.org/webservices")> _
```

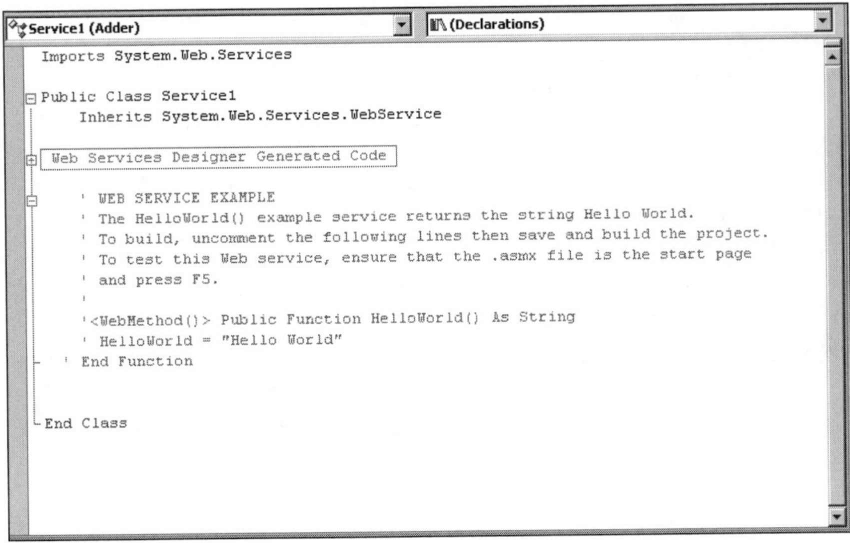

Service1 (Adder)
(Declarations)
Imports System.Web.Services
Public Class Service1
Inherits System.Web.Services.WebService
Web Services Designer Generated Code
' WEB SERVICE EXAMPLE
' The HelloWorld() example service returns the string Hello World.
' To build, uncomment the following lines then save and build the project.
' To test this Web service, ensure that the .asmx file is the start page
' and press F5.
'
'<WebMethod()> Public Function HelloWorld() As String
' HelloWorld = "Hello World"
' End Function
End Class

Figure 23.1
The default Web service code inserted by Visual Studio.

Note the underscore at the end, which is needed because the preceding code is supposed to be on the same line as the **Public Class** statement, and the underscore permits them to be logically on the same line while split in the editor for easier viewing.

Then, add the following code inside the class:

```
<WebMethod()> Public Function AddTwoNumbers(ByVal num1 As Double, _
    ByVal num2 As Double) As Double

  AddTwoNumbers = num1 + num2

End Function
```

The first code addition defines the namespace for the Web service. This is essential, because each Web service needs a unique namespace to distinguish it from other services. The namespace used here is one that has been set aside for use by Web services that are under development. It is also the default namespace, and will be used if you omit the **<WebService>** attribute. When your Web service is finished and ready to be published, you will need to assign your own unique namespace.

The second code addition defines an operation, a method that the service exposes. You can see that for the most part this is no different from a regular class method. The only addition is the **<WebMethod()>** tag that identifies it as a Web method.

The next step in creating the Web service is to navigate to the ASMX file you just created using a browser. ASP.NET will create and display a page with information about the service and include a link that lets you test it. In this case, you would point your browser to **http://localhost/adder/service1.asmx**. The resulting page is shown in Figure 23.2.

Most of the page is taken up with general information, such as a reminder to change the service's namespace before publishing it and a few links to useful information. At the top of the page is the name of the service, Service1, as well as a list of the operations it provides—in this case, only a single operation named AddTwoNumbers. Click on that link to test the service, as shown in Figure 23.3. Enter two numbers in the Num1 and Num2 boxes and click the Invoke button. Note that the test page also shows, in the bottom portion, a sample Simple Object Access Protocol (SOAP) request. SOAP is the protocol that is used to transmit Web service requests and responses; you'll learn more about it later. For now, however, the Web service is ready to use.

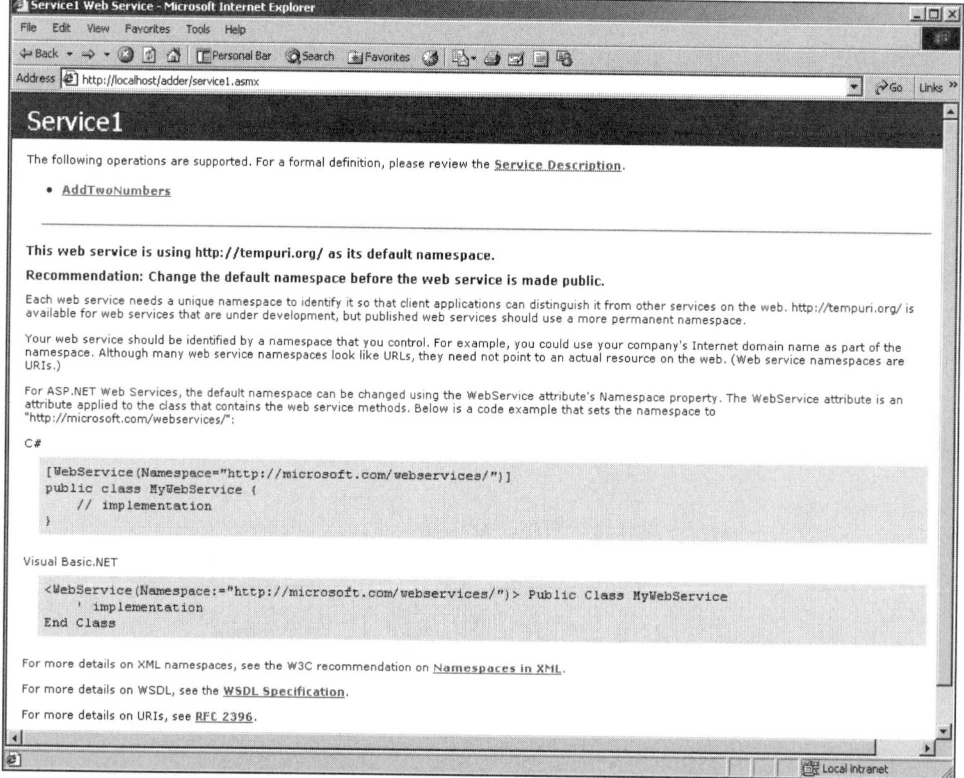

Figure 23.2
The test page created by ASP.NET for the Web service.

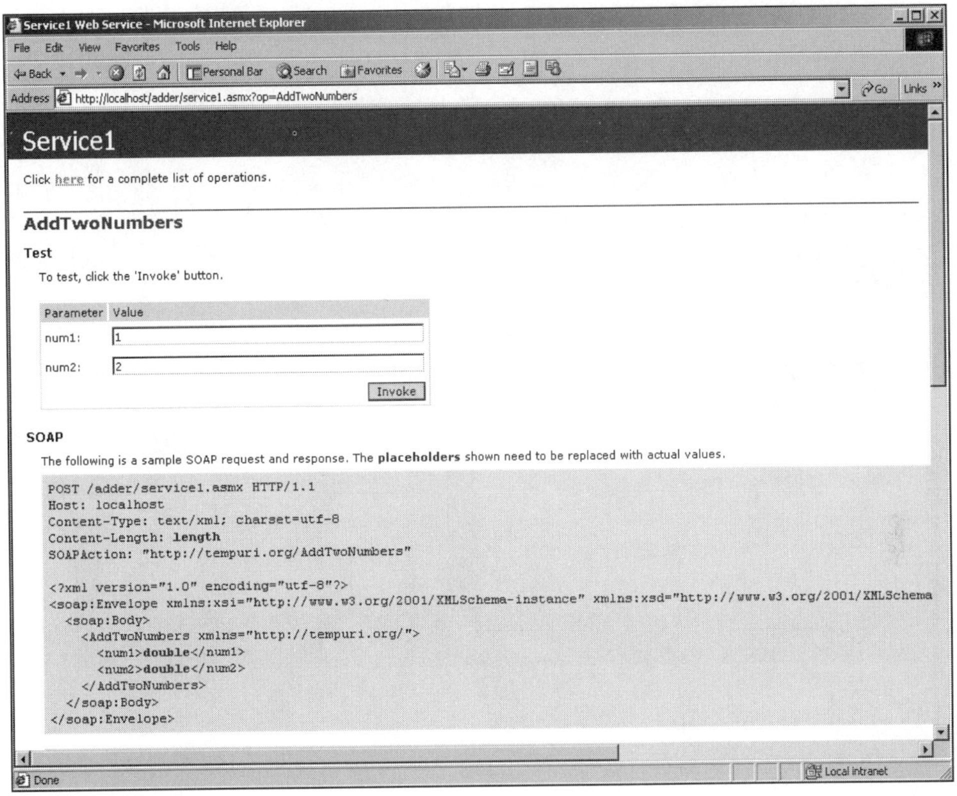

Figure 23.3
Testing the Web service.

Creating the Client

Essentially any type of program can use a Web service. In fact, one Web service can use another Web service, a configuration that opens up some very interesting possibilities. For now, however, I will keep things simple. This client will be a Windows application.

To create the client, start a new Windows application. If the service application is still open, it can be closed. In order for a client program to use a Web service, it must of course "know" about the service. This is done by adding a reference to the service to your project. To do so, select Add Web Reference from the Project menu. The Add Web Reference dialog box will appear, as shown in Figure 23.4. I will explain the other parts of this dialog box later in the chapter; for now, click the Web References On Local Web Server link at the lower left.

After a few seconds, the dialog box will display in its right panel a list of available Web references. You'll note that quite a few references appear, which reflects the fact that things

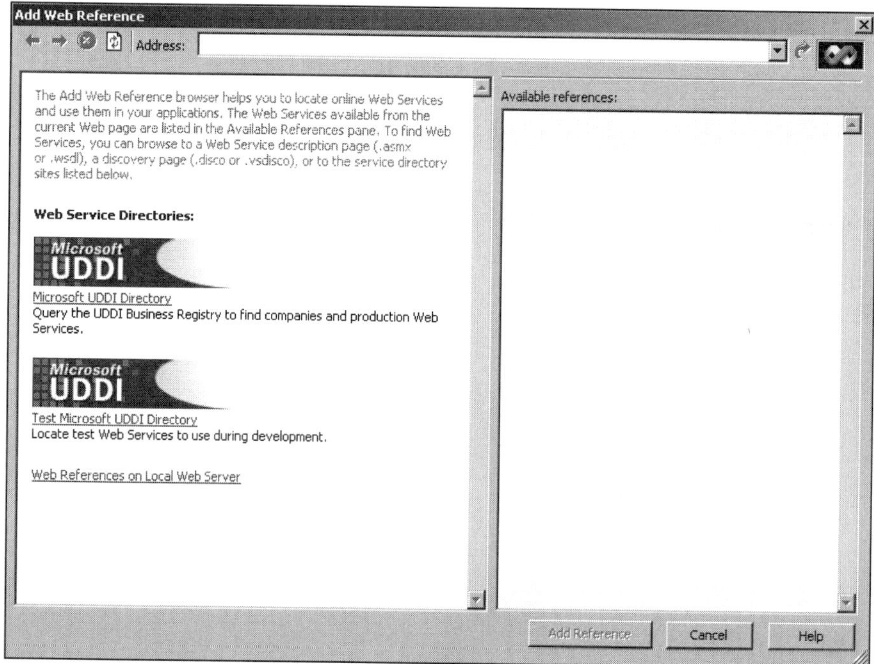

Figure 23.4
The Add Web Reference dialog box.

other than Web services are considered Web references. For now you are interested in the entry "http://localhost/adder/adder.vsdisco," which should be located at the top of the list. Click this entry, and then, in the next dialog box, click the Add Reference button.

When a Web reference is added to your project, it shows up in the Solution Explorer. For example, Figure 23.5 shows how the "Adder" reference is displayed in the Solution Explorer. Note that the reference includes a file named Adder.disco and another one named Service1.wsdl. I'll explain these files later in the chapter.

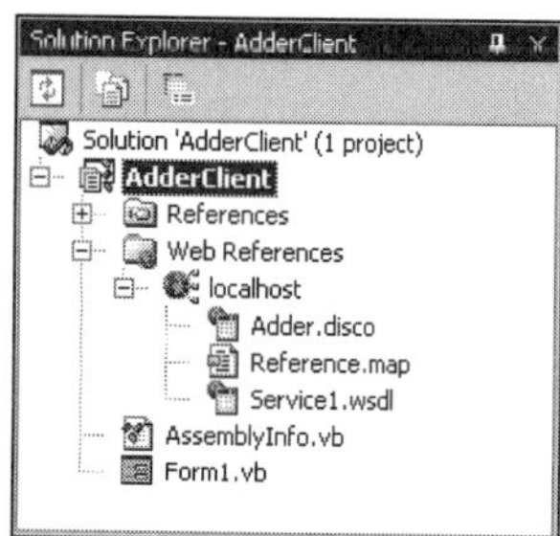

Figure 23.5
Selecting a reference from those available on the local host.

Now that your client project has a reference to the service, you can create an instance of the service to use in your program. This is done using the standard Visual Basic syntax:

```
Dim MyAdder As New localhost.Adder
```

Note that the service is referenced by its location, in this case "localhost", and also by the service name. Now, the name MyAdder references the service. If you type this name in the program followed by a period, the autolist feature will display a list of the service members, including the **AddTwoNumbers()** method. There are also members called **BeginAddTwoNumbers()** and **EndAddTwoNumbers()**, which I will discuss later in the chapter. The other members you see are all inherited by your service from its base class **System.Web.Services.WebService**.

To complete the client, place two TextBox controls on the project's form, plus a Label control and a Button control. At this point, I am sure that I do not have to provide you with detailed instructions for these tasks. Open the code window and add the declaration of MyAdder shown above. Then, place the code shown in Listing 23.1 into the **Click()** event procedure for the Button control. When you run the program (see Figure 23.6), you can enter numbers in the two TextBox controls and click the Add button, and the sum will be displayed as shown.

Listing 23.1 Code in the Click() event procedure calls the Web service.

```
Private Sub Button1_Click(ByVal sender As System.Object, _
    ByVal e As System.EventArgs) Handles Button1.Click

    Dim num1 As Double
    Dim num2 As Double
    Dim sum As Double

    num1 = Double.Parse(TextBox1.Text)
    num2 = Double.Parse(TextBox2.Text)
    sum = MyAdder.AddTwoNumbers(num1, num2)
    Label1.Text = "The sum is " & sum.ToString

End Sub
```

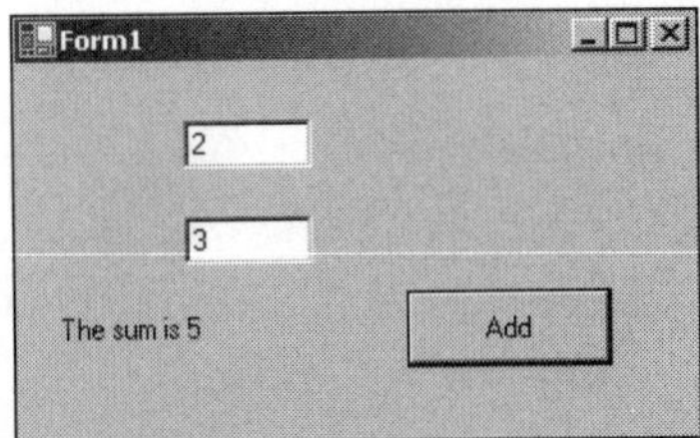

Figure 23.6
Running the Web service client.

The first time you run the client and click the Add button, you may notice a pause before the result is displayed. This is the time required for the Web server to compile and cache the service. Subsequent hits occur much more quickly.

You can see that creating and consuming Web services with the .NET framework is pretty easy. Now it's time to explore some of the details.

SOAP

The Simple Object Access Protocol (SOAP) is a protocol that defines a vocabulary for communication between computers. More specifically, SOAP defines a way for requests and responses to be exchanged. It is relevant to the present discussion because the .NET Web services model uses SOAP for communication between client and service.

SOAP uses Extensible Markup Language (XML) syntax to structure the content of its messages. As such, a SOAP message consists of plain text, which offers several advantages. SOAP messages can be transported easily using widely used Web protocols, particularly HTTP. In addition, SOAP messages can be passed through firewalls without difficulty. Being plain text, they are operating system independent. Finally, a SOAP message can be read and edited by a person using a standard text editor—something that is not needed all that often, however.

What does a SOAP message look like? Listing 23.2 shows a template for the SOAP message that would be used by the Adder client developed earlier to call the Adder Web service. To be exact, this listing shows the entire HTTP POST request, which includes the SOAP message. The lines are numbered for reference.

Listing 23.2 An HTTP POST request containing a SOAP message.

```
POST /adder/service1.asmx HTTP/1.1
Host: localhost
Content-Type: text/xml; charset=utf-8
Content-Length: length
SOAPAction: "http://tempuri.org/AddTwoNumbers"

<?xml version="1.0" encoding="utf-8"?>
<soap:Envelope
    xmlns:xsi="http://www.w3.org/2001/XMLSchema-instance"
    xmlns:xsd="http://www.w3.org/2001/XMLSchema"
    xmlns:soap="http://schemas.xmlsoap.org/soap/envelope/">
  <soap:Body>
    <AddTwoNumbers xmlns="http://tempuri.org/">
      <num1>double</num1>
      <num2>double</num2>
    </AddTwoNumbers>
  </soap:Body>
</soap:Envelope>
```

Lines 1 through 5 are the HTTP POST header, and are not directly connected to the content of the POST. Note that line 4 includes a placeholder for length, which in a real request would contain the total length of the POST request.

Lines 7 through 18 comprise the SOAP message itself. If you have worked with XML before, you will recognize line 7 as the standard XML definition element. The content of the SOAP message is contained between the envelope tags, and in particular lines 13 through 16:

- Line 13 identifies the service method being called, namely **AddTwoNumbers**. It also identifies the namespace that the method is contained in.
- Line 14 passes one argument, num1, to the method. Here, there is a placeholder for the type **double** that would be passed in a real request. In a real request, for example, this line might read **<num1>2.09</num1>**.
- Line 15 passes the second argument, num2.
- Line 16 marks the end of the information passed to the method.

For the most part, you need not be concerned with the details of the SOAP messages; Visual Studio and the .NET framework will take care of everything. If needed, however, you can customize SOAP messages following the instructions provided in the online documentation.

Describing Web Services with WSDL Files

When you created and ran the Web service client demonstration, you may have noticed that the client seems to know all about the Web service provider. It knew, for example, that the service exposed a method named **AddTwoNumbers()**, and it also knew the details of how to call the service. Of course, in this case the service was on the local computer, but the same would have been true if the service was on a remote computer. This information is made available by means of a Web Services Description Language (WSDL) file. These files are sometimes called *contract* files because they define an agreement, or contract, that the Web service promises to fulfill.

When you create a Web service, Visual Studio automatically creates a WSDL file for it. This is a good thing, because WSDL files are quite complex and you would not want to create one manually (nor should you even modify a WSDL file created by Visual Studio). To examine a WSDL file, in Solution Explorer right-click the file name (Service1.wsdl in this example) and select Open.

A WSDL file uses XML to organize its contents. Even for a very simple Web service like the one we created, the WSDL file is quite long and complex. Within all this information are the details about how a client program should call service methods, and how the response will come back. For example, look at this section of the Adder service's WSDL file:

```
<s:element name="AddTwoNumbers">
  <s:complexType>
    <s:sequence>
      <s:element minOccurs="1" maxOccurs="1" name="num1"
         type="s:double" />
      <s:element minOccurs="1" maxOccurs="1" name="num2"
         type="s:double" />
    </s:sequence>
  </s:complexType>
</s:element>
```

This defines part of the format of the message used by the client to call the service. The important information is in the two lines that start with "<s:element". The first such line specifies that:

- The request will contain a data element named "num1".
- The data element will be type **double**.
- It will occur exactly one time in the request.

The next line defines an element named "num2" with the same restrictions. Clearly, these elements match up with the two parameters that the **AddTwoNumbers()** method requires.

Look next at this part of the WSDL file:

```
<s:element name="AddTwoNumbersResponse">
  <s:complexType>
    <s:sequence>
      <s:element minOccurs="1" maxOccurs="1" name="AddTwoNumbersResult"
          type="s:double" />
    </s:sequence>
  </s:complexType>
</s:element>
```

Here, the WSDL file defines the response of the Web service—in other words, the return data from the **AddTwoNumbers()** method. You can see that it specifies one type **double** as the response, which is exactly correct. By reading this WSDL file, your client program can determine exactly how it should interact with the Web service. There are more details than I have discussed here, of course, but fortunately you can ignore them because Visual Studio handles them automatically.

Proxy Classes and WSDL.EXE

When you add a reference to a Web service to a Visual Studio program, what goes on behind the scenes is that Visual Studio creates a *proxy class* for the service, based on information in its WSDL file. In your client program, you are actually referencing this proxy class, which in turn contains all the "plumbing" required to access the Web service (for example, generating SOAP requests). This arrangement is illustrated in Figure 23.7. All of this happens behind the scenes and is invisible to the programmer. For most situations, there is no reason to do otherwise.

Sometimes, however, you may wish to explicitly create your proxy class. This will be the case if the Web service is not accessible from the computer you are using for development or if you have need to customize the proxy class. Visual Studio provides a tool for this: WSDL.EXE. This command-line utility takes the service's WSDL file as input and outputs a source code file in the language of your choice. You then compile the file and add the class to your client project in lieu of a Web reference.

The WSDL utility runs at the Visual Studio command prompt, accessed from the Windows Start menu. This command prompt is configured with the path and other settings needed to run the .NET framework's command-line tools, including WSDL.EXE. This utility has many options, which are explained in detail in the documentation. The ones you'll need most often are

```
wsdl /l:lang /n:namespace /o:outfile url
```

Here, *lang* specifies the language of the output file: vb for Visual basic, cs for C# (the default), and js for JavaScript.

namespace specifies the namespace for the generated proxy. If this argument is omitted, the global namespace is used.

outfile is the name of the output file.

url is the URL of the WSDL contract file or, if the file is local, its path and name. You can reference a service's WSDL file by using the URL to its WSMX file followed by "?WSDL".

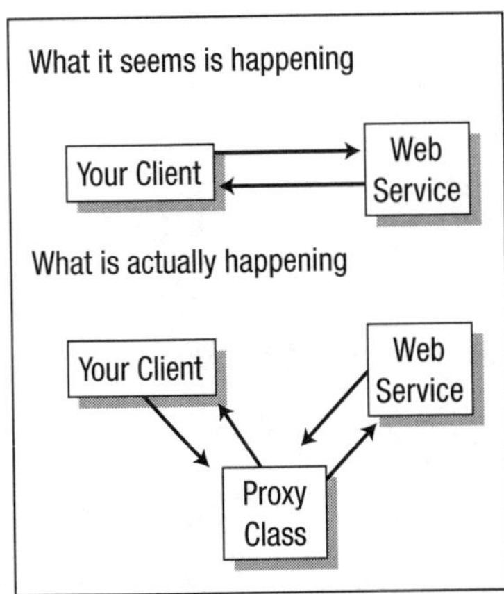

Figure 23.7
The proxy class connects the client and the Web service.

To create a proxy class for the Adder service that was created earlier in the chapter, open a Visual Studio Command Prompt window and change to the client project directory (not the directory for the service project). If you have not started programming the client yet, you may want to create a new directory for it at this point. Then, enter the following command line:

```
wsdl /l:vb /n:http://tempuri.org/webservices /o:adder.vb
    http://localhost/adder/service1.asmx?WSDL
```

Assuming that there are no errors, the WSDL utility will generate the file Adder.vb, which is shown in Listing 23.3.

Listing 23.3 The proxy class source code generated by WSDL.EXE.

```
'----------------------------------------------------------------------
' <autogenerated>
'     This code was generated by a tool.
'     Runtime Version: 1.0.2914.16
'
'     Changes to this file may cause incorrect behavior and
'     will be lost if the code is regenerated.
' </autogenerated>
'----------------------------------------------------------------------

Option Strict Off
Option Explicit On

Imports System
Imports System.Diagnostics
Imports System.Web.Services
Imports System.Web.Services.Protocols
Imports System.Xml.Serialization
'
'This source code was auto-generated by wsdl, Version=1.0.2914.16.
'
Namespace http://tempuri.org
   <System.Web.Services.WebServiceBindingAttribute(Name:="Service1Soap",
      [Namespace]:="http://tempuri.org/")>
  Public Class Service1
    Inherits System.Web.Services.Protocols.SoapHttpClientProtocol

      <System.Diagnostics.DebuggerStepThroughAttribute()>  _
      Public Sub New()
        MyBase.New
        Me.Url = "http://localhost/adder/service1.asmx"
      End Sub
```

```
<System.Diagnostics.DebuggerStepThroughAttribute(),  _
    System.Web.Services.Protocols.SoapDocumentMethodAttribute
   ("http://tempuri.org/AddTwoNumbers",
   Use:=System.Web.Services.Description.SoapBindingUse.Literal,
   ParameterStyle:=System.Web.Services.
   Protocols.SoapParameterStyle.Wrapped)>

 Public Function AddTwoNumbers(ByVal num1 As Double, _
     ByVal num2 As Double) As Double

    Dim results() As Object = Me.Invoke("AddTwoNumbers", _
       New Object() {num1, num2})
     Return CType(results(0),Double)

 End Function

<System.Diagnostics.DebuggerStepThroughAttribute()>

 Public Function BeginAddTwoNumbers(ByVal num1 As Double, _
       ByVal num2 As Double, ByVal callback As System.AsyncCallback, _
       ByVal asyncState As Object) As System.IAsyncResult

   Return Me.BeginInvoke("AddTwoNumbers", New Object() _
      {num1, num2}, callback, asyncState)

 End Function

<System.Diagnostics.DebuggerStepThroughAttribute()>

  Public Function EndAddTwoNumbers(ByVal asyncResult As _
     System.IAsyncResult) As Double

    Dim results() As Object = Me.EndInvoke(asyncResult)
    Return CType(results(0),Double)

  End Function

End Class
End Namespace
```

You will see that there are a lot of special syntax elements in this source code file, but you should note one thing in particular. First, you will notice a method named **AddTwoNumbers()**, which corresponds to the Web service method of the same name. When your client program calls **AddTwoNumbers()**, it is this method in the proxy class that is called; it in turn sends the method request to the Web service, receives the response, and returns the result to the client program.

Now that you have your proxy class source code, what's next? You can compile it with the command-line compiler, or more likely add it to the client project in Visual Studio. You can also modify its source code, but I strongly recommend against doing so unless you know exactly what you are doing.

Calling Web Services Asynchronously

The default method for calling Web services is synchronous, which means that the client program makes the request and then waits for the response before proceeding. What if the Web service is slow? It may be a slow Internet connection, or a service that is inherently time consuming, such as searching a huge database of airline flights. In any case, you probably do not want your client program to be "frozen" while waiting for the Web service to respond. The answer lies in calling the service asynchronously. This involves the **Begin*XXXX*()** and **End*XXXX*()** methods that I mentioned in Chapter 22. The procedure in broad outline is as follows:

1. Create a callback method that calls the **End*XXXX*()** method, where *XXXX* is the name of the Web service method. The **End*XXXX*()** method returns the results from the Web service.

2. Create an **AsyncCallback** object that wraps the callback method that you created in Step 1.

3. Invoke the Web service method using the **Begin*XXXX*()** method, passing it the **AsyncCallback** object created in Step 2 (along with any other parameters needed by the service).

After Step 3, your program can go about other tasks. When the Web service method finally completes, it invokes the callback method that you created in Step 1. This in turn calls the service's **End*XXXX*()** method and retrieves the information returned by the method. To demonstrate this, the first step is to create a "slow" Web service.

Creating a Slow Web Service

For demonstration purposes, it is easy to create a Web service that is slow simply because it is designed to be slow. It uses a method called **Sleep()**, part of the **System.Threading** namespace, that pauses the program for a specified number of milliseconds. The service will be designed so the client can specify the length of the pause.

Start by creating a new Web Service project named MySlowService. Open the Service1.asmx file and add the code shown in Listing 23.4 (some of the code will already be present in the file).

Listing 23.4 The method for mimicking a slow Web service.

```
Imports System.Web.Services
Imports System.Threading
```

```
<WebService(Namespace:="http://pgacon.com/webservices/")> _
Public Class Service1
  Inherits System.Web.Services.WebService

  <WebMethod()> _
  Public Function Delay(ByVal msec As Long) As String

    Thread.Sleep(msec)
    Return "You paused " & msec.ToString & " milliseconds."

  End Function

End Class
```

Note that I am using the **<WebService>** tag to set the service's namespace; you use the development namespace or your own namespace in your own projects.

At this point, the Web service is complete, and you should test it using the technique described earlier in this chapter. To reiterate, save the project files, then create an IIS virtual directory for the Web service's directory, and finally (with your Web browser) navigate to **http://localhost/*VirtualDirectoryName*/Service1.asmx**. After you have confirmed that the service is working properly, close the project in preparation for creating the asynchronous client project.

Creating the Asynchronous Client

After closing the Web service project, start a new Windows application project called AsynchClient. Use the Project | Add Web Reference command, as described earlier in this chapter, to add a reference to the MySlowService Web service to the project.

The program's visual interface is quite simple. The four controls that are required are described here:

- A Timer control, all properties at default values.
- A Button control: **Text** = Call Service; **Name** = btnCall
- A TextBox control: **Text** = 5000; **Name** = txtDelay
- A Label control: **Text** = Delay in milliseconds
- A second Label control: **Text** = (blank string); **Name** = lblOutput

The next step is to write the callback procedure. The rules that this procedure must follow are that it take one argument of type **IAsyncResult** and that it not return a value—in other words, it must be a **Sub** procedure. In this procedure, call the service's **End*XXXX*()** method, which will return the result from the Web service. The code for the demo program's callback is shown in Listing 23.5. Note the use of a **Try...Catch** block. The reason for this will be explained soon. You also need to declare a variable to reference the Web service at the global level:

```
Dim SlowService As localhost.Service1
```

Listing 23.5 The callback procedure for the asynchronous service call.

```
Public Sub TheCallBack(ByVal ar As IAsyncResult)

  Try
    Dim reply As String
    reply = SlowService.EndDelay(ar)
    lblOutput.Text = reply
    Timer1.Enabled = False
  Catch ex As Exception
    lblOutput.Text = "The Web service timed out."
  End Try

End Sub
```

Calling the service asynchronously is a little bit more complicated. First you must create an instance of **AsyncCallback** that contains information about your callback procedure—specifically, its address, obtained with the **AddressOf** operator. This is the information used to call the callback procedure. The syntax is as follows:

```
Dim name As New IAsyncCallback(AddressOf callbackproc)
```

For the demo program, you will write the following (I'll explain where to put this code in a minute):

```
Dim cb As New IAsyncCallback(AddressOf TheCallBack)
```

The next statement you need will actually call the service, using the **Begin*XXXX*()** method. This method is passed all the parameters that the Web service method requires plus a reference to the **IAsyncCallback** object created previously. There is a final parameter that is not being used here, so pass the value **Nothing**. The code will look like this:

```
Dim ar As IAsyncResult = SlowService.BeginDelay(Val(txtDelay.Text), _
        cb, Nothing)
```

After this line is executed, the Web service has been called and, when the service returns, your callback procedure will be called automatically. What does the program do in the meanwhile? It depends on your needs. In many cases, the program really does not have anything else to do except wait for the result. However, you do not want to wait forever, but would like to define a waiting period after which the program will abort the service call and display a message to the user such as "Sorry—try again later." One way to do this is to use the **AsyncWaitHandle.WaitOne()** method of the **IAsyncResult** object that was returned by the call to **BeginXXXX()**. Call this method, passing it the number of milliseconds you want to wait, as shown here for a 5,000-millisecond wait:

```
ar.AsyncWaitHandle.WaitOne(5000, False)
```

This method returns after the specified wait. Then, test the **IsCompleted** property to determine whether the service has returned. If this property returns False, you know the service has not returned and you can call the service's **Abort()** method to abort the service call. Calling **Abort()** raises an exception, and you catch this exception in the callback function.

Another way to implement a "time out" is to use the Timer control. When the service is called, set the timer's interval to the desired time out period and enable it. In the **Timer_Tick()** event procedure, call the service's **Abort()** method and catch the resulting exception. This technique, using a Timer control, is used in the demo program. All this code is contained in the **Click()** event procedure for the demo program's Button control, as shown in Listing 23.6.

Listing 23.6 Code in the Click() event procedure calls the service asynchronously and waits for it to complete.

```
Private Sub btnCall_Click(ByVal sender As System.Object, _
    ByVal e As System.EventArgs) Handles btnCall.Click

  SlowService = New localhost.Service1()
  Dim cb As New AsyncCallback(AddressOf TheCallBack)

  lblOutput.Text = "Waiting for the Web service..."

  Dim ar As IAsyncResult = SlowService.BeginDelay(Val(txtDelay.Text), _
      cb, Nothing)

  ' Change this value for different timeout periods.
  Dim wait as Integer = 3000
  Timer1.Interval - wait
  Timer1.Enabled = True

End Sub
```

When you run the program, enter in the text box the amount of time that you want the Web service to take, then click the button. If the Web service delay is shorter than the timeout delay specified in the program, the service will complete and the program will display a message like that shown in Figure 23.8. Otherwise, the Web service will be aborted and a message to that effect will be displayed.

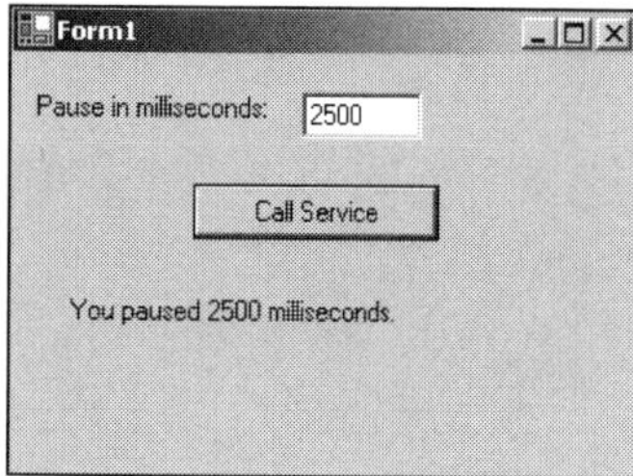

Figure 23.8
Testing the asynchronous Web service client.

Note that if you want your program to do something during the waiting period, you cannot use the technique of calling the **WaitOne()** method. Rather, you must use the Timer control, as was done in the example program.

Web References and Discovery Files

Unlike with a resource that is located on your local computer, there is no obvious way to find out about the presence of a Web service that may exist on a server halfway across the country. The disconnected nature of Web services brings up two related questions:

1. How do I find out about Web services published by others?
2. How do I publish my Web service so that others can use it?

Related to these questions is the way in which the Web References dialog box in Visual Studio works. Let's look at that first.

Discovery Files

When you select Add Web Reference from the Project menu, the Add Web Reference dialog box is displayed (shown earlier in Figure 23.4). Then, clicking the Web References On Local Web Server link calls up information on all the local references. Where does this information come from? The answer lies in so-called *discovery* files. When you create a Web service, or add a reference to a Web service to a project, you'll see a file with the .disco extension in the Solution Explorer. A discovery file uses XML format to provide certain information about the service, most importantly identifying its contract (WSDL) file and the service source code (ASMX) file. In general, each directory that contains a Web service will also contain a discovery file that points to the service's contract file; the discovery file will be named *xxxx*.disco, where *xxxx* is the name of the Web service. The server will also have a "master" discovery file that is used to find all the individual discovery files on the server. This master file is located in the virtual root and is named default.vsdisco. Visual Studio takes care of creating and managing discovery files, and also provides ways to "hide" a Web service if you do not want to make it publicly available. You can refer to the Visual Studio documentation for information on how to do this.

Thus, when you enable Web References On Web Local Server in the Add Web Reference dialog box, a request is made to the local Web server, which is in turn handed off to ASP.NET. Starting with the master discovery file, the process examines all the DISCO files on the local server and, based on this information, displays a list of locally available services from which you can choose.

Likewise, if you know the URL of a remote server, you can type it into the Address box in the Add Web Reference dialog box and then click the adjacent arrow. Visual Studio will look for default.vsdisco on the specified server and use the same process to list any Web services that the remote server makes available. This is fine if you know the URL for a remote service, but you may not. What then? That's my next topic.

UDDI

Universal Description Discovery and Integration (UDDI) is a technology that has been proposed as a means for discovering and publishing Web services. UDDI provides a global registry where providers can publish information about Web services that they make available. In this context, the term *Web service* is used in a broader sense than referring only to the type of service that has been covered in this chapter. With UDDI, a "Web service" can be nothing more than a site that provides travel listings. Microsoft, IBM, and Ariba jointly maintain the UDDI registry. As of this writing, the UDDI project is in its early stages, but it shows a lot of promise. You can find more information at **www.uddi.org**.

For the Visual Studio developer, the Add Web Reference dialog box provides a way to use UDDI to locate Web services. When you first display this dialog box, two UDDI links are available, one to find "test" services that you can use during development, and the other to find "real" Web services. When you click either of these links, you are asked to enter the name of the company providing the service. Then, follow the prompts to locate a specific service.

Publishing Your Web Service

You can publish your Web service by entering the relevant information into the UDDI directory. To do so, go to **www.uddi.org/register.html**. The first step is to choose a node, with the current choices being IBM and Microsoft. Because the various nodes have the same registration information, this choice does not have any real impact. Then, follow the prompts to enter the information for your service. You are required to register with a username and password, which you will need should you ever want to remove or modify your information.

Passing Objects to and from Web Services

The Web service examples you have seen so far are rather simple in terms of the information that is passed to and returned from the service: strings, individual numbers, and so on. Is this all you can do? Not at all—in fact, much of the real power of Web services comes from the fact that you can pass essentially any object from a client to a service, and back from the service to the client. For example, consider a Web service that lets the user search for books by topic. The Web service can open the relevant database, perform the search, and place the matching records in a **DataTable** object. Then, that **DataTable** can be returned to the client and used as needed—for example, by binding it to a DataGrid control.

How does this work? At the server end of the process, the object to be returned—in this case a **DataTable**—is *serialized* into XML format. The resulting XML is enclosed in the SOAP message that is returned to the client, where the proxy class reverses the procedure and converts the XML into an instance of the object that the client program can use. As you might imagine, serializing an object such as a **DataTable** into XML is a complex process, but fortunately the details need not concern you because ASP.NET takes care of all the details. There are really no "tricks" to this. You only need to define a Web service that returns an object, and write a client that makes use of the object. This works both ways—objects can be passed as parameters to Web services.

Summary

Web services provide a way for you to create programming functionality and make it available remotely via the Web. At one level, a Web service is nothing more than a method that can accept parameters from the calling program and returns a result that can be anything from a single number to a complex object such as a DataTable. By employing standard Internet data-transfer protocols, Web services avoid potential problems with firewalls and other security measures. If you create such methods as Web services, they can be made available from a central location and accessed from anywhere on the Web.

Chapter 24
Developing Customized Web Controls

ASP.NET provides quite a few controls for you to use on your Web pages. Occasionally, however, none of these controls will meet your needs. You can then design your own Web control that is precisely tailored to the requirements of your program. Custom Web controls, called user controls, can present a customized visual interface and can also have their own properties and events. This chapter shows you how to create customized Web controls by using Visual Studio .NET.

User Control Basics

A user control is made up of ASP.NET code and HTML. In some ways, it is like an ASP.NET page, and in fact you can easily convert an existing ASP.NET page into a user control (as will be covered later in this chapter). By encapsulating HTML and ASP.NET code in a separate unit, user controls provide numerous advantages, including improved code reusability, easier program maintenance, and reduced errors. User controls are compiled the first time they are requested and cached in the server's memory for rapid response on later requests.

Employing user controls involves two parts: creating them and using them. The creating part is easy, because a user control is simply some HTML and/or ASP.NET code saved in a separate file with the .ascx extension. The HTML can contain just about anything you want, including ASP.NET controls. EnterPhone.ascx in Listing 24.1 shows a very simple example, a control that is made up of some text and an ASP.NET TextBox control displayed between two horizontal lines (that are created with the **<hr>** HTML tag).

What About the #include Directive?

Readers who have programmed with earlier versions of ASP might be wondering about the **#include** directive, which appears to do the same thing as a user control. With a tag such as

```
<!-- #include "mycode.asp" -->
```

you could insert any existing ASP file into another one. This certainly worked as a means of reusing code, but it could become a maintenance nightmare. User controls provide an easier and less troublesome technique, and should always be used instead of **#include**.

Listing 24.1 EnterPhone.ascx is a simple user control.

```
<hr><p>Please enter your phone number:
<asp:TextBox id="Phone" runat="server" /></p><hr>
```

To use a user control in an ASP.NET page, you must follow two steps. First, you must register it in your page using the **@Register** directive. The syntax is as follows:

```
<%@ Register tagprefix="prefix" TagName="tagname" Src="pathname"%>
```

Prefix is the prefix that will be used for this control. ***Tagname*** is the name by which the control will be referred to. ***Pathname*** is the path and name of the ASCX file where the control is located.

After the control is registered, you display it with a tag in the page's HTML, as follows:

```
<tagprefix:tagname runat="server"/>
```

The tag should be placed within a form as defined by **<form runat="server">. . .</form>** tags. An example is presented in Listing 24.2. In this code, I have used my initials, "pga", for the prefix. You can use any prefix you want, but generally the prefix is used to organize controls. This is a very simple Web page, with the body consisting of only the control from Listing 24.1. Its appearance in a browser is shown in Figure 24.1.

Listing 24.2 UserControlDemo1.aspx displays the user control defined in Listing 24.1.

```
<%@ Register TagPrefix="pga" TagName="GetPhoneControl"
    src="EnterPhone.ascx" %>
<html>
<body>
<form runat="server">
<pga:GetPhoneControl id="MyPhone" runat="server"/>
</form>
</body>
</html>
```

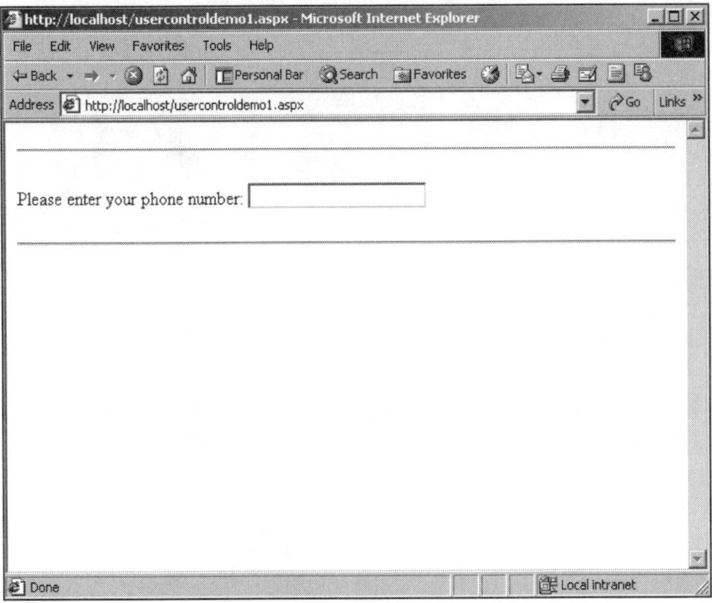

Figure 24.1
The user control EnterPhone.ascx displayed in a Web page.

This basic user control is not all that useful. You need to add some properties and code for it to show its true potential.

User Control Properties

A user control can have properties. You create a property by placing the usual code—that is, a property procedure—inside **<SCRIPT>** tags in the control. (A user control can also use the code behind feature, and I will cover that soon.) To illustrate defining a property for a user control, I will add a read-only type **Boolean** property called **IsValid** to the EnterPhone control. I will also add a property **PhoneNum** for the phone number itself. The latter property will be connected to the **Text** property of the TextBox control in the user control. What about the **IsValid** property? In order to validate the text that the user has entered, to ensure that it is a valid phone number, the control will use a RegularExpressionValidator control. You learned about this control in Chapter 21, and you can turn to that chapter if needed for the details. In brief, this control compares the contents of another control, in this case a TextBox, against a regular expression (a regular expression is a pattern that defines certain characteristics that a string must have). Validation succeeds only if there is a match. A phone number must have the form *xxx-xxx-xxxx*, where each x represents a digit, and the regular expression to match this is as follows:

```
\d\d\d-\d\d\d-\d\d\d\d
```

Thus, the tag to define the validation control that we will use is shown in the following snippet:

```
<asp:RegularExpressionValidator
     ASPClass="RegularExpressionValidator"
     EnableClientScript="false"
     id="PhoneValidator" runat="server"
     ControlToValidate="Phone"
     ValidationExpression="\d\d\d-\d\d\d-\d\d\d\d"
     Display="None">
     </asp:RegularExpressionValidator>
```

The plan is to give the user control a read-only property that in turn uses the RegularExpressionValidator control to determine whether the TextBox has a valid phone number in it and return True or False accordingly. The code for the new user control, called EnterPhone2.ascx, is shown in Listing 24.3. This user control is presented as an integrated file in which the HTML and the code are together. You can also design user controls using .NET's code behind capability, and I'll show you how later in the chapter.

Listing 24.3 EnterPhone2.ascx has two properties and a validation control added.

```
<script language="vb" runat="server">

public readonly property IsValid() As boolean
  get
    return PhoneValidator.IsValid
  end get
end property

public property PhoneNum() As string
  get
    return Phone.Text
  end get
  set(byval v as string)
    Phone.Text = v
  end set

end property

</script>
<asp:RegularExpressionValidator
     ASPClass="RegularExpressionValidator"
     EnableClientScript="false"
     id="PhoneValidator" runat="server"
     ControlToValidate="Phone"
     ValidationExpression="\d\d\d-\d\d\d-\d\d\d\d"
```

```
    Display="None">
    </asp:RegularExpressionValidator>

<hr><p>Please enter your phone number:
<asp:TextBox id="Phone" runat="server" /></p><hr>
```

To make use of the new features of this user control, a page should check the **IsValid** property at the appropriate time, such as when the page is being submitted. If the return value is True, you can be confident that a valid phone number was entered, which can then be retrieved from the **PhoneNum** property. Otherwise, the program must take appropriate action, such as displaying an "invalid phone number" message to the user. The ASP.NET page in Listing 24.4 demonstrates these steps. When you run this page and enter a valid phone number, you'll see something like Figure 24.2.

Listing 24.4 UserControlDemo2.aspx demonstrates the improved user control.

```
<%@ Register TagPrefix="pga" TagName="GetPhoneControl"
    src="EnterPhone2.ascx" %>
<html>
<script language="vb" runat="server">
public sub Submit_Click(Sender as Object, e as EventArgs)
  if MyPhone.IsValid then
    Response.Write("You entered a valid phone number: " & _
        MyPhone.PhoneNum)
  else
    Response.Write("That is not a valid phone number.")
  end if
end sub
</script>
<body>
<form runat="server">
<pga:GetPhoneControl id="MyPhone" runat="server"/>
<asp:Button Text="Submit" OnClick="Submit_Click" runat="server"/>
</form>
</body>
</html>
```

To assign an initial value to a property, place an attribute in the control's tag using the following format:

```
propertyname="initialvalue"
```

For example, the following tag would display the EnterPhone control with a phone number initially displayed:

```
<pga:GetPhoneControl id="MyPhone" PhoneNum="555-555-1212" runat="server"/>
```

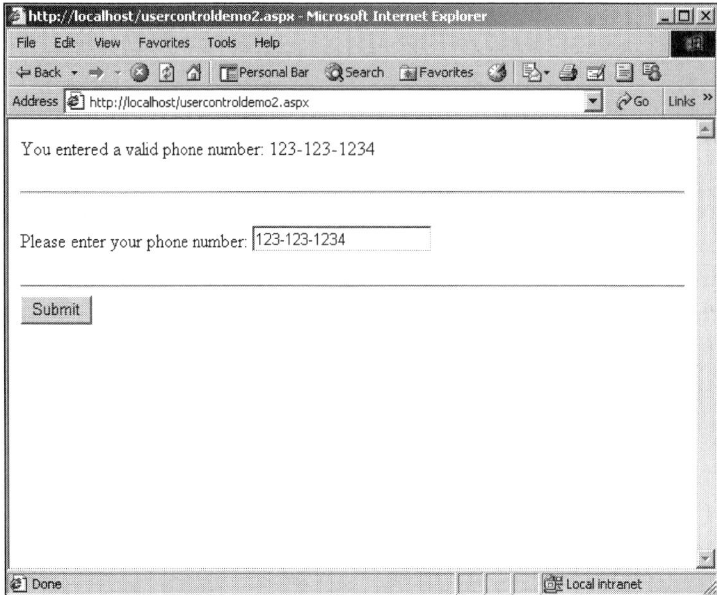

Figure 24.2
The user has entered a valid phone number.

Events in User Controls

So far, you have seen that a user control can have properties. This is very important, but often it is not enough. Particularly with more involved user controls, you will want them to handle events as well. An event in a user control can be contained within the control, or it can be "bubbled up" up to the containing page (or both). For example, you could create a data entry user control that includes several TextBox controls as well as a Clear button control that clears all the data entry fields when clicked. This is an example of an event being handled within the control. You could also "send" that event to the containing page, permitting it to respond if needed.

Some of the events that you can respond to in a user control are inherited from the **Control** class. These are **Init()**, **Load()**, **DataBinding()**, **PreRender()**, and **UnLoad()**. If your control needs to respond to any of these events, you will have to override them in your code. Many user controls do not make use of these events at all.

Other events you can work with are associated with the individual ASP.NET controls that are part of your user control. Thus, if your user control contains a Button control, you have available all of the events detected by the Button control, such as **Click()**. To connect these events with code in your control, follow these two steps:

1. Write the event handler. This is a **Sub** procedure that has exactly the same signature (number and types of arguments) as required by the event. In most cases, this is **sender as Object, e as EventArgs**. The name of the procedure can be anything you like within

the normal VB naming rules. For the sake of code readability, however, the traditional *controlname_eventname* convention is often used.

2. In the tag that defines the ASP.NET control, connect the event to the event handler written in Step 1 by including an attribute of the following format:

```
OnEventName="procedurename"
```

For example, the following tag defines an ASP.NET Button control whose **Click()** event will be handled by the procedure named **Clear_Click()**:

```
<asp:Button Text="Clear" OnClick="Clear_Click" runat="server"/>
```

Listing 24.5 demonstrates by adding a Clear button to the EnterPhone control. The additions to the code, as compared with EnterPhone2.ascx, include the **Clear_Click()** procedure and a tag for the ASP.NET Button control. You can test this modified control by changing the **<Register>** tag of UserControlDemo2.aspx to point at EnterPhone3.ascx.

Listing 24.5 EnterPhone3.ascx adds an internal event to the EnterPhone control.

```
<script language="vb" runat="server">

public readonly property IsValid() As boolean
  get
    return PhoneValidator.IsValid
  end get
end property

public property PhoneNum() As string
  get
    return Phone.Text
  end get
  set(byval v as string)
    Phone.Text = v
  end set

end property

public sub Clear_Click(sender as Object, e as EventArgs)
  Phone.Text = ""
end sub

</script>
<asp:RegularExpressionValidator
     ASPClass="RegularExpressionValidator"
     EnableClientScript="false"
```

```
        id="PhoneValidator" runat="server"
        ControlToValidate="Phone"
        ValidationExpression="\d\d\d-\d\d\d-\d\d\d\d"
        Display="None">
        </asp:RegularExpressionValidator>

<hr><p>Please enter your phone number:
<asp:TextBox id="Phone" runat="server" />
<asp:button Text="Clear" OnClick="Clear_Click" runat="server"/>
</p><hr>
```

To bubble an event up to the containing page, a user control calls the **RaiseBubbleEvent()** method. The syntax is as follows:

```
RaiseBubbleEvent(sender as Object, e as EventArgs)
```

Then, the containing page (or other parent container) can detect the event with the **OnBubbleEvent()** handler, which has the following syntax:

```
Protected Function OnBubbleEvent(sender as Object, e as EventArgs) _
    As Boolean
```

The return value of the **OnBubbleEvent()** handler determines whether the event continues bubbling further up the hierarchy (return value = False) or whether bubbling stops (return value = True). The container can do one of three things with a bubbled event:

- Ignore it by not implementing the **OnBubbleEvent()** handler. The event will continue to bubble up the hierarchy (if additional levels exist).
- It handles the event but continues bubbling it by returning False from the **OnBubbleEvent()** handler.
- It handles the event and stops the bubbling by returning True from the **OnBubbleEvent()** handler.

When you are designing an application with user controls and various levels of containment, the capability to bubble events can provide a great deal of flexibility to your application.

Code Behind in User Controls

So far, I have been presenting user controls as integrated ASCX files that contain both the HTML and the ASP.NET code. You can also use Visual Studio's code behind approach, where the HTML and the code are located in separate files. The end result is the same, but some programmers find the use of code behind to be more convenient. To use code behind, create a separate file that contains all of the control's code, and save this file with the .vb extension. Specifically, this file must do the following:

- Import the required namespaces **System.Web.UI** and **System.Web.UI.WebControls** as well as any other namespaces that the control requires.
- Define a public class that inherits from the **UserControl** class.
- Declare each event handler as **Public**.

Also, in the class, you must declare a public variable of the appropriate type for each of the ASP.NET controls (if any) that the user control contains. The variable names must match the **ID** attribute of each control. For example, if your user control contains an ASP.NET Calendar control with an **ID** of **cal**, you would declare a variable as follows:

```
Public cal As Calendar
```

Within the code behind file, you will use the name **cal** to reference the Calendar control.

The remainder of the user control, namely the HTML, remains in an ASCX file. To connect the ASCX file to its code behind file, you use the **codebehind** and **inherits** attributes in the **<Control>** tag at the start of the ASCX file. The syntax is as follows:

```
<%@ Control Inherits="classname" CodeBehind="filename" %>
```

Classname is the name of the class that you defined in the code behind file, and ***filename*** is the name of the file itself.

To demonstrate, the following section takes the user control that was presented as a single file in Listing 24.5 and splits it into two files using the code behind feature. Listing 24.6 shows the code behind portion of the control, and Listing 24.7 shows the HTML portion. You can test this version of the control by modifying the **<REGISTER>** tag in the file UserControlDemo2.aspx in Listing 24.4 to point at EnterPhone_cb.ascx.

Listing 24.6 EnterPhone_cb.vb is the code behind file for the user control.

```
Imports System
Imports System.Web.UI
Imports System.Web.UI.WebControls

public class EnterPhone
   Inherits UserControl

public PhoneValidator as RegularExpressionValidator
public phone as TextBox
public clearbtn as Button

public readonly property IsValid() As boolean
  get
    return PhoneValidator.IsValid
```

```
    end get
  end property

  public property PhoneNum() As string
    get
      return Phone.Text
    end get
    set(byval v as string)
      Phone.Text = v
    end set

  end property

  public sub Clear_Click(sender as Object, e as EventArgs)
    Phone.Text = ""
  end sub

  end class
```

Listing 24.7 EnterPhone_cb.ascx contains the HTML for the User Control.

```
<%@ Control inherits="EnterPhone" codebehind="EnterPhone_cb.vb" %>
<asp:RegularExpressionValidator
     ASPClass="RegularExpressionValidator"
     EnableClientScript="false"
     id="PhoneValidator" runat="server"
     ControlToValidate="Phone"
     ValidationExpression="\d\d\d-\d\d\d-\d\d\d\d"
     Display="None">
     </asp:RegularExpressionValidator>

<hr><p>Please enter your phone number:
<asp:TextBox id="Phone" runat="server" />
<asp:button Text="Clear" id="clearbtn" OnClick="Clear_Click" runat="server"/>
</p><hr>
```

Converting ASP.NET Pages to User Controls

You have seen how user controls are similar to ASP.NET pages in many respects. This means that it is fairly easy to convert an existing Web Form page into a user control, a technique that can be useful if you have already encapsulated some needed functionality in a Web Form and now want to make use of it as a control.

The first step in converting a Web Form to a user control is to remove all **<HTML>**, **<BODY>**, and **<FORM>** tags from the code. These tags are not permitted inside a user control.

The second step is required only if the page was associated with a code behind file. You must place a **<@CONTROL>** directive at the start of the file to identify the class and the file name of the code behind. If the original page has a **<@PAGE>** directive, the **<@CONTROL>** directive will replace it.

Finally, save the file with the .ascx extension to identify it as a user control.

Summary

Support for user controls provides the VB.NET Web programmer with a lot of additional flexibility. You can define custom controls that contain HTML, ASP.NET controls, properties, and events, and then use these controls in your Web Form pages just like you use the controls that are part of .NET. The ability to encapsulate functionality in this manner provides advantages in many areas, including code reusability, program maintenance, and error prevention.

Chapter 25

Debugging and Deploying Your Applications

Writing a Visual Basic .NET program is not enough. You must also test and debug it to ensure that it works properly, and in most cases, you must distribute it to your end users. These are the topics of this chapter.

Debugging Your Programs

A *bug* is a code error that prevents your program from operating correctly. I am not talking about an error that prevents the program from executing or that can be caught by Visual Basic's error-trapping mechanisms—these are called *runtime errors* or *exceptions* and were covered in Chapter 5. Rather, a bug is a logical mistake in the program's source code that causes the program to behave incorrectly. Here are some examples of the kinds of problems bugs can cause:

- A financial program that calculates and displays incorrect loan payments
- A graphics program that applies improper colors to images
- Any program that does not respond properly to user commands

These are just a few examples; there are plenty more, and I can guarantee that you will run into some of them. Dealing with bugs is a two-part process that begins with avoiding them in the first place. No, it isn't feasible to avoid all bugs in all programs (at least I haven't been able to), but you can greatly decrease their frequency with good programming practice. (As you have probably noticed by now, teaching and encouraging good programming practices are among the major goals of this book.)

Here are some of the most essential programming guidelines to follow when it comes to avoiding program bugs:

- Always use Option Explicit, so variable declaration is required. This prevents the pernicious "misspelled variable name" error that is perhaps the most common cause of bugs in Visual Basic.
- Follow the tenets of object-oriented programming. By encapsulating your code in classes, you decrease the chance of bugs while also making them easier to track down and fix.
- Divide your code into relatively small, manageable procedures (methods). Large, complex procedures are more prone to bugs, and more difficult to debug, than short, simple ones.
- Use global and public variables sparingly. Stick with local variables within procedures and methods as much as possible, resorting to global and public variables only when unavoidable.
- Use the proper data type for your program's data. Using type **Integer** for certain calculations can result in rounding errors, which can cause bugs.

Regardless of how carefully you work, and how religiously you follow these guidelines, some bugs are likely to crop up in your programs—particularly as you move into more complex projects. Almost all bugs can be traced to one of two things: a program variable taking on an improper value, or program execution taking an unexpected path (or a combination of both). Visual Studio and Visual Basic provide debugging tools that help track down both kinds of problems.

Using the Debug Class

Debug is an abstract class that provides a set of members to aid you in your debugging. It is part of the **System.Diagnostics** namespace. The beauty of this class is that it is ignored when you create the final release version of your product, so you can use it freely without worrying about removing calls to **Debug** or compromising the performance of your final program.

Perhaps the most useful members of **Debug** are those that write information to Visual Studio's output window. As your program runs in Visual Studio, you can see what's going on in critical parts of the program. For example, you can display the value of variables and also simply display messages to identify the section of code that is executing. The **Debug.Write()** method has the following syntax:

```
Debug.Write(item)
```

If *item* is a type **String**, it is written to the output window. If *item* is a type **Object**, the result of its **ToString()** method is written. For example, placing the following statement in a procedure named **Calculate()** would provide evidence in the output window whenever execution enters the procedure:

```
Debug.Write("In Calculate procedure")
```

The **Debug.WriteLine()** method is identical to **Debug.Write()** except that each call places its output on a new line, whereas **Write()** does not start a new line. This line displays the value of the variable **Total** in the output window:

```
Debug.WriteLine("Total = " & Total.ToString())
```

Two related methods write their output only if a condition is True. The syntax is as follows:

```
debug.Write(condition, item)
debug.WriteLine(condition, item)
```

For example, this statement displays a message only if the variable **Count** is equal to 0:

```
Debug.WriteLine(count = 0, "Count is zero")
```

The Visual Studio output window is only one location where the **Debug** class can display information. Sending **Debug** output to other locations is based on the concept of *listeners*, which will be covered later in the chapter in the section on the **Trace** class.

The **Debug** class has a few additional members, as described in Table 25.1.

Table 25.1 Additional members of the Debug class.

Member	Description
IndentLevel	Specifies the number of indents that output is indented. The default is 0.
IndentSize	Specifies the number of spaces in an indent. The default is 4.
Indent()	Increases indentation by 1 indent.
Unindent()	Decreases indentation by 1 indent. Has no effect if Indent is already 0.
Assert(*condition*)	Outputs the call stack to the output window if *condition* is False.

The Call Stack

The Call Stack is a display of what procedures, or methods, have been called but not yet returned. For example, if **Sub Main()** calls **SubA()**, and then **SubA()** calls **SubB()**, the call stack is as follows:

- **Main**
- **SubA**
- **SubB**

The Call Stack is useful because it shows you not only where execution is at the time the stack is displayed, but how it got there.

Using the Trace Class

The **Trace** class is similar in most respects to the **Debug** class covered previously. It has the same members as were described in Table 25.1, and they are used in the same way. The difference is that **Trace** is functional in both debug and release versions of a program, whereas **Debug** is functional only in the debug version.

But how useful is this? When the final program is executing on its own, outside the Visual Studio environment, there is no output window for the **Trace** information to be displayed in. The answer lies in the use of *listeners* to direct output to other locations. Both the **Debug** and the **Trace** classes have a **Listeners** collection. By default, this collection contains one item, a **DefaultTraceListener** that directs output to the Visual Studio output window. You can include additional listeners as follows:

- Add a **TextWriterTraceListener** to direct output to an instance of the **TextWriter** class or to any stream.
- Add an **EventLogTraceListener** to direct output to an event log.

Here are some examples, which would work the same way for the **Debug** class. This statement directs output to the console:

```
Trace.Listeners.Add(New TextWriterTraceListener(System.Console.Out))
```

This code directs output to a file named TraceOutput.txt:

```
Dim OutFile As Stream = File.Create("TraceOutput.txt")
Dim NewListener As New TextWriterTraceListener(OutFile)
Trace.Listeners.Add(NewListener)
```

Tracing is automatically active within the Visual Studio environment. If you compile your program with the command-line compiler, you must include the switch **/d:Trace=True** on the compiler command line to activate tracing in the resulting executable.

Working with Breakpoints

A *breakpoint* causes program execution to pause when it reaches a specified line of code. You can set breakpoints on one or more lines of code in your program. When execution reaches a breakpoint, the program pauses and the line of code is highlighted in the code editor window (this is relevant only when you are executing within Visual Studio .NET, of course). While execution is paused, you can take several actions to help locate a program bug. I will describe these options soon.

To set a breakpoint, move the editing cursor to the line of code where you want execution to pause, then press F9. The line that a breakpoint has been set on is displayed with a

---

Breaking Program Execution

When you set a breakpoint on a line of code, execution pauses just *before* the statement on that line is executed. The statement where the breakpoint is located will be the first one executed when you continue execution.

---

different-colored background and a dot in the left margin. Press F9 again to remove the breakpoint from a line of code. You can set as many breakpoints as you need.

To clear all breakpoints from your program, press Ctrl+Shift+F9 or select Clear All Breakpoints from the Debug menu. Note that you cannot undo this command; your breakpoints are lost and can be reset only manually, one at a time. To temporarily disable all breakpoints, select Disable All Breakpoints from the Debug menu. Disabled breakpoints are displayed with a thin black border around them. Select Enable All Breakpoints to re-enable the breakpoints.

Another way to break program execution is based on the value of program variables rather than on specific code location. I'll explain this technique in the following section.

When a breakpoint is encountered, a Visual Basic program enters *break mode*. You can enter break mode manually while the program is executing by selecting Break All from the Debug menu or by clicking the Break All button on the toolbar. Entering break mode manually is useful when you realize you should have, but did not, set a breakpoint at a particular location in the code. If a Basic statement was executing at the moment, execution will pause at that statement. Quite often, however, no Basic statement will be executing; the program will be waiting for an event to occur. In this case, you cannot say "where" in your code execution halted, because the next Basic statement to be executed usually depends on the event that is received. As a result, the technique of entering break mode manually is of limited usefulness.

There are other ways of setting breakpoints, which you access by issuing the New Breakpoint command on the Debug menu or by pressing Ctrl+B. The New Breakpoint dialog box has four tabs in it, only one of which is likely to be useful to most programmers. This is the Function tab, shown in Figure 25.1, which lets you set a breakpoint at a specific location in a procedure. Make entries in this dialog box as follows:

- *Function*—The name of the procedure in which to break.
- *Line*—The number of the line at which to break.
- *Language*—Basic.
- *Character*—The character position on the line at which to break. Relevant only when you have multiple statements per line; otherwise leave set at 1.

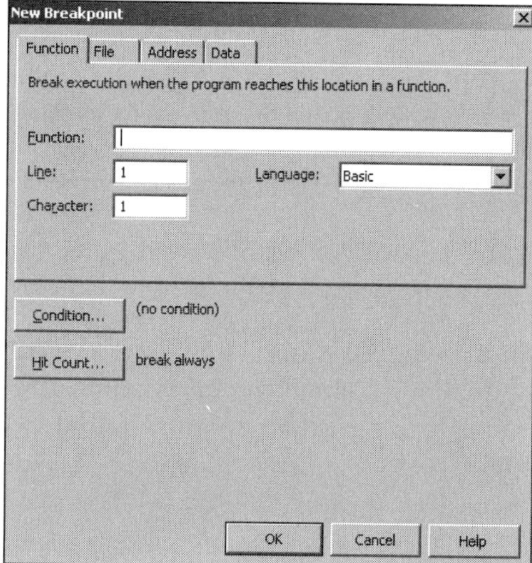

Figure 25.1
Setting a breakpoint at a location in a procedure.

You can set additional conditions on the break by using the Condition and Hit Count buttons in this dialog box. When you click the Condition button, you'll see the dialog box shown in Figure 25.2. Then, follow these steps:

- To break only if a condition is True, enter the condition (for example, x > y) in the Condition box and select the Is True option.
- To break only if the value of an expression has changed, enter the expression in the Condition box and select the Has Changed option.

Note that the conditions you enter here are applied along with the conditions entered on the Function tab. Thus, you could specify that execution break on the second line of the procedure **Foo()** only if X is greater than Y.

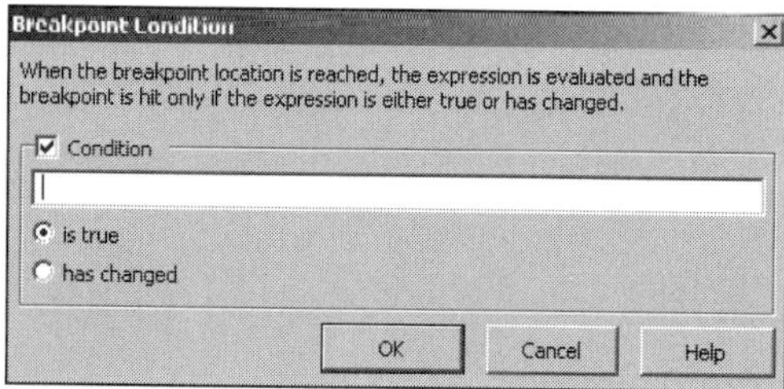

Figure 25.2
Setting an additional breakpoint condition.

While your program is paused at a breakpoint, you have the following execution commands available to you. They are located on the Debug menu, and are also represented by toolbar buttons:

- *Continue*—Resumes program execution with the next statement.
- *Stop Debugging*—Terminates program execution.
- *Restart*—Restarts the program. Selecting Restart has the same effect as selecting Stop Debugging followed by Run.

While a program is paused in break mode, you can track down bugs in a number of different ways. I will cover these methods in the following sections.

Using Watch Expressions

A *watch expression* is a Visual Basic expression whose value is monitored, or watched, during program debugging. A watch expression can be any Basic expression—a program variable, an object property, a function call, or a combination of these elements. You can use any of Visual Basic's mathematical and logical operators, as well as its built-in functions, to create a watch expression. As mentioned earlier, a prime cause of program bugs is a program variable or property taking on an inappropriate value. By setting a watch, you can keep an eye on the value of the variable or property to see if and when it changes. You use a watch expression by simply monitoring its value as the program runs. Visual Basic will display the expression value in the Watch window, which opens automatically when you define a watch expression. The displayed value is updated whenever the program enters break mode.

Another way to use a watch expression is to specify that the program enter break mode either when the value of the expression changes or when an expression becomes True. This technique was covered in the previous section of the chapter.

The program must be in break mode for you to set a watch expression. Then, select Debug | Windows | Watch and select one of the four available watch windows. These windows all work the same way and are provided as a means for you to organize and keep track of your watches. An empty watch window is shown in Figure 25.3. To add a watch, click the Name column and type in the variable name or expression you want to watch. Press Enter, and the other columns will display the current value and the type of the variable or expression. You can also drag a variable name from the code window and drop it in the watch window. If you use a variable name that is not in scope, the Value column will display a message to that effect. You can use object references in a watch window, but all the information you will see is the type of the object. To remove a watch, right-click and select Delete Watch from the context menu.

One valuable use of a watch is to modify the value of program variables during execution. While the program is paused, double-click the value of a variable in the window and change it to the desired new value. When you continue execution, the variable will have the new value.

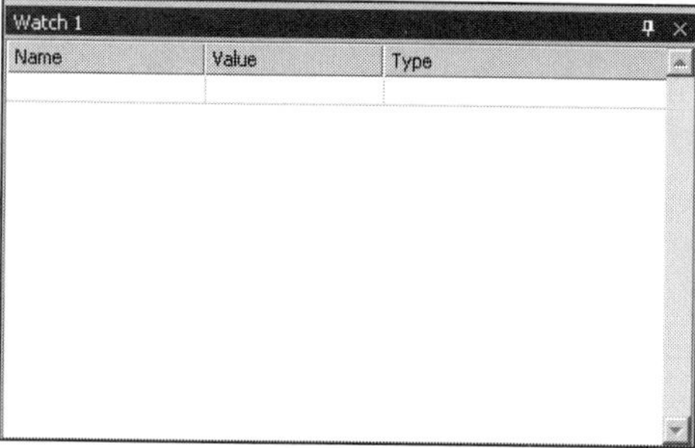

Figure 25.3
An empty watch window.

It is important to realize that variable scope is relevant to the watch window. When the program enters break mode, the window can display values for only those variables that are in scope.

Using Quick Watches

In some situations, a Quick Watch may be the most appropriate way to evaluate a variable or an expression. In break mode, right-click on a variable name in your source code and select Quick Watch from the context menu. The QuickWatch dialog box opens with the variable and its value and type displayed, as shown in Figure 25.4. Then, you can take the following steps:

- To evaluate a different variable or an expression, edit the entry in the Expression box, and then click Recalculate.
- To add the variable or expression to a regular watch window, click Add Watch.

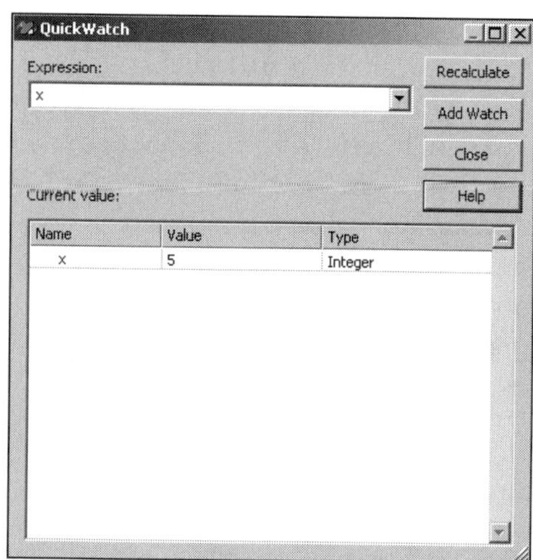

Figure 25.4
Using the QuickWatch dialog box.

Even-Quicker Watches

In break mode, you can rest the mouse cursor on the name of a variable in your code and a small window will open showing the current value of the variable.

- To change the value of a variable, edit the Value column.
- To close the QuickWatch dialog box, click Close.

Single-Stepping Your Program

When debugging a program, you are not limited to executing from breakpoint to breakpoint. You can also step your program so that it executes one statement at a time, which could be thought of as having a breakpoint on every line. The single-step command has three variants, whose actions differ depending on whether the program has not yet started or is paused at a breakpoint. These commands are summarized in Table 25.2.

Use of the single-step commands might proceed as follows:

1. Set a breakpoint on a line of code at the start of the section where you think the problem is located.
2. Start the program by pressing F5. It will run to the breakpoint and then pause.
3. Set up any needed watches.
4. Press F8 to execute the next statement. If the statement is a procedure call and you are sure the problem does not lie in the procedure, press Shift+F8 to execute the entire procedure. If you are already in a procedure and you are sure the problem does not lie in the procedure, press Ctrl+Shift+F8 to execute the remainder of the procedure.
5. Repeat as needed until finished.

Table 25.2 Visual Studio's single-step commands for debugging.

Command	When Program Has Not Yet Started	When Program Is Paused at Breakpoint	Shortcut Key
Step Into	Executes the first statement. If the first statement is a procedure call, pauses at the first statement in the procedure.	Executes the next statement. If the next statement is a procedure call, pauses at the first statement in the procedure.	F8
Step Over	Executes the first statement. If the first statement is a procedure call, executes all statements in the procedure, and pauses at the first statement following the procedure.	Executes the next statement. If next statement is a procedure call, executes all statements in the procedure and pauses at the first statement following the procedure.	Shift+F8

(continued)

Table 25.2 Visual Studio's single-step commands for debugging *(continued)*.

Command	When Program Has Not Yet Started	When Program Is Paused at Breakpoint	Shortcut Key
Step Out	Not available.	If execution is paused in a procedure, executes the remainder of the procedure and pauses at the first statement following the procedure.	Ctrl+Shift+F8

Deploying Your Applications

The final step in any software development project is usually the deployment of the finished application. This might involve creation of an installation program that can be put on CD-ROMs for sale or made available for download from a Web site. It might involve moving your Web application to the server where it will be hosted. In any case, you will be glad to hear that with .NET, program deployment is vastly easier than ever before. In fact, you can approach many deployment scenarios by simply copying the compiled project files to the target system. Gone are the days of complex install routines, problems with the Windows Registry, and the so-called "DLL hell" that could result from conflicts and confusion among DLL files.

It is important to note that .NET's simplicity of deployment is applicable only for projects that are "pure .NET" and use only the Visual Basic language and components from the .NET framework. Although it was not covered in this book, Visual Studio provides the capability to use legacy COM and COM+ objects in your projects, such as an ActiveX control that was developed with Visual Basic 6. In this case, some of the old deployment complexities come into play again, and you'll have to refer to the Visual Studio documentation for details on how they should be handled.

Deploying Web Applications

One way to deploy a Web application or a Web service is with Visual Studio's Copy Project command. This can work two ways. One uses the HTTP protocol and requires that the destination server have Microsoft FrontPage extensions installed. The other uses a file share and requires that the destination server be available on your LAN as a share. The end result is the same in both cases.

To copy a project, first load it into Visual Studio. You'll probably want to be sure that you have created a release build of the project for distribution. Then, select Copy Project from the Project menu to display the Copy Project dialog box, shown in Figure 25.5. Then select the Web access method you will be using and enter either the URL of the destination (for FrontPage access) or the full path to the destination (for file share access). Finally, choose

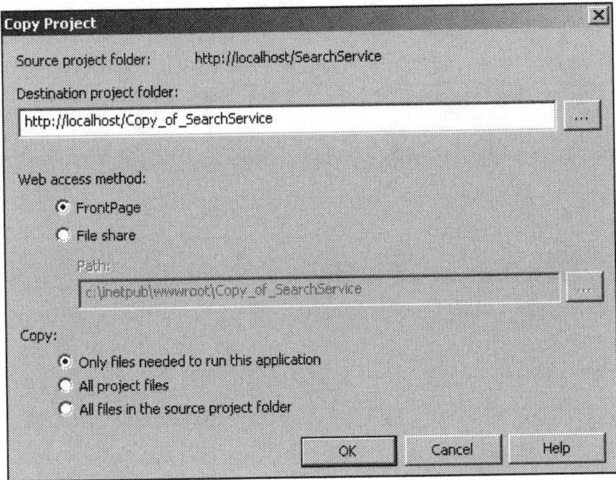

Figure 25.5
Deploying a Web application with the Copy Project command.

which files to copy and click OK. You may be prompted to log onto the server, and then the copy operation will proceed. There are three options for which files to copy:

- *Only Files Needed To Run This Application*—Copies the minimum set of files required for the application to execute.
- *All Project Files*—Copies all files needed to run the application plus all other files that are part of the project, including your source code files.
- *All Files In The Source Project Folder*—Copies all project files plus any non-project files that are located in the project folder.

The first option is usually appropriate. Select one of the other options only if you have a reason to make additional files available on the server. Remember that each Web application must be installed in a virtual directory under Internet Information Server. You might be able to do this yourself, or you might need to ask the Web site administrator.

The second way to deploy a Web application is to create a Web setup project. After building, the setup project is copied to the server computer and run, and it performs all the needed installation steps. Web setup projects create installation programs that use the Windows Installer, and they end in an .msi extension. The Windows Installer is widely used, including installation of all Microsoft programs, so you can be confident that your setup program will function properly on the target computer. The Windows Installer has several important features, including the capability to undo a partially complete setup and to repair an installed program.

To create a Web setup project, open the New Project dialog box and select Setup And Deployment Projects in the Project Types list. Then select Web Setup Project from the Templates selection. Finally, name your project and click OK.

When you are working on a setup project, Visual Studio provides you with a number of views. Each view is connected with a specific aspect of the setup program you are creating. To switch between views, select View | Editor and then select the desired view. The views are listed and described in Table 25.3. Note that some of these views, such as Registry and Custom Actions, are not used all that often for Web deployment of pure .NET applications.

The most important part of creating a Web setup project is defining the target file system. This means specifying the directories that will be created on the target system and the files that will be in those directories. You do this using the File System view, as shown in Figure 25.6. You can see that this view has two panes, similar to the Windows Explorer. The left pane lists the directories in the project, and the right pane lists the contents of whichever directory is selected in the left pane. By default, the project has three directories:

- *Global Assembly Cache Folder*—For shared assemblies (assemblies used by more than one Web application on the server).
- *Web Application Folder*—For the application's main files, such as ASPX and code behind files. This directory will be renamed on installation.
- *bin*—For application-specific assemblies (DLL files, and so on).

The first step is to specify any additional directories that your project requires, although many Web applications do not need more than the default ones. To do so, right-click a folder and then select Add | Web Folder. Enter the folder name and press Enter.

Next, you must add the project's files by selecting the target directory in the left panel of the File System view and then selecting Project | Add | File. You should add files in a specific

Table 25.3 Views in a Web setup project.

View	Shows This
File System	The files and assemblies that comprise your application. This includes .NET assemblies and files ending in an .aspx, .asmx, .asax, .ascx, .disco, or .config extension.
Registry	Additional Registry entries that your application requires.
File Types	Custom file types. You can associate file types (extensions) with specific programs so that if the user double-clicks a file the associated program is opened.
User Interface	Screens that the setup program will display. You can add custom screens here, such as splash screens, license agreements, and readme screens.
Custom Actions	Custom scripts or executables that the setup program should run.
Launch Conditions	Shows rules that must be satisfied before the installation can proceed, such as a requirement for a certain version of Windows.

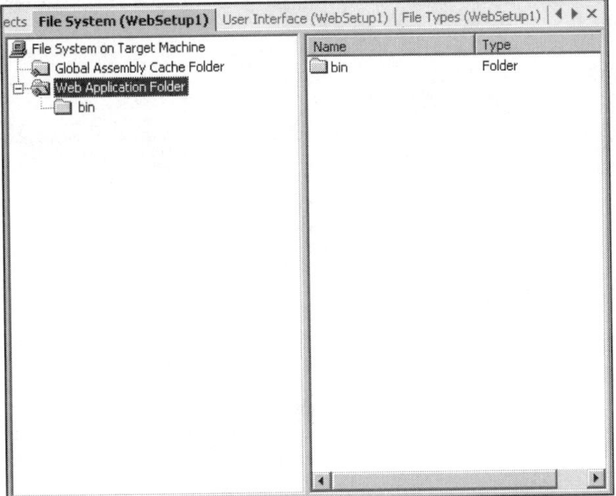

Figure 25.6
Defining the installation's file system.

order. First, add all .NET assemblies, Web forms, user controls, Web services, discovery files, and web.config files. As you add files, Visual Studio automatically identifies all file dependencies that your project requires and adds these files automatically. (This is why you should add files in a specific order, so these dependencies can be determined accurately.) Additionally, Visual Studio makes your application dependent on a file named dotnetfxredist_x86_enu.msm. This file is a merge module that contains the entire .NET framework installation, and it is required only if the target computer does not have .NET installed. You should remove this file if you know that the target computer already has the .NET framework installed because it is a big file.

The next step is to specify any additional files that are part of your project, such as Access database files, XML files, and help files.

At this point, your project may be finished, depending on whether you want to include any custom features.

Adding Launch Conditions

A launch condition is something that the Windows Installer checks for before it will proceed with installing your program. At a simple level, this can include such things as requiring a certain version of Windows to be installed and that the current user has administrative privileges. By default, Visual Studio adds one launch condition to every Web setup project, requiring that Internet Information Server version 4 or later be installed. You can see this in the Launch Conditions view, as shown in Figure 25.7. You can see in this figure that IIS Condition is selected in the Launch Conditions window and that the properties window shows that the **Condition** property is the following:

```
IISVERSION >= "#4"
```

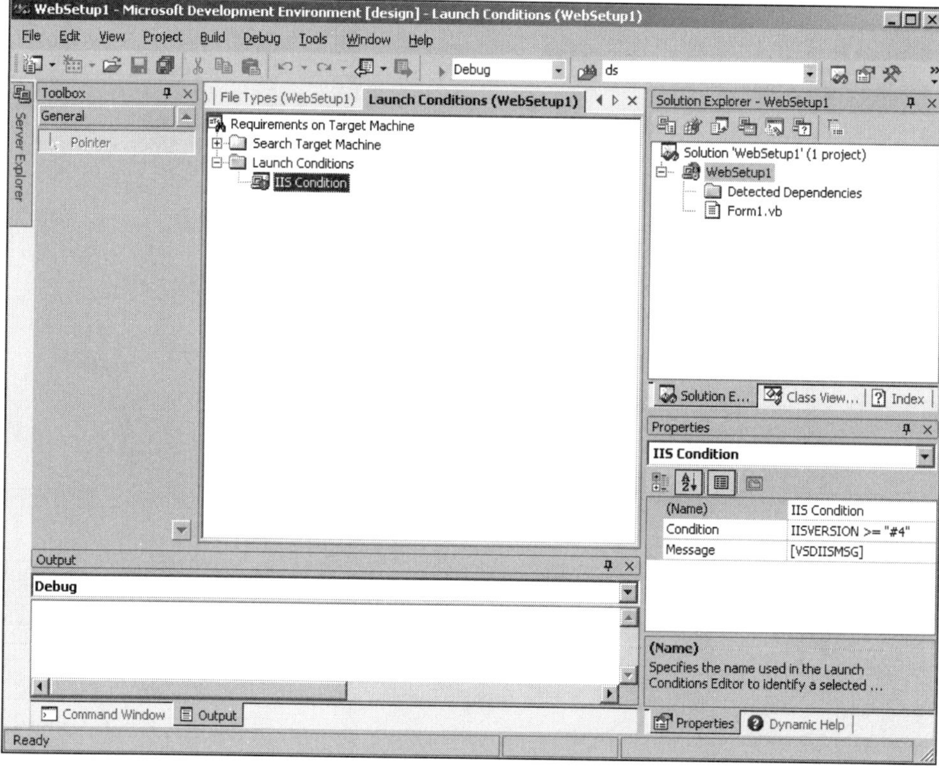

Figure 25.7
A default IIS Condition rule is added to every Web setup project.

This **Condition** property is evaluated by the Windows Installer when it starts, and if it evaluates as False the install is not permitted to continue. The condition has three parts:

- **IISVERSION** is a Windows Installer keyword that refers specifically to the version of Internet Information Server on the target machine.
- **>=** is the standard greater-than-or-equal-to operator.
- **"#4"** is the data to be compared against.

The Windows Installer has some other useful property keywords, as described in Table 25.4. This is not a complete list, but only the ones you are most likely to need.

To add a new launch condition, right-click the Launch Conditions folder in the main window, and then select Add Launch Condition. Specify a name for the condition; then in the properties window, enter the details of the condition that must be met, using the keywords presented previously.

Table 25.4 Keywords supported by the Windows Installer.

Keyword	Meaning
ADMINUSER	Will be True if the current user is logged on with administrative privileges.
WINDOWS9X	Version number of Windows if a non-NT version is installed (Windows 95,98, and Me).
WINDOWSNT	Version number of Windows if an NT version is installed (Windows NT, 2000, XP, and all Server/Datacenter versions).
SERVICEPACKLEVEL	The version of the latest installed Windows service pack.
WINDOWSBUILD	The Windows build number.

In addition to the keywords, you can specify a wide variety of custom conditions for a setup project. For example, you can require that certain files be present, that files meet requirements regarding their dates and lengths, that specific Registry entries are found, and so on. These advanced setup details are beyond the scope of this book, but if you need them you can find the relevant information in the Visual Studio documentation.

Building and Testing the Project

To build your setup project, select Build from the Build menu. You'll probably want to create a debug version during development and then a release version after you are ready to deploy the setup program. The build process will report any errors it finds.

Assuming the build completed with no errors, you need to test the setup program that was created. You must do this on a "naive" computer that does not have the application on it already. If the test computer has any of your program's components on it before you test the setup program, you will not know if the installed program works because the setup program did its job or because the components were already present.

Deploying Windows Applications

Like Web applications, most .NET Windows applications can be deployed by simply copying the relevant files to the target machine. However, Visual Studio does not have a Copy Project command for Windows applications, as it does for Web applications. This means that to deploy a Windows application by simply copying files, you will have to do it manually. Most people avoid this, however, because there are some extra factors to consider when deploying a Windows application, including whether program commands are placed on the user's Start menu and/or desktop. Although all these things can be done manually, it is a lot easier to create a setup project. To do so, open the New Project dialog box and then, from the Setup And Deployment Projects category, select Setup Project.

In many ways, creating a setup project for a Windows application is like creating one for a Web application. You have the same six views in Visual Studio, and you use the same procedures to add files and directories to the install, specify launch conditions, and add customized screens. Please read the section earlier in this chapter on creating Web setup projects for this information; I will not be repeating that information here.

A part of most installations is placing a shortcut to the program on the user's Start menu. You do this using the User's Programs Menu folder in the File System view. If you create a shortcut to a program (which I'll explain next) and drag it to this folder, the shortcut will appear on the user's Programs menu. If you want to create one or more levels of submenu for your program, you do so by creating subfolders within the User's Programs Menu folder. To add a subfolder to the User's Programs Menu folder (or to an existing subfolder), right-click the folder and select Add | Folder. Enter the name of the folder, which will also be the name of the submenu. For example, Figure 25.8 shows the File System view after adding a subfolder named My Programs to the User's Programs Menu.

To create a shortcut, you must have already added your program's files, particularly its EXE file, to the file system. Then, do the following:

1. Open the folder where the file is located, typically the Application folder.
2. Right-click the name of the file in the right pane and select Create Shortcut To *xxxx*, where *xxxx* is the name of the file. The shortcut will be added to the folder.
3. Rename the shortcut as you want it to appear on the user's menu.
4. Drag the shortcut to the User's Programs Menu folder or a subfolder that you have created.

If you want the shortcut on the user's desktop rather than on the Programs menu, drag it to the User's Desktop folder.

When you build the setup project, it will report any errors and warnings that occur. If successful, its output will be a file with the setup project's name and the .msi extension. This is the file you distribute. When it is executed, the Windows Installer starts and walks the user through the installations steps.

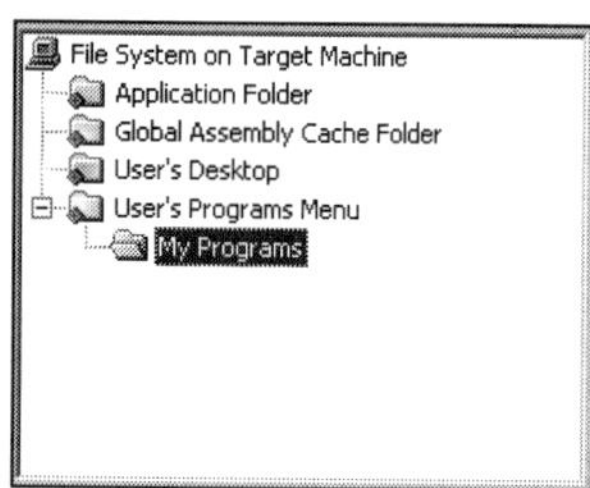

Figure 25.8
I added a subfolder named My Programs to the User's Programs Menu.

Summary

Many programmers do not enjoy debugging and deploying their applications. After all, the creating work goes into designing the program and writing the code, and that's where the fun and satisfaction are. Even so, debugging and deployment are essential steps in the development of any .NET application. Fortunately, Visual Studio provides you with a sophisticated set of tools for both tasks. The debugging tools let you track down the cause of just about any imaginable bug, and the deployment tools—particularly the two types of setup projects—make it a breeze to deploy both Web and Windows applications.

Appendix A
Changes in Visual Basic .NET

Like Visual Basic 6, Visual Basic .NET offers an easy-to-use WYSIWYG development environment. However, VB .NET contains many new features, changes to existing features, and even some features that have (or are about to) become obsolete.

New IDE Features

Visual Studio .NET introduces a common development environment for the primary languages within the .NET framework, such as VB, C++, and C#. The Integrated Development Environment (IDE) contains many new features related to this common environment, as well as productivity enhancements that stand on their own.

Home Page

The browser-like Home Page, which displays when Visual Studio .NET starts, provides links that let you edit your profile, access recently opened projects, open or create projects, or log a Visual Studio .NET bug report. The Home Page is completely customizable because it uses Dynamic HTML (DHTML) to define the layout.

Configuration Profiles

Within Visual Studio .NET, profiles provide the user with the ability to customize the development environment, including the keyboard scheme, window layout, help filter, and the items to show at startup. Standard profiles set options by type of developer, including Visual Studio, Visual Basic, C++, C#, Visual Interdev, and Student.

New Project Dialog Box

The New Project dialog box contains options for projects built with any language in the .NET framework, as well as specialized types of projects, such as setup, deployment, and database projects. The dialog box displays templates corresponding to the type of project selected.

Window Arrangement

Window docking and arrangement is more flexible. Multiple windows can dock in the same location. Visual Studio.NET then displays tabs so you can select the desired window.

Window Docking

Undocked windows are no longer Multiple Document Interface (MDI) children, so they even can reside outside the Visual Studio .NET main window.

Tabbed Child Windows

The MDI child windows for form layout, code, and help now appear with folder tabs along the top. The Home Page also appears as a tab.

Toolbox

The Toolbox stays hidden by default until you click on its tab to display it. Within the Toolbox, controls display vertically with an icon and a description. In addition, the tabs in the Toolbox change to correspond to the type of project.

Toolbox Clipboard Ring

Within the Toolbox, the Clipboard Ring contains items copied to your Clipboard, available to drag and drop into code.

Toolbox General Tab

Frequently used code fragments can reside in the General tab or other custom tabs. You can drag and drop code fragments from another source onto the General tab to store the code for later use.

Component Tray

Controls that are invisible at runtime resided on a form in VB 6. Now, they appear in the component tray, a new pane in the Designer window.

Task List

The Task List displays tasks to perform, such as syntax errors, build errors, and to-do items. Code generators add tasks automatically, and a developer can add a task manually by typing a comment. Clicking on a task in the Task List moves to the task's location in the code window.

Solution Explorer

The Solution Explorer replaces the Project Explorer in VB 6, and can include modules from more than one language, references (which are similar to the component references in VB 6), and other miscellaneous files.

Class View Window

The Class View window displays the classes, methods, and properties contained in a solution.

Server Explorer

The Server Explorer displays a tree view of the available server components. Dragging and dropping a server component from the Server Explorer onto the Designer automatically adds code to declare, instantiate, and set properties so the object is ready to use.

Code Editor Hide/Show

On the left side of the code editor window, you'll see plus and minus signs, which expand or collapse code elements. This feature can hide automatically generated code or code not relevant to the current task.

Breakpoints Window

The Breakpoints window displays all the breakpoints currently set with a checkbox to enable or disable them. Clicking on a breakpoint in the Breakpoint window moves to the location of the breakpoint in the code window.

OO

Visual Basic .NET introduces true object orientation with the addition of inheritance. Everything in Visual Basic .NET code is an object, which leads to changes in the implementation of some of the existing OO features, and other aspects of the language.

File Extensions

All source files use a file extension of vb, because the file content now defines the file type. Projects, code, classes, and forms all use the Visual Basic (.vb) file extension.

Files and Classes

Modules now can contain more than one class. The **Class** keyword differentiates classes within a file.

Namespaces

Namespaces are a flexible mechanism for organizing classes. One namespace can contain multiple assemblies, just as one assembly can contain multiple namespaces. Namespaces can nest within other namespaces, providing a hierarchy of classes. Class names must be unique within a namespace, whereas classes of the same name can reside in different namespaces. Class definitions reside within a namespace block, as shown in the following code:

```
Namespace AppNamespace
     Public Class AppClass1
     End class

     Public Class AppClass2
     End Class
End Namespace
```

A reference to a class within a namespace uses both the namespace and class name:

```
Private obj As AppNamespace.AppClass1
```

By default, namespaces are local to the application in which they reside. Namespaces can be global, available to all applications on a system, but they must meet stringent requirements in naming, versioning, digital signature, and registration.

An alias for a namespace can reduce the typing required to reference a namespace, as demonstrated in the following code:

```
Imports vb6 = Microsoft.VisualBasic.Compatibility.VB6
```

System Classes

The .NET Class Framework now provides many features that previously were part of a language. These class libraries include easily extendible classes, and provide those classes to all applications on a system, making application deployment simpler.

Inheritance

The **Inherits** keyword in Visual Basic .NET introduces inheritance, where a class can inherit the behaviors and interface of another class, and, in some cases, appearance of another class. Forms, which are now classes as well, can inherit controls, visual appearance, and code from another form:

```
Public Class CustomOrder
     Inherits Order
```

Inheritance and Overriding Methods

Subclasses inherit the methods and properties of their parent classes. However, a subclass can alter behavior from the parent class by overriding methods:

```
Public Class Employee
     Inherits Person

     Public Overrides Sub AddInfo()

     End Sub
End Class
```

By default, a subclass cannot override a method in the parent class, so the parent class must contain the **Overridable** keyword to allow overriding:

```
Public Class Person

     Public Overridable Sub AddInfo()

     End Sub
End Class
```

Encapsulation and Scope

Visual Basic .NET provides public, private, and protected scopes. Public elements are available to any classes as well as to client code. Elements defined as private are restricted to their own class. Subclasses can access protected elements, but client code cannot.

Polymorphism and Overloading Methods

With overloading, a class can contain multiple methods with the same name as long as each method uses a different list of parameters:

```
Public Overloads Function Sort(ByVal ID As Integer) As ArrayList
     'sort and return result
End Function

Public Overloads Function Sort(ByVal LastName As String) As ArrayList
     'sort and return result
End Function
```

Creating and Initializing Objects

Classes in Visual Basic .NET contain constructors, methods that create an object, accept parameters, and handle errors. The **New** method without parameters is similar to **Class_Initialize** in VB 6, whereas the **New** method with parameters creates and initializes an object at the same time:

```
Public Class Order
     Public Sub New(ByVal ID As Integer)
          'initialize the object with an ID
     End Sub
End Class
```

Declaring the object can include initial data:

```
Dim objOrder as New Order(17)
```

A subclass must define its own constructor, because it does not automatically inherit the **New** method from its parent class. However, the subclass can call the parent class constructor using the **MyBase** keyword as in the following:

```
Public Class Employee
     Inherits Person

     Public Sub New()
          MyBase.New()
          'additional construction code specific to Employee
     End Sub
End Class
```

Garbage Collection

Visual Basic .NET includes a garbage collection mechanism, which looks for objects without references, terminates them, and cleans up the garbage. This mechanism does not rely on counting the number of references (as in VB 6) and can handle objects with circular references that caused memory leaks in the past.

However, the exact timing of an object's termination is unknown using this collection mechanism. The **Finalize** method is comparable to the VB 6 **Class_Terminate** event in that garbage collection calls this method just before an object terminates. However, garbage collection calls this method, so it does not execute immediately upon an object losing its last reference. For example:

```
Protected Overrides Sub Finalize()
     'clean up the object
End Sub
```

If an object uses valuable resources that should release as soon as the object is dereferenced, the solution is to create a method, typically named **Dispose**, called by client code to force cleanup.

Shared Methods

Shared methods are methods in a class that are available without instantiating the class. For example:

```
Public Class Logic
     Shared Function EqualTest(ByVal I As Integer, J As Integer) As Boolean
          If I = J then
               Return True
          Else
               Return False
          End If
      End Function
End Class
```

With shared methods, the reference uses the class name because access to the method is directly through the class, not an instance of the class as in the following:

```
Dim test as Boolean

Test = Logic.EqualTest(4,3)
```

Shared Variables

The value of a shared variable applies to all instances of a class:

```
Public Class ClassCounter
     Private Shared mintCounter As Integer

     Public Sub New()
          mintCounter += 1
     End Sub
End Class
```

Interfaces

Visual Basic .NET provides a formal structure for interface declarations. Subs, functions, properties, and events can be part of the interface as in the following:

```
Public Interface Mgr
     Sub MgrSub()
     Function MgrFunction(ByVal Param1 As String) As Integer
     Property MgrProperty() As Short
     Event MgrEvent()
End Interface
```

Although implementing an interface remains the same, implementation of the elements of the interface now uses the **Implements** keyword:

```
Public Class Employee
    Inherits Person
    Implements MgrInterface

    Public Sub MgrMethod() Implements MgrInterface.MgrSub

    End Sub

    Public Function AssignMgr(ByVal Name As String) As Integer _
         Implements MgrInterface.MgrFunction

    End Function

    Public Property EmployeeMgr() As Short _
        Implements MgrInterface.MgrProperty

        Get

        End Get
        Set(ByVal Value As Short)

        End Set
    End Property

    Public Event EmployeeEvent() Implements MgrInterface.MgrEvent
```

Locking Controls

The Lock Controls option in VB 6 locked all controls on a form, even controls added after the option were enabled. In Visual Basic .NET, Lock Controls locks all existing controls in place, whereas new controls are not locked until Lock Controls is selected again.

Windows Forms

Windows Forms are similar to VB forms, although they are available to all languages in the .NET framework.

Forms as Classes

Windows forms are no longer FRM files, but classes that inherit their features from the .NET **System.Winforms.Form** class. A form can act like a template through inheritance, providing controls, visual appearance, and code to a sub-classed form.

The **Sub New** for a form is the equivalent to **Form Load** in VB 6, just as **Sub Dispose** is equivalent to **Form Unload.** Because forms are classes, code must instantiate and then show the form. The Form Designer now automatically inserts code that used to reside in the FRM file, to instantiate and manage the form and its controls.

Owned Forms

Owned forms simplify form management for forms that act as slaves to other forms. Owned forms minimize and close along with the owner form, and will not display behind the owner form. The owner can define the ownership using the **AddOwnedForm** method in code within the owner form class, whereas the slave can set ownership with the **Owner** property in the slave form class. For example:

```
'Setting ownership in the owner form
Me.AddOwnedForm SlaveForm

'Setting ownership in the slave form
Me.Owner = OwnerForm
```

An owner form uses the form property, **OwnedForms**, which contains a collection of forms that it owns.

Dialog Boxes

In Visual Basic .NET, the **ShowDialog** method replaces **Show** with the **vbModel** option for displaying dialog boxes. In VB 6, communicating the user's action on a dialog box to the calling form required writing code to store and pass the action. In Visual Basic .NET, a form shown using the **ShowDialog** method has a **DialogResult** property, which indicates the action taken. The form hides when the **DialogResult** property is set. For example:

```
Dim DialogBox As New Form()
DialogBox.ShowDialog()

Select Case DialogBox.DialogResult
Case DialogResult.OK
'process OK
Case DialogResult.Cancel
'process cancel
End Select
```

MDI Forms

In Visual Basic .NET, a form becomes an MDI parent by setting the **IsMDIContainer** property to True in the property window. Unlike VB 6, a parent form must explicitly receive a MainMenu control to provide a top-level menu.

In VB 6, only controls with Align properties could reside directly on an MDI parent. In Visual Basic .NET, MDI parents can contain any controls available to a regular form directly on the MDI surface.

In VB 6, the **MDIChild** property, which is set at design time, defines a form as an MDI child form. VB 6 MDI child forms can only function as MDI child forms and load only when an MDI parent is available. Visual Basic .NET sets MDI child forms at runtime by setting a form's **MDIParent** property to an MDI parent form, which allows forms to act as MDI children or standalone forms at different times.

Buttons Activated by Esc and Enter

In VB 6, pressing Enter activated the button whose **Cancel** property equaled True. Pressing Esc activated the button whose **Default** property equaled True. In Visual Basic .NET, the form's **CancelButton** and **AcceptButton** properties define which buttons the Esc and Enter keys activate. In the property window, selecting **CancelButton** or **AcceptButton** displays a drop-down list showing all the buttons on the form.

Controls as Classes

Controls belong to a hierarchy of classes ultimately inheriting from the **UserControl** class. A RichControl inherits from the **UserControl** class while adding visual properties. The Scrollable Control inherits from the **RichControl** class, adding scrolling features.

Adding Controls at Runtime

With controls as classes, adding a control at runtime involves instantiating a control class and setting the control object's properties. The only other step required is to add the control to the form's control collection. Here is the code:

```
Dim txtSpecialText as New TextBox()
TxtSpecialText.Size = New Size(35, 100)
TxtSpecialText.Location = New Point(30, 120)
TxtSpecialText.Text = "Default Text"
Me.Controls.Add(txtSpecialText)
```

Control Arrays

Control arrays are no longer available in Visual Basic .NET, although arrays and collections of controls can provide the same functionality.

Controls with New Names

Several controls have new names in Visual Basic .NET. These controls also receive new default names when added to the Designer. The names are as follows:

- Command buttons from VB 6 are now Buttons with a default name of Button1.
- Option buttons are RadioButtons with a default name of RadioButton1.
- Sliders are Trackbars with a default name of Trackbar1.

New Controls

Visual Basic .NET includes several new controls:

- The MainMenu control provides the menus that display along the top of a form and appears in the component tray in the Form Designer. A Menu Designer appears near the form's title bar when the MainMenu control is highlighted in the component tray.
- The ContextMenu control represents pop-up menus and appears in the component tray in the Form Designer. A Menu Designer appears when a ContextMenu control is highlighted in the component tray.
- The LinkLabel can appear as an image or hyperlink text and provides a link to a window or Web page.
- A CheckedListbox is a list box with checkboxes next to each item in the list. VB 6 provided this functionality in a list box with the **Style** property set to Checkbox.
- The DateTimePicker is a new control for selecting dates and times.
- The GroupBox control is similar to the VB 6 Frame control, except that it always has a border.
- The Panel control is also similar to a VB 6 Frame control. However, the Panel control does not have a title or caption. The **BorderStyle** property specifies the display of the border. The Panel control can scroll using the **AutoScroll** property.
- A TrayIcon control displays an icon in the Windows system tray, the set of icons usually displayed on the right side of the Windows taskbar.
- Provider controls provide new properties for all the controls on a form. For example, the ToolTip control adds the **Tooltip** property to each control. The HelpProvider control enables context-sensitive help with the **HelpString**, **HelpTopic**, and **ShowHelp** properties. The ErrorProvider control adds an **Error** property, which can contain text to display in a ToolTip to describe an error.
- The PrintDocument control sets a document to print and specifies the options for printing. The PrintDocument control's **Print** method initiates printing.
- The DataGrid control is similar to earlier grid controls, except that it supports hierarchical datasets used in ADO.NET.

Eliminated Controls

The Image control no longer exists in Visual Basic .NET; all its capabilities are provided by the PictureBox control.

Resizing Multiple Controls

With multiple controls selected (either by clicking and dragging a rectangle around the controls or selecting them individually with Ctrl-Click), resizing the control with the white resize handles resizes the other controls proportionately.

Layout Properties

In the property window, **Location**, which contains an x,y coordinate, replaces the **Top** and **Left** properties. The **Top** and **Left** properties are still available in code. The **Size** property replaces the **Height** and **Width** properties, although they also are still available in code.

Visual Basic .NET introduces two new properties that simplify resizing controls when the form changes size. The **Anchor** property defines the borders that stay a fixed distance from the closest border of the form. The **Dock** property attaches a control to one edge of the form.

Caption Property

The **Text** property defines text for all controls. Controls that used a **Caption** property in VB 6 now use the **Text** property.

Name Property

The **Name** property in controls and forms is not available at runtime, meaning that a loop through controls searching for a specific control name is no longer possible.

Tag Property

The **Tag** property is no longer available for controls in Visual Basic .NET.

Custom Properties and Methods

Controls are private by default in Visual Basic .NET. Instead of accessing control properties directly, you should store values from a control in custom properties.

Graphics Functions

GDI+, the new version of GDI graphics functions previously provided by the Windows API, now reside in the **System.Drawing** namespace. Some VB 6 keywords no longer exist, replaced by methods in the **System.Drawing** namespace. For example, **System.Drawing.Graphics.DrawEllipse** replaces the **Circle** keyword, and **System.Drawing.Graphics.DrawLine** replaces the **Line** keyword.

Data

Data access technology changes frequently in Visual Basic, and Visual Basic .NET is no exception.

ADO.NET

The newest data access technology, ADO.NET, provides the same methods for data access for local, network, and Internet connections. ADO.NET does not need continuous database connections; it passes data to any application tier. In addition, ADO.NET contains XML support.

The namespaces, **System.Data**, **System.Data.ADO** and **System.Data.SQL**, contain all the classes for ADO.NET.

Datasets

A dataset is much like a relational database containing one or more recordsets along with their relationships. Datasets reside in memory. ADO.NET converts data to XML, processes the data, and then posts it back to the original source, using XML as a means to pass data between application tiers. A dataset is a local copy of the data that accepts any required operation on the data, including changes to the data structure. After the data operations are complete, the dataset and the original data synchronize.

Managed Providers

Managed providers interface to the original data store and perform operations such as connecting to a database, obtaining data from the database, examining datasets for differences to record in the original data, and raising errors. Visual Basic .NET currently offers an ADO Managed Provider and an SQL Managed Provider. Both Managed Providers include **Connection**, **Command**, **Datareader**, and **Datasetcommand** classes.

Web Capabilities

Visual Basic .NET introduces ASP.NET, a new model for programming Internet user interfaces and interfacing to remote components.

Web Forms

Web Forms provide the visual development model of Visual Basic to Internet user interface development; layout emulates VB-style layout; controls on a Web Form act like VB controls. The IDE adds the additional files for a Web Form to a new project created as a Web application and stores the project folder in the root directory of your Web site by default. The IDE also displays two tabs: one for the visual layout and the other for the HTML to generate the visual layout. The ASP.NET runtime engine executes the file for a Web Form, which includes both HTML and code, and calls the Common Language Runtime to compile and execute any logic on the page.

Controls in Web Forms appear to maintain state. ASP.NET achieves this behavior by passing tokenized state information when a page posts.

Web Form Events

The ASP.NET runtime interprets HTTP posts and calls event-handling routines when it finds events. However, because of the overhead associated with handling events from remote clients, Web Forms offer a limited number of event types.

ASP.NET Server Controls

Server controls provide programmability on the server side, while projecting a standard HTML user interface. In addition to offering a familiar programming model, ASP.NET server controls create the HTML necessary to display their user interface and customize their output automatically to match the browser in use.

Validation Controls

Validation controls are Web Form server controls used to validate data entered in other controls. Attached to user input controls, the validation controls can validate the data when the user leaves the control or when the page posts.

Web Services

A Web Service is a mechanism for programs to communicate over the Internet. The **Web Method** attribute identifies a method in a Web Service as visible outside the Web service:

```
Public Function <WebMethod> MyFunction(MyVar as Integer) As Integer
End Function
```

To use a Web Service in another project, the project must contain a reference to the Web Service. Selecting Project | Add Web Reference opens the dialog box that lets you select a Web Service and add it to the project. After you declare an object as a Web service, code that uses the Web Service looks like a call to a method in a local object:

```
Dim objDistributedProcess as New localhost.Service1()
Dim intOption as Integer
Dim intResult as Integer

intResult = objDistributedProcess.MyFunction(intOption)
```

Language and Syntax

Visual Basic .NET includes a significant number of changes to the language and syntax, which help make Visual Basic .NET a more powerful and robust programming language.

Option Statement

When you set options in a project's properties, they become global for the entire project.

Option Explicit On, the default selection in Visual Basic .NET, forces variable declarations before using a variable in code.

Option Base is no longer available, because all arrays are zero based in Visual Basic .NET.

A new option in Visual Basic .NET, **Option Strict**, forces explicit type conversions when turned on. In the past, Visual Basic would convert data on-the-fly, such as converting an integer to a type **Long** in the following code:

```
Dim lngVar as Long
Dim intVar as Integer
intVar = 1
lngVar = intVar
```

With **Option Strict On**, Visual Basic .NET requires explicit conversions, as shown in the following code:

```
lngVar = CLng(intVar)
```

Data Types

Table A.1 summarizes the new, modified, and discontinued data types in Visual Basic .NET.

Table A.1 Visual Basic .NET data types.

Data Type	Status	Description
Byte	Unchanged	8-bit unsigned integer, 0 to 255.
Short	New	16-bit integer, -32768 to 32.767.
Integer	Changed	32-bit integer, formerly Long, -2,147,483,648 to 2,147,483,648.
Long	Changed	64-bit integer, formerly 32-bit integer, -9,223,372,036,854,775,808 to 9,223,372,036,854,775,808.
Currency	Discontinued	
Decimal	New	Decimal, a 128-bit data type consisting of a 96-bit integer and 32 bit integer. Decimal replaces the Currency data type and represents very large numbers with exponents of powers of 10.
Char	New	2-byte data type representing single characters, used for Unicode characters.

(continued)

Table A.1 Visual Basic .NET data types *(continued)*.

Data Type	Status	Description
String	Changed	Data type derived from the **System.String** class that cannot change. Changes to a string create a new string and destroy the old string. The syntax for creating a fixed length string is no longer valid: **Dim strVar As String * 1-**.
Variant	Discontinued	The Object data type replaces the **Variant** data type.

Declarations

Visual Basic .NET presents several changes to variable declarations.

Declaring Initial Values

Visual Basic .NET introduces syntax for declaring a variable and setting its initial value on the same line:

```
Dim intVar as Integer = 17
```

Declaring Arrays

The declaration statement can initialize values in arrays, although with this syntax, the declaration cannot contain an explicit array size:

```
Dim intArray() As Integer = {1, 1, 2, 3}
```

Arrays are all zero based in Visual Basic .NET, which makes the **To** keyword obsolete in declaring an array. The following code is no longer valid:

```
Dim intArray(1 To 5) As Integer
```

Declaring Constants

Declarations for constants must specify a data type, as shown in the following declaration statement:

```
Public Const MAX_THICKNESS As Double = .0125
```

Declaring Multiple Variables

The VB 6 syntax for declaring multiple variables on a single line behaves differently. A declaration statement cannot declare different data types. In VB 6, the declaration statement that follows would have declared **Var1** and **Var2** as Variants, while declaring **Var3** as a **Long**. In Visual Basic .NET, all three variables are declared as **Long**:

```
Dim Var1, Var2, Var3 As Long
```

Declaring with New Keyword

In VB 6, declaring an object variable with the **New** keyword did not create an object immediately. A declaration using the **New** keyword now creates an object immediately.

Block-Level Scope

Visual Basic .NET provides for variables with scope within a block of code, such as **If ... End If**, **For ... Next**, and other blocks. With block scope, the following code is no longer valid because the variable, **intLast**, does not exist outside the **For ... Next** loop:

```
For I = 1 To 5
     Dim intLast As Integer
     IntLast = I
Next
Obj.LastValue = intLast
```

User-Defined Types

Visual Basic .NET changes the syntax for defining a user-defined data type, using the keyword **Structure** instead of **Type** as in VB 6. In addition, elements within the structure include scope. For example:

```
Public Structure strEmployee
     Public strFirst As String
     Public strLast As String
     Private decSalary as Decimal
End Structure
```

Collections

The **System.Collections** namespace contains the functionality for collections in Visual Basic .NET. Collection types in Visual Basic .NET include **ArrayList**, **BitArray**, **Dictionary**, **HashTable** (equivalent to the Collection in VB 6), **ObjectList**, **Queue**, **SortedList**, **Stack**, and **StringCollection**. For example:

```
Dim colSort As New SortedList()
```

Custom Collections

In VB 6, custom collections required less than obvious techniques, such as the **NewEnum** property and setting a Procedure ID = -4. Visual Basic .NET implements custom collections by inheriting from one of the existing collection types included in the **System.Collections.Bases** namespace.

New Arithmetic Operators

Visual Basic .NET includes new shortcuts for existing arithmetic operators, similar to syntax available in C++ and Java. Table A.2 shows these shortcuts.

Table A.2 Shortcuts for arithmetic operators.

New Shortcut	Existing Arithmetic Operation
X += 2	X = X + 2
X -= 2	X = X - 2
X *= 2	X = X * 2
X /= 2	X = X / 2
X \= 2	X = X \ 2
X ^= 2	X = X ^ 2
X &= "More text"	X = X & "More text"

Floating-Point Division

Floating-point division behaves differently when you are dealing with division by zero. Dividing a non-zero value by zero now returns the word **Infinity**. Dividing zero by zero returns the text **NaN**, for Not a Number.

Boolean Operators

The operators **And**, **Or**, **Not** and **Xor** are now Boolean operators, not bitwise operators. The bitwise Boolean operators are **BitAnd**, **BitOr**, **BitNot**, and **BitXor**.

In Visual Basic .NET, True now equals 1, not –1, as in VB 6.

If ... Then Evaluation

VB 6 evaluated all expressions within an **If...Then** clause. Visual Basic .NET halts evaluation as soon as a part of the expression establishes the outcome of the entire expression. In the following example, Visual Basic .NET stops evaluation after the first test because the entire expression evaluates to False as soon as the first test returns False. The sample code takes advantage of this behavior to protect against division by zero:

```
If intVar <> 0 And intVar2 / intVar <> 2 Then
...
End If
```

Property Procedures

In VB 6, **Set**, **Get**, and **Let** each appeared in separate routines. In Visual Basic .NET, a property has one property routine, which contains blocks of code for **Set** and **Get**. **Property Let** is no longer available, subsumed by the functionality in **Property Set**. One side effect of this new syntax is that **Set** and **Get** always have the same scope. For example:

```
Private mintID as Integer
Public Property ID() as Integer
```

```
    Set
        mintID = Value
    End Set

    Get
        ID = mintID
    End Get
End Property
```

Shown in the sample code, **Value** is a new keyword automatically set to the value passed to the **Set** block.

ReadOnly and WriteOnly Properties

Visual Basic .NET includes a more explicit approach to creating **ReadOnly** and **WriteOnly** properties. The Compiler checks that a property procedure contains a **Get** block if the property declaration contains the **ReadOnly** keyword. The **WriteOnly** keyword restricts the property procedure to only a **Set** block. Here's an example of the ReadOnly property:

```
Public ReadOnly Property EditStatus() as Boolean
    Get
        EditStatus = True
    End Get
End Property
```

Default Properties

Unlike VB 6, where default properties required setting the procedure ID within procedure attributes, Visual Basic .NET assigns default properties with the **Default** keyword in the **Property Procedure** declaration. The sample code also demonstrates the new restriction that default properties must be a property array, and therefore must contain at least one required parameter:

```
Default Public Property Total(ByVal objID as Integer) As Integer
```

Sub New

Visual Basic .NET no longer offers **Class_Initialize**, replacing it with the **Sub New** procedure, a constructor that can accept parameters to initialize objects and can include error handling. Because forms are now objects in Visual Basic .NET, **Sub New** also replaces **Form_Load** for creating forms. The following code shows a class that accepts a parameter to initialize the object, as well as instantiating the object:

```
Public Class Part
    Public Sub New(ByVal ID As Integer)
        'initialize the object with ID
```

```
    End Sub
End Class

Dim objPart As New Part(intNextID)
```

Set Statement

With the move to full object orientation, Visual Basic .NET eliminates the **Set** statement when assigning an object to a variable. Object variables act like any other variable:

```
objEmployee = New Employee(intID)
objManager = objEmployee
```

Procedure Syntax

All method calls now require parentheses unless the method accepts no parameters. In addition, because object creation calls the constructor method in the class, the code to create an object also includes parentheses:

```
ObjEmployee = New Employee()
```

Returning Results

The **Return** keyword assigns the return value of a function to the value of the parameter following the keyword:

```
Public Function Divide(intNum As Integer, intDenom As Integer) As Integer
    Dim intResult As Integer
    IntResult = intNum / intDenom
    Return intResult
End Function
```

Parameters

Visual Basic .NET switches the default method for passing parameters from **ByRef** to **ByVal**. Optional parameters now require a default, used when a value is not passed:

```
Public Sub TestText(Optional ByVal strText As String = "")
```

Event Handling

Visual Basic .NET offers clearer and more flexible syntax for handling events. The **Handles** keyword associated with a procedure calls that procedure when the specified event occurs. With this keyword, a procedure to handle an event can have any scope and any name. This syntax also allows the same procedure to handle multiple events:

```
Private WithEvents objOrder1 As Order
Private WithEvents objOrder2 as Order

Private Sub CancelOrder(ByVal ID As Integer) _
    Handles objOrder1.OrderEvent, objOrder2.OrderEvent

End Sub
```

Delegate Functions

Delegate procedures are callable by other procedures and can act as parameters passed into other procedures. Any procedure or method is a valid delegate. The **Invoke** method calls a delegate procedure within another procedure. The **AddressOf** operator provides the address of a procedure for passing as a parameter. For example:

```
Delegate Function ValidProc(intVar As Integer, strVar As String) As Boolean

Public Sub ValidateData(ByVal InputData() As Integer, _
ByVal TestData As ValidProc)
      Dim intTest As Integer
      Dim strTest As String
      Dim blnVar As Boolean

      blnVar = TestData.Invoke(intTest, strTest)

End Sub

'calling subroutine and passing procedure
ValidateData(DataToTest, AddressOf MyTestDataProc)
```

Attributes

Visual Basic .NET provides attributes as a mechanism for adding tags to elements within code. Attributes can accept parameters, including named parameters:

```
Public Class <Description("Validates required data")> Required
```

Structured Error Handling

Although **On Error Goto** and **On Error Resume** are still available, Visual Basic .NET now provides new syntax for structured error handling. A series of blocks, including **Try- Catch-** and **Finally** provides the structure. In addition to the **Error** object, Visual Basic .NET includes an **Exception** class. The **Error** object now includes a **GetException** method to return the exception raised.

Try – Catch – Finally

The **Try** block contains the code to execute while watching for errors. The **Catch** block executes only if an error occurs. The optional **Finally** block executes code to clean up or execute any other actions. Here is the sample code:

```
Try
     'Code to execute

Catch e As FileNotFoundException
     'Code to execute if file is not found

Catch When Err.Number = 5
     'Code to execute if error occurs with number = 5

Catch
     'Catch all other errors

Finally
     'Code to clean up before exiting

End Try
```

Resume Functionality

The **Try – Catch** approach does not include an equivalent to **Resume** from VB 6. However, **Try** blocks can nest within other **Try** blocks. A nested block can emulate the functionality of **Resume** by catching and fixing an error before continuing with the rest of the code. For example:

```
Sub GetData()
     Try
         'Code to execute
         Try
             'Code to open a file
         Catch e As FileNotFoundException
             'Display dialog to select file to use
         End Try
           'Continue with code using specified file
       Catch
       End Try
   End Sub
```

Exit Try

Visual Basic .NET includes the **Exit Try** statement to leave the **Try – Catch – Finally** structure. **Exit Try** jumps to the code in the **Finally** block, if present, or to the first line of code after the **End Try** statement as in the following:

```
Try
    'Code within error trap
    If blnValid Then Exit Try
    'More code within error trapping
Catch
    'Error handling code
End Try
'Code execution continues here after Exit Try
```

Debug.Print

Visual Basic .NET replaces **Debug.Print** with **System.Diagnostics.Debug.Write** or **System.Diagnostics.Debug.Writeline**.

Language Change Summary

This section summarizes the language changes from VB 6 to Visual Basic .NET.

Unsupported Elements

The elements in Table A.3 do not exist in Visual Basic .NET. The Compatibility Library provides temporary substitutes for some of these elements, whereas other features in the Visual Basic .NET language replace the remainder.

Table A.3 VB 6 Elements Not Available in Visual Basic .NET

Discontinued Element	Type
As Any	Keyword
Atn	Function
Calendar	Property
Circle	Statement
Currency	Data Type
Date	Function and statement
Date$	Function
Debug.Assert	Method
Debug.Print	Method
DefType	Statement
DoEvents	Function
Empty	Keyword
Eqv	Operator
GoSub	Statement
Imp	Operator
Initialize	Event
Instancing	Property
IsEmpty	Function

(continued)

Table A.3 VB 6 Elements Not Available in Visual Basic .NET *(continued).*

Discontinued Element	Type
IsMissing	Function
IsNull	Function
IsObject	Function
Let	Statement
Line	Statement
Lset	Statement
MsgBox	Function
Now	Function
Null	Keyword
On ... GoSub	Construction
On ... GoTo	Construction
Option Base	Statement
Option Private Module	Statement
Property Get, Property Let, Property Set	Statements
Pset	Method
Rnd	Function
Round	Function
Rset	Statement
Scale	Method
Set	Statement
Sgn	Function
Sqr	Function
String	Function
Terminate	Event
Time	Function and Statement
Time$	Function
Timer	Function
Type	Statement
Variant	Data Type
VarType	Function
Wend	Keyword

New Elements

The elements in Table A.4 are new in Visual Basic .NET.

Table A.4 Elements Introduced in Visual Basic .NET

Element	Type
AddHandler	Keyword
Alias	Keyword

(continued)

Table A.4 Elements Introduced in Visual Basic .NET *(continued)*.

Element	Type
Assembly	Keyword
Char	Data Type
Class	Keyword
Handles	Keyword
Imports	Keyword
Inherits	Keyword
MustInherit	Keyword
MustOverride	Keyword
MyBase	Keyword
MyClass	Keyword
Namespace	Keyword
NotInheritable	Keyword
NotOverridable	Keyword
Overloads	Keyword
Overridable	Keyword
Overrides	Keyword
Protected	Keyword
Readonly	Keyword
RemoveHandler	Keyword
Shared	Keyword
Structure ... End Structure	Construction
Throw	Keyword
Try ... Catch ... Finally	Construction
Webmethod	Attribute
Writeonly	Keyword

The Visual Basic Compatibility Library

As shown in Table A.5, the **Microsoft.VisualBasic.Compatibility.VB6** namespace includes elements maintained to help migrate code from previous versions of VB to Visual Basic .NET. Even though the library exists, it is preferable to replace the obsolete code with new Visual Basic .NET features, because the length of time that Microsoft will support this namespace is unknown.

To use the Compatibility Library, add a reference to the Microsoft Visual Basic .NET Compatibility Runtime to the project. Add an **Imports** statement to the project with an alias. Then, reference the contents of the Library with the namespace alias:

```
Imports VB6 = Microsoft.VisualBasic.Compatibility.Vb6

Dim ctl As VB6.CheckBoxArray
```

Table A.5 Obsolete VB 6 Elements Provided Temporarily by the Compatibility Namespace.

Element	Type
AddControl	Method
And	Method
ArrayBase1	Method
BaseControlArray	Class
BaseOCXArray	Class
ButtonArray	Class
ByteArrayToString	Method
CheckBoxArray	Class
CheckedListBoxArray	Class
ComboBoxArray	Class
CopyArray	Method
DirDriveDrawing	Class
DirListBox	Class
DirListBoxArray	Class
DriveListBox	Class
DriveListBoxArray	Class
Eqv	Method
FileListBox	Class
FileListBoxArray	Class
FixedLengthString	Class
FontChangeBold	Method
FontChangeItalic	Method
FontChangeName	Method
FontChangeSize	Method
FontChangeStrikeout	Method
FontChangeUnderline	Method
Format	Method
FormShowConstants	Resource File
GetActiveControl	Method
GetCancel	Method
GetDefault	Method
GetEXEName	Method
GetHInstance	Method
GetItemData	Method
GetItemString	Method
GetListBoxColumns	Method
GetPath	Method
GetTag	Method
GetToolTipText	Method
GroupBoxArray	Class

(continued)

Table A.5 Obsolete VB 6 Elements Provided Temporarily by the Compatibility Namespace *(continued)*.

Element	Type
HscrollBarArray	Class
Imp	Method
LabelArray	Class
LateBoundAdd	Method
ListBoxArray	Class
ListBoxItem	Class
LoadResConstants	Resource File
LoadResData	Method
LoadResPicture	Method
LoadResString	Method
MenuItemArray	Class
MouseButtonConstants	Resource File
NewArray	Method
Not	Method
Or	Method
PanelArray	Class
PictureBoxArray	Class
PixelstoTwipsX	Method
PixelstoTwipsY	Method
RadioButtonArray	Class
ReDim	Method
ReDimPreserve	Method
SendKeys	Method
SetCancel	Method
SetDefault	Method
SetItemData	Method
SetItemString	Method
SetListBoxColumns	Method
SetResourceBaseName	Method
SetTag	Method
SetToolTipText	Method
ShiftConstants	Resource File
ShowForm	Method
StringtoByteArray	Method
Support	Module
TabLayout	Method
Tag	Class
TextboxArray	Class
TimerArray	Class

(continued)

Table A.5 Obsolete VB 6 Elements Provided Temporarily by the Compatibility Namespace *(continued)*.

Element	Type
TwipsPerPixelX	Method
TwipsPerPixelY	Method
TwipsToPixelsX	Method
TwipsToPixelsY	Method
ValidateControls	Method
VscrollBarArray	Class
WhatsThisMode	Method
Xor	Method
ZOrder	Method
ZOrderConstants	Resource File

Appendix B

The Upgrade Wizard

With the large number of changes between Visual Basic 6 and Visual Basic .NET, upgrading code requires significant changes. Microsoft provides the Upgrade Wizard to assist with upgrading code from VB 6 to Visual Basic .NET. Even with the Upgrade Wizard, upgrading usually requires additional code modifications after the wizard finishes.

To Upgrade or Not

Rebuilding applications from scratch using Visual Basic .NET will make the most of the new development platform but is usually not feasible for various reasons. With the interoperability features available in Visual Basic .NET, another approach is to develop new applications in Visual Basic .NET and use interoperability to access existing VB 6 code. In other cases, upgrading can provide benefits of the new platform without much work.

Running the Upgrade Wizard and reviewing the resulting Upgrade Report and Task List can indicate the level of effort to port code to Visual Basic .NET. For long Task Lists, interoperability might be the solution, while upgrading makes sense if the Task List is reasonably short.

What the Upgrade Wizard Does

The Upgrade Wizard creates a new VB .NET project, copies the original project files, and converts the files, leaving the original project intact in VB 6. The Upgrade Wizard modifies VB 6 code to reflect VB .NET syntax changes and modified element names, such as the following:

- Changes data types (**Integer** becomes **Short**; **Long** becomes **Integer**, **Variant** becomes **Object**)
- Adds a data type assignment to **Constant** declarations
- Removes **Set** in object assignment statements
- Reconfigures **Get** and **Set** routines into the new style **Property** procedure
- Replaces VB 6 keywords with Visual Basic .NET equivalents (**Type** becomes **Structure**, **Circle** becomes **System.Drawing.Graphics.DrawEllipse**, etc.)
- Adds parentheses to parameter lists as needed
- Explicitly identifies default properties
- Updates revised **Constant** names
- Updates revised **Function** names

The Upgrade Wizard converts VB 6 forms to Windows Application objects with a class for the form, declarations, constructor and destructor methods, and initialization. The wizard replaces VB 6 form properties and events with equivalent VB .NET properties and events.

During the upgrade, the wizard adds Option Strict Off to the top of all files in the project so that implied type coercions don't raise errors. The wizard uses the Compatibility Library to upgrade some unsupported features without VB .NET equivalents, such as obsolete keywords, functions, and control arrays. For projects using ADO for data access, the wizard takes advantage of interoperability to continue with ADO. The wizard can support non-zero bounded arrays by including an array wrapper.

What the Upgrade Wizard Doesn't Do

The Upgrade Wizard does not completely upgrade most VB 6 projects to Visual Basic .NET. Most items that the Upgrade Wizard cannot handle appear in the Upgrade Report and in the Task List. However, some issues with an upgraded project won't appear until application testing.

Visual Basic .NET does not support several VB 6 features, and also does not provide an equivalent replacement. Other features need rework because of behavioral, performance, or object model changes. Projects that depend on these features, listed below, either require reworking or should remain in VB 6.

- OLE Container Control
- Dynamic Data Exchange (use another communication method, or leave in VB 6)

- DAO or RDO Data Binding (update to ADO, or leave in VB 6)
- Visual Basic 5.0 Controls (update to 6.0 Controls, or leave in VB 6)
- ActiveX Documents (rewrite as User Controls, or leave in VB 6)
- Property Pages
- User Controls
- Web Classes
- Single-tier Database Applications (need reworking to address controls bound directly to databases)
- Visual Basic Add-Ins (need reworking to address the Visual Basic .NET extensibility object model)
- Games (need reworking due to different performance parameters)
- Graphics
- Drag and Drop (need reworking due to differences in drag-and-drop functionality)
- Variants (Need reworking to eliminate behavioral changes due to **Object** data type)
- Windows API Calls (replace calls with .NET framework functions)

The Upgrade Wizard also can't handle syntax and object differences between VB 6 and Visual Basic .NET that are too dissimilar.

Running the Upgrade Wizard

Opening a VB 6 project in Visual Basic .NET automatically runs the Upgrade Wizard. The Welcome window explains what the Upgrade Wizard does and provides a Next button to continue with the upgrade and a Cancel button to leave the Upgrade Wizard.

Setting the Upgrade Options

After the Welcome window, the Upgrade Wizard displays the dialog box (Step 2 of 5) that provides some options for the upgrade. The Upgrade Wizard automatically selects the type of project based on the original VB 6 project type, as shown in Figure B.1.

The wizard provides an option for generating default interfaces for public classes. When this option is deselected (the default), the upgrade generates only default interfaces for public classes implemented by other classes in the project. When this option is selected, the upgrade generates default interfaces for all public classes.

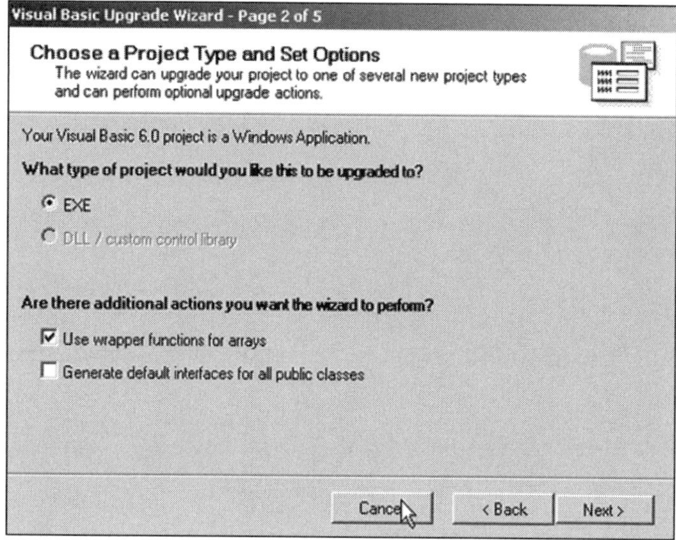

Figure B.1
Selecting options for the upgrade.

You also have an option for changing arrays to zero-based bounds. When this option is deselected (the default), the upgrade uses a wrapper function so that code runs without modification. However, the wrapped arrays are slower and incompatible with VB .NET arrays. Checking the option changes arrays to zero-based VB .NET arrays. However, this change might require code modification, particularly where variables and functions calculate index values.

Setting the .NET Project Location

The next dialog box (Step 3 of 5) asks for the location for the new VB .NET project. By default, the wizard creates the project in a subfolder within the existing project folder. The new project name is *ProjectName*.NET, where *ProjectName* is the name of the existing VB 6 project.

If the target folder does not exist, a dialog box appears asking if you want to create it.

Confirming the Upgrade

The next dialog box (Step 4 of 5) asks for confirmation to continue because the upgrade process can take a significant amount of time. The dialog box displays the progress of the upgrade and then shows a final message when the upgrade is complete.

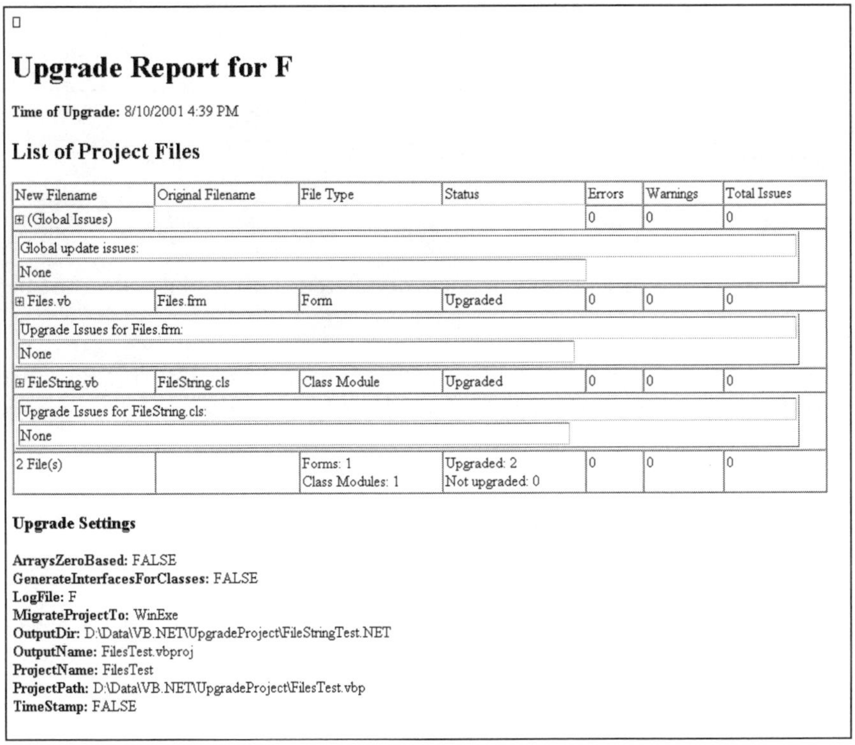

Upgrade Report for F

Time of Upgrade: 8/10/2001 4:39 PM

List of Project Files

New Filename	Original Filename	File Type	Status	Errors	Warnings	Total Issues
⊞ (Global Issues)				0	0	0
Global update issues: None						
⊞ Files.vb	Files.frm	Form	Upgraded	0	0	0
Upgrade Issues for Files.frm: None						
⊞ FileString.vb	FileString.cls	Class Module	Upgraded	0	0	0
Upgrade Issues for FileString.cls: None						
2 File(s)		Forms: 1 Class Modules: 1	Upgraded: 2 Not upgraded: 0	0	0	0

Upgrade Settings

ArraysZeroBased: FALSE
GenerateInterfacesForClasses: FALSE
LogFile: F
MigrateProjectTo: WinExe
OutputDir: D:\Data\VB.NET\UpgradeProject\FileStringTest.NET
OutputName: FilesTest.vbproj
ProjectName: FilesTest
ProjectPath: D:\Data\VB.NET\UpgradeProject\FilesTest.vbp
TimeStamp: FALSE

Figure B.2
The Upgrade Report.

Viewing the Upgrade Report and Upgrade Tasks

The Upgrade Report, shown in Figure B.2, includes information about the upgrade, such as the settings, the files upgraded and their status, and the issues that need manual intervention. The Upgrade Report is an HTML file located within the new .NET project folder.

When the new .NET project opens in Visual Studio .NET, the issues that need manual intervention appear in the Task List for the project. The Upgrade Report appears in the Solution Explorer. In addition to adding tasks to the Upgrade Report and the Task List, the Upgrade Wizard adds comments in the code identifying the type of issue and the work needed to correct the code. Comments in the code, as shown in Figure B.3, include links to the help topics that explain the issue with the code and how to resolve it.

- *UPGRADE_ISSUE*—An application will not compile unless these errors are corrected.
- *UPGRADE_TODO*—ToDo items don't prevent compilation, but do cause runtime errors.

```
Dim sFile As String
'UPGRADE_NOTE: Declaration of sArray was changed from sArray() As String. Click for more:
Dim sArray As System.Array
Dim i As Short
```

Figure B.3
Upgrade comments in the code.

- *UPGRADE_WARNING*—Warnings are items that might cause runtime errors.
- *UPGRADE_NOTE*—Notes identify changes or differences that could affect the behavior of the code.

To complete the upgrade, you must correct each item in the Task List. It is also wise to search the code for the string **UPGRADE_NOTE** and review those notes to determine whether code modifications are necessary.

Appendix C

VB.NET Exceptions

The **Exception** class includes the **HRESULT** property, a coded numerical value that identifies an exception. Error numbers are still available through **Err.Number**. Table C.1 includes error numbers to assist in migrating existing Visual Basic 6 applications to VB.NET.

Table C.1 Exceptions and equivalent error numbers in Visual Basic .NET.

Exception Name	Thrown By	Err.Number
ApplicationException	The application exception is the base class for any exception created for a user application. User programs, not the Common Language Runtime, throw application exceptions.	5
Types of Application Exceptions		
InvalidFilterCriteriaException	The filter criteria are not valid for the type of filter used in the **FindMembers** method.	5
TargetException	The target for a nonstatic method is a null object. Potential causes are the caller not having access to the member or the target not defining the member, among other reasons.	5
TargetInvocationException	Methods invoked by reflection throw this exception.	5
TargetParameterCountException	The number of parameters provided does not match the number expected.	5
CodeDomSerializationException	A line number is available when a serialization error occurs.	No number available at this time.
InvalidPrinterException	A program attempts to access a printer using invalid printer settings, often caused by attempting to access a nonexistent printer.	91
IO Exceptions	An IO error occurs.	57
Types of IO Exceptions		
DirectoryNotFoundException	Accessing a directory fails because the directory does not exist on disk.	76
EndofStreamException	A program attempts to read past the end of a stream.	5
FileLoadException	An error occurs while you're attempting to load a file.	5
FileNotFoundException	Accessing a file fails because the file does not exist on disk.	53
IsolatedStorageException	Isolated storage fails. Potential causes include missing evidence, which provides Information about an assembly and its origin, or use of **FileStream** operations not supported by isolated storage.	5
PathTooLongException	A pathname or file name is too long.	5
CookieException	No information on the CookieException available at this time.	5
ProtocolViolationException	Descendants of WebRequest and WebResponse throw this exception when an error occurs using a network protocol, such as HTTP.	5

(continued)

Table C.1 Exceptions and equivalent error numbers in Visual Basic .NET *(continued)*.

Exception Name	Thrown By	Err.Number
WebException	Descendants of WebRequest and WebResponse throw this exception when an error occurs accessing the network through a pluggable protocol.	5
MissingManifestResourceException	The main assembly does not contain a required neutral set of resources.	5
SUDSGeneratorException	No information available at this time.	No number available at this time.
SUDSParserException	No information available at this time.	No number available at this time.
SystemException	The Common Language Runtime throws this exception when nonfatal and recoverable errors, such as an array out-of-bound error, occur in user programs.	5
Types of System Exceptions (a subset of the system exceptions available)		
ArgumentException	A method passes an invalid argument. This class contains derived classes such as **ArgumentNullException** and **ArgumentOutofRangeException**.	5
ArithmeticException	An arithmetic error occurs. This class contains derived classes such as **DivideByZeroException** and **OverflowException**.	5
IndexOutofRangeException	A program attempts to access an element of an array with an index that is outside the bounds of the array	9
NullReferenceException	A program attempts to dereference a null object reference.	91
OutofMemoryException	There is insufficient memory to continue execution of a program.	7
StackOverflowException	Too many method calls are pending causing the execution stack to overflow.	5
URIFormatException	The Uri class constructor throws this exception if the supplied URI is invalid.	5
SOAPException	The Common Language Runtime throws this exception if a response to a request has an invalid format. Web Service methods can generate this exception by throwing an exception within the Web Service method.	No number available at this time.
Types of SOAP Exceptions		
SOAPHeaderException	An exception occurs while processing a SOAP header from a Web Service method called over Simple Object Access Protocol (SOAP).	No number available at this time.

Appendix D
Compiler Options

Some compiler options are available only when you are compiling from the command line, while others are available at the command line and within Visual Studio. Options available within Visual Studio are identified in the Purpose column of Table D.1.

Table D.1 Visual Basic .NET compiler options.

Option	Purpose
Optimization	
/optimize[+ | -]	Compiler optimizations include output files that are smaller, faster, and more efficient. The default, **/optimize+**, also represented by **/optimize**, enables optimizations, while **/optimize -** disables optimizations.
Output Files	
/out: *filename*	The compiler creates an output file created using the file name provided.
/target:<targettype>	**/target** specifies the format of the compiler output. The default, **/target:exe**, creates an .exe console application. **/target:library** creates a code library. **/target:module** creates a module. **/target:winexe** creates a Windows program.
.NET Assemblies	
/addmodule:*module*[*module2*]	The compiler makes available to the project being compiled all type information from the specified file(s).
/delaysign[+ | -]	The default, **/delaysign-**, creates a fully signed assembly, while **/delaysign+** places the public key in the assembly. **/delaysign** works in conjunction with either **/keyfile** or **/keycontainer**. This option is available in Visual Studio.
/imports:*namespace*[*namespace*]	**/imports** makes available a namespace to all source code files in the compilation from the current set of source files or any referenced assembly. This option is available in Visual Studio.
/keycontainer:*"container"*	**/keycontainer** specifies the name of the key container for the key pair that gives an assembly a strong name. This option is available in Visual Studio.
/keyfile:*"file"*	**/keyfile** specifies the name of the file containing a key or key pair that gives an assembly a strong name. This option is available in Visual Studio.
/libpath:*dir1*[*dir2*]	**/libpath** specifies the location of assemblies referenced through the **/reference** option. *dir1* is a directory to search if a referenced assembly is not found in the current working directory or in the Common Language Runtime's system directory. The compiler searches additional directories for assembly references if the option includes additional directory names separated with commas.
/reference:*file*[,*file2*]	**/reference** makes available type information in the specified assemblies to the project being compiled. This option is available in Visual Studio.
Debugging/Error Checking	
/bugreport:*file*	**/bugreport** creates a file useful for filing a bug report that contains a copy of all source code files, the compiler options used, version information about the compiler, Common Language Runtime, operating system, and any compiler output. This option prompts for a description of the problem, and your recommendation for fixing the problem.

(continued)

Table D.1 Visual Basic .NET compiler options *(continued)*.

Option	Purpose
/debug[+ | -] **/debug:[full | pdbonly]**	**/debug+** generates debugging information in a PDB file, while the default, **/debug-**, also represented by **/debug**, produces no debug information. This option is available in Visual Studio. **/debug:full** enables attaching a debugger to the running program. /debug:pdbonly provides source code debugging if a program is started in the debugger and displays assembler if a running program is attached to the debugger.
/nowarn	**/nowarn** suppresses the compiler's ability to generate warnings. This option is available in Visual Studio.
/quiet	**/quiet** outputs only the diagnostic text from a syntax-related error or warning.
/removeintchecks [+ | -]	The default, **/removeintchecks-**, checks all integer calculations for errors such as overflow or division by zero, while **/removeintchecks+**, also represented by **/removeintchecks**, prevents error checking and can speed up integer calculations. This option is available in Visual Studio.
/warnaserror[+ | -]	The default, **/warnaserror-**, treats the first occurrence of a warning as an error, while subsequent warnings appear as warnings. **/warnaserror+**, also represented by **/warnaserror**, treats warnings as errors. This option is available in Visual Studio.
/define:*symbol=value* [,*symbol=value*]	**/define** defines conditional compiler constants, which can be used to compile source files conditionally with the #If...Then...#Else directive. This option is available in Visual Studio.
Resources	
/linkresource:*filename*[,*identifier*]	**/linkresource** creates a link to a managed resource. The identifier parameter defines the logical name for the resource.
/resource:*filename*[,*identifier*]	**/resource** embeds a managed resource in an assembly. This option is available in Visual Studio.
/win32icon:*filename*	**/win32icon** includes an ICO file in the output file, which displays the icon for the output file in the Windows Explorer. This option is available in Visual Studio.
/win32resource:*filename*	**/win32resource** inserts a Win32 resource into the output file.
Miscellaneous	
@response_file	@ specifies a response file, which the compiler reads to obtain compiler options and source code files as if they had been entered on the command line.
/help or /?	**/help** displays the compiler options and does not compile code or produce output.
/baseaddress:*address*	**/baseaddress** specifies a default base address for a DLL. This option is available in Visual Studio.

(continued)

Table D.1 Visual Basic .NET compiler options *(continued).*

Option	Purpose
/main:*location*	When creating an executable or Windows executable program, **/main** specifies the class or module containing the **Sub Main** procedure. This option is available in Visual Studio.
/nologo	When compiling from the command line, **/nologo** suppresses display of the copyright banner and informational messages. By default, the copyright banner and informational messages display.
/optionexplicit[+ | -]	With **/optionexplicit+** the compiler reports errors when variables are not declared before use. The default, **/optionexplicit-**, also represented by /optionexplicit, does not check for variable declarations. This option is available in Visual Studio.
/optionstrict [+ | -]	**/optionstrict+** reports errors when conversions implicitly narrow type, such as assigning a **Decimal** type object to an **Integer** type object. The default, **/optionstrict-**, also represented by optionstrict, allows permissive type semantics. This option is available in Visual Studio.
/optioncompare	The default, **/optioncompare:binary**, specifies that string comparisons are binary while **/optioncompare:text** specifies text comparisons.
/recurse:[*dir*\\]*file*	**/recurse** searches all child directories of the project directory or the specified directory (*dir*). The parameter, file, specifies files to search for.
/rootnamespace:*namespace*	**/rootnamespace** specifies a namespace for all type declarations. This option is available in Visual Studio.
/utf8output[+ | -]	**/utf8output+**. Also represented by /utf8output, uses UTF-8 encoding to display compiler output. The default is **/utf8output-**.

Index

C

D

E

F

G

H

I

J

K

L

M

N

P

Q

R

S

T

V

W

X

Z

What's On The CD-ROM

The *Visual Basic .NET Programming with Peter G. Aitken*'s companion CD-ROM contains elements specifically selected to enhance the usefulness of this book, including:

- *The .NET SDK*—The SDK features:
  - The complete CLR class library
  - The most current version of the command-line C# compiler
  - Complete debugging libraries and symbol files
  - Documentation for the .NET class libraries
  - Complete example applications ready to compile and run
  - Up-to-date documentation for the .NET system

Note: This program was reproduced by The Coriolis Group under a special arrangement with Microsoft Corporation. For this reason, The Coriolis Group is responsible for the product warranty and for support. If your diskette is defective, please return it to The Coriolis Group, which will arrange for its replacement. PLEASE DO NOT RETURN IT TO MICROSOFT CORPORATION. Any product support will be provided, if at all, by The Coriolis Group. PLEASE DO NOT CONTACT MICROSOFT CORPORATION FOR PRODUCT SUPPORT. End users of this Microsoft program shall not be considered "registered owners" of a Microsoft product and therefore shall not be eligible for upgrades, promotions or other benefits available to "registered owners" of Microsoft products.

Please note that Coriolis is providing the .NET SDK under license from Microsoft Corporation. While we are happy to assist you with defective, damaged or unusable CDs, we are unable to address any technical or product support issues associated with the Microsoft SDK.

The CD-ROM contains a folder for each chapter in the book that contains numbered listings. There is a file for each listing, named as follows:

- Most code files are in the form List*xxyy*.txt where *xx* is the chapter number and *yy* is the listing number. You can open the file and copy and paste the code into your project as needed.
- A few files are given the same name as assigned in the book, such as Checkbook xml.
- *TextPad Text Editor*—TextPad is an extremely powerful text editor that can be used for many tasks including editing of source code files. It permits extensive customization and provides many time, and work-saving features , it's my favorite. To install: go to the TextPad folder on the CD-ROM and run the program txpeng450.exe.
- *Tal Technologies Bar Code Software*—The TAL BarCode ActiveX Control has all the features necessary to easily add professional quality barcodes to any Windows application including Web pages, database reporting and labeling, product packaging, document tracking, postal bar coding and special purpose barcode labeling applications. It works with Visual Basic .NET as well as many other software development tools. To install: go to the TalTech folder on the CD-ROM and run the program OcxDemo.exe.
- *Visual UML*—Visual UML is an object modeling tool that can be great help when designing the structure of object-oriented programs as well as other processes. By laying out program stucture diagrammatically before you start coding, you can avoid problems that are time-sonsuming to fix later during development. The product supports all 10 diagram types defined in the Unified Modeling Language specification. To install: Go to the VisualUML folder on the CD-ROM and execute Vuml282.exe. Leave the serial number field empty when installing. After the Visual UML components have been installed, the Windows Script 5.5 component and the VBScript 5.5 and JScript 5.5 documentation installers are run in sequence. If you choose to install these, it is recommended that you accept the default directories for these components.
- *ImagXpress*—ImagExpress provides a set of development tools for creation of document and image processing applications. They work with Visual Basic .NET as well as with some earlier versions. To install, go to the folder ImagXpress on the CD-ROM and execute the program XpressPE.exe.

Note: The following software (not included on this CD-ROM) is required to complete the projects in this book:

- Visual Studio.NET (Visual Studio 7.0)

Software Requirements

- Windows ME, Windows NT 4, Windows 2000, or Windows XP.
- Internet Explorer 5.5 or higher to view some of the newer documentation.

Hardware Requirements

- An Intel (or equivalent) Pentium 300MHz processor (500MHz recommended)
- 64MB of RAM required (128MB recommended)
- The .NET CLR requires approx. 200MB of disk storage space.
- A color monitor (256 colors) is recommended.